PURDEY

Gun & Rifle Makers

The Millennium Gun, No. 30,000, a 28-bore, round-bodied sidelock ejector, engraved by Ken Hunt.

PURDEY

Gun & Rifle Makers

THE DEFINITIVE HISTORY

DONALD DALLAS

Quiller Press
London

To my son Donald, 'finder' of Purdey gun No. 14, and my daughter Katie.

Copyright © 2000 James Purdey & Sons

First published 2000 by Quiller Press Limited
46, Lillie Road, London SW6 1TN

ISBN 1 899163 63 8
Designed by Jo Lee
Printed by Colorcraft Ltd, Hong Kong

All rights reserved.
No part of this book may be reproduced by any means
without prior written permission of the publishers or copyright holders.

CONTENTS

	Acknowledgements	*vi*
	Preface	*vii*
Chapter 1	BLACKSMITH IN THE MINORIES	1
Chapter 2	'A SMALL SHOP IN PRINCES STREET'	7
Chapter 3	314 ½ OXFORD STREET	17
Chapter 4	MUZZLE-LOADING GUNS, RIFLES AND PISTOLS	35
Chapter 5	BOLT AND BEESLEY	49
Chapter 6	EARLY BREECH-LOADING GUNS AND RIFLES	89
Chapter 7	'A PALACE AMONGST GUN MANUFACTURIES'	100
Chapter 8	BOOM, BUST AND BELLIGERENCE	130
Chapter 9	FROM AUSTERITY TO RENAISSANCE	145
Chapter 10	THE PURDEY WAY	155
Chapter 11	LATER BREECH-LOADING GUNS AND RIFLES	165

Appendices

1	Purdey Family Tree	185
2	Diary of Events in Purdey History	186
3a	Purdey Serial Numbers and Dating	190
3b	Woodward Serial Numbers and Dating	196
4a	Muzzle-Loading Gun, Rifle and Pistol Production	197
4b	Early Breech-Loading Gun and Rifle Production 1857-79	199
4c	Breech-Loading Gun and Rifle Production 1880-2000	200
5	Analysis of Gun Demand 1816-2000	201
6	Purdey Gunmakers	203
7	Trade Labels	209
8	James Purdey & Sons Patents	218
9	Tom Purdey's Notebook 1921	231
10	Purdey Masters of the Worshipful Company of Gunmakers	240
	Select bibliography and sources	241
	Index	242

ACKNOWLEDGEMENTS

I would like to thank all the staff of James Purdey & Sons, in particular, Richard Purdey, Nigel Beaumont, Tony Sinnett, Robin Nathan and Peter Blaine for their full co-operation in researching and producing this book. They encouraged open access to all the Purdey archives and materials and were most helpful in answering all queries and offering much pertinent advice.

Special thanks must be given to Tricia Bruce for undertaking much of the research, suggesting improvements to the manuscript and for her constant enthusiasm for the project.

Several gunmakers and writers also gave me assistance and offered help. David Baker, David Trevallion, David Dryhurst of W W Greener Ltd. and Mike Clarkson in particular gave a great deal of technical and historical advice. Lawrence Salter, retired managing-director of Purdey's advised me on various issues and Ken Hunt, the engraver, discussed engraving styles with me.

Harry Lawrence's two daughters, Pamela and Audrey Lawrence, were of great help in providing details about their family involvement with Purdey's and for producing the Lawrence family tree.

I would like to thank Marion Murray for her many hours of work in typing and preparing the manuscript.

Several private collectors offered guns from their collections and thanks must go to them for their co-operation and effort. For reasons of confidentiality and security, they requested not to be identified with their collections. Specific thanks must be given to the following as here:

The Royal Museum of Scotland	Pages 9, 36; and Plates 3, 4, 5.
Boss & Co.	Pages 16, 120.
David Trevallion	Pages 15, 62.
Geoffrey Boothroyd	Plate 16.
Robert Balfour	
John Ormiston	
George Yannaghas	
Brian Hyde	
J P Hall	

PHOTOGRAPHIC ACKNOWLEDGEMENTS

Chris Austyn of the Sporting Gun Department at Christies deserves special thanks for allowing me full access to Christies' photographs. In addition Roger Lake of Butterfield & Butterfield did likewise. Adrian Weller of the Sporting Gun department at Sothebys kindly allowed use of Sothebys' photographs. Peter L Hughes of Photo View produced superb photographs of several guns and did the bulk of the photography for the book. He deserves great credit for his skill and artistry in creating these photographs.

Christies' Images: Plates 1, 15, 23, 26, 29, 30, 31, 34, 35, 37, 40, 42, 45, 48, 51, 55, 60, 63, 74, 75, 79, 80, 81, 82, 83, 84, 87, 88, 89, 90, 92, 93, 94, 95, 96.

Sothebys: Page 109; Plates 32, 56.

Butterfield & Butterfield: Plates 12, 13, 18, 49, 50, 85, 86.

Peter Hughes: Pages 11, 22, 37, 38, 44, 45, 46, 47, 56, 57, 75, 90, 91, 92, 94, 105, 128, 152, 153, 161, 162, 163, 164.
Plates 6, 7, 9, 10, 14, 19, 20, 28, 33, 36, 38, 39, 41, 43, 52, 58, 67, 68, 69, 70, 72, 73, 97, 98, 101, 108, 109. Front and back cover and frontispiece.

PREFACE

James Purdey & Sons are the most famous gunmakers in the world. The name 'Purdey' is a by-word for quality and excellence of workmanship, a quality and excellence that has stood the test of time since the establishment of the firm in 1816.

Not only are Purdey's renowned for quality, they are also highly regarded for their contribution to gunmaking. The Purdey bolt of 1863 is the standard closing action used on countless guns and rifles throughout the world.

Probably more articles have been written on Purdey's than on any other gunmaker, published in all languages and in all countries in the world. Yet the Purdey archives still had much to yield. Purdey's are fortunate in that they possess a vast archive dating back to their beginnings. This is in part due to the firm making only two moves in its entire history, the last move taking place in 1882-3.

In my researches I uncovered a fascinating array of material never previously published, the special relationship between W C Scott and Purdey's that created the combination of the Purdey bolt and top lever, the Purdey engravers who introduced the traditional rose and scroll engraving, the makers of the second quality guns at the end of the 19th century, the Wem ejector, the 'move' to 287-289 Oxford Street, etc.

It was my privilege to be asked by James Purdey & Sons to write a definitive history of their firm. Being an historian, such a vast archive source gave me great satisfaction; to examine metal boxes and letters unopened for scores of years, to search the cellars of Audley House and to complete a giant historical jigsaw. My research has been considerable and hopefully will add to the aura of Purdey Gun and Rifle Makers.

Donald Dallas,
BSc (ECON) London.

Blacksmith in the Minories – James Purdey 1739-96

James Purdey the Elder 1784-1863

James Purdey the Younger 1828-1909

Athol Purdey 1858-1939

James Purdey IV 1891-1963

Tom Purdey 1897-1957

Richard Purdey 1942

Chapter one

BLACKSMITH IN THE MINORIES

'Heredity counts for something, and if the first gunmaking Purdey was a workman of consummate skill, his descendant has consummate skill in the selection of workmen… Men do not go to Purdey because they want to economise; they go to him and pay his best price with the utmost cheerfulness, because they are well aware that by doing so, they will have done for them all that the art of smooth bore making can do.'

The above quote is taken from an article on Purdey's published in the magazine *Land and Water* in the 1880s, an article that noted 'heredity counts for something'. From blacksmith to best gun is the heredity of James Purdey & Sons, a heredity that stretches back over 250 years to metamorphose the rough iron work of the blacksmith into the fine workmanship of the gunmaker.

The Purdey family has its origins in Scotland. The name Purdey, variously spelled over the centuries, Purdie, Purdy, Purde, Prade, Proude is not an uncommon name in the southern half of Scotland. No satisfactory explanation has ever been offered as to the derivation of the name. One such Purdey, a John Purdey, was born most probably in south Scotland around the year 1700. For unknown reasons, this John Purdey decided in the early part of the 18th century to travel to London. In this period, a journey such as this would not be undertaken lightly due to the distance involved, the difficulties of transport and the danger of travelling. As with many before and after him, it is probable that the lure of the capital beckoned in the form of regular employment as opposed to the harsh reality of agrarian life in pre-Industrial Revolution Britain. Perhaps he was attempting to escape the political uncertainties of the time regarding the early 18th century Jacobite uprisings in Scotland against the reigning British monarchs. It is also possible that any existing relatives in London would beckon him and provide him with support in his transient phase. All this is conjecture. But we do know that John Purdey moved from Scotland to the Whitechapel area of London in the early decades of the 18th century.

John Purdey married and had three sons; the first, George, born in 1735 and the third, Robert, born in 1740, in Colchester Street, Whitechapel. His second son, named James Purdey, is the son of interest, for he would become a blacksmith in the Minories and would begin the Purdey gunmaking connection that still exists, in direct line, to this day. Early details about this James Purdey are sparse. He was born on 27 November 1739 to parents John and Anne. Where is difficult to locate, although most probably in the Whitechapel area.

This James Purdey became a blacksmith in the Minories. A blacksmith is a general term for a craftsman who worked in 'black' or iron metal. The term 'gunmaker' was not used a great deal in the early 18th century and the trade 'blacksmith' was often a generic classification that encompassed gunmakers, rather like 'wright' was a very general term for a builder.

The Minories was a street just to the north of the Tower of London that housed a large number of gunmakers and gun-related tradesmen. An abbey of nuns of the order of St. Clare, called the Minories, gave the street its name. John Stow, writing in the 1720s related, 'in place of this House, is now built divers, fair and large storehouses for armour and habiliments of war with divers workhouses serving to the same purpose'. In James Purdey's time the Minories was almost entirely taken over as a gunmaking and trades related area. Even as late as 1891, a commentator, Wheatley, wrote that it was 'a place of general trade with a gunsmith from end to end'.

There were named gunmakers in the Minories in the 18th century such as Brander and Potts, John Bumford and William Henshaw. However, it was the 'blacksmiths' who conducted the bulk of the Minories gun-related work. These blacksmiths would be involved in barrel-making, using their lathes, forges and hammers. They would produce rough castings for trigger guards, tangs and butt plates and they would finish many items for both military and private gunmakers. James Purdey the blacksmith would therefore become very conversant with all aspects of gun manufacture; hence it is not surprising that his lifestyle would have a major influence on future happenings.

Most probably in the 1770s, the blacksmith married a woman called Ann and they went on to raise the normal large family of the period. However, as befitted the trials and tribulations of the 18th century, few survived to adulthood. Their first son, James, born at All Hallows, Barking, near the

Blacksmith in the Minories – James Purdey, born 27 November 1739, died Lambeth Street, Whitechapel aged 56, buried 10 January 1796 St. Mary's, Whitechapel. The silhouette bears the inscription in the black label below, 'J Purdey, Gunsmith, 1780'.

Tower of London, in 1772, died a year later. In the year 1774 the Purdey family moved to Worley's Court, the Minories, and later in 1776 a second son, William, was born. This son died, at the age of four, from 'convulsions'. The Purdey family moved again to Lambeth Street in Whitechapel and in 1778 Ann was born, followed in 1782 by Maria. Both Ann and Maria fell victim to one of the great scourges of the 18th century, smallpox, Ann succumbing in 1781 and Maria in 1783. Before Edward Jenners's vaccinations gave protection in the early 19th century, smallpox, an acute and highly-infectious disease, occurred in great epidemics. A further daughter, Susannah, born in 1786, died just a few months later. Such high mortality was the norm in an era of inadequate diet, housing and medical knowledge. Of the seven children born to James and Ann Purdey, only two survived – two that were responsible for the establishment of the gunmaking firm, James Purdey.

The blacksmith's second daughter Martha was born on 30 September 1774 at Worley's Court, Minories and baptised on 30 October at St. Botolph's without Aldgate. She survived infancy and went on to live to the advanced age of 79, dying in 1853. Martha's importance to the history of the firm is that she married a local gunmaker, Thomas Keck Hutchinson.

Thomas Keck Hutchinson was born about 1771 and around the age of fourteen, on 1 April 1785, began his gunmaking apprenticeship with the relatively unknown London gunmaker, Stephen Sandwell. This was the typical age at which to begin an apprenticeship that normally lasted seven years – this period considered necessary to become competent in all aspects of the trade. Either due to Sandwell's death or retirement, or perhaps through disharmony, Hutchinson's indenture was transferred to another unknown gunmaker, Matthew Limberry, to complete. Shortly after he completed his apprenticeship in mid-1792, Hutchinson set up business on his own. The following year, on the 30 June 1793, at St. Mary's Whitechapel, he married eighteen-year-old Martha Purdey

It was this direct family connection to gunmaking, combined with the existing tentative blacksmith connection, that helped her brother, the future James Purdey and founder of the firm, to embark on his gunmaking career.

The second of the seven children to survive to James and Ann Purdey was their sixth child, whom they named James. This is the James Purdey in Purdey's history – either James Purdey the Founder or James Purdey the Elder – the James Purdey who would found the gunmaking dynasty. James was born on 21 August 1784 in Lambeth Street, Whitechapel, and

A page from a notebook of James Purdey the Blacksmith recording the birth of his son James Purdey the Founder on 21 August 1784.

christened in St. Mary's, Whitechapel, on 19 September 1784. It is interesting to note the continuation of the family name James. His father called his first-born son, born in 1772, James, after himself. Due to the death in infancy of his first-born son, he resolved to re-use the name James for his third-born son. This re-use of family names, in the event of death, was a common occurrence at the time and shows how pragmatic families were in their dealings with high child mortality. It is also interesting to note that James was born shortly after the smallpox epidemics that killed his sisters and interesting to speculate how gunmaking history might have been very different if fate had played a different hand.

Young James would have been brought up with a blacksmith-gunmaking background in the area around the Minories. He would absorb his father's work and become familiar with the techniques of metalwork and how they applied to the gun trade. In addition he probably had a close affinity to his only surviving sibling, his sister Martha, married to Thomas Keck Hutchinson, the gunmaker. James was eight years old when this marriage took place and no doubt their gunmaking business would greatly influence an impressionable young mind.

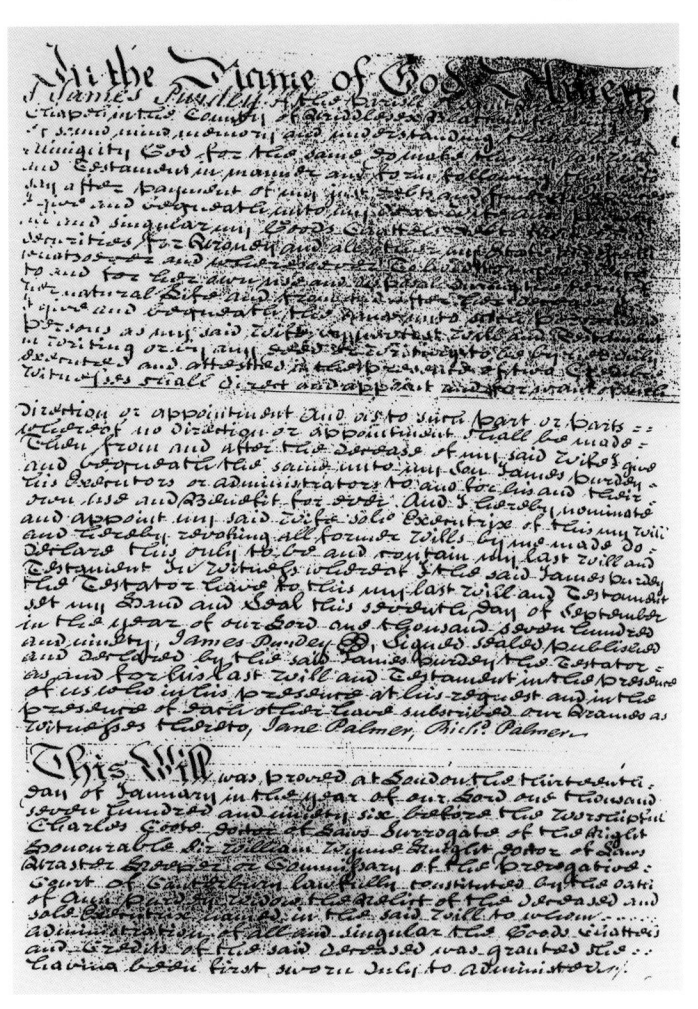

Young James's father had been quite advanced in years, at the age of forty-four, to sire a son. Unfortunately, he would not survive long and would die relatively young, leaving his young son fatherless. In January 1796 he became ill with what is described on his burial certificate as the 'fever', a term that could denote any of the virulent diseases of the time. He died in his house in Lambeth Street, Whitechapel, aged fifty-six and was buried on 10 January 1796 in the graveyard of St. Mary's, Whitechapel. Although leaving a will was relatively uncommon for a tradesman in this period, it is fortunate that James Purdey made such a will, proved at London on 13 January 1796, in which he left everything to his wife with the proviso that if she died everything would go to his young son James.

The will of James Purdey, blacksmith, 1739-96 proved 13 January 1796.

> In the Name of God Amen, I James Purdey of the Parish of St. Mary's, Whitechapel in the County of Middlesex, Blacksmith, being of sound mind, memory and understanding, thanks be to Almighty God for the same, so make this my last Will and Testament in manner and form following that is to say after payment of my just debts and funeral expenses I give and bequeath unto my dear wife Ann Purdey all and singular, my goods, chattels, credits,   and securities for her own and all other my estate and effects whatsoever and whosoever to give to my said wife to and for her own use and disposal during the passing of her natural life and I dispose, give and bequeath that   and persons as my said wife my first, last Will and Testament in writing for by any   and attested in the presence of two credible witnesses shall direct and appoint and for want of such direction or appointment and as to such part or parts which have no direction or appointment shall be made in from and after the decease of my said wife and bequeath the same unto my son James Purdey his Executors or Administrators to for his and their own use and benefit for ever. And I hereby nominate and appoint my said wife sole Executrix of this my Will and hereby revoking all former Wills by me made so declare this only to be remain my last Will and Testament set my hand and seal the Seventh Day of September in the year of our Lord One Thousand Seven Hundred and Ninety. James Purdey, signed, sealed, published and declared by the said James Purdey the testator as and for his last Will and Testament in the presence of us who in his presence at his request and in the presence of each other have to subscribe our hands as witnesses thereto Jane Palmer, Richard Palmer.
>
> This Will was proved at London on the Thirteenth Day of January in the year of our Lord One Thousand Seven Hundred and Ninety Six before the Worshipful Court Surrogated of the Knight Honourable Sir William Wynne, Knight of Laws Keeper of Commissary of the Prerogative Court of Canterbury lawfully constituted by the oath of Ann Purdey widow, the wife of the deceased and sole Executrix named in the said Will to whom administration of all and singular the goods, chattels and credits of the said deceased was granted she having been first sworn duly to administer.'

N.B. Blanks are illegible parts of the will.

Young James Purdey was only eleven and still at school when his father died. The prior deaths of all his brothers and sisters, and the fact that his elder sister had already married and moved away, left only James and his mother in the house in Lambeth Street. The decline in income of the Purdey family must have been traumatic and it became imperative to find young James immediate employment as soon as he reached the apprenticeship age of fourteen.

JAMES PURDEY, APPRENTICE AND JOURNEYMAN

It seemed obvious that James would go into gunmaking, bearing in mind the two direct influences on his life: his father's blacksmithing activities and his brother-in-law's gunmaking business. Family kinship prevailed and notwithstanding the fact that his sister, Martha, and brother-in-law, Thomas, had existing children, James was taken on as an apprentice in the family firm. The 'Register of Apprentice Bindings 1745-1902' in the Records of the Worshipful Company of Gunmakers held in the Guildhall Library, London, state:

> James Purdey, son of James Purdey, late of The Parish of St. Mary's, Whitechapel in the County of Middlesex deceased, puts to Thomas Keck Hutchinson Citizen and Gunmaker of London for seven years by Indentures dated this day (21 August 1798).

Due to the fact that apprentices lived with their master during their period of apprenticeship, James would go to the house of his sister and brother-in-law. During this period, the Hutchinsons and Purdeys lived in the Parish of St. Botolph, Bishopsgate, very close to James's family house in St. Mary's, Whitechapel. After a short move to Whitechapel *circa* 1801-02, the Hutchinsons and Purdeys moved south of the river Thames to Southwark *circa* 1803. Usually in an apprenticeship 'Consideration money' was stipulated. An apprentice had to agree to a certain sum of money to be paid to his master, a type of fee 'in consideration' for the tutelage and lodgings. However, in Purdey's apprenticeship, family connections negated this.

Hutchinson's gunmaking business was conducted in the early years of the 19th century at 232 Borough High Street, Southwark, and it would be here that James Purdey was taught all aspects of gun manufacture. Conditions regarding an apprenticeship indenture were strict – such as not being able to marry – but the most important part of the contract was that the master would feed, clothe and teach the apprentice in return for the apprentice's work. Apprentices were paid no wages at all. James Purdey completed his apprenticeship in August 1805, the year of the Battle of Trafalgar, aged 21, and was now a journeyman gunmaker in his own right. Journeyman denoted that an apprenticeship was complete and the young man qualified in his trade.

Shortly after he completed his apprenticeship James Purdey married. Unfortunately, despite considerable research, it has not been possible at present to discover exactly whom he married. All that is known is that he married 'Mary', surname unknown, in the year 1806. He most probably married her in one of the myriad of parishes close to his own in Whitechapel. It is also known that Mary was born on 21 July 1790. This fact is given in the Purdey family Bible. Mary was a mere sixteen years of age when they married and James, twenty-one or twenty-two. People then tended to get married earlier than today due to lower life expectancy and the desire to raise a family at an early age as a form of 'old-age insurance'. Soon after they were married, James Purdey returned, not only to Whitechapel, but directly to his old street, Lambeth Street. It is highly probable that the newly-weds went to live with James's widowed mother in his original house. Very soon after they were married, their first child was born in Lambeth Street in May 1807. They named her Mary in time-honoured tradition of the first-born having the same Christian name as the parent.

Having completed his apprenticeship, Purdey intended to secure work in another gunmaking firm. Hutchinson's business was small, he had a large family to feed and by the time James Purdey had completed his indenture, he had already taken on another apprentice. Purdey couldn't remain and in any case he had set his sights on a far higher plane.

James Purdey went straight to the top of his trade and in 1805 joined the king of the London gunmakers, Joseph Manton. Joseph Manton was born in April 1766 at Grantham in Lincolnshire. He was first apprenticed to a Grantham gunsmith, Newton, and then to his elder brother, John Manton, in business at 6 Dover Street, London. By 1789 he had established his own business at Davies Street, Berkeley Square, London, where Purdey would travel every day to work, primarily as a stocker, for his new employer.

Manton has been quite rightly eulogised by most commentators and writers. He produced guns of the highest quality and established the form and style of the double-barrel sporting gun that to all intents and purposes is basically the same today. He perfected the flintlock to such an extent that he made this ignition system fire rapidly. He was also 'in the van' with the new percussion system, experimenting with early detonating systems. His 1816 pelletlock didn't succeed, yet his tubelock of 1818 was an immediate success, due to its certainty of ignition. It was primarily the consistent high quality of his guns, coupled with the quick ignition of his flintlocks, that was the guarantee of his success. Sportsmen essentially became better shots. Manton also had a patron in the shape of Colonel Peter Hawker, a redoubtable sportsman of his day, whose book *Instructions to Young Sportsmen* became a standard of its time. In this book he consistently refers to Manton in somewhat hagiographical terms, in a quite unusual relationship between patron and tradesman for the time: 'The only man whom any first-rate judge of work could consider as qualified for a leader or king among the gunmakers.' James Purdey himself would later comment on Manton in the oft-repeated quote, 'but for him we should all have been a parcel of blacksmiths'. This quote is no doubt in direct reference to the early days of his father, the blacksmith in the Minories. Joseph Manton, with such a business, was fortunate in being able to choose top-rate journeymen, and he must have had a high opinion of Purdey to select him at the age of 21.

Working with Manton had a terrific influence on Purdey's future career. He would be involved in a top-class gunmaking establishment and would absorb the ethos surrounding it. The consistent high quality of Manton's guns would serve as a yardstick. He would make a great many contacts in the business – such as barrel-makers and lock-makers – that would enable discerning choices to be made in the future. And he would work alongside other journeymen with exacting standards that could only further his skills.

Perhaps the most famous journeyman Purdey worked alongside was Thomas Boss, born in 1790, who almost mirrors Purdey's early career. Boss was apprenticed to his father, William, in 1804. At this time his father was working, until his death in 1809, for Joseph Manton. It is interesting to note that many books repeat the assertion that Manton would take no apprentices, yet it is positively established that Thomas Boss was an apprentice at Joseph Manton's between 1804 and 1812, as was his elder brother, William, between 1801 and 1808. On completion of his apprenticeship in 1812, Boss continued to work for Manton until 1816. This is when he left to set up his own business that went on to achieve the highest standards of gunmaking and innovation and still exists today as Boss & Co. now also at 16 Mount Street, London. Consequently, Thomas Boss and James Purdey would have been colleagues and it is no surprise that when Purdey set up on his own in 1816, he contracted a large amount of his work out to Thomas Boss.

Manton's was a large concern. At the time of Purdey's stay there, they were producing around 250 weapons per year, a considerable output compared to other businesses of the period. Purdey would become familiar with a business on this scale and would also gain a great knowledge of its customers, many of whom transferred their allegiance to Purdey after Manton was forced into bankruptcy in 1826. Manton made various vain attempts at setting up businesses again before he died in 1835.

THE ADVENT OF THE PERCUSSION SYSTEM

It was while Purdey was working for Joseph Manton that a major metamorphosis was to occur in gun development – the introduction of the percussion system of ignition. The flintlock, having been around for over two centuries, was a relatively crude form of ignition and had reached the zenith of its development in the hands of makers like Manton and Nock by the early 19th century. Its main drawbacks were that it was unreliable in ignition and slow to re-load. Even with the advent of the waterproof pan, moisture could still permeate the pan on damp, rainy days to hinder ignition. The flash in the pan as the priming powder burned could cause wary birds to jink, the flintlock was time-consuming and tricky to load and finally the mechanism required a certain expertise in adjusting and trimming the flint to maintain its efficiency.

The percussion system that came into general use in the 1820s – the basic system that is still used today – solved most of the flintlock's defects. In a percussion system, a hammer hits a detonating compound of fulminates that instantaneously explode to ignite the main charge in the gun. Fulminates had been known for centuries, culminating in various experiments in the 18th century to use them in

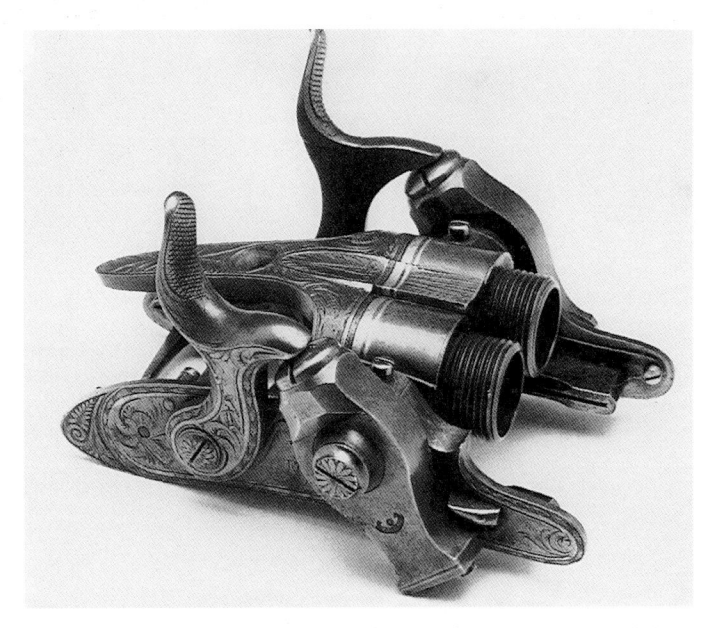

A pair of Forsyth locks and breeches showing the magazines containing the fulminate powder. These locks were constructed around 1813, most likely for the conversion of a flintlock gun. Due to the fact that James Purdey was a lock filer at Forsyth's, it is highly probable that he worked on them.

firearms. The Reverend Alexander Forsyth, Minister of the Parish of Belhelvie, near Aberdeen, had conducted experiments over a number of years to use fulminates in a percussion system of ignition. In 1807 he patented a lock mechanism in which fulminates of mercury, silver and gold could be used to detonate charges in guns. In the Forsyth percussion lock, a small magazine on the outside of the lock held a quantity of fulminating powder. When this magazine was rotated it would deposit a small amount of fulminate powder into a channel connected to the breech of the gun. Upon firing, the hammer would hit a striker in the channel causing detonation of the fulminating powder that in turn would ignite the main charge in the breech. Hence the term 'percussion system'. The advantages were great over the flintlock system because ignition was instantaneous, enclosed, impervious to water and certain.

Forsyth realised the importance of his invention and in June 1808 set up the Forsyth Patent Gun Company at 10 Piccadilly, London. Forsyth locks were very tricky to build and required a high degree of workmanship. They had to be exceptionally well made to work properly and be safe. It had to be ensured that the contents of the magazine would not come into contact with the primary charge when percussion took place.

Three years after he had joined Manton's, in 1808, Purdey left to join the new firm of 'Forsyth' as a stocker and lock filer. One can only guess as to why he left Joseph Manton – a new challenge, an interest in the new percussion system, a smaller firm with better advancement possibilities? Whatever the reason, Forsyth was obviously impressed with Purdey's prowess and before long made him foreman of the firm.

On 31 December 1812, Purdey was admitted to the Freedom of the Gunmakers' Company. *The Gunmakers Company Freedom Admissions 1749-1949* held in the Guildhall Library, London state:

James Purdey's scroll admitting him to the Freedom of the Gunmakers Company hangs in the Long Room. It states 'James Purdey, Son of James & late App. of Thos Keck Hutchinson was Admitted into the Freedom aforesaid and sworn in the Mayoralty of George Scholey Esq. Mayor and Richard Clark Esq. Chamberlain and is Entered in the Book signed with the letter E relating to the Purchasing of Freedoms and the Admissions of Freedom (to wit) The 12th day of January in the 53rd Year of the Reign of King GEORGE the Third and in the Year of our Lord 1813. In Witness whereof the Seal of the Office of Chamberlain of the said City is hereunto affixed Dated in the Chamber of the Guild – hall in the same City the day and Year abovesaid'

> James Purdey, apprentice to Thomas Keck Hutchinson, Citizen and Gunmaker of London for seven years by Indentures dated the Twenty First day of August, One Thousand Seven Hundred and Ninety Eight was admitted into the Freedom of the Company by the Master here present – 31st December, 1812.

Admission to the Gunmakers' Company was essential if a journeyman desired to set up his own business or take on an apprentice. In Purdey's case, his immediate concern was to indenture an apprentice. On 15 January 1813 he took on such an apprentice.

> William Williams the younger, son of William Williams Citizen and Cordwainer of London puts to James Purdey Citizen and Gunmaker of London for seven years by Indentures dated this day. Consideration – £60. The Master is a Gunmaker and lives at 15 New Grey Coat Place, Tothill Fields. Bound Out of Court by the Master.

Although the Consideration money appears high it must be remembered that this was a time of high inflation during the Napoleonic wars.

Purdey had in fact moved house and area before his admission to the Gunmakers' Company in 1812 and the taking on of his apprentice in 1813. Around 1808 he had left his old house in Lambeth Street, Whitechapel, and moved to a better residential area – a house at 15 New Grey Coat Place, Westminster. Grey Coat Place was roughly equidistant between the Houses of Parliament and Buckingham Palace and, more importantly for Purdey, much closer to his place of work at Forsyth's in Piccadilly. In the meantime Purdey's family was expanding and a second daughter, Eliza, was born in May 1811. Later on, this second daughter would further augment the Purdey gunmaking tradition by marrying the gunmaker Joseph Lang, in 1828. A third daughter, Elizabeth, was born in January 1814, the place of birth being recorded as 'Piccadilly'. It is highly possible that, due either to convenience or to the elevated position Purdey had with Forsyth, the Purdey family actually lived above Forsyth's shop at 10 Piccadilly.

Forsyth was under a great deal of business pressure at this time. His percussion system, so innovative and far ahead of its time, was greeted with scepticism by sportsmen and other gunmakers. To procure a more constant trade, Forsyth also made conventional flintlocks. In addition to these difficulties, he was also engaged in long and expensive law suits over this new system, such as with Joseph Manton, 1816-18, over Manton's pelletlock. To ease this financial pressure, Forsyth moved to smaller, less expensive premises at 8 Leicester Street, Leicester Square in September 1816. Here the business would continue until 1852.

Purdey had worked for Joseph Manton, the king of the gunmakers, from 1805 to 1808, then for Forsyth, the leading exponent of the percussion system since 1808. He had risen to the position of Forsyth's foreman. How circumstances had changed from Purdey the blacksmith in the Minories, to Purdey the foreman at Forsyth's!

Chapter two

A SMALL SHOP IN PRINCES STREET

The year 1816 was a watershed in the life of James Purdey. This was the year in which he decided to take the big step and set up his own business. Since completing his apprenticeship in August 1805 Purdey had worked as a journeyman gunmaker until 1816. He had worked in two first-class establishments – Manton's and Forsyth's – and had built up considerable experience in the running of such businesses. By the time of the Battle of Waterloo, in 1815, Purdey had decided to set up his own business. He also foresaw the business and legal difficulties facing Forsyth and realised that his future was not secure there.

Setting up a business in the immediate post-Napoleonic war period was not easy – *circa* 1815 to 1820 was a time of acute dislocation. Prices rapidly fell from their inflationary, unnatural high levels during the war period, de-stabilising businesses. The interim income tax introduced during the war was abolished in 1816, with a corresponding increase in indirect taxations. There was a general post-war slump with rioting among the lower classes, such as the Spa Field Riots in London in 1816. The gunmaker's shop of W A Beckwith was broken into during this riot, weapons were stolen and a customer shot. Shortly afterwards, other gunmaker's shops in the Minories were set upon and looted. Although the times were turbulent, the rich still remained rich and it was to these clients that Purdey would owe his business.

James Purdey looked around and eventually found suitable premises at 4 Princes Street, Leicester Square, parallel to Forsyth's future gunmaker's shop at Leicester Street. There are no drawings or descriptions of Purdey's first shop. The only description comes from Colonel Hawker who refers to it as 'a small shop in Princes Street'. The London County Council renamed Princes Street as Wardour Street in 1878, probably because there were at least ten Princes Streets in London in the 19th century. As such, the site of Purdey's first shop, although re-built, still exists today. The map illustrated dates from 1813 and helps to locate the present day site of the old shop. (Shaftesbury Avenue was not in existence when the map was produced in 1813.)

Richard Horwood's map of London 1792-99, updated by Richard Faden in 1813, showing 4 Princes Street, Leicester Square. Princes Street was renamed Wardour Street in 1878.

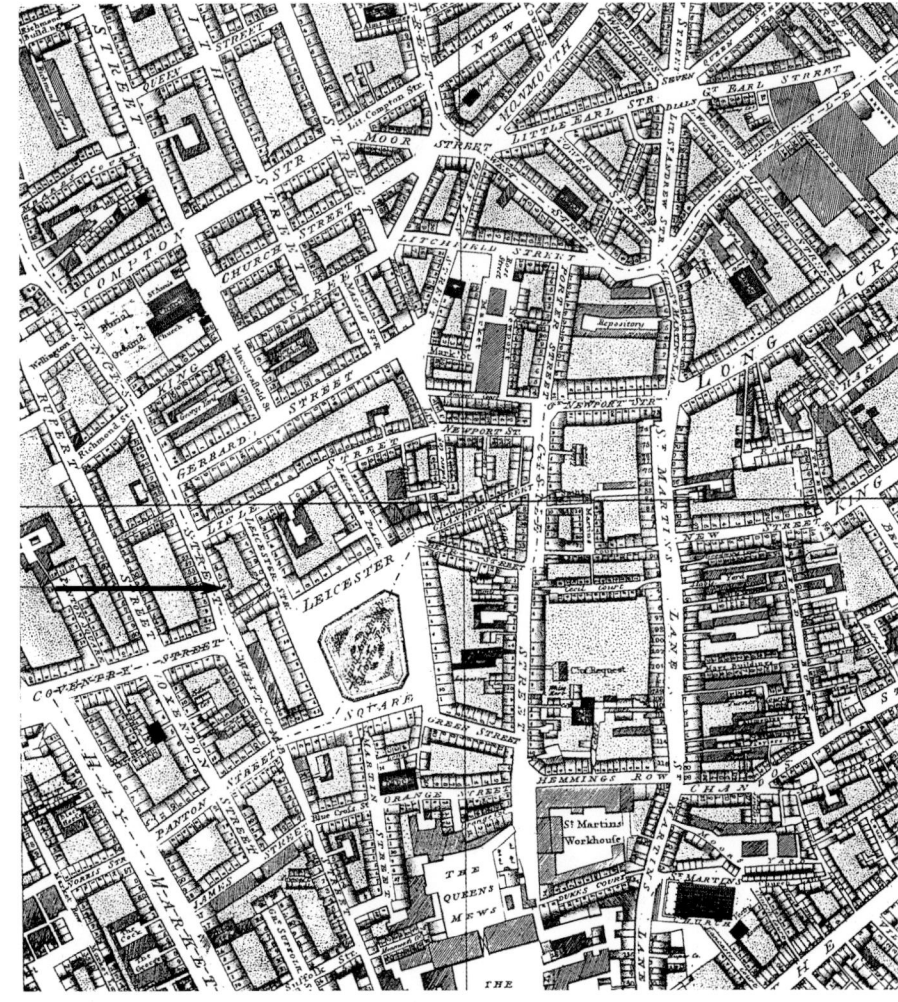

Purdey most probably moved into these premises in the spring of 1816. The ratebooks for 4 Princes Street are contained within the Leicester Fields West ward, St. Anne, Soho (*Land Tax Collectors Book*). It is recorded that Purdey had an assessed rent of £36 and paid a Land Tax of £3. 3s. This sum was assessed on 23 October 1816 and it was shown that Purdey had paid four instalments commencing Lady Day (25 March1816), so it must be assumed that he began his business close to this date.

It has always been assumed and quoted in many books that James Purdey set himself up in business in 1814. Although the ratebooks of the period are difficult to read and do not include street numbers, it is apparent from a study of the 1814 and 1815 ratebooks that 4 Princes Street was occupied by Samuel and Thomas Greatorex, not Purdey. Ratebooks are very accurate, so the establishment of James Purdey's 'small shop' most probably was in early 1816, not 1814. Purdey's themselves have always quoted 1814 as the date of the beginnings of their business. It is quite possible that James Purdey rented the shop from Greatorex in 1814 and did not pay rates, but this is not recorded and is merely speculation.

James Purdey, his wife, Mary, and their three daughters, Mary, Eliza and Elizabeth, set up home at the Princes Street address and lived alongside his gunmaking business. This is known because, when his fourth daughter, Jane, was born on 19 September 1819 the baptismal records of St. James's, Westminster, record her abode as 'Princes Street (between Piccadilly and Oxford Street)'. Out of interest, the Purdey's next door neighbour was the famous painter, Benjamin Robert Haydon (1786-1846), who painted grand historical and religious work and, closely linked with the Romantic movement in literature, painted portraits of Wordsworth and Keats – the former writing a sonnet to him.

One of the first things Purdey had to organise was the printing of a trade label for his cased guns. By 1800, most of the established makers had their own trade labels printed and pasted on to the baize in the lid of the case. Trade labels were important to gunmakers in this period due to the very limited use of advertising. When a case was opened the labels immediately proclaimed the maker where barrel and lock-engraving could not, and the finely engraved labels looked good in a cased outfit. There was an incredible variety of label designs in the early 19th century. Some were quite flamboyant with Royal Coats of Arms, patent drawings and sportsmen out shooting. Unusually, Purdey's Princes Street label was restrained and modest in appearance, merely stating:

J Purdey,
Gun Manufacturer,
4 Princes Street,
Leicester Square,
From J Mantons.

There is little comparison with his previous two employers, Manton and Forsyth, who both utilised very visual labels. Purdey's first label was very small, measuring just 3 inches by 1 1/2 inches. Why he adopted such a small simple label is open to speculation. The use of the last line 'From J Mantons' is interesting. It is simply an attempt to give added respect to his products. The majority of sportsmen would have revered

The first Purdey trade label, measuring only 3 inches by 1 1/2 inches. In use from 1816 to 1826.

Manton's firearms and to proclaim that he came from Manton's stable would give Purdey kudos. Such a practice was not uncommon. Thomas Boss's label in the early-mid 19th century stated, 'Many Years with the late Joseph Manton'. More recently in the late 19th century, the clock turned full cycle when the ex-Purdey employee, William Evans, consistently advertised himself as 'William Evans from Purdey'.

Setting up a gunmaking business was expensive. Rates had to be paid, workmen employed, barrelmakers, lockmakers and engravers paid and raw materials bought in. Coupled with the difficulty of enforcing 'gentlemen' to pay their bills, cash flow problems could unsettle a fledgling gunmaker. Purdey very sensibly attempted to found his business upon the established familiarity of the flintlock. It might be thought that after his long experience at Forsyth's, he would be in the forefront of percussion development. But he was aware of the conservatism of shooters and the expensive litigation that was occurring between Forsyth and Manton. His object was to sell guns, as many as possible, and in the second decade of the 19th century that meant flintlocks.

The establishment of Purdey's business coincided with the flintlock's swansong. Upon the rapid and universal adoption of the percussion system between 1820 and 1825 flintlock production diminished rapidly. The history of gun development shows how quickly major innovative changes occur. Although flintlocks had been the norm for over two centuries, this half decade – 1820 to 1825 – was the watershed for the changeover to percussion. The same thing occurred between 1860 and 1865 when breech-loaders took over from muzzle-loaders. Anachronisms always occur, however, due to the eccentricities of life. Purdey's last recorded flintlock shotgun No. 3205 was sold on 3 September 1838.

As well as founding his business on the flintlock, Purdey intended right from the start to build guns of the highest quality only – a precedent that has stood the test of time for two centuries and has made the name Purdey a by-word throughout the world for excellence of workmanship. What is remarkable is how quickly Purdey's gunmaking business became established. From small beginnings in 1816, producing around 12 guns a year, his production rate rose to around 180 guns a year a decade later. In the 1833 edition of *Instructions to Young Sportsmen*, Hawker gives us the famous comment, 'I once asked Joe Manton who he considered to be the best maker in town (of course excepting himself); and his answer was "Purdey gets up the best work, next to mine." This was when Purdey occupied a small shop in Princes Street.' It is no coincidence that Purdey produced such high quality work from the start, having worked with the first-class establishments of Manton and Forsyth. He himself was competent at such work and was astute enough to realise that quality sells.

In the first two or three years of the establishment of the business Purdey's production was flintlock only. Purdey probably produced around 300-400 flintlock guns. Only one flintlock rifle is listed in the records – No. 1186, built in 1827, whereabouts unknown today. The earliest Purdey flint gun known is No. 14, a single-barrel 12-bore sporting gun built in 1816-17 and now part of the National Museums of Scotland collection. This gun is described and illustrated in detail in Chapter 4. Of all the flintlock sporting guns made, only ten are known to have survived; hence Purdey flintlock sporting guns are very rare. With the advent of percussion in the 1820s, the flintlock rapidly went out of production, yet some were still being produced for the diehards even into the 1830s. A great many of these obsolete flintlocks were simply discarded while others were converted to percussion. This explains their rarity today.

Even though Purdey produced a very limited number of flintlocks, the design is very distinctive. Sea monsters were often engraved on the lock plates, cocks and trigger guards. The name 'Purdey' and sometimes the address '4 Princes Street, Leicester Square' was inlaid in gold in Gothic script on the barrel.

The barrel address of No. 14 of 1816-17:
'Princes Str t
Purdey
Leicester Squ re'

Single-barrel 12-bore flintlock shotgun No. 14, built 1816-17, the earliest known surviving Purdey gun.

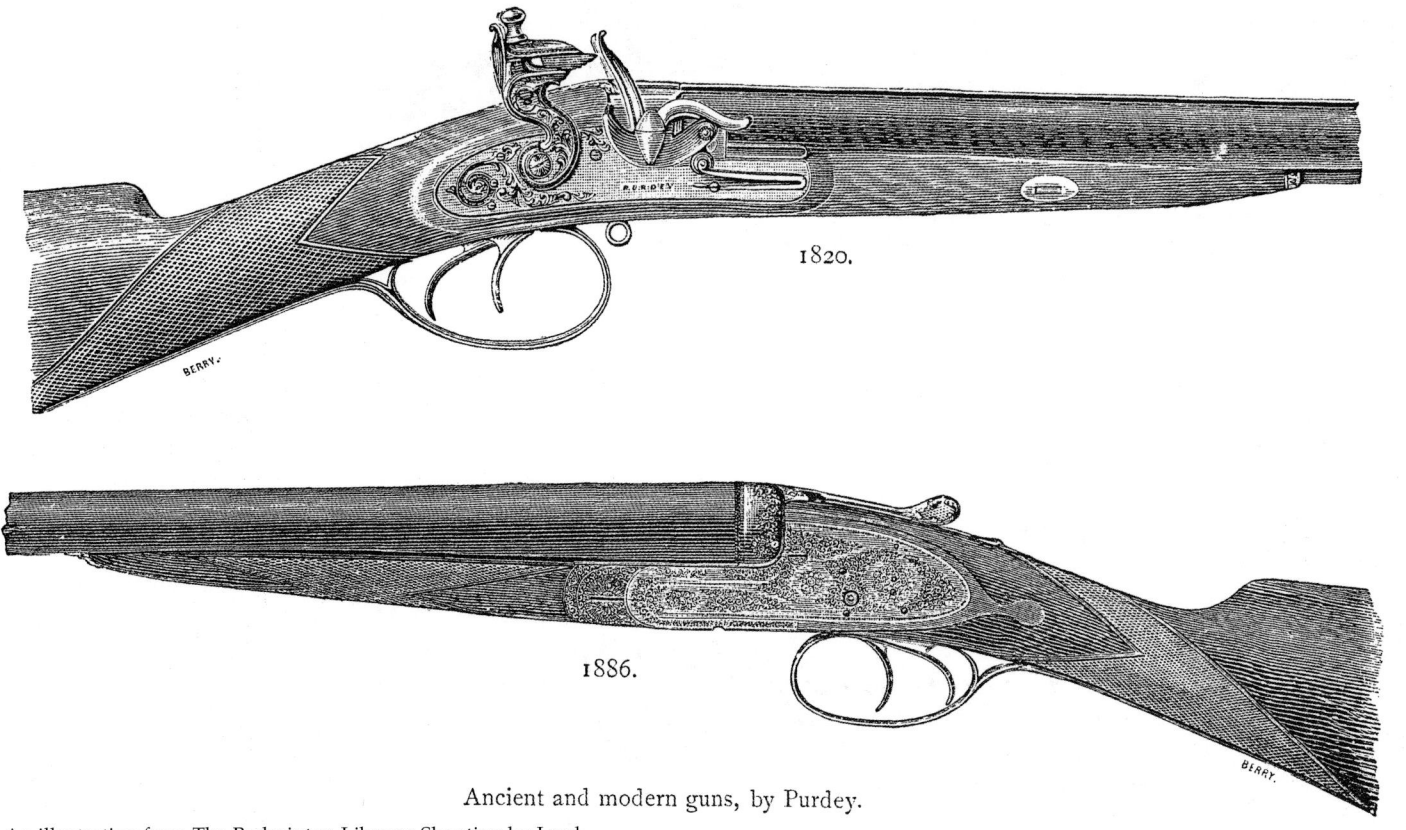

1820.

1886.

Ancient and modern guns, by Purdey.

An illustration from The Badminton Library: Shooting by Lord Walsingham and Sir Ralph Payne-Gallwey, 1900, comparing a Purdey flint gun c1820 with a hammerless gun c1886.

Other factors that gave a distinctive Purdey look to his flint guns were his improvements to the actual flintlock mechanism. Purdey made no fundamental changes – he merely refined the design to ensure rapid, certain ignition. He altered the flashpan slightly by angling the pan downwards towards the cock. When the frizzen flew back upon being struck by the flint, the priming powder in the pan was more directly in line with the shower of sparks. Due to the forward angle of the frizzen, while sitting upon the pan, a longer and higher limb on the frizzen was required. As was common in the last vestiges of flint development, 'throat hole' cocks were used, often embodying a lip on the lower jaw to give greater protection to the cock when it struck the flash guard.

A flintlock from shotgun No.200 *circa* 1820, showing sea serpent engraving, angled flashpan and long limbed frizzen.

PURDEY'S PATENT SAFEGUARD 1818

With the flintlock at the acme of perfection in the early 19th century, various makers attempted to improve upon it. One such improvement, much in vogue at the time, was a safety device to prevent accidental discharge. Some of these devices were sops, others more serious. They became such a fashion that most good makers were obliged to design and fit them to match the contemporary mood. In the 1790s and later, Joseph Manton used a safety guard that consisted of a pivoted lever over the tang of the trigger guard to bolt the trigger. When the lever was depressed, as the sportsman gripped the gun to fire, the locking mechanism disengaged to free the triggers. It wasn't a real safety device in that the locks were not bolted, only the triggers. Later Manton patented another device, patent no. 3558 of 30 April 1812. This was Manton's 'gravitating stop', an external rotating weight that fell into position by gravity and locked the cocks at full cock when the gun was placed vertically for loading. It wasn't a real safety device either, merely a means of preventing discharge if a foolhardy shooter attempted to load his gun with the locks at full cock. Unfortunately, it did the same thing if a sportsman had his gun in a vertical position when attempting to take a high bird.

Having worked with Manton, Purdey would be only too aware of the safety guard and the commercial necessity to produce one to satisfy contemporary demand. Purdey's device was patented by Matthew Cotes Wyatt on 3 February 1818, patent no. 4218 entitled *Safeguard to Prevent Accidental Discharge of Firearms*. It is interesting to note that apart from Purdey's name shown on the lock illustration, there is no mention of Purdey in the specification. Why this should be so is open to speculation. Wyatt had no connection with the gun trade, being described as an 'artist' or 'gentleman'. He may have been a friend of Purdey, he may have done the drawings, or invented the mechanism itself. It is interesting to speculate that since Wyatt was an 'artist', Purdey may have come into contact with him through his neighbour, the painter Benjamin Robert Haydon.

Purdey's safety was an improvement over Manton's and was a combination of two types of safety. There was a trigger guard grip safety similar to Manton's that locked the trigger blade, but there were also external sears on the lock plates that locked the cocks at half-cock. When the gun was ready to fire, the cocks were drawn back to full cock. This released the external sears. Upon gripping the gun to fire, the safety lever was depressed, unbolting the triggers and pre-venting the external sears from re-engaging in the cocks. Purdey's guard was a real safety with the use of the external sears to lock the cocks. The locking of the trigger blades only, as used by most contemporary makers, failed to render a gun safe in the way Purdey's did. Purdey fitted this safety device throughout the 1820s to some of his guns, until the safety guard went out of fashion in the 1830s. The word 'Patent' is usually engraved on either the grip lever or lock plate.

In the November 1818 edition of *The Sporting Magazine*, an article was published entitled *Purdey's Patent Safeguard*. This extoled the virtues of Purdey's new safety lock and quoted from advertising material written by James Purdey. It begins:

> A Gentleman has called our especial attention to the invention of a new Patent Safeguard for preventing the accidental discharge of firearms. We are given to understand it has excited very great interest in the sporting world and that from those who have inspected it, has received unqualified approbation. The following is a copy of a hand bill circulated making known its uses and merits:
>
> Purdey's Patent Safeguard, to prevent the accidental discharge of guns – J Purdey, Gunmaker, No. 4, Princes Street, Leicester Square (from J Manton's) respectfully solicits the attention of the nobility, gentry and sportsmen, to his new invented Patent Safeguard, for preventing the recurrence of those lamentable

misfortunes that are unhappily almost daily recorded, in consequence of the accidental discharge of guns; trusting that its great simplicity, and perfect security, will upon inspection recommend it to their patronage...'

The article is considerably longer than this and goes on to describe the Safeguard in great detail. Although Purdey terms his device 'Patent Safeguard', he also used the description 'Safety Gun Lock' on his trade labels.

THE CHANGEOVER TO PERCUSSION

That Purdey's early business at 4 Princes Street prospered rapidly there is no doubt. Although the early records until about 1825 are very sparse, they do show how the business was flourishing. Around 50 firearms were produced in the year 1818, yet this rose to around 165 by the year 1825. Neal and Back's book, *The Mantons*, states that Joseph Manton was producing around 200 guns per year in the early 1820s and John Manton, although more variable, around the same. Considering that these two establishments were among the premier gunmakers of the time and long-established to boot, it does show the acclaim that Purdey's early products had. In comparison, Thomas Boss in his early business days in the 1830s produced around 30 to 40 guns per year.

Purdey's lack of experi-mentation with the early detonating system has been remarked on earlier, despite the fact that he worked for Forsyth for so long. However, whenever the percussion system had been adapted for general use in the early 1820s and all the initial snags and interim developments ironed out, Purdey constructed his guns upon the percussion principle with acclaim. Indeed from an early date James Purdey was championed by Colonel Hawker who, in his 1824 edition of *Instructions to Young Sportsmen*, states, 'Mr. Purdey, a rising gunmaker of extraordinary merit is acquitting himself most admirably in the detonating system as well as in neat and elegantly finished style of his work.'

Hawker's comment summarises Purdey's success in this period on two counts. Firstly he remarks on the quality of Purdey's work and secondly he praises Purdey's prowess with the new detonating or percussion system. This successful early use of the perfected percussion system helps to explain the continued expansion of Purdey's Princes Street business in the early 1820s.

Forsyth's detonating lock had been complicated to make and dangerous to operate. However, the principle was well established and other makers sought to improve upon it. Chief among the innovators was Joseph Manton who brought out his pelletlock patent no. 3985 of 29 February 1816. A 'pellet' of fulminates was placed inside a detachable striker on the hammer. It was a fussy system in that the detachable striker was made in two parts

The underside of double flintlock gun No. 86, built in 1818, showing the deep engraving of the safety lever.

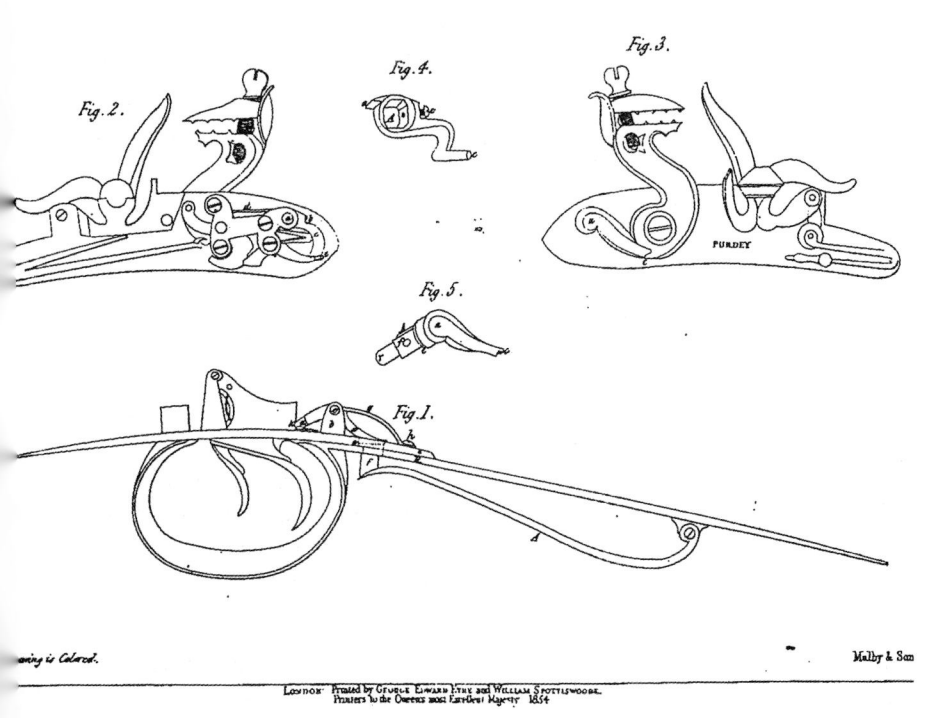

The patent drawing for Wyatt's Safeguard dated 3 February 1818 as used by Purdey on many of his early guns. Note the safety lever over the trigger guard and the external sear on the lock plate to secure the cock in the half-cock position.

and had to be detached from the hammer every time the gun was primed. It was Manton's first foray into the field of percussion, yet it was a failure, resulting in expensive and time-consuming litigation with Forsyth. Purdey had little to do with it, however, concentrating in that period on building flintlocks.

Manton's other percussion development, the tubelock, patent no. 4285 of 3 August 1818 was, on the other hand, a great success. A thin, copper tube filled with detonating compound was inserted into a vent in the breech. It was held in place by a spring clip. When the hammer struck the tube, the compound exploded and ignited the main charge. Because the tube had a relatively large amount of detonating compound contained within it, detonation was violent and ignition certain. Long after the copper cap came into use in the 1820s, many wildfowlers and live pigeon-shooters continued with it for that very reason. It was the cessation of mis-fires that gave the tubelock its immediate success. The principle drawback of the tubelock was that the tube was not completely enclosed – it could blow out upon detonation, injuring bystanders.

As with the pelletlock, Purdey had little to do with the tubelock. It is interesting to note that Neal and Back in *The Mantons* state that Joseph Manton's production for 1817-18 fell away by half from the preceding two years, as he experimented with the early percussion systems. An average of 400 guns per annum were produced in 1815 and 1816, yet this declined to an average of 200 guns a year in 1817 and 1818. Due to the fact that Purdey had just set himself up in business in 1816, it is no wonder that he concentrated on the proven flintlock in his fledgling years and left the early experimentation to others.

The tubelock was rapidly superseded around 1820 by the familiar copper cap. It has never been firmly established as to who invented the copper cap. Lewis Winant in his book *Early Percussion Firearms* could come to no satisfactory conclusion. It is highly probable, as is so often the case in the history of invention, that several gunmakers hit on roughly the same idea at the same time. A similar thing happened with the 'three pull' single-trigger system in the closing decades of the 19th century. A number of people, including Manton and Colonel Hawker, have claimed to be the originator of the copper cap, but with dubious authenticity. Purdey never claimed to be the inventor, yet Captain Lacy in his book *The Modern Shooter*, published in 1842, suggested he was.

> That Purdey was 'the great original' of this tidy little contrivance – this bit of 'thimble-rig' in the art of gunnery – I by no means intend to assert; but that he himself, ever since the copper cap appeared, has been of that opinion, I am most thoroughly persuaded. Having, for some years previous to that event, been the leading man in Forsyth's establishment, Purdey was early and well schooled in the detonating system; no man, therefore, more likely than he who had become so conversant with the defects of Forsyth's lock – to strike out a new plan on the percussion principle. Be that as it may, the following is entirely in substance, and nearly verbatim et literatim, what he related to me some eighteen and twenty years ago.

> 'I was,' said Purdey, 'sitting one evening with a friend named Prior, who had just returned from a very wet day's shooting; the detonating patches were then very much in vogue, and Prior complained that he 'found them too much exposed to be waterproof' and suggested the idea of "enclosing them in some substance impervious to the wet."
> "Yes," replied I, inverting an empty tumbler. 'A metallic cap in this form, with a perforated peg to communicate with the charge.' "The day following," continued Purdey, 'at the request of Prior, I set to work to realise this new idea, and, from the tag of an old umbrella, produced a brass cap, which was handed about for some time, and a year or two afterwards, Mr. Egg brought out the copper cap.'

> These surely give strong indications, on the part of Purdey, of a PRIOR-ity of claim. But, if Purdey was not the inventor of the copper cap, most certainly he was the first to bring it to the highest pitch of perfection.

There is no actual hard evidence for believing what Lacy writes. Perhaps his last sentence invalidates his claim, 'but if Purdey was not the inventor of the copper cap, most certainly he was the first to bring it to the highest pitch of perfection'. It must be remembered that just as Hawker had eulogised Manton, Lacy eulogised Purdey and wanted Purdey to be the inventor.

The inventor of the copper cap is not known, but what is certain is that once Purdey had seen the practical merit of the copper cap, he put a great deal of effort into producing such arms. The first known existing percussion Purdey gun is a double-barrel 14-bore shotgun, No. 349, produced in 1822, closely followed by a single-barrel 6-bore gun, No. 374, produced in the same year.

The main record of Purdey guns are the Dimension Books, used from the earliest times to the present day. Although the first Dimension Book begins officially at No. 273 of 1821 there is a small list of a variety of early serial numbers written on the inside of the front cover. The earliest, No. 206, is described as 'D', denoting a 'double gun.' Other contemporary serial

Single-barrel 6-bore percussion gun No. 374 *circa* 1822 – a very early Purdey percussion gun.

numbers in the list are described as 'D Flint ', so it is reasonable to assume that No. 206 is a percussion gun. If this is so, then No. 206 of 1820 is the earliest recorded Purdey percussion gun. Indeed No. 206 is the earliest serial number to feature in any of the Purdey records.

This early use of the copper cap percussion system and high-quality workmanship, resulted in a buoyant demand for Purdey guns. From producing around 100 guns in 1822, production went up to around 165 in 1824 and to around 180 in 1826.

In 1826, Purdey published a small booklet, *Observations on the Proper Management and Cleaning Detonating Guns*. It is obvious from the instructions given in his booklet, that percussion guns were in their infancy. 'Never put the cocks down on the copper caps when the gun is loaded'; 'Detonating locks should not be snapt either with or without copper caps, but in the act of shooting'; 'Detonating guns should be cleaned the same day they are used'; 'Clean those parts of the breech and locks that the detonating powder acts on with a wet rag'.

A page from a notebook written in James Purdey's hand, dating from the early 1820s, containing details of guns ordered. 'DD' represents 'Double Detonator'. Hardly any serial numbers or dates are recorded. Is this the 'lost small black book'?

The first and second pages of the small booklet published by James Purdey in 1826 entitled Observations on the Proper Management and Cleaning Detonating Guns.

PURDEY GUNMAKERS AND SUPPLIERS IN THE 1820S

Purdey have today in their archives a series of registers known as 'Dimension Books' which contain records dating back to 1821. They give the serial number of each weapon with a description of it, the gunmakers involved in its production and who it was built for. The first Dimension Book covers the period from near the beginning of production – gun No. 273 of 1821 to gun No. 9165 of 1874. At first glance the Dimension Book appears to contain a wealth of information about individual Purdey guns, yet it is tantalising in its paucity of real information. Firstly, the information given is virtually non-existent until the late 1820s, secondly no credible dates are given to assist with dating guns, thirdly gun details are sparse and finally, although all the gunmakers are listed for their respective work on each individual gun, only an initial is given for the gunmaker.

The other main records that Purdey possess are ledgers detailing Purdey's customers and their accounts. These ledgers began in the year 1818, yet again the early years contain little detail. When more detailed information appears later, it is apparent that the ledgers are basically sales ledgers giving the customer's name, gun and related items purchased and the date of sale. No technical information is given. Where the ledgers are useful is in confirming sale dates to assist the dating of Purdey guns. The first gun number to appear in the ledgers is No. 567 sold on 15 January 1824 'To a Dble. Gun with Mah. case to complete No. 567 £52. 10, Leather cover £2.2, 1000 caps £1. 15.' This gun was sold to Dr. H Vachell Esq., Stock Lodge, Ingatestone, Essex.

A 'small black book' filled in by James Purdey has assumed legendary status on account of the fact that it is 'lost'. James Purdey is supposed to have entered into the book all the details of the earliest Purdey guns from serial No. 1 in 1816. A 'small black book' has been found at Purdey's but it contains the barest details and dates for the 1820s. Virtually no serial numbers and dates are given.

The headings of the Dimension Book illustrated in the

A part page from the Dimension Book recording weapons from serial Nos. 1925-35. The shotguns were sold in 1830, and rifles 1931, 1932 and 1933 in 1831. The date '1830' has been written in a considerable time later.

Such 'dates' in the Dimension Books are often inaccurate. Note 'Gumbrell' written in full in the Engraving column for rifle No. 1932.

photograph are typical of late 1820s and 1830s entries. The headings are as follows:

- Description
- Length
- Bore
- Charge
- Barrels
- Locks jointed
- Stocked
- Screwed together
- Making off Checkering and Escutcheons
- Cocks fitted
- Detonated and finished
- Polishing
- Engraving
- Varnishing and Pegs
- Brown'g and Case

In the 'Description' column, 'D' refers to a double gun, 'S' to a single gun, 'R' to a single rifle, 'DR' to a double rifle, 'P' to a pistol. ('P' can often cause confusion, as it sometimes refers to a weapon with a Patent Safety. A check on the barrel length will help identification in this instance.) Later the word 'Pistol' was used to avoid confusion.

The London gunmakers of the 19th Century used some fairly quaint terminology. In 'Locks Jointed' and 'Stocked', the stocker would inlet the lock, barrel, trigger plate, etc. and roughly shape the stock. In 'Making off' the stock would be finely finished and shaped precisely. 'Detonating' was in reference to fitting the percussion hammers. A nipple was known as a 'Peg' and hence 'Pegs' meant making and fitting the nipples. The last column headed 'Brown'g & Case' refers to browning and case hardening.

It should be noted that the column headings in the Dimension Books varied over the decades. In giving column headings for reference throughout the book, discrepancies will occur on account of this.

It will be noted from the photograph that only the initial of the gunmaker appears. No wage books survive pre-1863, so it is difficult to ascertain who the gunmakers were. A further complication is that it is difficult to read many of the initials. Interestingly, the barrel column is never filled in. Purdey began producing his own barrels in the mid-1820s. Until then Purdey bought in barrels from specialist barrel manufacturers. The majority of barrels Purdey used at this time came from Charles Lancaster. Before he set himself up in business as a gunmaker in his own right, in 1826, at 151 New Bond Street, Charles Lancaster was a barrel-maker to the trade. During Purdey's Princes Street era, until around 1818, he had a workshop at 10 Craven Buildings, Drury Lane, before moving to Great Titchfield Street in the early 1820s. Lancaster barrels are easily identifiable, having 'CL' stamped underneath them. Occasionally Purdey used another barrel manufacturer, William Fullerd of 56/57 Compton Street, Clerkenwell. His barrels are again readily identifiable, bearing a 'WF' stamp. Many top makers of the period, such as the Mantons, used both these barrel-makers. Some barrels have no stamps and they were possibly removed when they were finished or struck up, or were barrels by other makers and not stamped.

If the barrel-makers are relatively easy to identify, the same cannot be said for the rest of the workmen. One who can be positively identified is Thomas Boss because 'Boss' is occasionally written in full. Boss was involved in 'stocking', 'screwing together' and 'making off'. Born in Blackfriars, London, in 1790, Thomas Boss had completed his apprenticeship by 1812 under his father William Boss at Joseph Manton's. He stayed on at Joseph Manton's until around 1816 and then commenced his own business at 3 Bridge Road, Lambeth. He combined the seemingly unconnected trades of a truss manufacturer and gunmaker. For the next ten years or so he worked for the trade as an outworker, concentrating upon the specialities mentioned above. Around 1827, he set himself up as a gunmaker in his own right at 33 Edgware Road.

The majority of work he did in the 1820s was for James Purdey, although he did work for other makers, such as Moore, Beckwith and Lancaster. When he set himself up as an independent gunmaker later on, he frequently stated that he had worked for Purdey. Boss's assertion led to the fallacy that he was solely employed by Purdey but we now know that he was an independent outworker. It was not unusual for Purdey to employ outworkers. Having set up his own business, it would be expensive to take on men on a regular basis. It was far easier to use an outworker on a demand-only basis, especially where Purdey personally knew someone such as Boss, with whom he had worked at Joseph Manton's.

Another stocker who can be identified is 'B', later written in full in the Dimension Book as 'Bagnl'. This is Robert Bagnall who had previously worked with Joseph Manton and whom Purdey would have known. Robert Bagnall went on to work for James Wilkinson in the early 1840s. 'R' in polishing and hardening most probably refers to Abbe Robins who began his career with Purdey around 1825, retiring in 1901, aged 92, after some 75 years service to Purdey's.

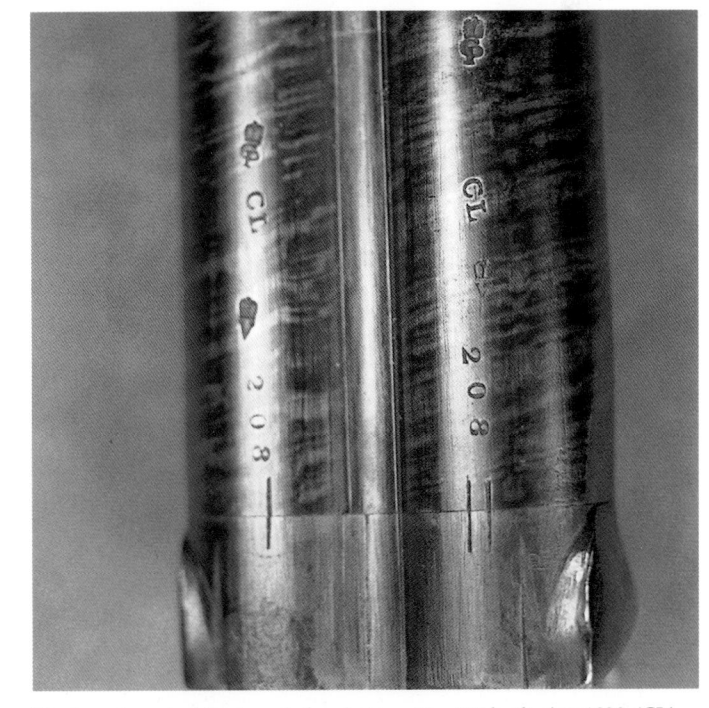

The breech end of the barrels for shotgun No. 208 built *circa* 1820. 'CL' stamp shows that the barrels were forged by Charles Lancaster.

The initial 'A' can be positively identified as Henry Atkin. There is no record of Henry Atkin's apprenticeship and indeed little is known of his early career. His initial is to be found in the Locks Jointed, Stocked, Screwed Together and Making Off columns. He remained with Purdey for a considerable length of time, beginning his career there. An 'Atkin', either himself or his son, was still being listed in Purdey's Stockers' Workbook in the late 1860s. His son, also known as Henry, served his apprenticeship with his father, worked for Purdey then left to go to Moore and Grey and subsequently set up his own business, at Oxendon Street in 1877.

There is no doubt that the initial 'G' represents Peter Gumbrell, the engraver of King Street, Golden Square. Like Boss, his name occasionally appears in full in the Dimension Book. He had previously worked for Joseph Manton and it is most probable that he was an independent outworker. It is possible that 'L' refers to Henry Lewis in the Locks Jointed column as later, in the 1850s and 1860s he was the head stocker.

Due to the lack of wage books from the period, it is impossible to ascertain reliably who the other workers were.

A page from the Ledger Book of Thomas Boss dated 1820 entitled 'Mr. Purdey to Thos. Boss'. It details various work on Purdey guns, such as 'screwing together', 'filing sets of furniture', 'making off' etc. Note the comment of 29 June 1820 at the bottom: 'Mr. Purdey put the escutcheons in himself, Fancy Ones'.

Chapter three

314 ½ OXFORD STREET

By the mid-1820s, Purdey had outgrown the 'small shop in Princes Street'. From 1816, his production rate had increased yearly from around 50 weapons a year in 1818, to around 85 in 1820 and around 165 in 1824. From this date his production stagnated, remaining at around 165 in 1825. Although it is possible that the change over to percussion had an effect on gun production, it is highly likely that the small Princes Street premises precluded any further real rise in output. Larger premises were required if the Purdey business was to achieve its full potential. Also, Princes Street, Leicester Square, was a minor street, not suited to attract the business that Purdey wanted.

Accordingly, Purdey began to seek out suitable premises to fulfil both necessities. He found them in 1826 in the shape of Joseph Manton's old shop at 315 Oxford Street. Manton had moved here in March 1820, retaining recently acquired premises nearby at 11 Hanover Square as his own house. At his Oxford Street premises, Manton produced around 200 guns per year. However, by late 1825, Manton's business was in trouble. He had accumulated big debts and even spent a period in a debtors' prison. On 24 January 1826, a Commission of Bankrupt was issued. On 31 January and 1 February the contents of Manton's house at Hanover Square were sold at auction. On 25 March the lease on his Oxford Street premises was terminated.

To Purdey, Manton's premises were ideal. They were far bigger than his Princes Street shop and could allow production to expand. As a previous gunmaker had been resident there, the accommodation and attendant organisation were ideal. In addition, customers of the type that Purdey's business was based upon were well used to visiting Manton's shop in Oxford Street, probably the most famous gunshop in London. And Oxford Street itself was an excellent location from which to conduct a first-class gunmaking business.

In the early to the mid-19th century, Oxford Street cut a very different image from today's. It was originally on the route of a Roman road which ran from Hampshire to the Suffolk coast. It was variously known as the 'King's Highway' in 1678, the 'Road to Oxford' in 1682 and the 'Acton Road' in 1691. 'Oxford Street' became its established name in the 18th century when the land to the north side of the street was acquired by Edward Harley, Second Earl of Oxford. Real development of the street began in the mid-18th century and by 1800 it stretched unbroken from St. Giles Circus to Park Lane. It became both a residential area and a centre for a multiplicity of small businesses such as fur manufacturers, hosiery and glove warehouses, tea dealers, millinery warehouses, trunk makers, etc. The buildings were Georgian in design, each of no more than four storeys. By the late 19th century, the character of the street had changed completely on account of the 'March of the Multiples' that give it its character today.

In 1826 Purdey found it a perfect location and he negotiated with Mr. Hulme, the freeholder, to acquire the lease. The deeds were dated 21 August 1826 and the lease ran from 29 September 1826 for 14 years at £260 per annum. Interestingly, on the original deeds, the actual number of Oxford Street has been left blank and filled in retrospectively. On the first deed '315' is written retrospectively and on a copy '314 ½' is written retrospectively. This shows that there was confusion right from the start over Purdey's occupancy. The rate books for Purdey's share of the Oxford Street premises show that, as a result of Manton's bankruptcy, the premises were empty in the first half of the year and that Purdey paid rates of £2.15s at Christmas 1826. Purdey's assessed rental was £120, the same as Joseph Manton's in 1825, so Purdey must have taken over exactly the same premises as Manton had. Accordingly, in late 1826 James Purdey moved his business to 315 Oxford Street, where it would remain until 1882. In 1828, the clock turned full cycle when Joseph Manton, pursued by creditors and in dire financial straits, rented a room from Purdey in his old premises. The Purdey family moved into living accommodation on the premises, a fact recorded on James Purdey the Younger's Birth Certificate of 19 March 1828 stating that his abode was 'Oxford Street'.

Unfortunately, there seem to be no photographs in existence of the Oxford Street shop. The only illustrations available are the architectural drawings of Oxford Street drawn by John Tallis around 1838. Although not specifically named, Purdey's premises encompassed two blocks, the block to the right of Henry Clarke, the seed merchant, that is numbered 315 and the block to the right of this, numbered

314. No. 314 was in fact the workshop where the guns were made and No. 315 the shop. These premises were large, enabling all aspects of gun manufacture to take place on site.

The general street view shows that the numbering system in Oxford Street at this time was haphazard, to say the least. Due to recent expansion and a primitive postal service, the street numbering was anything but official and appears to have been at the whims of the inhabitant. Even the rate books of 1825, 1826 and 1827 give a different number. They state that both Manton and Purdey paid rates on No. 313. Just after Purdey left his Oxford Street building in 1882, the premises were knocked down and re-developed. In the 1960s the re-developed No. 314 was again demolished and a new building erected. The site of Purdey's original shop can easily be located today on the south side of Oxford Street to the left of Harewood Place, numbered 287 and 289 Oxford Street.

A few months after he had moved into No. 315, Purdey changed his address to No. 314 $^1/_2$, the number that would remain throughout his stay in Oxford Street. This change is always put down to Purdey's superstitious determination not to allow the ghost of Joseph Manton's bankruptcy to haunt him– a good story but apocryphal. The real reasons are logical. As we have seen, the numbering system in Oxford Street in the early 19th century was chaotic. There were three separate No. 314 blocks and four separate No. 315 blocks. The creation of a 314 $^1/_2$ would give Purdey his very own address. In addition, the gunmaker Isaac Riviere was at one of the No. 315s. Obviously, two separate gunmakers, both with the same address would cause confusion. The only description that exists of the premises is one from an article in *Land and Water* of 6 July 1889 that states 'although fine weapons were sent out from this place, it was somewhat confined in space and rather dark and inconvenient'.

Below: The site of 314 $^1/_2$ Oxford Street today re-numbered 287/289. The building on the left is No. 315 (present day No. 287) that was re-developed in the 1880s after Purdey left and the building on the right, re-developed again in the 1960s, No. 314 (present day No. 289).

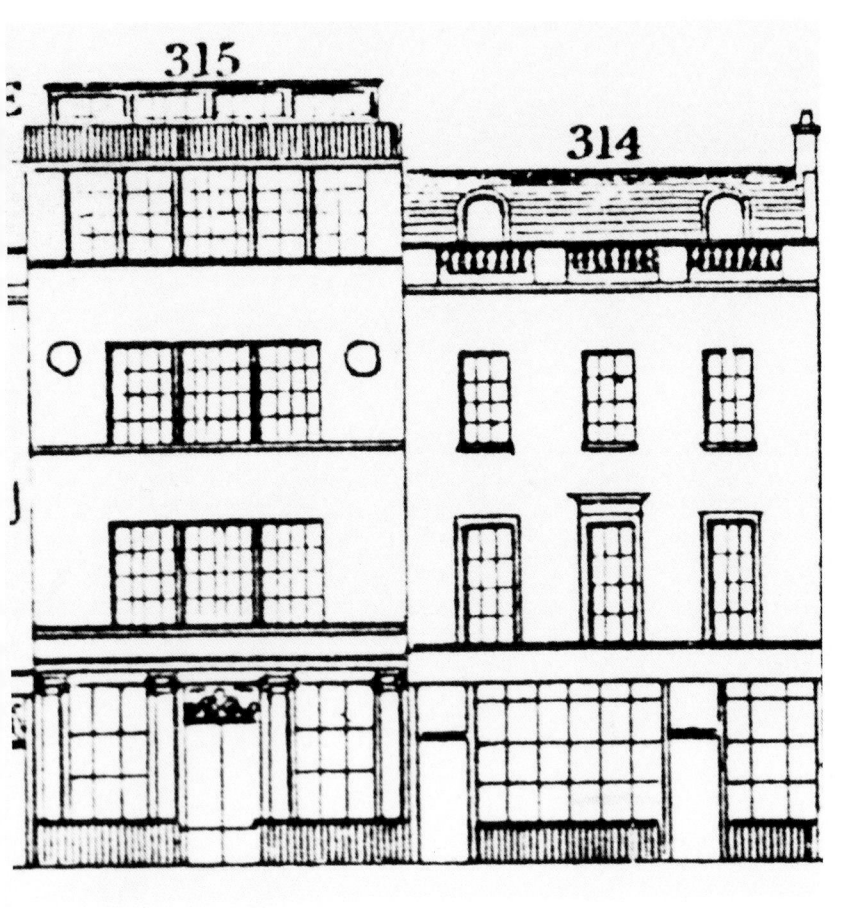

Purdey's shop and workshops at 314 $^1/_2$ Oxford Street. No. 315 housed the shop and No. 314 the workshops. Note the more decorative front of the shop.

Below: Oxford Street in the late 1830s, showing the haphazard numbering of premises. Purdey's premises encompassed the two blocks to the right of Henry Clarke, No. 315 and 314. From John Tallis's *Street Views of London 1838 to 1840*.

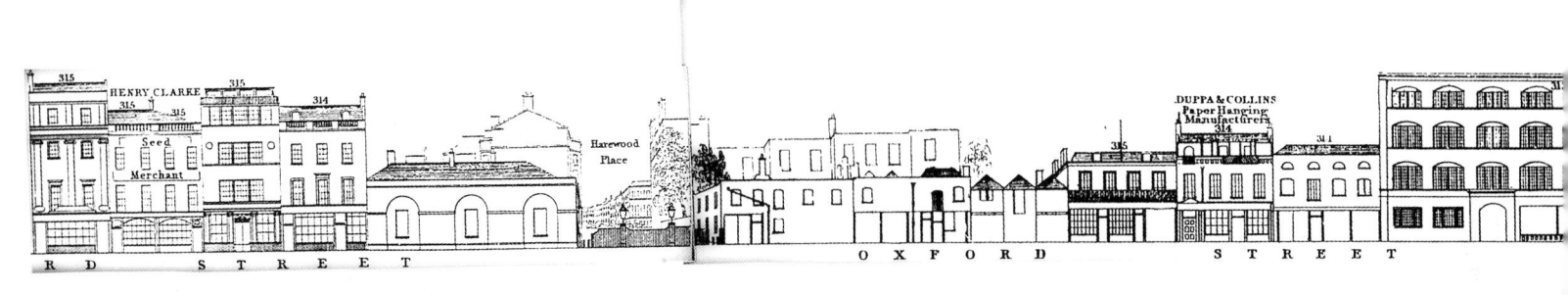

314 ½ OXFORD STREET

Purdey's move to 315 Oxford Street in late 1826 necessitated a new design of trade label. His second trade label was larger than the first, measuring some 7 ½ in. by 5 ¾ in. and more conventional in appearance. The label states:

J Purdey
315 Oxford Street
(Near Hanover Square)
London
Gun Manufacturer
Patentee of the safety Gun Locks
(NB Removed from Princes Street, Leicester Square)

Purdey probably inserted 'Near Hanover Square' for two reasons. Firstly, Joseph Manton had given the address '11 Hanover Square' on his labels from 1819 until 1826. Sportsmen would be familiar with this address and it would help them to locate Purdey's new shop more easily. Secondly, because Oxford Street was so long and the numbering system inadequate, customers would be given a pointer to the shop's position. He also made sure customers knew he was the same Purdey who had been at Princes Street. The label also indicates that his 1818 Patent Safety was still relevant and in demand. By using the Royal Coat of Arms, Purdey was following the tradition of many other gunmakers in adopting a more flamboyant label to proclaim the superiority of his product. Where Purdey's label was unusual was in his use of blue ink, against the more conventional black ink. This blue ink was obviously not fast as its colour often ran and permeated the rest of the label.

When Purdey decided after a few months to re-number 315 Oxford Street as 314 ½, a new label had to be introduced. Before this new label was printed, the new number was handwritten over the old. No doubt Purdey had a fair supply of 315 labels and there was no point in wasting them over such a small detail! Such overprinting was common on many gunmakers' labels when they moved location for the same reason.

By late 1827, the engraver of Purdey's label had altered the copper-plate from '315' to '314 ½'. There is a variation in the sizes of many labels because they were hand cut. From the 1840s, the label was usually cropped to remove the bottom two lines, by then irrelevant.

The trade label used by Purdey when he moved to 315 Oxford Street in late 1826. In use until early 1827. A very rare item.

The handwritten alteration to Purdey's 315 Oxford Street label when he decided to re-number his premises 314 ½ Oxford Street. In use mid-to-late 1827.

The re-engraved trade label changed to 314 ½ Oxford Street, in use from late 1827 to 1877. This label was often cropped from the 1840s by removing the last two lines. By then the safety gunlock was obsolete and Purdey was well established in Oxford Street.

THE BIRTH AND APPRENTICESHIP OF JAMES PURDEY THE YOUNGER

With the move to Oxford Street, Purdey's annual production began to rise. The records for 1826 show that he was producing around 200 guns a year and by 1827 even more. A great many customers part-exchanged their old guns for new Purdeys. Consequently, Purdey had a great many second-hand guns by various other makers to sell. Some of these he sold through his shop, but most went to other gunmakers and dealers. Many of these second-hand dealers described their business in the parlance of the time as a 'gun repository'. Such dealers who dealt in second-hand guns supplied by Purdey were D Gass, who had a 'Gun and Pistol Repository' at 42 and 43 Oxford Street, Isaac Blissett of 'Blissett's Repository' at 69 Leadenhall Street; John Baker of 2 Princes Street, and James Collins of Vigo Lane.

However, the main purchaser of Purdey's second-hand weapons was Joseph Lang who had been established at 7 Haymarket since 1821. Lang is listed in the trade directory and newspaper adverts of the time as having a 'repository', meaning that he was primarily a gun dealer. Later, he would produce guns bearing his own name. Joseph Lang also dealt in brand new Purdey guns. The sales ledgers show that in 1826, for example, Purdey was selling new percussion guns to Lang for £40, against Purdey's retail price of around £52. Lang, therefore, received a good profit and Purdey increased sales of his own guns while still maintaining an adequate profit margin. Lang also bought accessories and had guns repaired by Purdey.

This flourishing business between Lang and Purdey took on a different slant when Joseph Lang fell in love with James Purdey's second daughter, Eliza, born in 1811. The couple were married in St. George's Church, Hanover Square on 12 January 1828. The marriage register states:

> Joseph Lang, a Batchelor of the Parish of St. Martin-in-the-Fields and Eliza Purdey, a Spinster and Minor of this parish were married in this church by licence and with the consent of James Purdey the natural and lawful father of the said Minor this Twelfth Day of January,1828 by me James Glen, Curate in the presence of James Purdey and Elizabeth Purdey.

Eliza had been living at 314 ½ Oxford Street and upon her marriage set up home at another gunmaker's – her husband Joseph Lang's shop at 7 Haymarket. Lang still continued to conduct business with Purdey, yet by the early 1830s his purchases fell off probably denoting that he had established his own gunmaking business.

So far James Purdey the Elder had sired four daughters, the fourth, Jane, being born at 4 Princes Street in 1819. A considerable gap ensued before his fifth and final child – a boy – was born in 1828. The parish records for St. George's, Hanover Square for 1828 state:

> James Purdey, Baptised August 3rd, 1828, son to James and Mary. Abode, Oxford Street.

This was the future James Purdey the Younger, destined to take over the family firm from his father James Purdey the Elder in 1858. James Purdey the Younger would run the firm in the second half of the 19th century until his death in 1909.

He was born on 19 March 1828 at 314 ½ Oxford Street – 'born 25 minutes past 2 o'clock in the morning' as recorded in the Purdey family Bible. His father must have felt a great deal of pride in that the excellent business he had established could now continue securely down the direct family line. James Purdey the Elder was now in middle age (for these days) at 43 and his wife, Mary, was 37.

Joseph Lang in 1828 – the year of his marriage to Eliza Purdey.

Young James spent his early childhood in Oxford Street right next to the shop, and since that is where the Purdey guns were built as well as sold, he was immersed in gunmaking right from the start. At the age of fourteen, he began his apprenticeship. The *Register of Apprentice Bindings*, 1745-1902 in the Records of the Worshipful Company of Gunmakers, states:

> James Purdey the Younger, son of James Purdey of Oxford Street in the County of Middlesex, Gunmaker was bound apprentice to his father the said James Purdey for seven years by Indentures dated this day. Bound out of Court by Order of the Master.
> Consideration; Natural love and affection.
> Fourteenth day of July, 1843.

The charming term 'natural love and affection' was much used in this period to denote a close family relationship in an apprenticeship that would render any Consideration of money superfluous.

Another family apprenticeship occurred shortly afterwards. Young James's elder sister, Eliza, who had married the gunmaker Joseph Lang in 1828, had given birth to a son christened on 17 May 1829 and named Joseph after his father. When young Joseph reached apprenticeship age, his grandfather, James Purdey, took him on, as an apprentice. Again the *Register of Apprentice Bindings* 1745-1902 records this for 28 June 1845.

> Joseph Lang the Younger, son of Joseph Lang of Haymarket in the Parish of St. Martin-in-the-Field in the County of Middlesex, Gunmaker, was bound apprentice to James Purdey, Citizen and Gunmaker of London for seven years by Indentures dated this day.
> No Consideration. Bound out of Court by Order of the Master.

The direct family connection prevailed once more with no Consideration of money being paid. Consequently, both boys – James Purdey the Younger and Joseph Lang the Younger – would spend roughly the same years in apprenticeship together at Purdey's.

When James Purdey the Younger was born in 1828, production rates remained high. From 1826 until 1830, around 265 weapons were being produced annually, a very high output. In the early 1830s the annual production rate dropped slightly and by the mid-1830s averaged around 150 weapons. The most probable reason for the drop was that output had been unnaturally high in the 1820s due to the advent of the new percussion system. There would be terrific demand from sportsmen to acquire the new system, benefiting Purdey in his early Oxford Street years. This high production rate and best gun principles placed Purdey among the higher echelon of makers, if not the highest. In his 1833 edition of *Instructions to Young Sportsmen*, Colonel Hawker again refers to Purdey's position at this time. 'Who is now to be called the leading gunmaker I hardly know and there are so many competitors for the title, that it would be an unthankful office to name anyone in particular. Mr. Manton and Son, in partnership with Mr. Hudson carry on the old established house at No. 6 Dover Street in the best possible manner. Mr. Purdey has at this moment perhaps the first business in London and no man better deserves it.' Such praise from Hawker who had so expounded the now bankrupt Joseph Manton, must have been of great benefit to Purdey in the days before real advertising.

Although very faint, the bill illustrated is a very early example, dated 28 March 1831. It was sent to J Newham who had previously bought a double 15-bore sporting gun, No. 1224 on 17 November 1827. The bill states:

1830
Sept. 13	Double Gun Cleaned	-	5	-
	4 Pegs	-	16	-
	1000 Caps	1	15	-

1831
March 28	P.Pistols Cleaned & done up	-	10	-
	Barrels Browned	-	12	-
	Stocks repaired	-	7	6
	Mahogany Case repaired			
	New Partitions Lined and done as New	1	7	-
	Bullet Mould	-	5	6
	Powder Flask	-	7	6
	New Leather Cover	1	11	6
		£7	17	-

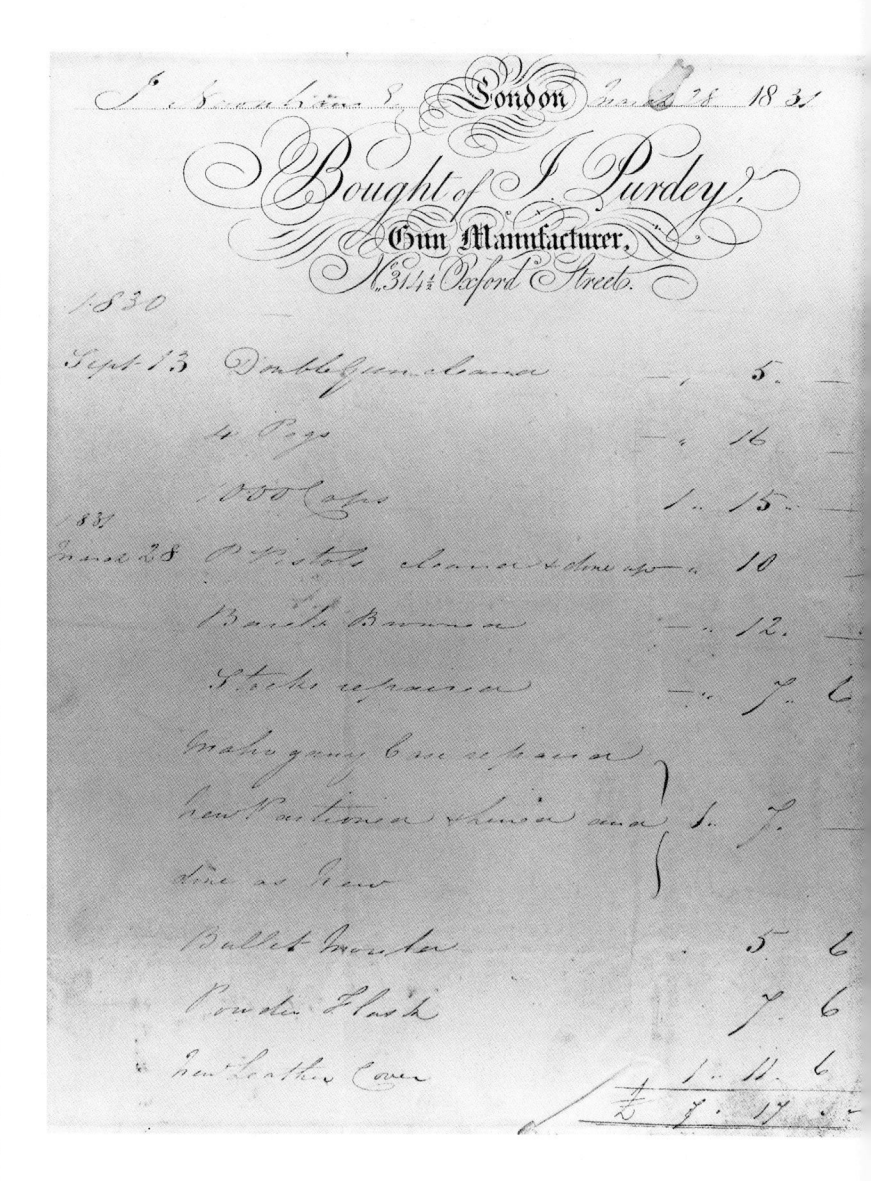

THE DIVERSITY OF ARMS IN THE PERCUSSION PERIOD

Writing in the 1860s in response to some ill-informed criticism of Purdey's, James Purdey the Younger commented: 'Purdey's have produced a greater variety (to such various tastes) of guns and introduced more improvements successfully than most in our trade.' Until the mid-19th century, Purdey's produced an incredible variety of weapons of all types and descriptions. The 18th century had seen a far greater range of arms produced than the century that followed. Pistols were made in large quantities for personal protection in a more lawless age, duelling pistols were constructed to settle disputes in contemporary fashion and sporting guns produced to pursue game. By the opening decades of the 19th century, demand for

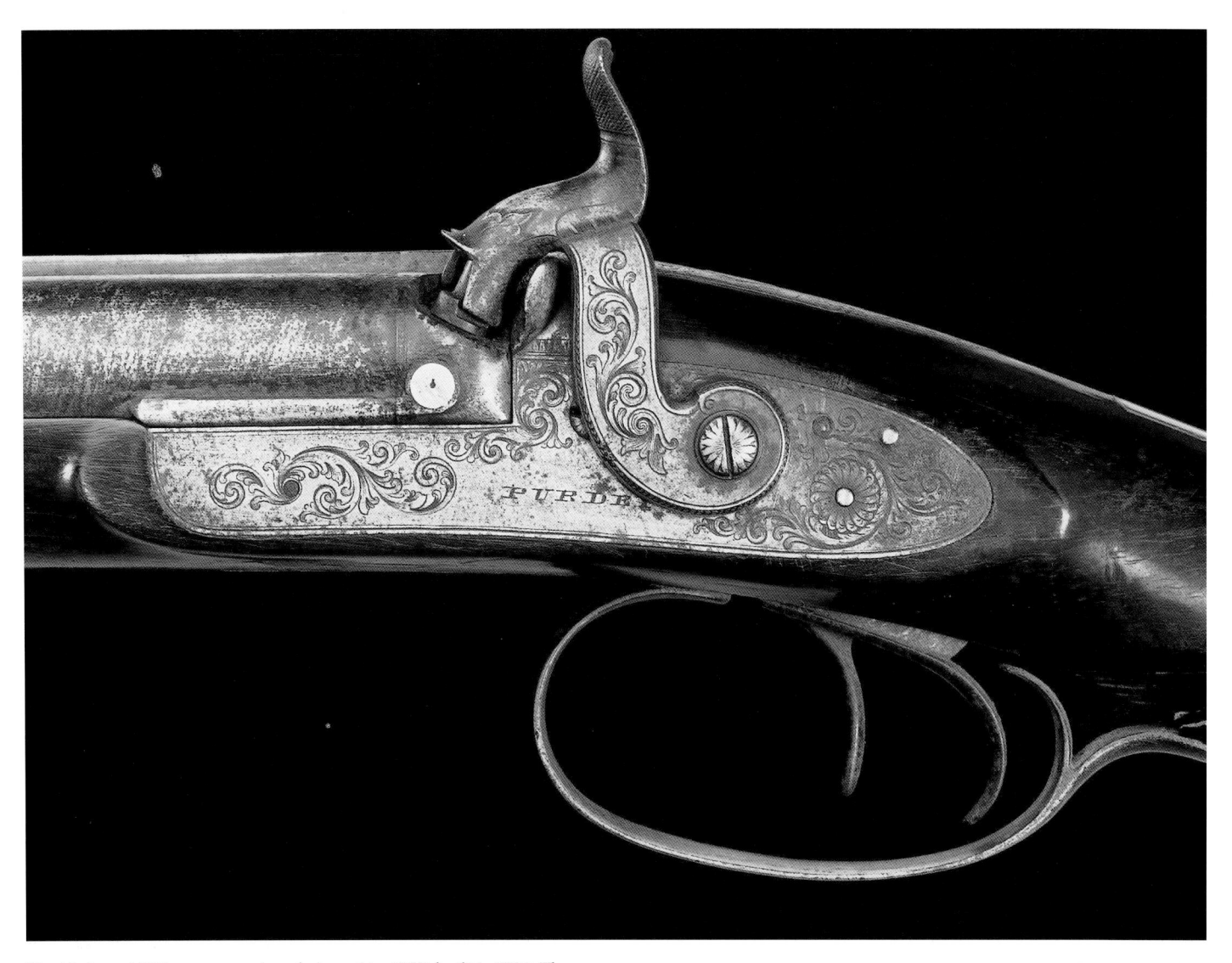

Double-barrel 19-bore percussion shotgun No. 1939, built in 1830. The 29-in. twist barrels are stamped 'J P'. This gun displays the typical engraving of the late 1820s and early 1830s.

pistols was in decline due to better transportation facilities and a more efficient police force. Only the sporting gun and rifle remained in high demand and a great many gunmakers concentrated upon such firearms. Yet Purdey's continued in the early-mid-19th century to produce a rich diversity of arms.

The most numerous weapon produced by Purdey's was the sporting gun, due to the amount of shooting that took place and the subsequent real demand created for a 'working' gun. By the time the percussion system was well established in the late 1820s, the Purdey double percussion gun did not vary greatly. Locks were invariably front action and compared with today's sporting guns came in many different bore sizes. 14-bore tended to be the most common. The ratio of single guns to double guns diminished as the decades of the early 19th century progressed, the double gun becoming the norm by mid-century. Purdey's produced some lesser quality guns, recorded as 'Keepers' Guns' that sold for around £20 against the best gun price of around £55. Pairs of guns became more common due to the changing nature of shooting with the advent of driven game, although it was not until the breech-loading era that the pair assumed big demand. Some shotguns are described as 'Rifle and Shot' – combination guns. This is reflected in the price of around £68 in comparison to the average price of £55 for a shotgun. A great many of these muzzle-loaders were converted to breech-loaders in the 1860s and 1870s – not a simple job as it involved rebuilding the entire gun. Just how big an undertaking this was is illustrated by Purdey's usual charge for conversion – around £21.

The next most common type of weapon made by Purdey's was the rifle. Rifles were far more difficult to make and hence more expensive. Demand was more limited and many makers shied away from them. James Purdey made something of a speciality of his rifles producing around 1400 muzzle-loaders – an enormous output. Before around 1840 single-barrel rifles were the most common, but as barrel-makers became more proficient in the art of laying rifle barrels and sporting fashion changed, the double-barrel rifle rose in prominence and overtook the single. Purdey's first recorded double rifle is No. 1031 sold in 1827. The sales ledger states:

Feb. 5, 1827.
To a best finished double gun, not numbered, with a pr. of extra Rifle Barrels, 1031.

Although rifle demand was more limited compared to

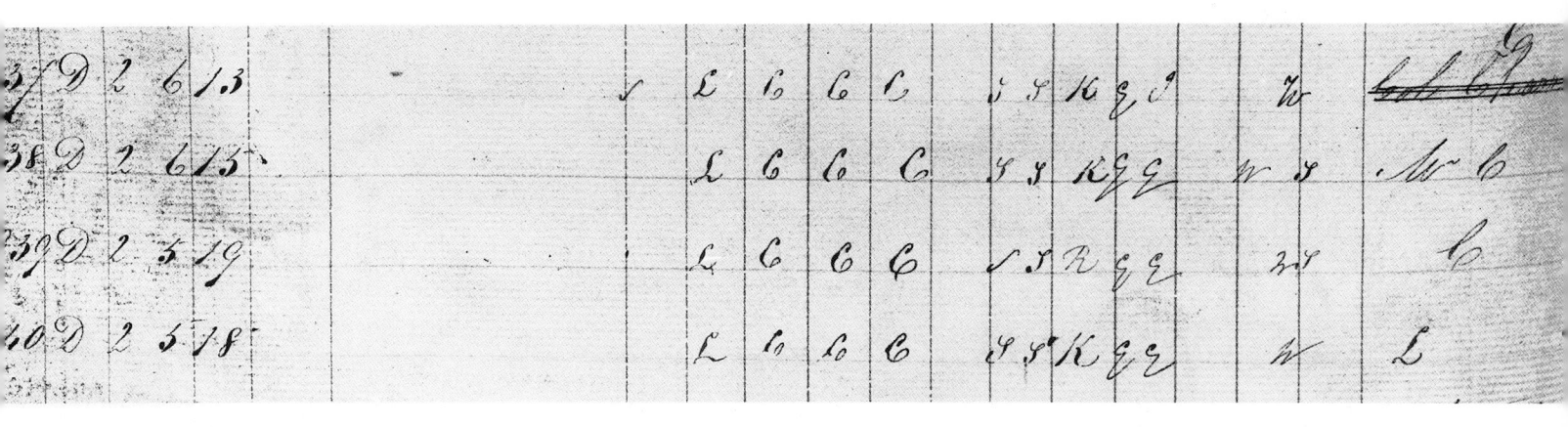

The record in the Dimension Book for shotgun No. 1939. 'G' is Peter Gumbrell, engraver; 'L' is possibly Henry Lewis, locks jointed; 'R' is Abbe Robins, polishing and hardening. See page 14 for the column headings.

shotguns, it remained steady, due to better transportation facilities. The British Empire was being created and new sporting opportunities presented themselves in areas such as Africa and India. At home the combination of the railway and Queen Victoria's love for the Highlands meant that deer stalking became very popular in Scotland.

Larger bore sizes, right up to 8-bore, were built for sport abroad, but the 16-bore rifle built primarily for deer stalking was the most common. In the early decades of the 19th century, two single rifles were often used for stalking deer. The sportsman carried one and the stalker another. After the sportsman fired, he could then take the second rifle if another shot presented itself while the stalker re-loaded the first. However, many sportsmen only had one single rifle – a handicap if a second shot was required. To overcome this, the double rifle was built in increasing numbers in the 1830s and 1840s. Building double rifle barrels was extremely difficult as it was tricky to align two rifle barrels to the one set of sights. The barrels had to converge at the muzzle, the degree of convergence depending on the range at which the barrels were to zero, usually one hundred yards. For the shooter, the powder charge and weight of ball had to be strictly maintained to ensure that the gun operated properly.

Most rifles built had multi-groove rifling of ten grooves. Forcing the lead-patched ball down the rifling with the ramrod required a fair degree of effort, particularly if the barrel was fouled up. Charges were relatively light, usually one and a half drams of slow-burning No. 6 powder for a 16-bore. Too high a powder charge would cause the ball to strip across the rifling rendering the shot inaccurate. These rifles were accurate at ranges of 100 to 150 yards and to make up for the lack of velocity, due to the low charge, the relatively large 16-bore size was needed to ensure sufficient stopping power. Purdey would remedy these defects in the 1850s with his famous 'Express' rifles. Hair triggers were common on single-barrel rifles, far less common on double rifles due to the jar on discharge of the first barrel.

Smaller bore rifles, termed 'Pea' rifles of 60- or 80-bore, later known as 'Rook and Rabbit' rifles were also made, intended for far smaller game. They usually had a very small charge of about three-quarters of a dram of powder and were normally used at ranges of 50 to 75 yards.

Purdey double percussion rifles are very distinctive and display a style all of their own. This is due primarily to the design of the hammer. Hammer design evolved gradually. Early Purdey hammers were conventional in appearance, and in use until around 1832. They were retained for the duration of production on most of the single rifles throughout the percussion period. In the early 1830s, the hammer design was changed to a unique Purdey pattern and at the same time, the safety bolt was moved in front of the hammer. This first pattern was modified over the years to create a second pattern of lighter style, more in keeping with the reduction in bore sizes. The second pattern was further modified into a third pattern, even lighter in design.

A single-barrel 16-bore rifle No. 2932 sold on the 30 August 1839. Rifled with ten grooves and sighted to 200 yds. The lock and furniture are engraved with stag, hinds and boar. In its original mahogany case with accessories. (*See plate 1 in colour section.*)

The record in the Dimension Book for No. 2932. See column headings on page 28. 'L' is Henry Lewis, locks jointed; 'B' is probably Robert Bagnall, stocked; 'A' is Henry Atkin, screwed, making off; 'R' is Robins, polishing and hardening; 'G' is Gumbrell, engraving.

Nothing better illustrates the variety of arms produced by Purdey until the mid-19th-century than the production of pistols. Single-barrel, double-barrel, multi-barrel, carriage, duelling, target, pocket and holster pistols were all produced in Oxford Street. Such description of pistols as used today is not apparent in Purdey's records. 'Duelling pistols' is often recorded to mean target pistols, 'double pistol' has a wide interpretation. Over 400 muzzle-loading pistols were produced by Purdey, a considerable output bearing in mind the very limited use of a pistol.

Duelling pistols with heavy, smooth-bore barrels were produced, even though duelling was illegal. Duelling was nonetheless condoned by society and protagonists were rarely prosecuted, a state of affairs that led to a demand for duelling

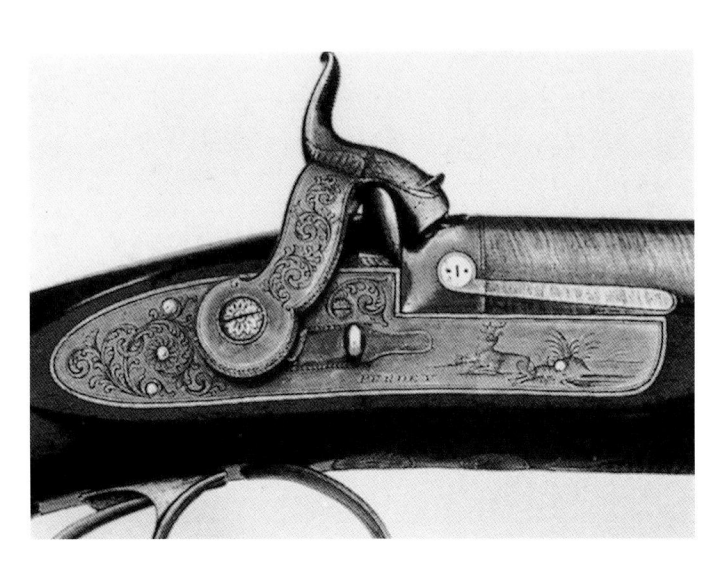

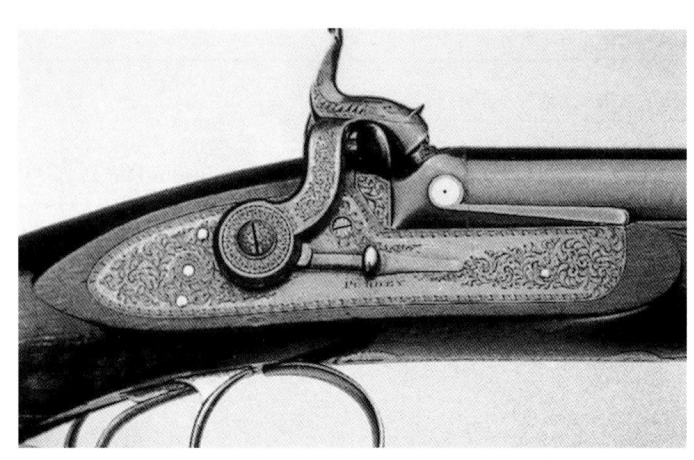

The changing style of the Purdey percussion hammer on the double rifle. From top to bottom, *left*: the conventional hammer, the first pattern, *right*: the second pattern, the third pattern.

pistols. Public opinion turned, however, during the percussion period and towards mid-century duelling had virtually ceased. The successor to the duelling pistol – and very similar in appearance – was the target pistol. These pistols had lighter barrels and were rifled, usually multi-groove rifling with 12 or 16 rifling grooves. Competition target shooting was popular, involving a fair degree of gambling.

Purdey duelling and target pistols are very distinctive. The pistols of the 1820s were more conventional in appearance, with ramrods and more heavily built. During the 1830s, as the target pistol came into use, the ramrod and bottom rib were left out to create a lighter style. However, it is the butt design that denotes the Purdey duelling or target pistol. In the early 1820s, Purdey's butts were almost vertical with a horizontal base. The second style, introduced in the late 1820s and referred to in the records as 'new pattern handles', are butts angled backwards with an oval metal base cap. By the early 1830s the sweep of the butt was angled further backwards. Trigger guards likewise changed from the late 1820s, the more rounded style of the early 1820s giving way to a deeper guard to give greater support. Hair triggers were usually fitted. This was the final form of the Purdey target pistol, destined to remain until production died out in the 1860s.

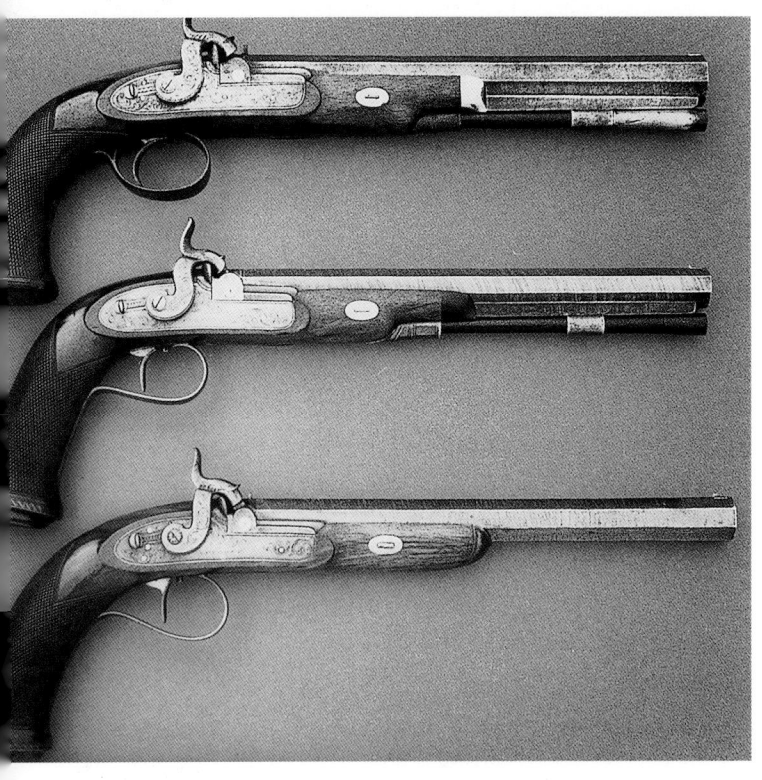

Another type of pistol in good demand was the large double-barrel percussion pistol. These were of smooth bore, varying from 12- to 17-bore, commonly termed today 'campaign' or 'cavalry' pistols. Built mainly for army officers, they had back action locks, swivel ramrods and sometimes a detachable stock.

The last recorded muzzle-loading pistols were Nos. 17071/2, a pair of double 40-bore muzzle-loading back action pistols with Whitworth barrels, sold to the eccentric Charles Gordon in December 1901.

Other pistols will be found bearing the company name, but they are not strictly Purdey's in that they were not entirely built by Purdey's. Pocket pistols are a good example. These simple pistols were bought in from other manufacturers and finished to a high standard by Purdey's. Consequently, most do not bear Purdey serial numbers and do not appear in Purdey's ledgers. Prices ranged between £7.7s and £15 for double-barrel examples and from £3.13s.6d to £7 for single-barrel examples, the price variation being reflected in the degree of engraving and finish. Other weapons in this category are multi-barrel, turnover, revolvers and holster pistols again bought in and finished in Oxford Street. Some bear serial numbers, but not in line with Purdey's normal serial number classification. Perhaps these numbers were put on by the supplier.

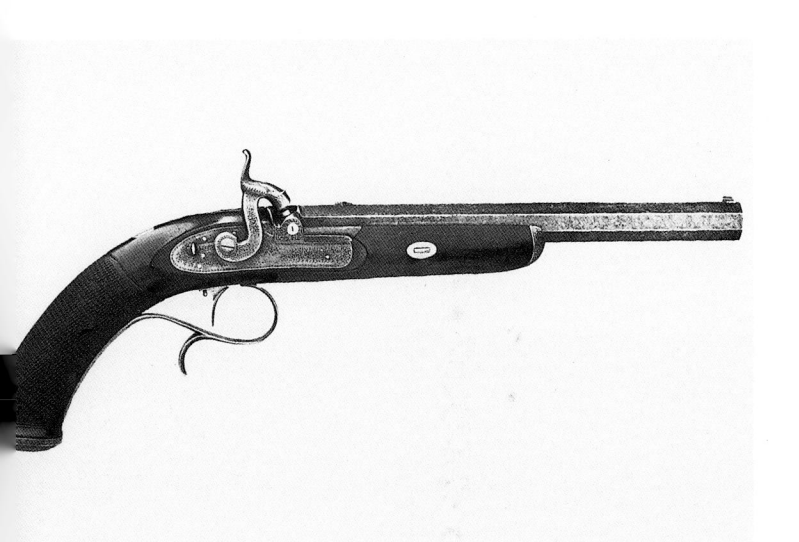

A decade of Purdey pistols to show the evolution of the 'new pattern butt'. From top to bottom, duelling pistol No. 968 of 1826, target pistol No. 1166 of 1827, target pistol No. 1768 of 1829.

Probably the last target pistols built by Purdey's. One of the pair Nos. 6674/5 of 100-bore rifled (2 groove) target pistols with black lacquered stocks and leaf sights for 20, 40, 60, 80 and 100 yards sold on 15 June 1864 to the Maharajah of Bulrampore.

A double hammer, 88-bore, 6-barrel, turnover pistol numbered '26'. This is one of a small number of pistols bought in from suppliers 'in the white' and finished by Purdey's. Built in the 1830s.

That Purdey guns in this period had a distinctive Purdey style, there is no doubt. The hammers on the double percussion rifles and the shape of the butts on the pistols proclaim 'Purdey' in no uncertain terms. The black lacquered stock gave another dimension to the Purdey look.

Black was the fashion colour to the Regency style. Black japanning or finishing, particularly on furniture, was much in vogue in the early decades of the 19th century and was much used as a protective for metal in the days before plating. James Purdey aped contemporary fashion and introduced an 'ebonised' finish to his firearms. He applied a black lacquer to many of his stocks fairly soon after the move to Oxford Street in 1826. He was probably the first gunmaker to offer such a finish. There is no real mention of it in the records so it is difficult to judge the popularity of the finish. On the other hand, the use of maple wood – the other fashion for stocks in this period – is always recorded in the Dimension Books. The 'ebonised' finish was applied to all manner of weapons. It appears to be more common on pistols, but this could be accounted for by their higher survival rate. There was no extra cost to the customer for this particular finish. When brand new, the black lacquer looked superb, giving a sumptuous appearance to an already top quality firearm, and it was used frequently on presentation pieces. The black-lacquered finish was in use for around 40 years, the last recorded example being the pair of target pistols built in 1864 as illustrated on page 25.

As well as guns, Purdey sold in large quantities such shooting accessories as gun cases, powder flasks, shot belts, cartridges, wads, percussion caps, etc. Other goods associated with sport were knives, daggers, fishing lines, fish hooks, targets, etc.

Purdey's customers were a veritable Who's Who of the era. The British nobility from all corners of the island featured in large numbers as shooting on their estates played an important part of their leisure activities. Many clergymen bought sporting guns from Purdey's as their role in the establishment allowed them to indulge in shooting as a sport. Royalty were also frequent customers.

The first royal customer to appear in the records is probably His Serene Highness The Prince of Leinegen who purchased double-barrel 14-bore percussion gun No. 817 in 1825 (see page 13). The Duke of Gloucester, brother to King George IV, bought double-barrel 16-bore percussion gun No. 856 in 1825. European royalty, such as the Crown Prince of Bavaria and the Prince of Orange, also feature in the records.

Shortly after her accession to the throne, Queen Victoria purchased on 23 October 1838 a pair of 'double pistols, 8 1/2 inches, carbine' Nos. 3151/2 for presentation to the Imam of Muscat. In the ledger they are described as 'Pr. of Double Barrel Pistols, with Rosewood case inlaid with Buhl, lined with crimson silk velvet'. Price £73. On 22 November 1838 she bought a gold-mounted double 16-bore percussion gun, No. 3039, cased with a gold-mounted single 17-bore percussion rifle, No. 3027, the gun costing £53 and the rifle £45. Such presentation guns and rifles were regularly made by Purdey's and illustrate the workings of the British Empire. Lavish gifts were a system of smoothing and furthering diplomatic relations to help expand the tentacles of Empire.

On 11 July 1840 Prince Albert purchased double percussion gun, No. 3309, for £68.5s, the ledger stating 'Barrels Richly Inlaid in Gold, with Mahogany case lined with Handsome Blue Silk Velvet'. He followed this up on 11 March 1841 with No. 3259, a small pea rifle, price £36.15s. On 19 December 1848 he purchased Nos. 4382/3, a pair of 14-bore double rifles for £168.

Trade with India was brisk. Due to the conversion of the East India Company into a vast administrative machine with consequent territorial expansion, Britain came to control an enormous area in India. Many Indian princes were in alliance with the company and it was these who demanded the best English guns. They usually ordered flamboyant Purdey guns, with much gold inlay, gold plating and richly applied cases.

In this period guns were tested and could be tried out at Norlands Shooting Ground leased by Purdey at Notting Hill. Here Purdey constructed a 'magnificent' target, referred to in Captain Lacy's book *The Modern Shooter*, published in 1842. 'I would recommend him to inspect, with Mr. Purdey's permission, his magnificent target at Norlands Shooting Ground, Notting Hill. This target fronted with slabs of iron, 2 inches thick, and powerfully supported behind a vast mass of brickwork, is so lofty, and so wide as to defy almost all possibility of danger'. Guns could also be tried out at the live pigeon shooting clubs – The Red House, Old Hats Club or Hornsey Wood House – that were so popular at this time. In 1857, the leasehold on a six-acre plot of land in Harrow named 'Foxholes' was taken as a shooting ground and for rifle testing. This ground, just off the Harrow Road, was leased for 21 years.

The entry in the Dimension Book for Queen Victoria's first order for a pair of 'Double Pistols 8 1/2 inch Carbine'. Sold on 23 October 1838. Note No. 3150, a small rifle for Lord Henry Bentinck, and that the stocking, screwing etc. of No. 3153 was by 'An' in reference to Atkin.

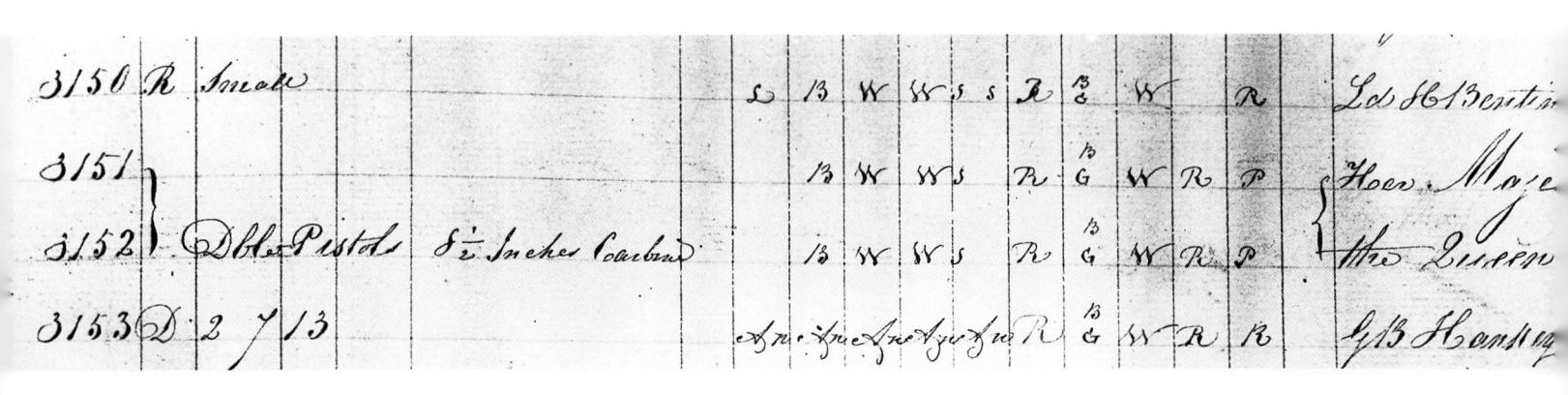

In 1841, James Purdey received due acclaim when he was elected Master of the Gunmakers' Company, which had been formed in response to much petitioning by the gunmakers with the grant of a Charter on 14 March 1638. Prior to that date, guns were manufactured by all manner of tradesmen – blacksmiths, armourers, etc. With the development of the handgun in the 16th century, a more specialist craftsman, the gunmaker, had evolved. These gunmakers complained about inferior standards and lack of proof of guns with subsequent safety issues involved. In one such petition in 1588, the gunmakers complained, 'some [guns] were not wrought and boared straight within and some beinge made crooked'.

The creation of the Gunmakers' Company in 1638 brought greater control and higher standards of firearms manufacture. The company had the right to view and prove all handguns made or sold in London and apprentices had to serve seven years. In 1657, a permanent proofhouse was built near Aldgate, moving in 1675 to its present site at Commercial Road. The company was given the authority to stamp all weapons with its mark, 'the letters G.P. Crowned' to show they had passed proof.

The Gunmakers' Company was organised along hierarchical lines with an annually elected Master, Upper Warden and Renter Warden, and a Court of Assistants comprising of around 10 gunmakers. Having been elected to the Livery of the Company in 1820, James Purdey was admitted to the Court of Assistants in 1838, elected Renter Warden in 1839, Upper Warden in 1840, and finally to the pinnacle of the Gunmakers' Company, Master in 1841. Upon his election to each of these offices, Purdey chose Samuel Nock as his deputy.

Since 1841, the Purdey family or members of the Purdey firm have provided 28 Masters of the Gunmakers' Company, a record only surpassed by the Barnett family of gunmakers who provided 30 Masters between 1761 and 1843 (see Appendix 10).

PURDEY GUNMAKERS AND SUPPLIERS IN THE 1840s AND 1850s

The Dimension Book again records which gunmaker was responsible for each piece of work, but as usual only an initial is given. By this period the barrel column had disappeared – it was never filled in anyway. In the Princes Street period, 1816-26, Purdey had used the barrels of Charles Lancaster and to a lesser extent William Fullerd. The year 1826 is the first recorded use of Purdey's own barrels being used, with their attendant 'JP' stamp and the last recorded use of Lancaster barrels. It is no coincidence that the year 1826 saw Purdey in far bigger premises and Charles Lancaster setting up in his own right as a gunmaker at 151 New Bond Street. Purdey would buy in rough tubes and finish them in his larger Oxford Street premises, stamping them 'JP' upon completion.

Occasionally, Purdey would buy in finished barrels from other suppliers. Thomas Evans of Cirencester Place, Paddington, had previously supplied barrels to Joseph Manton and was listed as a creditor during Manton's bankruptcy proceedings of 1826. His barrels are stamped 'TE'.

The stamp 'J P' denoting James Purdey barrels as used after 1826.

Later, as Thomas Evans and Son, he was in business from 1859-75 at 9 Charlotte Mews, Tottenham Court Road. In the 1870s, Purdey acquired the Evans barrel-making business and produced their own barrels from that address.

Another barrel-maker used by Purdey's was Thomas Parkin of 5 Meards Court, Soho, London. Parkin supplied barrels to many top makers such as Joseph Manton, Alexander Forsyth and Thomas Boss. His barrels are identifiable by a 'TP' stamp. By the late 1850s Parkin's business had ceased.

The other gunmakers employed are difficult to identify due to the lack of wage books. The following workers can be identified in the 'Locks Jointed', 'Stocked', 'Screwed' and 'Making Off' columns. 'G' is either F or H Glaysher, 'A' is Henry Atkin, 'T' is Tregale. 'L' is Henry Lewis. In the 'Polishing' column, 'R' is Abbe Robins. In the 'Engraving' column, 'G' refers again to Peter Gumbrell and 'S' is Jack Sumner of 10 Queen Street, Soho. Sumner's name occasionally appears in full or as the abbreviation 'Smr'. Sumner began his own business in the 1830s at 10 Queen Street, Soho as an outworker to the trade. His son, Jack Sumner, took over the firm and after World War I went to work for Boss. The other gunmakers, initials cannot be positively identified.

James Purdey the Younger had completed his apprenticeship in 1850. At this time the Purdeys lived at Royal Hill Cottage, Queen's Road, Bayswater, having moved from Oxford Street in the 1830s. Purdey the Elder had named the place Rifle Cottage, reflecting his great affection for the sporting rifle. Purdey had also purchased a seaside retreat, 5 Upper Clifton Terrace, Margate, and he named this Rifle House. It was at Rifle House that his sister Martha, who had married Thomas Keck Hutchinson to whom Purdey had been apprenticed, died in early 1853.

Purdey the Younger had been born on 19 March 1828 and he celebrated his 23rd birthday by getting married in the Parish Church of St. George's, Hanover Square. His bride was Caroline Thomas, age nineteen from 3 Bolton Road. Her

A part page from the Dimension Book recording weapons from serial No. 4424 to 4435. This page illustrates the difficulty in dating Purdey guns. No. 4424 was sold in 1848; No. 4425 is listed only as a second-hand sale in 1865; No. 4426 was sold in 1850; No. 4427 in 1849; No. 4428 in 1849 and No. 4429 in 1850. Hence the date '1850' written far later on is inaccurate. In the 'Description' columns, 'D' again refers to a double gun; 'DR' to a double rifle. Note Nos. 4434/5, a pair of double 'pea rifles'.

father, George Thomas, described himself on the marriage certificate as a 'Gentleman'. The couple went to live at 17 Warwick Crescent, Paddington, and their first child, James, was born on 11 June 1854. This son, James III, would die at the tragically young age of 36 from consumption. A sister, Florence Caroline Purdey, was born on 23 July 1855, followed by Athol Stuart Purdey on 27 January 1858. Both Athol and James III were taken into the firm on 21 December 1877 and the firm renamed 'James Purdey and Sons'.

'THE SELF-EXPANDING PURDEY BULLET 1852'

In January 1852 Purdey's were asked by the Board of Ordnance to submit a rifle for use with the army for trial. In this period the rifles then available to the army were unsatisfactory, mainly due to a lack of standardisation. In 1851, rifles used by the army were the newly-introduced .702-inch Pattern 1851 Minié rifle, the .758-inch Sea Service Pattern rifle and the .758-inch Minié Pattern 1842 rifle.

The Master General of Ordnance, Viscount Hardinge, asked five well-known gunmakers – Westley Richards, Lancaster, Purdey, Wilkinson and Greener – to submit rifles to trial against three Government rifles, the Minié, the Brunswick and an individual rifle designed by the Inspector of Small Arms, Lovell.

Muzzle-loading rifles presented the designer with a problem. If the ball was made a tight fit to grip the rifling, it was difficult to force the ball down the barrel with the ramrod, particularly if fouling was present and in the heat of battle. If the ball had a lesser interference, then the rifling might not grip the bullet, affecting accuracy. Following upon a design principle established by a Captain Gustave Delvigne in 1826, a Frenchman, Captain Claude-Etienne Minié, designed a self-expanding bullet. He produced a lead bullet with a hollow base into which was fitted a small iron cup. When the bullet was driven forward by the expanding gas, the iron cup was pushed into the base broadening it sufficiently to grip the rifling. His rifle, 'The Minié' .702-inch calibre with four grooves, was adopted by the British army in 1851. The Minié's attraction was that it was easy to load, and upon expansion the ball was spun by the rifling. In recognition of his services Minié received £20,000 by the British Government in 1852. W W Greener complained and was awarded £1,000 in 1857 as he had already proved the principle of expansion to the army in 1836.

Purdey designed and submitted four rifles, two 32-bores and two 17-bores for the Board of Ordnance Trials in 1852. The rifles appear in the ledgers on 16 February 1852, priced £20 each. The 17-bore rifle, of .650 inches calibre, weighed 9lb 1 1/2 oz with bayonet and had four-groove rifling. These rifles were designed to be used with 'The Self- Expanding Purdey Bullet,' protected by Registered Design No. 3135 of 24 February 1852 granted to 'James Purdey, 314 1/2 Oxford St., London.' A patent which covers an original discovery was not applied for. A registered design is applied to a variation of an existing design or patent, and Purdey's design was a variation on the existing Minié bullet.

In the Purdey bullet, a conical metal plug was fitted into a corresponding cavity in the bullet, projecting slightly from the base. The two portions were secured together by a normal greased rifle patch. Upon firing, the metal plug drove into the bullet causing it to expand and grip the rifling. The only part of the bullet that Purdey claimed as his own design was the metal plug, hence the reason for the Registered Design and not Patent.

Purdey used two bullets in the test, a Minié bullet of 487 grains and Purdey's own plug bullet of 610 grains. The Minié bullet differed from the standard Minié projectile in its exterior shape only.

The 1851 expanding Minié bullet, showing the recess in the base and iron cup.

The Self-Expanding Purdey Bullet, Registered Design No. 3135 of 24 February 1852. Figure 4 shows the bullet before firing and figure 5 shows it after firing.

On 1 August 1852, *The Report on Experiment with Muskets* was submitted upon the conclusion of the trials. Purdey's musket was said to be of 'superior workmanship', 'the shooting is very accurate', but that 'the hardened metal plug separates from a leaden bullet when the latter strikes against iron'. In conclusion, the report stated that none of the private gunmakers' rifles was really satisfactory for the military. The end result was that in 1853 the Enfield rifle of .577-inch calibre with three grooves produced at the Royal Manufactury in Enfield was adopted by the military. In reality, Purdey's rifle was too well made and too civilian, ideal as a sporting weapon, yet not applicable to the rigours of military life. In particular, the plug bullet, made in two parts secured together with a patch, was too finicky for army use.

THE TWO-GROOVE 'EXPRESS' RIFLE

It has already been remarked upon how both Purdeys had a penchant for rifle-making, to such an extent that James Purdey the Elder called his house in the Queen's Road, Bayswater, London, 'Rifle Cottage' and his house in Margate

'Rifle House'. He had also developed a terrace, nos. 1-8 in the Queen's Road, Bayswater, which he named 'Rifle Terrace'! In the late 1840s and early 1850s, Purdey's developed a weapon that achieved outstanding success with an exciting soubriquet that will forever be associated with Purdey's – the Express rifle.

Prior to the Express, muzzle-loading rifles were usually of large calibre, multi-grooved and loaded with a small powder charge. They had to be so designed due to the problem of bullet-stripping. These low-velocity rifles were very accurate, but had a poor trajectory with a subsequent short effective range of about 100 yards.

The Express rifle is usually associated with James Purdey the Younger in the early 1850s. Purdey the Elder would have been in his mid-60s and close to handing over the firm to his son in 1858, so it seems reasonable to assume that Purdey the Younger played the major role in its development. To overcome the inadequacies of the conventional multi-grooved large-bore sporting rifle, Purdey built a two groove rifle with grooves broad and deep of smaller bore size and with a far slower rifling spiral, of one turn in six feet. A conical bullet was cast with two 'wings' to 'lock' securely into the rifling to prevent stripping. A far higher powder charge was used, for example, 2 ½ drams for a 40-bore. The end result was a distinctly different type of rifle. The two-winged bullet, the deep two groove rifling and slow spiral meant that the rifling gripped the bullet and enabled a far higher powder charge to be used. The rifle had a much greater velocity, longer point blank range, lower trajectory and greater range. Purdey caught the contemporary mood of the era perfectly in describing it unofficially as an 'Express Train' to identify it with speed, power and straight direction. Shortened to 'Express' this name remained into the 20th century to describe rifles with long point blank ranges, low trajectories and high velocity.

The probable first Express rifle to be found in the Dimension Book is No. 4700, a single-barrel 16-bore rifle built in 1851. It is recorded as 'Experiment Two-groove New Pointed Ball'. This rifle was obviously retained by Purdey for development work as it was not sold until 22 October 1856. It was not a true Express rifle on account of its large bore size. The first rifle to fit the accepted description of the Express was No. 4703, a double-barrel 40-bore, sold on 8 October 1852 for £84.

From this day on the two-groove Express was made in increasing quantities. Its adoption saw the disappearance of the larger calibres and the virtual end of multi-groove rifling

The muzzle end of a Purdey Express rifle showing the two deep grooves.

in muzzle-loaders. The 40-bore was the more popular bore size although the rifle was produced in calibres from 12-to 140-bore. The two-groove Express fell into disuse with the advent of the breech-loader, because it could not be adapted to breech-loading.

It would be entirely wrong to assume that Purdey invented two-groove rifling. It had been in use many years previously and even adopted by the military in the Brunswick rifle of 1837. However, those rifles used a belted ball with a fairly fast rifling turn and small powder charge. W W Greener claimed to be the inventor of the Express in 1855 with a winged conical bullet, two grooves and a large powder charge. However, his rifling turn was far faster, one turn in 30 inches, and, as we now know, Purdey was producing Express rifles in 1851-52. Greener termed his rifle the 'Cape' rifle.

The success of the Express rifle can be gauged from the comment made by J W Walsh ('Stonehenge') in his book *The Shotgun and Sporting Rifle*, published in 1859:

The entry in the Dimension Book for rifle No. 4700, probably the first Express rifle, built in 1851. See page 28 for column headings. 'G' is Henry Glaysher, locks jointed, 'A' is Henry Atkin, stocked, screwed, making off.

MR. PURDEY'S TWO GROOVED RIFLE.
Foremost in simplicity and in established fame stand Mr Purdey's rifles, to possess one of which has been the object of most deerstalkers and rifle shots for many years… These rifles are all made with two grooves, the balls being a sugarloafed form and cast with two wings to fit the grooves… On the wing itself there is a very slight shoulder, three-eighths of an inch from the base, and this giving way beneath the ramrod ensures an exact fitting of the ball to the groove, so as to avoid windage altogether. The turn is one in six feet, and for sporting purposes at sporting ranges – that is, at anything not exceeding 300 yards – this variety is, in my opinion, one of the best, as it gives a sufficient spin without any unnecessary friction, and very little elevation of the sights is required. The weight of the whole rifle is is $8\,^{1}/_{4}$ lbs; length of barrel 32 inches; bore 40. Weight of ball $^{1}/_{2}$ ounce; charge of powder $2\,^{1}/_{2}$ drams.

James Purdey the Founder or Elder. Born 21 August 1784, Lambeth Street, Whitechapel, died 6 November 1863, Rifle House, 5 Upper Clifton Terrace, Margate. An oil painting in the Long Room attributed to Sir William Beechey, RA. *(See plate 2 in colour section.)*

Lord Henry Bentinck who gave assistance to Purdey's in 1847. The dark label at the bottom states, in James Purdey's handwriting, 'Lord Henry Bentinck My Earliest And Best Customer And Friend When I Was A Youth. JP'.

1 JANUARY 1858 – JAMES PURDEY THE YOUNGER TAKES FULL CONTROL

In the 1820s, Purdey's produced around 200 weapons per year and in the 1830s around 150 weapons, but in the 1840s production dropped to around 120 weapons per year and remained so in the early 1850s. Why production rates in the 1840s should be nearly half those of the 1820s is difficult to answer. Purdey's was by this period well established with a loyal clientele. Perhaps an output of 120 guns a year satisfied the demand of the era, bearing in mind the large number of other quality London makers at this time. In the 1820s Purdey's had been prominent with the new percussion system, thereby creating a buoyant demand – the same thing happened with the success of the Purdey bolt in the early breech-loading period of the 1870s and the Beesley hammerless action in the 1880s.

Part of Purdey legend in this period is the intervention of Lord Henry Bentinck, younger brother of the 4th Duke of Portland. According to Purdey family tradition, Purdey's experienced severe financial problems in 1847. No credible reasons are given for this, but it is assumed that a cash flow problem occurred. By matching entries in the Dimension Book with the sales ledgers, it is apparent that several customers often took years to pay. Outlays such as wages and rates had to be paid immediately and bearing in mind the considerable price of a Purdey gun, if payment was not received in a reasonable timescale, cash flow problems could result.

44 – A bill dated Christmas 1875 showing the potential cash flow problem. Original account delivered 1873 yet paid July 1876. Signed by G Lubbock, the Purdey shop manager in this period.

'Gentlemen' often adopted a cavalier attitude to settling their accounts with 'tradesmen' and due to the social divisions of the era it was difficult for 'trade' to enforce payment legally.

Whatever the reasons for the 1847 financial problem, it is known that Lord Henry Bentinck intervened and put the finances of the firm on a sounder footing. Purdey's were obviously grateful, for there is a note in James Purdey the Younger's writing on a photograph of Bentinck in the Long Room stating: 'Lord Henry Bentinck. My Earliest And Best Customer And Friend When I Was A Youth. JP'. On the back of the photograph there is a further note: 'The Best and Truest Friend and Patron to James Purdey the Elder and Younger'.

Another factor that could have created financial instability in this period was the lifestyle of James Purdey the Elder. He had come from humble origins yet had by dint of his own skill and achievement created a renowned gunmaking establishment in London. Naturally, he wanted to enjoy the fruits of his endeavours, and he spent and invested a great deal of money. Not only had he bought Rifle Cottage in the Queen's Road, and Rifle House in Margate, he had also purchased or

A very early photograph of James Purdey the Younger taken around 1860.

leased nos. 1-8 Rifle Terrace, Queen's Road, Bayswater, two cottages, garden ground and a brewery at Hendon, farmland at Lower Cumberworth at Silestone, York, seven houses at Inverness Terrace, Kensington Gardens, and a house at 8 Coburg Place, Bayswater. He also spent a great deal of money on horses, carriages and stabling.

Either due to his expenditure or advancing years and subsequent inability to run the business efficiently, Purdey the Elder had built up substantial debts by the 1850s. The Purdey archives note that on 31 December 1860 his debts amounted to £10,902.15s.11d, a considerable sum of money at this time. Of this, £1,187.15s.6d are recorded as 'doubtful and bad', in reference to the problem of enforcing customers to pay their bills. Further credence to the problem of his advancing years is given in the Records of the Court Minutes of the Worshipful Company of Gunmakers. He had been elected to the Proof House Committee in 1858, yet had to be excused from serving, 'due to inability to attend and loss of hearing'. Purdey was by this time 73 or 74 years old.

On account of all these factors, father and son agreed that it would be best for James Purdey the Younger to take over the running of the business. An indenture was drawn up between them in October 1857 giving James Purdey the Younger full ownership and control as from 1 January 1858. On that date Purdey the Elder would be 73 years of age and Purdey the Younger 29.

The final agreement between father and son was legalised on 25 August 1860. Various negotiations and arrangements had preceded this final agreement, culminating in a mutual agreement by mid-1860. James Purdey the Younger wrote the following letter on 23 July 1860 from 314 ½ Oxford Street.

> My dear Father,
> I am very glad you agree to the arrangement proposed and shall be glad to complete it as early as can be.
> I fear I cannot get one to join me as security but I am sure the Lawyers can make it safe enough for you – by my giving a Bill of Sale in case I fail to pay up which is not likely.
>
> The Amount of your Debts were about £10,902.15s.11d with about £1,187.15s.6d bad or doubtful – of these £9,300 have been collected. The amount owing to me I could not get at much before Xmas as we are so pressed. The amount would be I should think about £14,000 and more than that a good bit at Xmas – but the word all will comprise everything.
>
> If you give me the lease, goodwill, tools, fixtures together with all the Book debts and in consideration of the same I agree and bind myself to allow you an annuity of £1,000 a year for your life payable as you please, these were the terms mentioned and if they are said to the Lawyer with instruction to make them as binding upon me as possible, I am sure it can be soon and easily done.
>
> I am Dear Father
> your faithful Son
> James

These arrangements were legalised in a Grant of Annuity dated 25 August 1860. Basically, Purdey the Younger received the business and the lease 're-negotiated for a further 21 years from September 1861 to expire at Michaelmas 1882' in return for an annuity of £1,000 to Purdey the Elder for the rest of his life.

And so came to an end the direct involvement of James Purdey the Founder. The son of a blacksmith had established a business, succeeded to the crown of Joseph Manton and developed his business into the best-known and respected gunmaker in Britain. His son, James Purdey the Younger, would build upon these principles to such an extent that Sir Ralph Payne-Gallwey writing in 1893 described the firm as the 'Emperor of Gunmakers'.

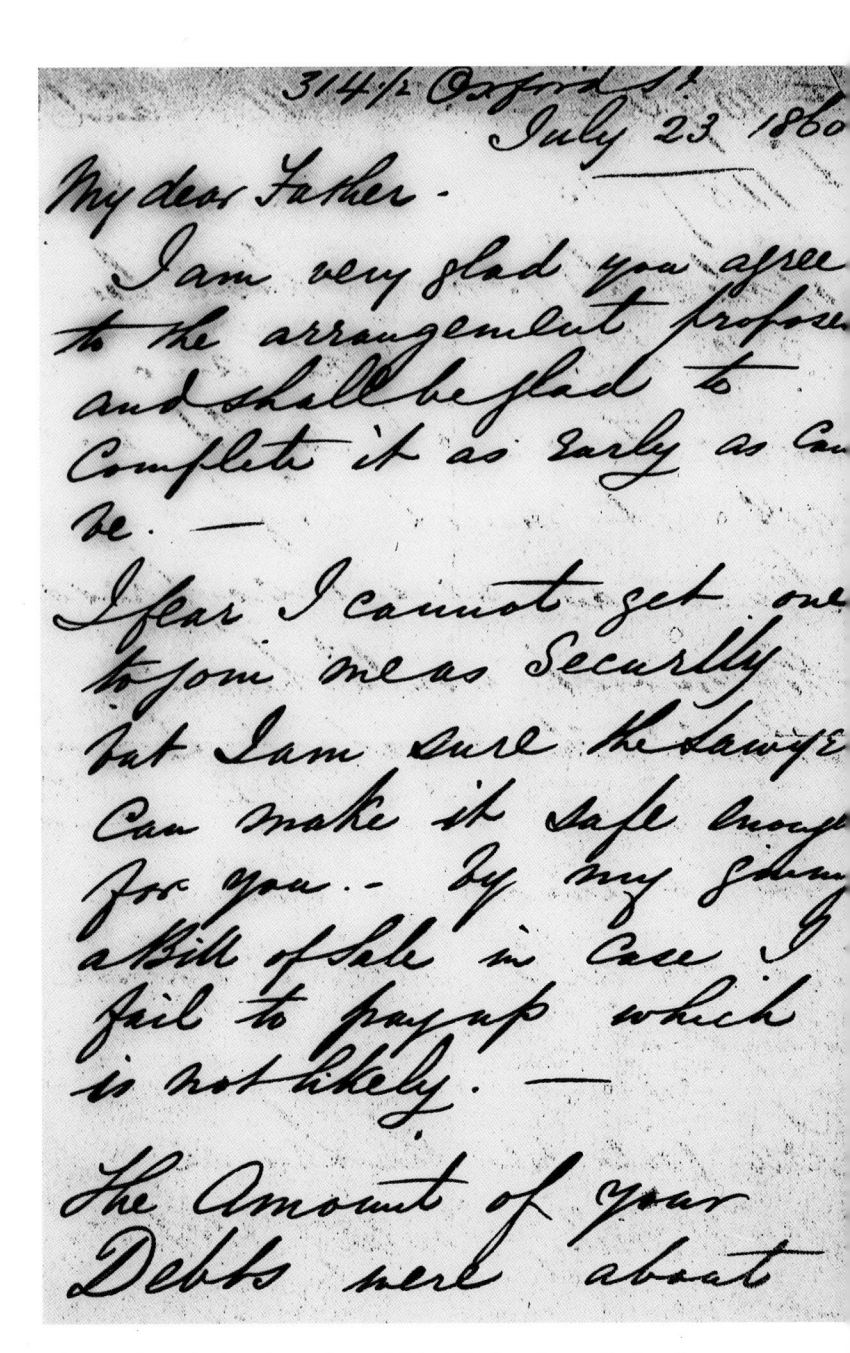

Above and overleaf – A letter dated 23 July 1860 from James Purdey the Younger to his father, finalising details about the transfer of the business from father to son.

£10902 - 15 - 11, with about £1187. 15. 6 bad & Doubtful of these £300 - have been Collected. — The amount owing to me I could not get at much before Xmas, as we are so pressed the amount would be I should think about £14,000 and more than that a good bit at Xmas — but the word all will Comprise everything. —

You give me the Lease, good will, Tools, fixtures, together with all the Book debts and in Consideration of the same, I agree and bind myself to allow You an annuity of £1000, a year for your life, payable as you please. These were the terms mentioned and if they are sent to the Lawyer with instructions to make them as binding upon me as it is possible I am sure it can be soon & easily done

I am Dear Father
Your faithful Son
James.

Chapter four

MUZZLE-LOADING GUNS, RIFLES AND PISTOLS

It has already been noted how Purdey produced a wide diversity of arms in the muzzle-loading era. Not only was a good variety of arms of the finest quality being turned out, but the volume of production for a West End London gunmaker was also considerable, with 100-150 weapons being constructed annually between 1830 and 1860 (see Appendix 5).

As befitted their quality, Purdey guns were expensive. It is interesting to note the virtual non-existence of inflation in the muzzle-loading period. Shotgun prices remained basically the same from 1820 to 1860.

Shotgun Prices

Double gun in case	£52.10s. 0d (usually written as 50 gns.)

Many double guns cost as much as £55 or £57.15s. 0d, usually because of extra finish being stipulated such as, having the case lined in Russian leather or purple velvet.

Single gun in case	£29. 8s. 0d
Double keeper's gun	£20. 0s. 0d
Double duck gun (no case)	£42. 0s. 0d
Extra barrels	£15.15s. 0d

Rifle Prices

In comparison to shotguns, rifle prices gently rose in the period.

Single rifle c1828	£36.15s. 0d
Single rifle c1830	£39.18s. 0d
Single rifle c1840	£42. 0s. 0d
Double rifle and shot	£68. 5s. 0d
Double rifle c1830	£73.10s. 0d
Double rifle c1836	£84. 0s. 0d
Pair of double rifles c1860	£186.0s. 0d
Single keeper's rifle	£26. 5s. 0d

Pistol Prices

Pistol prices varied, due to the wide divergence of pistol types.

Pair of single-barrel target pistols	£52.10s. 0d
Single-barrel pistol	£22.10s. 0d
Pair of double-barrel pistols	£45. 0s. 0d
Double-barrel pistol	£25. 0s. 0d
Pair of double-barrel rifle pistols	£63. 0s. 0d

The first gun illustrated is single-barrel 12-bore flintlock shotgun No. 14, by far the earliest Purdey known to date. The gun is part of the National Museum of Scotland collection in Edinburgh. It is not on display at present. I am indebted to my ten-year-old son for locating this gun, a fact he will not let me forget! The gun was originally in the collection of William Grieve, Langholm, Dumfrieshire. Upon his death, it was given to the Museum in 1927, along with many other items in his collection.

No.14 (see plate 3) is an original flintlock gun in its original case, constructed in late 1816 or early 1817, in the first year of the establishment of James Purdey's business. The 31-inch twist barrel is in two stages. The breech has a platinum poincon 'Purdey London', a platinum vent and two platinum bands. The top flat is engraved in flamboyant Gothic scroll 'Purdey'. The flats on either side are similarly engraved 'Princes Str't' and 'Leicester Squ're' (see plate 4). Under the barrel, apart from the proof marks, is a very small '14'. So insignificant looking was this '14', that I first took it to mean the bore size! However '14' is also engraved on top of the lock, leaving us in no doubt that this is indeed gun No. 14.

The lock has a roller frizzen and throat-hole cock. The engraving appears to pre-date the 'sea-serpent' style with simpler, more conventional engraving of the period *circa* 1815. 'Purdey' is engraved in large Gothic script in comparison to the later more restrained engraving of the name. The number '14' is engraved on the top flat of the lock, behind the flashguard.

The stock has a cheek-piece carved out of the walnut, silver barrel bolt escutcheons and a silver fore-end cap. The hickory ramrod has a brass tip. The trigger guard has no number on it.

The gun is contained in its original mahogany case with brass carrying ring in the centre (see plate 5). The case is lined in blue velvet, now faded to a green colour. Interestingly, the case has the 314 $^1/_2$ Oxford St. label of the late 1820s-1840s. I presume this was added when the gun went back to Purdey for service or repair. This was not an uncommon occurrence. The case is a typical flintlock case of the era. The lock has to be detached before the stock is placed in the case and there is a special compartment to accommodate the lock to the left.

Between the barrel and the stock is a long compartment to house the shot belt.

Very few original accessories remain in the case. Apart from a few cleaning rod ends, the only major original accessory is a fine kid leather shot belt by Sykes. The brass charger is engraved 'Sykes Patent' and has graduated ounces. No details exist of this gun in the records as is the case in most of the pre-1820s records.

This flintlock sporting gun is certainly a historic weapon. The entire quality is superb and shows from the outset that Purdey intended to build one quality – the best.

A very early original double-barrel flintlock gun, No. 86, has been in the Purdey collection at Audley House for many, many years (see plate 6). It is a 16-bore gun constructed in 1818 at 4 Princes Street. The twist barrels are 29 inches long and have an elevated rib in the style of Joseph Manton, inlaid in gold with Gothic lettering, 'Purdey'. There are gold poincons proclaiming 'Purdey' and two gold lines in the breech plugs (see plate 7). The flintlocks show one of the first uses of Wyatt's Patent Safety of 1818, the external sears being engraved 'Patent'. Throat hole cocks and roller frizzen springs are fitted. The lockplates and cocks are engraved with sea serpents and marked 'Purdey'. The pans are long and narrow. There is a large bow trigger guard, fashionable in this period with the long safety lever behind. A leather cheek-piece is

No. 14 in its original mahogany case, lined in blue velvet, now faded to green. A later label of the 1826-40s period has been added. (*See plate 5 in colour section.*)

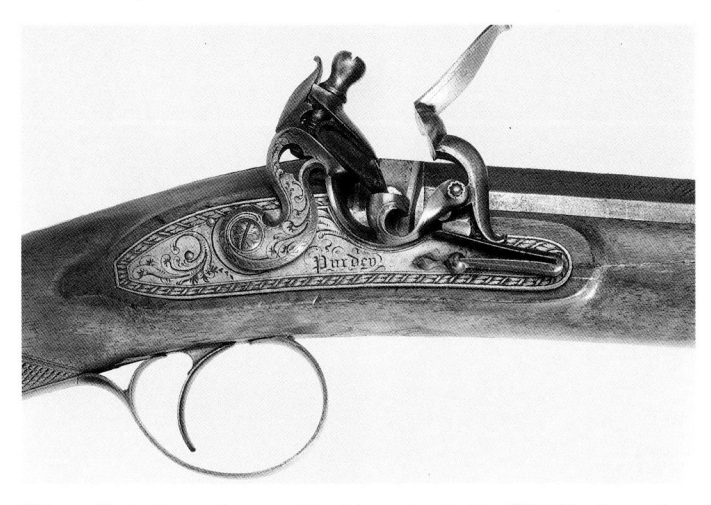

12-bore flintlock sporting gun No. 14 constructed in 1816-17 – the earliest known surviving Purdey gun. It is in original, unrestored condition. Note the simpler engraving predating the sea serpent/monster style. (*See plate 3 in colour section*)

The number 14 stamped on the bottom barrel flat. Note how small it is in comparison with the proof mark.

No. 14 showing the top barrel flats engraved:
'Princes Str't
Purdey
Leicester Squ re'
Note the platinum poincon 'Purdey London' (*See plate 4 in colour section*)

The trigger guard and finial of No. 14.

The number 14 stamped on the upper edge of the lockplate.

fitted to the comb of the butt. In common with the early records, no details at all are given on this gun. It is most probable that Thomas Boss, working at 3 Bridge Road, Lambeth, did the stocking and screwing together because the bulk of his work at this time was for Purdey.

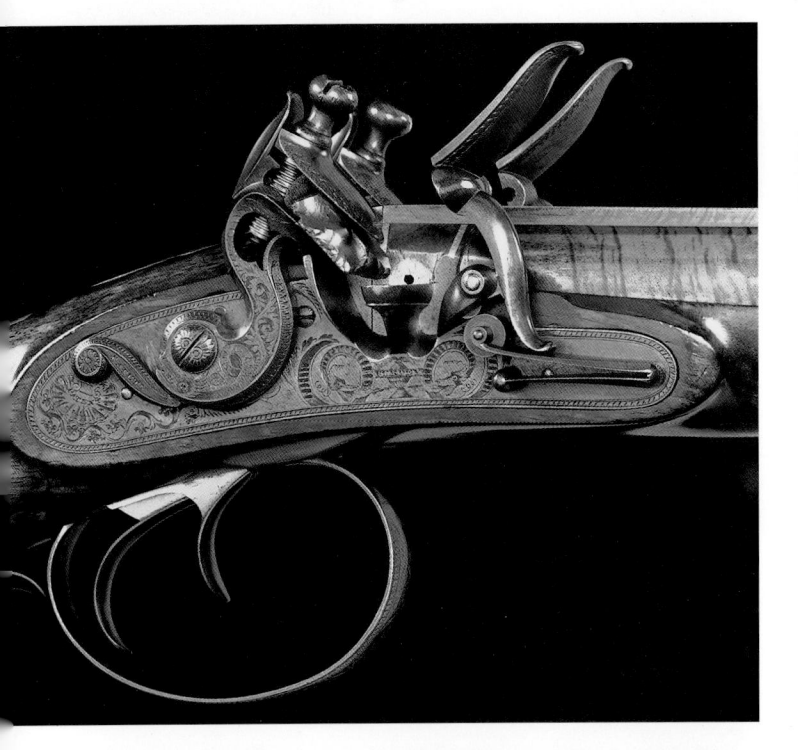

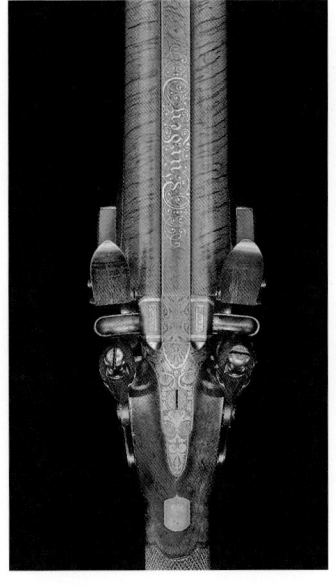

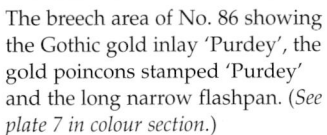

The breech area of No. 86 showing the Gothic gold inlay 'Purdey', the gold poincons stamped 'Purdey' and the long narrow flashpan. (*See plate 7 in colour section*.)

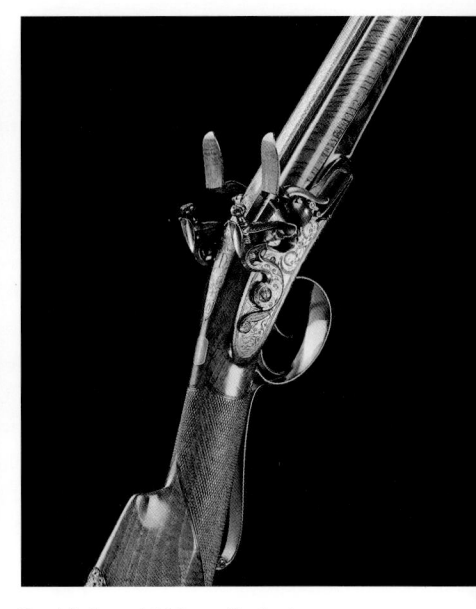

Double-barrel 16-bore flintlock sporting gun No. 86 built in 1818. (*See plate 6 in colour section*.)

Left: The lock of No. 86 showing the external sears of the Patent Safety of 1818. Note the engraving of sea serpents.

Below: A photograph taken in the Long Room in 1928, showing Athol Purdey holding double flint gun No. 86.

A double-barrel 14-bore percussion shotgun, No. 287, converted from flintlock is illustrated right. This gun was built in Princes Street around 1821 and converted some time later. The quality of the conversion is excellent and it is highly possible that it was converted by Purdey. The twist barrels have an elevated rib and are stamped 'CL' being built by Charles Lancaster. They have the Princes Street address on the top rib. The cut down lockplates still retain the 1818 Patent Safety and the word 'Patent' is engraved behind the external sear on the lockplate. 'Purdey' is engraved with flowing scrolls on the lockplate. The gun is contained in its original mahogany case with the small Princes Street label and another label with instructions on how to prevent barrel corrosion. Accessories in the case are a planished tin powder-flask, leather wallet with a two-piece turnscrew/nipple key, steel double-ended shot chargers and a two-piece cleaning rod in a leather case. As it was originally a flintlock, the locks have their own separate compartments within the case.

Plate 9 shows a very early percussion gun, No. 473, a single-barrel 12-bore sporting weapon constructed *circa* 1823. The 30-inch twist, two-stage barrel is part round part octagonal, with a gold poincon at the breech stamped, 'Purdey, London'. A platinum vent and a Purdey threaded nipple (to secure the percussion cap firmly) are fitted. The 1818 Patent Safety is engraved 'Patent' on the external sear. The grip lever of the safety has been modified to a far smaller lever. The lockplate and percussion hammer are engraved with sea monsters and 'Purdey' is engraved within a sunburst on the lock. The stock is of bird's eye maple of a wonderful

Double-barrel 14-bore flintlock converted gun No. 287 built in 1821. (*See plate 8 in colour section.*)

Below: The bird's eye maple stock of percussion gun No. 473. (*See plate 10 in colour section.*)

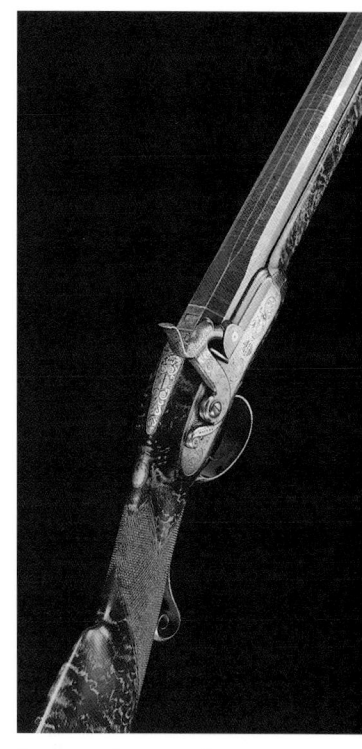

A very early percussion gun, single-barrel 12-bore sporting gun, No. 473, *circa* 1823 with Patent Safety and modified lever. (*See plate 9 in colour section.*)

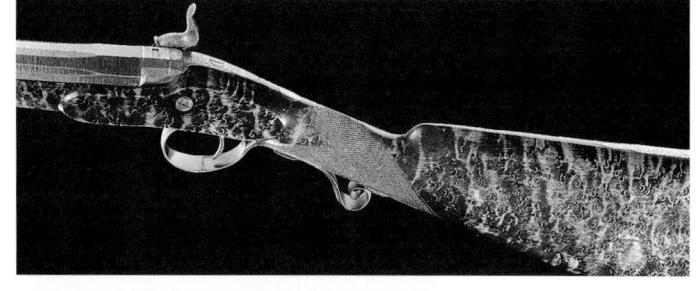

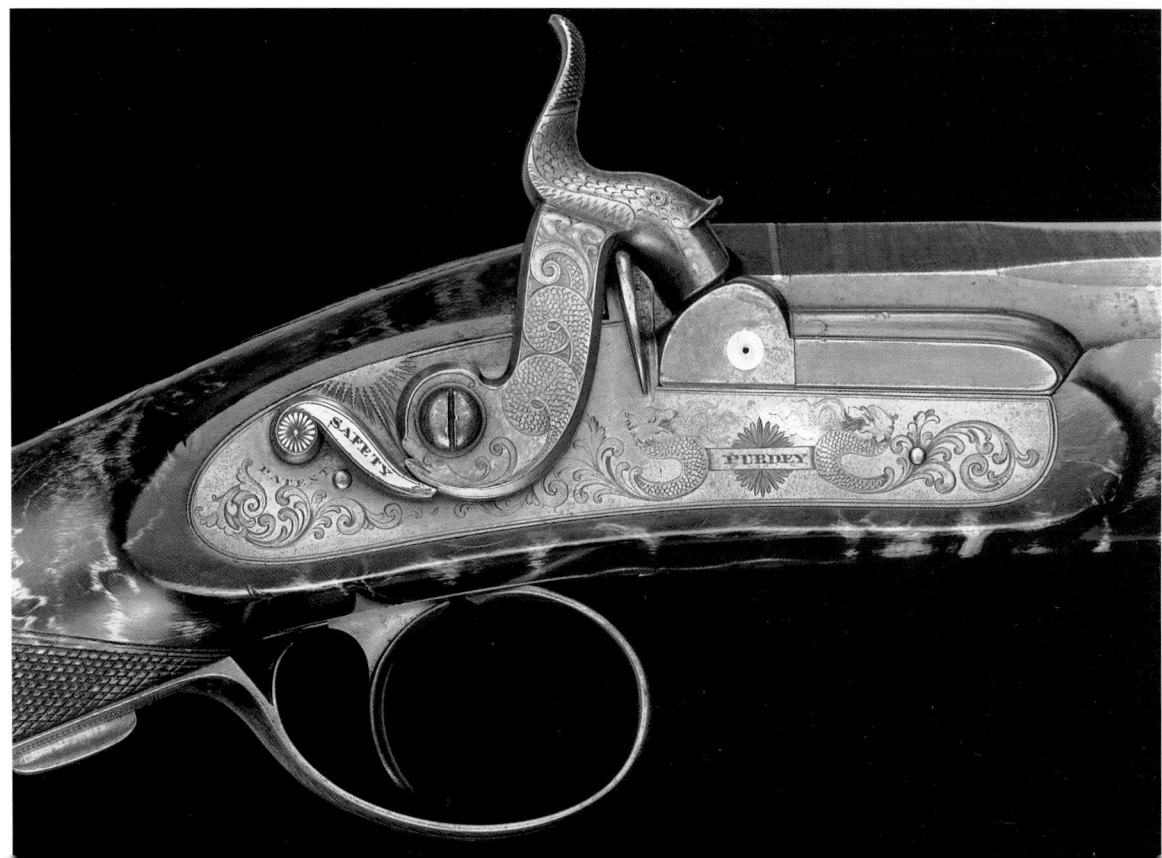

The lockplate of No. 473, showing the sea monster engraving and the sunburst around 'Purdey' still used today as part of the Purdey logo.

colour (see plate 10). No details of this gun are given in the Dimension Book.

Another very early double percussion gun is No. 544 built in 1823 (see plate 11). Apart from the fact that it was built for W Stuart, no other details of this gun are given in the Dimension Book. The twist barrels have a raised rib and platinum vents. The locks are engraved flamboyantly with double sunbursts and a scroll-embellished shell. Wyatt's 1818 Patent Safety is fitted and the word 'Patent' is engraved behind the external sear.

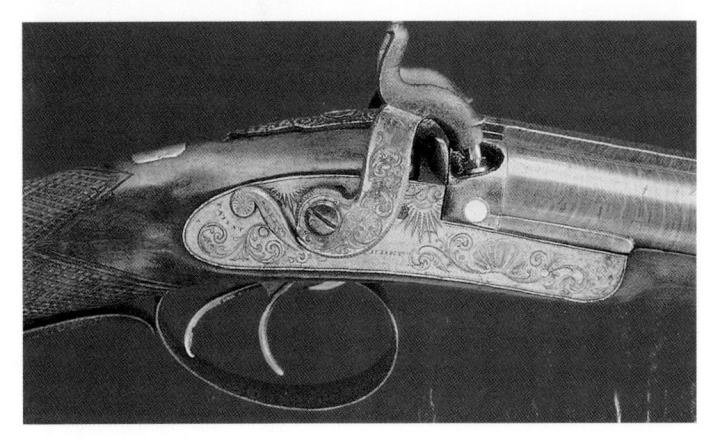

Double percussion gun No. 544 built in 1823 with the 1818 Patent Safety. (*See plate 11 in colour section.*)

A superb pair of percussion pistols, Nos. 1629/30 in a two-tier mahogany case (see plate 12) was sold originally on 28 February 1829 for £52. 10s to Sir James South. On 13 July 1835 they were resold for £25 and an extra pair of smooth-bore barrels costing £8. 8s were supplied at this time. On 23 June 1836 the new owner bought a new mahogany case, price £3. 13s. 6d., to house the entire outfit. Both rifled and smooth-bore barrels are 9 inches long, octagonal and have platinum vents and platinum bands. The locks have half-cock safeties and set triggers are fitted. The wrists of the butts have slots cut to accommodate the skeletal shoulder stock. The pistols are contained in a green baize-lined mahogany two-tier case fitted with full accessories. The upper tray contains a shoulder stock with tang marked 'J Purdey London', a loading mallet, a mainspring cramp, a cleaning brush, an ebony-handled powder measure, a bullet mould, an ebony handled turnscrew, a combination turnscrew/nipple key, a patch box, an ivory nipple box and a black japanned tin painted 'Gunpowder' in gold. The lower tier contains the pistols plus extra barrels, a loading rod, an oil bottle, a leather-covered Dixon powder flask, a wad punch, two horn percussion cap boxes and a bag of Westley-Richards percussion caps. These pistols were stocked by either Boss or Bagnall and engraved by Gumbrell.

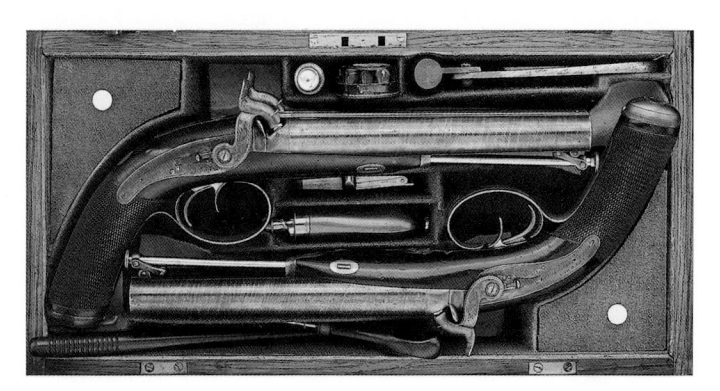

A pair of double-barrel back-action percussion pistols, Nos. 2114/5, in original oak case sold on 21 March 1831. (*See plate 13 in colour section.*)

A pair of 12-bore double-barrel percussion cavalry pistols. The pistols, numbered 2114/5 (see plate 13), sold on 21 March 1831 for £45 are listed in the Dimension Book simply as 'DP Back-Action'. The 7 1/2-inch barrels have silver foresights and swivel ramrods. The back-action locks have half-cock safeties and are engraved 'J Purdey 314 1/2 Oxford Street, London'. The stocks have the ebonised finish and domed butt-caps with traps. The pistols are contained in their original green baize-lined oak case complete with powder flask, cleaning rod, turnscrew, bullet mould marked 'No. 14', oil bottle, mainspring cramp and cap box. They were stocked by Atkin, hardened by Robins and engraved by Gumbrell.

Plate 14 shows a small double-barrel 32-bore percussion pistol, No. 2320, sold on 9 March 1832 for £23 to F Lumley. These small double pistols were for self-protection. They were light and convenient to carry and having two barrels offered extra protection. The twist barrels are 5 1/2 inches long but are not fitted with platinum vents. There is a small brass bead foresight on the muzzle end of the barrels. The locks are back action, with safety bolt, of the type found on many of the Purdey self-protection pistols. They are engraved 'J Purdey, 314 1/2 Oxford Street, London'. The stocks have the black lacquer ebonised finish and the butt is finished off with a domed steel pistol grip cap with a trap lid. Originally a steel stirrup ramrod would have been fitted.

The gun illustrated on plate 15 is an interesting example of an early percussion muzzle-loader converted to a centre-fire breech-loader. No. 3210 is a 16-bore sold as a percussion gun for £53. 15s. on 6 September 1838 to H W Heathcote. Its early

A pair of percussion pistols, Nos. 1629/30, sold on the 28 February 1829. These pistols have extra smooth bore barrels and are contained in a mahogany two tier case. (*See plate 12 in colour section.*)

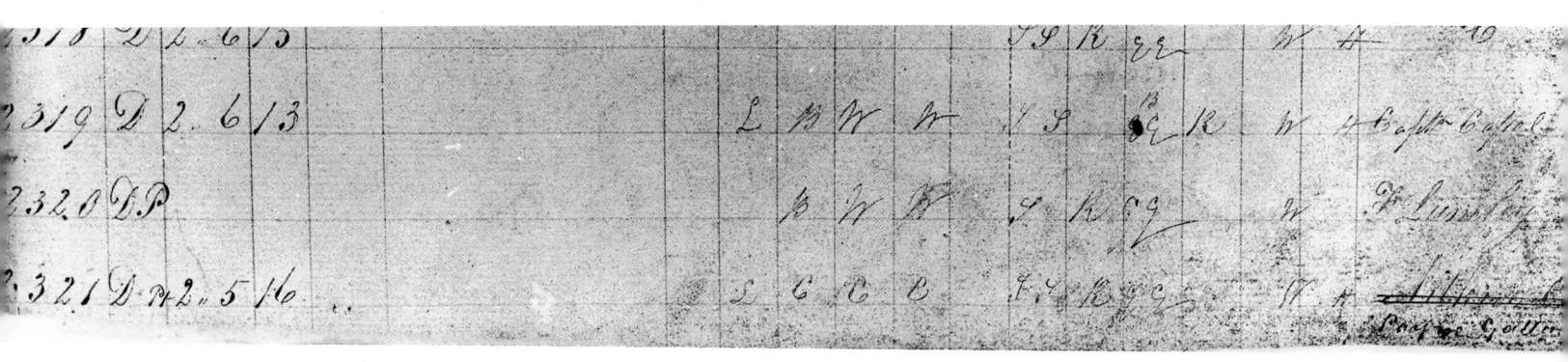

The record in the Dimension Book of No. 2320. See column headings on page 14. 'B' is either Boss or Bagnall, stocked; 'R' is Robins, polishing; 'G' is Gumbrell, engraving.

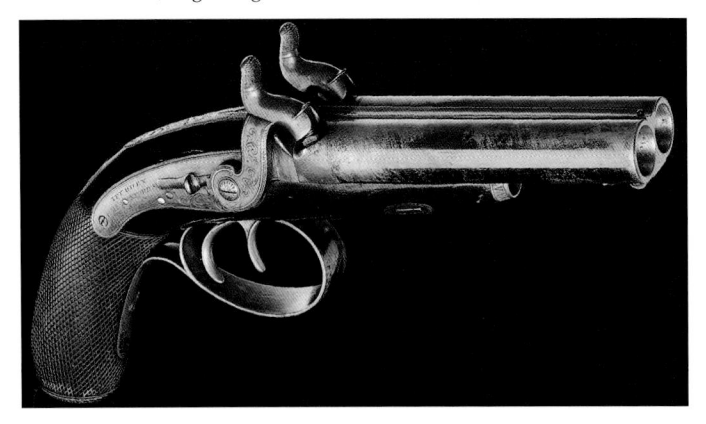

A small double-barrel 32-bore percussion pistol, No. 2320, sold on 9 March 1832. (*See plate 14 in colour section.*)

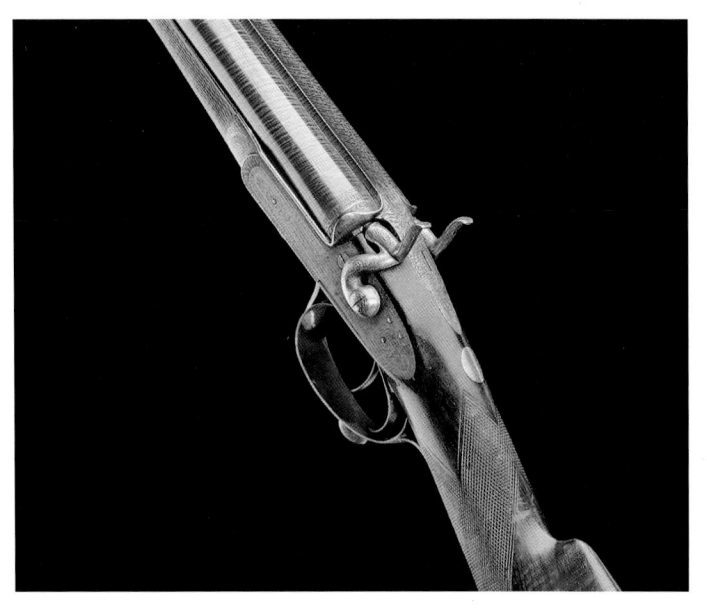

16-bore percussion muzzle-loader No. 3210 sold on 6 September 1838 and subsequently converted in the 1870s or 80s to an underlever centre-fire breech-loader. (*See plate 15 in colour section.*)

ancestry is obvious with its twist barrels, raised rib, open engraving, substantial stock and bow trigger guard. The stock has a cheek-piece. At some time in the 1870s or 1880s this gun was converted to a centre-fire breech-loader with non-rebounding locks and Jones underlever. Conversion was complex and expensive, involving a major re-construction of the gun, yet was quite popular in the late 19th century.

Double-barrel percussion rifle No. 3845 (see plate 16) is a 16-bore rifle sold on 5 July 1844 for £84 to Lord Blantyre. The rifle was most probably intended for deer-stalking and is an excellent example of the double Purdey percussion rifle before the Express was introduced in the early 1850s. James Purdey the Elder had a great interest and love of percussion rifles, to such an extent that Purdey produced a vast number – around 1,400 in total. The barrels are 30 inches long and have multi-groove rifling of 10 deep grooves. These early rifles, with their low velocity and poor trajectory, had a short range, born out by the fact that the sight on the barrel is ranged for 80 yards.

The top rib is engraved 'James Purdey, 314 1/2, Oxford Street, London'. Underneath the barrels is the stamp 'JP', denoting that they are Purdey barrels. Platinum vents are fitted. The locks are engraved 'Purdey' and have safety bolts. The percussion hammers are of the second Purdey pattern. The interior of the locks display no maker's initials. A grip tail trigger guard is present as was common on many rifles to steady the trigger pull. A patch box is fitted into the right-hand side of the stock.

Rifle No. 4826 is the type of Purdey (see plate 17) most collectors would give their hind teeth for. It is virtually

The record in the Dimension Book for No. 3210. See column headings on page 14. 'L' is Henry Lewis, locks jointed; 'B' is Bagnall, stocked; 'R' is Robins, polishing; 'G' is Gumbrell, engraving.

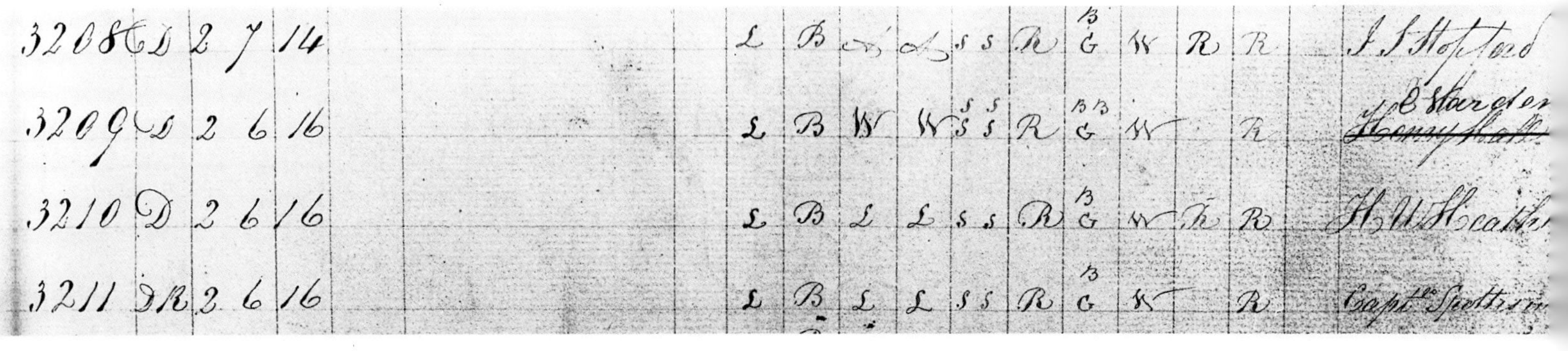

The record in the Dimensions Book for No. 3845. See column headings on page 28. 'L' is Henry Lewis, locks jointed, stocked, screwed, making off; 'R' is Robins, hardening.

Double-barrel percussion 16-bore rifle No. 3845, rifled with 10 grooves, sold on 5 July 1844. (*See plate 16 in colour section.*)

untouched from the day it was made, having lain in the same gun room for over a century and is cased with all accessories. Unfortunately, both hammer spurs have broken off, a not uncommon occurrence on percussion weapons. No. 4826 is a double-barrel 32-bore Express rifle sold on 18 June 1853 for £84 to J Balfour of Balbirnie House, Fife. It is an excellent example of the Purdey Express rifle, particularly since virtually all the accessories are present in the case.

The 31-inch barrels are engraved 'J Purdey, 314 1/2 Oxford Street, London' and are stamped 'JP' underneath. A flap sight has a fixed 'V' sight to 75 yds. and folding flaps to 150 yards. and 200 yards. The barrels have two-groove rifling with a pitch of one turn in six feet and there are engraved platinum vents in the breeches. The hickory ramrod is numbered '4826' to the gun and the brass tip has a deep recess to accommodate the nose of the bullet. The locks are engraved 'Purdey', have safety bolts and the hammers are of the second Purdey pattern. The locks are engraved '4826' on the inside but no maker's mark is present. The trigger guard is of the grip tail variety and an extended trigger plate finial is employed for extra strength. '4826' is engraved on the guard. The patch-box in the butt has simple engraving with the original owner's crest in the centre. The stock has a cheek-piece.

The gun is contained in its original mahogany case with brass carrying ring in the centre. Originally it had a leather outer cover. On the right-hand side of the lid, a handwritten set of loading instructions state, 'The Rifle shoots best with 2 1/2 drms. of No. 6 Powder. Sighted coarse for 75, 150, 200 yds., by taking the Sights fine, they answer for 50, 100 and 180 yds.'. The cropped 314 1/2 Oxford Street label is pasted in the lid.

The following original accessories are present in the case. An enamelled black tin powder canister with 'Rifle Powder' painted on it, also has a handwritten paper label 'No. 6 Powder'. When the lid is opened a brass screw cap is revealed. There are two bronze bullet moulds for casting winged bullets. The moulds have the same serial number as the rifle, are engraved with the original owner's name and have string wound round the handles to dissipate the heat when casting bullets. Each mould is slightly different: one is engraved with a '1' and the other is left blank. The reason for the slight difference in the moulds is that one mould casts, by a few thousands on an inch, a slightly smaller bullet than the other. This was necessary when the barrels became fouled and the original bullets could not be forced down.

When the bullets were cast from these moulds, there was always swarf and extraneous lead present and this had to be removed to create a perfect bullet. A bullet swage was provided for this purpose. This is a piece of hardwood shaped like a small stool with a metal top into which a hole and two grooves have been cut to exactly the same dimensions as the barrel bore. The bullet was forced through this swage to size it perfectly. The top of the swage is engraved with the original owner's name and the serial No. '4826'. Very similar to the bullet swage is a circular brass, patch/bullet aligning tool. In the centre, a hole with two grooves is cut, again to the same dimension as the barrels. A circular recess surrounds the central hole to the exact diameter of a 32-bore patch. The greased patch was placed in this recess and the bullet pushed through the central hole taking the patch with it. In this way the bullet would be perfectly centred in the patch for accurate shooting. There is a patch punch for stamping out the patches from pieces of Cambric muslin. This fabric is very thin and care had to be taken not to put two patches stuck together round the bullet.

There is a nickel powder measure with '2 1/2 drms.' engraved on the side to ensure an exact measure – rifles had to be loaded precisely to ensure accurate shooting. One very rare accessory present is a steel funnel. One end of the funnel has a screw thread identical in size to the nipple thread. If a sportsman omitted to load a bullet without a powder charge, he removed the nipple and screwed the small funnel in place. At the other end the funnel opened out and powder could be poured down the funnel into the breech. The nipple would then be replaced and the gun fired. Cleaning equipment consists of a rod with a detachable rounded knob and various bronze turksheads and jags. A spare locknail and spare nipples complete a very comprehensive outfit.

The record in the Dimension Book for No. 4826. See column headings on page 28. 'G' is Henry Glaysher, locks jointed; 'L' is Henry Lewis, stocked, screwed together, making off; 'R' is Robins, polishing and hardening. Note No. 4828, a rifle for Lord Henry Bentinck.

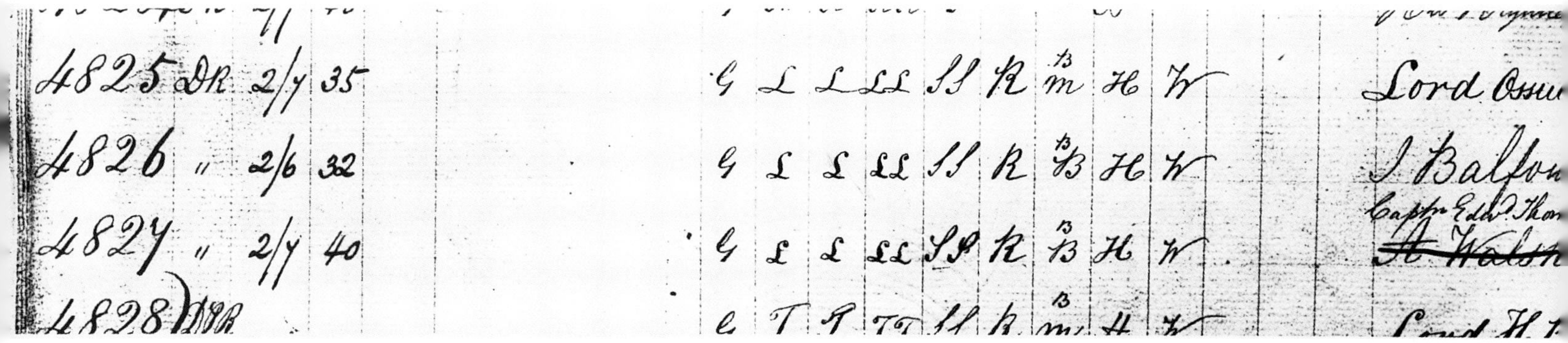

Double-barrel percussion, 32-bore, two-groove Express rifle No. 4826, cased with all accessories, sold on 18 June 1853. (*See plate 17 in colour section.*)

The enamelled black tin powder canister with 'Rifle Powder' painted on it and handwritten label 'No. 6 Powder'.

The extended trigger plate finial of Express rifle No. 4826.

Bronze bullet moulds for casting the winged bullets.

MUZZLE-LOADING GUNS, RIFLES AND PISTOLS

Original oxidised winged bullets, wads, patch and patch punch.

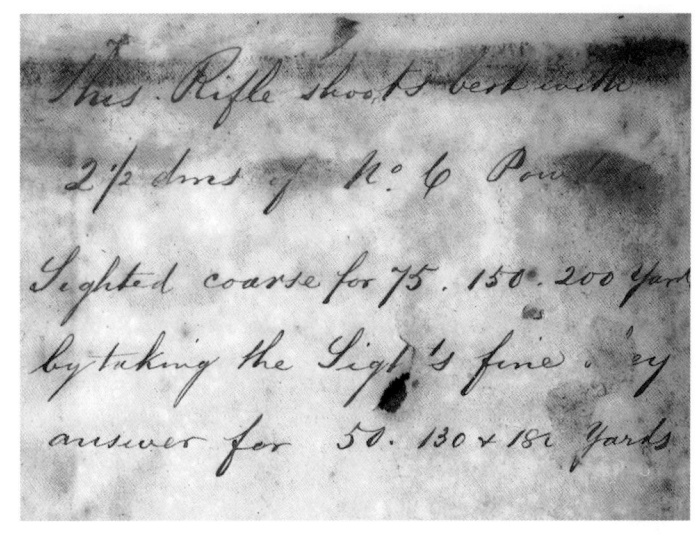

Loading and sighting instructions for rifle No. 4826 pasted into the lid.

The very rare steel funnel for pouring powder into the breech should a sportsman forget to charge the gun with powder; circular brass patch/bullet aligning tool showing the two grooves in the centre and circular recess exactly the same size as the patch in the foreground; nickel powder measure; bullet swage for accurately sizing the bullet after casting. All from rifle No. 4826.

Two-groove 40-bore Express rifle No. 7463 is illustrated on plate 19. This Express rifle is in superb condition, retaining much of its original colouring. It is a late-built muzzle-loading Express rifle sold on 8 August 1867 for £84 to H Wood. Interestingly, No. 7464 was identical to a rifle sold to C Wood, presumably a relative. The 30-inch Damascus barrels have a matt file cut rib and engraved platinum vents. The locks have the very slim fourth pattern hammer. The patch-box is finely scroll engraved as is the tang, the work of Lucas. The stock has a pistol-grip.

Bronze cleaning tools for rifle No. 4826.

A two-groove 40-bore Express rifle No. 7463 sold on 8 August 1867 to H Wood (*See plate 19 in colour section.*)

43

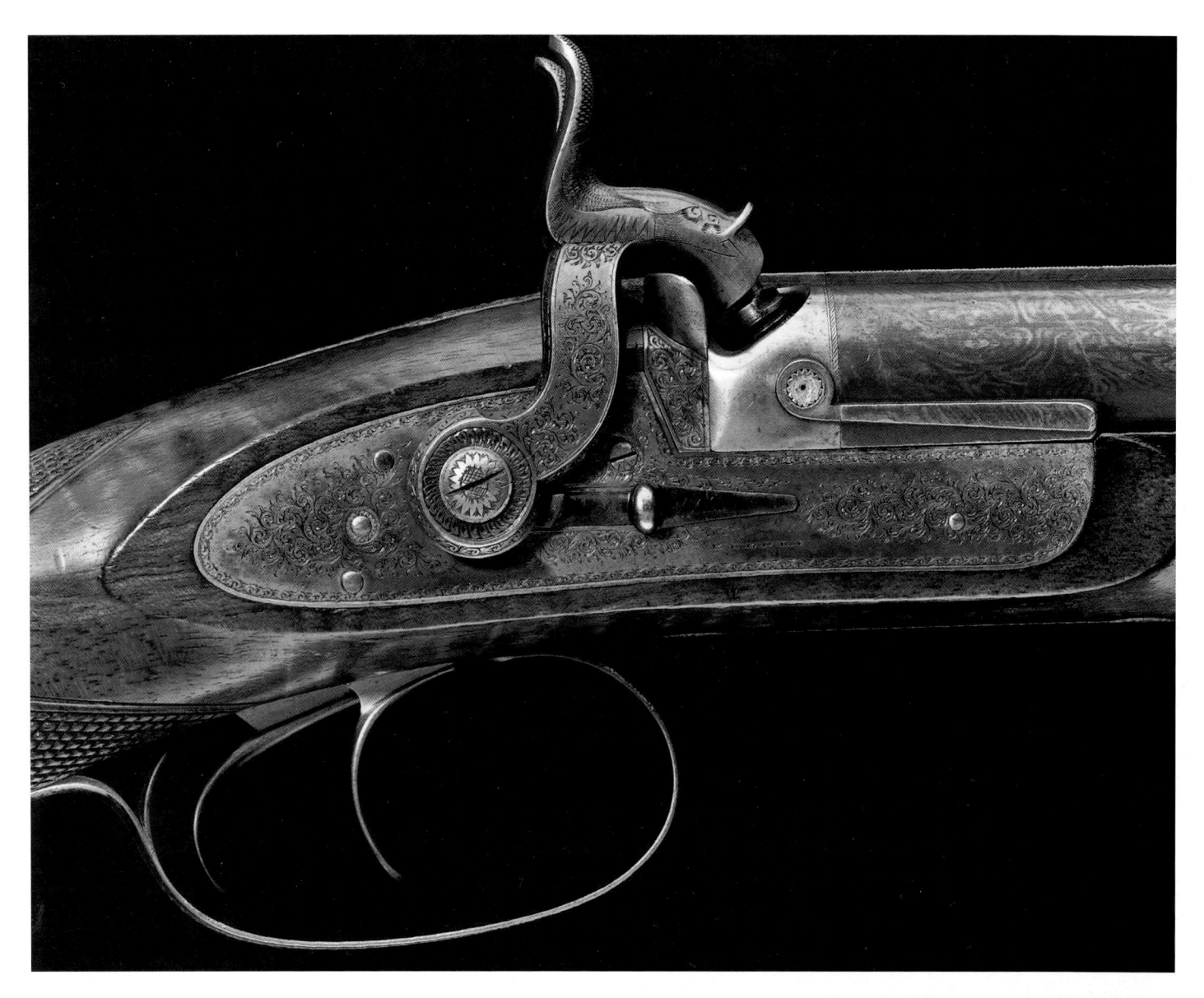

The lockplate of No. 7463.

The fine Lucas scroll engraved patch-box of No. 7463.

The record in the Dimension Book for No. 7463. See column headings on page 84. 'C' is Carver, jointing, stocking and screwing; 'GP' is G Prentice, cocking; 'L' is Lucas, engraving; 'R' is Robins, hardening.

MUZZLE-LOADING GUNS, RIFLES AND PISTOLS

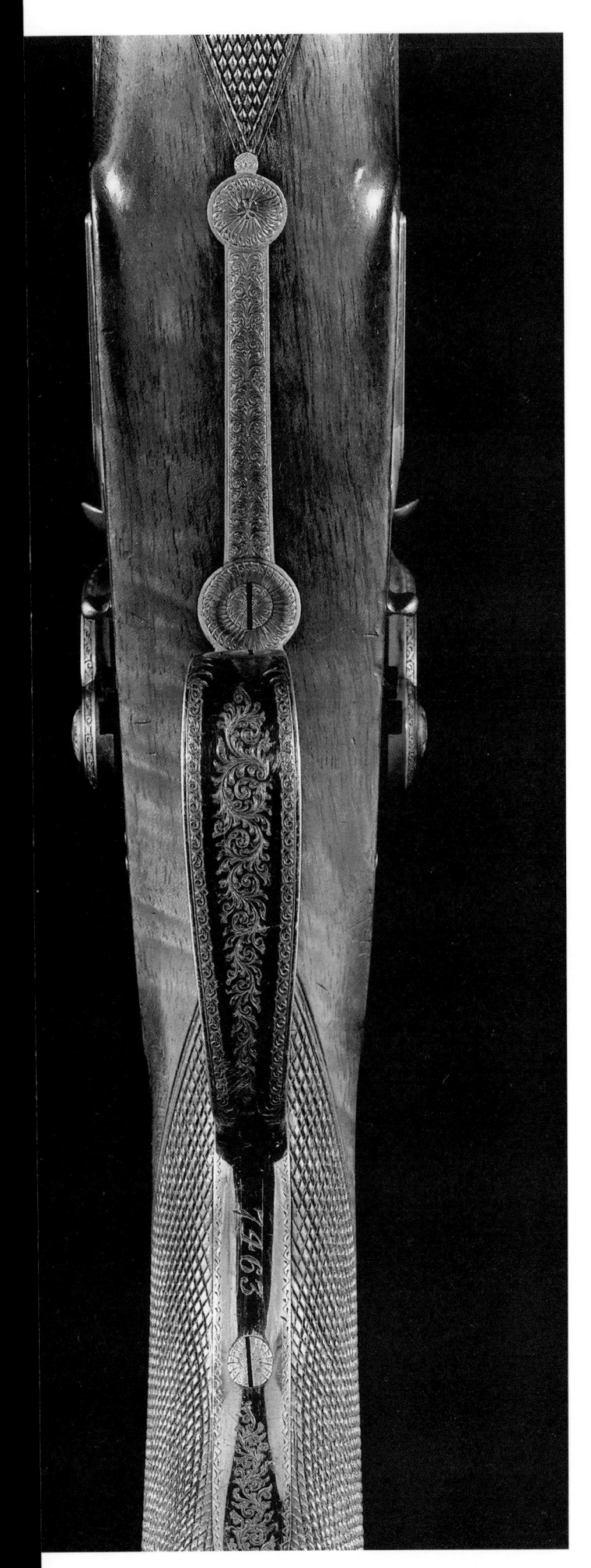

The tang of No. 7463.

The trigger guard and extended trigger plate finial of No. 7463.

A very late built muzzle-loading shotgun, No. 7902 (see plate 20) is a double-barrel 12-bore gun tested on 1 March 1869. By this date, centre-fire breech-loaders were well established and very few muzzle-loaders were constructed. The gun was supplied to the gunmakers Moore & Sons. The 12-bore Damascus barrels are 32 inches long with engraved platinum vents. The percussion hammers are far slimmer than the more conventional design and closely mirror the elegant hammers of the breech-loaders of this era. The gun is unusual in its display of game scene engraving, quite uncommon on a Purdey in this period. The lockplates and trigger guard show a setter and pheasant engraved by Lucas and Mace.

A very late-built 12-bore muzzle-loading gun No. 14987 (see plate 18) was sold in November 1894 to Charles Gordon, a muzzle-loading diehard who ordered large numbers of muzzle-loaders in the late 19th century from various makers. Purdey built several shotguns, rifles and pistols for him at the turn of the century. The Gordon guns all follow a similar vein. Their specifications are slightly unusual and they are all housed in ostentatious cases with every conceivable accessory. Most have never been fired.

No. 14987 has 32-inch Whitworth steel barrels, back action locks and platinum vents. The gun is contained in a lavish green baize-lined oak case with a full complement of accessories, including two leather-covered powder flasks, two

Double-barrel 12-bore percussion sporting gun No. 7902 tested on 1 March 1869. A late built muzzle-loader. (*See plate 20 in colour section.*)

The record in the Dimension Book for No. 7902. See column headings on page 84. 'J' is Jones, jointing. stocking and screwing; 'GP' is G Prentice, cocking; 'L' and 'M' are Lucas and Mace, engraving; 'R' is Robins, hardening.

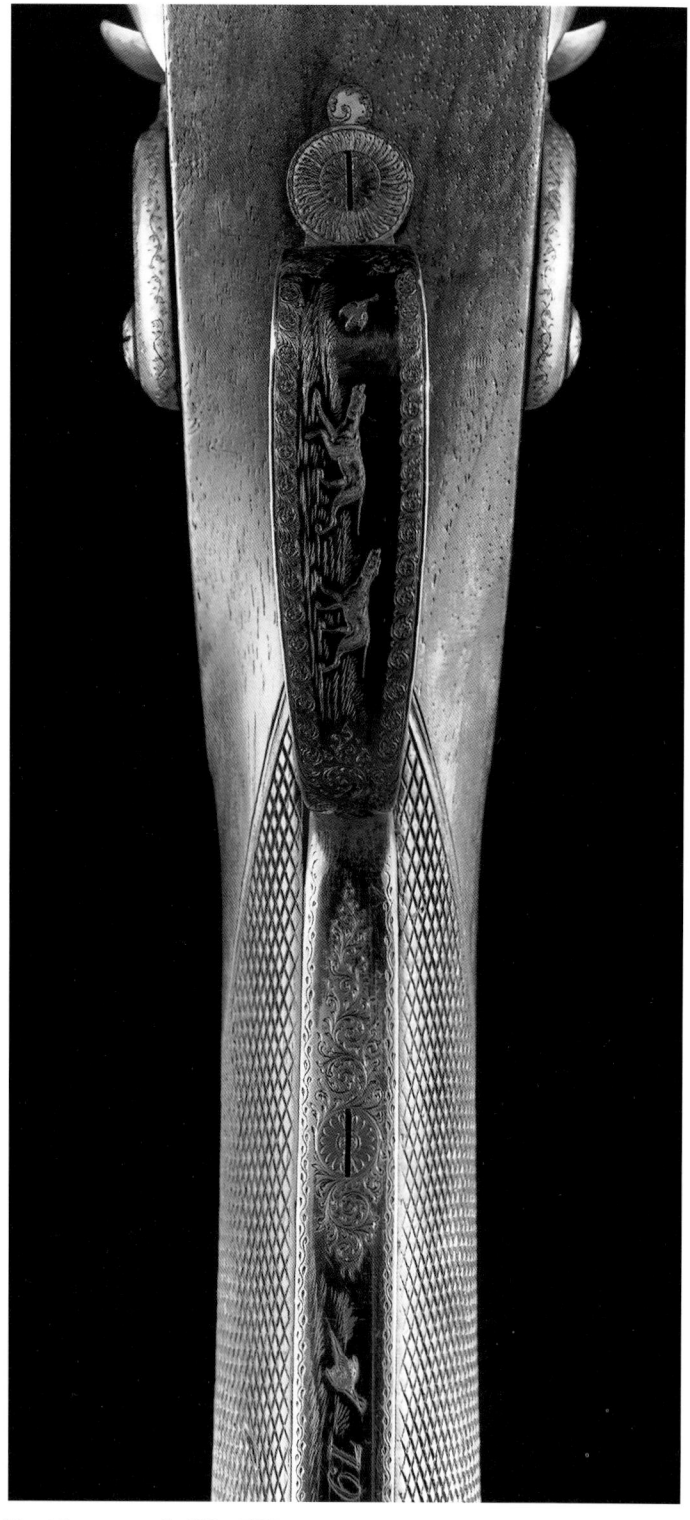

The trigger guard of No. 7902.

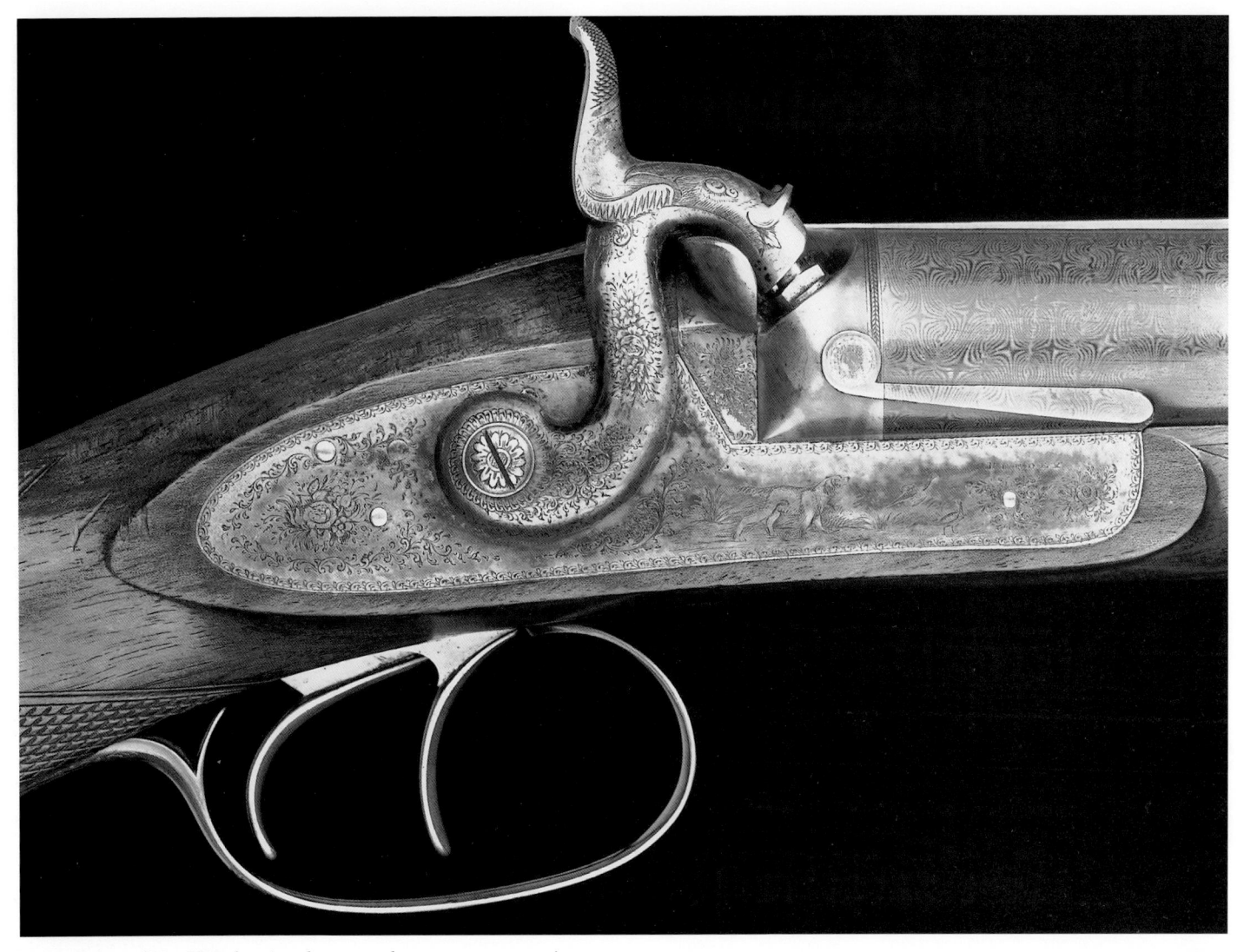

The lockplate of No. 7902 showing the unusual game scene engraving.

shot pouches, two nipple cleaning tools, a nipple key, two turnscrews, oil bottle, ivory container with two spare nipples, a mainspring cramp, wad punch, oak wad container, leather case containing a two piece rosewood cleaning rod and a spare rosewood ramrod. This gun was stocked by James Lumsden and put together by Apted.

The second last muzzle-loader built by Purdey's was No. 17766, again to the order of Charles Gordon (see plate 21). The actual last Purdey muzzle-loader was yet another Gordon gun, a 14-bore, No. 18198 sold on 3 July 1904. No. 17766 is a double-barrel 14-bore percussion gun sold on 16 March 1904. The back action locks hark back to the very early percussion period and have a 'steel nose with shield to prevent blowback to hammers'. The gun has 36-inch Whitworth steel barrels and weighs in at 10 lbs. 2oz., a very heavy weight for a 14-bore. Double-barrel bolts are used on account of the length of the barrels. The gun is contained in a green velvet-lined oak case with a plethora of accessories to cover all needs and eventualities. No. 17766 was stocked by Lumsden and put together be Hopewell. I wonder what the Purdey gunmakers in 1904 thought about this gun, when hammerless ejectors had been the norm for twenty years?

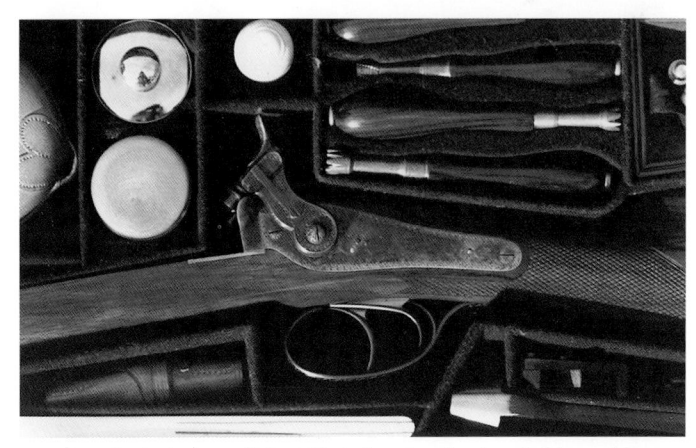

Detail on the lockwork of No. 17766, showing the detachable steel hammer noses evocative of a far earlier era.

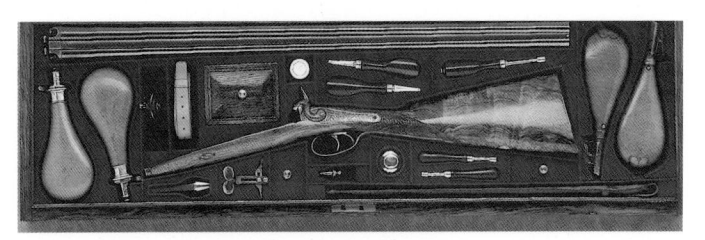

A late-built 12-bore percussion gun No. 14987 sold in November 1894 to Charles Gordon. (*See plate 18 in colour section.*)

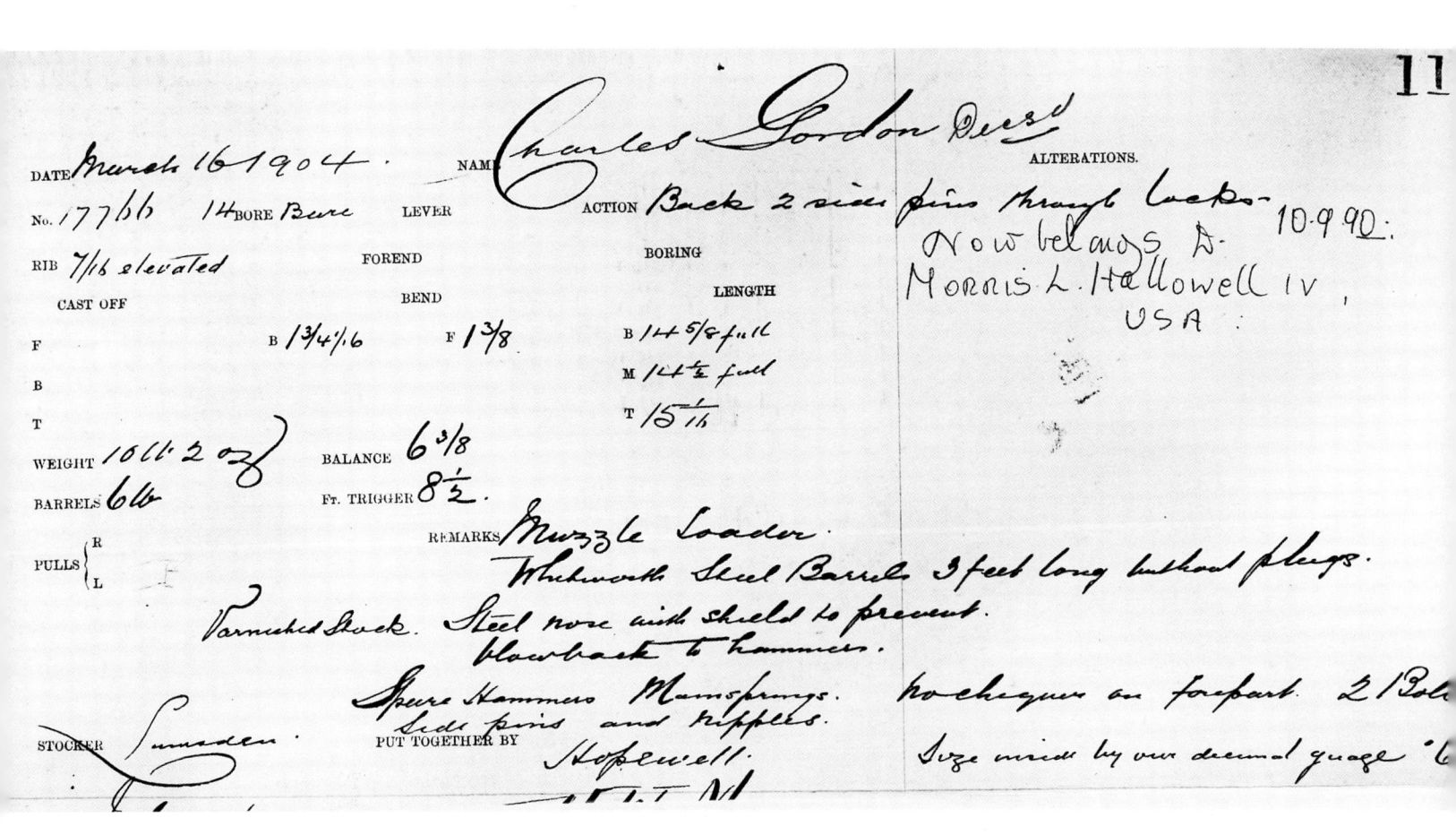

The record in the Dimension Book for No. 17766. Note beside 'Remarks', 'Muzzle-loader. Whitworth steel barrels 3 feet long without plugs. Varnished stock. Steel nose with shield to prevent blowback to hammers. Spare hammers. Mainsprings. Side pins and nipples. No chequer on forepart. 2 Bolts. Stocked by Lumsden and put together by Hopewell.

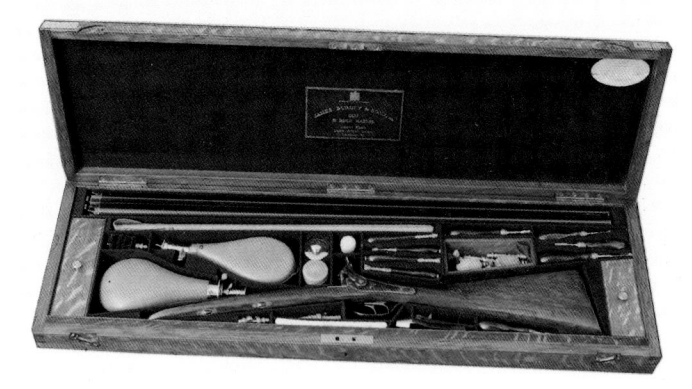

The second last muzzle-loader constructed by Purdey, No. 17766 sold on 16 March 1904 to Charles Gordon. 14-bore with 36-inch Whitworth barrels cased with every accessory. (*See plate 21 in colour section.*)

Chapter five

BOLT AND BEESLEY

In the 1850s a major metamorphosis occurred in gun development – the introduction and public awareness of the breech-loader. Breech-loading guns had been around ever since the invention of guns themselves but had never previously proved to be reliable or superior to muzzle-loaders.

The development of the effective breech-loader originated in France. On 29 September 1812, Samuel Pauly obtained French patent no. 843 for a breech-loading system. In Pauly's system, the barrels were fixed, the breech block lifted up and a paper cartridge, very similar to a modern day cartridge, inserted. Bearing in mind that Forsyth's percussion system had just been introduced a few years earlier, this gun was really too advanced for its time to gain public acceptance. A successor to Pauly, Casimir Lefaucheux in the 1830s utilised the now conventional method of barrels pivoting down to accept a pinfire cartridge at the breech and developed an efficient breech locking mechanism.

The breech-loading action had by now been developed but the cartridges used were far from gas-tight. In 1846 a Parisian gunmaker, Houllier, in patent no. 1963, invented the gas-tight cartridge that would transform the breech-loader. The essential feature of Houllier's invention was that he introduced the base wad. Upon detonation the base wad expanded to seal the chamber and after firing returned to its original size to permit the removal of the spent case.

These developments in France appear to have had little impact in Britain until the Great Exhibition opened in Hyde Park, London on 1 May 1851. This 'Great Exhibition of the Works of Industry of All Nations' had originated in the mind of Queen Victoria's husband, Prince Albert. Industrialisation had proceeded so rapidly that countries were keen to exhibit the great strides that had taken place. Even the building itself was revolutionary, constructed in glass, iron and prefabricated. Sixty-five British, 22 French, 18 German and 14 Belgian gunmakers exhibited, in addition to various other smaller contingents from other countries. Interestingly, Purdey's did not exhibit, although they played a big part in later 19th century exhibitions.

With the benefit of hindsight, the most important exhibit in the Small Arms section was 'No. 1308 Lefaucheux Paris:

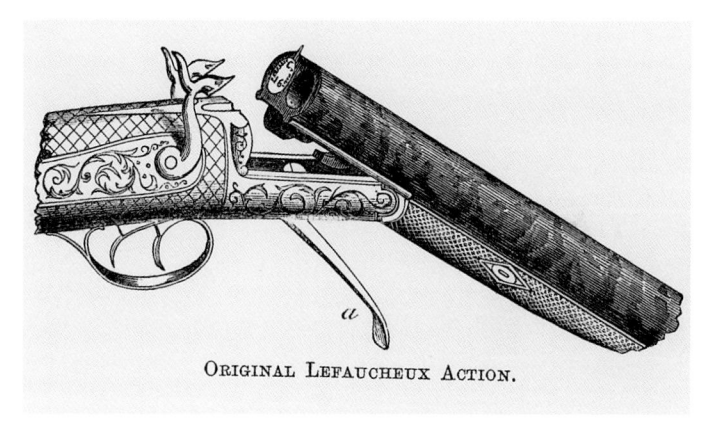

ORIGINAL LEFAUCHEUX ACTION.

The Lefaucheux pinfire breech-loader *circa* 1840 with pinfire cartridges.

different sorts of guns'. This was the breech-loading pinfire gun and cartridge. This exhibit would prove to be a watershed in the history of gun development in Britain. An efficient breech-loading gun and cartridge was brought to the attention of a great many gunmakers in Britain.

It is generally acknowledged that Purdey's son-in-law, Joseph Lang, the gunmaker of 22 Cockspur Street, was one of the few gunmakers to attempt to improve on the Lefaucheux breech-loader and one of the first to build breech-loaders in Britain. This must have been a major talking point between the Lang and Purdey families and it is tempting to suggest that James Purdey the Younger had such knowledge of the early breech-loaders that he improved upon them with his famous snap action patent no. 1104 of 2 May 1863.

The pinfire guns of the early 1850s were dangerous on account of their poor closing mechanisms and very thin standing breeches. Like most established gunmakers, Purdey waited until the manufacturing techniques of the breech-loader were better understood. A firm like Purdey's had a great deal to lose by producing an unreliable or dangerous weapon. The first breech-loader to appear in Purdey's records is a double-barrel 13-bore pinfire shotgun, No. 5305, produced in 1857. It was not sold until 26 October 1864, at a second-hand sale for £27, plus 250 loaded cartridges at £2.2s.6d. It was sold to F Soames. It is probable that this breech-loader was experimental, and this might explain its later sale. The first

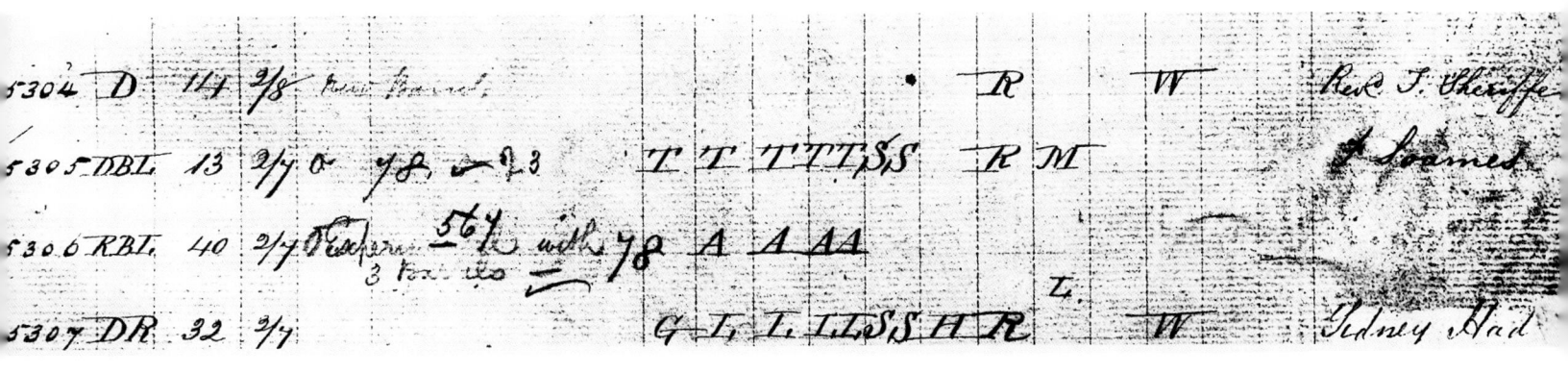

The record in the Dimension Book for the first recorded Purdey pinfire breech-loading gun, No. 5305, and the first recorded pinfire breech-loading rifle, No. 5306, both built in 1857, probably as experiments. No. 5305 was stocked and screwed by Tregale, hardened by A Robins and engraved by J Mace. No. 5306 was stocked and screwed by H Atkin. For some reason an 'Experiment with 3 Barrels' has been written in later on.

breech-loading pinfire rifle recorded is No. 5306, a single-barrel 40-bore rifle with a 31-inch barrel produced in 1857. No sale is recorded of this rifle. The probable reason for the consecutive serial numbers is that both weapons were experimental, both shotgun and rifle construction being tried out. The first double-barrel breech-loading pinfire rifle recorded is No. 5323, a 40-bore with 31-inch barrels sold to W Bromley-Davenport who lived close to Purdey's at his London address of Grosvenor Square. Although the rifle was built in 1857, it was not sold until 1862. The sales ledger records:

> June 6 1862
> A Best finished B/Ldg.
> Dble Rifle No. 5323 complete £84.0s.0d
> 100 Loaded cartridges for d.b. £1.6s.0d
> 100 Unloaded do. 7s.0d
> 100 Prepared felt for do. 1s.6d
> 1lb No. 6 Powder 3s.6d

The first actual sale of a Purdey pinfire breech-loader recorded is No. 5462 purchased for £57.15s. on 3 May 1858.

The very early Purdey pinfire breech-loaders of 1857-61, in common with various other makers, used a single grip worked by an underlever, or lever lying forward beneath the fore-end. This locking method was unsound and not robust enough and could result in a loose action. It must be remembered that breech-loading was in its infancy and that the mechanisms and pressures of the system were not properly understood. Relatively few Purdey's were built with this action.

The problem was solved by a gunmaker Henry Jones who invented the double grip screw underlever. He patented this with patent no. 2040 of 7 September 1859. This double grip screw underlever was used on guns of all qualities and types and made in massive quantities in the second half of the 19th century. It was relatively simple to make, very reliable, involving no springs, and offered a safe and secure method of locking the breech. Henry Jones should have made his fortune from this but was in such dire financial straits that he let the

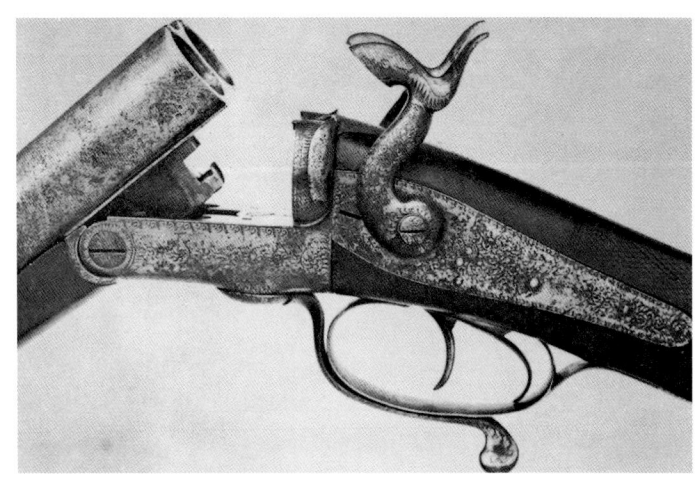

One of the first pinfire breech-loading shotguns built by Purdey. No 6039 of 1861 uses an unsatisfactory single-grip screw underlever. This gun was built for the Hon. Chas. Howard, was stocked by Henry Atkin and engraved by J Mace.

patent lapse on 19 September 1862 for want of payment of the £50 stamp duty necessary to prolong it. In the Jones double grip there are two bites with inclines cut in the barrel lump. A coarse screw underlever engages these bites and as the lever closes, progressively tightens to draw the barrels tight to the action face.

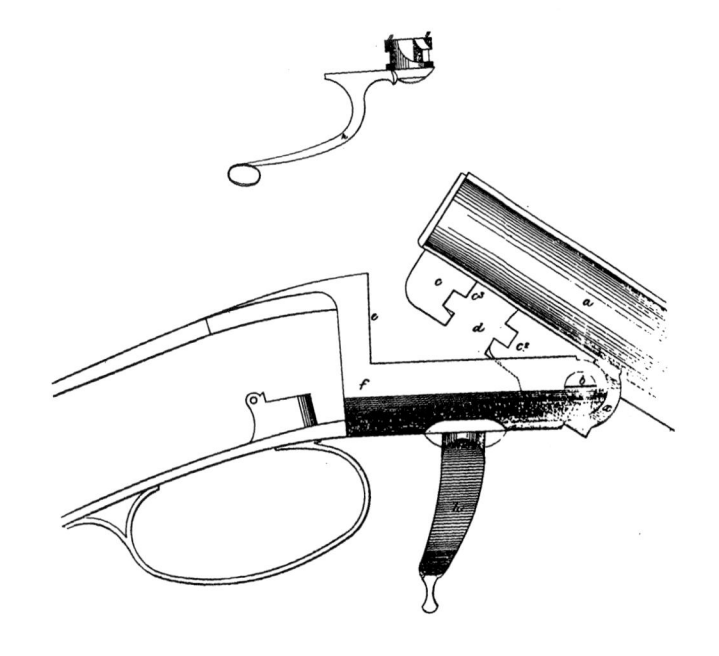

Henry Jones double-grip screw underlever patent no. 2040 of 7 September 1859.

Purdey's, like most other makers, understood the merits of this invention and adopted it for their breech-loaders. Although universally known today as the 'underlever', it was always referred to in the 19th century as the 'Lever Over Guard' and this is the terminology that will be found in Purdey's records. This lever over guard was the main closing system used by Purdey's until the introduction of the snap action patent no. 1104 of 1863. Upon the adoption of this snap action and the subsequent use of the Scott top lever of 1865, Purdey's rarely used the lever over guard. It tended to be used more often in rifles where greater pressures were exerted and on guns used abroad where it was more reliable. The snap action was far faster and combined with the early thumb-hole and the later top lever system of opening, made for a far lighter and more elegant gun that served to enhance the Purdey reputation even more.

Purdey's introduced their own variant of the lever over guard, referred to in the records as 'Long Guard Lever'. In this design the underlever is combined with a moveable trigger guard to give more leverage to the grip. The long guard lever is far more prevalent on rifles where a stronger locking action is required (see plate 22).

THE BASTIN/PURDEY SLIDE ACTION

Purdey produced in the 1860s to another design from the continent, a small number of Bastin slide action pinfire breech-loaders on the slide forward principle. A total of 41 slide actions, 34 shotguns and 7 rifles were produced, the first recorded being No. 6122 of 1861 and the last recorded No. 7933 in 1869. In the records they are referred to as 'slide action' or 'slide forward action'.

In the Bastin system, the barrels do not drop but slide backwards and forwards in a metal fore-end that is a direct extension of the action body. The barrels were moved forward by a lever linked to the underside of the fore-end, to receive the cartridges. Upon closing, a catch upon the lever bolted the barrels tight against the action face.

Purdey appeared to have produced the two varieties of the Bastin system. In one version the long lever is pulled backwards to open the mechanism and upon closure locks at the fore-end and in the other the lever is pushed forwards to open the mechanism and upon closure, locks near the trigger guard (see plate 23). In Purdey's patent no. 424 of 14 February 1865, he illustrates a slide action gun with the lever fastening at the trigger guard. (This patent is partly concerned with an extractor system for centre-fire cartridges to be used in the slide action). Just what arrangement Purdey had with Bastin is open to speculation. The name 'Bastin' is not written in any of the records, nor is there any stamp as such on Purdey's weapons. The Bastin system was complicated to make and created a heavy gun. It rapidly fell into disuse when the underlever and snap action proved their superiority.

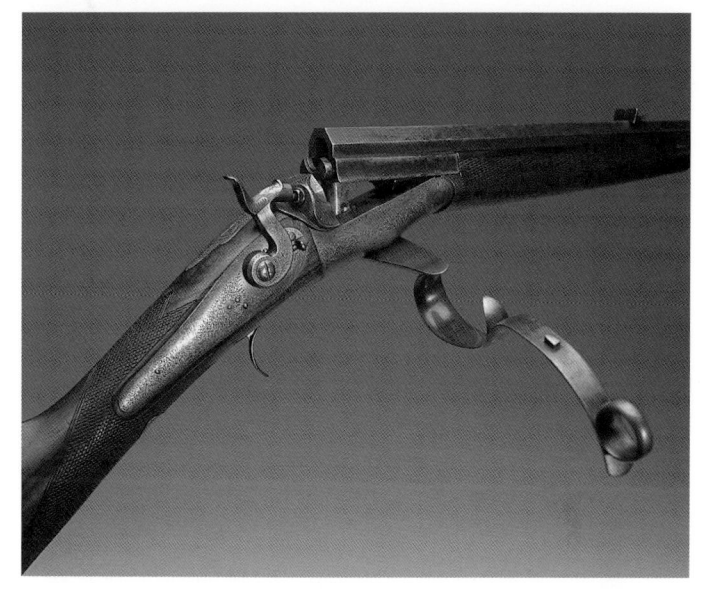

A single-barrel .450 rifle, No. 9223 of 1874, showing the 'Long Guard Lever'. (*See plate 22 in colour section.*)

A 12-bore Bastin pinfire sporting gun No. 6424 tested on 21 October 1863. This gun has the forward opening lever. (*See plate 23 in colour section.*)

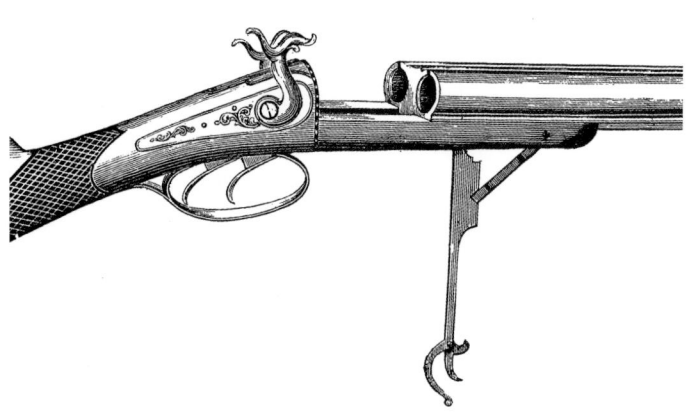

Bastin slide action breech-loader.

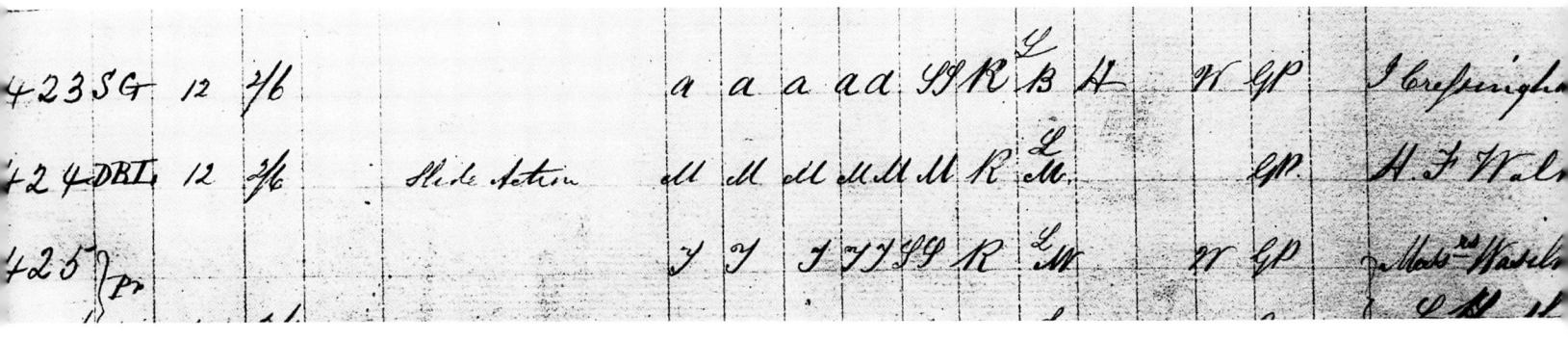

The record in the Dimension Book for slide action gun No. 6424. See column headings on page 66. 'R' is A Robins, hardening. 'L' is J Lucas and 'M' is J Mace, engraving. 'GP' is G Prentice, cocks.

THE ADOPTION OF THE BREECH-LOADER

During the 1850s, the introduction of the breech-loader caused great debate among sportsmen and gunmakers. The new system created many new gunmaking challenges that would result in a flurry of activity in the second half of the 19th century to produce a plethora of patents of all varieties and designs. Purdey's alone took out nine patents in this period.

The relative merits of the muzzle-loader and breech-loader caused much controversy and J H Walsh, editor of *The Field*, in response to lively debate in his columns, announced a trial involving both types of weapon. The first *Field* trial was held on 9 and 10 April 1858 and the results were indecisive. A second trial was held at the well-known live pigeon shooting ground at Hornsey Wood House on 4 and 5 July 1859. This showed the great improvement that had been made to breech-loaders in the space of a year and proved them to be the equal of muzzle-loaders. Interestingly, none of the great gunmakers including Purdey's took part in these trials, having more to lose if public failure occurred.

These trials are of great importance to the acceptance of the breech-loader. The trials proved that breech-loaders were on a par with the muzzle-loader. Coupled with the constant rapid improvements on the technical side of breech-loading and the far greater ease of use of the system, it is no wonder that the demands for breech-loaders grew rapidly in the late 1850s and early 1860s. Purdey's Dimension Books and Sales Ledgers show just how rapid the changeover to breech-loading was.

Date	Muzzle-loading shotguns	Breech-loading shotguns	Muzzle-loading rifles	Breech-loading rifles
1859	109	67	27	1
1860	69	117	34	4
1861	49	121	31	9
1862	35	115	16	27

It can be seen from the above table that the watershed year for shotguns was 1860 and the similar occurrence for rifles slightly later at 1862. The reasons behind the belated acceptance of the breech-loading rifle, were fears that early breech-loading mechanisms could not withstand the greater pressures and the lack of need for a rifle to be re-loaded quickly. From the early 1860s, therefore, the breech-loader rose to prominence and the muzzle-loader declined thereafter. By around 1870, the muzzle-loader had had its day at Purdey's, although occasional examples were still being made right up to the turn of the century. Probably the last muzzle-loading gun made by Purdey's was 14-bore gun, No. 18198, sold on 3 July 1904. This gun was sold to Charles Gordon, the great buyer of muzzle-loaders of all descriptions in this period, John Dickson of Edinburgh being his principal choice.

THE DEATH OF JAMES PURDEY THE FOUNDER – 6 NOVEMBER 1863

By the time the breech-loader was making its appearance, James Purdey the Elder was well into his seventies. The day-to-day running of the business had been in the capable hands of his son James the Younger since 1 January 1858, and the elder Purdey tended to spend a great deal of his time at his seaside retreat, Rifle House in Margate. His health was ailing and it was only right that he should enjoy his well-earned retirement at a seaside resort.

His wife Mary, pre-deceased him, dying, aged 69, on 5 February 1860 at their home, Rifle Cottage in the Queen's Road, Bayswater. Her death certificate states that she died of 'Fever Three Weeks' and refers to her husband's retirement: 'Wife of James Purdey formerly a gunmaker'. She left no will. Mary was interred in Paddington Cemetery, Willesden Lane. Her husband had purchased a vault in the cemetery and by the beginning of World War 1, this Purdey vault contained the remains of eleven family members. In addition to Mary, the prominent Purdeys interred in the vault are:

> James Purdey the Elder, died 6 November 1863.
> Caroline Purdey, first wife of James Purdey the Younger, died 7 January 1870.
> James Purdey III, son of James Purdey the Younger, died 9 September 1890.
> James Purdey the Younger, died 13 March 1909.
> Julia Purdey, second wife of James Purdey the Younger, died 5 January 1911.

Paddington Cemetery was later re-named Willesden Cemetery and today the Purdey vault can be located in row 1H, No. 756. Unfortunately for the casual visitor, there is absolutely no evidence to denote the importance of the grave or even identify it. Until the 1970s, the vault was embellished by an elaborately carved marble tomb, but this had to be dismantled due to its deteriorating state and danger to the public. All the other vaults in the cemetery have suffered the

The Purdey vault in Willesden (old Paddington) Cemetery today, row 1H, No. 756. Nothing remains of the tomb that adorned the stone slabs and there is no evidence left to record the Purdey interments. The vault is in the foreground with other vaults in similar condition in the background.

same fate. Today, all that remains are the enormous horizontal stone slabs that seal the vault, with no carving or inscription. Later, in 1897, James Purdey purchased another burial plot in the same cemetery for Sarah Davies, a servant of very long standing who had looked after 314 1/2 Oxford Street since the 1840s. Sarah had died on 8 May 1897, after some fifty years service.

After his wife's death, James Purdey the Elder found a companion by the name of Martha Hatch, a widow. Little is known about Martha, but it was important to James Purdey that he didn't experience solitude and that he enjoyed companionship in his advancing years. He makes reference to their active relationship in various letters of the period, such as the one he wrote to his son James from Margate on 3 November 1862.

Rifle House Nov 3rd 1862

Dear James,
I have to thank you for a Most Beautiful Leg of Mutton and two Birds I never had a tender and sutch Rich flavoured Mutton Before, the Gravy was a rich dark colour that shewd the quality of the Meat the Birds we are Going to cook today. The weather is fine warm summer weather here there has been a great quantity of herrings and the bloters is considered very Good. I will send you a Small Basket if you like them. We are Going for the morning Ride the country is Beautiful we intend to stop here til cold weather drives us home your Sailor went out to fish and Brought us some Rock Whiting we Put a Little salt on them and cooked them next day they were excellent I think the thief that stole the gun did not Get Punishment enough for the crime the judg is not severe enough.

I will sign the Banker's Receipt when I come up.

I am truly yours Jas Purdey Snr.

Although Purdey's writing is robust and it is apparent that he was enjoying life to the full, he was already 78 at the time of writing the letter. The inevitable happened and the following year on the 6 November 1863, James Purdey the Founder died, at Rifle House, Margate. Interestingly, his death certificate records inaccurately that he was 80. Had Purdey in time-honoured fashion being deliberately advancing his years? There is an addendum to the certificate making the correction back to 78 some two weeks later. The certificate also records that his occupation was 'gentleman' – a term much used in this gracious era to denote 'retired'– and that he died of 'affection of the liver with severe jaundice'. His remains were brought to London and he was interred in the Purdey vault in Paddington Cemetery.

James Purdey's will was proved on 14 July 1864. He left around £7,000 net and his legacies bear witness to the amount of business activity he had been involved in. The gunmaking business was not specifically mentioned since it had been transferred to his son, James, in 1860. James Purdey the Younger was left 4 and 5 Rifle Terrace, Queen's Road, Bayswater, two cottage gardens and a brewery at Hendon, farmlands at Lower Cumberworth, Silestone, York, and seven dwellinghouses at Inverness Terrace. He also received all his horses and harness. Purdey the Elder's daughter, Elizabeth,

James Purdey the Elder photographed in 1863 – the year of his death.

received the income for life from 7 and 8 Rifle Terrace and his other daughter, Jane, the income for life from 1 and 2 Rifle Terrace. These properties would then pass in trust to their respective children.

On 29 October 1863 Purdey made a codicil to his will that was of great benefit to 'my kind and faithful friend Martha Hatch Widow'. Martha received outright Rifle House at 5 Upper Clifton Terrace, Margate. Rifle Cottage, Queen's Road, Bayswater, the seven houses in Inverness Terrace, 3 and 6 Rifle Terrace and 8 Coburg Place, Bayswater, were given to Martha for her life, thereupon these properties would pass to James Purdey's children. Martha also received £100 and all the furniture, linen, plates, china, etc. A servant, John Purvis, received £100 and Rifle Lodge, a small cottage. Another servant, Edward Jermyn, also received £100.

So ended the life and career of James Purdey the Founder. We must laud him for creating the Purdey business, style and name that is revered throughout the world today. Schooled by Joseph Manton, James Purdey had set up his business based on the principle of the highest quality only and had acceded to Manton's mantle. He established a reputation, second to none, with the 'first business in London' (Hawker, 1833) and attracted the most influential clientele of the day. He maintained the highest production output of any of the best West End gunmakers and remained at the van in gun design and development with his black lacquered stocks, rifles, etc. He created a style that was distinctly Purdey, a by-word for elegance with his new pattern butts, repeated use of front action locks and slimness of design in all his weapons. James Purdey the Younger had inherited the most famous gunmaking house in Britain.

THE PURDEY BOLT 1863

James Purdey the Younger had been in control of the firm since 1858, five years before his father's death. It would be James Purdey the Younger who would control the destinies of Purdey from the second half of the 19 century until his death in 1909. His obituary, published in *The Field* in 1909, states:

> Mr. James Purdey was in his day a man of extraordinary energy and vitality. Throughout the sporting world he was the unchallenged maker of guns for those who were in a position to appreciate and to afford the best work. This reputation amongst users was enhanced to an equally flattering degree by the estimation in which he was held by the workmen who carried out his orders and by these of his rivals who were able to judge the perfection of his method. Always a man of commanding presence and convincing manner…

James Purdey was a gunmaker who had served his apprenticeship in Oxford Street from 1843 to 1850 and as such had great technical knowledge of the construction and manufacture of guns. He developed the percussion Express rifle, invented the famous Purdey bolt snap action of 1863 and registered eight patents between 1861 and 1894. He was also a shrewd businessman. The financial arrangements with leading gunmakers over the Purdey bolt in the 1860s and a similar arrangement with Frederick Beesley over his hammerless action of 1880 accrued big profits to Purdey. By the 1880s he had doubled Purdey gun production to over 300 weapons a year and by the time of his death the papers could proclaim:

> Gunmaker's Fortune
> Mr. James Purdey, dean of the London gunmakers and first maker and namer of the Express rifle, has left an estate valued at £200,289.

James Purdey the Younger, around 1870.

On 27 December 1860, James Purdey was admitted to the Freedom of the Gunmakers' Company. The Gunmakers' Company, Freedom Admissions 1746-1949 held in the Guildhall Library, London state:

> James Purdey the Younger, Apprentice to his Father, James Purdey, Citizen and Gunmaker London by Indentures dated the fourteenth day of July, One Thousand Eight Hundred and Forty Three was admitted into the Freedom of this Company by Servitude.

He played an important part in the gunmakers' company. In 1864 he was elected as an Assistant in View and Proof and became a member of the Court of Assistants in 1867. He achieved the supreme accolade in 1874, 1882 and 1892 when he was elected Master of the Gunmakers' Company.

James Purdey the Younger's scroll admitting him to the Freedom of the Gunmakers' Company. The scroll is placed beneath the oil painting of him by Stuart-Wortley in the Long Room. It states 'James Purdey Son and late Apprentice of James Purdey, Citizen and Gunmaker of London was admitted into the freedom aforesaid and made the Declaration Required by Law in the Mayoralty of William Cubitt Esquire M.P. Mayor and Benjamin Scott Esquire Chamberlain and is entered in the book signed with the letter R relating to the purchasing of Freedoms and Admission of Freemen (to wit) the thirteenth day of April – the twenty-fourth year of the reign of Queen VICTORIA, And in the Year of our Lord 1861. In Witness whereof the Seal of the Office of Chamberlain of the said City and here and to affixed Dated in the Chamber of the Guild Hall of the same City the day and year above said.'

The first patent granted to James Purdey (indeed the very first Purdey patent, since the 1818 safety was not in Purdey's name) was no. 302 of 5 February 1861, *Improved Apparatus For Ramming and Turning Over Breech-Loading Cartridges* (see Appendix 8). The rolled turnover of early pinfire cartridges was inadequate resulting in unequal patterns and velocity. This would help to explain why muzzle-loaders were equal or superior, even by the late 1850s. In Purdey's invention (see plates 24 and 25), the previously loaded cartridge was placed in the machine and rammed by a lever to compress the charge. The cartridge was then reversed and the open end placed in the head of a revolving circular spindle. The head of this spindle had a groove cut in it containing a small steel projection. The cartridge was compressed and the spindle cranked round via bevel gears. The small steel projection then turned over the head of the cartridge 'with a burnishing action' to effect the turnover. Purdey's machine ensured consistency in cartridge loading and was of great importance in creating a reliable cartridge that would allow breech-loading development to proceed apace.

James Purdey's next patent is probably one of the most famous gun inventions of all time – the famous Purdey bolt of patent no. 1104 of 2 May 1863 entitled *Improvements In Breech-Loading Firearms*. (Patent titles were often deliberately vague to keep secret the nature of the invention from potential competitors whilst the patent was being applied for.)

This action has been used on millions of weapons, from the cheapest to the best, on double-barrel, single-barrel, over-and-under, rifle and shotgun. It has been in continuous production from its inception in 1863 to the present day. Its importance to

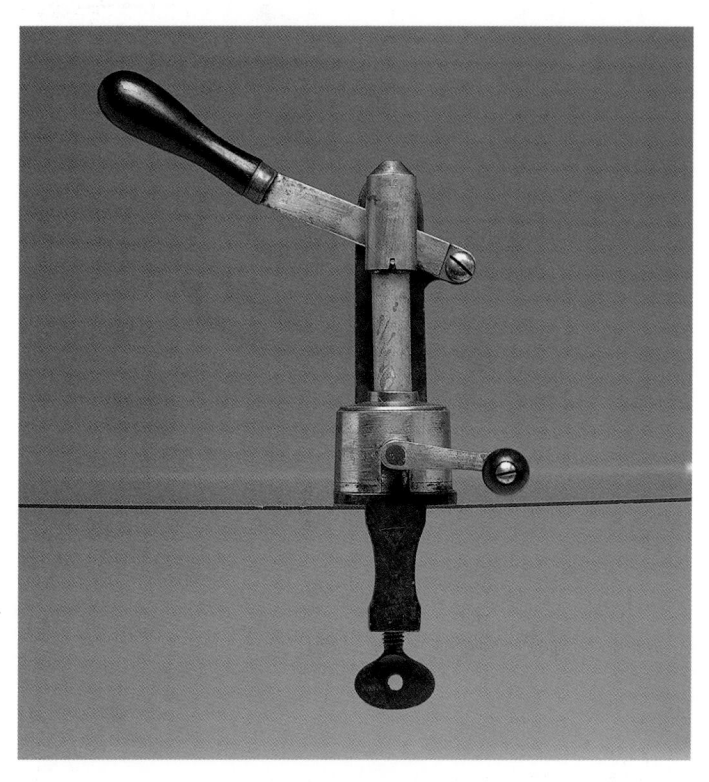

James Purdey's cartridge reloading machine built to patent no. 302 of 5 February 1861. Shown with a pinfire case about to receive a rolled turnover. This was the first patent granted to Purdey's. (*See plate 24 in colour section.*)

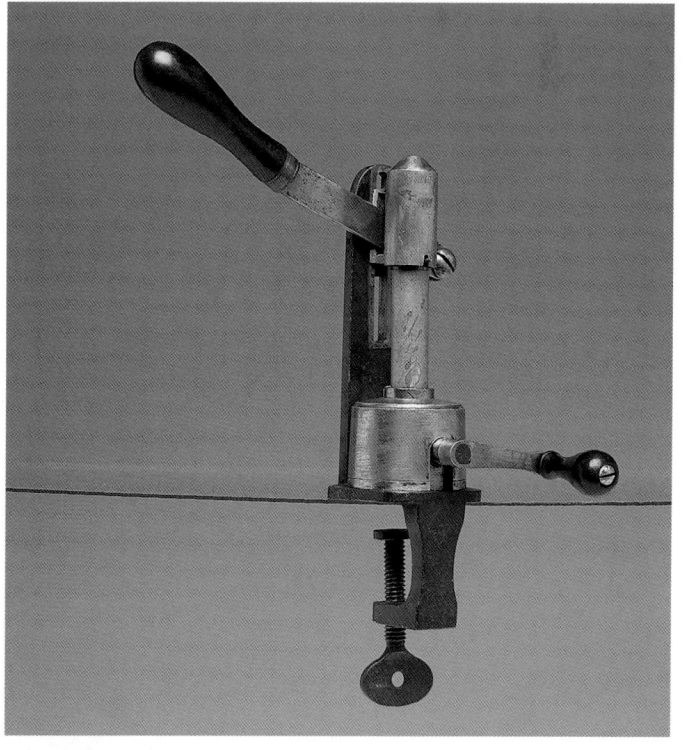

The cartridge reloading machine of 1861 showing the top lever for compressing the cartridge and the bottom crank for turning the spindle to effect the turnover. (*See plate 25 in colour section.*)

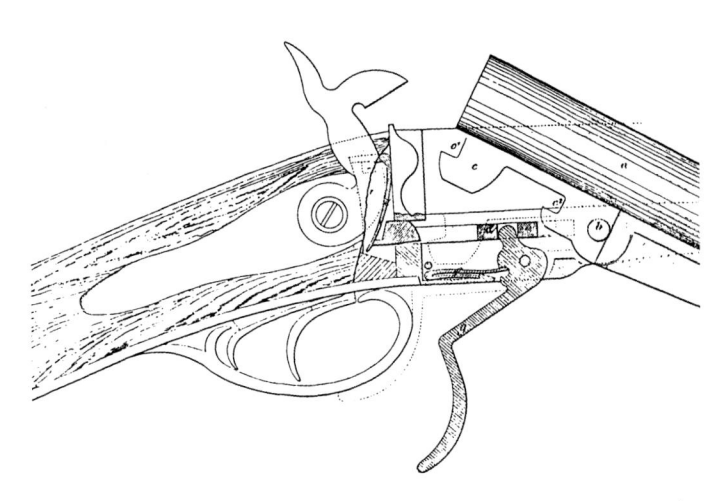

One of the patent drawings for the Purdey bolt from patent no. 1104 of 2 May 1863. The patent shows the First Pattern of underlever and two springs, one working the lever and the other in the head of the stock to assist the bolt.

Purdey was two-fold. Firstly, it demonstrated that not only were Purdey builders of the highest quality guns, they were also in the forefront of breech-loading development. Its importance was not immediately apparent to the gun grade. However, after a few years when its merits became known, particularly when it was used in the conjunction with the Scott spindle of 1865, it became widely used and set the standard to which all other actions aspired. Secondly, Purdey licensed the rights to manufacture it to a large number of makers and so created considerable revenue for the firm.

The double bite action of the type patented by Henry Jones in 1859 in his screw underlever had proved how secure a double bite action was. The problem with this type of inert action was that it required three separate motions to fire the gun. First, the barrels had to be closed, then the underlever closed to the lock the action, finally the hammers pulled back to full cock. The great advantage of breech-loaders that had excited everyone, was their rapidity of fire over muzzle-loaders. In their search for an even faster system, it became apparent to many inventors that, if upon closing the barrels the gun would automatically lock, the rapidity of fire could be increased further. Pairs of guns and driven game shooting were becoming far more popular and hence a fast action was in demand.

Weapons that closed automatically were termed 'snap actions'. They all used springs of varying degrees and at first this was a criticism of them. Ingenuity knew no bounds in the early 1860s and there were literally scores of patents regarding snap actions, mostly of the single bite variety. But the single bite snap action was not robust enough to withstand constant hard usage. So if one bite was not sufficient, why not use two as had been proved to be so secure in the double bite inert action?

This is exactly what James Purdey invented in one of the first of the double bite snap actions. He was granted a Provisional Specification No. 1104 of 2 May 1863 (see Appendix 8) – 'A novel method of securing or locking the barrel when it is brought down into a horizontal position on the stock ready for being discharged.' One of its main virtues lay in its simplicity. A bolt with two bites slid in grooves cut in each side of the action. The bolt itself had slots cut in it to accept the barrel lumps. Both barrel lumps had notches cut at the top to accept the bolt as it slid forward when the barrels became shut. The bolt itself was driven by a spring under tension to snap the action shut. When the gun was closed, the rear of the front lump pushed back the bolt. The barrels could now close, the barrel lumps projecting through the slots in the bolt. When the barrels closed tight upon the action, the spring-powered bolt moved forward entering the notches in the barrel lumps, securely locking the action. One of the beauties of the Purdey bolt is its ease of action. The rear of the front lump close to the hinge pin forces back the bolt under tension as the gun closes. This exerts a far greater leverage than if the rear lump had been used and makes closing virtually effortless.

Before the adoption of the Scott top lever spindle in the later 1860s, Purdey used another method of operating the snap action that has long been associated with Purdey – the elegant 'thumb-hole'. This used a lever in front of the trigger guard that pushed forward to open the gun. The trigger guard itself is bifurcated to enable the thumb to be inserted to operate the lever. In Purdey's records the mechanism was termed 'under-snap'. There are two main variations on the thumb-hole. The earliest is the one shown on the patent drawing. In the early version, the lever is pivoted near the front of the action and is then projected rearwards to curve round the front of the trigger guard. When the lever is pushed forward, the upper part of it pushes the sliding bolt backwards. Two springs are shown in the drawing, a V-spring set close to the pivot of the lever and a leaf spring in the head

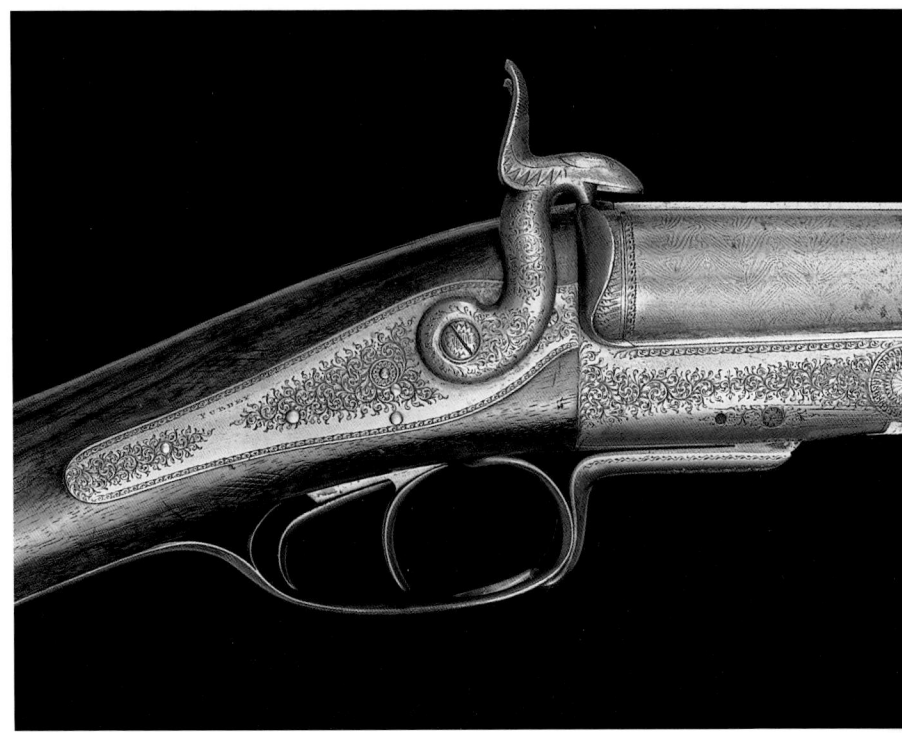

The First Pattern thumb-hole as used on pin-fire gun No. 6829 tested on 17 September 1864.

The more common Second Pattern thumb-hole as used on 12-bore gun No. 7745 of 1868.

The Second Pattern thumb-hole with the variation 'de Brante lever' as used on gun No. 10008. The de Brante lever is something of an enigma. It is variously spelled in Purdey's records de Brante, de Brantes, de Brantz, but there is no Purdey gunmaker or Purdey assocciation bearing this name. This gun was sold on 23 July 1880 and was one of the last guns Frederick Beesley stocked while at Purdey's.

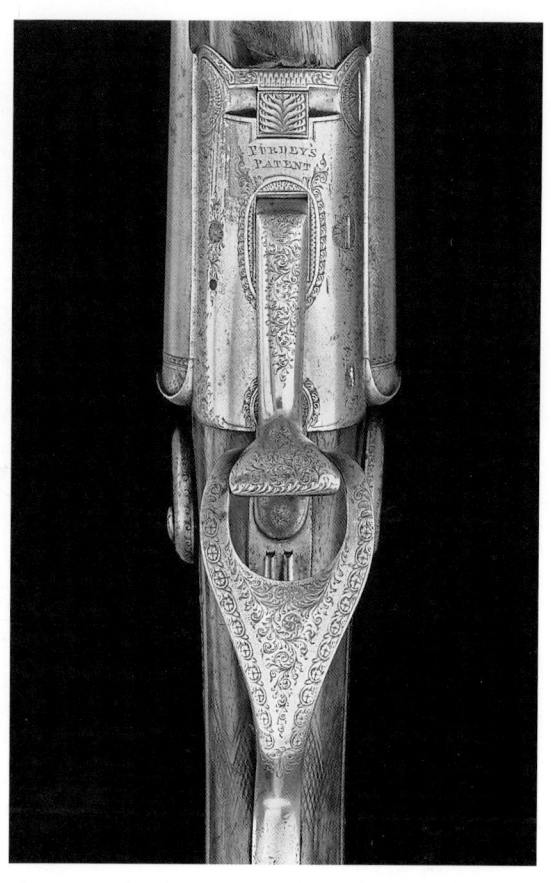

The bifurcated trigger-guard and First Pattern lever of No. 6829 showing the engraving 'Purdey's Patent' referring to patent no. 1104 of 2 May 1863. 'Purdey's Patent' appeared on Purdey guns long after the patent expired in 1877.

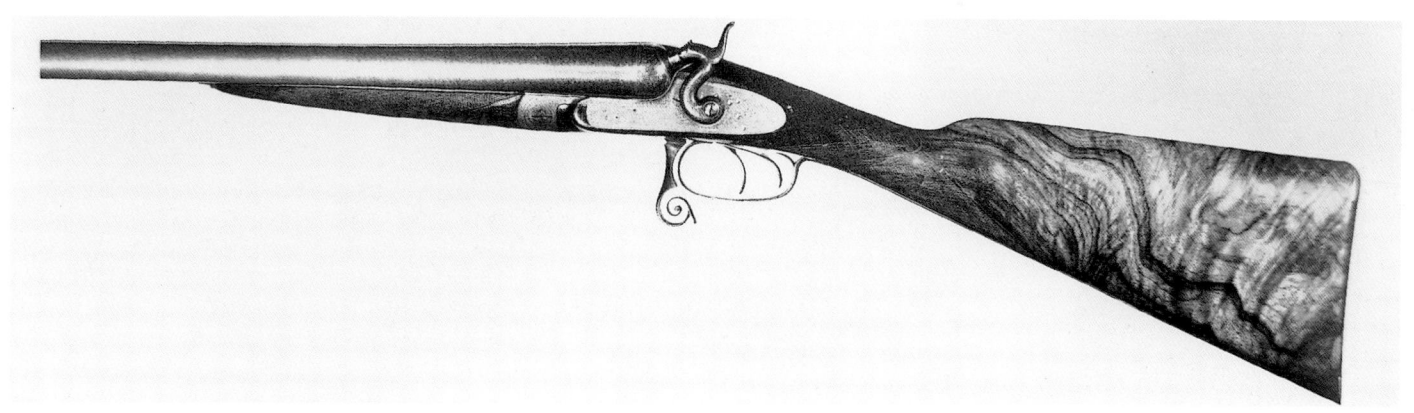

of the stock to assist the sliding bolt. This early type of thumb-hole is generally known as the 'First Pattern'.

The second variation is by far the most common. A short lever pivots just above the trigger guard. A single spring with two limbs lies backwards on either side of the trigger plate. Relying on one spring, and with better leverage, it was easier to make and operate. It also looked more elegant. This type of thumb-hole is generally known as the 'Second Pattern'. Another variation far less encountered is very similar to the Second Pattern. In this third variation, although the mechanism is identical, the lever design is different. A more flamboyant lever was used with a curving scroll type lever. In Purdey's records they are referred to as 'scroll-lever'. There are yet more variations on this design, such as a long lever that curved right round the trigger guard and was operated by its rear end, the 'Daw lever' and a more uncommon variant, the 'de Brante lever'.

It is difficult to ascertain which gun was the first built by Purdey to his patent. In the Dimension Book, 12-bore shotgun No. 6516 is described as 'Spring Action'. This gun was sold on 3 July 1863. Two more 'Spring Actions' are subsequently listed, No. 6541 sold on 11 June 1863 and No. 6565 with no record of sale. 12-bore gun No. 6572 sold to Lord Kenlis and tested on 21 August 1863 is described as 'Patent Action'. Thereafter, several guns are described as 'New Patent'.

From the late 1860s onwards, the Purdey bolt is usually found in conjunction with the Scott top lever and spindle. Scott's were founded in 1834 at 79 Weaman Street, Birmingham. On 25 October 1865, William Middleditch Scott was granted patent no. 2752 for his invention of top lever and spindle. There were actually two parts to the patent, one was an indicator to show if a gun was loaded and the other was the more important part regarding the top lever and spindle. In this patent, Scott used a top lever attached to a vertical

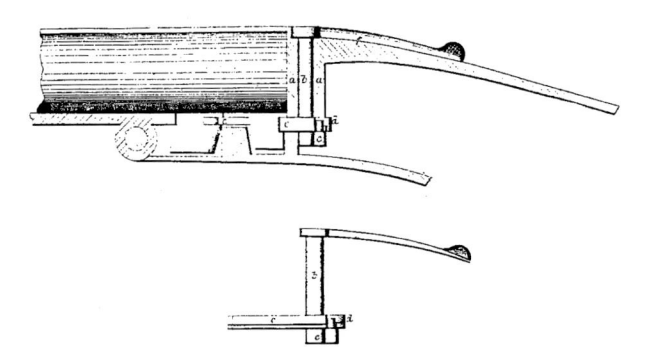

One of the patent drawings for patent no. 2752 of 25 October 1865 – the Scott top lever and spindle.

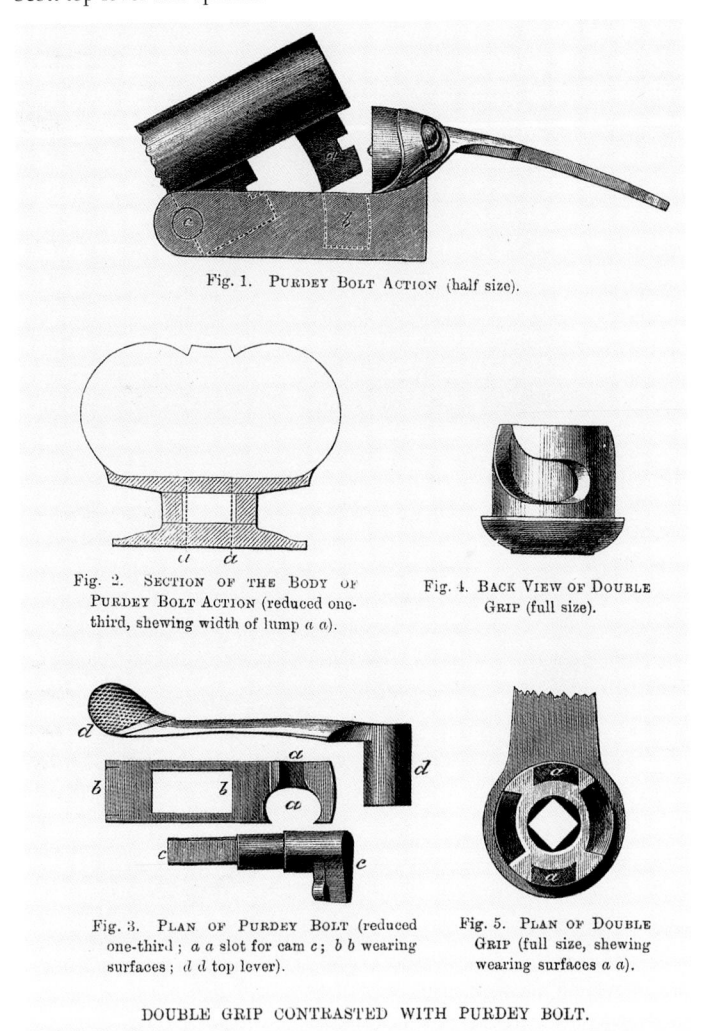

Fig. 1. PURDEY BOLT ACTION (half size).

Fig. 2. SECTION OF THE BODY OF PURDEY BOLT ACTION (reduced one-third, shewing width of lump *a a*).

Fig. 4. BACK VIEW OF DOUBLE GRIP (full size).

Fig. 3. PLAN OF PURDEY BOLT (reduced one-third; *a a* slot for cam *c*; *b b* wearing surfaces; *d d* top lever).

Fig. 5. PLAN OF DOUBLE GRIP (full size, shewing wearing surfaces *a a*).

DOUBLE GRIP CONTRASTED WITH PURDEY BOLT.

Drawings of the Purdey bolt in *The Modern Sportsman's Gun and Rifle* by J H Walsh, 1884. Illustrations like this gave rise to the fallacy that the Purdey bolt was an integral design of sliding bolt and top lever.

spindle. At the bottom of the spindle, a short lever drew back the sliding bolt in the action as the top lever was pushed to the right. Various types of spring were tried until design settled upon a V-spring under the top strap. The essence of the Scott spindle was its robustness, simplicity and convenience. Combined with the Purdey bolt, it would champion all other types of closing action – the reason why it has been in continuous production since its invention.

A great many people, including writers, assume the Purdey bolt was an integral design of sliding bolt and top lever, both invented by James Purdey. The combination is often referred to as the 'Purdey lever', or 'Purdey action', in ignorance of the two separate parts, taken out by two separate gunmakers, two years apart. The obvious reason for this misinterpretation is that Purdey's from the earliest days of both inventions, used the combination of Purdey bolt and Scott lever in preference to all other types of closing action. As has been previously remarked, they reserved the lever over guard for rifles and larger bore shotguns and very rarely used the side lever. This is in contrast to a firm like Boss, who much preferred the lever over guard and side snap in the second half of the 19th century and hardly made any top levers. And when one takes into account the far bigger production of Purdey's than their contemporaries and the engraving 'Purdey's Patent', it is no wonder that it became assumed that bolt and lever were one and the same.

Another reason for the misinterpretation concerns the licencing and royalty agreements Purdey's had with Scott's. It will be noted from the Scott patent drawing of 1865, that the top lever and spindle are shown in conjunction with the Purdey double bolt. There are several licensing agreements and all are of great interest in showing the workings of the gun trade in the second half of the 19th century.

The original agreement with W & C Scott & Son (William Scott, Charles Scott, William Middleditch Scott) of Bagot Street, Lancaster Street, Birmingham, to licence Purdey's patent no. 1104 of 2 May 1863, was dated 5 April 1867 and had three main conditions. (1) The licence would run for three years; (2) there would be a 20 shillings; (£1) royalty payment per gun; (3) each gun had to be engraved 'JP Patent'. A reciprocal agreement with Scotts for use of their patent no. 2752 of 25 October 1865 created the bond of Purdey bolt and top lever. On 5 December 1868, this agreement was amended, backdated to 1 July 1868.

> James Purdey do hereby agree to grant unto the said W & C Scott & Son, full and free liberty, licence and authority to make, work, use, exercise and authority to make, work, use, exercise and practice the said Invention granted by the said letter Patent....

The subtle changes to the agreement were that guns had to be engraved 'Purdey's Patent Bolt' and that Scott were not to supply guns or actions to Alfred Lancaster, Boss & Co., Stephen Grant, Moore & Grey, Rigby, Thomas Jackson, G H Daw, Alexander Henry, Edward Paton, Wilkinson, J D Dougall, Westley-Richards, H J Holland, George Smith, S & C Smith. Obviously Purdey's were licencing these makers as well.

A further agreement followed to run for five years and ten months (to the expiry of the Purdey patent) from 1 July 1871. Purdey's agreed not to licence any makers in Birmingham or elsewhere, apart from London (any licences so issued would be agreed with Scott and royalties split 50-50). Scott's guns had to be marked:

◇ JP Patent 1104 ◇

Again, Scott's were not allowed to supply London makers. Purdey's licenced a great many London makers at 40 shillings (£2) royalty per gun.

These licencing agreements created not only a bond between Purdey's and W & C Scott, they also created the constant combination of Purdey's snap action patent 1104 and Scott's top lever spindle patent no. 2752. It is no wonder that the misnomer 'Purdey lever' has come about. It was a clever business arrangement. The successful combination of bolt and lever was divided into two patches – Scott's controlling Birmingham and the rest of the country and Purdey's controlling the London gunmakers.

It must be a great testament to James Purdey the Younger that not only did he make a large income out of the Purdey bolt but that it has stood the test of time since the mid-1860s. With the top lever, the sportsmen now had an action that could be conveniently opened without having to relax his grip on the rest of the gun. It required little pressure to open and snapped shut easily. Also, the action was totally secure and easily able to withstand the thousands of rounds individual guns expended yearly in the late Victorian battue. To conclude on the action, I can do no better than quote Sir Ralph Payne-Gallwey in his *Letters to Young Shooters*, 1892 edition.

> The strongest, neatest and simplest fastening for a gun ever devised is Mr. Purdey's. It is one now utilised by nearly every gunmaker in the kingdom; and a gun properly fitted with his 'snap bolt action' will stand as hard work and last as long a time as any can do. I have known many guns with the Purdey action, and without any projection on the breech to add to their safety that have fired 5,000 shots a season for years without a symptom of the slackness or other necessity for repair which the advocates of the doll's head and top fastenings declare is sure to take place without these ugly and fanciful encumbrances.

The first recorded top levers in the Dimension Book are Nos. 7726-7 of 1868.

After his marriage in 1851, James Purdey the Younger sired a large family, as was normal at that time. James Purdey III was born on 11 June 1854, a sister, Florence, on 23 July 1855 and another son, Athol Stuart, on 27 January 1858. Both James and Athol were to join the firm as gunmakers, although James died a sick young man in 1890. It would be left to Athol Purdey primarily to carry on the business in the early 20th century. Four more children were born to James Purdey the Younger and his wife Caroline in the 1860s. Algernon George Ingle Purdey was born on 25 May 1859 at 17 Warwick Crescent, but died the following year on 10 May 1860. Constance was born at the new family home of 1 Manchester Square on 28 December 1863 and Cecil Onslow Purdey was born there on 8 July 1865. At first, Cecil had not intended to go into gunmaking. However, due to the illness of James Purdey III in the 1880s, Cecil entered the business. A further son, Percy John, was born at yet another new house, 28 Devonshire Place, on 24 August 1869. Percy never entered gunmaking, but started his own business as a stockbroker, 'Purdey & Wilson', at 10 Throgmorton Avenue in the City.

The gunmaking business was doing so well that the Purdey family had been able to move from their home at 1 Manchester Square to a substantial property in Marylebone –

28 Devonshire Place today – the home of James Purdey the Younger and family *circa* 1868-1909.

28 Devonshire Place. This was a highly desirable residential area, parallel to Harley Street and Portland Place. The move occurred around 1868. The property was a magnificent townhouse on five floors with a basement, and stables were nearby in Harley Street. The Purdey family would remain here for the remainder of the century and it would be at this address that James Purdey the Younger would die in 1909.

In the late 1860s, Purdey the Younger's eldest son, James III was apprenticed into the firm. Unfortunately, the Gunmakers' Company Records, Register of Apprentices, ceased to be used on a regular basis after 1851. I can find no record of his apprenticeship and I can only assume that it took place in his early teenage years in the late 1860s. During the latter stages of his apprenticeship, or in his early days as a gunmaker, he unfortunately fell victim to consumption, one of the great scourges of the time, and died in 1890, aged 36.

THE ARRIVAL OF THE CENTRE-FIRE

The pin-fire system of breech-loading could never be more than in interim development. Care had to be taken in loading guns due to sportsmen having to make sure that the pin of the cartridge was in the correct vertical position in the chamber. Cartridges were difficult to store on account of their protruding pins and safety was always an additional issue. Hand re-loading of pin-fire cartridges, popular in this era, was also a tricky and time-consuming business. In addition, pin-fire guns had an ungainly look with their high hammers protruding forwards. Even though the centre-fire, developed in 1861, was a better system, it is easy to see why the pin-fires soldiered on into the 1860s. The pin-fire was in many respects a direct progression from the percussion gun with its high hammers and pins reminiscent of nipples protruding from the breeches.

Purdey's built a large number of pin-fire guns from No. 5305 the first one built in 1857, to the probable last pin-fire, a 12-bore shotgun, No. 16056, sold in May 1898 to Charles Gordon. In total, 1,110 pin-fire shotguns were built, as were 134 pin-fire rifles. Many of these guns were converted to centre-fire in the 1870s and 1880s and Purdey's Dimension Book records such conversions. The first probable centre-fire shotgun, No. 6992, was produced in 1865 and the first probable centre-fire rifle, No. 7207, was produced in 1866, so any breech-loading weapons prior to these serial numbers would originally have been pin-fires. Apart from a serial number check, later converted pin-fires can usually be identified by the fact that the grooves cut into the top end of the barrel chambers will have been welded up.

Most Purdey pin-fires had back action locks. The pressures generated at the breech and new developments in barrel closing mechanisms made it easier to fit back action locks, whereby wood from the head of the stock could be removed and not metal from the action body. Later, when the workings of the breech-loader became better understood, front action locks would be fitted to culminate in what many regard as the most elegant Purdey's of all – the bar-in-wood hammer guns.

As in the case of early breech-loading weapons, the centre-fire was a French development. It has already been noted how Samuel Pauly introduced the breech-loading gun in 1812 with a very modern cartridge, containing priming powder in its head. For some reason, Lefaucheux, in his 1834 patent breech-loader that established the form of the modern breech-loader, used pin-fire cartridges. Lefaucheux's influence was such that breech-loading development from now on tended to go down the pin-fire line. On 12 March 1829 another Frenchman, Clement Pottet, developed a centre-fire cartridge with the percussion cap on a central nipple.

However, it was up to yet another French gunmaker, Francois Eugene Schneider, at 13 Rue Gaillon, Paris, to create the real foundations of the centre-fire. In his French patent no. 46957 of 4 October 1860, taken out in Britain as no. 1487 of 11 June 1861, Schneider invented a snap-action gun with centre-fire cartridge and extractor. The London gunmaker, G H Daw, of 57 Threadneedle Street, realised the importance of this and bought the patent rights to it. In a minor way he improved upon the design in his patent no. 1594 of 27 May 1862. (Incidentally, G H Daw will feature later on as Purdey's used the 'Daw lever' in their early hammerless guns.) In Britain the Daw guns, with their centre-fire cartridges, caused great interest due to their far easier loading system and operation. Any makers who attempted to copy the centre-fire system were threatened with legal action by Daw. However, the big cartridge manufacturers, Eley Bros, made such cartridges and Daw took them to court for alleged patent infringement. Daw lost because it was ruled that he had the rights to the Schneider patent but not the centre-fire system itself. This decision cleared the way for gunmakers to develop the centre-fire.

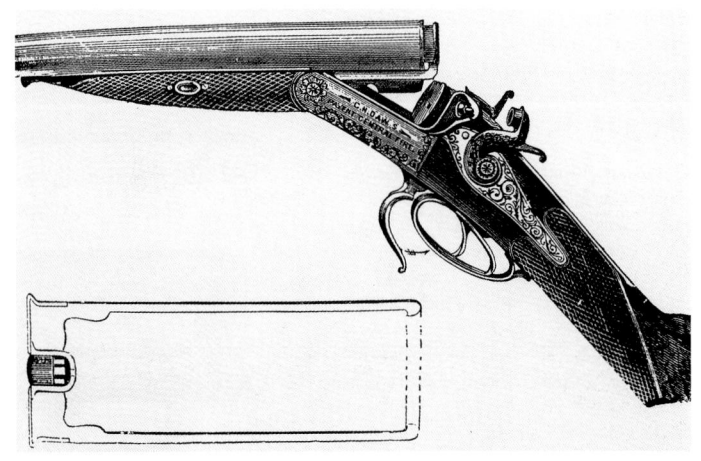

G H Daw's 1861 centre-fire breech-loader and cartridge. Note the under-lever – 'the Daw Lever' Purdey would use later on hammer guns and hammerless guns, including early Beesley actions.

The first recorded centre-fire gun built by Purdey's was a double-barrel 12-bore shotgun, No. 6992, built for F J Parkes in 1865. There is, unfortunately, no record of its test. The first recorded centre-fire rifle was No. 7207, a double-barrel 70-bore built in 1866 for Colonel H Johnson.

The changeover to centre-fire from pin-fire was incredibly rapid as the following figures show. The watershed year for shotguns was 1866 when the centre-fire instantly overtook the pinfire – remarkable when it is considered that the first centre-fire was built only one year earlier. As usual rifle

The record in the Dimension Book for the first recorded centre-fire, No. 6992 of 1865 (see column headings on page 84). 'J' is T Jones, jointing and stocking, screwing, finishing. 'GP' is G Prentice, cocking. 'L' is J Lucas, engraving. 'R' is A Robins, hardening.

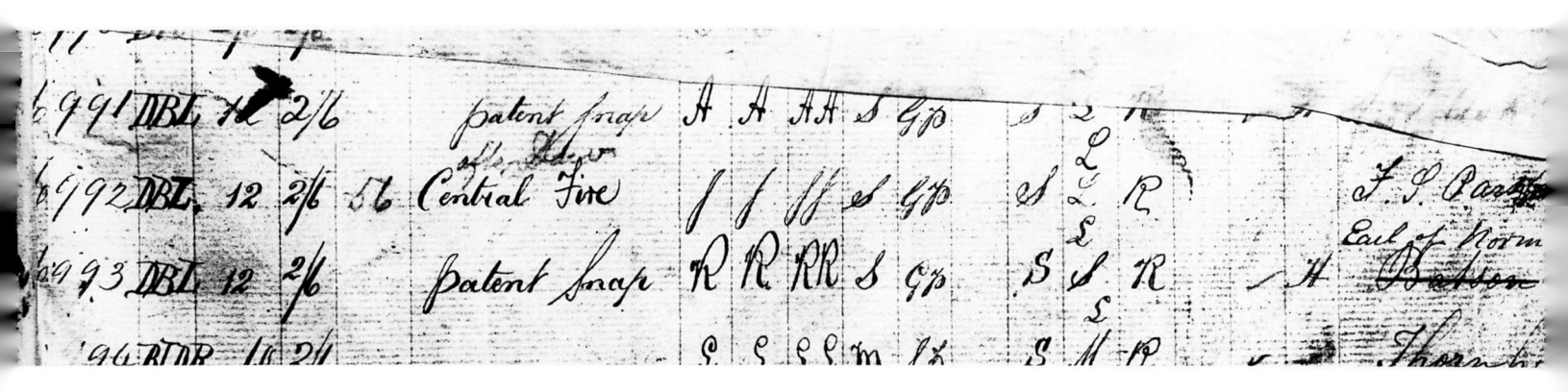

change lagged behind. Again, it was equally rapid with 1867 as the watershed year. It is also interesting to note from the statistics that a fair number of muzzle-loaders were still being constructed.

Year	Shotguns		Percussion Guns & Rifles	Rifles	
	Pin-fire	Centre-fire		Pin-fire	Centre-fire
1865	172	10	72	30	0
1866	51	150	21	14	2
1867	33	158	20	1	20

Soon after the arrival of the centre-fire, the Purdey hammer gun evolved in the late 1860s into the elegant and distinctive guns we know today.

The first factor to create such a distinctive style, was the shape of the hammer – small, slim and lean with a beautifully designed curve. They are not really to be found on other makers' guns. The second factor was the design of the back action locks used on such guns. The lockplates were rounded at the front with a small area of wood left between the lock and the rear of the action, usually known as 'isolated locks'. This created an area of handsome curves. Most other makers made the front of the lock about the action, which Purdey did on rifles and large bore guns for extra strength. A third factor was the style of engraving. Purdey's were the first gunmakers to develop the very fine rose-and-scroll engraving that came into fashion in the late 1860s. This fine engraving style provided great elegance. A final factor was Purdey's frequent use of bar-in-wood actions, in which the stock is carried forward past the locks and up to the barrel hinge bolt, in much the same style as a muzzle-loader. These bar-in-wood guns have a grace and elegance second to none and are highly regarded by collectors today. Purdey's even carried bar-in-wood actions over into their very early hammerless guns. The defect of the bar-in-wood was that metal had to be cut away from the action body, thereby weakening it. The mechanism of the hammerless action was not really compatible with the bar-in-wood and it never reappeared.

12-bore hammer gun No. 7983, the No. 2 gun of trio Nos. 7982/3/4 built for the Earl of Sefton. Tested on 16 February 1869. Typical Purdey back action locks. (*See plate 27 in colour section.*)

The record in the Dimension Book for Nos. 8998-9000 built in 1873 (see column headings page 84). 'JH' is J Harris, nipples and plungers. 'G' is Henry Glaysher and 'B' is Frederick Beesley, jointing and stocking, screwing, finishing; 'FP' is F Phillips, percussioning; 'GP' is G Prentice, cocking; 'JA' is J Apted, levering. 'L' is J Lucas, engraving; 'R' is A Robins, hardening; 'HS' is H Schmidt, luggers.

The Purdey hammer gun at its finest. Nos. 8998/9000, the No. 1 and No. 3 guns of a trio of 12-bore top lever bar-in-wood hammer guns sold on 19 September 1873 to Lord Stourton for £189. (*See plate 26 in colour section.*)

The record in the Dimension Book for Nos. 7982-7984 built in 1869 (see column headings on page 84). 'G' is Henry Glaysher, jointing and stocking, screwing, finishing; 'GP' is G Prentice, cocking; 'L' is J Lucas, engraving. 'R' is A Robins, hardening. 'HS' is H Schmidt, luggers.

Further James Purdey the Younger patents followed after the famous Purdey bolt of 1863. On 14 February 1865 James Purdey took out his third patent, No. 424, 'Improvements in Breech-Loading Firearms' (see Appendix 8). This was a long patent comprising five distinct parts. The first dealt with a snap bolt action totally different from patent no. 1104 of 1863. A locking bolt situated at the bottom of the action had cut-outs that matched the rear of the barrel lump. When the barrels closed, a wedge came into position behind the locking bolt, locking the barrels. This wedge was connected to a rocking lever, the rear of which carried a button that projected through the top strap. On pushing the button, the wedge was released and the barrels could be opened. Another version in the patent used an underlever to release the wedge. This was a fussy, complicated, single-bite snap action, inferior to the earlier 1863 double-bite snap action. I don't believe it was ever used.

The second part of the patent concerns improved centre-fire firing pins which were connected to the hammers. When the hammers were drawn back to half cock, the firing pins were automatically retracted. This part of the patent was used on some early centre-fire guns.

The third part of the patent showed centre-fire cartridges with protruding pins for manual extraction. The fourth part showed spring-loaded extractors, and the fifth part extractors for use in the slide action Bastin gun. None of these improvements would have any lasting effect.

His next patent, no. 1464 of 25 May 1866, 'An Improvement In Breech-Loading Firearms', did have more practical use and was used on many early Purdey breech-loaders (see Appendix 8). With a pin-fire, it was apparent when the gun was loaded because the cartridge pins protruded from the breech. However, this was not the case with the new centre-fire system. Such was the rapidity of the introduction of the centre-fire, it seemed logical to provide some sort of indicator as to whether or not the gun was loaded. Although James Purdey was not the first to do so, he invented in patent no. 1464 of 1866 a loaded indicator, 'to indicate by the protruding of a pin or stud, or its equivalent from the barrel or breech, whether the arm is loaded or not'. Crank levers were fitted set in the breech above the strikers. When the gun was closed, the rim of the cartridge pushed one end of the lever backwards until the other end protruded slightly from the top of the breech. In this way it could be seen at a glance whether the gun was loaded. The first recorded use of 'Indicators' in Purdey's Dimension Book are Nos.7500/1 of 1867.

Two years later Purdey patented another gadget in patent no. 2319 of 23 July 1868 (see Appendix 8). Again, the title is bland: 'Improvement In Firearms'. This was a somewhat curious invention 'this Invention relates to the obtaining for firearms a moveable and adjustable elevation for the breech to

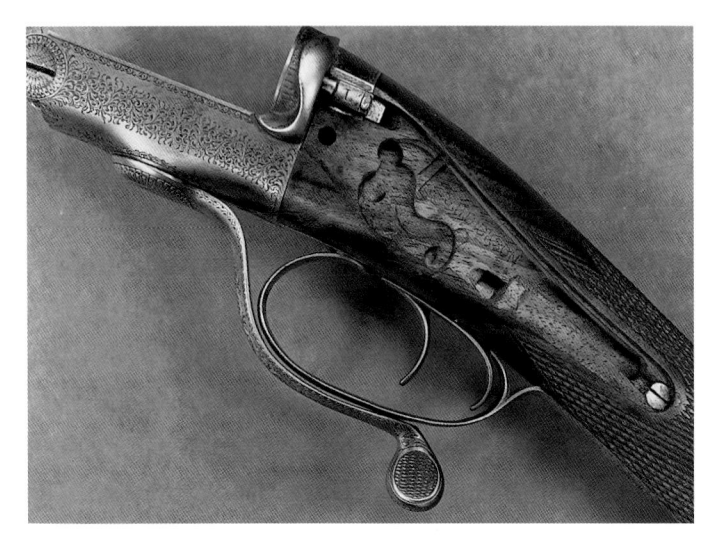

An early Purdey centre-fire gun, No. 7390 of 1866, showing the retractable firing pins of patent no. 424 of 14 February 1865. The swellings on the breasts of the hammers hit the pins. Notice the early use of J Lucas's very fine scroll engraving.

suit the varying requirements of the user'. A plate was placed on top of the tang that had an adjustment screw to raise or lower it. The patent drawing is very plain and there is certainly no sight shown. The object appears to be an attempt to provide an alternative to an elevated rib on a shotgun.

Indicators would be no more than a passing fad as sportsmen learned to adapt to the centre-fire. Stanton's rebounding lock of 1867 had a great deal to do with improving safety in centre-fire hammer guns and negating the need for indicators. The early hammer guns had the same half cock, full cock system as used on muzzle-loaders. The hammers rested on the firing pins when the gun was not cocked, resulting in the firing pins protruding into the breech. If the hammers were not drawn back to half cock when the gun was loaded and closed, an accident could occur when the pins came into contact with the primers. Similarly, if a hammer was released to rest upon the pin in ignorance of a cartridge in the chamber, detonation could result. The system was also inconvenient because the hammers had to be drawn back to half cock to release the firing pins before opening.

A thumb-hole hammer gun showing the indicators of patent no. 1464 of 25 May 1866. The levers can be seen beside the firing pins on the action face.

John Stanton, the lockmaker of 13 Clifton Street, Wolverhampton, invented a rebounding lock in 1867 to overcome these problems. Rebounding locks do not have the two positions, half cock and full cock. When the gun is cocked and fired, the hammer flies forward, utilising the lower half of the main spring, and hits the firing pin. The top half of the main spring then rebounds the hammer back from the firing pin. It was very simple but very effective. It meant that the hammer never rested against the firing pin, making for a far safer gun. It was also very convenient because the gun could be opened and closed with no concern about hammer position. A great many earlier guns were converted to rebounders and Purdey's Dimension Book records several such conversions. The first recorded use of the rebounding lock listed in the Dimension Book are Nos. 7679/80 of 1868.

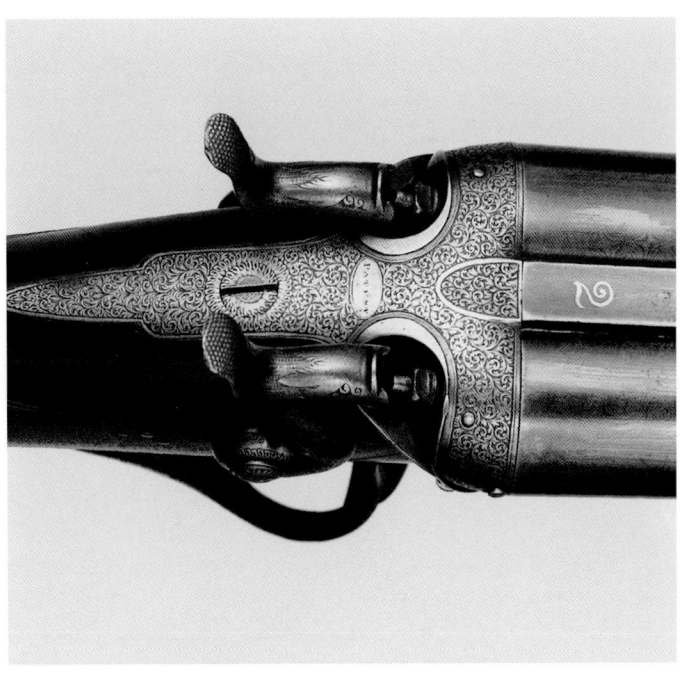

The pop-up pins flush with the breech in the unloaded position. Notice Lucas's beautiful scroll engraving.

PURDEY GUNMAKERS IN THE 1860s

We are fortunate that from the 1860s onwards, Purdey's possess wage books that progress to the present day. They list all Purdey's gunmakers, but unfortunately do not list Christian names or specialisation. Appendix 6 lists such details where known.

In the 1861 census James Purdey the Younger describes himself as a 'Gunmaker Master employing forty men and six boys'. The 1863 wage book confirms this. For a West End gunmaker building best guns, this was the largest establishment of its kind. The Purdey gunmakers would all be working on the premises at 314 $^1/_2$ Oxford Street. The wage book of June 1863 lists the gunmakers employed. If the wage payments are studied, then the degree of importance of a gunmaker can be deduced. Aston was the head barrel maker on £8-£11 per week, an excellent wage for its time. There must be some connection with the barrel-making firm of Christopher Aston, of 26 Little Windmill Street, Golden Square, who had a barrel-making business in the mid-19th century. Henry Lewis was the head stocker. Lewis had been with Purdey since the 1840s and had trained James Purdey the Younger. His name ceases to be mentioned in the wage books by the late 1870s.

Perhaps the most interesting name is that of J Lucas, Purdey's head engraver. Lucas is something of an enigma. Nothing is known of his origins, history or even his Christian name. He joined Purdey's around 1855 and retired after some 60 years' continuous service on the 23 October 1915. To whom he was apprenticed and from where he came is not known. He died in 1920 with no written record of his significance. There is no mention of Lucas in any of the myriad books on British gunmaking, yet his contribution to the style of the traditional best British gun is immense. Lucas engraved a very large number of Purdey guns and rifles during his service with the firm. He was assisted by J Mace who had begun with Purdey around 1850, the initials 'L' and 'M' appearing consistently in the Dimension Books. Mace left Purdey's in the 1870s and was replaced by another skilled engraver, Walter Warren. Warren completed over 50 years' service with Purdey's, retiring in the 1930's. Their output was prodigious when it is borne in mind that Purdey's in the second half of the 19th century were producing on average 300 guns per year, not far off one a day. The gunmakers were on piece work and the wage books continually show Lucas achieving a very high rate of pay.

Until the mid-19th century gun engraving was relatively sparse. By the early 1860s a new type of engraving came into fashion, a far more delicate floral style known today as rose-and-scroll or bouquet-and-scroll. This classic engraving style is synonymous with the traditional best British gun which has an elegance and fineness second to none. Purdey's were the first gunmakers to use this type of engraving, frequently referred to as 'Purdey engraving'. It enhanced the Purdey 'style' and its use on their guns from the 1860s was yet another factor in making the Purdey gun instantly recognisable. It is no coincidence that Lucas began his career at Purdey's in 1855 when the new style began to emerge. Lucas introduced and developed the rose-and-scroll and along with Mace and Warren executed it to the highest standards possible. Lucas must be given recognition for his skill and artistry and must be revered along with the likes of Jack Sumner and Harry Kell.

J Lucas, head engraver at Purdey's between 1855 and 1915. He was responsible for developing and executing the traditional bouquet-and-scroll engraving, the so-called 'Purdey engraving', typical of the best British gun.

A group of gunmakers on a Purdey 'beanfeast' around 1890, all dressed in their very best clothes. J Lucas is No. 7. Other gunmakers are – 1. Aston, head barrel-maker; 2. William Nobbs who invented the first Purdey ejector in 1883 and the first Purdey single-trigger in 1894, actioner; 3. H Horsley, stocker; 4. H Dean, stocker; 5. Charlie Butler, front shop; 6. H Johnson, stocker; 8. Howell, actioner; 9. H Blanton, finisher; 10. Abbe Robins, hardener.

A Purdey wage book of June 1863. The specialisations of the gunmakers where known are listed in Appendix 6.

	Name	June 6. 1863 £176. 0. 0			June 13. 1863 £146. 0. 0			June 20. 1863 £146. 0. 0			June 27. 1863 £164. 0. 0		
40 JJJJ	Aston	8	15	.	10	4	.	11	3	.	11	16	0
65 JJJJ	Atkins	2	.	.	2	3	6	2	.	.	2	.	.
	Apted	2	8	9	2	17	.	2	13	10	2	5	7
57 JJ	Bissell							4	3	6	4	1	.
	Batham	2	.	.	2	.	.	2	.	.	2	.	.
	Boulter	1	18	6	2	2	.	2	2	.	1	18	6
	Denholm	2	10	.	2	10	.	2	10	.	3	2	.
94 JJ	Goff	3	"	"	3	.	.				3	2	.
33 JJ	Hewson	2	6	8	2	4	6	2	7	6	2	7	6
	Harbroe	2	2	"	2	2	.	2	2	.	2	2	.
	Hawkes	1	7	6	1	4	0	1	4	.	1	4	.
22 JJJJ	Lewis	7	5	.	6	6	.	6	12	.	8	2	.
	Lewis James	1	12	.	1	12	.	1	12	.	1	12	.
67 JJ	Lucas	1	6	6	4	10	.	4	16	6	6	.	.
244 JJJJ / 120	Mayo	2	10	"	3	11	6	3	.	.	4	2	.
		3	3	"									
64 JJJJ	Martin	3	"	"	3	14	6	3	10	.	3	.	.
	Milsted	2	10	"	2	10	.	2	10	.	2	16	.
	Mace	2	"	"	2	.	.	2	.	.	2	.	.
	Norman	2	4	"	2	4	.	2	4	.	2	4	.
28 JJJ	J. Prentice	3	7	.	3	7	8	3	11	6	4	"	10
30 JJJJ	Th. Prentice	4	7	.	4	5	4	4	9	4	4	5	4
	Phillips	2	10	.	2	10	.	2	10	.	2	10	.
116 JJJJ	Portlock	1	6	.	3	4	6	8	.	.	3	11	.
	Purves	1	4	.	5	4	.	1	4	.	5	4	.
	Pike	"	17	6	1	.	.	1	.	.	1	.	.
	Ridley	2	10	.	2	5	10	2	10	.	2	10	.
55 JJJJ	Robins	3	10	.	3	10	.	5	.	6	4	4	6
	Sanger	2	6	.	2	7	.	2	7	.	2	7	.
63 JJJJ	E. Sanger	3	18	.	3	10	.	4	11	.	3	10	.
. J	Smith Junr.	2	10	.	2	10	"	2	10	.	2	11	.
66 JJJ	John Smith	2	12	.	4	1	"	2	11	.	3	.	6
15 JJJJ	Schofield	4	19	.	3	6	"	3	6	.	3	6	.
	Suffolk		7	.		7	"		8	.		8	.
	Titterton	1	7	.	1	7	.	1	7	.	1	7	.
62 JJJJ	Tregale	5	.	.	4	5	6	4	5	6	5	10	6
39 JJJJ	Wm Webster	3	.	"	3	.	.	4	15	.	5	2	.
59 JJJJ	Weston	3	2	.	2	10	.	2	10	.	4	6	.
	Webster John	2	.	.	2	.	.	2	.	.	2	.	.
	Wasdell	2	10	.	2	10	.	2	10	.	3	2	.
	Wyburn	1	4	.	1	4	.	1	4	.	1	4	.
		114	18	5	115	17	4	121	9	2	131	19	9
79 JJJ	Sarah	.	10	.	1	5	.	1	"	"	1	6	.
10 JJJ	Mr. Lump	2	13	6	2	.	.	2	3	.	2	2	6
6 JJJ	W. Miller	12	3	6									
		130	.	5	119	5	4	124	12	2	135	2	3

Henry Lewis, the head stocker, who worked for the firm from the 1840s to the 1870s. A photograph taken around 1865.

With the advent of breech-loading, manufacturing terminology changed slightly. The following headings are from the 1859 page in the Dimension Book (illustrated below).

Number
Description
Bore
Length
Jointing
Stocking
Screwing
Making off, chequering, finishing
Tapping, finishing
Polishing, hardening
Barrels named Engrd
Rods
Varnishing
Pegs
Levers to B loaders
Filling and fitting
Cocks

Below: A page from the Dimension Book showing guns No. 5748-5759, built in 1859. 'D' = double percussion gun. 'DBL' = double breech-loader. In 'jointing, stocking and screwing', 'L' = Lewis, 'GL' = Glaysher, 'A' = Atkin, 'T' = Tregale. In 'polishing and hardening', 'R' = Robins and in 'Barrels named and Engraved', 'L' = Lucas and 'M' = Mace. In 'cocks', 'GP' = G Prentice.

Number	Description	Bore	Length	Jointing	Stocking	Screwing	making off chequering finishing	Tapping finishing	Polishing hardening	Barrels named Engrd	Rods	Varnishing	Pegs Levers to B loaders filling & fitting	Cocks	
5748	D	16	2/6		G	M	M	M	SS	R	L		W	GP	Earl of Antr
5749	Pr				L	L	L	LL	M	R	M		M	GP	
5750	DBL	12	2/6		L	L	L	LL	M	R	M		M	GP	Lord Guydr
5751	DBL	12	2/6		GL	GL	GL	GLGL	M	R	B		M	GP	Revd H D Ing
5752	Pr				G	T	T	TT	SS	R	L		W	GP	
5753	D	12	2/8		T	T	T	TT	SS	R	L		W	GP	Earl Strade
5754	D	12	2/6		G	A	A	AA	SS	R	M	H		GP	Honble Capt A
5755	DBL	12	2/6	safety	B	B	B	BB	M	R	L		M	GP	Col Madock
5756	D	13	2/6*		L	L	L	LL	SS	R	L	H	W	GP	Alan Gulsto
5757	Pr				G	T	T	TT	SS	R	L	H	W	GP	
5758	D	12	2/7		T	T	T	TT	SS	R	L	H	W	GP	F Mickleth

BOLT AND BEESLEY

With the adoption of the breech-loader and the recognition of the Purdey bolt in the 1860s, Purdey's continued to attract more and more influential customers. Production doubled from 112 weapons in 1855 to 228 in 1860. By 1865, 284 weapons were produced, an incredible rise in output. The Prince of Wales bought his first pair of pin-fire breech-loaders, Nos. 6236/7 tested on 23 January 1862 and sold for £115 on 1 February of the same year. Purdey's success did breed some jealousy and criticism, but James Purdey would have none of it. Further along the street at 502 New Oxford Street, E M Reilly, the gunmaker, experienced the wrath of Purdey the Younger over untrue allegations.

(Copy)
314 1/2 Oxford Street W
May 29th, 1866

Dear Sir,
I must beg your immediate attention to the following matter.

A gentleman was in your shop in Oxford Street and was shewn two guns, both of which were represented as being made by you. The price of one was 20 the other 40 guineas and the difference in price was accounted for by the person who showed them saying that 'one had been proved and stamped by Purdey for which you had to pay him'.

Now as you know that the foregoing statement is not only perfectly untrue, but malicious and injurious to my trade and reputation, I must request that you will give me an explanation respecting the same, with your assurance that the statement is untrue in every way and made without your sanction or knowledge (which I presume is the case) and that you will take steps to prevent a repetition of such reports being made.

I am Dear Sir
Yours truly
James Purdey

E M Reilly, Esq.
502 New Oxford Street.

E M Reilly apparently denied the accusation and in a subsequent letter to the gentleman who had first brought Purdey's attention to the matter James Purdey stated:

> I get up only one quality of work 'the best' have my *own men*, make my guns upon *my own premises*, pay a *larger price*, and have men to *overlook* and *perfect* work in the *finishing state* such as are employed I believe nowhere else. Since 1858 when I took sole management of my business, I executed more work and increased my business to a larger size than was ever done (even by Joe Manton). I have produced a greater variety (to such various tastes) of guns and introduced more improvement successfully than most in my trade….

Right: The letter dated 29 May 1866 sent by James Purdey to E M Reilly, the gunmaker, accusing him of impugning the reputation of Purdey's.

JAMES PURDEY AND SONS 1877

During the late 1860s, the Purdey gunmaking business under the leadership of James Purdey the Younger was going from strength to strength and a mood of confident optimism heralded the new decade of the 1870s. However, life never runs its intended course and personal disaster hit the Purdey family. James Purdey's wife Caroline, died on 7 January 1870, aged just 37, following complications after the birth of her seventh child, Percy Purdey, who had been born on 24 August 1869 at 28 Devonshire Place. Her death certificate records that she died of 'Puerperal Mania, One Month, Exhaustion' and that she died in the Kensington House Asylum, Kensington. How tragic this must have been for James Purdey. Not only had he to cope with the trauma of her untimely death, he also had six very young children to look after. The eldest, James III, was only fifteen and the youngest, Percy, a mere four months old. There is no record as to how James Purdey coped with these problems and one can only speculate on the extent of his troubles. Caroline Purdey was buried in the family vault in Paddington Cemetery.

James Purdey was only 41 when his wife died. However, fortune intervened and some three years later he married Julia Haverson, aged nineteen. Julia had been born on 10 July 1854 at Barking Road, Plaistow, a small village near Horsham, West Sussex. Her father was a printer and stationer. By the time of her marriage, the family had moved northwards to Penge on the southern outskirts of London. The couple were married on 12 August 1873 in the Church of St. John the Evangelist in Penge.

James Purdey III (1854-90), the eldest son of James Purdey the Younger. Both James and his brother Athol are the 'Sons' referred to when the firm was renamed 'James Purdey and Sons' in 1877. James Purdey III's personal gun was a 16-bore hammer gun, No. 8703, built in 1872.

Julia must have had great fortitude, as she now had to cope with six step-children, the youngest, Percy, being four and the eldest, James III, nineteen – the same age as herself! She went to live in the family home at 28 Devonshire Place. Far from being daunted by the prospect of inheriting such a large ready-made family, Julia went on to produce another six Purdey's! By the time of her last confinement in 1886, James Purdey the Younger had sired thirteen children in all.

The first of the children from the second marriage, Ada, was born in 1875 but died within a month. Others followed: Talfourd, born 1876, died 1885; Sefton, born 1877, died 1916; Mabel, born 1880, died the same year; Archie, born 1881, died 1885 and Lionel, born 1886, died 1959. Neither Sefton nor Lionel, the longest surviving children, entered the gunmaking business. Out of the thirteen children in total, only eight achieved their age of majority. James III died from tuberculosis at 36. This high mortality rate is typical of the era. Although the Purdeys enjoyed a privileged lifestyle with a substantial house in an excellent residential area and a high income, medical care and knowledge had not advanced sufficiently to tackle divergent illness.

Meanwhile, in 1874 James Purdey's second son Athol, aged sixteen, was sent to a school in St. Germain-en-Laye, France, to receive a final educational polish before entering the business in 1875. Again, we have no record of his apprenticeship. James Purdey the Younger must have felt satisfaction that he now had both his sons – his eldest boy, James III, and now Athol – involved in the business to ensure

Julia Haverson 1854-1911, the second wife of James Purdey the Younger. A photograph of her aged nineteen in 1873 at the time of her marriage.

continuity. On 28 June 1877, James Purdey III, aged 23 (opposite), was admitted into the Gunmakers' Company. The Gunmakers' Company, Freedom Admissions 1746-1949 state that 'James Purdey the Younger was admitted into the freedom of this Company by Redemption 28th June, 1877'. This use of the term 'Younger' is very confusing. It is used on official documents in the late 19th century and no doubt is technically correct in terming James Purdey III 'The Younger' in this period. However, use of the term certainly makes life difficult for the researcher! His younger brother Athol, aged 21, was admitted into the Gunmakers' Company on 13 November 1879.

Athol Purdey, 1858-1939, second son of James Purdey the Younger. He was primarily responsible for running the firm in the early part of the 20th century. A photograph taken *circa* 1880.

James Purdey the Younger himself played a major role in the Gunmakers' Company, being nominated Master of the Company on three occasions – in 1874, 1882 and 1892. With both his sons secure in the business, on 21 December 1877 James Purdey changed the name of the firm to 'James Purdey and Sons'.

James Purdey was quite specific in his objectives behind doing this. At some time his sons would share in and run the business so the name was altered 'to familiarise his Business Customers' with their existence in the firm. Purdey was adamant that the Deed of Agreement referred to a change of name only – "adding his sons names to his own is not to be taken as conferring any partnership rights, powers or interests upon them". The agreement was cautious but pragmatic. On the one hand, he acknowledged his sons future stake in the business but on the other he had to ensure that they were worthy and capable of running the business. Remember, that they were both young – James aged 24 and Athol, 19. There were also the continuing health worries over James. Consequently from 1878 onwards, all guns and rifles had the engraving 'J Purdey & Sons' as opposed to the simpler 'Purdey'.

The early part of the agreement states:

> … it is hereby understood and agreed between James Purdey of No. 314 $^1/_2$ Oxford Street, Gun Maker and his sons James Purdey the Younger and Athol Stuart Purdey as follows. The said James Purdey having in contemplation certain arrangements which he may hereafter make for admitting his said Two Sons to a share in his business of a Gun Manufacturer carried on by him 314 $^1/_2$ Oxford Street aforesaid has with a view to that possibility and with a desire to benefit the said sons by familiarising his Business Customers atonce with the step so contemplated, decided upon adding his sons' names to his own by changing thename of James Purdey in which the said Business has hitherto been carried on to 'Purdey & Sons' but on the distinct understanding and agreement with his said sons that the steps so taken by him and the change of name under which the said Business is carried on shall only be for so long as the said James Purdey shall think fit and that the adding his sons' names to his own is not to be taken as conferring any partnership rights, powers or interests upon them….

Athol's scroll admitting him to the Freedom of the Gunmakers' Company. Placed beneath his oil portrait in the Long Room, it states: 'Athol Stuart Purdey, Citizen and Gunmaker of London, was admitted into the Freedom aforesaid and made the Declaration required by Law in the Mayoralty of William McArthur, Esq. M.P., Mayor and Benjamin Scott, Esq., Chamberlain and was entered in the book signed with the letter B1 dating to the purchasing of Freedoms and the Admission of Freeman (to wit) the 11th Day of January in the 44th Year of the reign of Queen VICTORIA and in the Year of our Lord 1881. In Witness Whereof the Seal of the Office of Chamberlain of the said City as hereunto affixed dated in the Chamber of the Guild Hall of the same City the date and Year abovesaid.'

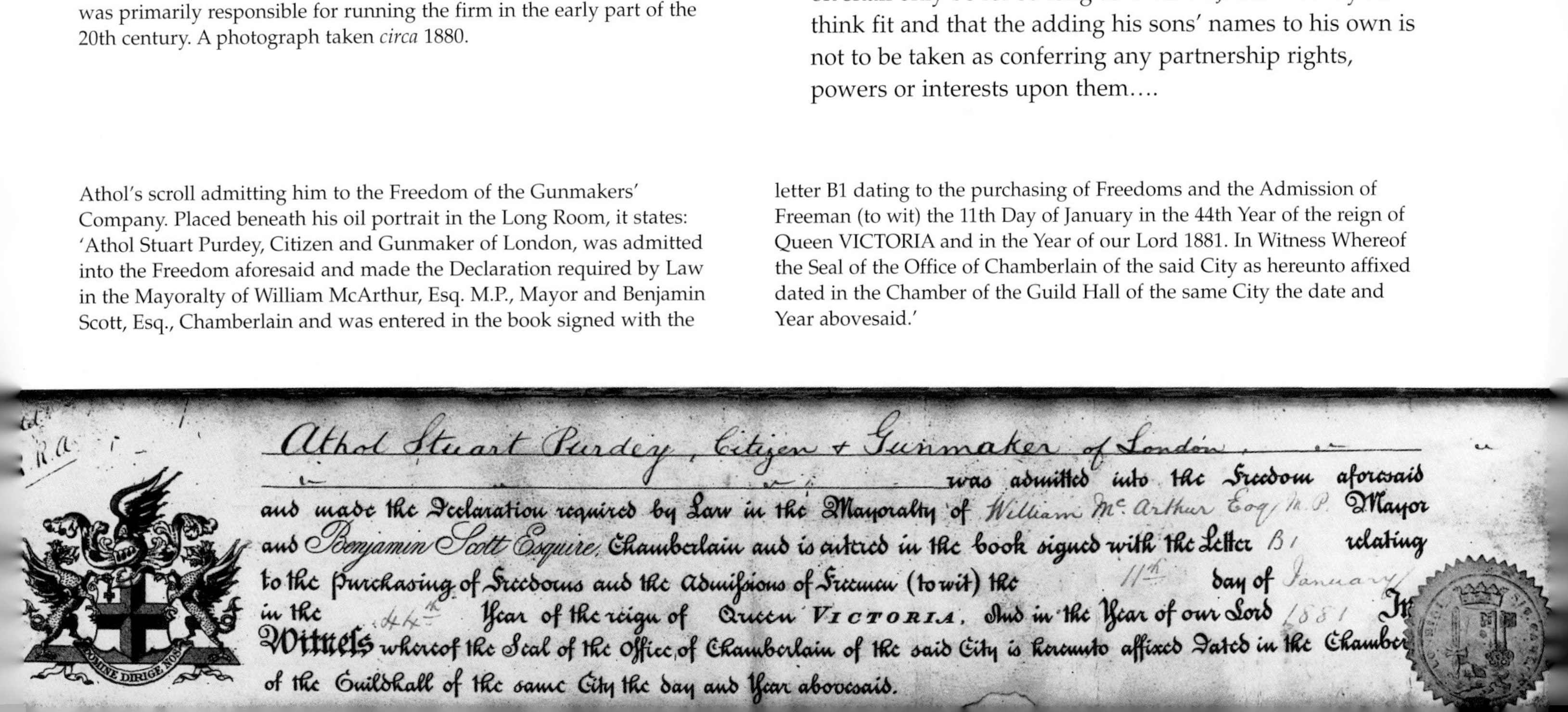

[handwritten deed of agreement image]

The introduction of the deed of agreement of 21 December 1877, renaming the firm 'James Purdey & Sons'.

FURTHER PATENTS

On 28 November 1870 James Purdey took out patent no. 3118 'An Improvement in the Action of Break-down Guns with a Snap Fastening' (see Appendix 8). This was a clever, simple patent means of preventing a gun from being fired until it was properly shut. It was primarily intended to apply to thumb-hole guns, although a top lever method is also mentioned. As previously mentioned, the thumb-hole snap action used a bifurcated spring with two limbs on either side of the trigger blades. In patent no. 3118, Purdey fitted a connection between these two limbs of the spring. When the gun was opened, the spring compressed and lowered and this connection came into contact with recesses in the trigger blades, effectively preventing the triggers from being pulled. Whenever the gun was snapped shut, the spring would return to its original position and the connection would rise free of the triggers, allowing them to be pulled.

Purdey's next patent, no. 2952 of 3 November 1871 – 'An Improvement in the Construction of Rifled Breech-loading Firearms' – remained only as a Provisional Specification and was never proceeded with (see Appendix 8). A Provisional Specification was a general statement of what was intended by the inventor who then had to submit a Complete Specification within nine months. The Complete Specification would fully describe the invention, usually with accompanying drawings. For some reason, Purdey never proceeded with a Complete Specification. This patent applied to breech-loading rifles. For the first three-quarters of its length, the barrel was smooth bore. For the last quarter of its length, a rifled tube, about six inches long was screwed into the barrel, tapered at the end where it met the smooth bore part of the barrel. The idea was that the smooth bore would enable the bullet to achieve a far greater velocity before reaching the rifling grooves. In 1885 Holland and Holland patented such a device – the Paradox, invented by Colonel Fosberry, using much the same principle as Purdey invented in 1871.

Purdey's final patent of the 1870s was no. 397 of 30 January 1878 'Improvements in Breech-loading Firearms' (see Appendix 8). This invention created an additional short bolt to lock the breech above the extractors on the barrels. Both top snap and under snap are shown in the patent drawing. Both mechanisms employ much the same method of using a small bolt attached to the vertical spindle. As the top lever was pushed to the side, this vertical spindle turned and withdrew the small bolt from the projection on the barrels just above the extractors. Upon closure, the small bolt would come into contact with this projection and lock it. The double bolt in the bottom of the action was of course still used and was the main barrel-locking bolt. This small bolt is often termed a 'third bite' or a 'secret bite'. Purdey termed this extra bolt a 'Patent Third Fastening' and charged £1.8s. extra per gun. This third fastening tended to be used on guns where there were greater pressures, such as pigeon guns or large-bore guns. The third fastening is still offered on Purdey guns today.

A drawing showing the 'Third Fastening' of patent no. 397, 30 January 1878.

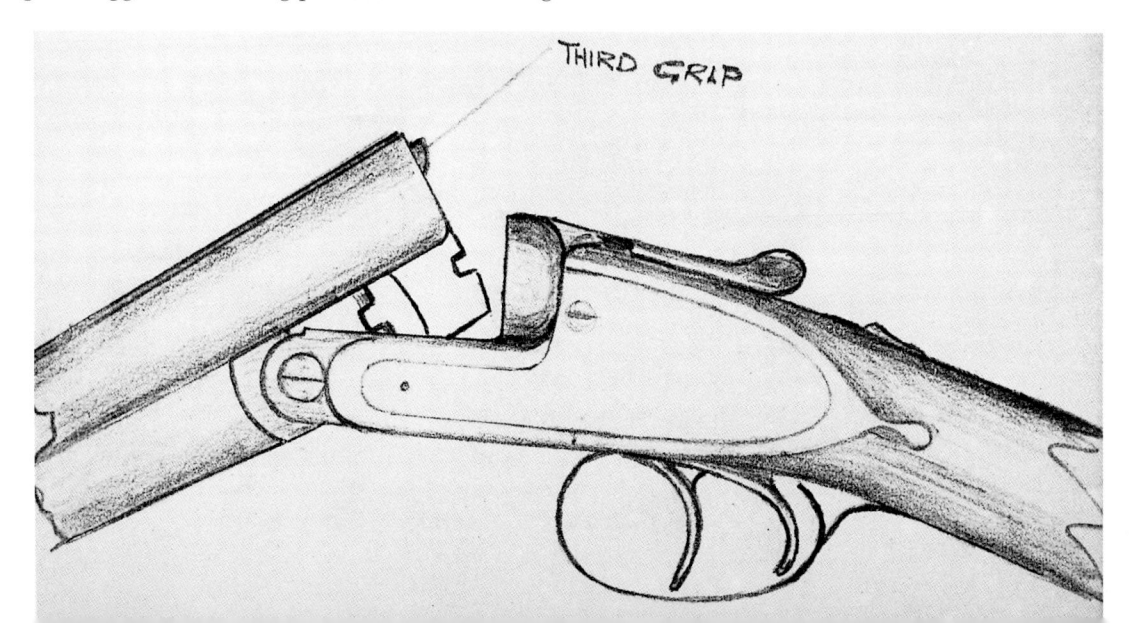

LIVE PIGEON SHOOTING

In the 19th century live pigeon shooting was a very popular pastime – a professional sport taken very seriously, involving a high degree of gambling. The leading gunmakers took great cognisance of this and when the results were published weekly in the press in contemporary periodicals like *Land and Water* and *The Field* it gave them great publicity if their guns came out on top. Consequently, Purdey's took a keen interest in the competitions.

James Purdey the Elder was one of the first gunmakers to take such an interest and he regularly organised such events at his shooting ground from the 1850s onwards. Purdey's continued to attend live pigeon events until the sport was banned in Britain in 1922. They donated several of their guns for prizes, e.g. single-barrel 6-bore percussion gun No. 5793, donated 'as a prize to be shot for at Hornsey Wood 1865 and won by William Page'.

The unfortunate pigeons were reared in their thousands and were not cheap – a dozen Blue Rock Pigeons cost 14s. The pigeon was placed in a metal trap and released on command. The trap was about 25 yards in front of the shooter and the pigeon had to fall within the boundary line, about 80 yards in front of the trap. Several live pigeon venues grew up in and around London, such as Hornsey Wood House; the Gun Club, Notting Hill; the Red House, Battersea Fields, and the Hurlingham Gun Club.

The muzzle-loaders tended to fire heavier loads than usual and many of them were bereft of ramrod, a loading rod being used instead. The charge would be from $2^{3/4}$ to 3 drams of powder and $1^{1/8}$ to $1^{1/4}$ oz. of shot. Rules regarding pigeon shooting at the clubs were very lax until the 1860s when some consensus was established and the 12-bore gun became the norm. Centre-fire hammer guns took over eventually from these muzzle-loaders and Purdey's built many such guns. These differed from the standard game gun in that they were built to shoot the heavier charges demanded in live pigeon shooting. Such guns often used $2^{3/4}$-inch cartridges, weighed in at between $7^{1/2}$ to 8lbs and were stocked and ribbed to throw the centre of the shot pattern high of the point of aim. Many Purdey pigeon guns had the third fastening on account of the heavier loads used and barrels were never less than 30 inches.

Towards the end of the century, live pigeon shooting declined as public opinion changed, and old established clubs like the Hurlingham closed. The inanimate bird or clay pigeon and trap replaced the live bird and in 1922 the Captive Birds Act banned live pigeon shooting in Britain.

Long after the introduction of the hammerless gun in the 1880s, hammer guns were preferred by live pigeon shooters. Purdey's records are full of orders for pigeon hammer guns, usually hammer ejectors, in the late 19th and early 20th centuries. The last recorded hammer gun is No. 25015, a 12-bore back action with side clips, built in 1935, and most probably a pigeon gun.

Of great importance to the live pigeon shooter, was the introduction of choke-boring in the 1870s. The idea of constricting a gun barrel to hold shot closer together in flight was not new. The principle was known by the beginning of the 19th century. W R Pape, of Newcastle, in patent no. 1501 of

A live pigeon competition at the Gun Club, Notting Hill, London 1870-80.

An interesting comparison with the 1880 engraving of the Gun Club, this photopgraph is of the International Meeting in 1894. The ornate tower can easily be recognised. Note the baskets for pigeons and a trap control lever. James Purdey the Younger is in this photograph, dead centre, third row back wearing a top hat with his trademark large moustache.

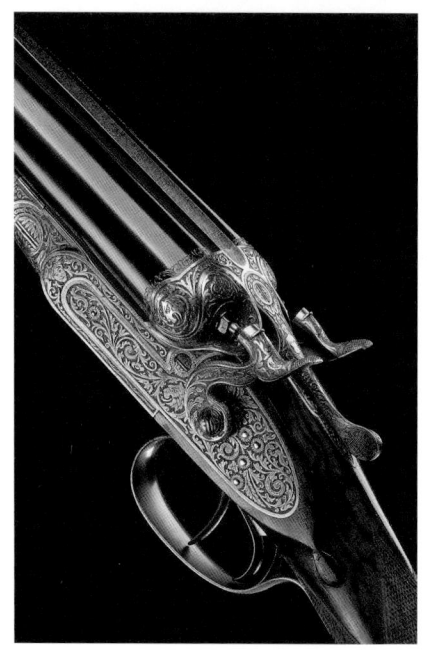

A typical pigeon gun, a late built double 12-bore hammer ejector gun, No. 22182, the No. 2 of a pair built in 1922. This gun displays all the classic pigeon gun features. A third fastening and side clips are employed for extra strength. The 32-inch barrels are full choke, 2 3/4-inch chambers and with raised matt rib. The gun weighs 7lbs 12oz. Probably engraved by Harry Kell with the heads of mythical beasts and grotesques amidst foliate scrollwork. Large numbers of hammer guns were built in the early 20th century for live pigeon shooting, usually for foreign customers. (*See plate 29 in colour section.*)

Name of Gunmaker.	Number of Chances.	Wins.	Divided Counts Half.	Proportion of Wins to Chances.
Guyot	14	2	—	·14
Powell	201	16	18	·12
Ducasse	25	2	1	·10
Reilly	432	28	18	·08
Lang	74	2	7	·07
Churchill	248	15	7	·07
Atkin	119	5	5	·06
Purdey	1161	48	35	·05
Holland	106	4	4	·05
Chapu	23	1	—	·04
Parker	25	—	2	·04
Greener	82	2	3	·04
Rennette	27	1	—	·03
Bonehill	16	—	1	·03
Bodson	44	1	1	·03
Grant	53	1	—	·01
Westley Richards	1	—	—	—
Horsley	1	—	—	—
Evans	2	—	—	—
Boswell	3	—	—	—
Leeson	5	—	—	—
Baker	7	—	—	—
Cririck	7	—	—	—
Lancaster	8	—	—	—
Cogswell and Harrison	8	—	—	—
Boss	9	—	—	—
Dougall	9	—	—	—
Janson	10	—	—	—

The table showing the pigeon shooting results of 1894 showing the prolific use of Purdeys.

The record in the Dimension Book for Nos. 2218 1/2. Stocked by Shackell and put together by Packman. Note 'Chased work & Guns Blued, Gold Ovals.'

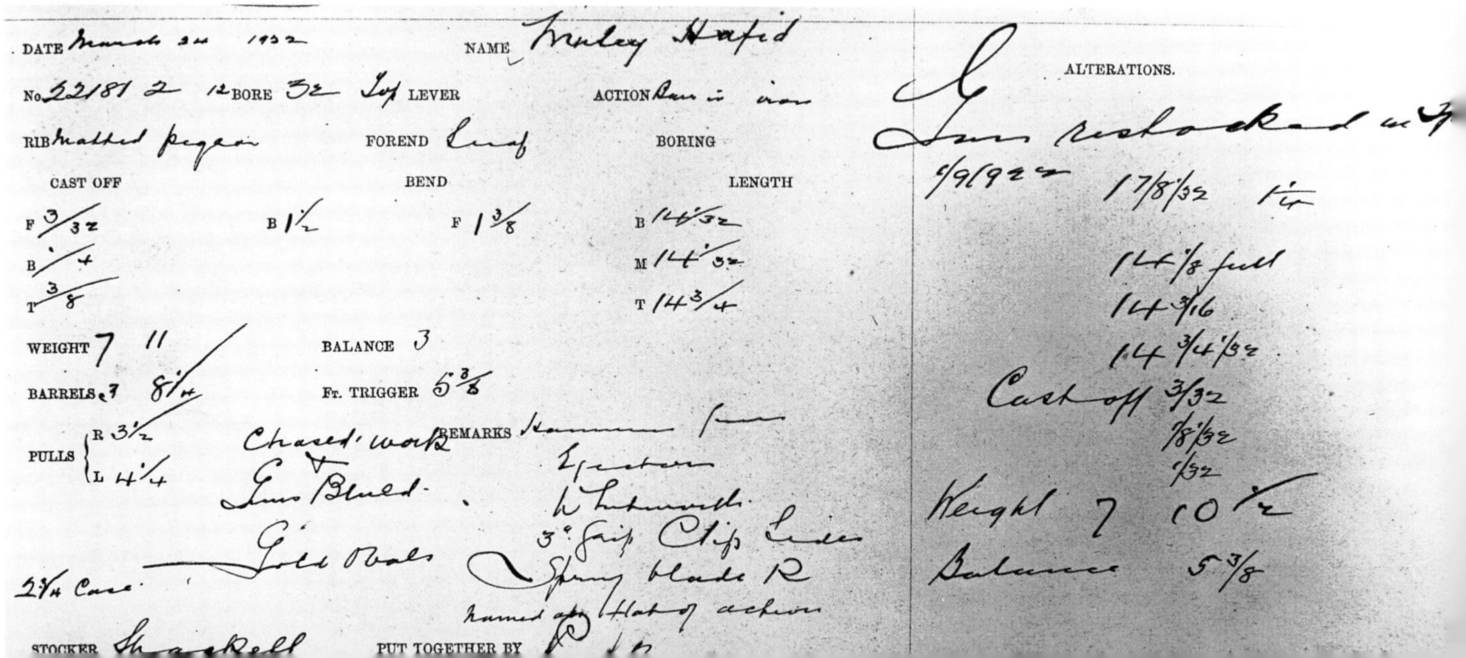

1866 claimed to be the inventor of the choke-bore. As with many inventions, the true originator can probably never be established. W W Greener of Newcastle was aware of the choke-bore and was responsible for popularising it with his advertisements in *The Field* in 1874.

Just as had happened in the controversy over muzzle *versus* breech-loaders in the 1850s the same debate occurred over choke *versus* cylinder-bores in the 1870s. Again *The Field* stepped in and organised a trial of the two systems in 1875. The trials proved conclusively that choke-boring produced tighter patterns at long range. A further trial was demanded in 1876 under field conditions to imitate actual shooting practice. This took place against live pigeons on 21 July 1876 at The Gun Club, Notting Hill. There were two teams of shooters, cylinder-bores *versus* choke-bores. On the cylinder side were guns by Purdey, Boss, Lancaster and Grant. The cylinder guns won by two birds at 27 yards rise and seven birds at 33 yards rise. Yet again, the established makers were erring on the conservative side. The trials were not particularly satisfactory and the cylinder guns did win, but they had the best shots on their side.

This advertisement appeared in the American periodical *The Turf, Field and Farm* of 15 January 1875. Note mention of the 'Factory' at 314 ½ Oxford Street.

A year later another trial under more realistic rules was held. This time, the choke-bore guns were victorious. Purdey's had put up a sweepstake of 50 guineas and a silver cup and this prize was won by a Greener choke-bore gun in the hands of Mr. H C Pennell using a 3 ¼ dram powder charge to bring down the birds at some 60 to 70 yards distance. This trial proved that choke-bores were the best for this shooting and from then on they became increasingly used at the gun clubs, and Purdey's began to build choke-bored guns as game shooters began to appreciate their merit.

The silver Purdey Cup presented by the firm plus £50 sweepstake in the 1877 trial of choke *versus* cylinder-bores.

The 1875 advertisement states that Purdey's were 'By Special Appointment to H.R.H. The Prince of Wales and the Crowned Heads of Europe and makers to nearly all the most noted game shots in England'. This was no idle boast. By this period Purdey's Dimension Book could record such customers as: H.M. Queen Victoria, H.R.H. Prince Albert, H.R.H. The Prince of Wales, H.R.H. The Duke of Cambridge, H.I.M. The Emperor of Russia, H.M. The King of Prussia, H.M. The King of Italy, H.H. Maharajah Prince Duleep Singh, Crown Prince of Portugal, Prince Hassan, Prince Furstenburg, The Maharajah of Patallah, Prince Hassan Pasha, Prince Hohenloke, Grand Duke of Vladimar, H.M. The King of Siam, Prince Metternich, Prince of Teck, Prince Edward of Saxe Weimar, Prince Wittgenstein, Prince Charles de Ligne, Count Romanoff, H.R.H. Duke of Brunswick, Duke of Wellington, Lord Walsingham and Lord de Grey.

Purdey's had received the Royal Warrant of Appointment to the Prince of Wales on the 12 February 1868. Queen Victoria

The first Royal Warrant, granted to James Purdey dated 1868. From the Prince of Wales, it states: 'Mr James Purdey, You are hereby appointed Gun and Rifle Maker to His Royal Highness, the Prince of Wales. Given under my hand and seal at Marlborough House this Twelfth day of February 1868.'

had purchased many guns, rifles and pistols from the firm and on the 29 March 1878 she granted the Royal Warrant to the firm. From that time Purdey's have consistently received the Royal Warrants of Appointment from all the reigning British monarchs as the following list shows:

Prince of Wales 12th February 1868, Queen Victoria 29 March 1878, King Edward VII 29 May 1901, Prince of Wales 1 March

1902, King George V 1 February 1911, Prince of Wales 26 May 1920, King George VI 30 June 1938, Queen Elizabeth II 15 July 1955, Duke of Edinburgh 2 January 1956, Prince of Wales 1 January 1981

Queen Victoria's Royal Warrant of Appointment to Purdey's 1878. The Warrant states 'These are to Certify that I have Appointed Mr James Purdey into the Place and Quality of Gun and Rifle Maker in ordinary to Her Majesty. To have, hold, exercise and enjoy the said Place together with all Rights, Profits, Privileges and Advantages thereunto belonging. Given under my Hand and Seal this Twenty ninth day of March 1878 in the Forty first Year of Her Majesty's Reign.'

THE ARRIVAL OF A, B, C, D AND E QUALITY

In the late 1870s, Purdey's made an entirely new departure from their normal standard of gunmaking. The firm introduced differing grades of guns, offering different qualities and at different prices. From this period, Purdey guns would be on sale from the best grade A, to the cheapest grade E. These graded guns would be sold from the late 1870s right through the 1880s and 1890s, tailing off before World War I, never to reappear after the war. The 1880s saw the greatest amount being constructed. The grades can be summarised as follows:

Grade A – Best Gun
Finest work and finish throughout – Hammer £56, Hammerless £58.10s.

Grade B – Approaching a Best Gun
Hammer £40.10s, Hammerless £45.

Grade C – Central-Fire Double Gun
Hammer £32.8s., Hammerless (boxlock) £35.15s.

Grade D – Central-Fire Double Gun
Hammer £25.13s., Hammerless (boxlock) £26.10s.

Grade E – Central-Fire Double Gun
Hammer £20.14s, Hammerless (boxlock) £22.

Customers could choose in all types either a top lever or under lever. In the hammerless guns, C, D and E Quality were boxlocks. In the hammer guns, E Quality were primarily made with back action locks. Rifles likewise were made in various qualities.

The grade A guns, were still entirely built by Purdey to the highest standards. The other grades of gun were not built by Purdey's. Depending upon the grade, Purdey's would finish and engrave the guns to a greater or lesser extent. The principal makers of the lower grade guns were:

W & C Scott, Birmingham. They were the major makers of the guns, no doubt due to the working business relationship Purdey's had with them.
A Smith & Son.
Richard Ellis, Birmingham.
Richard Redman, Birmingham.
Samuel B Allport, Birmingham.
William Jones, Birmingham.
Charles Osborne & Co., Birmingham.
Thomas Perkes, London.

A C Quality double .500 boxlock hammerless rifle No. 12992 built for Hugh Morrison. The breeches are stamped 'C Quality'. The 27 3/4-inch barrels have folding flaps to 100, 200 and 250 yards and are engraved 'J Purdey & Sons, Audley House, South Audley Street, London'. The sides of the action are engraved 'J Purdey & Sons'. (See plate 28 in colour section.)

Most of the pea rifles or rook and rabbit rifles were built by Redman.

There was absolutely no intention on the part of the Purdey to deceive customers with their varying grades of gun. The lower grade weapons were distinctly marked, usually on the action flats or on the underside of the breeches with the grade in question. In a *Land and Water* article 'Crack Gunmakers' of 6 July 1899, the writer states:

> … in reference to the guns themselves, Mr. Purdey used formerly to make but one quality the highest, and had but one price – viz, between £60 and £70, if with case and fittings. These guns were handmade throughout. He has latterly however set up an extensive plant of machinery, and can now supply a second quality, in the manufacture of which machinery bears a principal part. Indeed it is said that orders flow in so fast that even London machinery cannot go fast enough, and that therefore, Birmingham contributes to Mr. Purdey's bank balance.

The action flat of a C Quality double .500 rifle No. 12992 sold in October 1890 marked 'C Quality'.

The record in the Dimension Book for rifle No. 12992. The 'Remarks' state 'Anson & Deeley Hammerless'. The Stocker 'RE' refers to Richard Ellis of Birmingham who made the rifle, which was regulated by a Purdey gunmaker, Warren Jr., who normally did repairs.

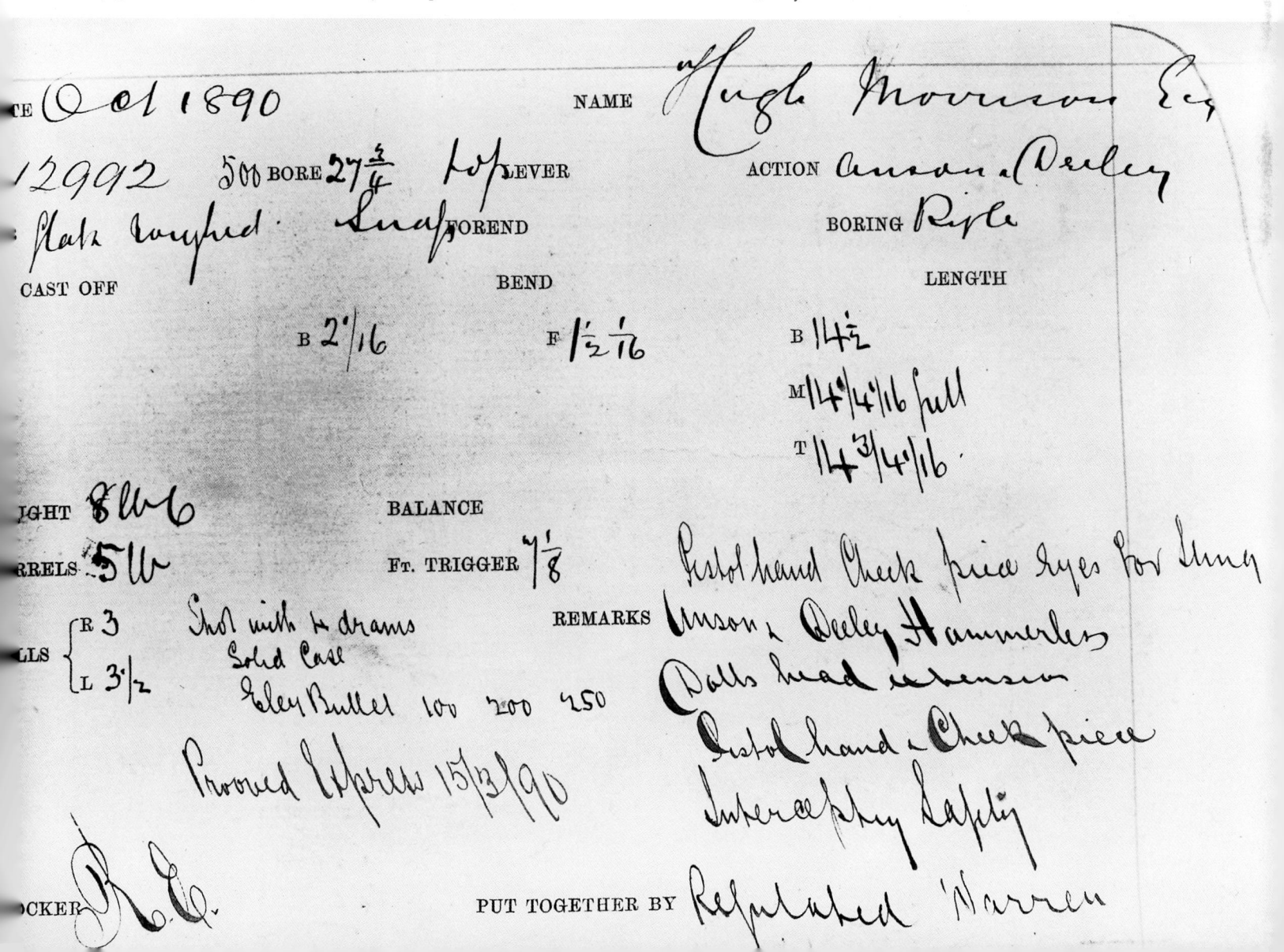

With the benefit of hindsight, Purdey's have been condemned for the introduction of these grades of gun. They have been accused of demeaning the Purdey name and of creating a scepticism about where the best guns were being built and what standard of finish was applied to them. However, this is unfair. Purdey's action must be viewed in the context of the era and in that light seems to be perfectly logical.

The demand for guns in the late 19th century was immense. In the 1870s, Purdey's were producing around 230 best guns a year. It was difficult to expand best gun output, finding skilled gunmakers and all in the confines of 314 ½ Oxford Street. To satisfy demand – not always for best weapons – guns had to be built elsewhere. The 'sun never set' on the British Empire and many sportsmen in far off climes, such as Africa and India, didn't want best guns – they wanted servicable weapons to withstand the rigours of colonial life. Purdey's were following the contemporary fashion of many makers in producing various grades of gun. In many respects, it wasn't an entirely new step for Purdey's. 'Keepers' guns' and 'cheap guns' had been produced from muzzle-loading days in response to demand, although Purdey's never promoted them as they did with the A to E Quality. In addition, the extra sales generated healthy profits. By the mid-1880s, sales of weapons were running at around 350 guns a year. During the 1890s, sales of the lower quality guns had dropped off as Purdey's began to distance themselves from them. They were seen as tarnishing a reputation built up over some 60 years. Best gun production was what the firm excelled at and once again after World War I, Purdey built only one grade – the best.

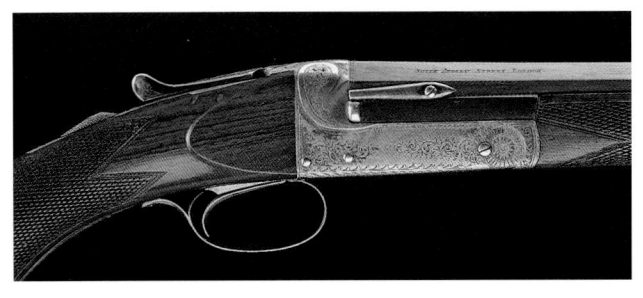

An 'E' Quality .300 hammerless top-lever boxlock rook rifle, No. 17242; sold in 1901, constructed probably by Redman and finished by Purdey's. The barrel is 26 inches long with a folding leafsight to 150 yards. Automatic ejector and stock with cheek-piece and pistol grip. (*See plate 32 in colour section.*)

To advertise the many grades of gun and types of gun built, Purdey's produced an advertising booklet in the 1880s. The booklet illustrated dates from 1885. Several points are of interest. The Grade E hammer gun is suitable 'for colonial use'. Best guns 'are made throughout on the premises by the most skilful workmen'. Beesley sidelock guns were made in only two qualities, the 'Best' and 'Grade B'.

Another type of weapon that was bought in and finished by Purdey during the 1870s only, was the 'Purdey-Henry' rifle. These were falling block single-barrel rifles, as patented by Alexander Henry, the riflemaker. The breech was closed by a sliding vertical block. Upon pushing forward a lever under the trigger-guard, the breech opened and a cartridge could be inserted. These rifles were made by S B Allport in Birmingham and finished by Purdey's. They all have Purdey serial numbers.

A 'C' Quality boxlock .450/.400 (3 ¼-inch nitro Express) non-ejector rifle No. 13963 sold on 15 March 1891 to W P Rylands. The gun was made by Samuel Allport of Birmingham and regulated by the Purdey gunmaker, Warren. Patent third fastening with intercepting safeties. Stock with pistol grip, pistol grip cap and cheek-piece. 28-inch barrels with matt rib and open sights. Weight, 7lb. 9oz. (*See plate 30 in colour section.*)

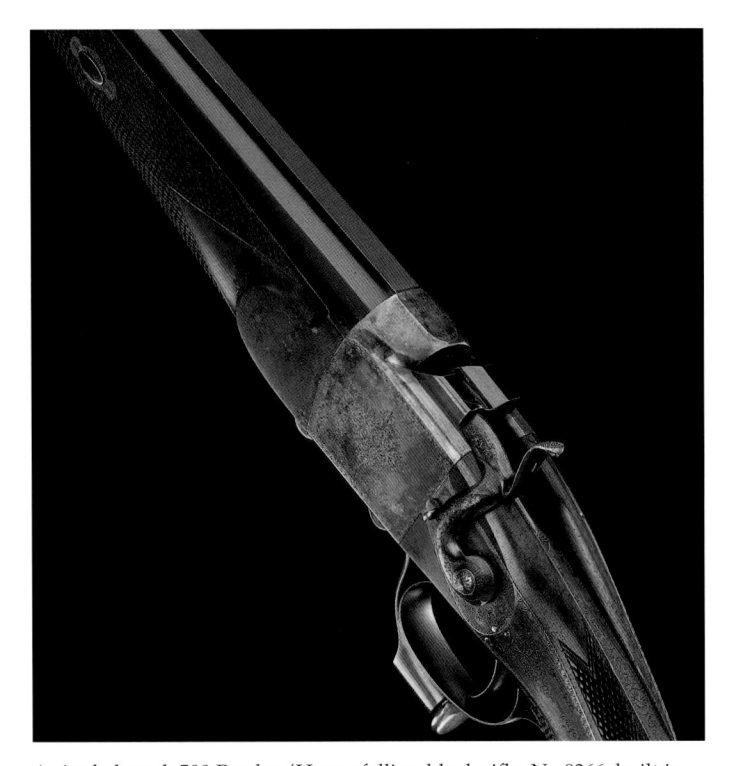

A single-barrel .500 Purdey/Henry falling-block rifle, No.9366, built in 1875 for B H Buxton. Although the records do not state it, Purdey probably bought in the rifle from S B Allport and finished it to a high standard. Alexander Henry patent falling-block action with left hand, faceted back action lockplate and bolted hammer. Pistol grip stock with horn tipped cap. The 28-inch barrel has nine groove rifling, open sights and a matt rib. A total of 41 Purdey/Henrys were sold by Purdey's. (*See plate 31 in colour section.*)

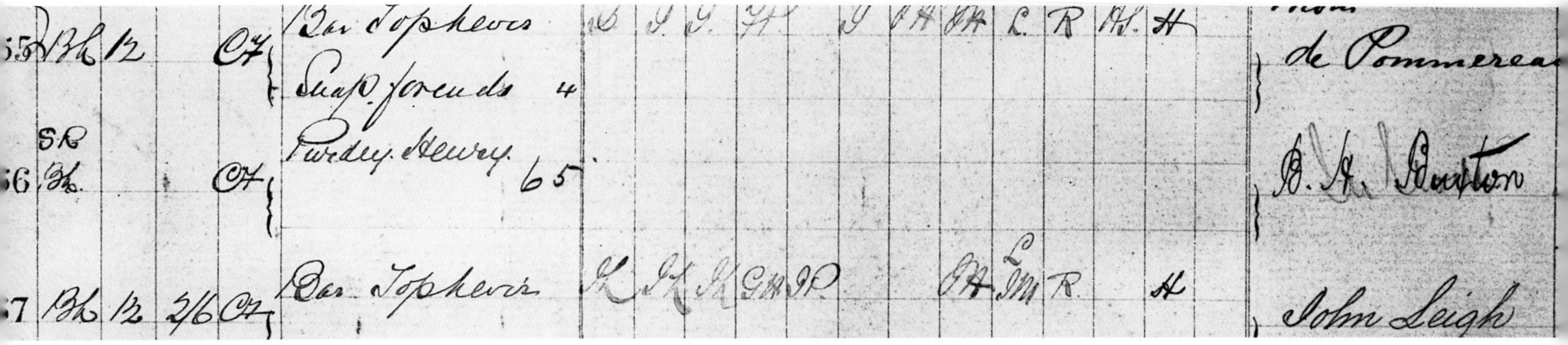

The record in the Dimension Book for No. 9366. No gunmakers' initials are recorded as the rifle was not built by Purdey's.

The following illustrations are taken from the 1885 catalogue of Purdey guns. Not all pages are reproduced, as the catalogue is lengthy.

JAMES PURDEY & SONS,

SOLE GUNMAKERS TO

Her Majesty the Queen

AND BY SPECIAL APPOINTMENT TO

H.R.H. The Prince of Wales.

GUNMAKERS TO

H.E. THE VICEROY OF INDIA

AND

H.E. THE LATE VICEROY.

GOLD MEDALLISTS, CALCUTTA, 1883-4.

MELBOURNE, 1880–1881.

PARIS, 1878.

HIGHEST AWARD, PHILADELPHIA, 1876.

INVENTORS OF THE EXPRESS RIFLE.

AUDLEY HOUSE, SOUTH AUDLEY STREET,

LONDON.

TERMS.

All prices in this List having been reduced 10 per cent., are Net and for Cash only, one third with Order, and balance paid in London on Goods being ready, and from this rule no departure can be made.

The Prices quoted for Guns include measures for Powder and Shot, and those for Rifles, a bullet mould and powder measure, excepting only the Repeating and Rook Rifles.

Weapons made to order take from three to five months.

GUNS WITH HAMMERS.
PRICES.

Grade E.—Central Fire Double Gun, choke or cylinder, top lever or lever over guard action, rebounding locks, snap forepart. A strong serviceable weapon, suitable for Colonial use. (*Fig.* I.) ... £20 14 0

Stout Waterproof Case with fittings ... 3 10 0

Grade D. do. do. better locks, make and finish ... 25 13 0

Leather Case and fittings ... 4 1 0

Grade C. do. do. do. choke, cylinder, or one-barrel choke and one-barrel cylinder. Hammers below line of sight if desired. (*Fig.* II.) ... 32 8 0

Oak and Leather Case and fittings ... 4 10 0

JAMES PURDEY & SONS make a large number of Guns of the last-mentioned quality, and strongly recommend it as *excellent value* to those who do not wish to go to a higher price.

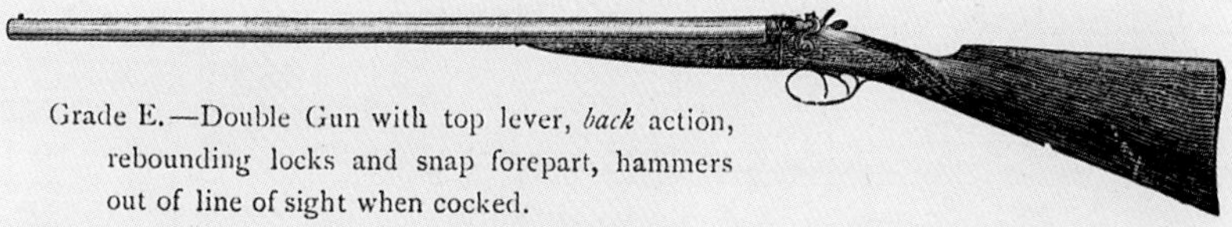

Grade E.—Double Gun with top lever, *back* action, rebounding locks and snap forepart, hammers out of line of sight when cocked.

Fig. II.

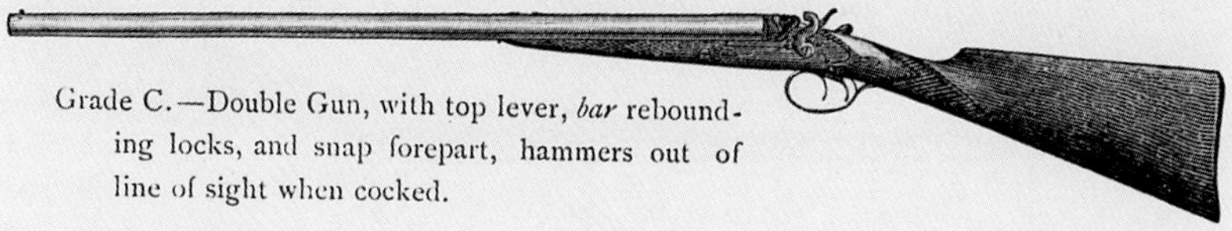

Grade C.—Double Gun, with top lever, *bar* rebounding locks, and snap forepart, hammers out of line of sight when cocked.

Fig. III. — Best Gun, with top lever, bar rebounding locks in wood, snap forepart and barrels of Whitworth steel, hammers out of line of sight when cocked.

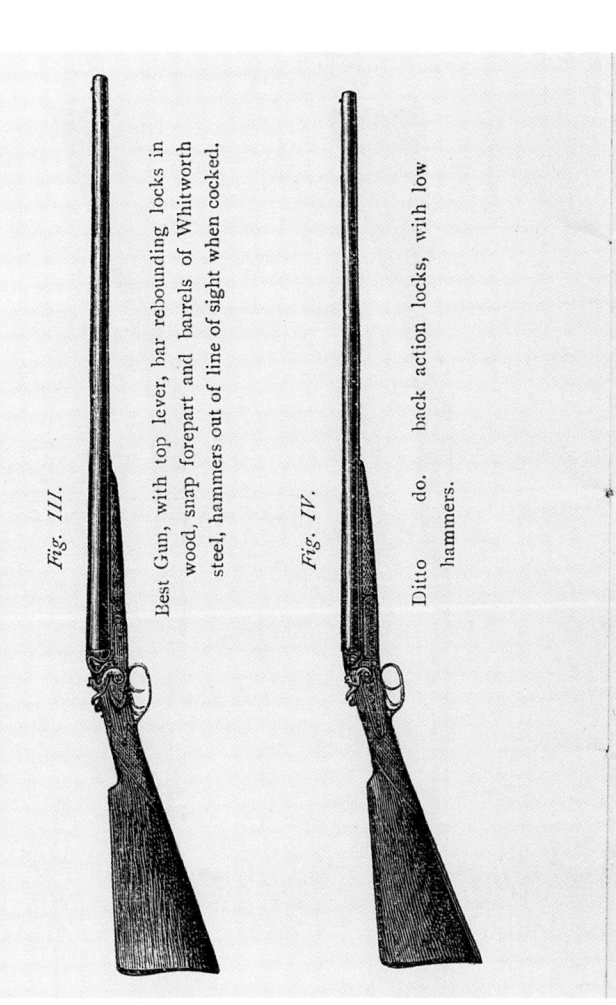

Fig. IV. — Ditto do. back action locks, with low hammers.

GUNS WITH HAMMERS—Continued.

Grade B.—Central Fire Double Gun, picked stock, fine Damascus barrels, superior make, balance and finish; approaching Best Gun in style .. £40 10 0

Oak and Leather Case and fittings... 5 0 0

Best Gun (*Figs*. III. and IV.)—Finest work and finish throughout 56 0 0

Best Oak and Leather Case and fittings 6 0 0

Best Guns are made throughout on the premises by the most skilful workmen, and are distinguished by the perfection of balance, shape, finish, and shooting power, for which they have obtained world-wide celebrity.

JAMES PURDEY & SONS' principal trade is in weapons of the best quality. They recommend intending Customers to order this quality in all cases where possible, and where not to have as high a grade weapon as they can. It should be borne in mind that a good Gun or Rifle lasts many years, and the outlay of a few pounds extra on its purchase may prove a source of satisfaction during the whole time of its use.

Double Guns of 28 bore, suitable for Ladies, in all qualities.

Single C.F. Guns for Youths 12, 16 and 20 bore, with snap action. (*Fig*. XIV.) ... ... from £10 10 0

Case and fittings 2 15 0

9

HAMMERLESS GUNS
ON
JAMES PURDEY & SONS' Successful Patent,
The SIMPLEST, SAFEST and BEST,

have now had four seasons' trial and in proof of the satisfaction they give J. P. & S. may mention that while in 1881 (their first year) they formed 20 per cent. of the Guns made, the proportion increased in 1882 to 35 per cent., in 1883 to 53 per cent., and in 1884 to nearly 65 per cent.

While J. P. & S. have no hesitation in recommending their hammerless Guns as by far the simplest made and least likely to get out of order, they must remind their Indian readers that hammerless Guns are necessarily somewhat more delicate than those with hammers, and for this reason they recommend the latter as preferable for India.

JAMES PURDEY & SONS' Patent Hammerless Gun is at present only made in two qualities, **The Best.** (*Fig*. V.)

price £58 10 0

Best Oak and Leather Case with fittings 6 0 0

AND

Grade B. ... ... price £45 0 0

Case and fittings 5 0 0

These Guns can be made with either the top or under-lever action, the former being generally preferred.

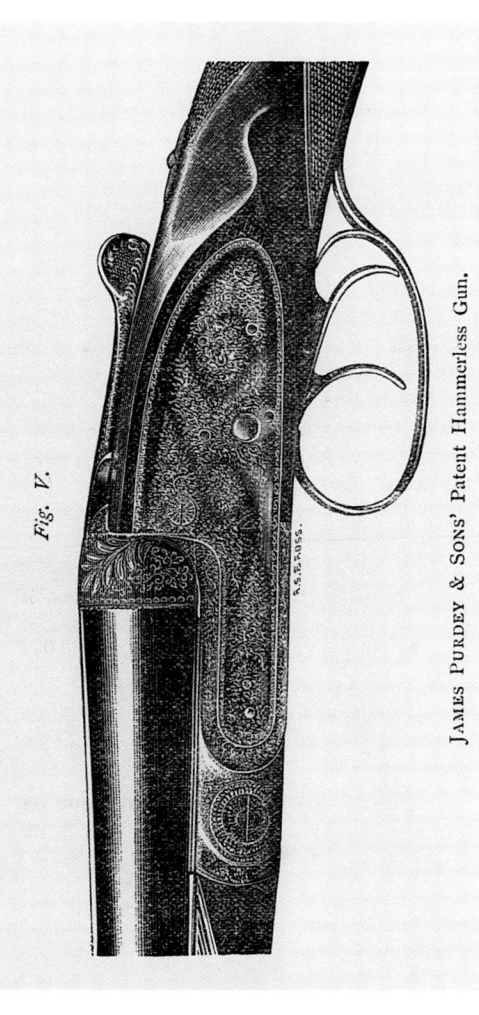

10

Fig. V. — JAMES PURDEY & SONS' Patent Hammerless Gun.

HAMMERLESS GUNS—Continued.

J. P. & S. also make hammerless Guns on a different though strong and simple system at the following prices:—

Grade C.	£35 15 0
Oak and Leather Case and fittings	4 10 0
Grade D (*Fig.* VI.)	26 10 0
Leather Case and fittings	4 1 0
Grade E.	22 0 0
Case and fittings	3 10 0

NOTE.—The foregoing prices both for hammerless Guns and those with hammers are for bores of 12 and smaller. Larger bores than 12 are extra. The barrels of best Guns can if desired be made of Sir JOSEPH WHITWORTH & Co.'s fluid pressed steel at an extra cost of £2 10s. per gun. This metal is stronger under excessive strain than Damascus, is harder and more durable and keeps its brown better. Best Guns can also be made with J. PURDEY & SONS' *Patent Third Fastening*, which in conjunction with their well-known and widely used double bolt, makes the strongest of all snap fastenings: extra cost £1 8s. per gun.

GUNS MADE ESPECIALLY TO SHOOT SHOT OR BALL (cylinder bore) with sight lying flush in rib when not in use,

£2 2s. extra.

An exceedingly useful weapon for India.

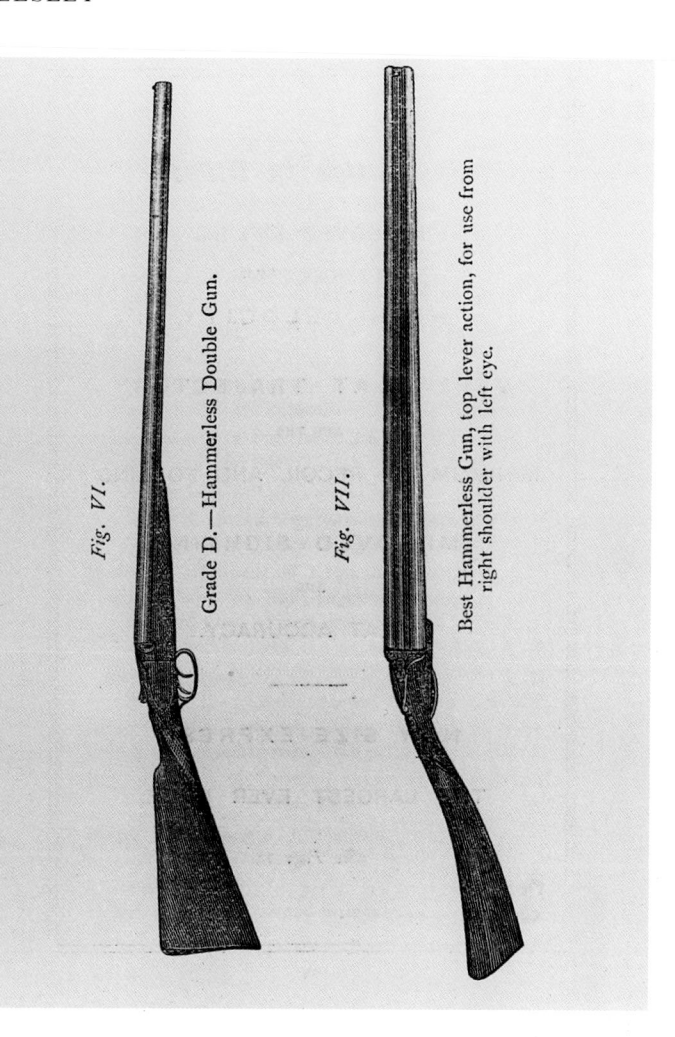

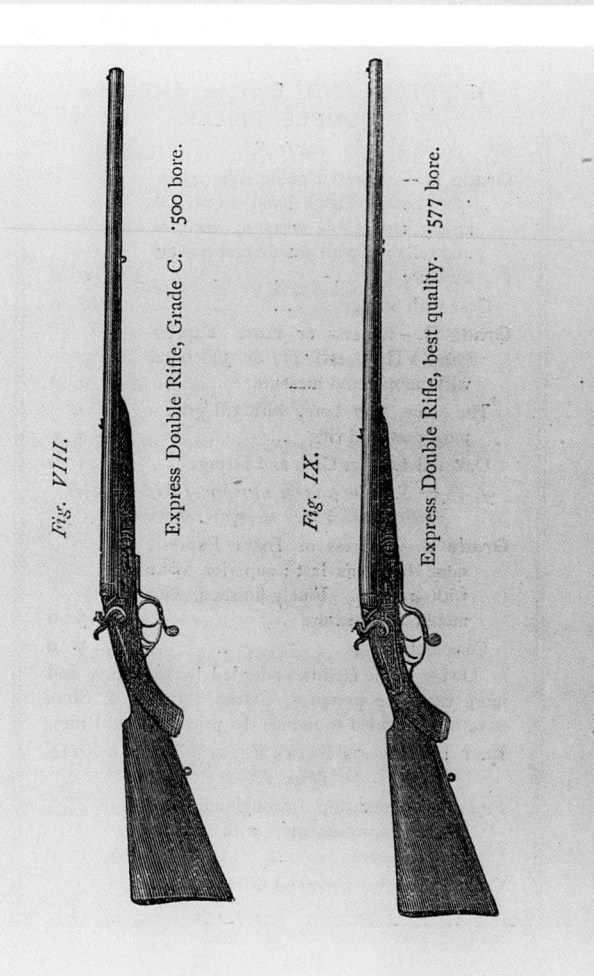

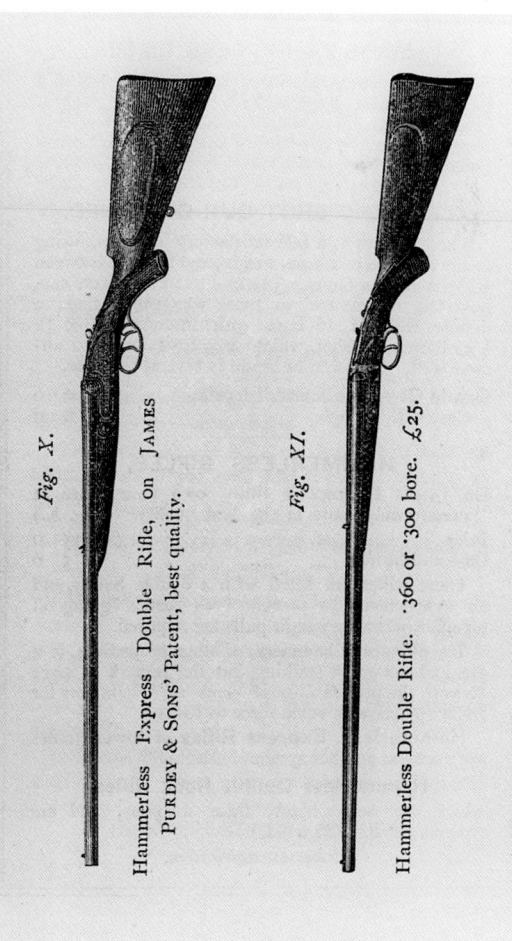

Fig. VI. Grade D.—Hammerless Double Gun.

Fig. VII. Best Hammerless Gun, top lever action, for use from right shoulder with left eye.

Fig. VIII. Express Double Rifle, Grade C. ·500 bore.

Fig. IX. Express Double Rifle, best quality. ·577 bore.

Fig. X. Hammerless Express Double Rifle, on JAMES PURDEY & SONS' Patent, best quality.

Fig. XI. Hammerless Double Rifle. ·360 or ·300 bore. £25.

NEW SIZE EXPRESS RIFLE.

JAMES PURDEY & SONS have just perfected a new size Double Express Rifle of terrific power for large and dangerous Game Shooting. It is of ·639 bore, and shoots 7 drachms of powder and an express bullet.

RIFLE AND SHOT GUN COMBINED.

These are not as a rule satisfactory weapons, owing to the difference in bore, weight, and balance between Rifles and Shot Guns. JAMES PURDEY & SONS can, however, recommend to those who prefer them a double Rifle of 16 bore, with interchangeable 12 bore barrels for shot, which they have found to answer well. This can be made in several qualities.

Grade C.—is recommended, price	£43	0 0
Case with fittings	5	0 0

HAMMERLESS RIFLES,

On JAMES PURDEY & SONS' own Patent, are at present only made in the best quality. (*Fig.* X.)

Price	£69	15 0
Case and fittings	6	5 0

These Rifles are fitted with a double Safety and an arrangement to prevent both barrels going off together, when very light pulls are required.

The absence of hammers, or other projections, is a great advantage in stalking, but the remark at page 10 as to the preferability of Guns *with* hammers for India applies with equal force to Rifles.

Hammerless Express Rifles of lower grades are made on another system. Also

Hammerless Double Rook Rifles,
which are neat, handy little weapons, and are recommended. (*Fig.* XI.)

Prices on application.

RIFLES—Continued.

Large Bore Double and Single Rifles, of great power, for Big Game, 4, 8, 10, and 12-bore, made especially handy for their weight and size. Prices according to requirements furnished on application. Shells and steel-pointed bullets for the above.

The **Grade C.** 8-bore Double Rifle with anti-recoil heel-plate, &c., including moulds and measures. *Fig.* XII.	£43	0 0
is recommended.		
Case and fittings	5	0 0

PUNT GUNS OF ALL SIZES.

Collectors' Guns (Double) ·360, ·410 and other bores, for shot, in all qualities.

Combined Gun and Rifle, one barrel ·410 bore for shot, the other ·360 bore and rifled for ball, in all qualities.

WEAPONS SUITABLE FOR PRESENTATION.
A SPECIALTY.

Guns and Rifles, chased in *Champ levé* style, are works of the highest art, and are most suitable for presentation, being quite unique.

In the best quality only. Extra cost of chasing, from £40 to £50 per Gun or Rifle. Photographs on application.

Guns and Rifles inlaid with gold, with ebonised or maple stocks. Particulars and prices on application.

SINGLE EXPRESS RIFLES.
At various prices.

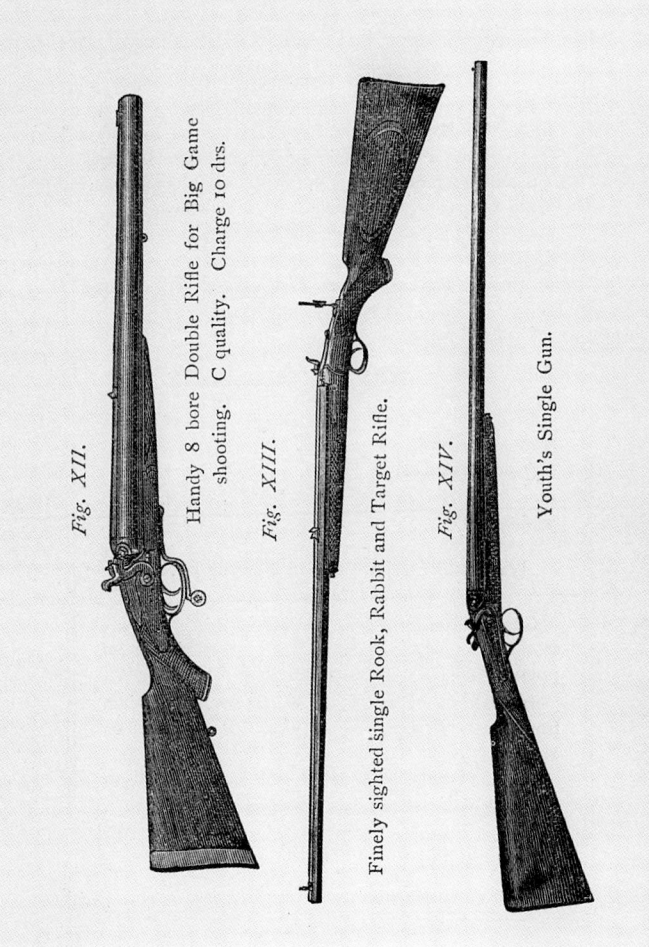

Fig. XII. Handy 8 bore Double Rifle for Big Game shooting. C quality. Charge 10 drs.

Fig. XIII. Finely sighted single Rook, Rabbit and Target Rifle.

Fig. XIV. Youth's Single Gun.

ROOK AND RABBIT RIFLES.

Finely sighted single Rook, Rabbit and Target Rifle, ·360-bore, fitted with orthoptic sight to fold down, Beach Combination foresight for Snap or fine target shooting. Top lever action, spring cartridge ejector and pistol hand stock. (*Fig.* XIII.) … price	£12	0 0
Case and fittings	3	0 0
Single C. F. Rook and Rabbit Rifles from	4	10 0
Single Hammerless ditto ditto ·300 or ·360 bore, with spring ejector	10	0 0

REPEATING RIFLES.
WINCHESTER'S.

Model 76, ·450-bore, Sporting Pattern, 9 Shots, 75 grs. Powder :—

Round Barrel	£5	10 0
Octagon ,,	5	18 0
Extra Quality	9	0 0
Express Model, ·500-bore, 95 gr. Powder, 300 gr. bullet, 5 Shots	6	10 0
Extra Quality	11	0 0
New Model, ·320-bore, 14 Shots	5	0 0
Extra Quality	9	0 0
New ·220 Rook Rifle, for long or short ·220 Cartridge, 5 or 3 grs. of Powder, Magazine carries 20 or 25 Cartridges	5	0 0
Extra Quality	9	0 0

THE INTRODUCTION OF THE HAMMERLESS GUN

During the first half of the century, most Purdey guns were built for and sold to customers in Britain. Due to better transportation facilities and better communication systems in the second half of the century, demand increased for Purdey guns from all over the world. James Purdey actively began to promote the company's weapons in far off lands. The fashion for exhibitions played an important part in this promotion. Following the success of the 1851 Great Exhibition (in which Purdey's did not participate), other countries began to stage similar events. Purdey's exhibited at the following exhibitions and acquitted themselves with just rewards.

1876:	International Exhibition Philadelphia. Gold medal plus highest award.
1878:	Paris Exhibition. Gold medal.
1879:	International Exhibition, Sydney, N.S.W. Gold medal.
1880/81:	Melbourne International Exhibition. Gold medal.
1883/84:	Calcutta International Exhibition. Gold medal.

Such awards were wonderful advertising and helped further the Purdey reputation for quality and ingenuity. The American market was developing to such an extent in the 1870s that Purdey's appointed an agent in Philadelphia – Messrs. Joseph G Grubb of Market Street. Messrs. Grubb were given a 20 percent discount on Purdey guns and, from this period, more and more weapons began to be produced for American customers.

Gold medals won by Purdey's in the late 19th-century exhibitions. Shown are, Philadelphia 1876, Sydney 1879, Melbourne 1880/81, Calcutta 1883/84 and Paris 1900. (*See plate 33 in colour section.*)

The guns illustrated are a pair of 20-bore hammer guns, Nos. 10140/1, that helped win the gold medal for Purdey's in the Paris Exhibition, 1878. They use the uncommon de Brante lever, a version of the second pattern thumb-hole. The action, locks, lever, trigger-guard, toe and heel plates and fore-end tip are all chiselled with continental-style relief foliage work. The records do not list who the engraver was. The 30-inch Damascus barrels are choked. The superb walnut stocks are of incomparable quality and perfectly matched. The fore-ends are inlaid with a gold diamond and engraved '1' and '2'. The guns are contained in a magnificent oak and leather case lined with blue leather, the lid tooled around the border in gold with Purdey's name and address, and the coat of arms of Queen Victoria and the Prince of Wales, all stamped in gold. The case is fitted with two ivory-handled turnscrews, an ivory striker removal tool, ivory-handled powder and shot measures with gilded metal work, ivory handled hogs hair brush, ivory wad seater, ivory and gilt hand turn-over tool, ivory box containing spare strikers and springs, a spring clamp and blue leather pouches with brushes. They were later sold to a Dr. Gowlland. Jones was the stocker on these guns.

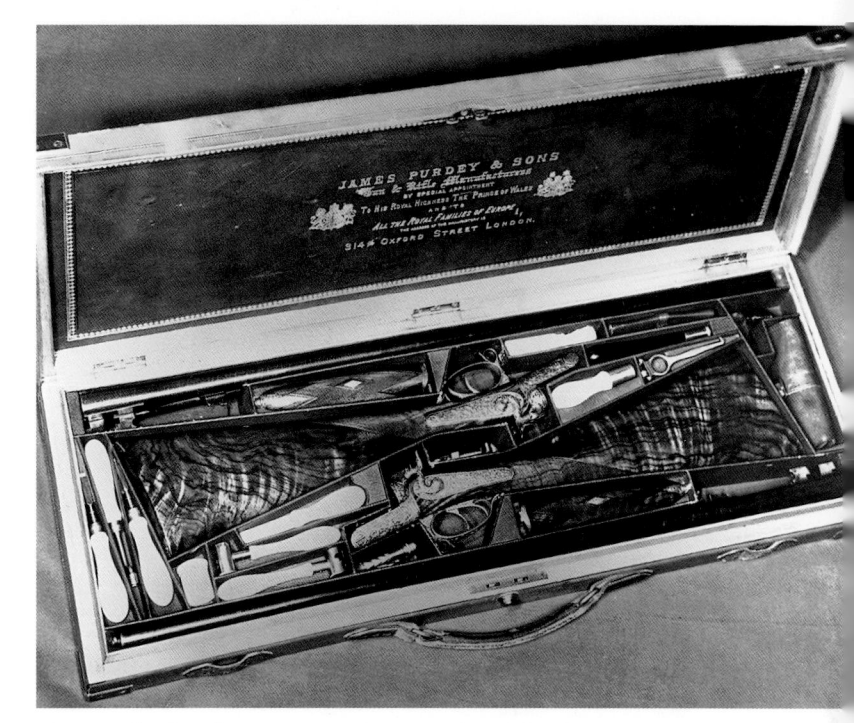

The pair of 20-bore hammer guns, Nos. 10140/1, exhibited at the Paris Exhibition, 1878, that helped Purdey win the gold medal. These guns, tested on 23 and 24 January 1878, were built to Exhibition standards, profusely carved and inlaid. They feature the very uncommon de Brante lever (sometimes spelled de Brantz), a variation on the second pattern thumb-hole.

Just as breech-loaders had been around for centuries, so had hammerless guns. There were even flintlocks in the 18th century that had enclosed mechanisms. The effective hammerless action, introduced in the 1870s, could be accredited to the newly developed centre-fire cartridges. The first successful hammerless guns of the 1870s used an under-lever cocking system. When the lever was pushed forward, the tumblers were cocked. As early as 1862, G H Daw had introduced such a gun, but it was too far ahead of its time and ugly to boot.

The first hammerless action to achieve real success was the lever cocked gun invented by Theophilus Murcott of 68 The Haymarket, London in patent no. 1003 of 15 April 1871. This gun used bar-action side-locks, the Purdey bolt and achieved a good deal of success. The next successful hammerless action became one of the most successful of all the lever-cocked hammerless guns. This was a gun invented by Gibbs & Pitt in patent no. 284 of 1873. From then on patents for hammerless guns abounded. Even a Purdey gunmaker, John Apted in patent no. 2328 of 1873, invented a push forward lever-cocking hammerless gun similar to the Gibbs & Pitt. The first recorded hammerless gun in the Dimension Books was a 12-bore double gun No. 10106 tested on 26 September 1877 and sold to G W Amory on 27 July 1880. Unfortunately, the Dimension Book does not record the type of action. This is

The record in the Dimension Book for Nos. 10140/1. Note beside Lever 'under de Brantes'.

common to all the early hammerless guns built by Purdey, there being no mention of the mechanism employed.

Before the Beesley hammerless action of 1880, Purdey's used various actions for their hammerless guns. Most seem to have been on the lever-cocking principal and examples exist of Purdey's built to Gibbs & Pitt patent. There are also examples of early hammerless guns built to William Adams patent no. 1128 of 20 March 1879. Interestingly, the address given on the patent is simply 'Oxford Street'. This was because William Adams was a Purdey gunmaker in this period and Purdey had made an agreement with him whereby they would apply for the patent and incur all costs, in addition giving Adams £5 for his invention. Purdey's would then have the rights to the patent. Adams later went on to work for Stephen Grant, then Boss, where he achieved due

The record in the Dimension Book for the first recorded hammerless gun, No. 10106, tested on 26 September 1877 but not sold until 27 July 1880.

FIG. 2.

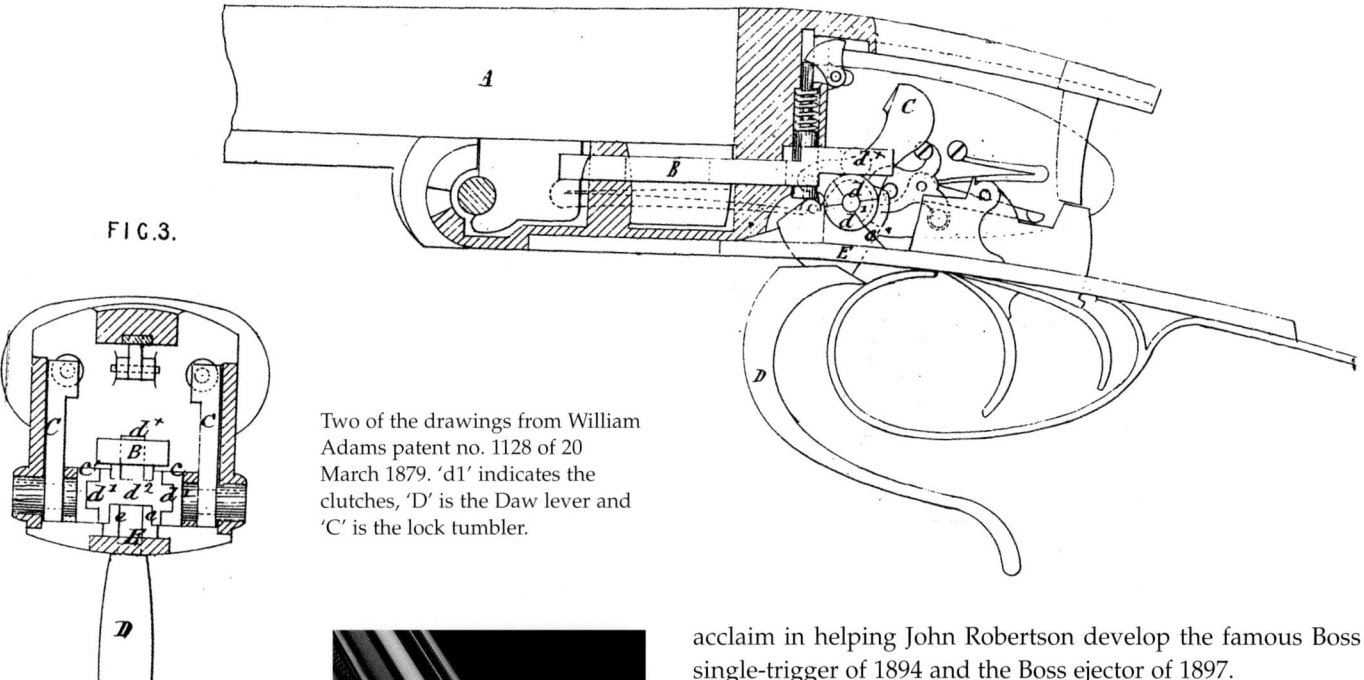

FIG. 3.

Two of the drawings from William Adams patent no. 1128 of 20 March 1879. 'd1' indicates the clutches, 'D' is the Daw lever and 'C' is the lock tumbler.

Right: Pre-Beesley 16-bore bar-in-wood, lever-cocking hammerless gun No. 10606, built to William Adams patent no. 1128 of 1879. This is the No. 2 gun of a pair built in 1879 and sold on 21 April 1880 for £68.5s. to Eyre Coote of West Park, Damersham, Salisbury. Daw lever, cocking indicators and finely carved fences. Notice the very fine rose-and-scroll engraving of J Lucas and also the lockplate engraving changed to 'J Purdey & Sons' after the 1877 agreement. (*See plate 34 in colour section.*)

Below: The record in the Dimension Book for No. 10606. Notice the mention of the 'Daw Lever'. Stocked by James Lumsden and put together by L Wasdell.

acclaim in helping John Robertson develop the famous Boss single-trigger of 1894 and the Boss ejector of 1897.

In patent no. 1128, Adams designed a lever-cocking gun in which a clutch pushed the tumblers to full cock when the lever was pushed forward. The standard Purdey bolt was used. Further drawings showed how the mechanism could be applied to a top lever gun.

Purdey's Dimension Books never record what type of hammerless action was employed. The only details given in Purdey's records are that many of these guns used the 'Daw Lever' in reference to the push forward under-lever as used by G H Daw in his 1861 Daw/Schneider gun. This lever is illustrated in patent no. 397 of 1878 regarding the 'Third Fastening' and in Adam's patent no. 1128 of 1879. Not a great many hammerless guns were built in the late 1870s, only 31 being listed before 1880 (see Appendix 4b).

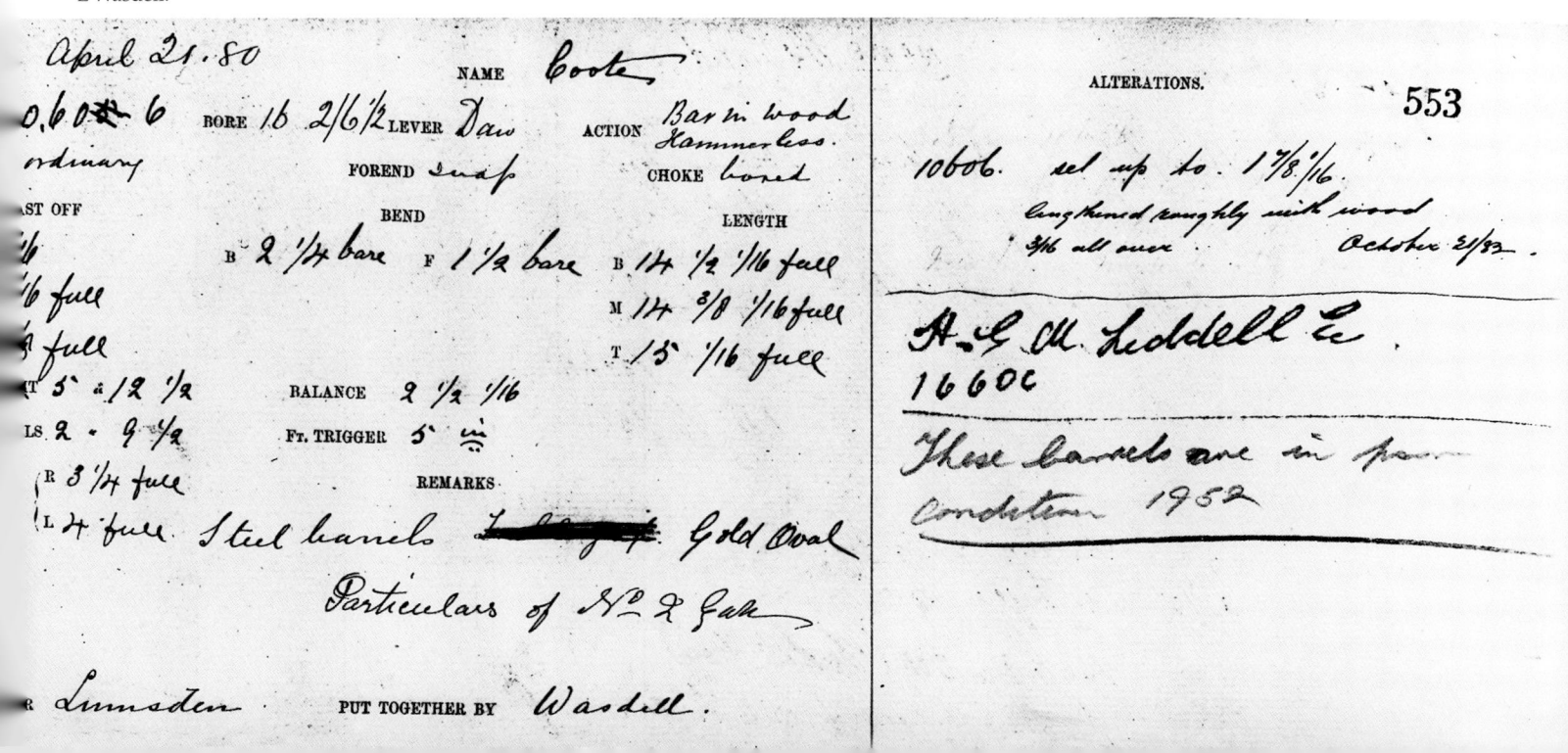

To cope with the increased demand for the breech-loader, extra gunmakers had to be employed. In the mid-1860s around 40 gunmakers were employed. By the mid-1870s this number had risen to around 65, again all working in 314 1/2 Oxford Street (see Appendix 6). New names that appeared and would feature prominently in the future were George Lubbock, who would become the shop manager, and S Wheatley who would become the factory manager, when the new factory opened in the 1880s at North Row. By far the most important addition to the workforce was the employment of Frederick Beesley who joined Purdey as a stocker on 4 September 1869 and left to set up his own business on 4 May 1878. The illustration of a page from the Dimension Book in 1870 shows the changes taking place. The headings on the right are from the 1870 Dimension Book page illustrated.

Column headings (right side):
Description
Bore
Length
Nipples and plunges
Jointing stocking
Screwing
Finishing
Percussioning
Cocking
rifling
Levering
Engraving
Hardened
Rods
Lugggers
Rubbing-off and buffing-up

Below: A page from the Dimension Book showing guns Nos. 8247 to 8258, all built in 1870. In 'Nipples and Plungers', 'JH' = J Harris, in 'Jointing, Stocking and Screwing', 'J' = Jones, 'R' = J Robertson, 'L' = H Lewis, 'A' = Atkin, 'B' = F Beesley, 'G' = H Glaysher, 'JL' = J Lumsden. In 'Cocking', 'GP' = G Prentice. In 'Levering', 'V' = Virgo. In 'Engraving', 'L' = J Lucas and 'M' = J Mace. In 'Hardening', 'R' = A Robins. In 'Luggers', 'HS' = H Schmidt. 'Luggers' is a Purdey term for extractors. Notice that 'Rods', in reference to ramrods, still exists as a few muzzle-loaders were still being built.

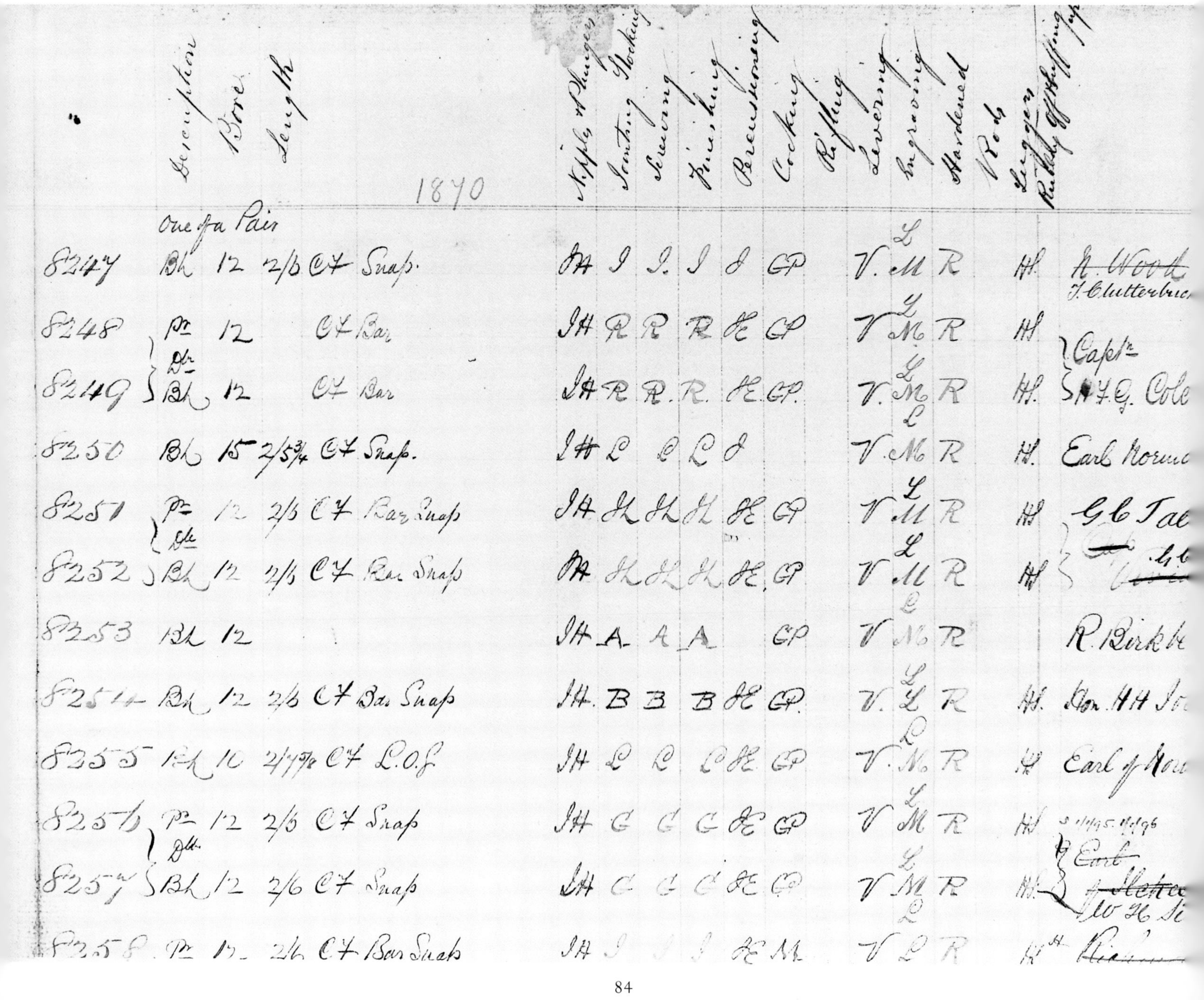

THE BEESLEY SELF-OPENING ACTION 1880

During 1879, Frederick Beesley invented a spring-cocked hammerless gun, patented in early 1880. He immediately sold the patent to Purdey's who have continued to manufacture it to the virtual exclusion of all other types of hammerless action right up to the present day. It was an ingenious design and has received widespread recognition throughout the world as one of the best hammerless actions ever devised. It has been used in all bore sizes of shotgun and all calibres of rifles.

Frederick Beesley (1846-1928) was a farmer's son from Model Farm, Hampton Poyle, Oxfordshire, who was apprenticed, aged fifteen, to Moore and Grey at Old Bond Street, London. He then worked for many great London firms, joining Purdey's as a stocker in 1869. He remained with Purdey's until 1878, then left to set up his own business at 22 Queen Street, Edgeware Road. Around 1884 he moved to 85 Edgeware Road and finally in 1891 to 2 St. James's Street, remaining there until 1939.

Frederick Beesley, inventor of the Purdey self-opening hammerless action of 1880.

Most hammerless guns of the 1870s used lever-cocking actions. However, it soon became apparent that the leverage of the barrels could provide the means whereby hammerless actions could be cocked, either upon closing or opening the barrels. One of the most famous barrel-cocking hammerless guns was produced in this period, the Anson and Deeley boxlock of patent no. 1756 of 11 May 1875. The 1870s abounded with such patents for hammerless actions.

On 3 January 1880, in patent no. 31, 'Improvement in the Construction of Break Down Guns', Frederick Beesley invented a spring-cocked hammerless gun. There were two main factors as to why this mechanism would achieve such status. Firstly, Beesley utilised the power of the mainspring to ease the opening of the gun and cock the tumblers. Secondly, he produced a very neat and graceful external appearance that complemented the existing Purdey style. Many of the hammerless actions of this period were anything but this.

In patent no. 31, Beesley primarily showed how his invention applied to back-action locks. He described many variations of the design, and the mechanism actually used by Purdey's was the last one shown in the patent. The essential feature of the action is a powerful V mainspring, the upper arm cocking the lock and assisting in opening the gun, the lower arm firing it. Figure 1 shows the gun open. The mainspring is free of tension. When the barrels are closed, the rod B drives the cam C backwards. This cam passes over a roller on the mainspring and compresses it. The gun is ready to fire as is shown in Figure 2. When the gun is fired, as in Figure 3, the lower half of the mainspring E throws the tumbler forward, rebounding backwards after hitting the firing pin. When the gun is opened, the upper half of the main spring D, being under tension, drives cam C forward, thereby assisting the opening of the gun, and at the same time cocking the tumbler. A vent was fitted to prevent any escape of gas from the cartridge into the lockwork. A bonus of the self-opening action was that when the barrels were removed and the gun dismantled, the mainsprings were not under tension.

Frederick Beesley had no intention of using this patent for himself. He had just set himself up in business and immediate money was probably what he required. On 18 December 1879 he wrote the following letter to Purdey's offering them his invention:

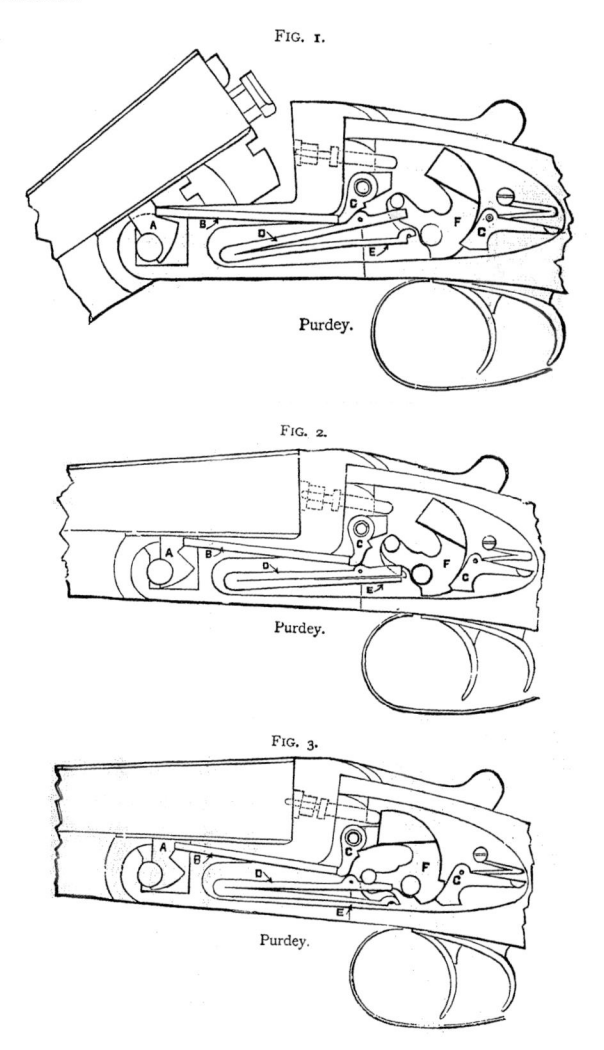

FIG. 1.

Purdey.

FIG. 2.

Purdey.

FIG. 3.

Purdey.

Purdey's Hammerless Gun.

The drawing of the Beesley action that appeared in W W Greener's *The Gun and its Development*, 1910.

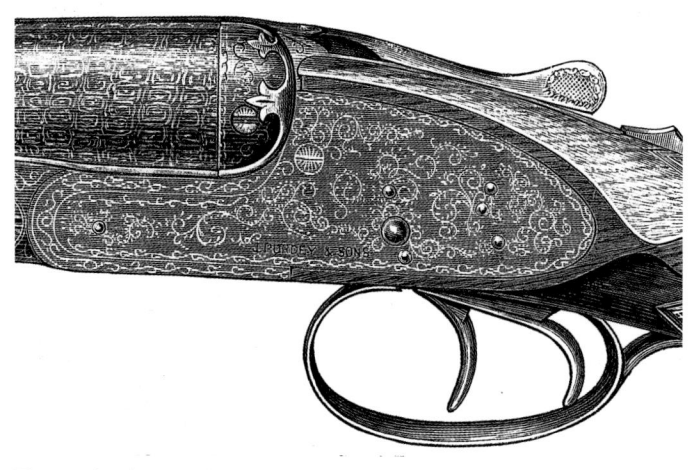

The Purdey hammerless gun as illustrated in *The Modern Sportsman's Gun and Rifle* by J H Walsh, 1884

22 Queen Street,
Edgeware Rd. W
18.12.79

Sir,
Having invented a Hammerless gun which I believe to be equal to, if not superior, to anything of its kind yet produced, I am desirous of meeting with a purchase of the right to the same. It is on a principle, *entirely different* to any other on the market, and also possessed a *peculiar* advantage as any old gun may be converted to a hammerless one at moderate expense. I offer it to your notice first in the trade, and should esteem the favor of a personal interview if worth your attention when I can submit a working conversion.

I beg to remain
Your Obdt. Servant
Fredck Beesley

James Purdey immediately recognised the merits of the Beesley action and bought the rights to the patent. They made an agreement on 2 January 1880, the day before the patent was published. The agreement was formalised on 29 July 1880. Beesley sold his patent to Purdey's for £20 plus a five-shilling royalty payable to Beesley for every gun made until 200 had been constructed. Alternatively, Purdey's could pay £35

Right: The letter written by Frederick Beesley to James Purdey, offering the invention of his new hammerless action that would shortly be registered as patent no. 31 of 3 January 1880.

instead of royalty payments within four months when they would then be discharged from all other claims Beesley might make. Purdey and Beesley agreed to the latter, and on 16 November 1880, Frederick Beesley received the £35. In total, Purdey's had spent £55 on acquiring the Beesley patent and now had full right to manufacture and licence the building of it for fourteen years. The first Beesley gun to appear in the Dimension Book was 12-bore gun No. 10743, built in 1880. Unfortunately, there is no record of a test. The first recorded hammerless rifle with a Beesley action to appear in the Dimension Book is a .450 rifle, No. 10905, built in late 1880, early 1881.

After the agreement with Beesley in 1880, various licensing agreements were made with other makers. The most notable, again as in the case of the Purdey bolt of 1863, was with W & C Scott of Birmingham. This agreement was dated 29 September 1882 and ran initially for three years. For a £1 royalty per gun, Scotts were granted exclusive manufacturing rights in Birmingham. Purdey's retained the right to licence London makers at £2 royalty per gun and also abroad. Guns produced by Scott had to be marked

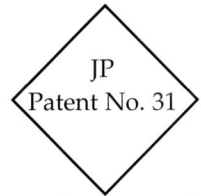

⟨ JP Patent No. 31 ⟩

and any guns for the foreign market had to be marked 'Purdey's Patent Rebounding Hammerless'.

Beesley was known as 'the inventor to the London trade'. In the 1880s alone he patented eleven inventions and always made great play out of the fact that he had invented Purdey's hammerless action. His shop front in St. James's Street proudly proclaimed, 'Beesley, Inventor and Patentee of Purdey's Hammerless Gun'. His advertisements likewise boasted of his association. All through his life he continued to invent. He died on 14 January 1928, aged 82.

Unlike the changeover to breech-loaders in the 1860s, the switch to hammerless guns was relatively pedestrian. The advantages of the hammerless gun over the hammer gun were not so great that the customers had to have the new design. The change in the 1880s was very gradual and it was only with the advent of the ejector gun in the late 1880s, that hammerlesss guns were ordered with greater frequency. The watershed year was 1886 when more hammerlesss guns were produced than hammer guns. Even then, large numbers of hammer guns continued to be built right up to World War I. The following figures show the slow pace of change from the introduction of the Beesley action.

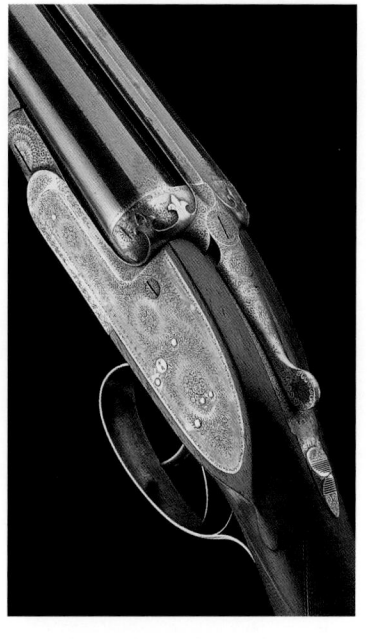

An early Beesley self-opening, 16-bore non-ejector gun, No. 11181, the No. 2 of a pair sold on 14 July 1882. Carved fleur-de-lys fences and cocking indicators (*See plate 35 in colour section.*)

Date	Hammer guns	Hammerless guns
1880	208	33
1881	181	45
1882	213	95
1883	192	165
1884	148	140
1885	160	116
1886	123	147
1887	112	197

The record in the Dimension Book for No. 10743, built in 1880, the first Beesley gun to appear in the Dimension book. Note 'Remarks': 'Beesly Early hammerless' and under 'Alterations': 'Nearly the 1st hammerless on present system'. The gun was sold in August 1897 to Evan Edwards.

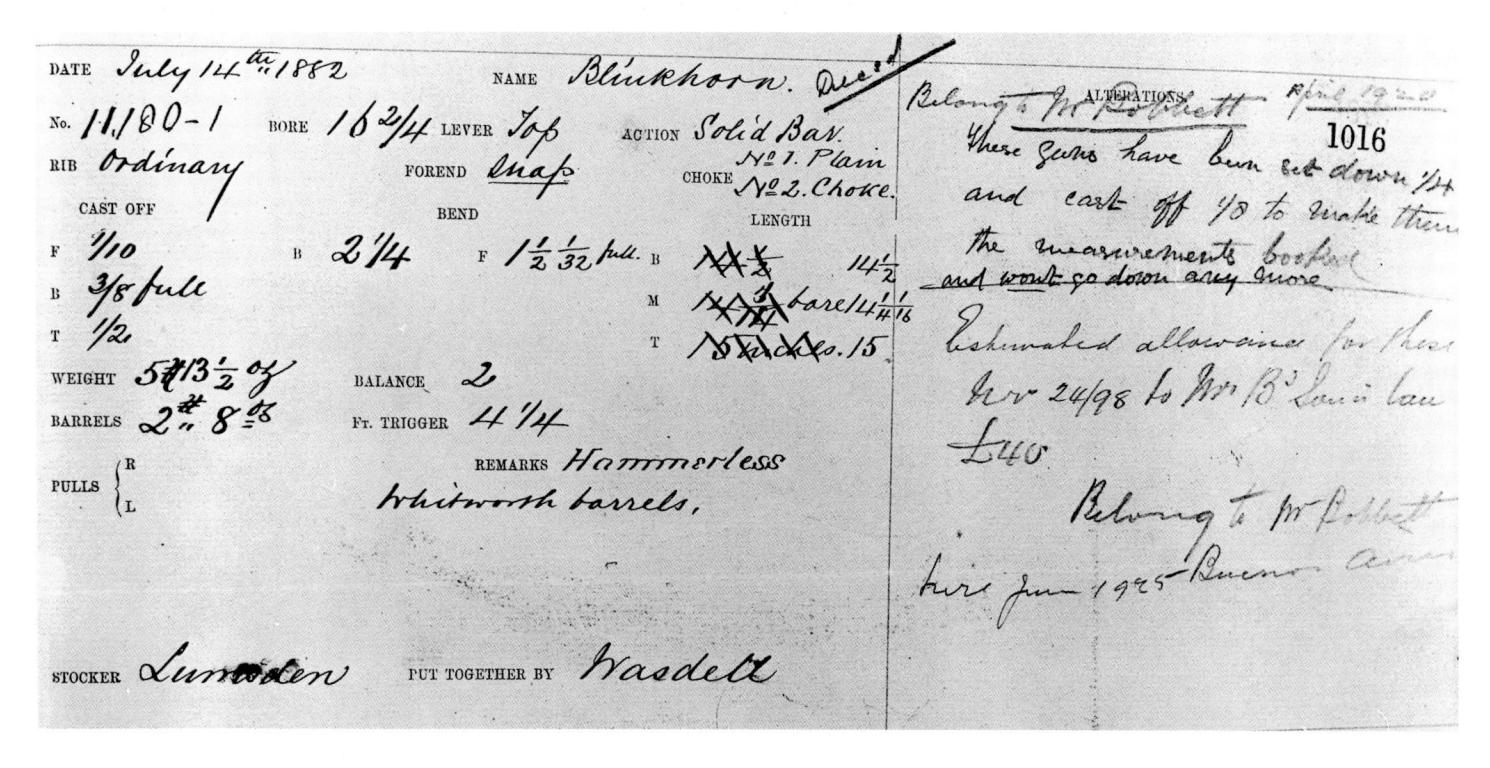

The record in the Dimension Book for Nos. 11180/1. Stocked by James Lumsden and put together by L Wasdell.

From Bolt to Beesley, a period of only seventeen years had seen the most incredible changes. At the beginning of the period, the breech-loader had only just come into use and James Purdey the Younger had made his valuable contribution to it with the 1863 Purdey bolt. By 1880, Purdey's had a hammerless action that once again, like the Purdey bolt, would stand the test of time to be produced in enormous quantities. Purdey's had gone from strength to strength, doubling their output and receiving more and more orders from royalty and the influential. To further enhance their reputation and to enjoy the profits from their enterprise, the firm would move in 1883 to the prestigious address that they still conduct business from to this day – Audley House, South Audley Street, in the heart of Mayfair.

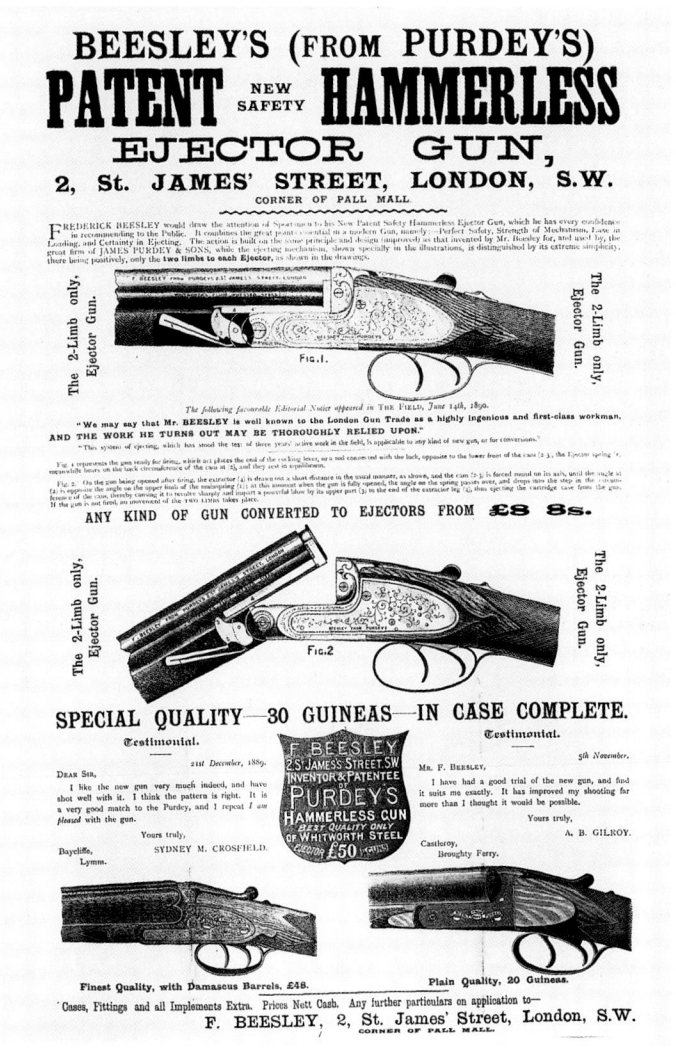

A Frederick Beesley advertisement of the 1890s.

The Beesley hammerless gun, advertised in *The Sporting Mirror Advertiser*, June 1883.

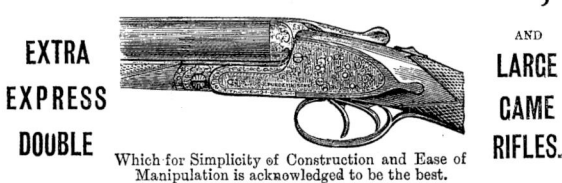

Chapter six

EARLY BREECH-LOADING GUNS AND RIFLES

The first breech-loading gun was built in 1857 and the first Beesley hammerless gun in 1880. There was no great rush to buy hammerless guns immediately after this, consequently hammer guns continued to be made into the 1880s and well into the 1890s. By the mid 1880s, hammerless guns were increasingly being made and, on account of this, I feel it is an appropriate date to conclude 'Early Breech-loading Guns and Rifles'.

Compared to the muzzle-loading period, a more straightforward variety of weapons was built by Purdey's. Pin-fire guns and rifles, centre-fire guns and rifles and hammerless guns and rifles were the principal types sold. The big change was in pistols. Purdey's made very few breech-loading pistols, although they would retail various familiar types. A mere handful are listed in the Dimension Book. Mechanisation had proceeded to such an extent that pistol production was not a realistic proposition. Breech-loaders were slightly more expensive than muzzle-loaders. The following list gives typical prices in the period (Best guns only). Prices include cases:

Double-barrel pin-fire shotgun 1864	£60. 0s. 0d.
Double-barrel pin-fire rifle 1863	£88. 0s. 0d.
Double-barrel centre-fire hammer gun 1880	£62. 0s. 0d.
Double-barrel hammerless gun 1885	£64.10s. 0d.
Double-barrel centre-fire hammer rifle 1880	£88. 0s. 0d.
Single-barrel centre-fire hammer rifle 1880	£39.18s. 0d.
Double-barrel hammerless rifle 1885	£76. 0s. 0d.

Lesser grade guns included:

Purdey-Henry rifle 1870	£34. 0s. 0d.
8-bore centre-fire double-hammer rifle 1880 (grade C)	£48. 0s. 0d.
Double-barrel centre-fire hammer rifle/shotgun 1880 (grade C)	£48. 0s. 0d.
Rook and rabbit rifle 1880	£15. 0s. 0d.
Double-barrel hammerless gun 1885 (grade B)	£50. 0s. 0d.
Double-barrel hammerless gun 1885 (grade C)	£40. 5s. 0d.
Double-barrel hammerless gun 1885 (grade D)	£30.11s. 0d.
Double-barrel hammerless gun 1885 (grade E)	£25.10s. 0d.
Double-barrel centre-fire hammer gun 1880 (grade B)	£45.10s. 0d.
Double-barrel centre-fire hammer gun 1880 (grade C)	£36.18s. 0d.
Double-barrel centre-fire hammer gun 1880 (grade D)	£29.14s. 0d.
Double-barrel centre-fire hammer gun 1880 (grade E)	£24. 4s. 0d.
Single-barrel centre-fire hammer gun 1880	£13. 5s. 0d.

Extras included:

Sir Joseph Whitworth's fluid compressed steel barrels 1885	£ 2.10s. 0d. extra
Patent third fastening 1885	£ 1. 6s. 0d.
Chasing in the Champ Levé style 1885	£40. to £50. extra
Ivory front sight 1870	11s. 6d
Patent cartridge machine 1860	£ 2. 5s. 0d.
Turnscrew 1870	3s. 0d.

Repair prices included:

New barrels 1870	£15. 0s. 0d.
Engraving a crest 1860	5s. 0d.
Trigger pulls regulated 1860	5s. 0d.
Cleaning gun 1860	5s. 0d.
Stocks shortened 1860	7s. 6d
Barrels browned 1860	£ 1. 4s. 0d.
New strikers 1870	£ 1. 5s. 0d.
New mainspring 1860	10s. 0d.
Double-rifle cleaned 1865	7s. 6d

The first weapon illustrated is a 38-bore double-barrel pin-fire rifle No. 6626 built in 1864 (see plate 36). This rifle is relatively rare – only 129 double pin-fire rifles are listed in the Dimension Books. No record of it exists in the sales ledgers. It was built for Sir John Ramsden who was MP for the West Riding of Yorkshire when he purchased this rifle. In addition to various estates, he also owned Ardverikie at Kingussie and no doubt intended to use the gun for deer stalking there. The

Damascus barrels are 29 inches long and secured by a Jones double grip underlever of the Purdey 'Long Guard Lever' pattern in which the entire trigger-guard forms the lever for extra strength. The back action locks abut the action and have high dolphin hammers. The action has slim breeches and percussion fences. The scroll engraving is of the more open style just pre-dating the fine work introduced by Lucas and Mace. An extended top strap is employed for extra strength. The stock has a cheek-piece.

A double-barrel 38-bore pin-fire rifle, No. 6626, built in 1864 for Sir John Ramsden. (*See plate 36 in colour section.*)

The underside of No. 6626, showing the Long Guard lever.

The extended top strap of No. 6626.

The record in the Dimension Book for No. 6626. See column headings on page 66. 'L' is Henry Lewis, jointing, stocking, screwing, making off; 'R' is Robins, hardening.

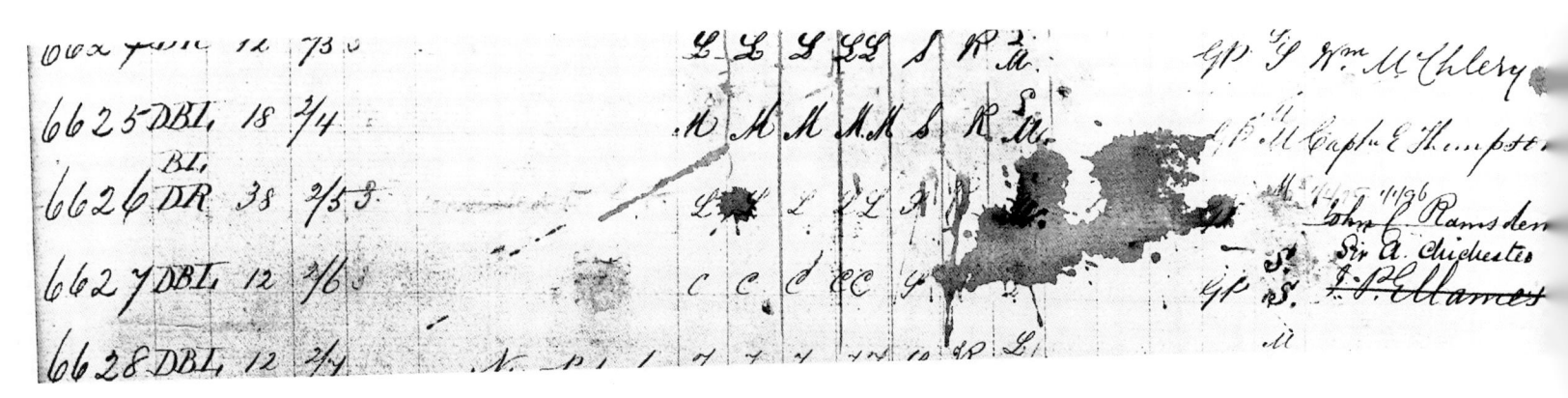

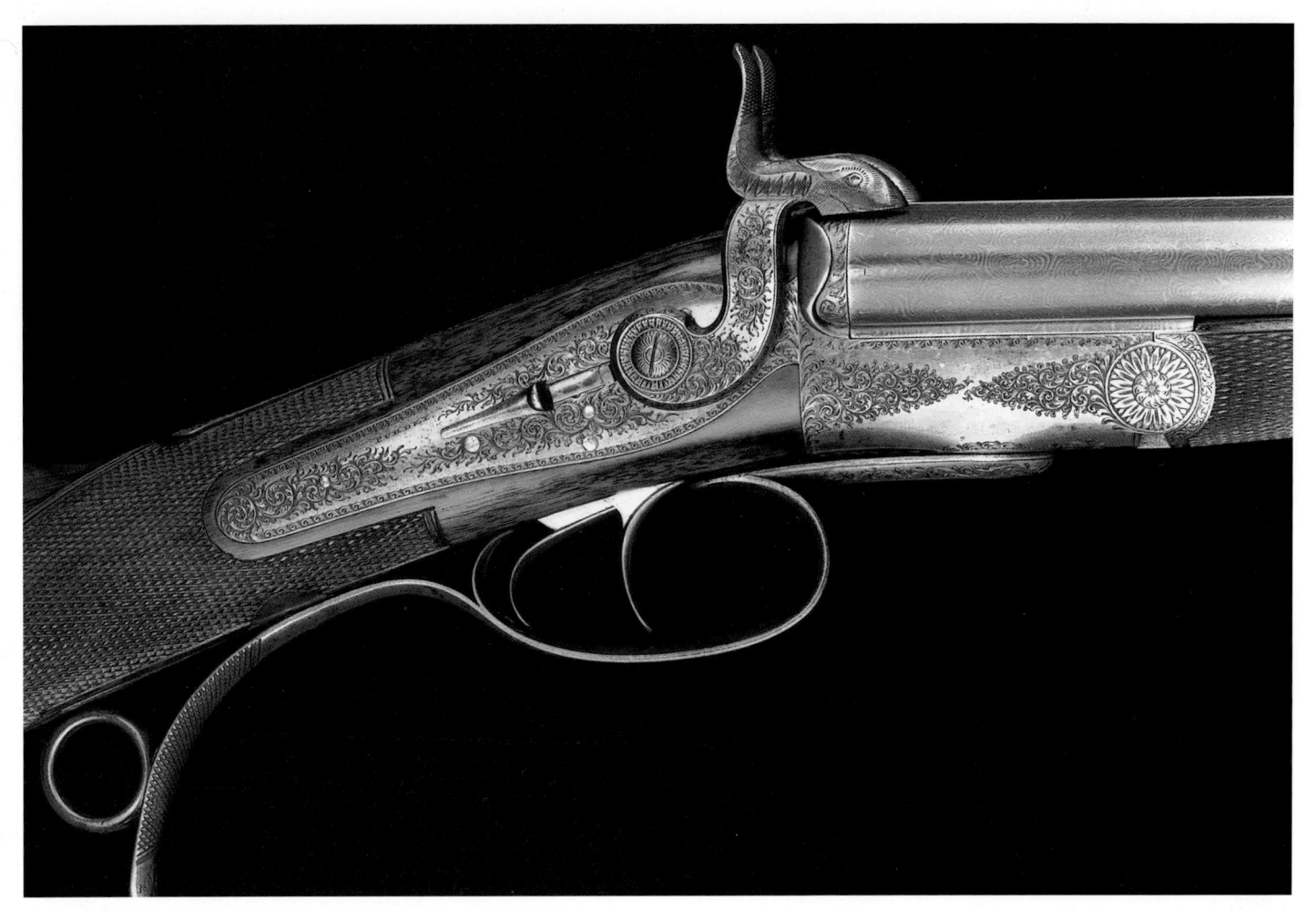

The action of No. 6626, with slim breech and percussion fences.

A very rare Purdey (see plate 37), No. 6746 is a 12-bore Bastin slide action pin-fire gun tested on 24 June 1864 and sold to Lord Wharncliffe of Wortley Hall, Sheffield. Only 34 Bastin/Purdey shotguns are listed in the Dimension Books. This gun uses one version of the Bastin system in which the long lever under the fore-end is pulled backwards to slide open the barrels. Upon closure, the lever locks at the fore-end. The back action locks have high spurred dolphin hammers and the action has serpentine fences. An extended top strap is used. The barrels are 30 inches long and the gun weighs 7lb. 1oz.

Plate 39 shows an early pin-fire 12-bore gun, No. 6829, tested on 17 September 1864 and sold to J H Barneby on 15 November 1864 for £60. The actual test is shown in Appendix 3. This gun displays all the characteristics of the early Purdey pin-fire breech-loader. The newly invented snap action bolt of patent no. 1104, 2 May 1863, is operated by a thumb-hole underlever of the first pattern. The pin to attach the lever can be seen in the centre of the action. Thumb-holes of the second pattern obviously did not require this pin. The standing breech, carved with percussion fences is very slim, the breech-loading pressures not being fully appreciated. The back action locks are finely scroll-engraved and marked 'Purdey'. The leading edge of the lockplate abuts the action as was the case in the very early breech-loaders. The gun weighs 6lb 14oz and has 30-inch Damascus barrels.

The record in the Dimension Book for No. 6746. See column headings on page 84. 'B' might be Bissell, jointing, stocking, screwing; 'GP' is G Prentice, cocking; 'L' and 'M' are Lucas and Mace, engraving; 'R' is Robins, hardening. Note the remark above dated March 1902: '6746 no longer fit to use'.

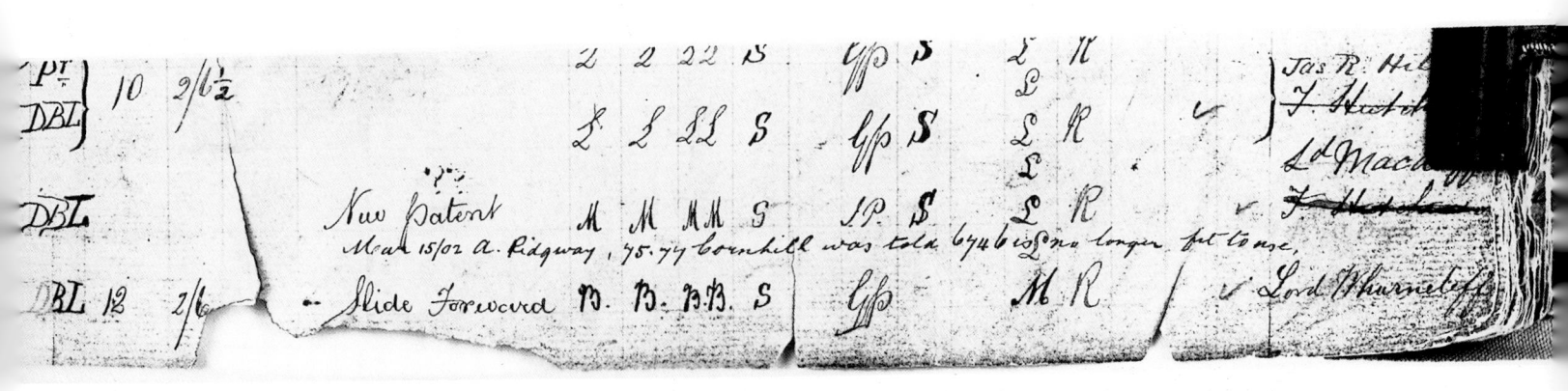

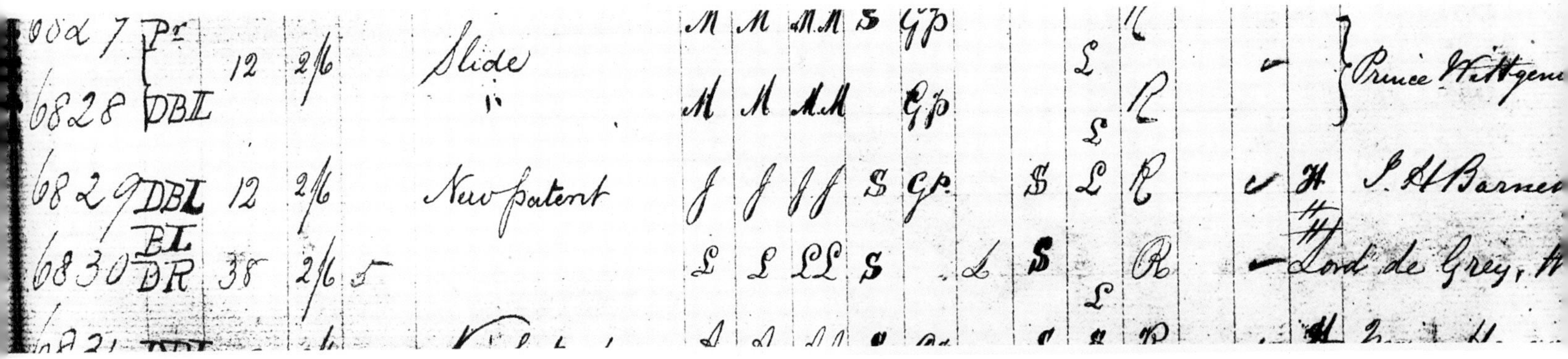

The record in the Dimension Book for No. 6829, built in 1864. See column headings on page 84. 'J' is T Jones, jointing, stocking, screwing, finishing. 'GP' is G Prentice, cocking. 'L' is J Lucas, engraving. 'R' is A Robins, hardening. Note Nos. 6827/8, a pair of Bastin slide action guns. 'New Patent' refers to patent no. 1104 of 2 May 1863, the Purdey bolt.

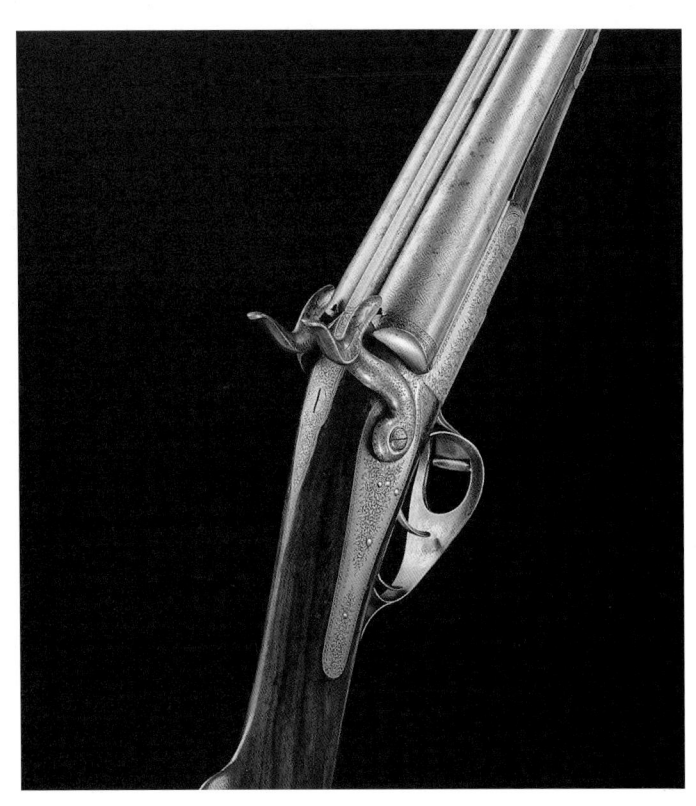

12-bore pin-fire gun No. 6829, sold to J H Barneby on 15 November 1864. First pattern thumb-hole underlever. (*See plate 39 in colour section.*)

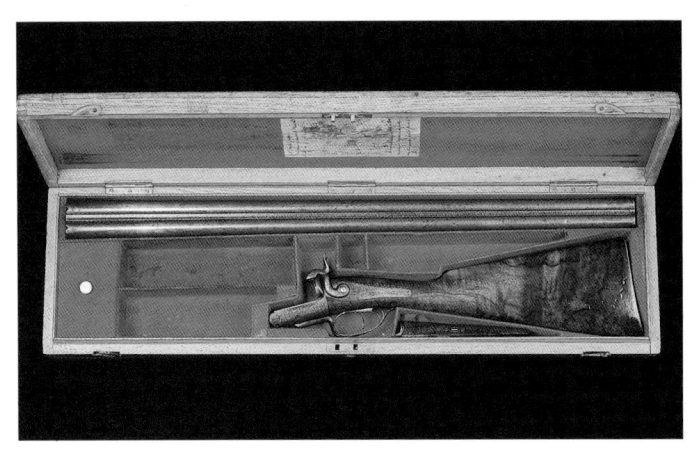

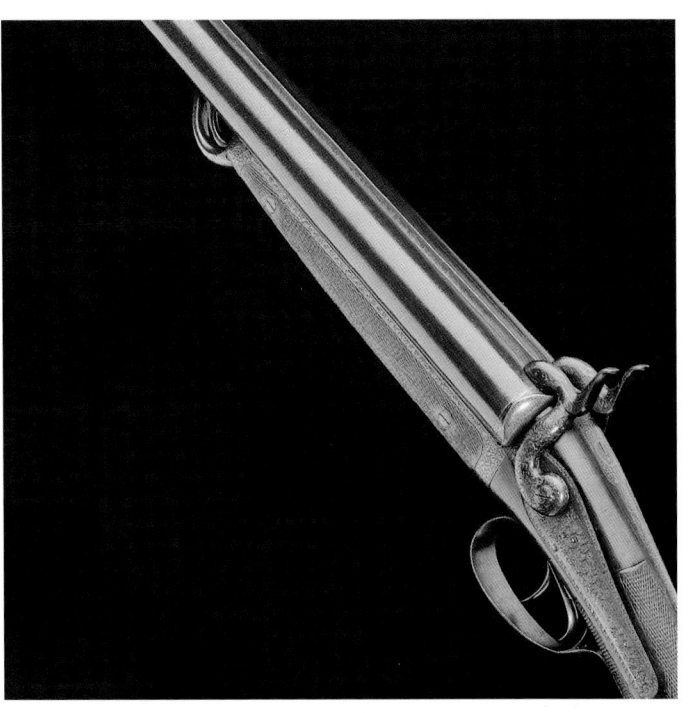

A 12-bore Bastin pin-fire slide action gun, No. 6746, tested on 24 June 1864 for Lord Wharncliffe. This model uses the rearward opening lever. (*See plate 37 in colour section.*)

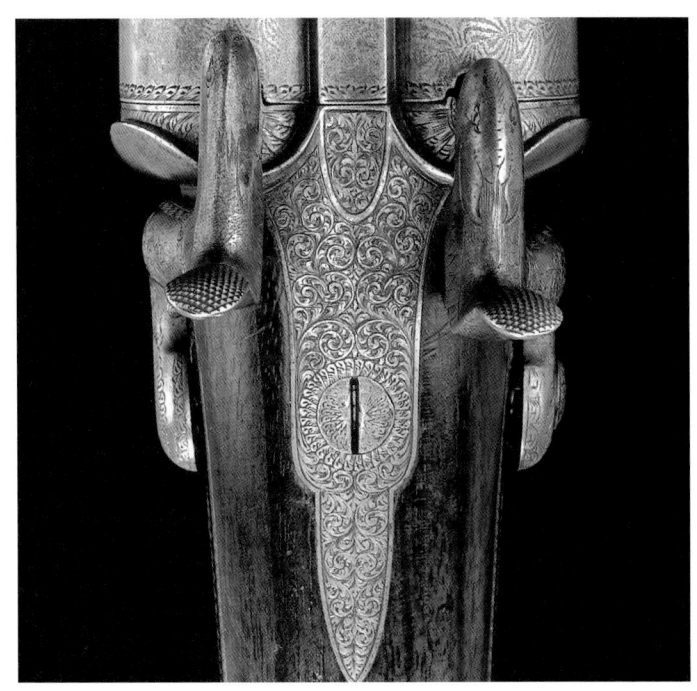

12-bore pin-fire gun No. 6845 tested on the 22 October 1864 and sold to George Hanbury. In its original red-baize-lined oak case. (*See plate 38 in colour section.*)

The tang of No. 6829, showing the fine Lucas scroll engraving and the slim standing breeches.

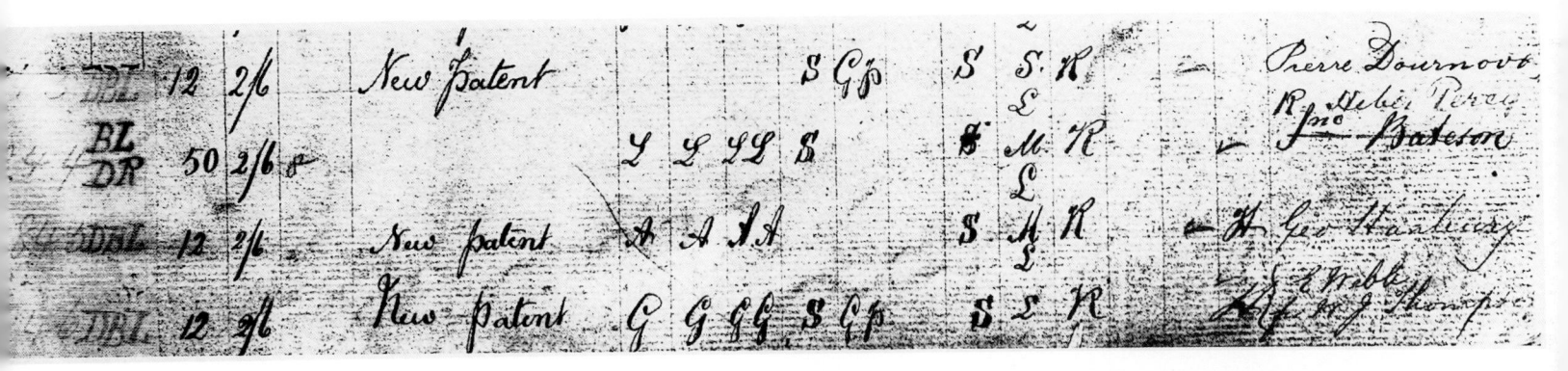

The record in the Dimension Book for No. 6845, built in 1864. See column headings on page 84. 'A' is Henry Atkin, jointing, stocking, screwing, finishing. 'L' is J Lucas, 'M' is J Mace, engraving. 'R' is A Robins, hardening.

Another early 12-bore pin-fire is illustrated (plate 38). This is gun No. 6845, tested by Smith on 22 October 1864 and sold to George Hanbury. The Damascus barrels are 30 inches long, a first pattern thumb-hole underlever is used and the slim breeches have percussion fences. The gun is contained in its original oak case. Early breech-loading Purdey cases were very similar to muzzle-loading cases. They were invariably of light oak, lined with red baize. The number '6845' is on a small circular label under the compartment lid.

No. 7225 (plate 40) is a good example, illustrating two of the early James Purdey patents. It is a very early 12-bore centre-fire gun, tested on 27 February 1866 and sold to Thomas Syme. The gun displays the First Pattern thumb-hole of patent no. 1104 of 1863 and also the retractable firing pins of patent no. 424 of 1865. The hammers are pin-fire style with the strikers attached to them. When drawn back, they pull out the strikers. The action has percussion fences and an elongated top strap. The fore-end is attached by a barrel bolt. The Damascus barrels are 30 inches long and the stock has a cheek-piece and an iron butt plate.

12-bore thumb-hole bar-in-wood hammer gun No. 7745 is shown (plates 41 and 43). No. 7745 was tested on 24 July 1868 and sold to Sir C Wingfield. The Damascus barrels are 30 inches long. The locks show one of the earliest uses of Stanton's rebounding lock and are stamped 'Patent' on the inside. The thumb-hole is of the Second Pattern and the action is engraved 'Patent' on the tang and 'Purdey's Patent' on the knuckle. The 1863 Purdey bolt patent no. 1104 remained well in force, not expiring until 1877. Even at this early date for a

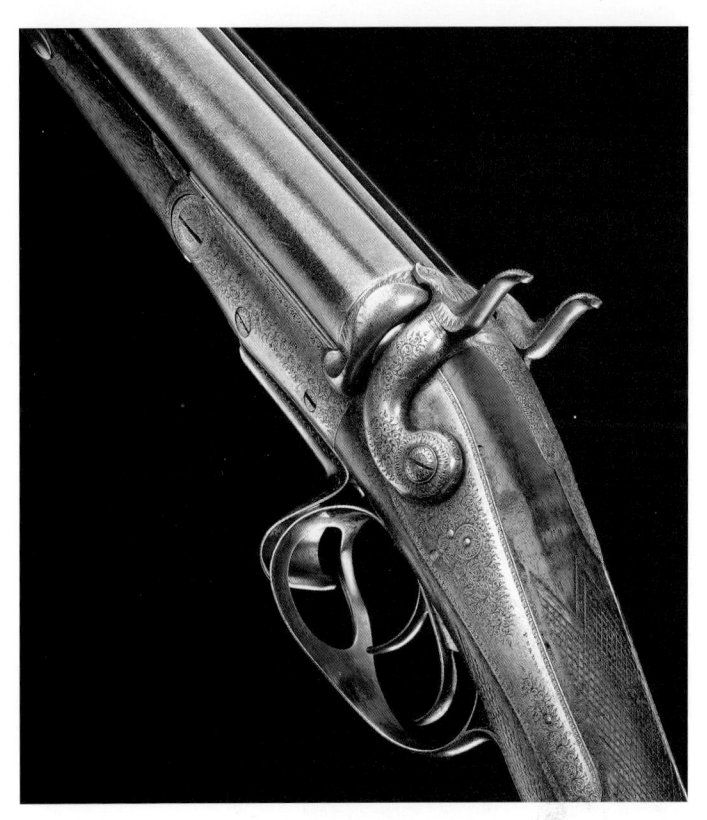

An early centre-fire gun, No. 7225 tested on 27 February 1866. It has pin-fire style hammers and retractable firing pins of patent no. 424 of 1865. (*See plate 40 in colour section.*)

The record in the Dimension Book for No. 7225. See column headings on page 84. 'R' is Robertson, jointing, stocking, screwing; 'GP' is G Prentice, cocking; 'L' is Lucas, engraving; 'R' is Robins, hardening; 'HS' is H Schmidt, luggers. Note that 'central fire' is recorded as most other guns in this period were pin-fires.

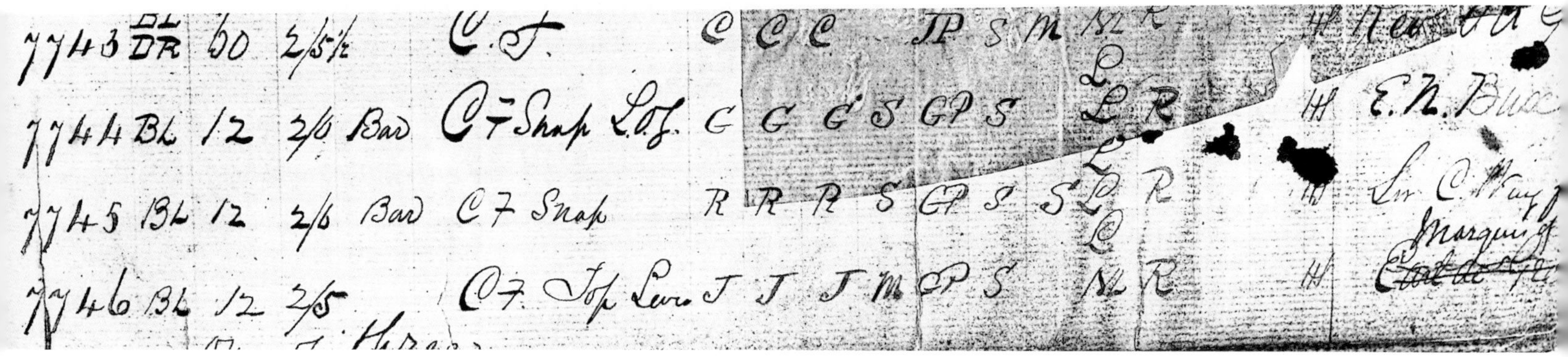

The record in the Dimension Book for No. 7745. See column headings on page 84. 'R' is Robertson, jointing, stocking, screwing; 'GP' is G Prentice, cocking; 'L' is Lucas, engraving; 'R' is Robins, hardening; 'HS' is H Schmidt, luggers. Note No. 7746 'one of three' for Earl de Grey.

Above: No. 7745 in its original oak case with many original accessories. (*See plate 41 in colour section.*)

12-bore bar-in-wood thumb-hole hammer gun No. 7745, tested on 24 July 1868 and sold to Sir C Wingfield. (*See plate 43 in colour section.*)

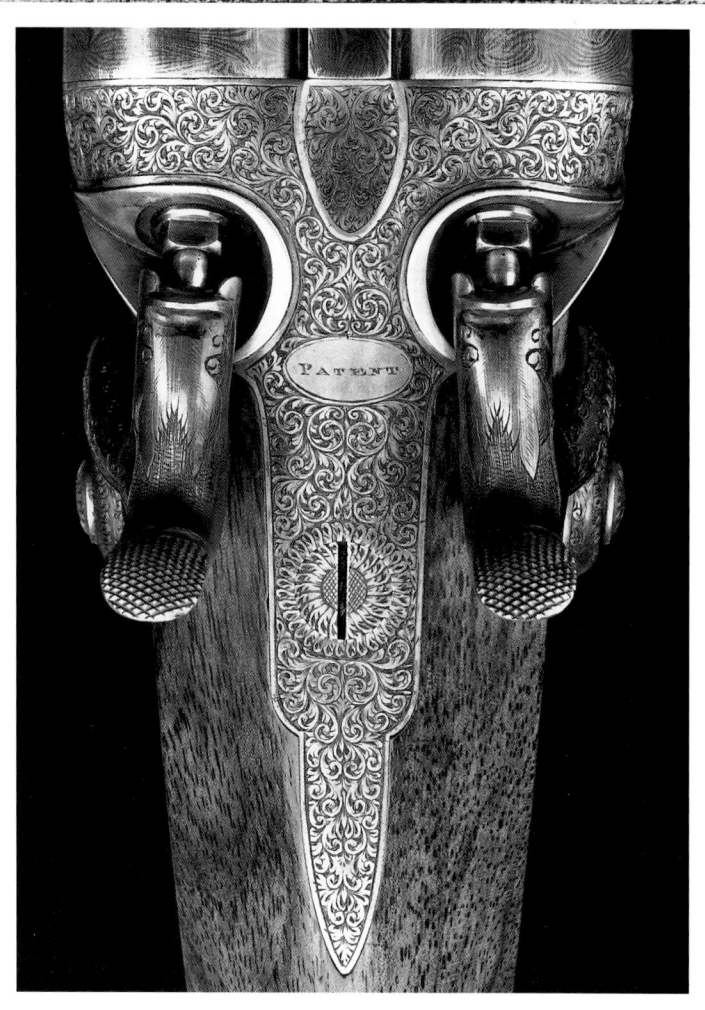

The tang of No. 7745 showing the engraving 'Patent' in reference to the Purdey bolt of patent no. 1104 of 1863.

centre-fire hammer gun, the gun displays all the stylistic Purdey features: the bar-in-wood action, the thumb-hole, the elegant hammers and the fine scroll engraving of Lucas. The gun is contained in its original red-baize-lined oak case. Two small round labels, one pasted under the trade label and the other under the compartment lid have the number '7745' written on them. A 'Charges' label on the inside of the lid states 'Light $3\,1/8$ drams powder, $1\,1/8$ oz. shot, Medium $3\,1/4$ drams powder, $1\,1/8$ oz. shot, Curtis and Harvey's No.2 size powder.' The following accessories are present in the case: cleaning rod, red Moroccan leather pouch with cleaning brushes, striker box, rosewood re-loading base, rosewood base for removing primer, oil bottle, two ebony-handled powder and shot measures and an ebony-handled rolled turnover tool.

An absolutely superb bar-in-wood hammer gun is shown in plate 42. No. 8623 is a centre-fire 10-bore bar-in-wood hammer gun, tested on 5 February 1872 and sold to Purdey's agent in America, Joseph G Grubb and Co., Philadelphia, on 11 May 1872 for £52.4s. (a discounted price). The gun is in remarkable original condition and displays all the features of the Purdey hammer gun at its finest. A second pattern thumb-hole underlever is used. The action is of the bar-in-wood type with the wood continuing right up to the hinge pin to produce a very attractive gun. The front action locks are very finely scroll-engraved by J Lucas and are marked 'Purdey'. The hammers are of the distinctive Purdey style and are also finely scroll-engraved. Percussion fences add to the graceful style. The 31-inch Damascus barrels are engraved 'J Purdey, $314\,1/2$ Oxford Street, London'. The gun weighs 8lb 1oz and has $2\,5/8$-inch

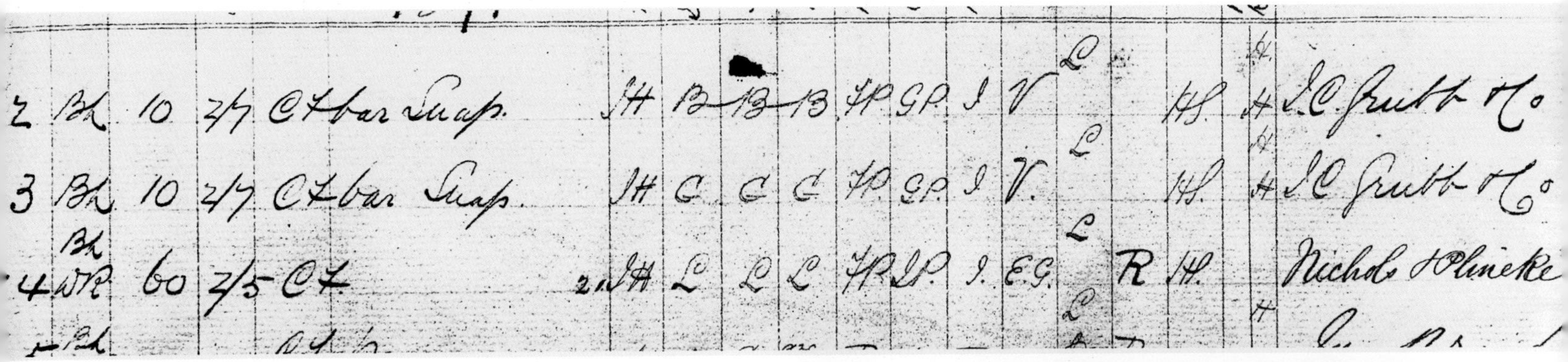

The record in the Dimension Book for No. 8623. See column headings on page 84. 'JH' is J Harris, nipples and plungers. 'G' is Henry Glaysher, jointing, stocking and making off. 'FP' is F Phillips, percussioning. 'GP' is G Prentice, cocking. 'V' is Virgo, levers. 'L' is J Lucas, engraving. 'R' is A Robins, hardening and 'HS' is H Schmidt, luggers.

chambers. The fore-end is attached by a barrel bolt. The strikers are gold-plated as was prevalent in many wildfowling guns.

A relatively rare single-barrel rifle, No. 9223 (see plate 44), is a .450 hammer rifle built for Lady Stamford in 1874. Pre-1880, Purdey's built only 27 single-barrel rifles. The barrel is octagonal and is engraved 'J Purdey, 314 1/2 Oxford Street, London'. A Henry Jones inert action with the Purdey 'Long Guard lever' is used as the bolting system. The back action lock, engraved 'Purdey' has a safety bolt and is rounded at the leading edge. As befits the early centre-fire hammer rifles, the hammer is flat. The fore-end has a horn cap and is attached by a barrel bolt.

12-bore top lever bar-in-wood hammer gun No. 11090 tested on 22 December 1881 and sold to Paul Fitter on 28 December is illustrated (plate 45). This very graceful gun has front action locks, typical Purdey hammers and fine scroll engraving. The 30-inch Damascus barrels are bored cylinder and full choke. The gun is contained in its original oak and leather case.

A unique four-barrel gun is illustrated (plates 46 and 47). Purdey's made only one four-barrel gun, possibly as a

A top-lever 12-bore bar-in-wood hammer gun No. 11090 sold on 28 December 1881 to Paul Fitter. *(See plate 45 in colour section.)*

10-bore bar-in-wood thumb-hole hammer gun No. 8623 tested on 5 February 1872. A superb example of the fine engraving style of J Lucas. *(See plate 42 in colour section.)*

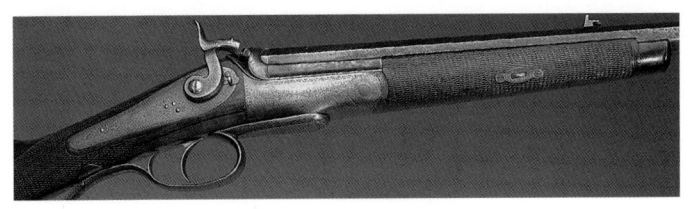

Single-barrel .450 rifle No. 9223 built for Lady Stamford in 1874. Single-barrel rifles are relatively rare. *(See plate 44 in colour section.)*

The record in the Dimension Book for No. 9223 – see column headings on page 84. 'GH' is Henson, jointing, stocking and making off. 'GP' is G Prentice, cocking. 'V' is Virgo, levers. 'JH' is J Harris, nipples and plungers. 'L' is J Lucas, engraving. 'R' is A Robins, hardening and 'HS' is H Schmidt, luggers. Notice the 'Scroll lever' on No. 9224, referring to the flamboyant variation of the Second Pattern thumb-hole.

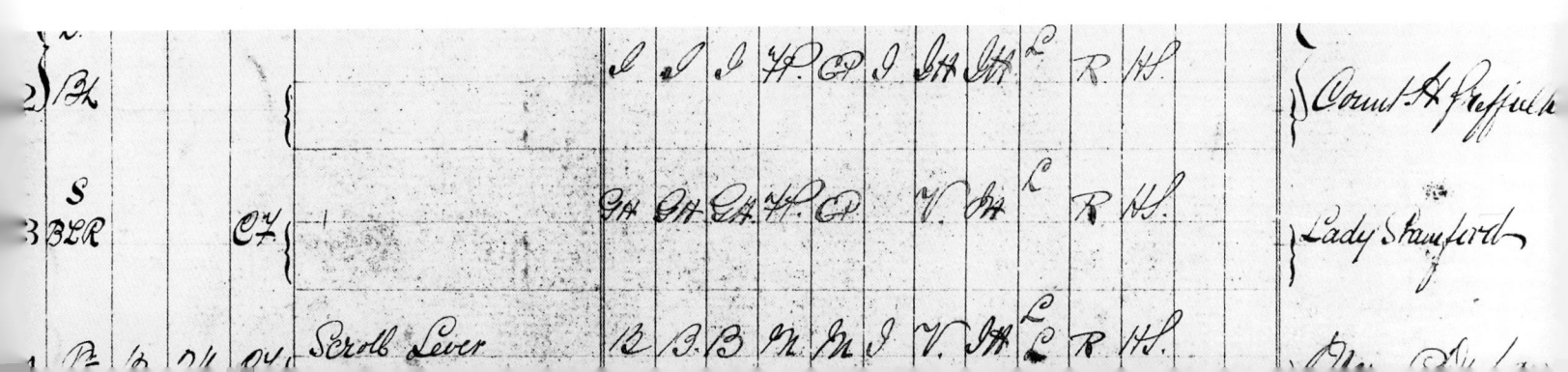

Dimension Book record (No. 11090):

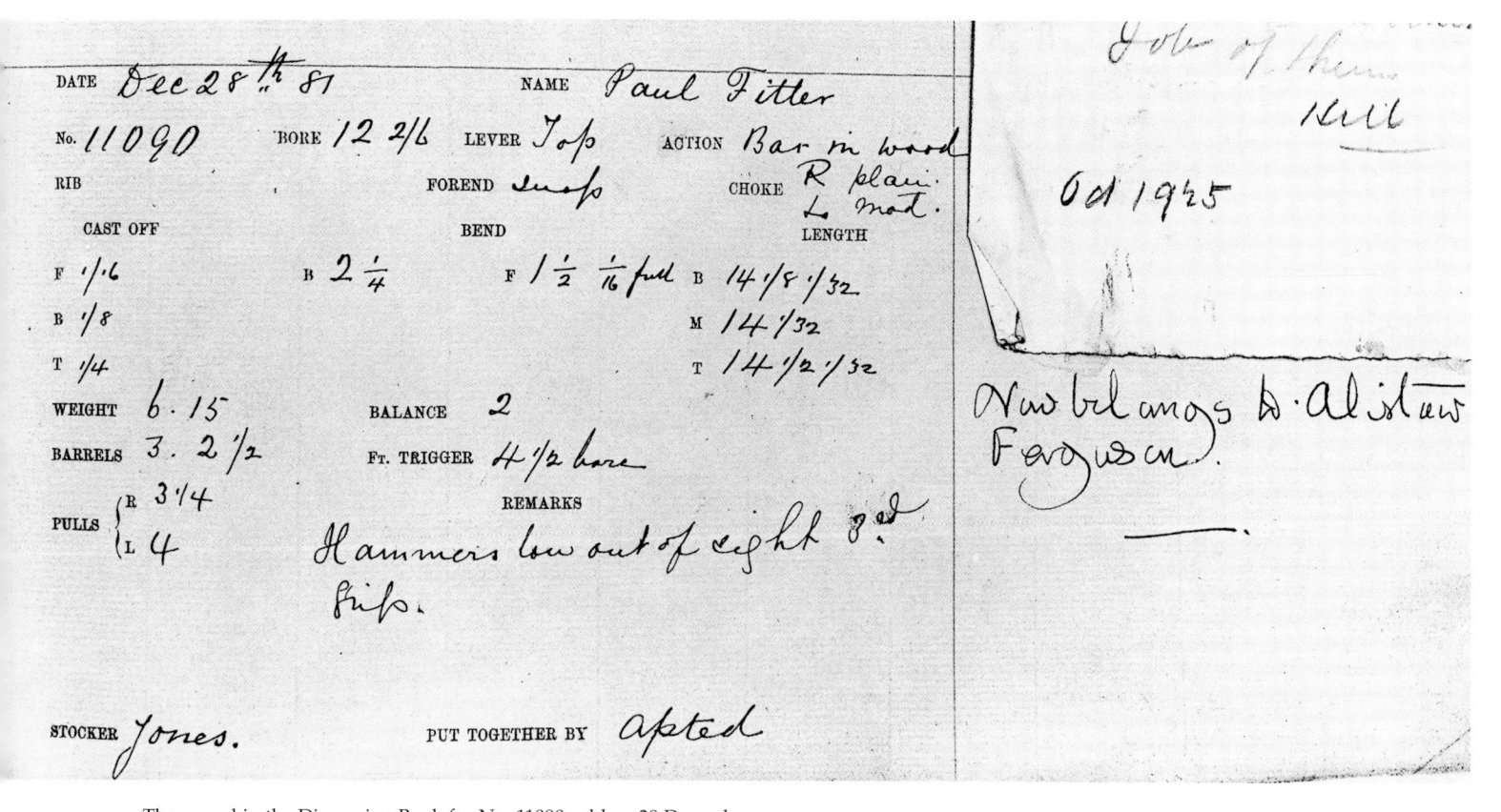

DATE	Dec 28th 81	NAME	Paul Fitter
No. 11090	BORE 12 2/6	LEVER Top	ACTION Bar in wood
RIB	FOREND snap	CHOKE	R plain L mod.

CAST OFF: F 1/16, B 1/8, T 1/4
BEND: B 2 1/4, F 1 1/2 1/16 full
LENGTH: B 14 1/8 1/32, M 14 1/32, T 14 1/2 1/32
WEIGHT 6.15 BALANCE 2
BARRELS 3. 2 1/2 FT. TRIGGER 4 1/2 bore
PULLS: R 3 1/4, L 4
REMARKS: Hammers low out of sight 8d fitted.
STOCKER Jones. PUT TOGETHER BY Apted

Alterations: Job of Thorn kill / Oct 1925 / Now belongs to Alistair Ferguson.

The record in the Dimension Book for No. 11090 sold on 28 December 1881. Stocked by T Jones and put together by J Apted. Note the 'hammers low out of sight'. An entirely different style of Dimension Book came in with No. 9841 at Christmas 1876. Only two gunmaking specialisations were recorded from now on, 'stocked' and 'put together by'. 'Put together' refers to the finishing of the gun.

demonstration piece for one of the exhibitions in the 1880s and 1890s, or perhaps as an experiment. Although multi-barrelled guns had always been constructed, there was a resurgence of interest in the second half of the 19th century due to the increase in popularity of driven game shooting. Probably the best known exponent of the multi-barrel gun was Charles Lancaster, 151 New Bond Street, London. Various mechanisms were patented by Henry Thorn, who controlled Lancasters in this period. The Purdey four-barrelled gun is very similar to Lancaster's second model of 1882.

The four-barrel gun is 20-bore and has the serial No. 11614, which would normally indicate a gun built in 1883. However, No. 11614 was not tested until 11 December 1886 and had in fact been sold the day before to Colonel de Tagnierres. This probably indicates that either the gun was experimental, or that, due to its novel method of construction, it took longer to make or sell than usual. The 20-bore Damascus barrels are

Below: The record in the Dimension Book for No. 11614. This gun was stocked by James Lumsden and put together by Apted.

Dimension Book record (No. 11614):

DATE 10/12/86 Damascus. NAME Col de Tignierres Decd ALTERATIONS
No. 11614 20 BORE 2 1/2 LEVER Top. ACTION Bar.
FOREND Roller BORING Choke
CAST OFF: B 17/8 16/7/32
BEND: F 1 1/2
LENGTH: B 14 3/4, M 14 1/2 16, T 15 5/8
WEIGHT 7.15 1/2 BALANCE 2 5/8
BARRELS 4. 2 1/2 FT. TRIGGER 4 1/2
REMARKS: 4 Barrelled Hammerless gun Pistol Hand
STOCKER Lumsden PUT TOGETHER BY Apted

Alterations: Belongs to C...
Sketch: Breech End of 4 Barrel 20 Bore

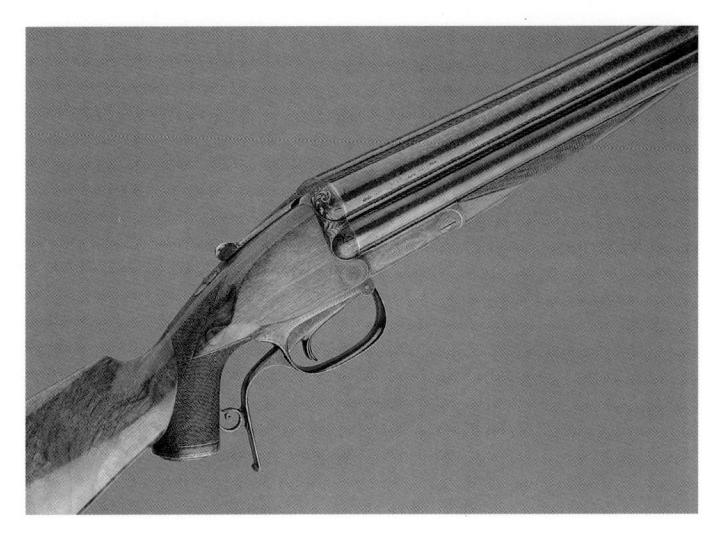

20-bore four-barrel hammerless gun No. 11614 tested on 11 December 1886. The only four-barrel produced by Purdey, this gun is of superb quality. (*See plate 46 in colour section.*)

25 1/2 inches long and are engraved 'J Purdey and Sons, Audley House, South Audley Street, London'. The lock work contained a rotating head to strike each individual striker. When the lever under the trigger-guard is squeezed, the head rotates to its next position and at the same time the mechanism is cocked. The figured walnut stock has a pistol grip and drop points. The action is finely carved and the gun is of the finest quality throughout, a superb piece of craftsmanship. The advent of ejectors in the 1880s made this type of weapon superfluous. These guns were heavy and cumbrous and the mechanism hard to operate.

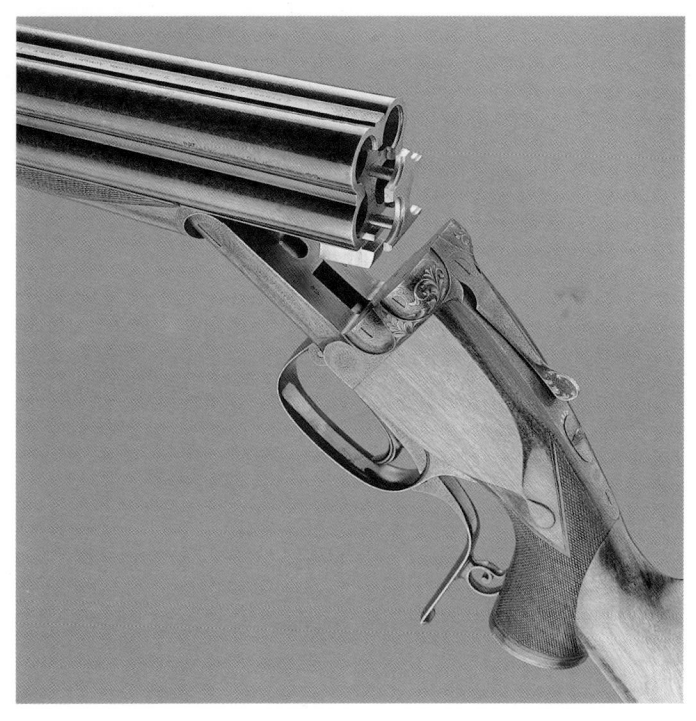

20-bore four-barrel hammerless gun No. 11614 of 1886. (*See plate 47 in colour section.*)

The pattern test for No. 11614 dated 11 December 1886.

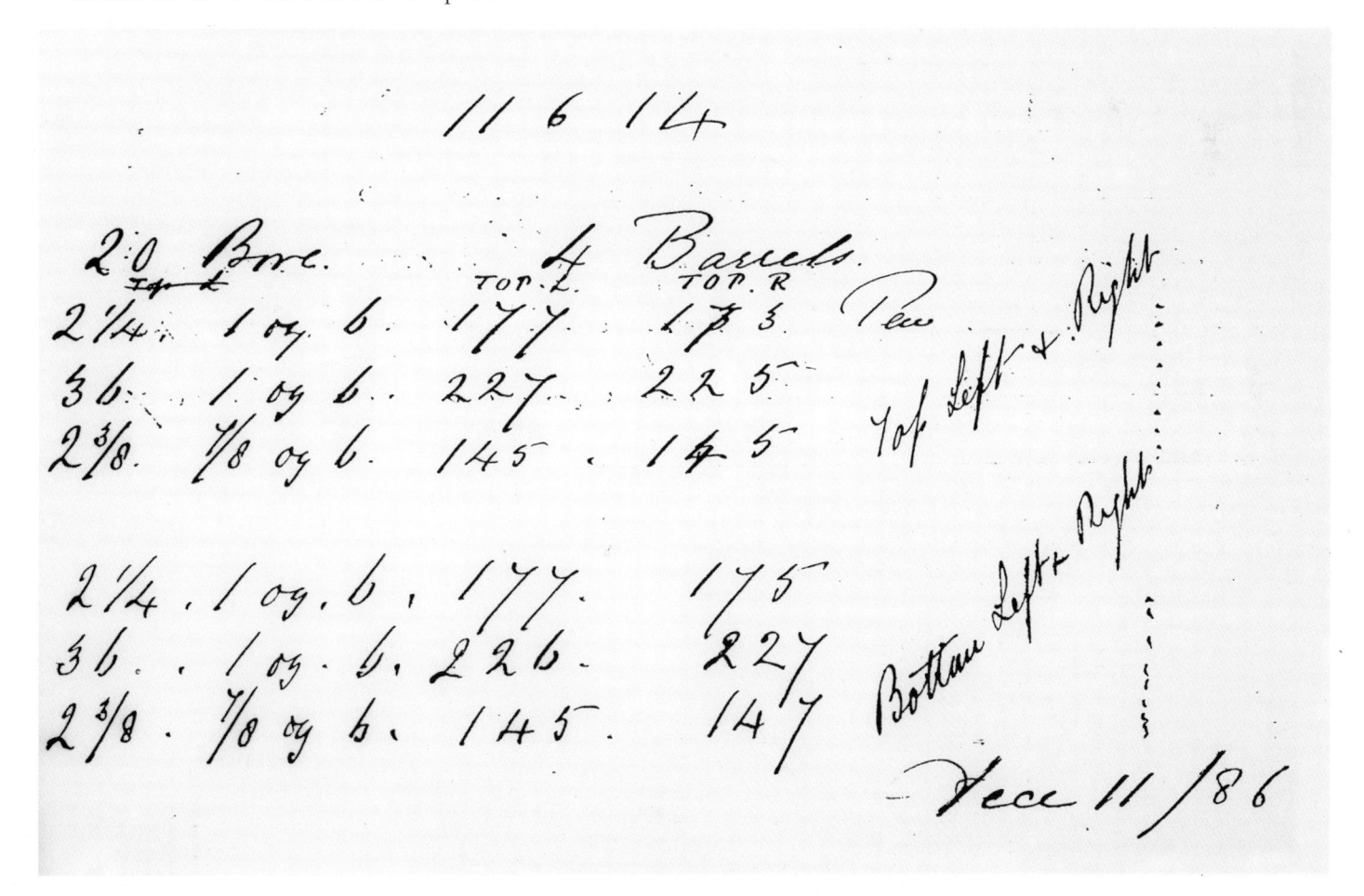

A C quality double-barrel .400 Black Powder Express rifle, No. 12022, was sold on 14 July 1885 to Lord Langford (see plate 48). The Jones underlever has a snap action. The rifle has isolated, bolted, re-bounding backlocks and gold-washed strikers. The 28 inch barrels have a matt file cut rib and open sights. The stock has a pistol grip with pistol grip cap, sling eyes and a horn buttplate.

A best quality double-barrel 8-bore rifle is shown in plates 49 and 50. This is No. 12371, weighing 17lbs. and sold on 8 July 1886. Very large bore double rifles by Purdey are fairly uncommon. The 24-inch Damascus barrels have a matt file cut rib, a fixed 50 yd. sight and three leaf sights to 100, 150 and 200 yds. A Jones underlever is employed and the action has side clips. The rifle is finely rose-and-scroll engraved, probably the work of Lucas. The stock has a pistol grip, cheek-piece and a Silvers recoil pad. The rifle is contained in its original red-baize-lined oak-and-leather case housing the following accessories: conical and spherical bullet moulds numbered to the rifle, cleaning rod, re-capper, turnover tool for round ball, powder measure, two ebony-handled striker removal tools, two horn containers for spare strikers, spare front sights, ebony-handled turnscrew, oil bottle, snap caps, leather pouch, pullthrough and leather sling. This rifle was stocked by Dean and put together by Blanton.

Plate 51 shows a double-barrel, top-lever .360 hammer rifle No. 12386 sold to Sir Henry Tichborne of Tichborne Park, Alresford, Hampshire, on 17 May 1886. He was nineteen when he took delivery of this rifle. The gun is an E quality – the lowest quality on sale at Purdey's – but it is still a fine weapon. It was constructed by Richard Ellis, Birmingham, and finished by Purdey. The rifle is chambered for the No. 5 black powder .360 cartridge and has 26-inch barrels with a matt top rib. The sights are for 30, 65 and 100 yards. The rebounding back locks are engraved 'J Purdey and Sons'. The action with percussion fences is sparsely engraved. The stock has a pistol hand, cheek-piece and eyes for a sling. Weight 6lb. 10oz.

Double-barrel .400 snap underlever C quality rifle No. 12022, sold on 14 July 1885 to Lord Langford. (*See plate 48 in colour section.*)

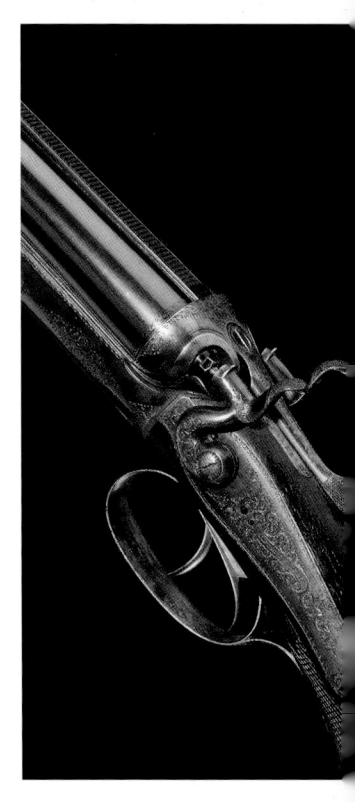

Double-barrel .360 top lever hammer rifle, E quality, No. 12386, sold to Sir Henry Tichborne on 17 May 1886. (*See plate 51 in colour section.*)

Double-barrel 8-bore underlever hammer rifle No. 12371 sold on 8 July 1886. (*See plate 49 in colour section.*)

8-bore rifle No. 12371 in its original oak-and-leather case with accessories. (*See plate 50 in colour section.*)

EARLY BREECH-LOADING GUNS AND RIFLES

DATE Dec 14/85   NAME LORD LANGFORD

No. 12022   400 BORE 2/14   LEVER over guard   ACTION Back

RIB flats Roughed   FOREND Snap   BORING Rifle

CAST OFF   BEND   LENGTH

F   B 2/16   F 1 3/8/16 1/32   B 14 2/16

B   M 14 1/2

T   T 15

WEIGHT 8. 4 1/4   BALANCE 4 1/4

BARRELS 4. 9 1/2   FT. TRIGGER 6 1/2/16

PULLS { R 1 3/4   L 2 1/2 }

REMARKS C.X. quality 3rd Sight
Rebounding Locks
Bolted in front
Pistol hand, Cheek piece
Silvers heel - Eyes for Sling
3/4 in × 50/400 case

STOCKER A Smith   PUT TOGETHER BY

The record in the Dimension Book for No. 12022. This rifle was built by A Smith & Son.

The record in the Dimension Book for No. 12386. Note that it was constructed by Richard Ellis of Birmingham.

DATE May 17/86   NAME Sir. H TICHBORNE   Dres'd

No. 12386   360 BORE 2/12 top LEVER   ACTION Back

RIB flats roughed   FOREND Snap   BORING Rifle

CAST OFF   BEND   LENGTH

F 1/16   B 2   F 1 1/2   B 14 5/8

B 3/16   M 14 1/2

T 3/8/16   T 15 5/8

WEIGHT 6 9 1/2   BALANCE 4 3/8

BARRELS 3 14 3/4   FT. TRIGGER 6 1/4

PULLS { R 2   L 2 3/4 }

REMARKS F. quality
Pistol hand Cheekpiece
Takes No 5. 360 cartridge
Eyes for Sling

STOCKER R Ellis   PUT TOGETHER BY R Ellis

Chapter seven

'A PALACE AMONGST GUN MANUFACTURERS'

The lease on 314½ Oxford Street was due to expire at Michaelmas (29 September), 1882. James Purdey had no intention of renewing the lease. He intended to find a far more prestigious location for Purdey's as befitted the product and clientele. Oxford Street had changed considerably in character since James Purdey the Founder had moved there in 1826. By the 1880s it was the major shopping street in London with end-to-end department stores selling all manner of merchandise. It was fast becoming a consumer's cornucopia, rather than the area of fashionable trade it used to be.

James Purdey had ample funds to finance a move. He set his sights on one of the most sought after areas in London – Mayfair, just south of Oxford Street. In this period there was scant regard for the buildings of the past and often when leases came up for renewal, they were offered to speculators who tore down the original property and re-erected a bigger building to generate a high profit or rent. South Audley Street in the late 1870s had several leases up for renewal from the freeholder, the Duke of Westminster.

In 1879, James Purdey bought the lease on a large draper's shop in South Audley Street that comprised a corner shop with Mount Street and two properties southwards. These properties were numbered 57-60 South Audley Street. The previous leaseholders had decided to sell their old leases to Purdey and remove, rather than undertake to rebuild for themselves. The Duke of Westminster approved as he wished the area to be inhabited by up-market trade.

It has always been stated in all histories of Purdey's, that the firm remained at 314½ Oxford Street until 1881, then moved to 287/289 Oxford Street in 1882, finally entering South Audley Street in 1883. I had always found it surprising how the move to 287/289 Oxford Street generated little comment, particularly when it would involve a major re-location of some 90 gunmakers and all their respective machinery, benches, etc. Also, to the best of my knowledge, there is no trade label or gun engraved '287/289 Oxford Street'. The answer to this puzzle was simple – Purdey's did not move to 287/289 Oxford Street at all. The council decided to re-number Oxford Street!

As we know, the numbering system in Oxford Street in the 19th century was quite chaotic. Due to the massive expansion of business in the street and the increasing sophistication of the postal service, this state of affairs could not be allowed to continue, so on 1 October 1880 London County Council decided to re-number the whole of Oxford Street. Consequently 314½ Oxford Street became 287/289 Oxford Street, the numbers the site still holds to the present day. ('314½' was transferred across the road to D H Evans and Co., causing some commentators to give the wrong present-day location of Purdey's old shop.) I wonder what James Purdey the Younger thought about this. He had been born in 314½ Oxford Street in 1828 and guns had been produced bearing this address for over fifty years. Official documentation of 1881-82 uses the new address, but I suspect that James Purdey never really recognised the new number.

In his re-building plans for South Audley Street, James Purdey never intended that the premises should house all the workshops, as had been the case at 314½ Oxford Street. The building in South Audley Street, to be named Audley House, would be more akin to a fashionable shop/gentlemen's club, and 90 gunmakers moving around with attendant machinery noise was not the atmosphere James Purdey wanted to create. Accordingly he acquired the lease on a property very close to South Audley Street – 37 North Row, just south of and parallel to Oxford Street. Here, for the first time, would be a specific Purdey factory where the heavy work of making guns and rifles would take place, such as barrel making and action filing. The lease on 37 North Row was acquired on 1 December 1881 and shortly afterwards, in 1882, the Purdey gunmakers and all their equipment began to move in. A fair amount of gun manufacture would still take place in Audley House, mostly the specialisations that did not generate grime and noise, such as stocking, finishing and engraving. Out of interest an 'insurance schedule' survives for this period showing the insurance value of the Purdey properties.

37 North Row – factory – £1,200
287 Oxford Street – stock – £17,200
289 Oxford Street – workshops – £2,500
Charlotte Mews – barrel making workshop – £750
28 Devonshire Place – James Purdey's residence – £3,000
28 Devonshire Place – furniture – £2,250

'A PALACE AMONGST GUN MANUFACTURERS'

30/32 Queen's Road – property bought to rent – £1,400
36/38 Queen's Road – property bought to rent – £3,100
42/44 Queen's Road – property bought to rent – £400
64 Harley Street – property bought to rent – £2,000
29 Green Street – a speculative development – £600
Stabling in Margate – £500

This insurance schedule gives a good description of the new workshops in 37 North Row.

> The insured building is now occupied by J Purdey and Sons, Gun and Rifle Makers. Ground and Floor – Office and Showroom/a hot water apparatus for warmth. First Floor – Barrel Maker's Shop/a gas engine for working two Boring Machines, a Portable Forge and a Blast Forge, sundry hand lathes. Second Floor – a forge for Rivets, sundry lathes. Future Annual Premium £3.00. A Carpenter's Bench for occasional use allowed. Gunpowder and cartridges are kept on iron safe on ground floor – the loading not to be done by artificial light.

Here the Purdey factory would remain until the lease ran out in 1900 and the factory moved to 2 Irongate Wharf, off Praed Street in the same year.

On 7 June 1882, the Zoological Society was given a short lease on 287 Oxford Street. By this time, much gun manufacture was taking place in North Row. Because the new building was not quite ready at South Audley Street, Purdey's remained in Oxford Street for the duration of 1882 and on 1 January 1883 they officially removed to Audley House, 57-58 South Audley Street, where they have remained to this day.

James Purdey had bought the leases of 57-60 South Audley Street in 1879 and submitted proposals to the Duke of Westminster to re-design the corner of Mount Street and the two properties southwards. James Purdey intended to have the corner of Mount Street and South Audley Street for his shop (nos. 57 and 58) and the rest of the building as a speculative venture for residential chambers (nos. 59 and 60). The building was designed by William Lambert, using red brick with dressings of red Mansfield stone in a vaguely Queen Anne style. In 1881, the old 18th-century buildings were demolished and work began on the new building, erected by the builder B E Nightingale. This is the date carved

The drawing by William Lambert, the architect of Audley House, 57-60 South Audley Street, 1881. To the left of Purdey's, are nos. 59 and 60, built as a speculative venture by James Purdey and, to the right, in Mount Street, is the original block that would be developed by James Purdey in 1892 as 84 Mount Street, to become part of the Purdey shop.

Audley House, February 2000. (*See plate 52 in colour section.*)

The Royal Coat of Arms above the front entrance of Audley House today. Note the date 1881, the year when work on the building began. (*See plate 53 in colour section.*)

on the front pediment of Audley House today (see plate 53). Construction took two years and it wasn't until the winter of 1882 that the building was ready for habitation. On 1 January 1883, James Purdey and Sons entered the building and so began a new phase in the history of the firm.

The rate books confirm this. No rates were paid at all for 1882, but rates were paid for the first instalment of the year 1883, between Christmas and Lady Day (25 March).

Purdey's speculation on 59 and 60 South Audley Street obviously paid dividends. Only one year later he attempted to buy the leases of the next building southwards to Aldford Street, nos. 61-63, as a speculation, but the occupying tenants wished to re-build themselves. To ensure harmony, the same architect, Lambert, was used and the buildings were completed in 1889-90. Purdey was successful in obtaining the lease to the west of his shop in Mount Street and in 1892 re-developed 84 Mount Street, again using Lambert as the architect. This is the present-day site of Purdey's accessories and clothing shop.

Purdey's new shop created great excitement – it was by far the most impressive and prestigious gun shop in the country, if not the world. An excellent description of the layout is given in the *Land and Water* article 'Crack Gunmakers' of 6 July 1889, some six years after the removal in which the new building is described as a 'Palace Amongst Gun Manufactories'.

… Mr. Purdey has built for himself a house which may be called a palace amongst gun manufactories, and no one can view it without conceding that it stands without a rival in the world amongst such establishments, and not only so, but one of the handsomest buildings of any description in London. This house, which is known as Audley House, stands at the junction of Mount-street with South Audley-street, and within two minutes' walk of Park-lane and Hyde-park. It is an imposing structure, rising to a considerable height, and graceful architectural design. The facings of Devonshire marbles, with marble columns, and the large plate glass windows, give to it a very elegant appearance, and more of the character of a West-end club-house than of a place wherein such work as the building of guns is carried forward. An entry into the house, however, and a moment's reflection, will prove that it possesses unrivalled advantages for that purpose. In the space at command, and the light and ventilation, far more of the work can be done on the premises than is done in the generality of London gunshops, and done better since the surroundings are so much more convenient and agreeable for the workmen. After passing the swing doors, we find ourselves in a capacious and

'A PALACE AMONGST GUN MANUFACTURERS'

lofty hall, down one side of which runs a long row of clerks' desks, which gives quite a banking-house look to the room, and testifies to the magnitude of the accounts that are kept. The sight of all these clerks would suggest to many the breaking of the tenth commandment, when they think for a moment of the sums which those clerks tick off to fortunate Mr. Purdey's credit. From this hall branch off passages, some into workshops, and others to various rooms, private rooms of members of the firm, etc., all of which, like the entrance-hall, are handsomely and substantially furnished and fitted. Passing through an elegant anteroom, we enter the large showroom. This room calls for something more than passing comment, since it is quite unique; and we must repeat that to compare it with anything that can be seen in any London gunmaker's establishment would give a misleading impression. Whoever designed this room was a genius, we very truly assert, when we keep in mind the purpose for which such room should be designed. Its character is that of a cross between the gun-room in a first-class country house and the luxurious smoking-room of a London club. Large, lofty, well lighted, comfortably carpeted, solidly furnished with dark mahogany and dark leather, with glazed cases of guns and rifles disposed around its walls, it furnishes the appropriate environments to display the beautiful and high-bred-looking productions of the establishment, as well as to properly impress the visitor, and to induce him to restore his equilibrium by giving an order for a pair of guns.

The 'large showroom' referred to is, of course, the famous Long Room. This was originally James Purdey's personal office but soon became a showroom and meeting room known worldwide to Purdey customers. It is in the Long Room that all the portraits of the generations of Purdey's are displayed along with an amazing array of memorabilia, guns and pictures of famous customers. One of the big changes that took place after the move to Audley House was that the bulk of gun manufacture now took place in the factory in North Row – such as cartridge manufacture, finishing, engraving and stocking – but the dirtier work involving machinery took place in the factory. Flats were built on the upper floors for family use.

Photographs of the Long Room in the 1880s as originally designed. Note the central well where the Purdey's could watch the activities in the gunroom below. The well was removed in 1938 and replaced by a large table.

THE PURDEY EJECTOR

The arrival of the hammerless gun in the 1870s increased the rapidity of fire. However, pulling out spent cases by hand was still time consuming, particularly on the organised driven game shoots. The addition of an ejector to get rid of these empty cases automatically would considerably enhance the firepower of the shooter. It was to this end that many gunmakers in the 1870s and 1880s devoted their energies.

The first ejector gun using the conventional method of barrels pivoting open was patented by Joseph Needham in patent no. 1205 of 1874. In this patent the ejector mechanism was contained within the action. The potential of the ejector was not fully realised and there were only a trickle of patents in the 1870s.

The ejector first used by Purdey was patented by one of their actioners, William Nobbs of Old Kent Road. This was patent no. 1137 of 2 March 1883. The Nobbs patent was an interrupter mechanism whereby a type of pop-up pin would prevent the unfired cartridge from being ejected. When a lock was fired, the lock sear moved a series of levers to activate a rocking lever in the standing breech. The rocking lever would be moved out of the way of the extractor. When the gun was opened a simple coil spring around the stem of the extractor/ejection rod was tripped by a lever on the knuckle allowing ejection to take place. When the gun was unfired and broken open, the rocking lever would be in its raised position blocking the extractor to prevent ejection. The system was crude with the extractor working against the action face.

Purdey made an agreement with Nobbs: firstly that Purdey would apply for the patent and pay all the patent costs, secondly that Nobbs would receive £5 for his patent. The Nobbs ejector was used for a short time in the 1880s.

Another Purdey gunmaker, William Wem of 21 Rothwell Buildings, Tottenham Court Road, patented an ejector in 1888. Wem's patent no. 3100 of 29 February 1888 created the Purdey ejector that has been in continual use since this time. From this date onwards the Dimension Books record with increasing frequency the 'Wem ejector'.

In the Wem ejector, a pair of very thin slides with 'D' shaped ends connected to the lock tumbler, work through the action body. The actual ejector mechanism is contained within the fore-end. An over centre tumbler of the Perkes/Southgate variety is used. This ejector tumbler is locked by a small side spring. When the gun is fired, the lock tumbler moves the slide forward to activate the ejector. The slide does this by pushing aside the small side spring locking the ejector tumbler. When the barrels are dropped, the ejector is tripped by a cam on the knuckle and the over centre tumbler fires out the empty case. The first important part of the patent is the adoption of a crossbar on the knuckle of the gun to cock the ejector tumblers when the gun is closed. Many of the early ejector systems used the extractors working in the action face.

The second important part of the patent is that the ejector tumblers contained within the fore-end work the extractors. The ejector tumblers are of a special shape and work on a cam in the knuckle. When the gun is opened unfired, the cam in the knuckle causes the ejector tumblers to turn about their axis

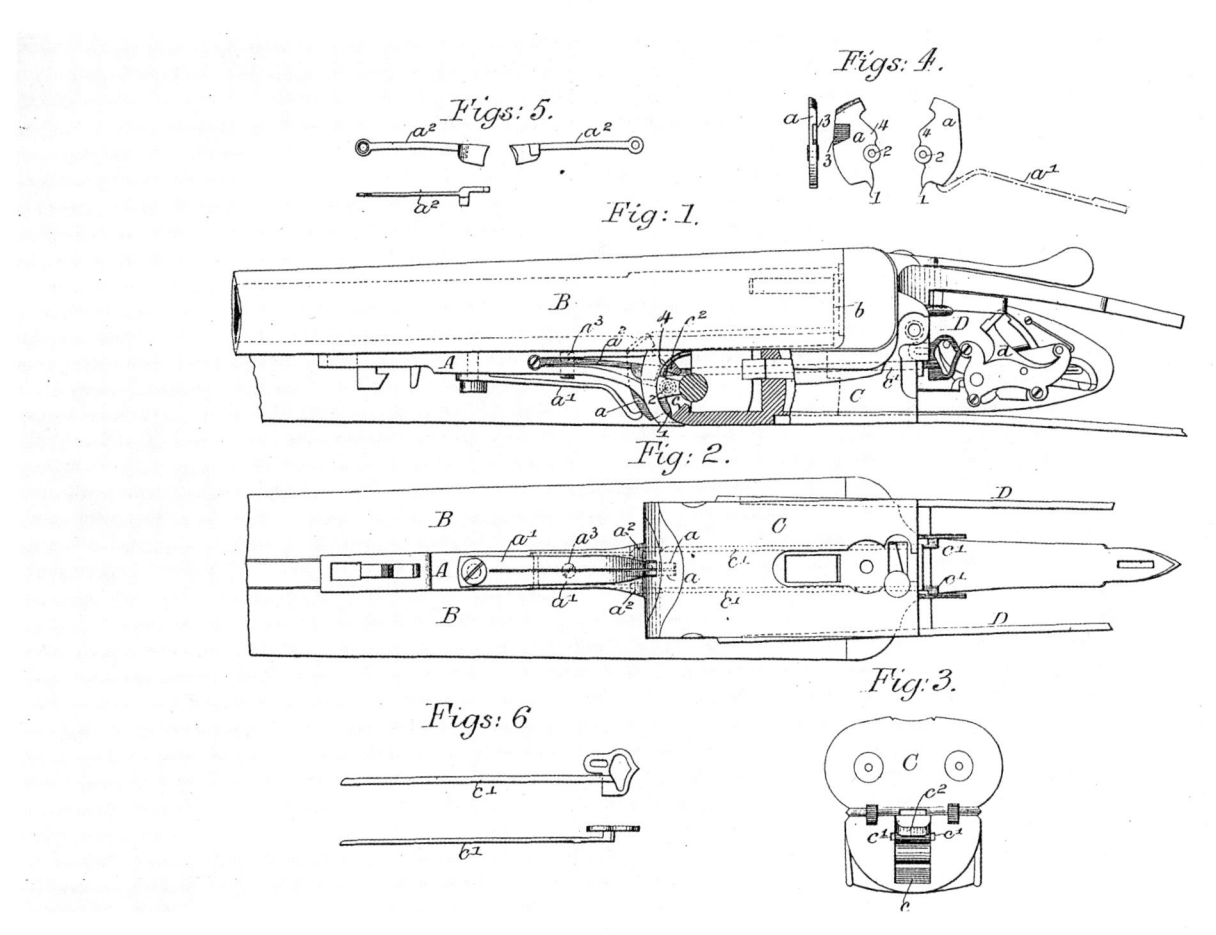

The Wem ejector, patent no. 3100 of 29 February 1888 – the Purdey ejector. Figure 5 illustates the side springs, Figure 4 shows the over centre tumbler, Figure 6, the ejector slides with 'D' shaped ends.

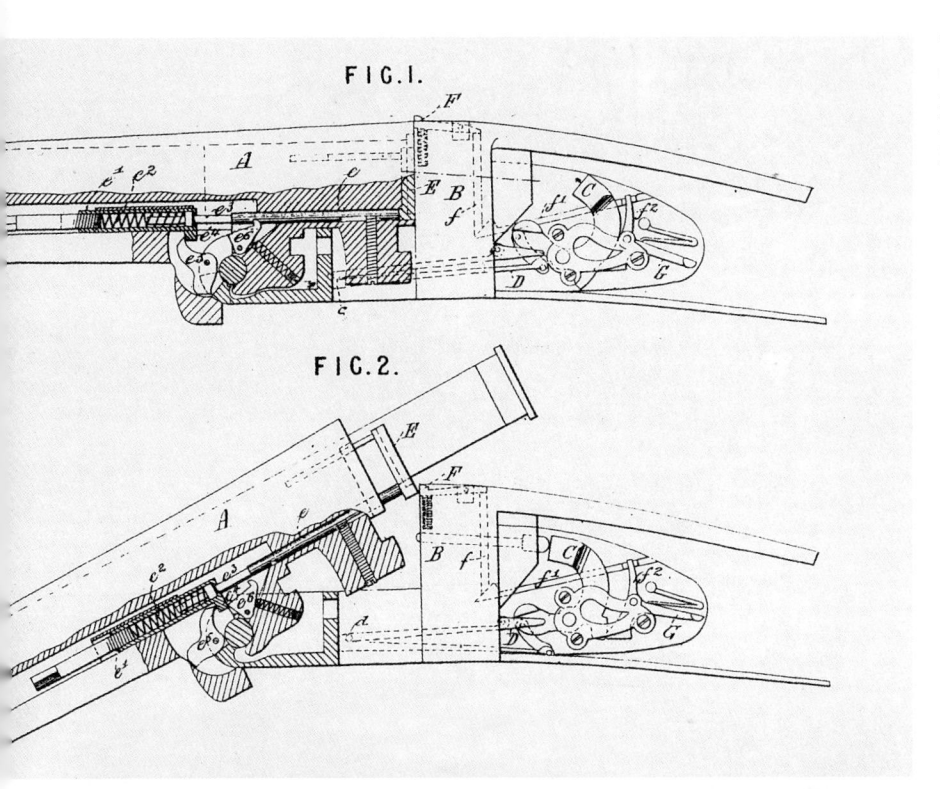

The first Purdey ejector, William Nobbs patent no. 1137 of 2 March 1883. Figure 1 shows the rocking lever 'F' raised in the unfired position to prevent ejection and Figure 2, the rocking lever lowered and ejection taking place.

The crossbar on the knuckle used in the original Wem/Purdey ejector that was done away with in the 1930s when Ernest Lawrence re-designed the ejector.

A demonstration gun 'in the white' dating from the early 1920s showing the 'D' shaped slide in the action body and the ejector mainspring and side spring (just above the ejector mainspring, held in place by the small screw) in the fore-end.

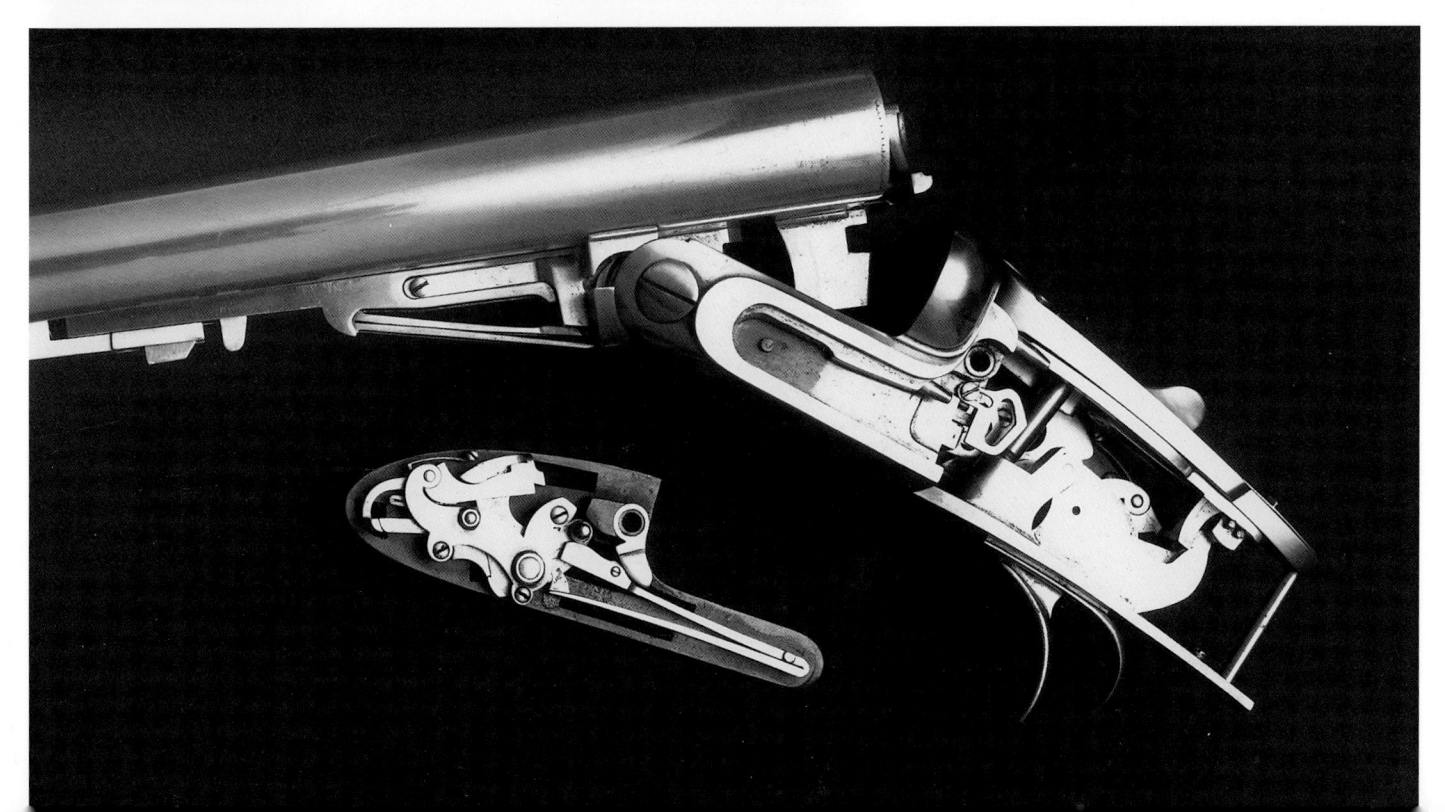

and push out the extractors. This same cam trips the ejector when it is activated by the 'D' slide. One of the great merits of the Wem ejector is the exceptional distance through which the gun opens, permitting the extractors to be drawn well out.

Purdey's made an agreement with William Wem over his ejector, once again buying the rights to the patent for a very small sum.

> 21 Rothwell Buildings,
> Tottenham Court Rd.
> 29th Feby 1888.
>
> To Mr James Purdey,
> Audley House,
> London.
>
> I the undersigned William Wem having worked out certain improvements in breakdown guns in your time and whilst receiving wages from you, hereby agree to apply for an English patent at your costs and charges and transfer the same to you when obtained in consideration of the sum of £5 (five pounds) over and above the amount I have received as wages during the time I have been working out the said invention.
>
> I am
> Yours Obedtly
> William Wem.

Evidently William Wem was about to move house and had to borrow £3 from Purdey a few months later:

> I the undersigned W Wem acknowledge the receipt of three pounds (£3) from James Purdey and promise to repay the said sum on his demand either by weekly instalments or as he may otherwise elect and I promise not to absent myself from work except through illness nor leave his employment till the amount has been repaid.
>
> W Wem
> May 26th 1888
>
> 21 Rothwell Builds. Fitzroy Sqr.
> about to move to Queen Park

Converting existing guns to this ejector was not simple. The following bill survives from the 1890s to show the stages and cost.

To alter ordinary hammerless guns to ejectors with old fore-end wood.

	£.	s.	d.
Fore-end forging		1	
Machining fore-end		3	
Fitting fore-end iron		7	
Machining luggers		2	
Luggering		10	
Chamber rims		1	
Machining action		6	
Fitting piece on back of action		2	
Fitting ejector	2		5
Regulating ejector		5	
Stocking		8	6
New tumblers	1		
Engraving		3	
Polish fore-end and tumbler		1	6
Finishing		5	
	6	0	0

It was found through time that the crossbar on the knuckle was a source of weakness. Constantly cocking the ejectors, it was prone to fracture. In the 1930s Ernest Lawrence redesigned the ejector mechanism and did away with the crossbar. In its place a central lifting arm contained within the fore-end compressed the ejector springs upon closure and from this time onwards the ejector mechanism was entirely satisfactory. The first mention of the Wem ejector in the Dimension Books is No. 13501 built in 1888.

During the 1880s, yet another major change occurred in gun development, the adoption of Sir Joseph Whitworth's fluid compressed steel in preference to the age old Damascus. Whitworth steel was proportionately stronger than Damascus and consequently barrels could be made that little bit lighter. The boring of rifle barrels was also easier as the material was far more even. 'Fluid compressed steel' derived its name from its manufacturing technique. In its molten state, the steel was compressed to remove any impurities.

James Purdey was the first gunmaker to use Whitworth's steel. In *The Gun and Its Development* W W Greener states, 'a leading London gunmaker decided to adopt it for shotgun barrels'. Whilst Greener must be applauded for his large and informed tome, it must be remembered that he was a master of self-aggrandisement and saw no reason to promote competition. An article in *Land and Water* in 1897 confirms the identity of the 'leading London gunmaker':

> They (Purdey) were the first to adopt Whitworth's steel for barrels. Purdey had a good many conversations with the late Sir Joseph Whitworth about the supply of rough tubes, which were at first made exclusively for him.

An earlier article of 6 July 1889, again in *Land and Water* gives more insight into Purdey's use of Whitworth's steel.

> Mr. Purdey is strongly biased in favour of steel for barrels, and prefers the fluid compressed steel of Sir Joseph Whitworth's manufacture. He declares that, weight-for-weight, it is stronger than iron, and shoots harder, though not so handsome an appearance of Damascus. Of all the leading makers with whom we are acquainted, Mr. Purdey is the staunchest advocate of steel.

Whitworth's steel was more expensive than Damascus, and Purdey's charged £2.10s extra per gun. The 1885 catalogue, previously shown, points out that:

> The barrels of best Guns can if desired be made of Sir Joseph Whitworth and Co.'s fluid pressed steel at an extra cost of £2.10s per gun. This metal is stronger under excessive strain than Damascus, is harder and more durable and keeps its brown better.

Whitworth barrels could be confused with inferior steel barrels and, to prevent this, they were always engraved 'Whitworth Fluid Compressed Steel'. At the turn of the century, Whitworth's steel began to be used less and less, as ordinary steel was developed and accepted for gun barrels. Credit must be given to Purdey for promoting the first real use of steel and in raising public awareness of its suitability for barrel manufacture. From this time onwards, Damascus barrels were rarely made.

For a short time in the late 1890s, Purdey used Krupp steel from Germany. On 27 August 1897, James Purdey wrote to his son Athol:

> The tubes of Krupp have been tested and are found <u>much</u> stronger and tougher so that we can use them satisfactorily and perhaps more than the Whitworth.

However by the early 1900s, Purdey had reverted to Whitworth steel.

THE DEATH OF JAMES PURDEY III – 1890

It had always been the intention of James Purdey the Younger to pass on the business to his two eldest sons, James III and Athol. He began this process with the Deed of Agreement in 1877 changing the name of the business to James Purdey and Sons. Unfortunately, his eldest son James had never been a well man. He had been ill for a considerable time with one of the feared diseases of the era. Tuberculosis, or consumption, was a wasting disease that only began to be understood in the 1880s and it was the 20th century before a cure was found. It killed people in their thousands. James Paddison, a partner in Boss and Co., died of it in 1873. In James Purdey's case it appears to have infected his leg and in the early 1870s he was operated on in an attempt to cure it.

On 5 August 1886, James married Ellen Peden, aged 22, of 39 Dulwich Road in the parish church of St. George's Hanover Square. He gave his address for the certificate as '58 South Audley Street'. Shortly after the marriage James and Nell (as she was known) gave birth to a daughter, Dorothy Irene.

It was known that tuberculosis was encouraged by damp conditions and polluted air and as young James Purdey's condition deteriorated, a long stay abroad was planned in a climate beneficial to his condition. In mid-1888, James and Nell set off for Bloemfontein in the Orange Free State, South Africa, leaving their daughter, Dorothy, in England. It must have been very obvious to James Purdey the Younger that his son was a sick man indeed, as he now made steps to bring his third son, Cecil, into the business.

Cecil Onslow Purdey, born in 1865, never envisaged Purdey's as a career, believing it to be the preserve of his elder brothers. He had begun a career in ship-building and by the time of James's sojourn in South Africa was aged 23. He entered the firm in the late 1880s. Cecil would have a one-third share of the business and Athol two-thirds in recognition of Athol's knowledge and leadership. Teasdale-Buckell in *Experts on Guns and Shooting* published in 1900, in reference to Athol and Cecil, states that 'one of his (Purdey the Younger) sons has been in the business for 24 years and is therefore well

Cecil Purdey 1865-1943, a photograph taken in the late 1880s around the time he joined the firm.

Athol Purdey *circa* 1890

Percy and Cecil (sitting) Purdey in the garden of Cecil's house at 'Highfield', The Ridgeway, Sutton, Surrey, *circa* 1890. Cecil entered the gunmaking business in the late 1880s due to the illness of his elder brother, James.

Mabel Field, wife of Athol Purdey, an oil painting, *circa* 1890 at the time of her marriage.

An oil painting of James Purdey the Younger by Archibald Stuart-Wortley. Completed in 1891 it hangs in the Long Room today. (*See plate 54 in colour section.*)

qualified to take his father's place in his absence, and another son is a good shot, superintends the rifle shooting and gives great assistance'.

It was apparent that James was not going to recover in South Africa and coupled with the fact that they were separated from their three-year-old daughter, James and Nell returned to Britain in the summer of 1890. James Purdey III died on 9 September that year, aged just 36. He died at his father's seaside home, 18 Marine Parade, Eastbourne, the cause of death being certified as 'Phthisis' (pulmonary tuberculosis) and was buried in the vault in Willesden Cemetery. He died intestate, letters of administration being granted to his wife Ellen Purdey. His personal estate was valued at £351. 17s. 5d.

Like Cecil, the youngest brother of all, Percy Purdey, born in 1869, was not intended to go into gunmaking. Percy set up a stockbroking business – Purdey and Wilson at 10 Throgmorton Avenue in the City. The business did not do well and the firm went bankrupt. James Purdey the Younger was forced to help his son out, a task he did not warm to as he was used to success in business. Percy eventually gave up his stockbroking career and became manager of The Grand theatre at Wolverhampton. In the will of James Purdey the Younger, dated 4 March 1903, he makes it quite plain that his son, Percy, had to take a more responsible attitude. Although he provided him with an income of £150 per annum out of the business, Percy was to receive nothing else out of the considerable estate left by James Purdey the Younger. 'I declare that my reason for not giving a share of the trust fund to my said son Percy John Purdey is that I have expended considerable sums for him and for his benefit.'

Shortly after the death of James Purdey III in September 1890, his brother, Athol Purdey, married on 1 December 1890 Mabel Field in St. Paul's Church, Hampstead. Athol was 32 and still living in the family home at 28 Devonshire Place. Mabel was 23, living in Hampstead and her father was a solicitor. Athol primarily ran the business in the early decades of the 20th century, and his sons – James Purdey IV and Tom Purdey – continued to conduct it in mid-century.

Athol and Mabel went to live at 67 Canfield Gardens, Hampstead, and bang on time, nine months later, their first child was born on 30 September 1891 christened James Alexander Purdey (James IV). Some six years later, at the same address, their second son, Thomas Donald Stuart Purdey, was born on 22 March 1897.

The Purdey business in the 1890s was considerable. In James Purdey the Younger's will of 1903, it was assessed at £90,000 – a very valuable business for the period. Over 300 guns and rifles per annum were being produced and when the royalties from the Beesley action, gun repairs, sub-contracted B-E quality weapons, cartridge sales and property speculation were taken into account, the business produced a very healthy profit. Cartridge sales were absolutely enormous, the volume dictating that they were loaded both in Audley House and in the factory in North Row. Sportsmen demanded their own

Earl de Grey with his trio of Purdey 12-bore hammer non-ejector guns, Nos. 10886/7/8, sold to him on 7 June 1887. The loader on the left is Charlie Day; on the right, James Hall.

individual loads and the cartridge sales in the sales ledgers of the late 19th century show just how popular shooting was. In 1890 approximately 363,000 Black Powder, 1,544,000 Schultze and 430,000 EC cartridges were sold. At the end of this decade the new nitro powders had rapidly gained favour and in 1898 approximately 34,000 Black Power, 1,813,000 Schultze and 329,000 EC cartridges were sold. Over 2,000,000 cartridges were sold annually by Purdey's in this period!

Three factors helped to explain the massive quantity of shooting that took place in the 19th century. Firstly, the development of the breech-loader allowed a very high rate of fire. Secondly, the trend towards the rearing of birds and the driving of game towards the guns created the opportunity for far more shots, and finally the increasing wealth of the *nouveau riche*, derived from industry, was invested in estates in imitation of their social superiors. The bags created were quite spectacular under such circumstances.

There were several notable shots in this period and virtually all used Purdey guns. The most famous was Earl de Grey, later Lord Ripon. De Grey was born on 29 January 1852 and had a large estate at Studley Royal, Ripon. He succeeded his father in 1909 to become the Marquess of Ripon. His shooting prowess was legendary, usually using a trio of Purdey's and two loaders. He preferred hammer guns long after the introduction of hammerless, having them passed to him at full cock (see plate 56). He held out in favour of Black Powder, changing to Schultze only in the late 1890s. He began shooting in 1867 and continued until he dropped dead with his gun in his hand on 22 September 1923, aged 71. His game book states 'on that date, Lord Ripon was shooting in Dullowgill Moor near Ripon and killed 165 grouse and 1 snipe – at 3.15 p.m., after a drive in which he had killed 51 grouse, Lord Ripon dropped dead in the heather'. In total, between 1867 and 1923 he bagged 556, 813 head of game.

Earl de Grey, 1852-1923, holding one of his Purdey hammer guns. A Spy cartoon dated 5 February 1890.

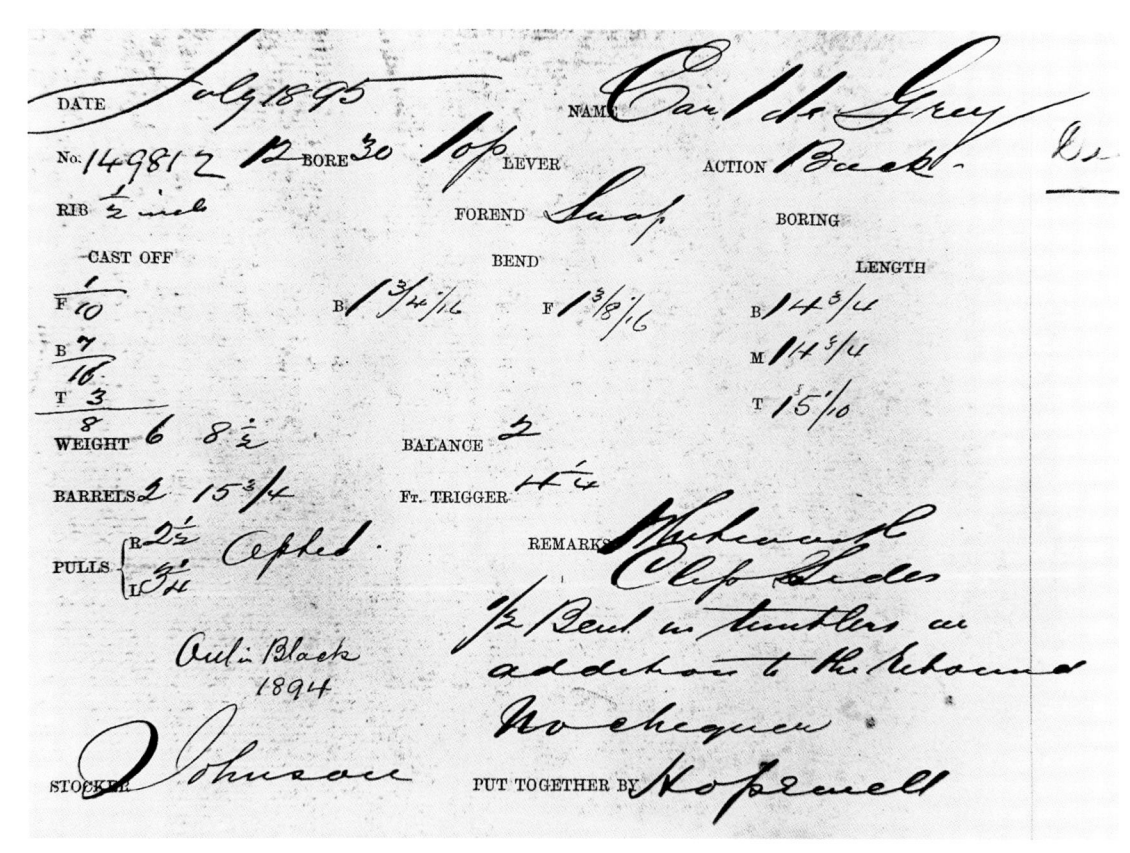

The record in the Dimension Book for No. 14981/2, sold in July 1895. Notice the '½ Bent on tumblers in addition to the Rebound' in reference to the unusual half-cock position. 'No chequer' is demanded as is 'out in black 1894' in reference to Earl de Grey testing the gun before it is finally finished. Stocked by H Johnstone and put together by W Hopewell.

Earl de Grey's 12-bore Purdey hammer ejector gun No. 14982, the No. 2 gun of the pair built in 1894/5. The gun was constructed with no chequering, a half-cock position on the locks and with Whitworth steel barrels. and engraving by Lucas. This gun was re-barrelled in 1928 by Henry Atkin. (*See plate 56 in colour section.*)

The record in the factory workbook for Nos. 14981/2. These workbooks, kept at the factory, detailed all the workmen involved in building a particular gun. Unfortunately many of the workbooks are missing. In this instance, Nos. 14981/2 were built by: Aston, barrel maker; Hughes, luggers; Howell, levers and detonating; Johnson, stocker; Gatrell ejectors; Lucas, engraving and Hopewell, finisher.

Another notable shot was Lord Walsingham. He was born on 29 July 1843 and before he succeeded in 1870 was the Hon. Thomas de Grey. Walsingham was involved in many shooting publications, especially notable being his contribution to the Badminton Library *Shooting* of 1887. His other great interest was lepidoptera and he was reputed to have one of the biggest collections in the world. He owned about 19,000 acres at Merton Hall, Thetford and his entry in *Who's Who* of 1906 under 'Recreation' states 'is a famous shot – his bag of 1,070 grouse to his own gun has never been surpassed; contributed the articles on the grouse, the pheasant and the partridge to the Badminton Library…'. Like the Marquess of Ripon, Walsingham favoured Purdey hammer guns.

Other famous shots referred to as excellent shots by their

Lord Walsingham, 1843-1919.

No. 15030, the No. 2 gun of a pair of 12-bore hammer ejector guns tested on 24 July 1894 and sold to Sir Harry Stonor in May 1895. This gun has sideclips, isolated locks, Whitworth barrels and weighs 6lb 10 oz. Harry Stonor was born on 17 November 1859, his mother being the youngest daughter of Sir Robert Peel. He became Gentleman Usher and Groom-in-Waiting to Queen Victoria, King Edward VII and King George V. *(See plate 55 in colour section.)*

Below: The record in the Dimension Book for Nos. 15029/30. Note 'Out in Black 1894', in reference to Harry Stonor testing the guns before they were finally finished. Stocked by Dean and put together by Apted.

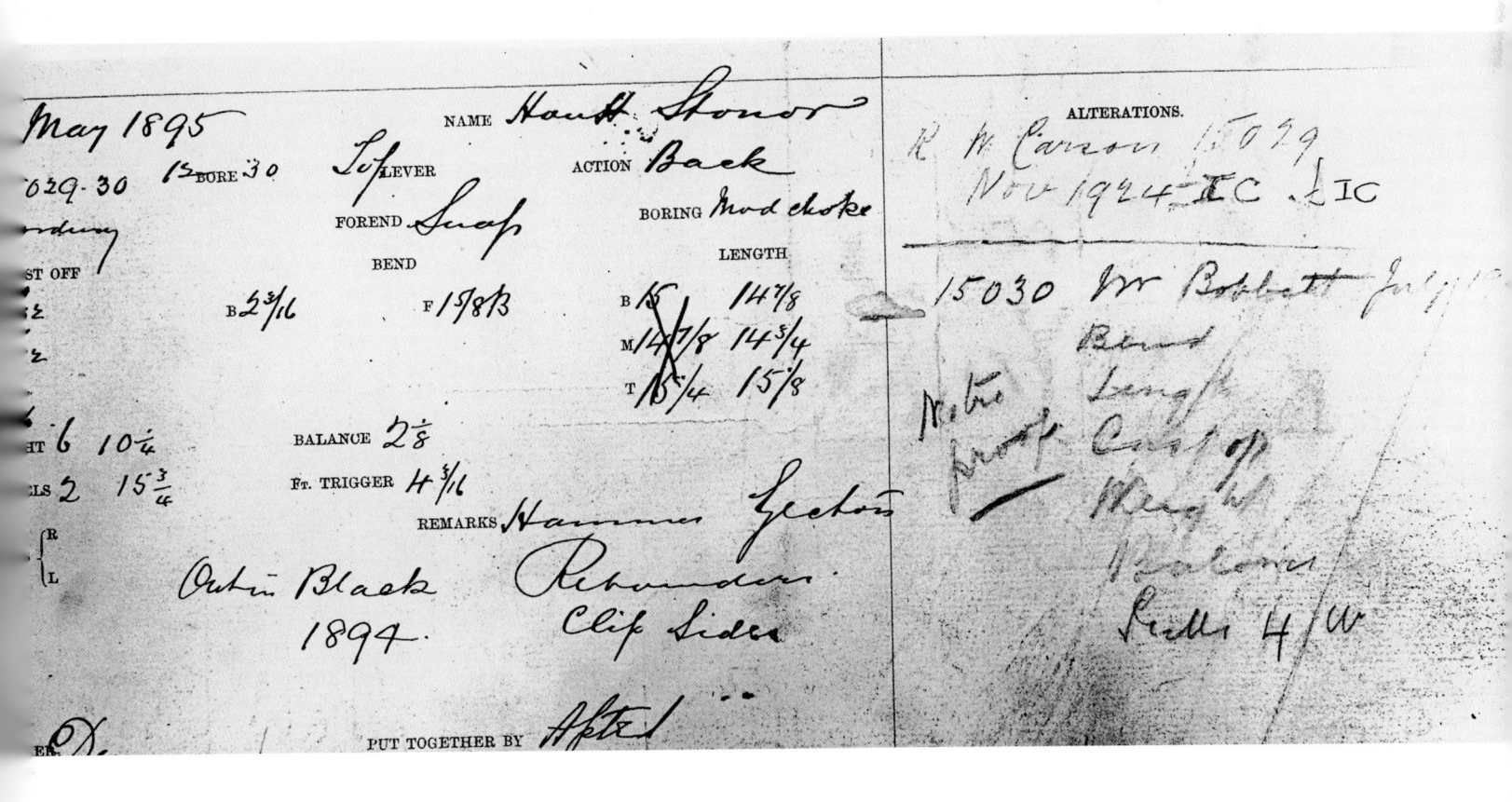

The record in the factory workbook for Nos. 15029/30. Gunmakers were Simons, barrels; Smith, luggers; Smith, levers and detonating; Dean, stocker; Gatrell, ejectors; Sanders, engraving and Apted, finishing.

Sir Harry Stonor with a pair of Purdeys, *circa* 1910.

No 12658, the No. 1 gun of a pair of 12-bore hammerless guns bought by Sir Ralph Payne-Gallwey on 7 July 1887. Payne-Gallwey, born 1848, was the author of many shooting books and an authority on wildfowling. Just before World War I, this gun was re-barrelled by Boss and fitted with their single-trigger. Stocked by H W Johnson and put together by J Apted and W Russell. Note the very unusual detonating.

Lord Ashburton holding his Purdey.

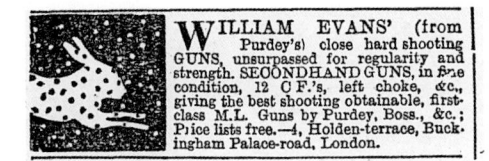

A William Evans advertisement.

King George V with one of his Purdey hammer ejectors.

contemporaries and featuring regularly in Purdey's ledgers, were Lord Ashburton of The Grange, Alresford, Hants; Sir Harry Stonor, Lord Huntingfield of Heveningham Hall, Yoxford; Prince Duleep Singh of Hockwold Hall, Brandon, Norfolk; R.H.R. Rimington-Wilson of Broomhead Hall, Sheffield, and Sir Ralph Payne-Gallwey of Thirkleby Park, Thirsk. And, of course, there was the Duke of York, later King George V, another sportsman who had a liking for Purdey hammer ejector guns (see plate 88).

These well-known shots, using Purdey guns, were of considerable significance to Purdey's. Building guns for most of European royalty gave the firm great pedigree and doing the same for the notable shots assured sportsmen that Purdey's were renowned for quality and reliability. In the era before the carnage and death of World War I, big bags were impressive and as many types of sportsmen are revered and respected today, those shooters and their prowess were emulated by others. Their feats were recorded and lauded by the press and since most used Purdey guns the name of Purdey achieved great status.

In 1897, Athol Purdey lodged his first patent 'An Improved Hand Protector for Sportsmen', patent no. 19027 of 17 August 1897 (see Appendix 8). He produced a padded left-hand glove to protect the hand holding the barrels from heat build-up due to rapid fire.

> I construct the sportsmen's left-hand glove with protecting pads at such parts of the fingers and thumb as will enable the sportsmen to grasp the gun firmly, notwithstanding the acquired heat of the barrel.

As production continued to increase in the late 19th century, more gunmakers had to be employed. There were 87 in 1889, 96 in 1894 and 108 by 1902, employed both in Audley House and in the factory at 37 North Row (until 1900) and at No. 2 Irongate Wharf (after 1900). (See names in Appendix 6.)

One ex-Purdey employee who caused concern was William Evans who was in business as a gunmaker at 4 Holden Terrace, Buckingham Palace Road. He always advertised himself as 'William Evans (from Purdey's).'

Most of the complaints about Evans's use of the Purdey

James Purdey the Younger in 1895.

name came from members of the public. The concern was due to the fact that Evans had never been employed by Purdey's as a gunmaker, but had worked in the shop for a very short time. A typical letter is quoted below, dated 22 August 1885, from T Shilston, Newton Abbot:

> Sir, I have in my possession a gun on it is engraved William Evans ('from Purdey's') would you kindly inform me what he was in your employ – I have reason to think not a practical man – but simply a shopman – if so he certainly ought not to make one of your name as is likely to mislead the public. I should be greatly obliged if you would give me the information.

It was the fact that Evans was not a gunmaker that rankled Purdey. Legal advice was taken, but little could be done. Frederick Beesley in the same period used the same terminology; however this did not generate the same rancour as he had worked as a gunmaker at Purdey's for many years.

Following 3 pages: A Purdey wage book of September 1902. Note the very high wage of Lucas, the engraver.

		1902.	SEP 6-1902				SEP 20 1902						OCT 4- 1902			OCT		
			£330			£330			£330			£330			£330			£3
	40/	Apted		2	·		2	·		1	16		2	·		2	·	2
50/	XX/	Anderson		2	4	5	2	7	4	2	7	6	2	6	6	2	7	5	2
		Aston		4	2	6	3	6	6	5	·	·	4	7	4	5	15	5
45/	40/	Bates		2	·		2	·		2	·		2	·		2	·	2
	34/	Barrell		1	14		1	14		1	14		1	14		1	14	1
	30/	Barnard		1	10		1	10		1	10		1	10		1	10	1
	24/	Blogg		1	4		1	4		1	4		1	4		1	4	1
	45/	Bratby		2	5		2	4	8	2	5		2	5		2	5	2
	30/	Bristow		1	10	3	1	10		1	10		1	10		1	10	
	55/	Clarke		2	15		2	13	1	2	15		2	13	1	2	13	2
		Colle		3	8		3	2		4	5		4	·		3	2	3
	38/	Cooper		1	17	4	1	17	4	1	14	8	1	18	·	1	16	1
		Cotton		5	5		2	3	6	5	5	6	5	10	·	3	5	4
		Dean Sen.		3	16	6	2	17	·	2	17	6	3	4	6	3	5	3
		do Jun		4	·	6	3	14	6	4	2	·	4	10	6	3	10	3
	26/	Donald		1	5	2	1	3	8	1	5	7	1	5	2	1	5	2	1
	45/	Edwards		2	5	6	2	5	·	2	5	·	2	5	·	2	4	3	2
		Field		3	7		3	11		3	10	·	4	3	6	3	17	6	3
		Fudalove		6	4		5	·		5	4	4	5	18	6	6	7	6	6
	43/	Flavell		2	13		2	·		2	2	3	2	12	6	2	1	6	2
		Gatrell		5	4		·	·		2	7	6	4	4	·	4	5	6	4
	35/	Gerrard		1	15		1	15		1	15		1	15		1	15	1
	30/	Gorman		1	8	6	1	8		1	7	·	1	8	·	1	8	1
	45/	Griffiths		2	16	6	2	10	11	2	11	4	2	1	6	2	7	2
	45/	Hawkes		2	3	10	2	5	·	2	5	·	2	5	·	2	5	2
		Henson		1	16	5				2	14	·	2	·	4	1	7	10	1
		Hill		3	6	6	3	9		3	10	6	3	18	·	3	7	3
		Hodges		3	5		2	3	6	2	·	·	3	7	6	2	2	6	2
	45/	Homer		2	5		3	·		2	5	·	2	5	·	3	5	·	2
	50/	Hopewell		2	10		2	10		2	10		2	10	·	2	10	2
		Horsley		4	4		3	·	6	1	11	·	3	6	6	2	10	3
		Hughes		5	11	6	4	1	·	4	6	·	5	8	·	5	16	6	5
		Johnson		3	8	6	3	2	6	3	6	·	3	10	·	3	1	6	3
		do Jun		4	7	10				2	·	·	2	15	·	2	17	·	3
	24/	Kippen		1	4		1	4		1	4	·	1	4	·	1	4	1
	35/	Horscroft		1	15		1	15		1	15	·	1	15	·	1	15	1
	40/	Lane		2	·		1	3	4	·	·	·	1	·	·	2	·	2
		Carried forward		105	15	9	83	5	4	92	11	2	101	10	5	97	7	5	98

	1902.	SEP 6-1902	SEP 1902	SEP 20 1902	SEP 1902	OCT 4-1902	OCT 1
		£330	£330	£330	£330	£330	£3
	Brot forward	106 159	83 5 4	92 11 2	101 10 5	97 7 5	98
50/-	Lawrence	√ 2 10	√ 2 9 2	√ 2 10	√ 2 10	√ 2 9 3	√ 2
45/-	Leeper Sen	√ 2 4 8	√ 2 4 8	√ 2 5	√ 2 5	√ 2 5	√ 2
28/-	do W.	√ 1 8	√ 1 8	√ 1 8	√ 1 8	√ 1 8	√ 1
27/-	do A.	√ 1 3 4	√ 1 7	√ 1 7	√ 1 6 7	√ 1 7	√ 1
55/-	Leggett Sen	√ 2 15	√ 2 15	√ 2 15	√ 2 15	√ 2 12 8	√ 2
	do Jun	√ 3 6 6	√ 2 17	√ 2 17 6	√ 9 19	√ 2 6 3	√ 2
	Lucas	√ 7 3	√ 8 6 6	√ 8 2 6	√ 7 7	√ 7 9	√ 8
	Lumsden Sen	√ 5 3 6	√ 3 18 6	√ 4 9	√ 4 4 6	√ 4 9	√ 6
	do Jun	√ 2 10	√ 2 10	√ 1 5	√ 4 19	√ 1 14	√ 2
45/-	Macfarlane	√ 2 5	√ 2 5	√ 2 5	√ 2 5	√ 2 5	√ 2
	Matthews	√ 3 14	√ 3 17	√ 3 17	√ 3 17	√ 3 11 9	√ 3
	Maddox	√ 2 12	√ 2 10	√ 2 16	√ 3 13	√ 3 9	√ 2
3/-	Mayo	√ 1 18	√ 1 14	√ 1 16 8	√ 1 17 8	√ 1 11 8	√ 1
55/-	Meers A	√ 2 15	√ 2 12	√ 2 15	√ 2 15	√ 2 15	√ 2
	" H.	√ 3 3	√ 3 5	√ 1 8 6	√ 4 16 8	√ 1 19	√ 3
31/-	Murray Sen	√ 1 11 3	√ 1 11	√ 1 11	√ 1 11	√ 1 11	√ 1
35/-	do Jun	√ 1 15	√ 1 15	√ 1 15	√ 1 15	√ 1 15	√ 1
	Nobbs W	√ 6 2	√ 6 8	√ 6 4	√ 6 8	√ 6 14	√ 6
45/-	do Wesley	√ 2 5	√ 2 4 3	√ 2 5	√ 2 5	√ 2 5	√ 2
	do S	√ 4 11	√ 2			√ 4 2 6	√ 4
	do J.	√ 2 10	√ 2 12 6	√ 2 10	√ 3	√ 2 12	√ 2
	Page	√ 3 10	√ 2 5	√ 2 10 8	√ 3	√ 4 3	√ 2
32/-	Palmer	√ 1 12	√ 1 12	√ 1 9 3	√ 1 12	√ 1 12	√ 1
	Phillips	√ 4 6	√ 3 8	√ 2 6 6	√ 3 16 6	√ 3 11 6	√ 3
45/-	Pike	√ 2 5	√ 2 5	√ 2 5	√ 2 5	√ 2 5	√ 2
45/-	Prentice J.	√ 2 10 4 5	√ 1 6	√ 1 5 1	√ 1 4 2 17	√ 1 12 9	√ 1
40/-	do R.	√ 1 16 8	√ 1 11 4	√ 1 18	√ 1 18	√ 1 18 4	√ 1
3/-	Price	√ 1 11 2 3 6	√ 1 11	√ 1 11	√ 1 10 6	√ 1 11	√ 1
32/-	Purvis	√ 1 12	√ 1 12	√ 1 12	√ 1 12	√ 1 12	√ 1
45/-	Roberts	√ 2 4 3	√ 2 5	√ 2 5	√ 2 4 3	√ 2 1	√ 2
	Robins	√ 4 5 6	√ 3 18 9	√ 3 9	√ 3 16	√ 4 6 6	√ 3
35/-	Rouse	√ 1 15 8 9	√ 1 12	√ 1 13 2	√ 1 15	√ 1 15	√ 1
50/-	Rose	√ 2 9 7	√ 2 10	√ 2 8 3	√ 2 9	√ 2 5	√ 2
45/-	Russell	√ 3 11 3	√ 2 16	√ 2 17 9	√ 2 16	√ 3	√ 2
	Simons	√ 3	√ 2	√ 3 10 6	√ 5 8	√ 5 2 6	√ 4
35/-	Smith C	√ 1 15	√ 1 15	√ 1 15	√ 1 15	√ 1 15	√ 1
	Carried forward	210 3 1	195 4 8	181 11 10	203 14 11	194 13 5	201

	1902.	SEP 6 1902	SEP 13 1902	SEP 20 1902	SEP 27 1902	OCT 4 1902	OCT 11 1902
		£330	£330	£330	£330	£330	£330
	Brot forwd	210 3 1	175 14 8	181 11 10	203 17 11	194 13 5	201 10 7
	Smith F.	4 2 6	3 6 ·	1 16 ·	4 14 6	4 1 ·	2 14 6
	Sparrow	3 12 ·	3 1 ·	2 15 6	2 14 ·	· · ·	2 17 ·
50/	Standley	2 5 8	2 10 ·	2 10 ·	2 10 ·	2 10 ·	2 10 ·
35/	Taylor F.	1 15 ·	1 15 ·	1 15 ·	1 15 ·	1 15 ·	1 15 ·
	do J	3 13 ·	3 5 ·	3 18 9	3 18 ·	· · ·	6 12 ·
	do E	1 15 6	1 13 6	1 13 6	1 13 6	1 13 6	1 16 ·
	Thompson	6 15 6	· · ·	3 · ·	4 · 6	4 15 6	5 16 6
	Warren Sen	3 1 2	2 18 3	2 9 7	2 18 8	3 15 10	2 13 3
46/	do Jun.	2 6 ·	2 6 ·	2 6 ·	2 6 ·	2 6 ·	2 6 ·
	Williams	3 14 ·	3 5 ·	4 1 ·	3 5 ·	4 3 ·	2 8 ·
45/	do Jun.	2 5 ·	2 5 ·	2 5 ·	2 5 ·	2 5 ·	2 5 ·
50/	Wilkes C	2 10 6	2 2 ·	1 5 ·	2 10 ·	2 3 ·	2 10 ·
52/	do W.	2 12 ·	2 12 ·	2 12 ·	2 12 ·	2 12 ·	2 12 ·
30/	do W Jun	1 9 ·	1 9 9	1 10 ·	1 9 ·	1 6 ·	1 8 ·
	Wilkin	3 13 ·	4 19 ·	5 5 10	· · ·	3 18 6	16 5 1
	Wheatley	4 · ·	4 · ·	8 · ·	· · ·	· · ·	4 · ·
	Butler	4 · ·	4 · ·	4 · ·	4 · ·	4 · ·	4 · ·
	Clarke	2 5 ·	2 5 ·	2 5 ·	2 5 ·	2 5 ·	2 5 ·
	Nash	2 5 ·	2 5 ·	2 5 ·	2 5 ·	2 5 ·	2 5 ·
	Page	3 · ·	3 · ·	3 · ·	3 · ·	3 · ·	3 · ·
	Tilson	3 15 ·	3 15 ·	3 15 ·	3 15 ·	3 15 ·	3 15 ·
	Ward	1 15 ·	1 15 ·	1 15 ·	1 15 ·	1 15 ·	1 15 ·
21/	Clarke G.	1 1 ·	17 6	1 1 ·	1 1 ·	1 1 ·	1 1 ·
22/	Field	1 2 ·	1 2 ·	1 2 ·	1 2 ·	1 2 ·	1 2 ·
22/20/	Hamilton	1 1 ·	1 1 ·	1 1 ·	1 1 ·	1 1 ·	1 1 ·
24/	Johnstone	1 4 ·	1 4 ·	1 4 ·	1 4 ·	1 4 ·	1 4 ·
18/6	Middlemas	17 10	17 2	17 6	17 2	17 ·	17 2
19/	Cole	18 ·	18 4	18 4	18 6	18 2	18 ·
14/	Coasley	13 8	13 10	13 1	13 5	13 ·	13 4
14/	Simpson	13 4	14 ·	14 ·	13 7	14 ·	13 8
50/	Virgo	2 10 ·	2 10 ·	2 18 ·	2 9 7	2 10 ·	2 10 ·
	Mens Book	· · ·	· · ·	· · ·	· · ·	2 · ·	· · ·
	Imbecil	5 · ·	5 · ·	5 · ·	5 · ·	5 · ·	5 · ·
45/	Lawley	· · ·	· · ·	2 5 ·	2 5 ·	2 5 ·	2 5 ·
	Carried forward	293 4 7	255 2 11	266 11 7	276 13 4	270 11 11	286 4 ·

THE SINGLE-TRIGGER PATENT DISPUTE 1906

The lease on the factory at 37 North Row expired in 1900 and new premises were found north-west of Audley Street at 2 Irongate Wharf Road, Paddington, formerly a china warehouse. The street itself was cobbled and was close to Praed Street. Here, the Purdey factory would remain until 1950. The gunmakers always referred to the factory as 'No. 2'. The building was rented from the proprietors of the Grand Junction Canal, which terminated at Paddington Basin, (hence the name Irongate Wharf). Purdey's did some alterations to the building and the gunmakers moved in during 1900. The insurance schedule of 2 June 1900 describes the premises as having:

> ... a 1HP Gas Engine used to work two boring machines, a Milling Machine, a lathe, two portable forges, a gas brazing hearth, sundry lathes and vices, a carpenter's bench and a vice bench, a gas syphon stove for warmth, and a gas stove for heating water on metal lined shelf therein. N.B. Gunpowder and other explosives are allowed to be kept in said workshops, but the Company will not be liable for any loss or damage caused by explosion to the premises hereby insured, but no Cartridges are allowed to be loaded on said premises.

In 1901 Athol's eldest son, James (James IV), aged nine, was sent to Praetoria House School, Folkestone, and in 1905 went on to Winchester College. His younger brother Tom went to West Downs Preparatory School in 1907, aged 10, and likewise went to Winchester College in 1910. Tom Purdey wrote a very detailed diary covering the period 1910-19 giving an excellent account of the family and himself during World War I. He didn't like Winchester and in 1912 transferred to Eton College where he thoroughly enjoyed himself.

Tom wrote an interesting aside in his diary in 1906. 'Boss - v - Purdey – over a single-trigger – we won the case.' A little biased perhaps, but indicative of the interest generated in the single-trigger patent dispute of 1906.

During the early decades of the 19th century, the hammerless gun was perfected. With the ejector mechanism of the late 1880s, any hammerless gun of this period would stand comparison with one produced today. Any further improvements would be additions or refinements. One such addition was the perfection of a single-trigger, whereby a shooter could discharge one barrel after the other using only one trigger. Single-triggers were nothing new, early examples being by James Templeman of Salisbury in patent no. 1707 of 1789 and John Manton of 6 Dover Street in patent no. 2178 of 1797. Most of these early single-triggers did not work properly as the principle was not understood – in any case, they offered few advantages over the muzzle-loader.

With the rapidity of fire now possible in the hammerless gun of the 1880s, gunmakers again looked to the single-trigger to increase the efficiency still further. One suspects that the mechanical problems encountered mounted yet another challenge to gunmakers in the heyday of the proliferation of patents.

Many gunmakers were puzzled as to why, in spite of well thought-out mechanisms, a double discharge took place in single-trigger actions. It then seemed to occur to various gunmakers in the 1880s and 1890s that three pulls were required in single-trigger mechanisms. The first pull discharges one barrel. Due to the recoil, the gun moves backwards and the shooter's finger comes off the trigger. Instinctively the shooter realises this and squeezes causing a second involuntary pull. It was this involuntary pull that had confused gunmakers and caused the double discharge problem. Upon the third pull the second barrel would discharge. To overcome the problem, two methods could be used. In the first method, a delay could be introduced between the firing of the first and second barrel to take account of the second involuntary pull. This is known as the 'delayed action system'. In the second method, 'the three-pull system', there are three distinct pulls, the first pull firing one barrel, the second being the involuntary pull and the third firing the second barrel.

William Nobbs, the actioner who had invented the first Purdey ejector mechanism in 1883, invented the first Purdey single-trigger mechanism in patent no. 13130 of 6 July 1894. As was by now the norm, Purdey bought the patent rights from Nobbs, paying for the patent application and giving Nobbs £5.

William Nobbs's £5 receipt for selling to Purdey the rights to his single-trigger patent no. 13130 of 6 July 1894.

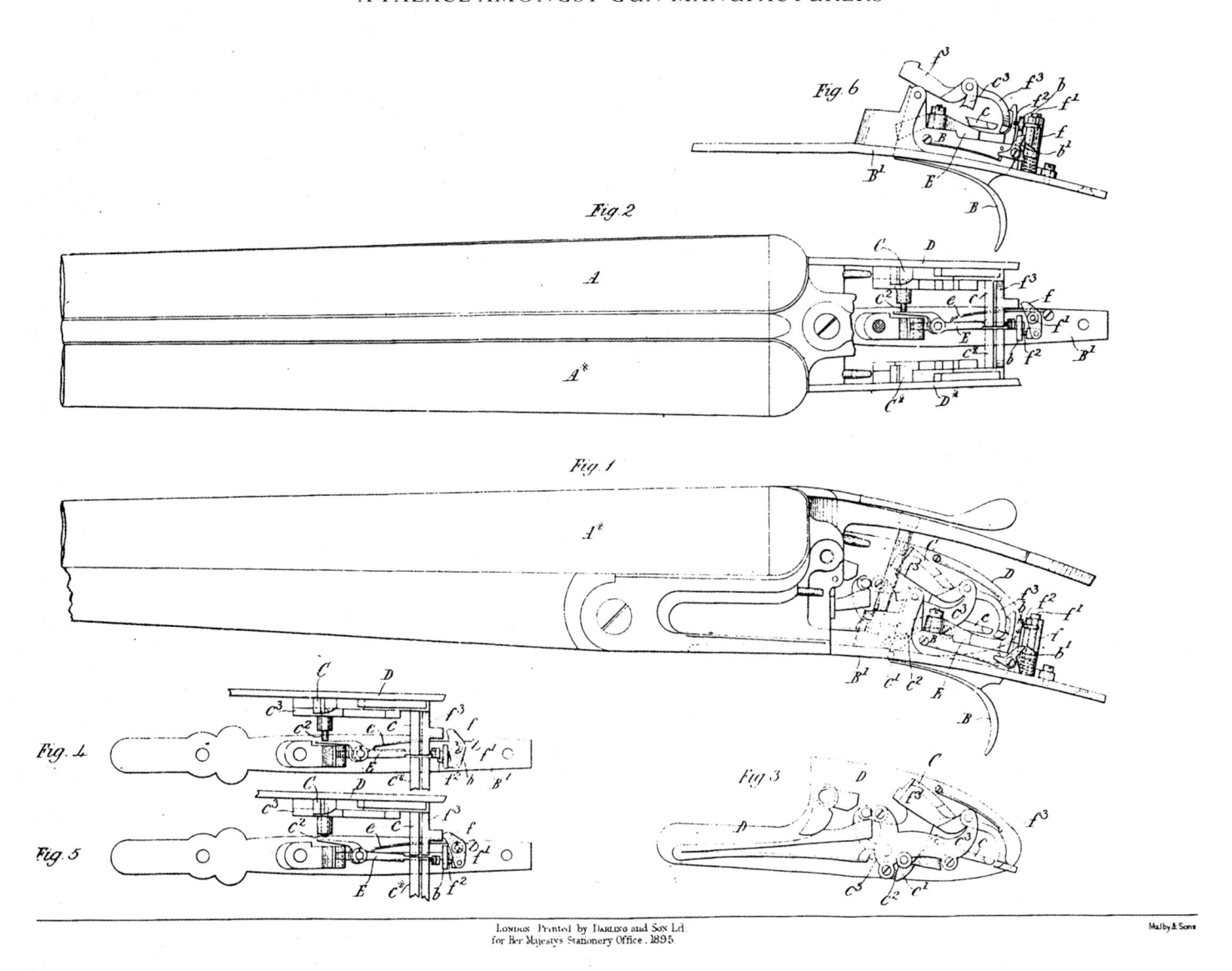

Some drawings from Nobbs's single-trigger patent no. 13130 of 6 July 1894.

Nobbs claimed that his single-trigger was a three-pull system, a fact strongly disputed in the 1906 patent dispute. This is open to question. I would regard it as a delayed action two-pull system, not very satisfactory and very complicated. A particular problem with the patent application was that the draughtsman who produced the drawings, working for Newton the patent agent, was blind and created inaccurate drawings. This fact played a major part in the dispute.

In Nobbs's patent a swinging bar (E) is employed. When the gun is cocked, the bar is under the right sear (c) and safety sear (f3). The swinging bar is held in position by (c2), a small pin attached to the lock tumbler. When the trigger is pulled, the right hand sear rises, the tumbler flies forward taking the small pin (c2) with it and discharges the barrel. The swinging bar is now in a position to the move to the left hand sear. However, to stop the discharge of the second barrel as would now happen on account of the second involuntary pull, the swinging bar is momentarily arrested by a stop. A horizontal rocking bolt (f) has a small bolt (f2) attached to it. As the safety sear (f3) is tripped in the right hand lock together with the ordinary sear (c), a projection on the safety sear will strike the rocking bolt causing the small bolt (f2) to contact the swinging bar to arrest it momentarily. The recoil of the gun (at the same time as the second pull) will cause the small bolt (f2) to disengage allowing the swinging bar to position itself under the left-hand sear ready for the third pull and second discharge. Other methods of arresting the rocking bolt during the second pull were shown in this long complicated patent, including a spring-loaded rod fitted right through the butt to the butt plate.

Purdey's at this time never placed a great deal of importance on the single-trigger believing it to be an unnecessary complication, its disadvantages far outweighing its advantages. Between 1894 and 1910, only three single-triggers are listed in the Dimension Books. They were, however, prepared to take action to protect their patent. On 29 July 1897, they forced John Rigby to pay 2s.6d royalties for every single-trigger Rigby made, as Rigby agreed that they had infringed Nobbs's patent no. 13130 of 1894 with their own patent, Rigby and Atkins patent no. 301 of 1897.

On 26 November 1894, John Robertson of Boss & Co. took out his famous three-pull single-trigger patent no. 22894. This three-pull system won general acclaim and popularity and established Boss as the leading manufacturer of completely reliable single-triggers. John Robertson claimed to be the inventor of the 'first reliable three-pull single-trigger' and was annoyed when Purdey's claimed they had patented such a three-pull trigger in the form of Nobbs's single-trigger some four months earlier than Boss.

There the matter simmered for some time. John Robertson wrote to *The Field* on 9 May 1896:

> As to Mr. Nobbs's patent, if your correspondents think there are three pulls in the mechanism therein described and specified, I should simply ask them to make a gun from the drawings and descriptions, when they will have absolute demonstration of the fact that the patent is decidedly on the two pull and not the three pull system. From the foregoing, I feel myself justified in saying it will be clearly seen that the first patented system of three pulls with a single trigger belongs to John Robertson (Boss & Co.), 73 St. James's Street, London.

The antagonism increased. On 26 September 1905, Purdey's wrote to Boss

> … now comes the point which you may perhaps have overlooked. On July 6th, 1894, or some three or four months before the date of your third patent (No. 22894, 26th November, 1894), Nobbs began his patent no. 13130. If you will examine the specification of this patent, you will see that the principle of the interceptor is there fully enunciated. That being so, it seems to us that instead of your complaining of infringement on our part, you had better consider whether or no you are infringing the patent of Nobbs which takes precedence of your patent as before pointed out…

Wooden models made by John Robertson for the court case in 1906. The lower model is built to Nobbs's patent no. 13130 of 6 July 1894 and the upper model to Robertson's patent no. 22894 of 26 November 1894. Note the patent nos. stamped in the wood on the trigger plate finials.

Nothing could be resolved. On Saturday 15 December 1906, John Robertson took Purdey's to law in the Chancery Division of the High Court for alleged patent infringement of the Boss single-trigger. The case excited considerable interest and contemporary periodicals like *Arms and Explosives*, *The Shooting Times, Land and Water*, etc. reported upon it with gusto. Purdey's were represented by Mr. A J Walker, KC, and Boss by Mr. T Terrell, KC. Robertson made wooden models to show the workings of the two patents.

John Robertson attempted to prove that Nobbs's patent no. 13130, being so poorly drafted, had been altered to a three-pull system like the Boss system, thereby infringing the Boss patent. Purdey's showed that the three-pull system had been invented in 1883 by William Baker, 87 Snow Hill, Birmingham, although he did not patent it because he did not have the money and did not think it would be a commercial success. Baker had made four or five such guns in 1883, some of which were produced in court. Consequently, it was argued, Robertson could not claim to be the inventor of the three-pull system.

It was not until Tuesday 26 February 1907 that Mr. Justice Parker delivered his judgement, which was regarded as being of 'historical importance'. There were two conclusions to the judgement: (1) Nobbs's patent was deemed to be invalid, 'the mechanism they describe being a two-pull mechanism which does not fulfil the object aimed at and is useless'; (2) Although the Baker three-pull system had not been patented in 1883 its existence was known and therefore Robertson could not claim to be the inventor of the three-pull system.

Although Tom Purdey, aged ten, thought otherwise, neither Purdey nor Boss won the case, although costs were awarded to Purdey. Robertson was judged not to have invented the three-pull system and Nobbs's patent was regarded as invalid. Such a conclusion was justified but it was unfortunate that two of the leading gunmakers had such a public disagreement, particularly when John Robertson had worked for Purdey's between 1864 and 1873.

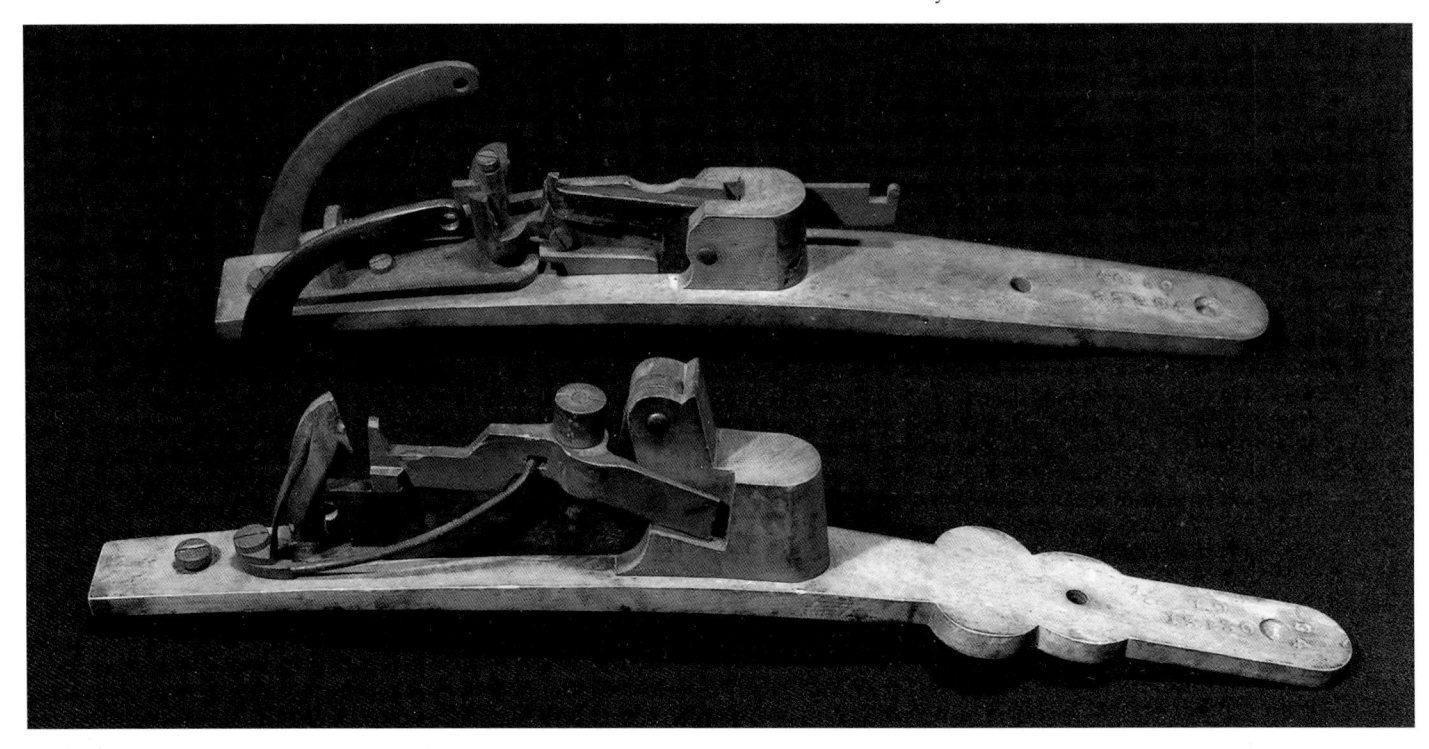

Plate 1 – Single-barrel percussion rifle No. 2932 of 1839.

Plate 2 – James Purdey the Elder, a painting attributed to Sir William Beechey.

Plate 3 – Flintlock sporting gun, No. 14 of 1816/17.

Plate 5 – No. 14 in its original mahogany case.

Plate 4 – The barrel address of No. 14.

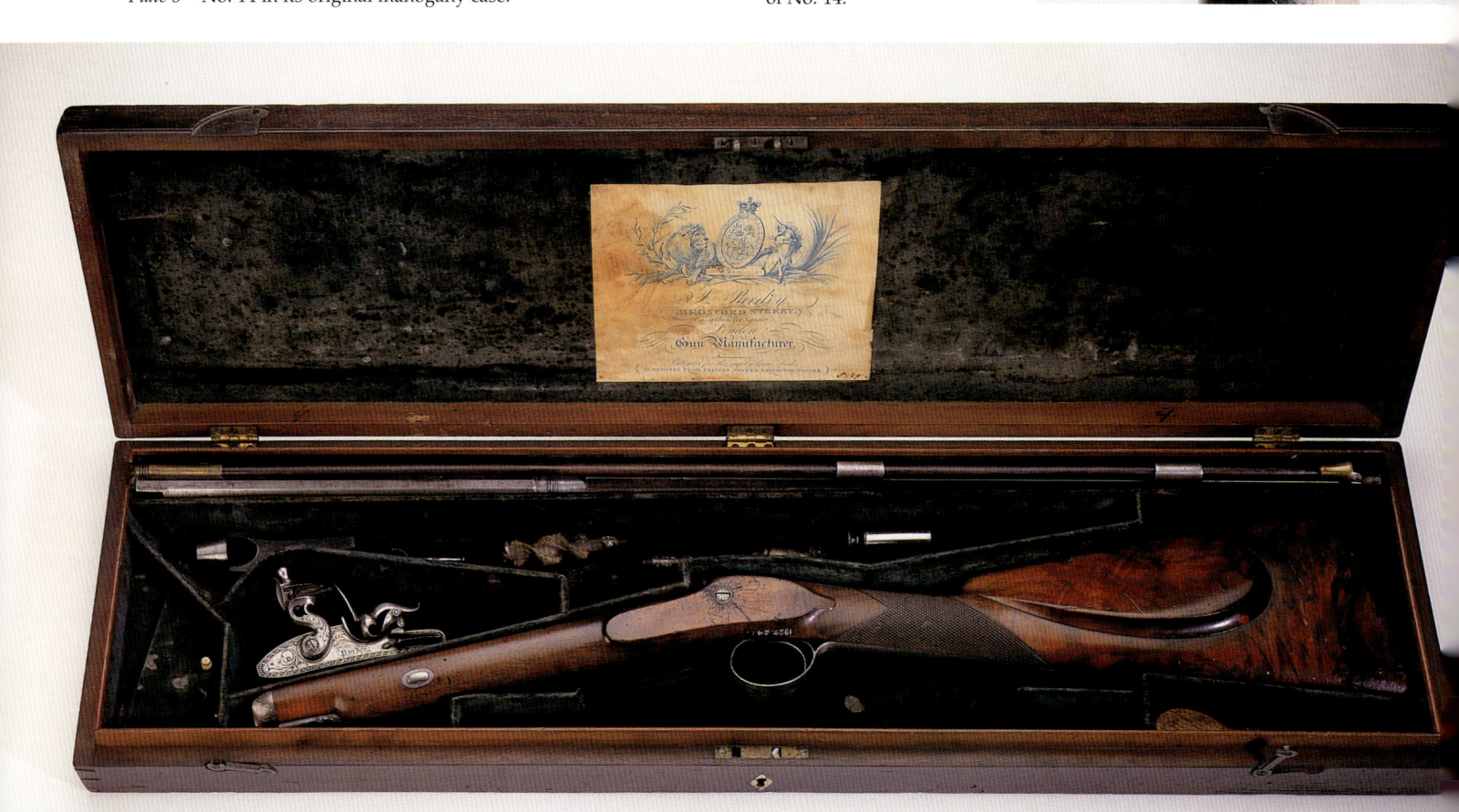

Plate 7 – The breech area of No. 86.

Plate 6 – Flintlock sporting gun No. 86 of 1818.

Plate 8 – Flintlock converted gun No. 287 of 1821.

Plate 9 – Early percussion gun No. 473 of 1823.

Plate 10 – The bird's eye maple stock of No. 473.

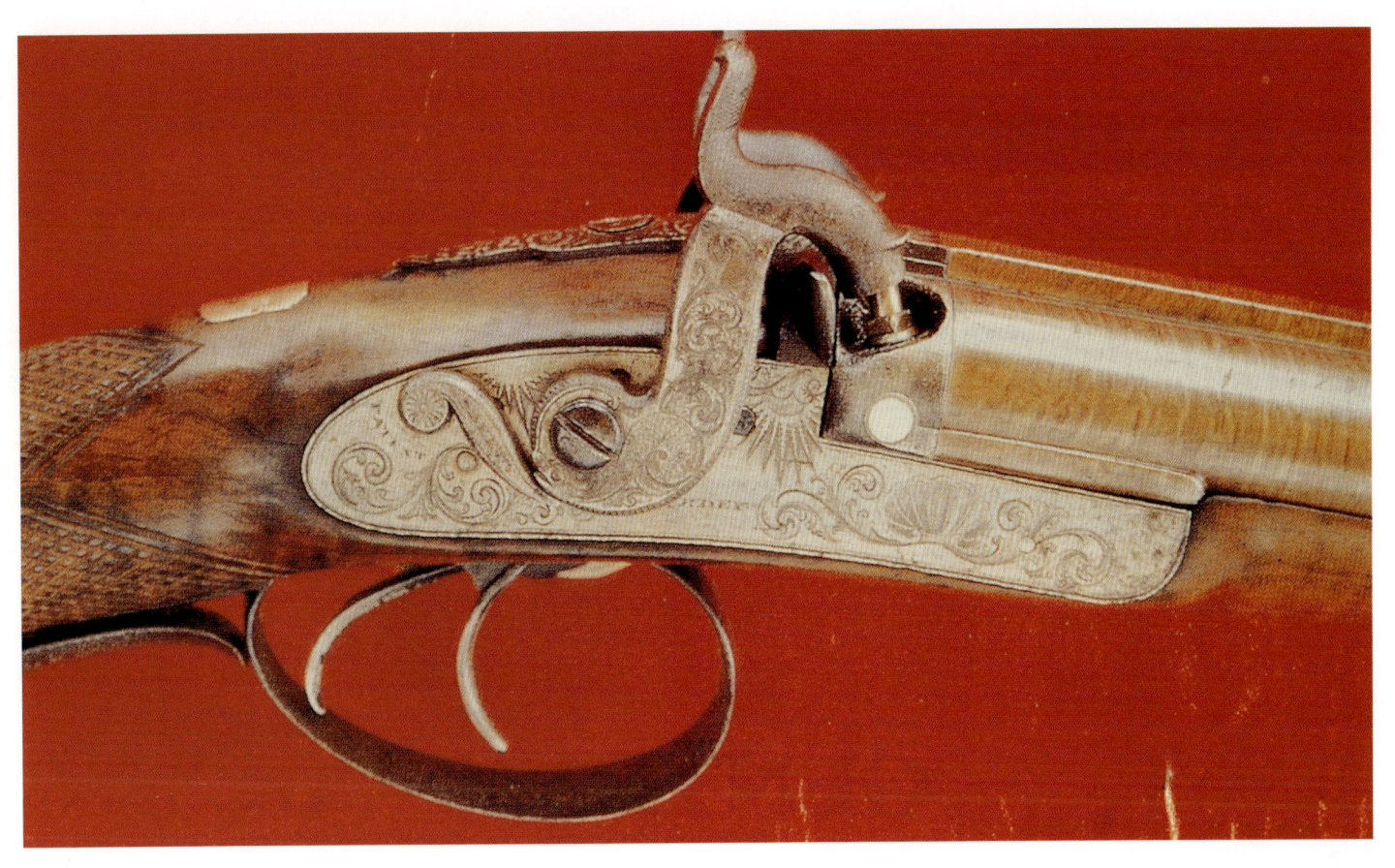

Plate 11 – Percussion gun No. 544 of 1823.

Plate 12 – Pair of percussion pistols Nos. 1629/30 of 1829.

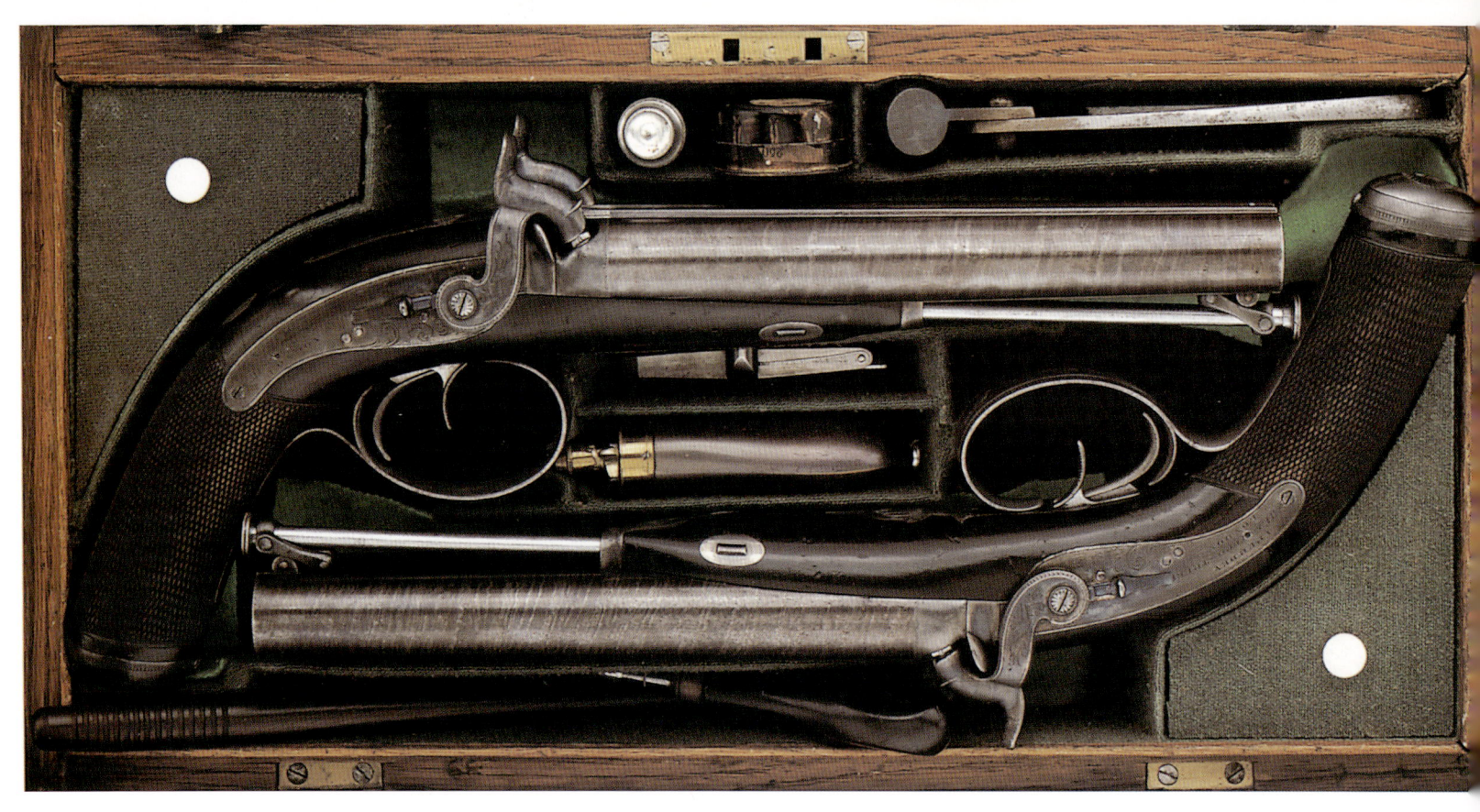

Plate 13 – Pair of double-barrel percussion pistols Nos. 2114/5 of 1831.

Plate 14 – Percussion pistol No. 2320 of 1832.

Plate 15 – No. 3210, a percussion gun built in 1838 converted to centre-fire breech-loader.

Plate 16 – 16-bore percussion rifle No. 3845 of 1844.

Plate 17 – 32-bore percussion Express rifle No. 4826 of 1853.

Plate 18 – Percussion gun No. 14987 of 1894.

Plate 19 – 40-bore percussion Express rifle No. 7463 of 1867.

Plate 20 – Percussion gun No. 7902 of 1869.

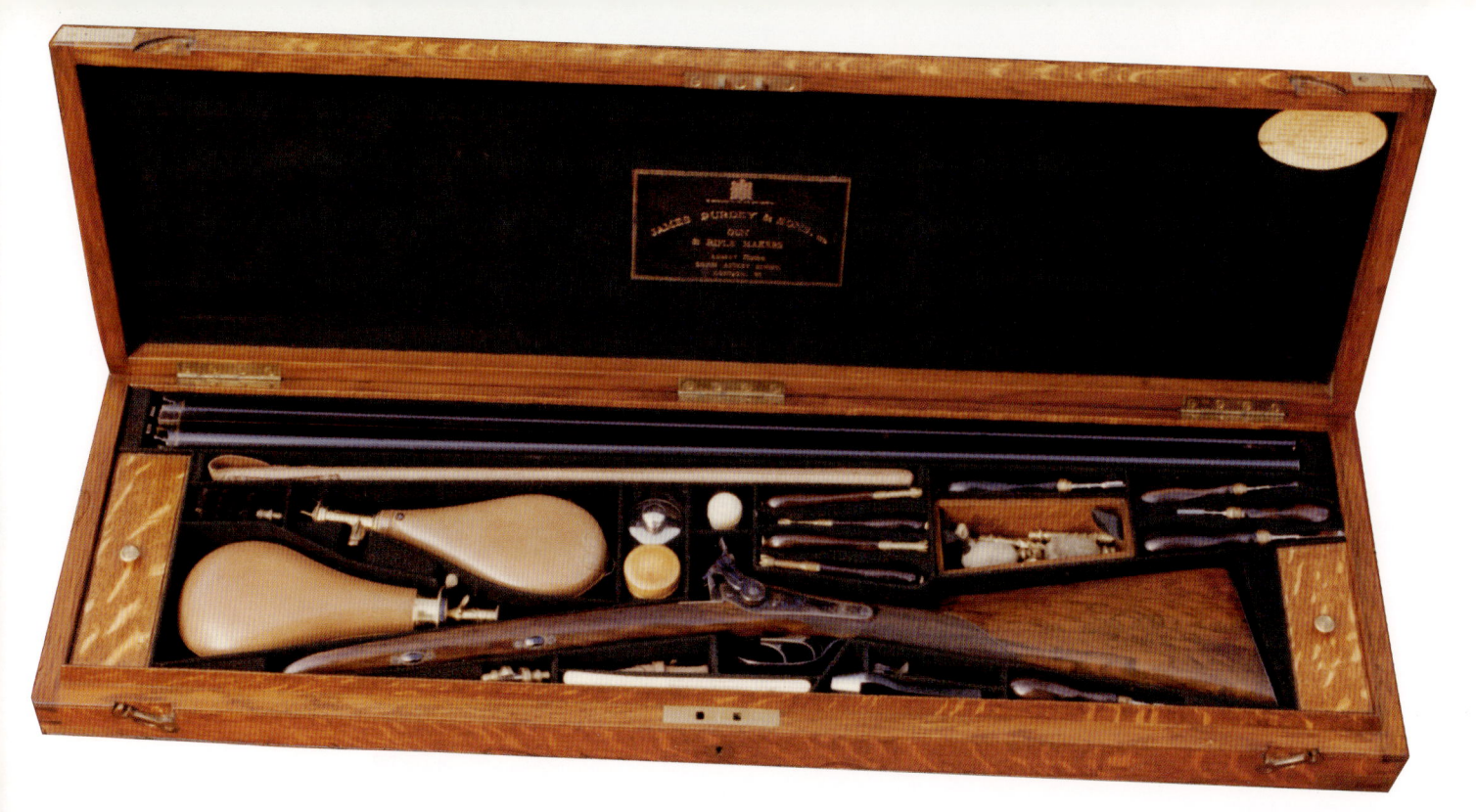

Plate 21 – Percussion gun No. 17766 of 1904.

Below: Plate 22 – The Long Guard Lever on rifle No. 9223 of 1874.

Plate 23 – Bastin pin-fire gun No. 6424 of 1863.

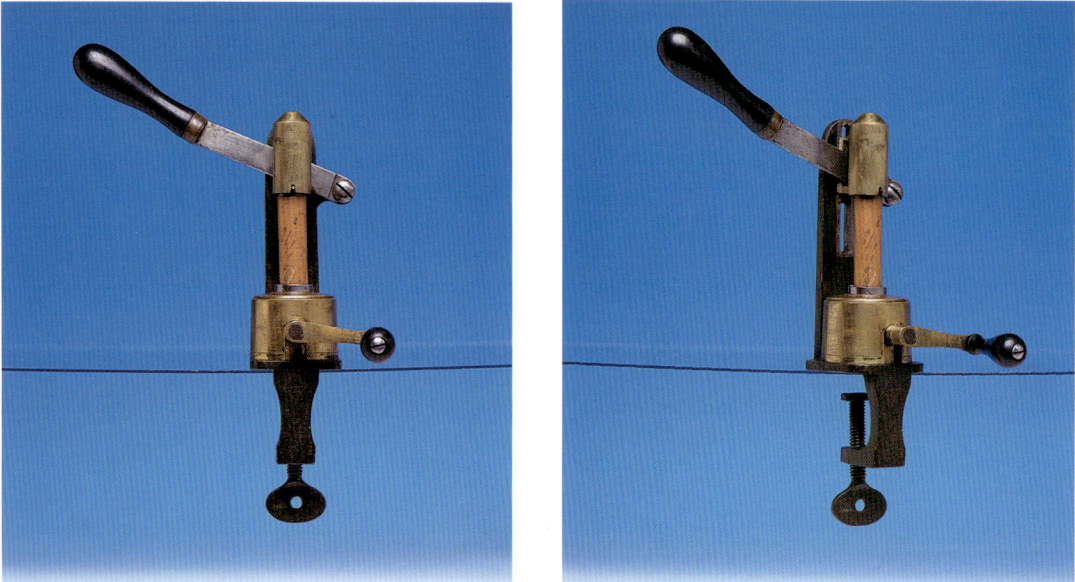

Plates 24 and 25 – Cartridge reloading machine to Purdey patent no. 302 of 1861.

Plate 26 – Pair of bar-in-wood hammer guns Nos. 8998/9000 of 1873.

Plate 27 – Hammer gun No. 7983 of 1869.

Plate 28 – C Quality boxlock hammerless rifle No. 12992 of 1890.

Plate 29 – Pigeon hammer ejector gun No. 22182 of 1922.

Plate 30 – C Quality boxlock hammerless rifle No. 13963 of 1891.

Plate 31 – Purdey/Henry rifle No. 9366 of 1875.

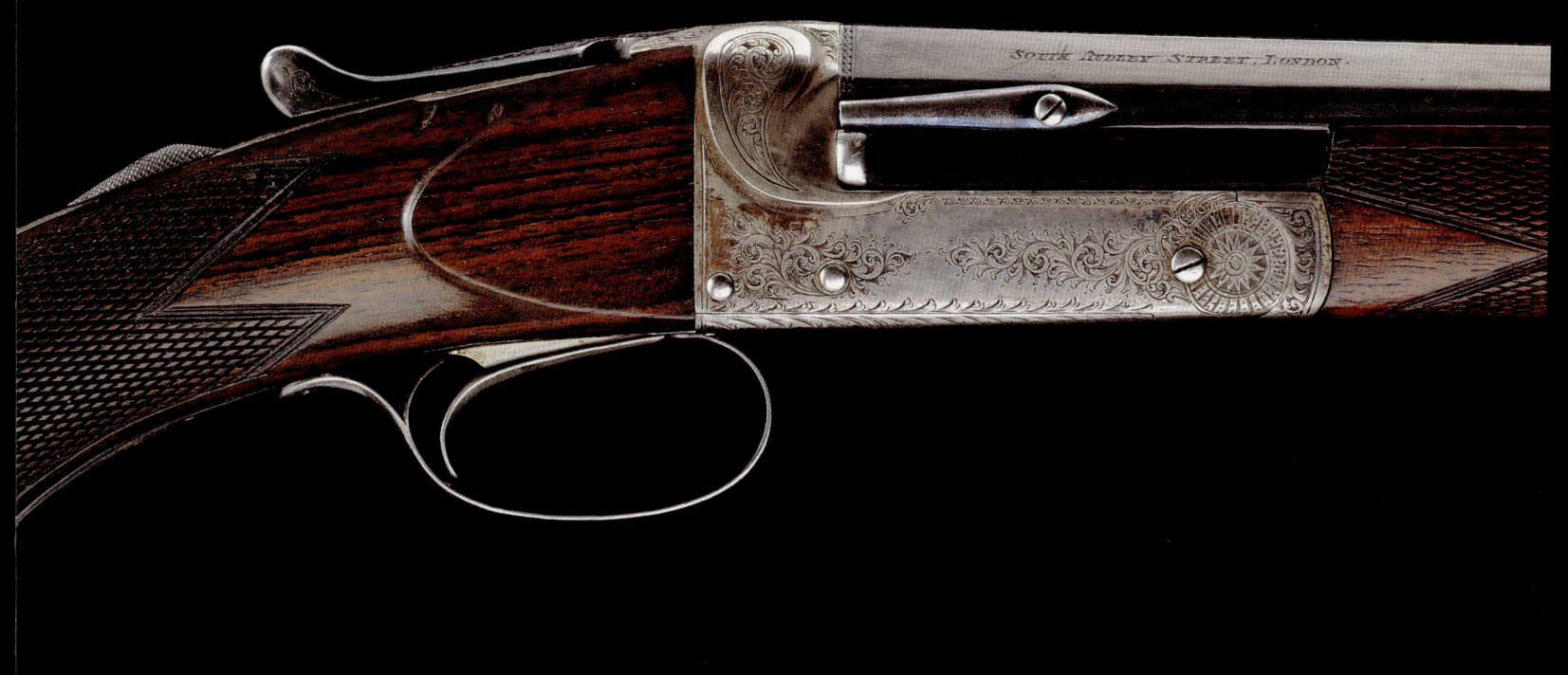

Plate 32 – E Quality hammerless rook rifle No. 17242 of 1901.

Plate 33 – Gold medals won by Purdey in late 19th-century exhibitions.

Plate 35 – Early Beesley hammerless gun No. 11181 of 1882.

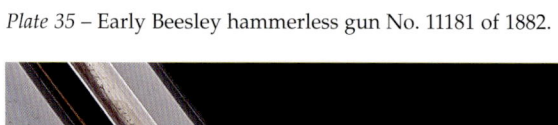

Plate 34 – Hammerless gun No. 10606 of 1879 to William Adams patent.

Plate 36 – 38-bore pin-fire rifle No. 6626 of 1864.

Plate 37 – Bastin pin-fire gun No. 6746 of 1864.

Plate 38 – Pin-fire gun No. 6845 of 1864.

Plate 39 – Pin-fire gun No. 6829 of 1864.

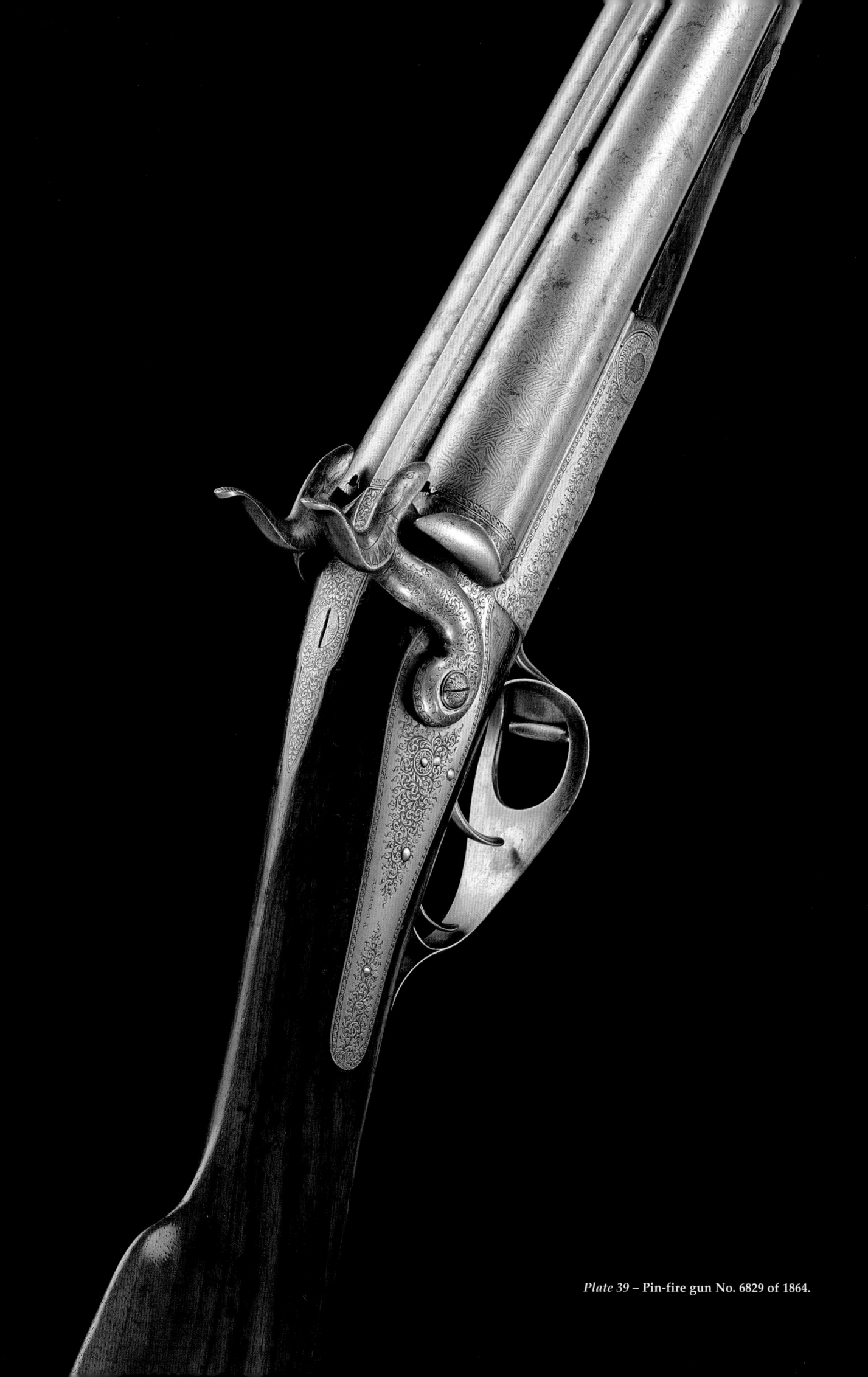

Plate 40 – Early centre-fire gun No. 7225 of 1866.

Plate 41 – Bar-in-wood hammer gun No. 7745 of 1868 in original case.

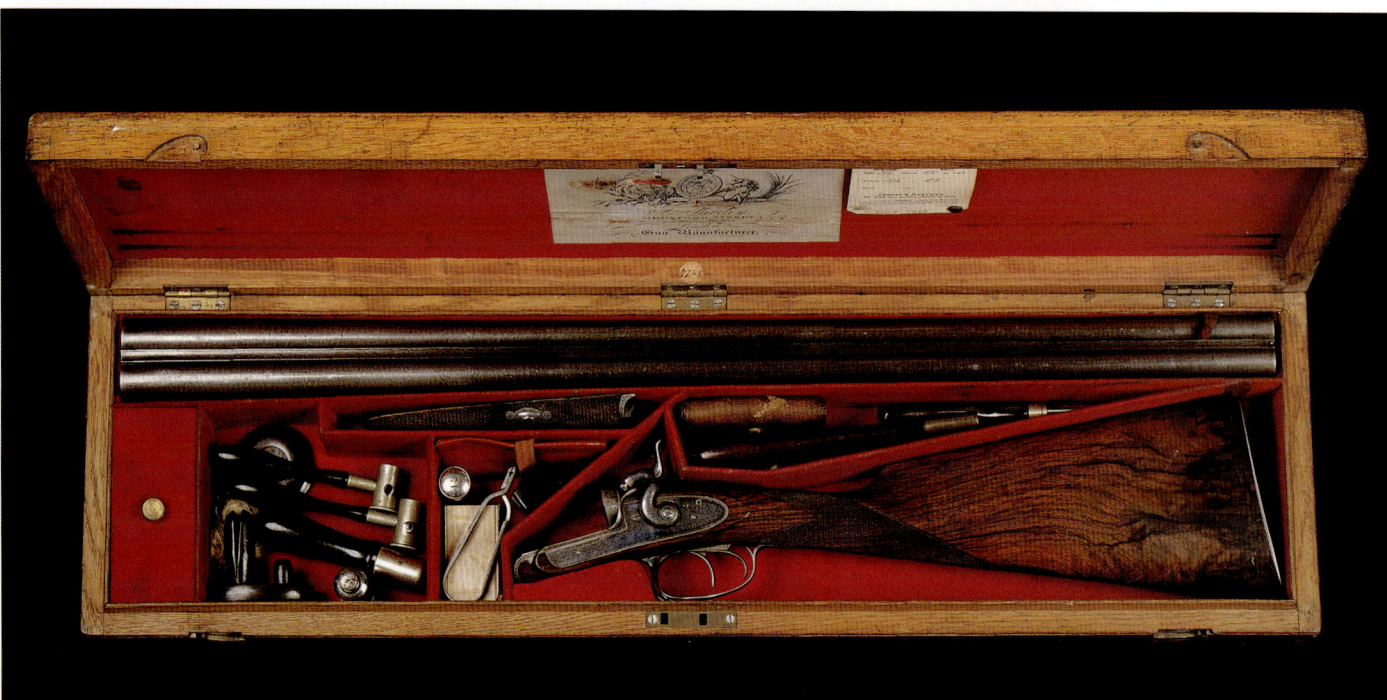

Plate 42 – 10-bore bar-in-wood hammer gun No. 8623 of 1872.

Plate 43 – No. 7745.

Plate 44 – Single barrel .450 rifle No. 9223 of 1874.

Plate 45 – Bar-in-wood hammer gun No. 11090 of 1881.

Plate 46 – 20-bore four-barrel hammerless gun No. 11614 of 1886.

Plate 47 – The action of No. 11614.

Plate 48 – C Quality hammer rifle No. 12022 of 1885.

Plate 49 – 8-bore hammer rifle No. 12371 of 1886.

Plate 50 – No. 12371 in original case.

Plate 51 – E Quality .360 hammer rifle No. 12386 of 1886.

Plate 52 – Audley House, February 2000.

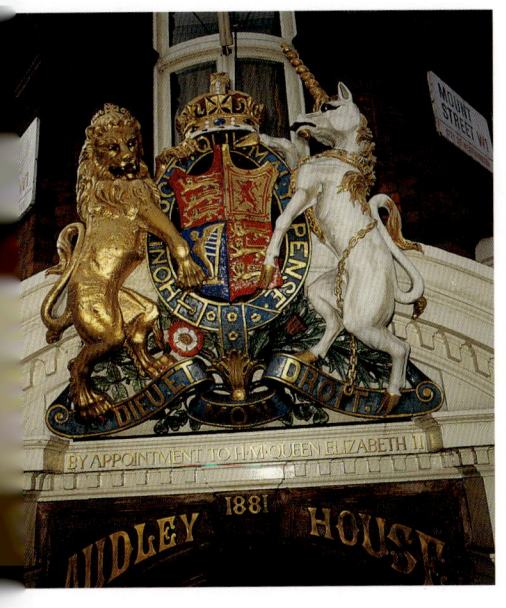

Plate 53 – The royal coat of arms above the front entrance.

Plate 54 – James Purdey the Younger, painted by Archibald Stuart-Wortley, 1891.

Plate 55 – **Sir Harry Stonor's hammer ejector gun No. 15030 of 1894.**

Plate 56 – Earl de Grey's hammer ejector gun No. 14982 of 1894.

Plate 57 – Athol Purdey, painted by Sir Oswald Birley, 1927.

Plate 59 – A Purdey cartridge catalogue 1931.

Plate 58 – The wooden electric gun built for King George V in 1929.

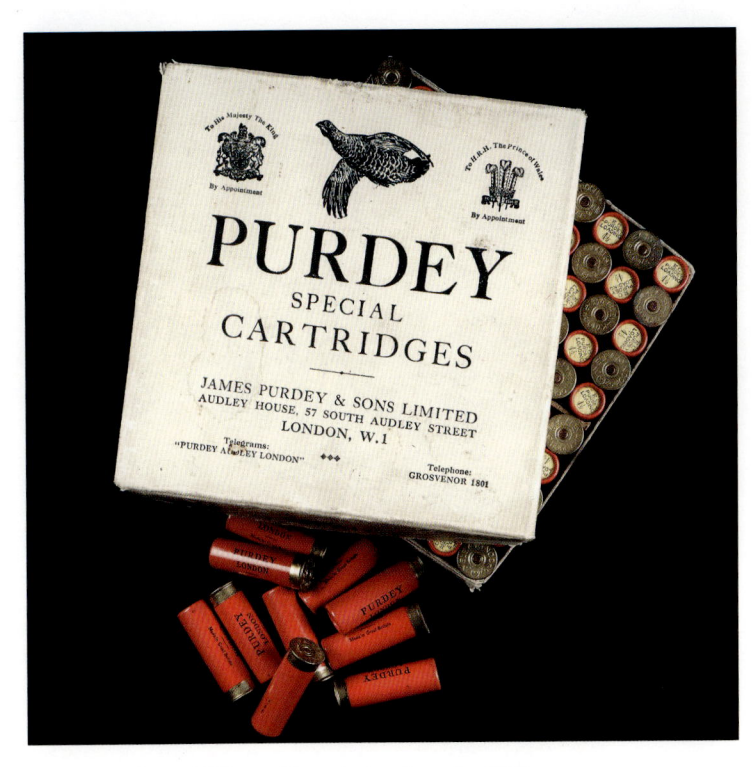

Plate 60 – A box of 100 cartridges dating from the 1930s.

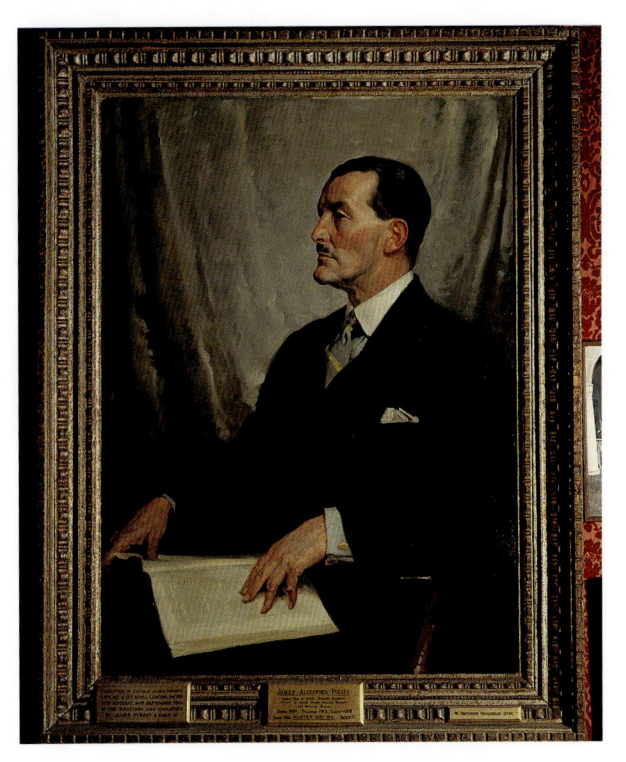

Plate 62 – James Purdey IV, painted by W Smithson-Broadhead, 1941.

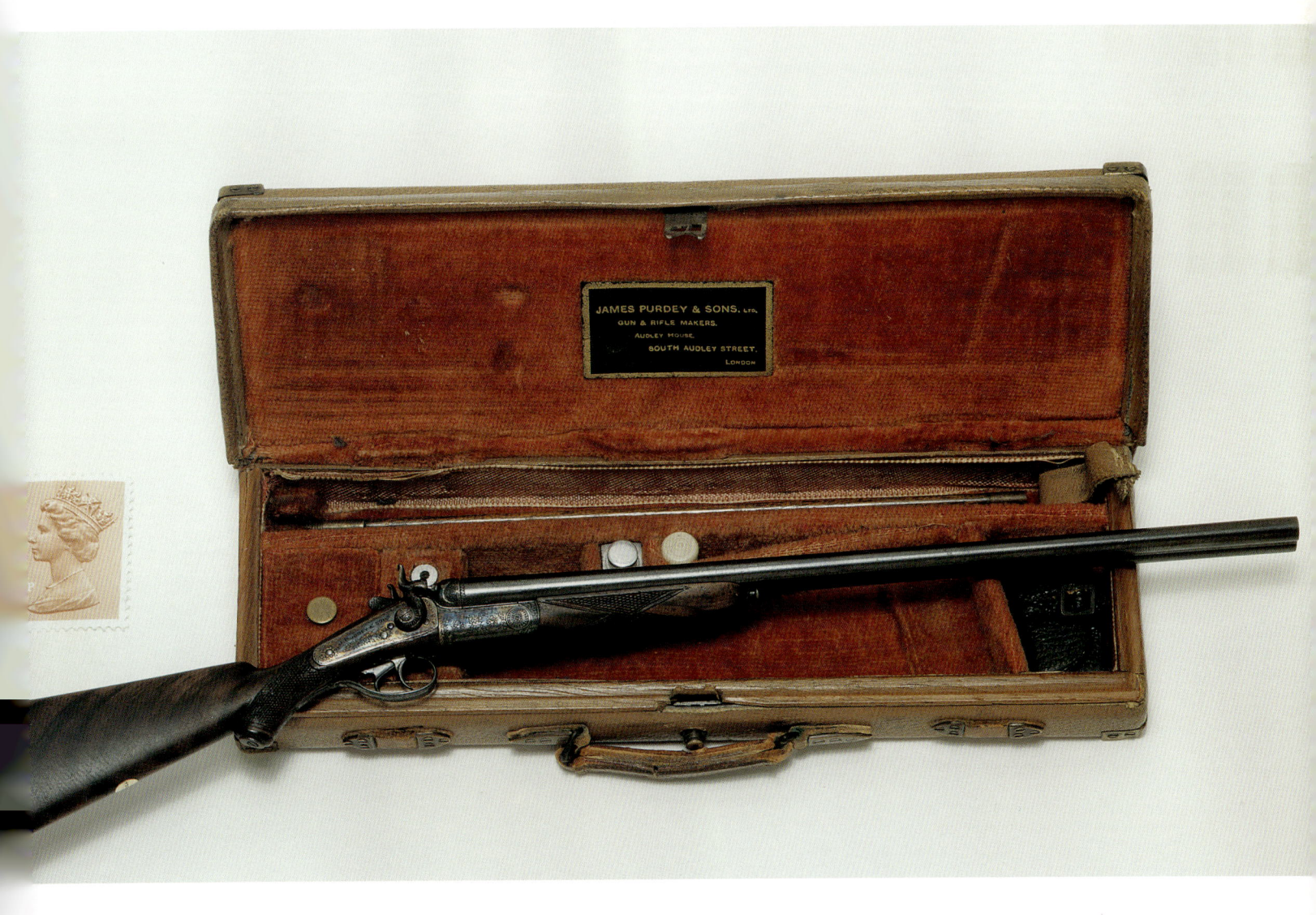

Plate 61 – The third of the miniature hammer guns No. 24707 of 1934/5.

Plate 63 – An early O/U gun No. 26212 of 1951.

Plate 64 – Tom Purdey, painted by Robert Swan, 1959.

Plate 65 – James Oliver Kinloch Purdey, 1918-84.

Plate 66 – Harry Lawrence MBE in the early 1980s.

Plate 67 – Richard Purdey, present chairman.

Plate 68 – Pin-fire gun No. 6829 with its relevant entry in the Dimension Book.

Plate 69 – Robin Nathan in the front shop, March 2000.

Plate 70 – Peter Blaine, Tony Sinnett, Nigel Beaumont, Long Room, March 2000.

Plate 71 – The Indenture of James Purdey the Younger, dated 14th July 1843.

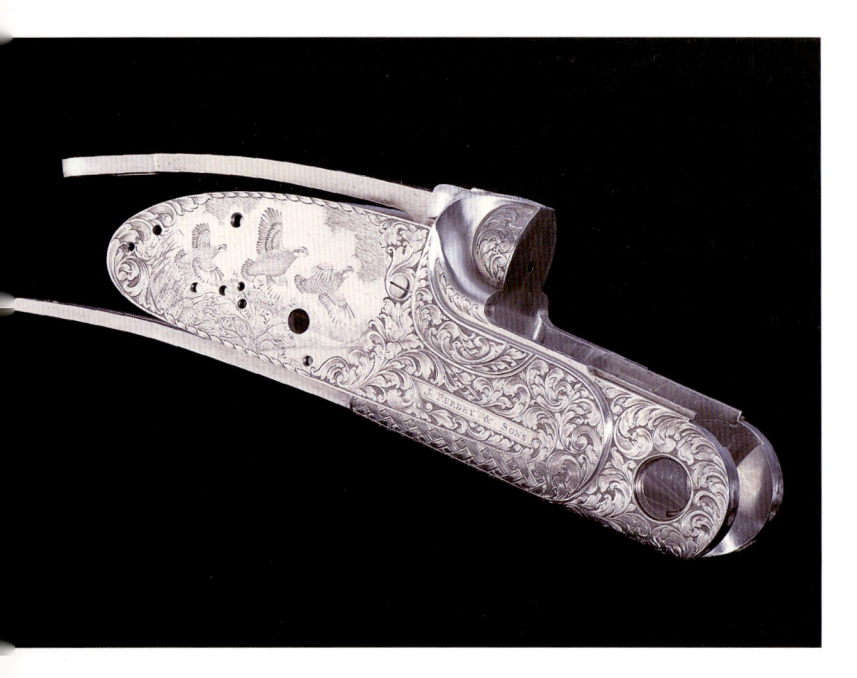

Plate 72 – O/U action No. 29596, engraved by Simon Coggan.

Plate 73 – Action No. 29687, engraved by Simon Coggan.

Plate 74 – Early Beesley gun No. 11837 of 1884.

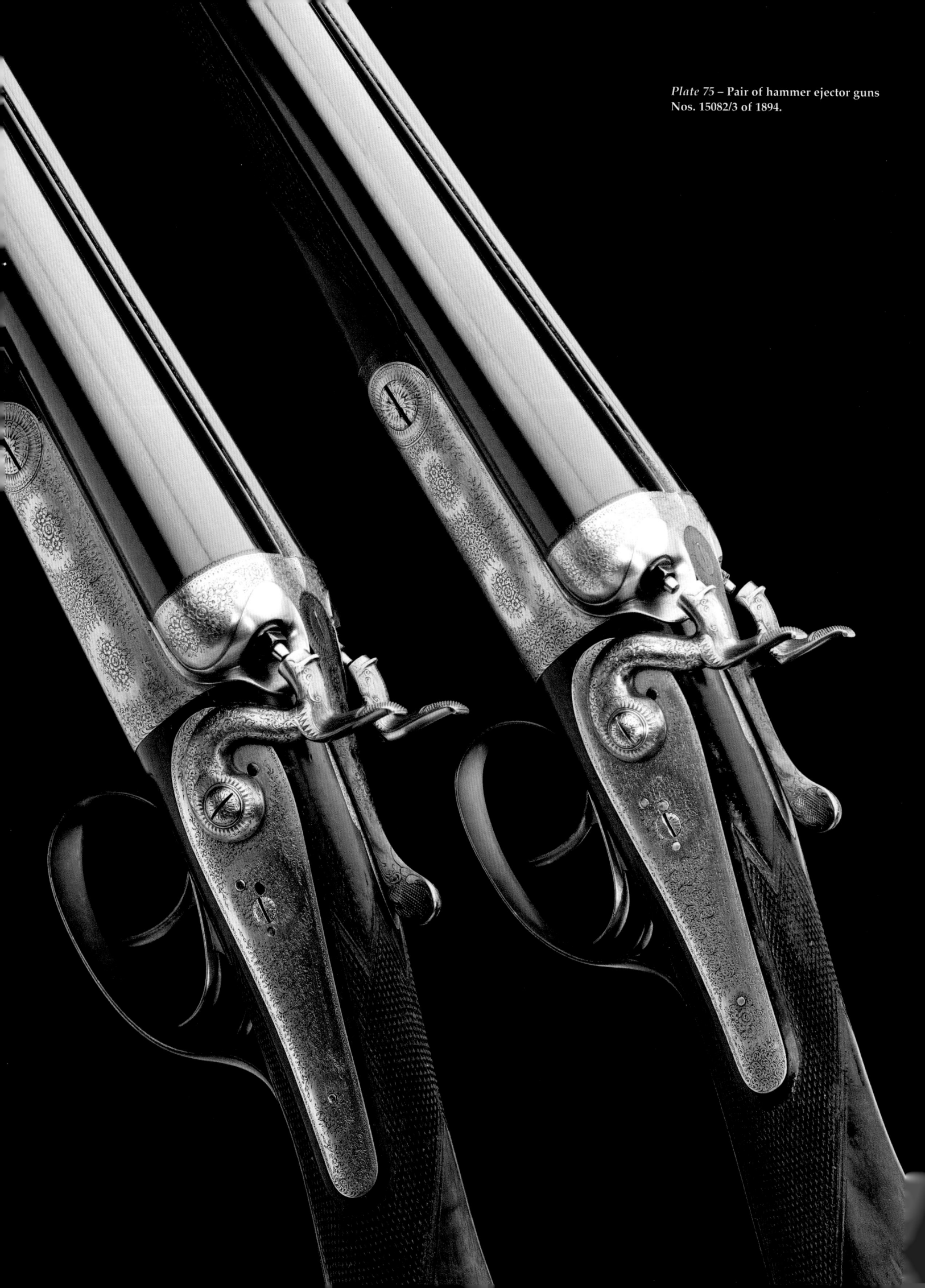

Plate 75 – Pair of hammer ejector guns Nos. 15082/3 of 1894.

Plate 76 – Single-barrel hammerless gun No. 15339 of 1895 in original case.

Plate 77 – No. 15339

Plate 78 – .303 hammerless rifle No. 15451 of 1896.

Plate 79 – Hammer ejector gun No. 15948 of 1897.

Plate 80 – .303 hammerless rifle No. 16472 of 1907.

Plate 81 – Combination gun/rifle No. 19658 of 1909.

Plate 82 – .400 hammerless rifle No. 20785 of 1913.

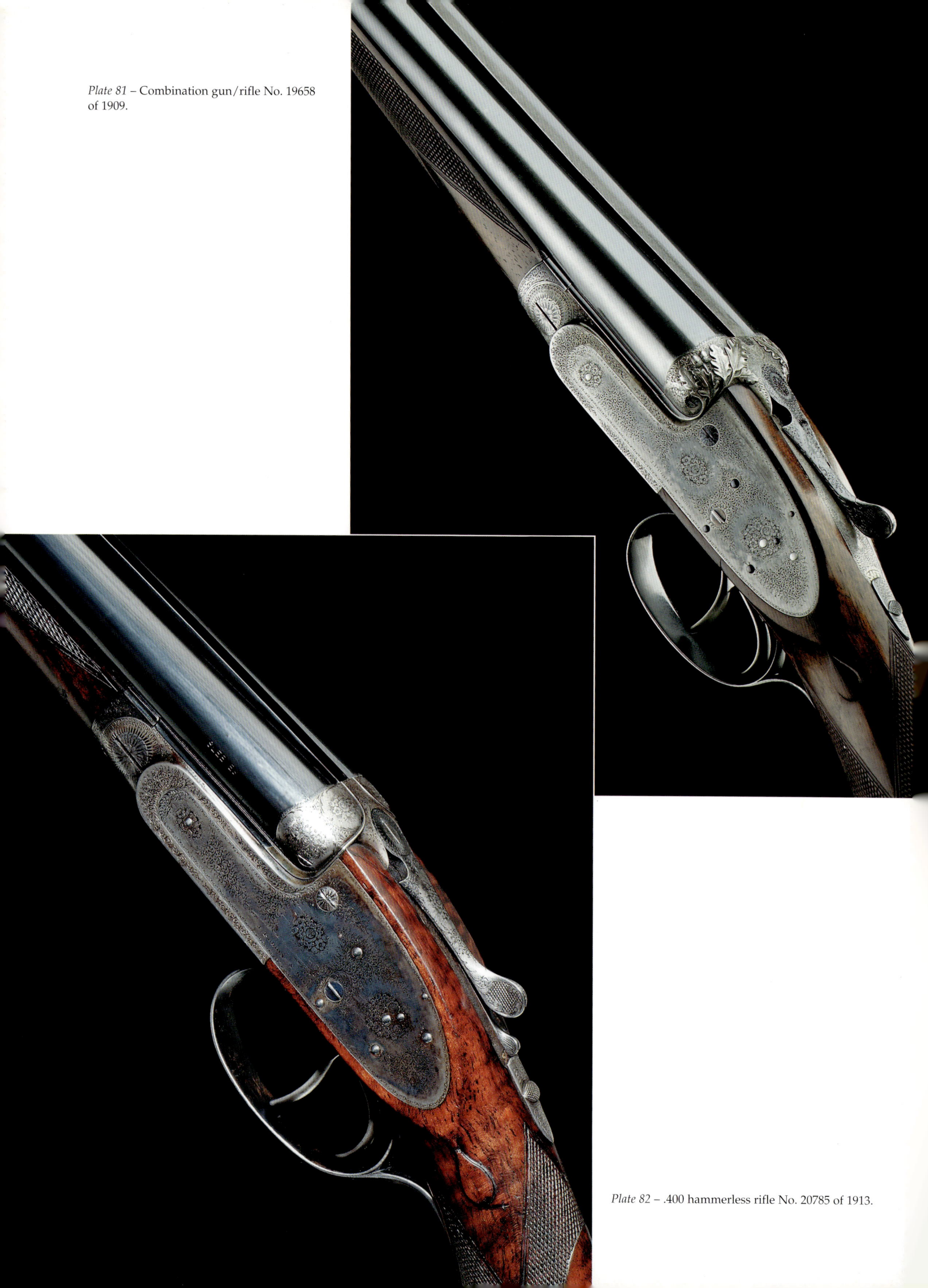

Plate 83 – Hammerless gun No. 20827 of 1913.

Plate 84 – Pair of hammerless guns
Nos. 22349/50 of 1923.

Plate 85 – .450 hammerless rifle with electric night sights No. 23289 of 1927.

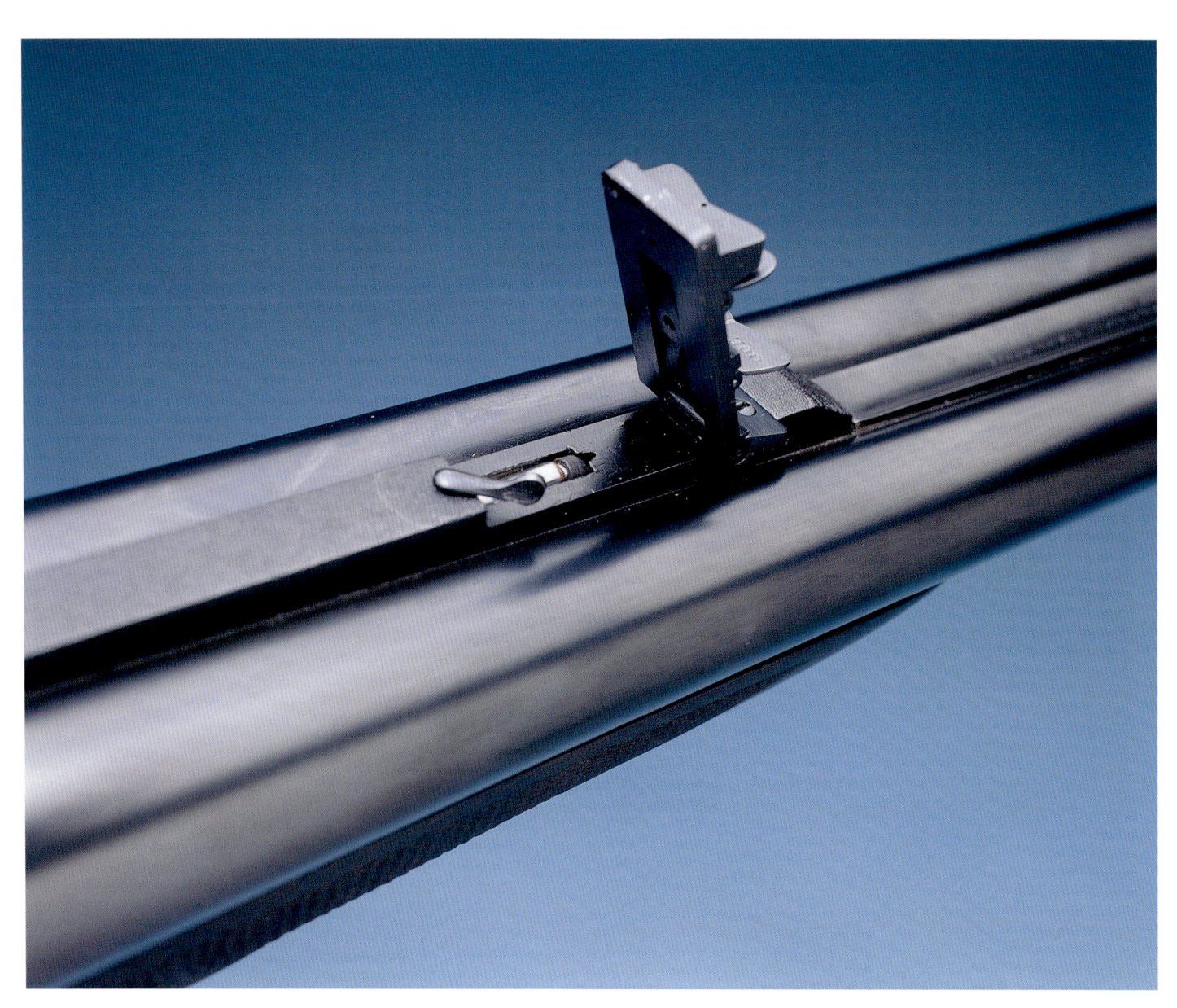

Plate 86 – The electric rear sight of No. 23289.

Plate 87 – Pigeon gun No. 23306 of 1927.

Plate 88 – King George V, 20-bore hammer guns Nos. 23891/2 of 1929.

Plate 89 – Hammerless gun No. 25968 of 1947.

Plate 90 – O/U gun No. 26619 of 1956.

Plate 91 – Pair of hammerless guns Nos. 27001/2 of 1963.

Plate 92 – O/U 20-bore gun No. 27379 of 1967.

Plate 93 – Hammerless gun No. 27699 of 1970.

Plate 94 – Hammerless gun No. 28147 of 1977.

Plate 95 – Two of a quartet of guns Nos. 28156/7/8/9 of 1976.

Plate 96 – O/U gun No. 28589 of 1986.

Plate 97 – .300 hammerless rifle No. 29181 of 1998.

Plate 98 – .300 hammerless rifle No. 29182 of 1998.

Plates 99 and 100 – O/U 20-bore gun No. 29424 of 1998.

Plate 101 – .375 hammerless rifle No. 29530 of 1997.

Plate 102 – .600 hammerless rifle No. 29601 of 1997.

Plate 103 – The action of No. 29601.

Plate 104 – Another view of .600 hammerless rifle No. 29601 of 1997.

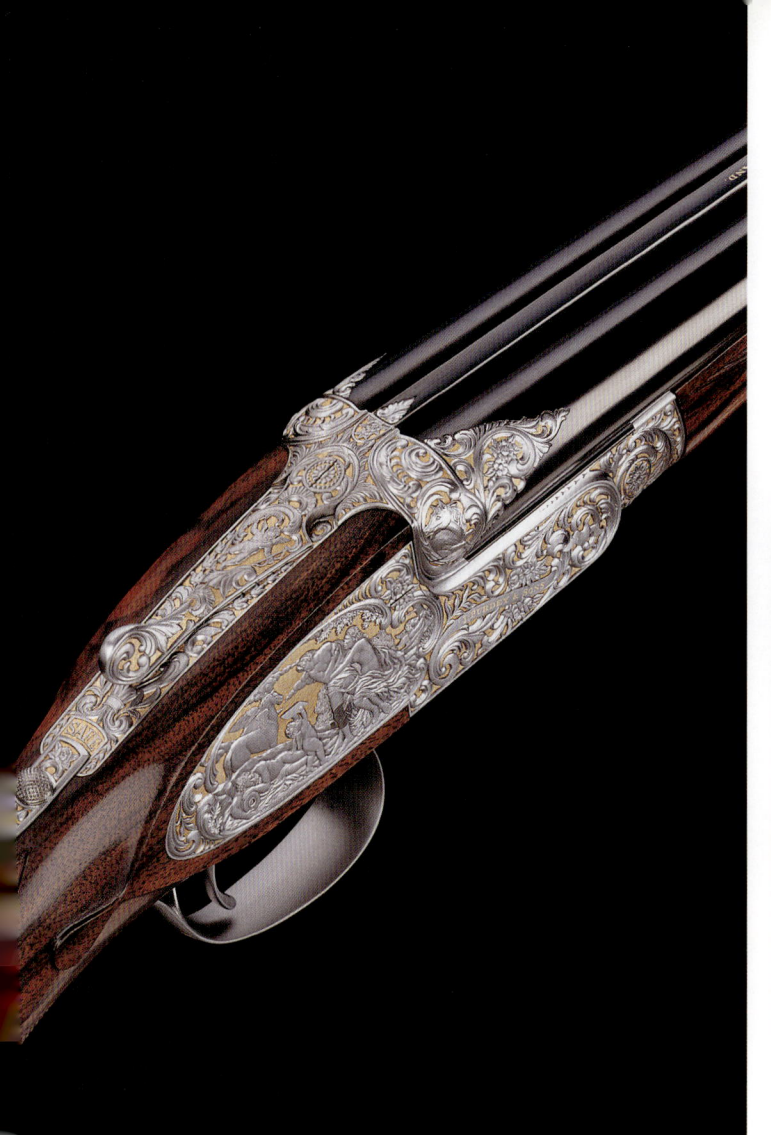

Plate 105 – 28-bore hammerless gun No. 29660 of 1997.

Plate 106 – No. 29660.

Plate 107 – No. 29660, in case complete.

Plate 108 and 109 – Millennium gun No. 30000 of 2000.

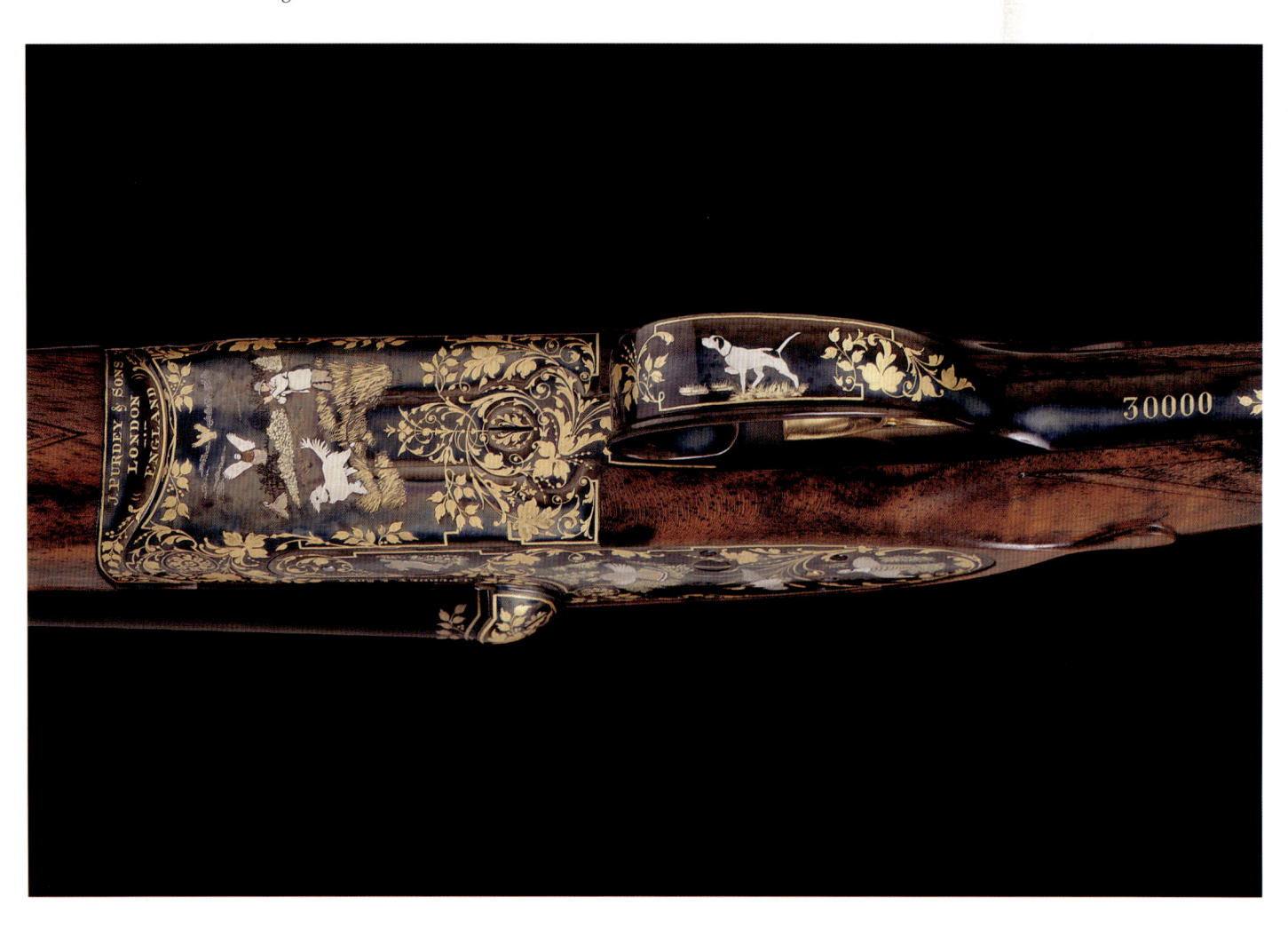

> I may add that though I have no doubt that the plaintiff and Nobbs independently invented the same thing at or about the same time, there being no satisfactory evidence as to which of them was really the prior inventor, I am not at all surprised that the plaintiff, having regard to Nobbs' specification, was not readily convinced of this. Indeed, the only way to explain the possibility of any draughtsman drawing these specifications with Nobbs' invention before him is on the hypothesis which we know to have been the fact that such person was blind, and did not grasp the intricacies of the gun he was describing, and could not verify or correct the drawings, which are exceedingly inaccurate by reference to the original. This would have been very unfortunate for Nobbs if the plaintiff's patent were not void on other grounds. As it is, both the plaintiff and Nobbs suffer the like misfortune in having been anticipated by Baker. In the result, therefore, the action fails.

Part of the conclusion from Mr. Justice Parker's summation of the 1906 patent dispute.

The Nobbs single-trigger was unsatisfactory and some four years later Purdey's patented another single-trigger mechanism. Patent no. 5150 of 1 March 1910 bears the names of James Purdey & Sons and William George Clark of 220 Canbury Park Road, Kingston-upon-Thames. In the patent specification, Clark described himself as an 'engineer'. William Clark was a Purdey gunmaker and although the term 'engineer' is sometimes used in the wage books of the period, he was more accurately a machinist and the foreman of the machinists to boot. No details exist of the financial arrangements he made with Purdey over this patent, but I suspect they were much the same as before.

Purdey and Clark's patent was a system employing a swinging arm (see Appendix 8). When the gun was fired right barrel first, the swinging arm was in the right-hand position under the right sear. After the first pull and discharge, the swinging arm moved to the centre position between the two sears. When the second involuntary pull took place nothing happened as the arm was between the two sears. The arm then swung over to the left under the left sear and upon the third pull, the second discharge took place. Purdey and Clark improved upon this patent one year later in patent no. 21822 of 3 October 1911 (see Appendix 8). The system was the same except that when the swinging arm was in the centre position, an interceptor locked the arm to prevent any possibility of a discharge on the second involuntary pull.

In the 1920s, Ernest and Harry Lawrence made certain modifications to this trigger. In Purdey parlance, it was known as the 'gate' trigger. Single triggers were relatively uncommon on Purdey guns until around 1950. With the production of the Woodward O/U gun from this date, single triggers became increasingly common. This gate trigger continued to be manufactured for side by sides until the late 1970s and for O/Us until the late 1980s when it was superceded by the Lawrence Salter bobweight inertia trigger that is the present-day Purdey single-trigger.

THE DEATH OF JAMES PURDEY THE YOUNGER

At the turn of the century control of Purdey's rested primarily with Athol Purdey, assisted by Cecil Purdey. By 1900, James Purdey the Younger was 72 and although enjoying his retirement his mind was wandering and he experienced some confusion. On his 79th birthday on 19 March 1907, his son Sefton completed a series of sketches of his father (see below). Sefton Purdey had been commissioned into the 18th Hussars in May 1898. He fought in the South African War 1899-1902 and saw action at Reitfontein, Lombard's Kop and the defence of Ladysmith. He was decorated with the Queen and King's medals with four clasps. He retired as a lt-colonel in 1895. When World War I broke out he re-enlisted as a temporary major in the Remount Service, yet died at the early age of 38 on 25 May 1916 from Bright's Disease (a disease of the kidneys.)

James and Julia Purdey sketched by Sefton Purdey 1907.

James Purdey sketched by Sefton Purdey 1907.

Some six days before his 81st birthday, James Purdey the Younger died at his home, 28 Devonshire Place, on 13 March 1909. His father, James Purdey the Elder, was 79 when he died, both Purdeys enjoying a considerable lifespan at a time when this was unusual. His death certificate records that he died of 'Senile Decay, many years, Influenza and Heart Failure'. He was buried in the Purdey family vault in Paddington Cemetery along with his mother, father, eldest son James and his first wife Caroline – plus various infant Purdey children.

He left a considerable sum of money. *The Times* printed:

GUNMAKER'S FORTUNE
Mr. James Purdey, dean of the London gunmakers and first maker and namer of the Express rifle, has left an estate valued at £200,289.

In his day he was known as a good shot with his weapons, and he was one of the oldest members of the Royal London Yacht Club.

His will, proved on 22 May 1909, bore witness to the fruits of his endeavours. He left the gunmaking business to Athol and Cecil, who would share it two-thirds and one-third respectively. £500 was to be given to his wife Julia immediately along with the house in 28 Devonshire Place, complete with all its possessions. £100 per annum was to be given to his granddaughter Dorothy, the daughter of his late son James, and £150 per annum to his son Percy. £750 each was given to his daughter Florence and son Lionel, and his wife Julia was to receive £1,750 per annum.

James Purdey's importance was such that most of the sporting periodicals of the day carried lengthy obituaries on him. Two are reproduced.

THE LATE MR JAMES PURDEY.

The greatest personality in the gun trade passed away last Saturday by the death of Mr James Purdey, who was in his eighty-first year. The business which bears his name, and of which he was the principal partner, has been run for many years on the hereditary principle. The father of the late Mr Purdey was a celebrated gunmaker in the time of Colonel Hawker. James, his son, entered the business immediately upon leaving school, and rapidly acquired a knowledge of guns and rifles, which enabled him to take an active share in the management at a very early age. In due course, when the efflux of time made him head of affairs, his own sons were coming along, and they in their turn passed through the various stages, first of acquiring knowledge, then utilising it, and finally practically running the business on behalf of the senior partner. Whilst, therefore, one cannot but deplore the death of one who will rank for all time as the greatest gunmaker of his day, the maintenance of the firm's ascendency is fully assured by the fact that Mr Athol Purdey has now completed thirty-four years of service with the firm, commencing first as a boy, and attaining of late years the entire control of the business jointly with his brother, Mr C. O. Purdey.

Mr James Purdey was in his day a man of extraordinary energy and vitality. Throughout the sporting world he was the unchallenged maker of guns for those who were in a position to appreciate and to afford the best work. This reputation amongst users was enhanced to an equally flattering degree by the estimation in which he was held by the workmen who carried out his orders, and by those of his rivals who were able to judge of the perfection of his methods. Always a man of commanding presence and convincing manner, he could carry out the instructions of his distinguished patrons, whilst reserving to himself a free hand to produce the required result in the manner which he deemed to be best. There naturally grew up around him an organisation for the making of best guns on a principle commensurate with the high price which they invariably commanded. Every workman was selected on account of his special skill and ability to perform some particular process or group of processes with an infinitude of care and precision of craftsmanship such as can only be acquired under conditions where the time taken is immaterial compared with the necessity to produce a perfect result. Purdey guns thus embody the sentiment of constantly striving towards the ideal, and it is a curious feature about guns, above all other things, that, although good workmanship is mostly hidden beneath a graceful, but not palpably ornate, exterior, its perfection is, nevertheless, clearly manifested. The handling properties disclose the advantageous arrangement of details; similarly, ease of manipulation is the outward sign of perfect mechanism within. Mr Purdey was an artist in his subtle appreciation of all these things, but nevertheless the desire to pay due tribute to the dead must not permit an injustice to be done to the living. Just, in fact, as Mr James Purdey proved himself the able successor of his father, so those who are now carrying on the business may be regarded as capable exponents of the family traditions of gunmaking.

The obituary published in *The Field* on 20 March 1909.

A considerable number of letters offering condolences were received by Athol . A typical letter was written by Lord Ashburton from Cairo:

Cairo
March 29th

Mr. Purdey,
I was very sorry to see the death of your Father reported in The Times. As you know, I knew him well and shall always remember the long talks I used to have with him on guns and shooting before his health broke down. He will be greatly missed by all the shooting world for

DEATH OF A FAMOUS GUNMAKER.

We regret to learn of the death, on Saturday last, of Mr. James Purdey, head of the well-known firm of gun manufacturers of James Purdey and Sons, Audley House, South Audley Street. He died somewhat unexpectedly within a few days of the completion of his 81st year. The firm was originally founded nearly one hundred years ago by the father of the deceased, who joined it in 1845. Thereafter its business increased very rapidly, and, as an expert in gun-making, Mr. James Purdey attained world-wide fame. Among its customers were a number of the crowned heads of Europe.

In his time the deceased may be said to have surpassed all his rivals in the making of the best gameguns, while his rifles to which he first gave the name of "Express," now so largely used, were to be found, along with his guns, in the hands of the best sportsmen in all quarters of the globe. He may be said to have raised the standing and reputation of his firm to a unique position among the gunmakers of England, and, in truth, of the whole sporting world, a reputation which is still maintained. The late Mr. Purdey was on three occasions elected Master of the Gunmakers' Company, and he was one of the oldest members of the Royal London Yacht Club. He was during his life not only the Prince of Gunmakers, but also a keen all-round sportsman; and many old sporting friends regretted sincerely to learn of his decease, even though dying full of years and honours. He is to be buried at Paddington Cemetery to-day (Saturday).

The obituary published in *Country Gentleman* on 20 March 1909.

whose interests he did so much, as well as in the profession of which he was the leading member and the master of the art in which he had no equal.

Yours faithfully,
Ashburton.'

A more poignant letter was received by Athol Purdey from his young son Tom Purdey, aged 11, at West Downs School.

West Downs
Winchester

My Dear Daddy,
I was very cut up about your Telephone message, I did not know Grandpar was even ill but of course it must have been a great relief that the poor old Gentleman was off your and your relations mind. For my birthday I want lots of small parsels you know what I mean any little novelty you see. See you Saturday lunch at George

Your loving son
Donald

In his book *Experts on Guns and Shooting*, published in 1900, G T Teasdale-Buckell began his chapter on James Purdey & Sons. 'There is no gunmaker personally better known than Mr. Purdey; there is none less written about.' To James Purdey's father, James Purdey the Elder, all credit must go to the business he founded upon best gun principles only, to create the best known and most respected gun establishment in Great Britain. To his son James Purdey the Younger, every acclaim must be given for building on his father's principles and retaining Purdey's position as the leading gun firm in the era of breech-loading development in the second half of the 19th century.

James Purdey the Younger had begun his career with his perfection of the double-barrel muzzle-loading Express rifle, which represented the pinnacle of muzzle-loading development in terms of accuracy and style. His invention of his cartridge re-loading machine in 1861 had a great deal to do with the increasing adoption of the breech-loader. His Purdey bolt of 1863 is probably the most famous invention in the history of modern sporting gun design, universally adopted the world over. He created a very handsome style for Purdey guns that made them instantly recognisable and attractive with their graceful hammers, wood-bar actions, bouquet and scroll engraving and flowing hammerless actions. He was also a shrewd businessman, acquiring patents and making licensing agreements with other makers. Under his leadership, Purdey sold enormous numbers of best guns, the year 1891 seeing more than 400 guns produced. He had built guns for most of European Royalty and the most influential sportsmen of the day. All truly remarkable achievements.

James Purdey the Younger's second wife, Julia, had never been particularly well. On 5 January 1911, aged only 54, she died in either a nursing home or hospital in Harrow Weald. She had suffered from rheumatic fever for 30 years, but her immediate cause of death was heart failure. She was interred in the Purdey family vault in Paddington Cemetery. Julia was the eleventh Purdey to be interred in the vault and after her interment, the vault was sealed. She had made a will dated 17 December 1909 leaving everything to her son Lionel Purdey.

However, the Purdey future was secure in the hands of James Purdey's sons, Athol and Cecil, who were now responsible for the business. Athol's eldest son, James IV, had decided upon a career in the army. In 1909 he left Winchester School and joined the Royal Military College at Sandhurst, aged eighteen. After training there for around a year, he joined the 21st Lancers on 25 March 1911 and sailed to Egypt to join them. By early 1914 his regiment had transferred to India and Jim went with them. On 8 May 1913 Jim was admitted to the Freedom of the Gunmakers' Company. The Register of Freedom Admissions 1746-1949 held in the Guildhall Library state:

Jim Purdey, August 1910.

James Alexander Purdey, Son of Athol Stuart Purdey, Citizen and Gunmaker of London was admitted into the Freedom of the Company by Patrimony.

On 7 March 1914, the factory manager, Mr. Wheatley, retired from the firm. Athol Purdey appointed Ernest Charles Lawrence in his place. The Lawrence family played a major role in Purdey's gunmaking business from the 1880s until the 1980s. In total, they have given 242 years service to the firm.

The Purdey connection began with Ernest Lawrence's elder brother, Thomas Lawrence, who joined the firm in the mid-1880s as an actioner. He experienced personal misfortune when his wife died in childbirth, closely followed by the child itself one month later. To escape this trauma, he left the country and became manager of the gun department in the

Jim Purdey's scroll admitting him to the Freedom of the Gunmakers' Company. Although admitted on 8 May 1913, for some reason the scroll was not issued until 4 March 1932. It states, 'James Alexander Purdey, Son of Athol Stuart Purdey, Citizen and Gunmaker of London, was admitted into the Freedom aforesaid and made the Declaration required by law in the Mayoralty of Sir Maurice Jenks Knt. Mayor and Sir Adrian Donald Wilde Pollock Kut., Chamberlain and is entered in the book signed with the letter G2 relating to the Purchasing of Freedoms and the Admissions of Freemen (to wit) the fourth day of March in the 22 Year of the reign of King George V. And in the Year of our Lord 1932. IN WITNESS whereof the Seal of the Office of Chamberlain of the said City is hereunto affixed. Dated in the Chamber of the Guildhall of the same City the day and year abovesaid.'.

London To Wit. James Alexander Purdey, Son of Athol Stuart Purdey, Citizen and Gunmaker of London was admitted into the Freedom aforesaid and made the Declaration required by Law in the Mayoralty of Sir Maurice Jenks Knt., Mayor and Sir Adrian Donald Wilde Pollock, Knt., Chamberlain and is entered in the book signed with the Letter G2 relating to the Purchasing of Freedoms and the Admissions of Freemen (to wit) the 4th day of March in the 22rd Year of the reign of King GEORGE V And in the Year of our Lord 1932. In Witness whereof the Seal of the Office of Chamberlain of the said City is hereunto affixed Dated in the Chamber of the Guildhall of the same City the day and Year abovesaid.

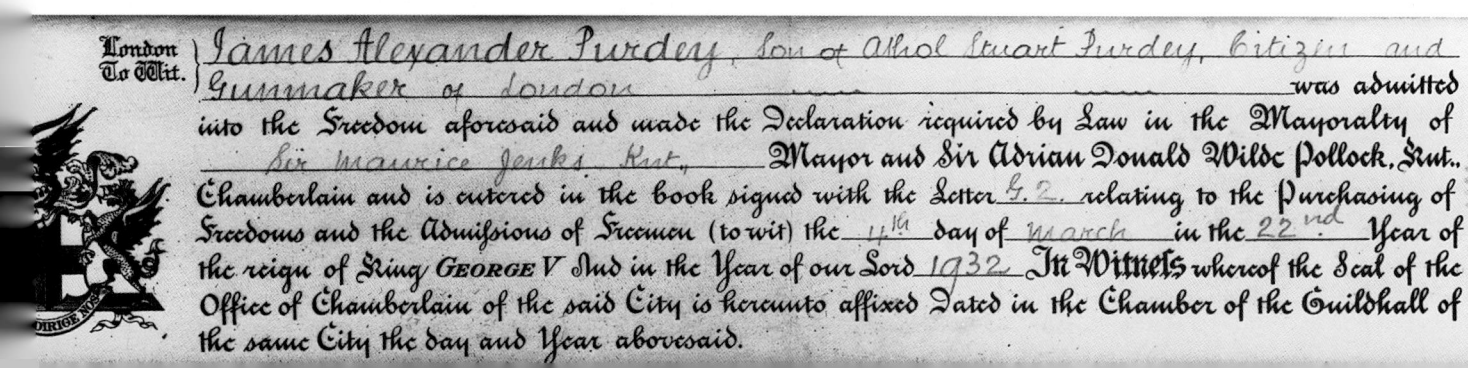

he joined Purdey's as a finisher. By 1912 he was assistant to Mr. Wheatley and by 1914 factory manager, a post he retained until 1948. Ernest Lawrence's contribution to Purdey's was immense. He organised and developed most of the 1914-18 war work, re-designed the ejector mechanism in the 1930s, patented the light projecting try gun in 1929, re-designed the third grip and developed the single-trigger. He died in 1953.

His son, Harry Lawrence, was apprenticed as an actioner under Alf Fullalove the first Monday after his 14th birthday on 27 January 1914. After army service during the war, he returned to Purdey's in 1919, completing his apprenticeship in 1921. He began actioning the single-barrel trap guns that were in demand from America in the 1920s. During 1923 he actioned the one-twelfth scale miniature guns for Queen Mary's dolls' house in Windsor. He re-designed and actioned the first Purdey O/U guns in the 1920s. By 1933 Harry had become assistant factory manager under his father. In 1935 he played a major part in building the three miniature hammer guns, seven inches long and working, which were presented to King George V on the occasion of his Silver Jubilee in 1935. During World War II he organised the production of war-related work, making gauges, moulds for aircraft and electrical equipment, special tools and gauges for cartridge manufacture and a pop rivet gun for aircraft construction. In recognition of his war work, Harry Lawrence was awarded the M.B.E. towards the end of the war. In 1951 Harry Lawrence became a director of Purdey's, in 1954 managing-director and in the same year Master of the Gunmakers' Company and chairman of the Proofhouse Committee. In 1970 he retired as managing-director but remained as director, never really retiring. He died in 1984. Like his father, Harry Lawrence made a major contribution to Purdey's in the 20th century. Apart from his superb technical expertise, he was to a

Captain James Purdey in dress uniform, 1919.

Army and Navy Stores in Bombay. His younger brother, Ernest Charles Lawrence, born 9 December 1870, was apprenticed to E C Hodges, the trade actioner, around 1886, then joined Woodwards as an actioner. He went on to make the Woodward single-trigger and to finish their guns. In 1898

LAWRENCE FAMILY TREE

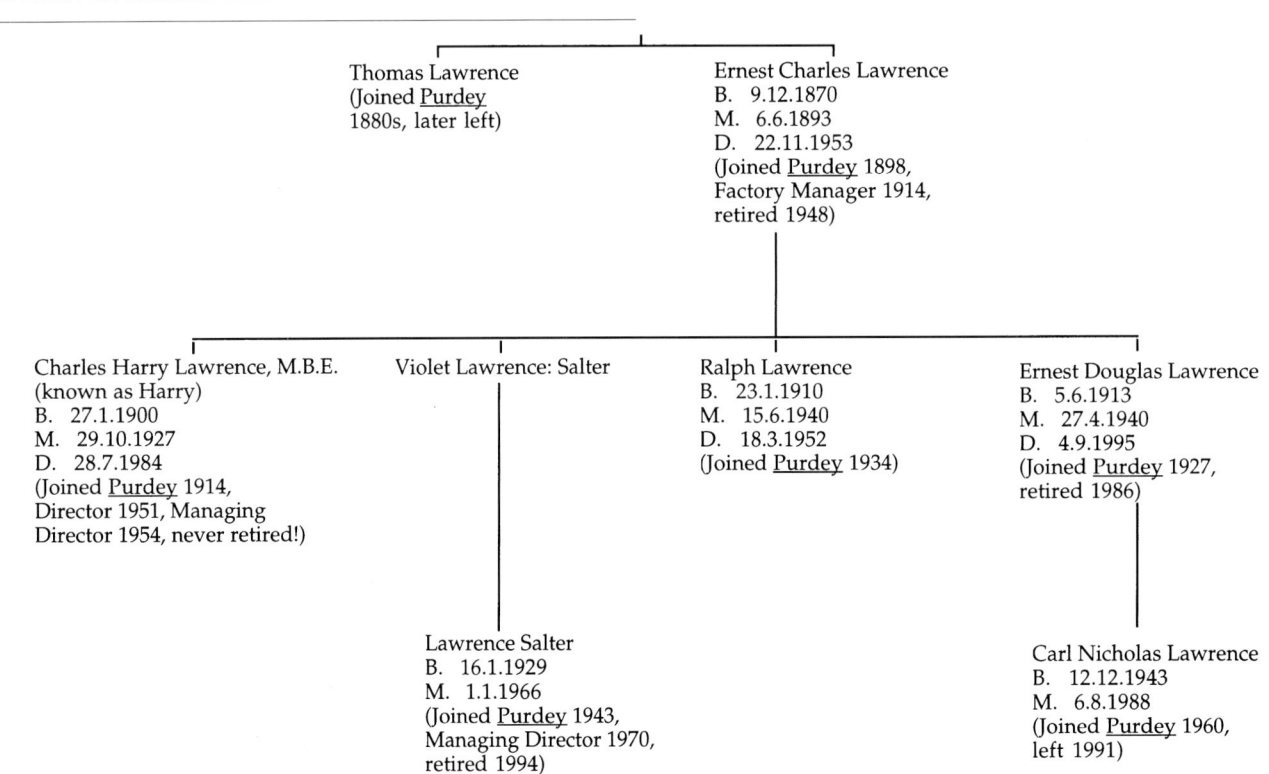

Thomas Lawrence (Joined Purdey 1880s, later left)

Ernest Charles Lawrence
B. 9.12.1870
M. 6.6.1893
D. 22.11.1953
(Joined Purdey 1898, Factory Manager 1914, retired 1948)

Charles Harry Lawrence, M.B.E. (known as Harry)
B. 27.1.1900
M. 29.10.1927
D. 28.7.1984
(Joined Purdey 1914, Director 1951, Managing Director 1954, never retired!)

Violet Lawrence: Salter

Ralph Lawrence
B. 23.1.1910
M. 15.6.1940
D. 18.3.1952
(Joined Purdey 1934)

Ernest Douglas Lawrence
B. 5.6.1913
M. 27.4.1940
D. 4.9.1995
(Joined Purdey 1927, retired 1986)

Lawrence Salter
B. 16.1.1929
M. 1.1.1966
(Joined Purdey 1943, Managing Director 1970, retired 1994)

Carl Nicholas Lawrence
B. 12.12.1943
M. 6.8.1988
(Joined Purdey 1960, left 1991)

large extent responsible for guiding the firm through the difficult period that followed World War II

Harry's brother, Ralph Lawrence, also worked for Purdey's, joining the cartridge loading shop in 1934. In 1950 Ralph went to the the London Proof House as Proof Master but later died in an accident there. Harry's other brother, Ernest Douglas Lawrence, began his apprenticeship at Purdey's in 1927 as an actioner. He assisted Harry in the building of the miniature hammer guns and specialised in the selective single-trigger. After war service in the Royal Navy, he returned to Purdey's in 1946 and upon the purchase of Woodward in 1948, took over the building of the O/U action and the ejector. In 1961 his son, Carl, joined Purdey's as an actioner and single-trigger specialist. Yet another Lawrence connection was made when Harry Lawrence's nephew, Lawrie Salter, joined Purdey's as a boy of fourteen in July 1943, learning his trade as an actioner. In 1967 he became a director, and joint managing-director in 1969.

HIGHLAND HANDLES, SPADE GRIPS, NORMAN SIGHTS AND MUZZLE PROTECTORS

The schoolboy assassination at Sarajevo on 28 June 1914 striking down the Heir Apparent to the Austro-Hungarian Empire, the Archduke Franz Ferdinand was but a relatively minor event in the summer of 1914. The gun order books were full and Purdey's prospered. (Incidentally, Franz Ferdinand was a customer of Purdey's – alongside his name in the Dimension Book is written in contemporary writing the single word that resulted in near apocalypse, 'Deceased'.)

However, the militarism of the first decade of the century, the re-opening of old animosities and the system of alliances combined to create a gradual drift to European war. As the European countries became embroiled in war like falling dominoes, the 'Splendid Isolation' of a Great Britain protected by the most powerful navy in the world did not seem appropriate. And as the German Schlieffen plan began its inexorable role, Britain had little option but to come to the assistance of her ally France and to honour her treaty obligations to Belgium. On 4 August 1914, Britain declared war on Germany.

Patriotism was intense, whipped up by a propaganda machine intent on milking every 'beastliness' perpetrated. There was a mad rush of men to join the colours – to participate in the excitement and to champion the underdog. This would, after all, be a short war and nobody wanted to miss it.

The Purdey gunmakers were no exception. By 1914 the company had around 108 employees, of whom 14 joined the army in the first month of the war. Due to their expertise, they were immediately given the rank of armourer staff sergeant and for most of the war were employed as armourers.

In total, around 32 Purdey gunmakers joined the Forces during World War I. Of these, Fred Eves, the finisher, who joined in the first month of the war, was killed in France in 1917.

The Purdey gunmakers who joined up in September 1914. All were given the rank of armourer staff sergeant. A photograph taken when they were being given instruction at the R.S.A.F. Enfield. Back Row L to R: Bob Thomson (finisher), Bill Geekie (finisher), Walter Forbes (stocker), Unknown, Fred Eves (finisher), Sam Smallwood (shooting coach), Frank Winter (actioner), Arthur 'Bung' Eves (finisher). Front Row L to R: Joe Hayes (repairs), A 'Topsy' Turvey (finisher), Jack Apted (stocker), Joe Watts (barrel filer), Joe Megroff (repairs), Percy Wilkes (actioner), Harry 'Titchy' Leggett (stocker).

Arthur Roberts, the son of George Roberts, the barrel borer, had been apprenticed to Alf Fullalove and upon completion of his apprenticeship had become an excellent actioner. He also did some of the fern and vine leaf carving on the actions which was popular at this time. He joined the army in 1914 as an armour staff sergeant, but was later commissioned and rose to the rank of captain. After the war he travelled to Turkey as a member of a Judicial Court which went around the country judging war criminals. He did not return to Purdey's.

Jim Purdey was already in the army, stationed in India. His younger brother, Tom, was not to be outdone and after leaving Eton joined the Royal Military College at Sandhurst on 12 November 1914, aged seventeen. Tom thoroughly enjoyed Sandhurst. He had 'a very comfortable room' and 'excellent food'. He put his name down for the Argyll and Sutherland Highlanders and had great excitement ordering his kit – 'above all my claymore and kilt and Glengarry'. On 17 February 1915 Tom was commissioned as a 2nd lieutenant in the Argyll and Sutherland Highlanders.

Philip Dean, a Purdey stocker, as an armourer staff sergeant during the war. Apprenticed to his father, Dean completed his apprenticeship in 1909 and worked as a stocker at Purdey's until his death in 1959.

Philip Dean in the Irongate Wharf factory, *circa* 1950.

Lieutenant Tom Purdey on his way to war, 1915. In his diary Tom states 'I went straight to see my father in Audley House – how proud I was crashing about with an enormous claymore with basket hilt complete!'

It wasn't long before Tom was posted to France and he sailed on 21 March 1915 to Rouen. 'I was exceedingly frightened, but with a little alcohol I carried on.' He went up the line on 20 May and experienced his first shelling at Poperinghe. 'Never felt more frightened.' At Ypres he experienced a gas attack, 'very unpleasant'. His regiment was in the line at Armentières with 'the Hun about eighty yards away – this seemed very close'. Tom then notes that 'my eyes were very bad, I could not see very well'. The Colonel decided that his eyes were not good enough and promptly sent Tom back to base camp at Rouen to the Medical Board. The doctors decided that Tom was unfit for action because of his vision. At the base camp 'we had one very amusing evening, two charming sisters, but I must not enlarge'.

On returning home, Tom was posted in early 1916 to Stirling Castle as adjutant to his regiment. He thoroughly enjoyed his eleven month stay there – 'I loved every moment of it, I learned so much from them all, how to behave, how to drink properly, how to fish'. There he met Major Sholto Douglas of 43 Squadron, Royal Flying Corps. This event had a big influence on Tom, for in late November 1916 he transferred to 43 Squadron R.F.C. as Sholto Douglas's adjutant at Netheravon. There Tom met his future great friend, Captain Harold Balfour. 'We have been the closest and greatest of friends ever since.' The squadron flew Sopwith Strutters and transferred to Northolt.

In January 1917 the squadron was posted to France. Only 'one fatal crash' ensued en-route. After a stop at Rouen, 'I was able to show them the town, including Madam Stephane!!', they arrived at their airfield, Trezannes, which they shared with 40 Squadron. Apart from intense cold and heavy casualties, Tom drew great support from the *esprit de corps* that existed. In May 1917 the squadron changed to Sopwith Camels and in January 1918 transferred to another aerodrome, La Gorgue. Due to the German spring offensives in 1918, the squadron was forced to go south to Avesnes le Compte just behind Arras. On 1 April 1918 the R.F.C. became the R.A.F. Tom was posted from 43 Squadron to 10th Wing at Wattignies, south of Lille. The German spring offensives had been halted and thoroughly exhausted, the tide turned against them.

At 8 a.m. on the morning of 11 November 1918 'my servant called me and gave me the message – all operations east of the Balloon Line to cease at 11.00 a.m.'. Tom went to see his friend Louis Strange. 'We just looked at each other, then he laughed and I cried – that is what life is.' The day consisted of 'tears, laughter, gin, more tears, more gin and memories that one cannot describe of all these friends whom we loved and could never be with us again'. The war was over. Tom was by now a captain and in February 1919 was posted to the Rhine in Germany. He applied for demobilisation and returned home shortly afterwards.

Tom had complained of his eyesight as a boy at school. How slender are the threads of fate. He had been at the front for only a few months in 1915 before he was pronounced unfit for active service. The average life of an infantry officer during World War I was measured in weeks – the future of Purdey could have taken a different turn.

His elder brother, Jim, had been involved in active service in India. On the North-West Frontier in 1915 the Germans and Turks encouraged a tribe of Afghan origin to attack the Punjab. Jim and his regiment, the 21st Lancers, attacked this force, successfully driving them back. One of the Lancers, Private Hull, was awarded the VC for saving the life of an officer in this attack. Later, in 1915, Jim was appointed ADC to the Governor of Bengal, carrying out his duties in Calcutta. The climate and disease affected Jim's health and in December

Tom Purdey and Louis Strange at Aachen in 1919.

1916, 'James arrived home from India – very sick with boils – Great Central Hospital – so glad to see him – almost a stranger', wrote Tom in his diary.

On 14 April 1917, Jim, aged 25, married Hariot Patricia Constance-Kinloch, aged 24, of Farm House, Old Windsor, in St. Paul's Church, Knightsbridge. Hariot's father, Harry Kinloch, was a major in the 60th Rifles. Their first and only child, James Oliver Kinloch Purdey, was born on 26 January 1918 in Farm House, Old Windsor. 'I went down to be with Jim at Farm House, Old Windsor – had to share a bed with Jim – too much White Port – restless night – Saturday 26 January Jim's boy was born', writes Tom again. Jim's boy was always known as J O K Purdey. For the rest of the war, Jim served in the War Office.

Even young Harry Lawrence did not escape military service. In 1917 he tried to join the army but was rejected for not being eighteen years old. When he reached enlistment age at the beginning of 1918, he had a medical and was accepted by the Queen's Westminster Rifles. He remained in the army until he was demobilised in August 1919, when he resumed his apprenticeship at Purdey's.

A firm like Purdey's, trading at the top end of the market,

were heavily dependent on the state of the economy and political events. A major European war would cause severe dislocation and, by early 1915, Purdey's experienced its full effect. A third of Purdey gunmakers were away on active service, and gun orders had diminished rapidly from a Europe embroiled in war. Athol Purdey realised that for the firm to survive, military work would be the key – and the skills inherent in the Purdey workforce made the firm eminently suitable for it.

Athol put his mind to work and designed a muzzle protector for the standard service issue Mk III Lee-Enfield rifle. He received patent no. 3188 of 27 February 1915, 'Improvements in Muzzle Protectors for Rifles' (see Appendix 8). Deadlock in trench warfare in France and Belgium had seen soldiers forced to live a subterranean existence in a sea of mud. Mud getting into the muzzle of a rifle could affect its accuracy, safety and operation. Athol's solution was to design a small, thin metal plate to clip over the muzzle of the rifle. If a soldier omitted to remove it, the clip would fly off when the gun was discharged. Hand presses were installed in the basement of 84 Mount Street and hundreds of thousands were produced. Harry Lawrence, as a young apprentice, did much of the work.

At the same time in 1915, Purdey's were asked by the War Office to fit telescopic sights to snipers' rifles. This was skilled work and thousands were fitted, tested and supplied with leather cases to be sent to the Western Front. Early in 1915, the Royal Flying Corps approached Purdey's to manufacture military items for their use. Gun jams on aircraft were a different matter from a jam on terra firma. Many RFC aircraft used the Vickers Gun and Purdey's produced 'The Highland Handle', a device for quickly clearing jams on the Vickers gun. Modifications were also made to the Lewis gun to enable a pilot to fly his plane with one hand and fire his gun with the other. This was the spade grip thumb trigger and again they

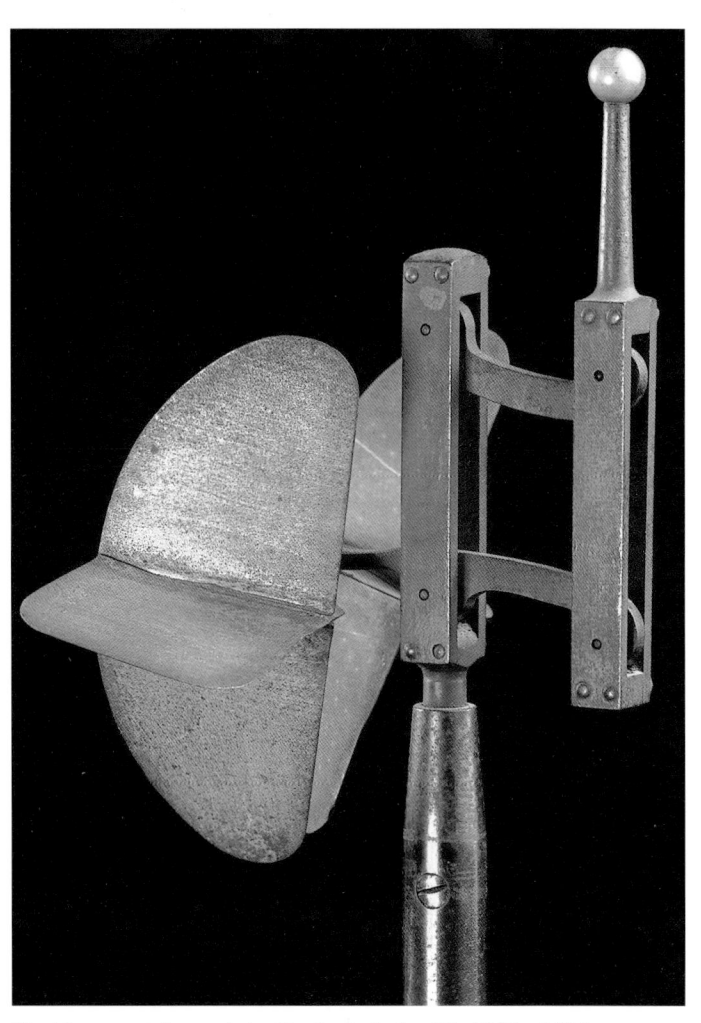

The Norman sight, made by Purdey's during World War I. This was a self-adjusting sight to be fitted to an aircraft machine gun, adjusting itself to angle of climb, dive, turning angle and wind pressure. Developmental work carried out by Ernest Lawrence.

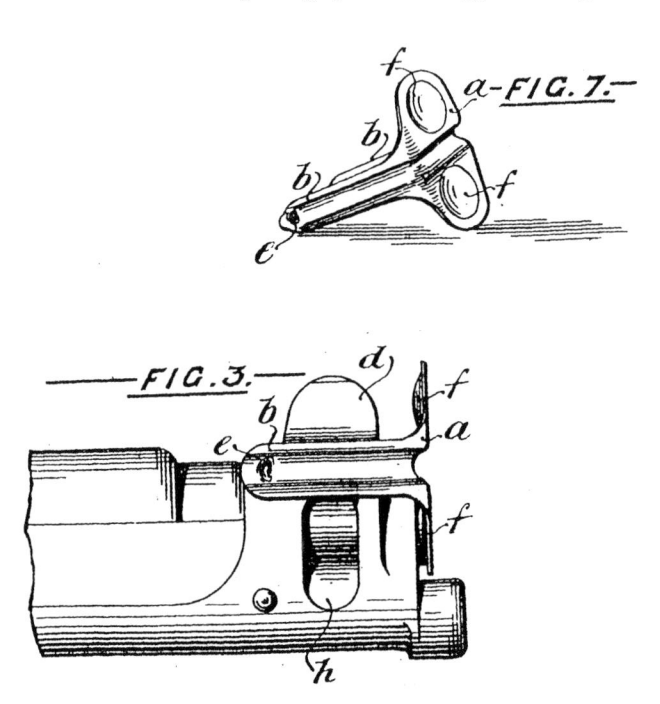

Athol Purdey's 1915 muzzle protector to prevent the ingress of mud into the barrel of the Lee-Enfield rifle in trench warfare conditions. Thousands were produced in the basement of 84 Mount Street.

were produced in their thousands. Magazines for the Mk II Lewis gun were machined and made as were Hutton sights for the same gun.

One of the most interesting developments of Purdey during the war was the development and manufacture of the Norman sight. Professor Norman of Cambridge had invented a self-adjusting sight for aircraft to take into account the angle of climb, dive, turning angle and wind pressure. Although Professor Norman invented the sight, it was Ernest Lawrence, the factory manager, who undertook the actual design and trials. It was a precision made sight involving small, moveable vanes. Lawrence developed it, eventually electrifying it for night fighting. By 1916 it was fitted to RFC aircraft and by the end of the war Purdey's had made over 4,500 of them. It was using one of these sights made by Purdey, that Lieutenant Leefe Robinson shot down a Zeppelin at Cuffley, near Potters Bar, in 1916, surely the most impressive bag ever made with a Purdey!

Robinson, of 39 Squadron RFC, encountered Zeppelin SL11, one of a massed attack of 16 airships bombing England on the night of 2-3 September 1916. At a height of 12, 500 ft. at 2.30 am, using the sight made by Purdey, he poured machine-gun fire into the Zeppelin and brought it down. For this feat he was awarded the VC.

Tom Purdey's Freedom Scroll admitting him to the Freedom of the Gunmakers' Company. Although admitted on 6 November 1919, for some reason, like his brother Jim's, the scroll was not issued until 4 March 1932. It states: 'Thomas Donald Stuart Purdey, Son of Athol Stuart Purdey, Citizen and Gunmaker of London was admitted into the Freedom aforesaid and made the Declaration required by Law in the Mayoralty of Sir Maurice Jenks Knut Mayor and Sir Adrian Donald Wilde Pollock, Kut; Chamberlain and is entered in the book signed with the capital letter G2 relating to the Purchasing of Freedoms and the Admissions of Freeman (to wit) the Fourth day of March in the Twenty second Year of the reign of KING GEORGE V And in the Year of our Lord 1932. IN WITNESS whereof the Seal of the Office of Chamberlain of the said City is hereunto affixed Dated in the Chamber of the Guildhall of the same City the day and Year above said.'

In the Dimension Book after the serial number 21573 of 1917, the following statement appears: '1918. There were no guns put in hand this year. Stopped by the Government under D O R A' (D O R A was the Defence of the Realm Act, first enacted in 1914 and repeatedly strengthened thereafter giving the Government dictatorial powers.) A small number of sporting guns had been produced in the early war years, but as the country converted to total war in 1917, Purdey's output was entirely given over to war production. Even women were employed for the first time to work some of the machinery in Audley House! To Ernest Lawrence, the factory manager, due credit must be given for his skill in converting the firm to war output and his developmental work for the military.

Immediately the war ended on 11 November 1918, the factory was re-organised for gunmaking. The majority of the gunmakers returned. Harry Lawrence returned from the army in August 1919, resumed his apprenticeship and completed it in January 1921. After leaving the army in 1919, Tom Purdey spent a short period as a guest of the navy, January-May 1920, then as his diary states 'joined James Purdey & Sons, June'. He had been admitted to the Gunmakers' Company on 6 November 1919. The Register of Freedom Admissions 1746-1949 held in the Guildhall Library states:

> Captain Thomas Donald Stuart Purdey, Son of Athol Stuart Purdey, Citizen and Gunmaker of London was admitted into the Freedom of this Company by Patrimony.

Mabel, Tom and Athol Purdey, Folkestone 1919.

Chapter eight

BOOM, BUST AND BELLIGERENCE

The post-war period was not a very easy time for Purdey's. Europe was suffering from the trauma of the Great War and orders were not as forthcoming as pre-war. The early 1920s saw around 200 guns on average being produced per annum in comparison to the average 300 guns in pre-war years. The American market, in a wealthy country relatively unscathed by war, was as yet an untapped source. In the closing decades of the 19th century many guns had been sold to America, but the potential had not been exploited.

With this in mind, Athol Purdey planned a sales trip to the U.S.A. in 1922. He visited New York, Pittsburgh and Chicago, created great interest and took several orders. Americans tended to specify more ostentatious weapons, deeply chased and carved, in comparison to the traditional bouquet and scroll. Athol also realised there was a good demand for a single-barrel trap gun and on his return entrusted Harry Lawrence with the job of making one with the assistance of his father. Vickers supplied the special barrel tubes. The first one produced was No. 22417 and was sold on 9 February 1923. These single-barrel guns were high quality, not to be confused with the lesser quality boys' and keepers' guns sold pre-war. Some 59 such guns were produced, the last being built in 1972.

Athol also saw in America how successful Woodward and Boss were with their O/U guns. Purdey's did not have an O/U gun and upon his return, Athol asked Harry Lawrence to experiment with a Purdey O/U based on the Edwinson Green of Cheltenham design, patent nos. 8225 and 14951 of 1912. Athol was concerned about the safety of O/U guns and was attracted to the Green design on account of its strength.

Harry Lawrence built the first Purdey O/U, No. 22564, to Green's design in 1923. This was an experimental gun and no details exist of it in the Dimension Books, although later it was sold to C B Vaughan. Athol insisted that the O/U should have six locking bolts, which created a very heavy gun at 8lbs 3oz. Also, due to the adoption by Green of the conventional Purdey underbolts, a very deep action resulted in comparison to the slim Boss/Woodward guns. The result was anything but satisfactory – a heavy clumsy gun not typical of the usual elegant Purdey style. In total, 27 Purdey O/Us were built to

An advertisement from the late 1920s showing the single-barrel hammerless ejector trap gun.

this design between 1923 and 1939. After the retirement of Athol in the 1930s, two of the barrel-locking bolts were removed and the weight dropped to around 7lbs 9oz. However, the gun was still ungainly. No Purdey O/Us were produced from 1940 to 1950. James Purdey's purchase of James Woodward & Sons in 1948 solved the problem of the O/U and from then on Purdey's produced their own version of the Woodward O/U – a superb gun and design.

Harry Lawrence was responsible for an entirely different type of gun in 1923. A very realistic dolls' house, designed by the architect, Sir Edward Lutyens, was being built for Queen Mary in 1922/3. The Queen's dolls' house was to be a replica of a grand country house and since her husband George V was a keen sportsman, Purdey's were asked to make a pair of miniature guns for the house. The guns were built to 1/12th scale. Harry made the drawings and was responsible for the major portion of their building. They were a pair of hammerless guns, Nos. 22491/2, complete in their case. They didn't actually fire but they were exact replicas in every detail.

130

JAMES PURDEY & SONS LTD.

Captain James Purdey's wartime marriage in 1917 to Patricia Kinloch, unfortunately, did not last long. In 1920 she obtained a divorce from Jim and obtained custody of their two-year-old son, Jok. She never married again, and Jok was brought up by her family. After the divorce, Jim was appointed ADC to the Governor of Dar-es-Salaam in Tanganyika (Tanzania), East Africa. It was here that he met and married his second wife, Bee Oliver. This marriage took place on 22 September 1923 and would have future implications for Purdey's.

JAMES PURDEY & SONS,
GUN and RIFLE MAKERS,
By Appointment to
His Majesty The King,
H.R.H. The Prince of Wales,
H.M. The King of Spain,
H.M. The King of Sweden.
Also by Appointment to His Majesty the late King Edward VII and Her Majesty the late Queen Victoria.
ONLY ONE QUALITY—THE BEST.
Audley House, 57 and 58, South Audley Street
LONDON, W.1.

An advertisement from the 1920s. Notice how Purdey's are determined to put the A-E quality era behind them – 'Only One Quality – The Best.'

married on 28 August 1930 in Riverfields, New Jersey, and returned shortly afterwards to London. Their son, William, was born in 1937. Jim at last found personal happiness, and the marriage was a success.

Mary La Boyteaux, third wife of James Purdey IV, and their son, William, outside their house, 5 Wellington Square, in 1939.

Shortly after their marriage, Jim and Bee returned from Dar-es-Salaam to London. The only problem was that Jim had no job. His father-in-law suggested farming and purchased a farm at Jedburgh in the Scottish Borders. The farm didn't work out and Jim's father-in-law's next proposal was for the Oliver family to invest in Purdey's if Jim could be taken on as a director. Athol and Tom agreed as the Purdey profits were low in this period. The year 1924-25 saw a distinct drop in the number of guns produced, from around 230 in 1923 to around 165 in 1925. The Oliver family were connected with Debenham and Freebody and well used to business practice. It became apparent that Purdey's required a greater injection of capital and the Olivers agreed to invest in the firm, provided Purdey's converted to limited liability status.

Athol and Cecil agreed to sell the business on 2 October 1925 to create a limited company. The consideration for the sale was £24,400. The first meeting of the new company, James Purdey & Sons Ltd. took place in the Long Room on 5 October 1925. Athol was chairman, and Cecil, Jim and Tom directors. As well as the Purdey family having shares in the firm, the Olivers also possessed shares. For the first time in the history of Purdey's, the family were not entirely in control.

Misfortune again intervened, and in 1929 Jim and Bee divorced. Jim was on a business trip to America in 1929 and travelled there on the cruise liner *Olympic*. On board, he met Mary Stuart La Boyteaux of Greenfields, New Jersey. They

Successful business with the USA saw Tom making various sales trips there in the 1920s. To help him on these trips, he compiled a notebook, accompanied by drawings from Harry Lawrence, of all the parts of the Purdey gun. The notebook also included details on charges, gun measurements and possible faults with guns. The drawings from this notebook are reproduced in Appendix 9. On one such trip, in 1926, Tom took over 40 orders for guns and rifles. America was enjoying a post-war boom and on a further trip in 1928 the orders generated resulted in extra gunmakers being taken on. Jim, who was in India during the war, returned there in 1928 to use his contacts to sell guns to the Maharajahs.

In 1926 Tom Purdey took out two similar patents for a shooting stick designed to hold cartridges. His first patent, no. 5523 of 26 February, remained as a provisional specification only (see Appendix 8). In shooting sticks with padded seats, the seat was formed with shallow holes to permit the insertion of cartridges, primer end uppermost. For leather seats, a flexible strip of leather with holes for cartridges cut out of it, was attached above the seat. The other patent, no. 19052 of 30 July 1926, was proceeded with as a complete specification (see Appendix 8). It differed slightly in that a piece of leather, again with holes cut out for cartridges, had clips on it for clipping over a shooting stick or shooting bag.

Due to the injection of capital in 1925 and the continuing prosperity of the American market, Purdey's finances were

The cover of a late-1920s Purdey catalogue.

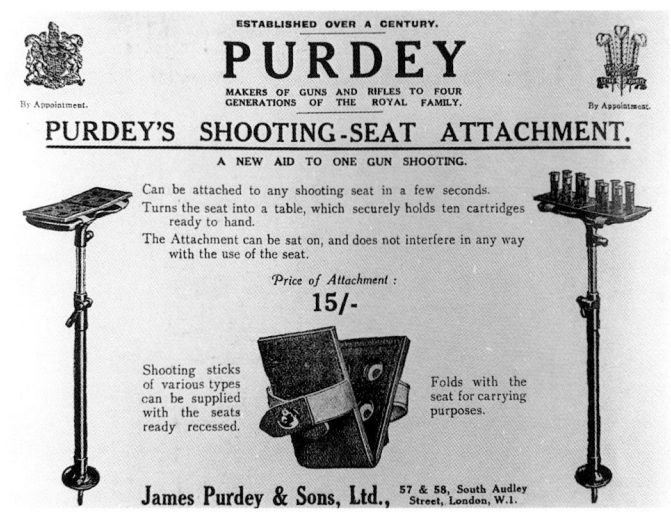

An advertisement for Tom Purdey's patent shooting stick, *circa* 1930.

back on a firm footing. Gun production had increased from around 165 in 1923 to 260 in 1927 and to 300 in 1928. The net profit for 1927 was nearly £10,000. Some of this went in 1927 into buying 36 acres of freehold property at Field End Road, Eastcote, South Harrow, the new Purdey shooting ground. A 1930 advert for the ground announced:

> James Purdey & Sons have the pleasure to announce that their new Shooting Ground, which is most conveniently situated at Eastcote near Harrow, and is reached in 25 minutes from Baker Street, Metropolitan Railway, or three

William Morgan, Purdey's head coach at the shooting ground from 1932 until his retirement in 1954. He had previously been at Lancasters. In addition, he tested all the new guns and rifles at the grounds.

quarters of an hour by car from the Marble Arch is available for general shooting practice and expert tuition. There are over thirty six acres of land and everything possible has been done to make the ground as up to date and as efficient as a shooting ground can be. Customers can have practice for driven grouse from a butt and for driven partridges coming over a very typical hedge. There is a 60 foot tower for pheasant practice…

Purdey's shooting grounds at Eastcote, 9 August 1929. Captain James Purdey, George Hirst (loader), Sam Smallwood (head coach).

On 27 January 1928, Athol Purdey celebrated his 70th birthday. To mark the occasion, a large dinner took place at the Holborn Restaurant, to which all the employees of James Purdey were invited. The company presented Athol with an oil portrait of himself by Sir Oswald Birley that hangs in the Long Room today. The employees presented him with a diamond tie-pin in the form of a flying grouse. Even *The Field* of 2 February 1928 paid tribute to his birthday.

> Mr. Athol Purdey
> We are sure that all readers of the Field will join us in congratulating Mr. Athol Purdey on attaining his 70th birthday which he celebrated on January 27th last. Mr. Purdey is happily in excellent health and is still a very active head of the famous firm which bears his name and with which he has worked continuously for 54 years.

Shortly after this, Athol retired from the firm around 1929. Although remaining head of the firm, he took little active part in the running of the business, leaving this to his two sons,

The portrait of Athol painted by Sir Oswald Birley. Sir Oswald had been a Purdey customer since 1897. The label beneath the painting states: 'ATHOL STUART PURDEY. Son of James Purdey the Younger, Father of James Alexander Purdey and Thomas Donald Stuart Purdey. Born 1858. Freedom 1879. Court 1887. Master 1890, 1899, 1908, 1921. Died 1939 aged 81 years. Sir Oswald Birley P.R.P. 1880-1952.' (*See plate 57 in colour section.*)

Tom and Jim. He spent much of his retirement at his seaside home in Folkestone.

In 1929 a fascinating patent was granted to Purdey's. Ernest Lawrence developed and patented an electric cartridge in patent no. 14943 of 13th May 1929 (see appendix 8). In this patent, a special electric cartridge could be inserted into the barrel of an ordinary gun. When the gun was fired, a beam of light was projected and the shooter could see his aiming point. As such, it was useful for indoor target practice. A long tube contained two batteries; at one end was a light bulb and lens and at the other end a contact device. The long tube fitted tightly into the barrel and when the trigger was pulled, the striker hit the contact causing illumination to take place.

There were variations on the electric gun. In 1929, King George V became ill and unable to shoot. Purdey's built a replica in wood of the King's hammer gun to his measurements that fired such a spot of light. It was considerably lighter than his normal gun and allowed the King to practise during his convalescence.

In the 1930s, Purdey's took such a wooden electric gun and developed it into a specialised try gun for use with customers in the Long Room to help when taking the gun measurements of a customer. This electric try gun was frequently used on selling trips abroad, but was unfortunately stolen on one such visit. Another one was constructed recently and is in use today.

The final patent of James Purdey was a curious device patented by Athol Purdey, aged 71, in patent no. 15985 of 23

May 1929 (see appendix 8). A normal walking-stick was fitted with a trigger for shooting practice – 'snapping at birds or other moving objects'. A folding trigger was employed which, when not in use, folded flush with the walking-stick. With the trigger pulled down, the walker, 'snapping at birds', could pull the trigger which made a realistic click.

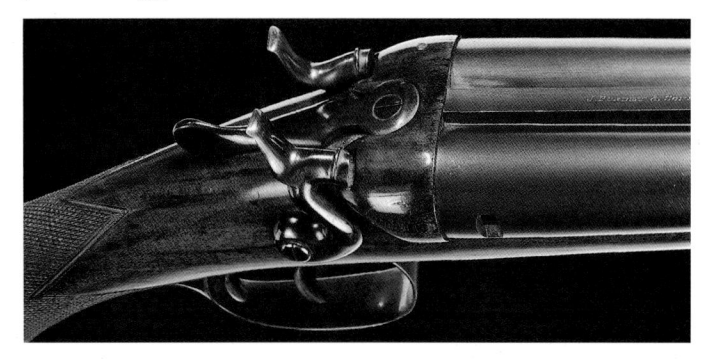

The wooden electric gun built for King George V in 1929 for indoor practice during his convalescence after illness. Other such wooden electric guns were built of far lesser quality, primarily as sophisticated toys for boys – although full-sized ones could also be made for 'grown up shooters'. (*See plate 58 in colour section.*)

AN IDEAL GIFT

A Purdey Electric Spotter Gun

FOR amusement and instruction. Will not fire cartridges. Quite harmless in the hands of a small boy, but it will teach how to take up a gun and will train his eye.

Has two barrels actuated by normal triggers and projecting, in broad daylight, a spot of light on the object aimed at, showing whether the aim is accurate.

Fitted with normal stock which can be lengthened or shortened.

Handle and balance like a Purdey Gun.

Also made for grown-up shooters for home practice in taking up a gun and keeping the eye in form. They can be stocked to the measurements of their own guns, and be made similar in weight, balance, and barrel length.

A DELIGHTFUL GIFT FOR A BOY AND AN EXCELLENT TRAINING FOR THE DAYS WHEN HE WILL USE A SERIOUS WEAPON

PRICE, WITH EXTRA BATTERIES & BULBS £5 The electric equipment is renewable for a few pence

An advertisement from a 1930 Purdey catalogue for the 'Electric Spotter Gun'.

Tom Purdey and Prince Frederick of Prussia on the road to Scotland for the opening of the grouse season, 10 August 1934.

THE GREAT DEPRESSION

Purdey's had come through the difficult post-war period and had gained a firm foothold in the lucrative American market due to the continuing prosperity of that country. However, trading at the luxury end of the market, the fortunes of the firm were a barometer to the world's economic and political vagrancies. Unfortunately, both situations were experienced in the 1930s – world economic recession and aggressive dictatorship resulting in total war.

'Boom and bust', the term often used to describe America in the 1920s and 1930s, could also be used to describe Purdey's in this period. The U.S.A. had experienced a fever of speculation leading first to the withdrawal of funds from Europe and later to panic ('The Wall Street Crash' of 1929), as confidence in the economy rapidly dissipated. The economic influence of the U.S.A. was so great that the tidal wave of depression engulfed all European countries. In the industrialised nations, exports fell and internal consumption dropped resulting from a shortage of capital. This led to reduced industrial production and mass unemployment.

Just as Purdey's had experienced prosperity in the 1920s, they suffered the full blast of world depression in the 1930s. The American market in particular essentially disappeared, only six guns being ordered in 1934. Gun production, running at around 300 guns per annum in 1928, dropped rapidly in 1930 to reach a real low of around 100 guns per annum 1931-34. Guns being built in the factory were put on hold, part finished and held as stock. This explains why dating of guns in the 1930s is a very difficult process. A gun might be started in 1930, given a serial no. and not delivered until 1938 or even later.

Rigorous economies had to be made at Purdey's to cope with the situation. The limited company created in 1925, with the Olivers having preference shares, meant that they had a say in the running of the company. At board meetings in 1932 the finances of the company were closely scrutinised. Austerity was to be rigidly enforced, no entertaining, personal expenses pruned severely, no dividends paid and the debts of Athol, Jim and Tom attended to. It was decided to cut the salaries of the clerical staff and more importantly to build only ten more stock guns. This could only mean one thing – laying off gunmakers in the factory. Twenty six gunmakers, about one-quarter of the workforce, were to be made redundant. It was decided that, although harsh, these redundancies would apply to the older craftsmen. If younger gunmakers had been dismissed, there was no guarantee that they would return when the situation improved and this could have long-standing implications for Purdey's. The whole business was unpleasant with long service gunmakers like Alf Fullalove being dismissed, but, as business picked up in the late 1930s, about three-quarters of them returned.

Right: A Purdey cartridge catalogue dated 1931. (*See plate 59 in colour section.*)

BOOM, BUST AND BELLIGERENCE

In 1935, the Olivers decided to sell their shares in the company. The shares were bought by Sir Wyndham Portal of Laverstock and Major Godfrey Miller-Mundy of Redrice in Hampshire.

As part of the rigid economies imposed, the recently purchased shooting ground at Eastcote was sold in 1936. In its place, Purdey's came to an agreement with the West London Shooting Grounds at Northolt to rent their ground for testing and instruction. This arrangement worked well and has continued to the present day.

King George V would celebrate his Silver Jubilee, twenty-five years on the throne, on 6 May 1935. Purdey's having such a close relationship with the royalty of Great Britain, decided to present the king with a very special present on the occasion of his silver jubilee. It was intended to build the king a pair of miniature hammer guns, $1/6$th exact copies of his own hammer guns Nos. 2418 1/2. The king's own guns, a pair of 12-bore hammer ejectors with Whitworth barrels, had been sold to him in July 1930.

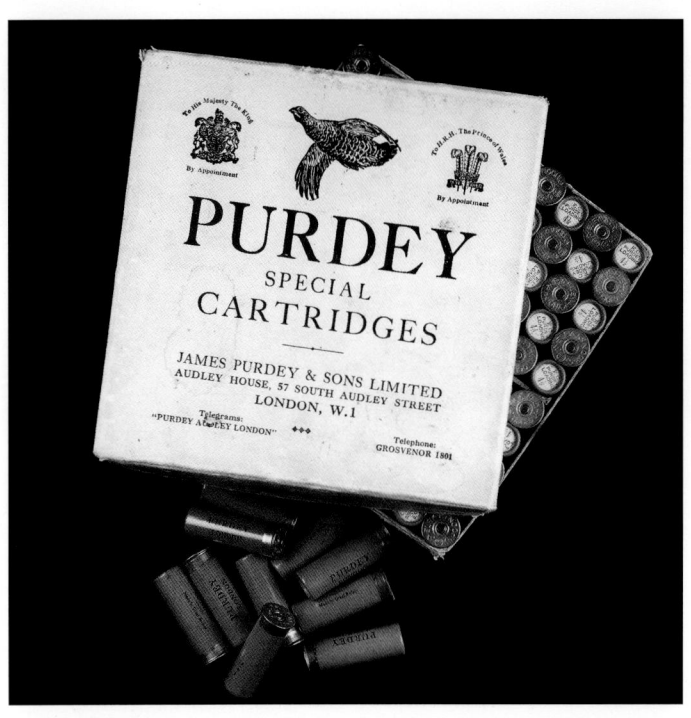

A box of 100 12-bore cartridges dating from the 1930s. (*See plate 60 in colour section.*)

The record in the Dimension Book for Nos. 2418 1/2. Stocked by Dean and put together by Turvey and Lane. They were very light guns weighing 5lbs. 15 $1/2$oz. each. Note beside 'Remarks': 'Hammer Ejectors Whitworth Clips, Sorbo heel plates, lea covered, Pistol hand, Spring blade R Crown & garter inlaid in stock.'

The record in the factory workbook for Nos. 2418 1/2. The gunmakers were: Simons, barrel maker; Fullalove, actioner; Williams, actioner; Sidney, luggers; Dean, stocker; Sumpter, barrel borer; Kell, engraver; Turvey and Lane, finishers.

Unlike the miniature hammerless guns built for Queen Mary's dolls' house in 1923, the Silver Jubilee guns would actually work. Three miniature guns were built in total, Nos. 25000/1 for presentation to the king and No. 24707 as a back-up in case of accident. Harry Lawrence played the major part in building these guns, Harold Delay stocked them and Fred Williams made the hammers. They were engraved by Harry Kell and browned by Alfred Jelffs. Len Howard made the case implements and all the Lawrences, Ernest Snr., Harry and Ernest Jnr. finished the guns. The silver and gold case was made by Garrard the Jewellers of Regent Street. Nos. 25000/1 are reckoned to be the last hammer guns built by Purdey, although there is a vague record of a later hammer gun, No. 25015 of 1935. This gun might not have been built. The miniature guns were 7 inches long, weighed 13 drams and had 69 parts. The cartridges were made by I.C.I. at their Eley plant in Birmingham with a powder charge of 1.62 grains and shot charge of 2.02 grains. The spare gun, No. 24707, was kept by Tom Purdey and had his initials engraved on the gold oval. The leather case was made by Harry Lawrence's mother. This gun remains in the Purdey collection at Audley House today.

The record in the Dimension Book for Nos. 25000/1.

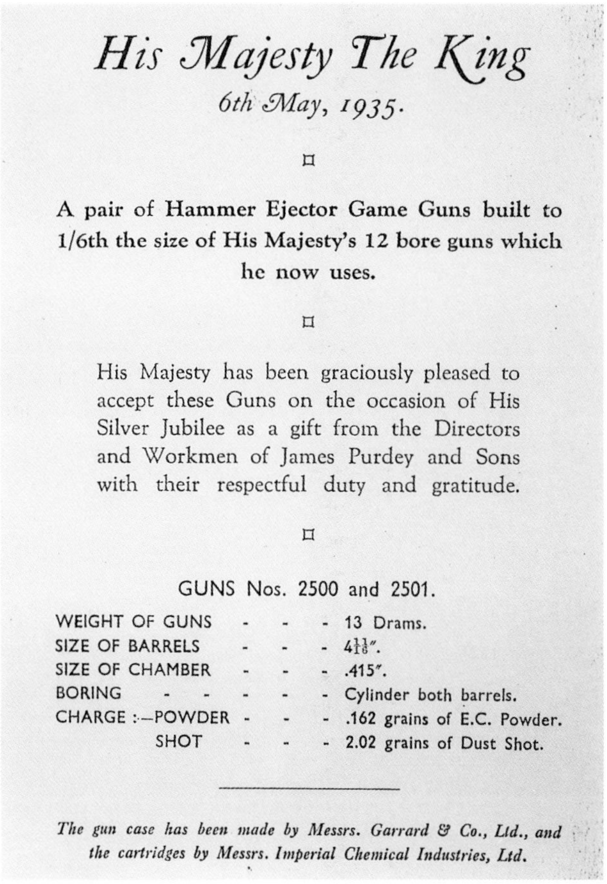

Just as James Purdey the Elder had delved into authorship with his *Observations on the Proper Management and Cleaning Detonating Guns,* 1826, so did his descendants Tom and Jim Purdey in 1936. *The Shot Gun* by T D S Purdey and Captain J A Purdey was published by Philip Allan as part of The Sportsman's Library. The book was 237 pages long, the earlier chapters giving advice on guns, fitting, cartridges, shooting schools etc. and the later chapters, hints on shooting and the care of guns.

A change took place in the design of the sidelocks in the 1920s and 30s. The original Beesley sidelocks of 1880 had no intercepting safety sears but, soon after the introduction of this action, such intercepting sears were invented. An intercepting sear will automatically bolt the tumbler to prevent the unintentional discharge of the gun if some mechanical malfunction should occur. In the normal course of events, when the trigger is pulled, the trigger will lift not only the lock sear to discharge the gun, but also the intercepting sear to clear it from the mechanism. These intercepting sears were fitted to all Purdey sidelocks.

In the 1920s and 30s Ernest Lawrence replaced the intercepting safety sear with a simpler version, the safety locking sear. This safety locking sear was simpler to use with the single trigger. From this period on safety locking sears were used up until very recent times when Purdey have reverted to the traditional intercepting safety sear.

His Majesty The King
6th May, 1935.

A pair of Hammer Ejector Game Guns built to 1/6th the size of His Majesty's 12 bore guns which he now uses.

His Majesty has been graciously pleased to accept these Guns on the occasion of His Silver Jubilee as a gift from the Directors and Workmen of James Purdey and Sons with their respectful duty and gratitude.

GUNS Nos. 2500 and 2501.

WEIGHT OF GUNS	13 Drams.
SIZE OF BARRELS	4$\frac{13}{16}$".
SIZE OF CHAMBER	.415".
BORING	Cylinder both barrels.
CHARGE :—POWDER	.162 grains of E.C. Powder.
SHOT	2.02 grains of Dust Shot.

The gun case has been made by Messrs. Garrard & Co., Ltd., and the cartridges by Messrs. Imperial Chemical Industries, Ltd.

The acceptance letter from King George V for the pair of miniature hammer ejector guns Nos. 25000/1.

The third of the miniature hammer ejector guns No. 24707 built in 1934/5. (*See plate 61 in colour section.*)

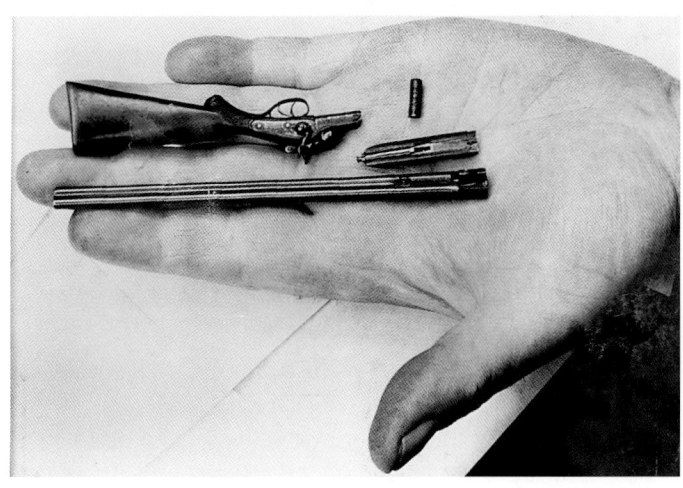

One of the miniature guns showing how small they were.

Jim Purdey and his son J O K Purdey outside Jim's house, 5 Wellington Square, *circa* 1935.

The Long Room in 1934 with Tom and Jim.

The Long Room in 1958 showing how the central well has been replaced by a table.

The second half of the 1930s saw the world climbing out of depression. Gun orders increased and many of the redundant gunmakers were re-employed. By 1937 gun output had doubled to around 200 guns per year from around 100 guns per year in 1934. Although economic recession was on the turn, the clouds of war were on the horizon, a war that would have the most far reaching consequences in the history of Purdey. However, appeasement, the perceived panacea to the belligerence of the dictators, created an atmosphere of nebulous optimism. Purdey's were no exception and upon the Coronation of King George VI on 12 May 1937, Audley House was decorated to patriotic excess. Red, white and blue bunting festooned the building, Union Jacks fluttered in the wind and 'God Save The King' placards emblazoned the railings on the first floor. In early 1938, the Long Room was re-built. The central well, whereby the activities in the gun room below could be watched, was covered over and in place of the central well, a large table and chairs were installed. The changes were designed to make the room more private for Tom and Jim.

Audley House in 1937, decorated for the coronation of King George VI.

Tom Purdey in July 1937.

WAR – GUNS OR MOULDS?

The optimism of the appeasers culminating in 'peace in our times' at Munich in 1938, rapidly gave way to the realism that the fascist dictators, Hitler and Mussolini, could only be stopped by military action. Reasoned diplomacy within the background of a guilt over the 1919 Versailles Treaty had been tried, tested and failed against aggressive megalomania and nationalism. Hitler's assurance at Munich in 1938, that the Sudetenland in Czechoslovakia was his 'last territorial demand in Europe', became worthless when a great deal of the rest of Czechoslovakia came under German 'protection' in March 1939. He could never be trusted again and this caused a complete reversal of British opinion. The inevitability of war was accepted, re-armament stepped up, the only imponderable being when. This spiral towards war had a great affect on Purdey's. Gun production rapidly dropped in 1938 and 1939, as American and European customers decided not to order in such an atmosphere of uncertainty.

As if to symbolise the closing of an era, Athol Purdey died, aged 81, at Folkestone in 1939. The generations of Purdey's had always enjoyed the sea, James Purdey the Elder having a seaside house at Margate. James Purdey the Younger had his own yacht and was a member of the Royal London Yacht Club. Athol Purdey had owned property for many years on the south coast at Folkestone and it was there on 30 April 1939 at 3 Shorecliffe Road that he died. He had been ill with pneumonia for a short length of time and, as it so often the case with elderly patients, it proved fatal. His son Jim Purdey was with him when he died. He was cremated in the Ashford Crematorium and his ashes interred in the grounds on 3 May. The following day, Thursday 4 May a memorial service took place at 12 noon at St. George's, Hanover Square.

Obituaries were published in a large number of periodicals, *The Field*, *The Times*, *Harpers*, the *Evening News*, the *Shooting Times*, etc. The obituary published in the *Shooting*

Times and British Sportsman of 6 May 1939 is reproduced below:

> It is with profound regret that we record the passing of a very eminent gunmaker, Mr. Athol S Purdey, who died at Folkstone, after a short illness, on Sunday April 30, in his 82nd year. Mr. Purdey was born in London on 1858 he was the son of the late James Purdey and grandson of the the founder of the firm of James Purdey and Sons. He was educated privately and in France.
>
> On completing his education he joined his father's firm and at the time of his death was Managing Director in the gunmaking business of James Purdey and Sons, Ltd., although for the last ten years he had taken no active part in business or public life.
>
> Mr. Purdey was admitted to the Livery of the Worshipful Company of Gunmakers in 1879 and was master of the Company for the first time in 1890 and on three subsequent occasions (1899, 1908 and 1921). During his long connection with the gunmakers' Company, he was prominent in assisting in the settlement of many questions vital to the interests of the British gunmaking industry, and all questions dealing with the re-drafting of The Gun Barrel Proof Act.
>
> During his sixty-four years with his firm he was recognised as a figure that stood for all that was best in practicing and influencing this world-famous British industry.
>
> He was as equally a familiar figure on the continent of Europe and the United States as he was to the great shooting fraternity of the '70s and '90s and those of the present in Great Britain.
>
> With the passing of this doyen of British gunmakers we lose a link between the great shooters and memories of the past and their modern descendants.
>
> He married, in 1890, Mabel Field, daughter of Alan Field Roscoe, and leaves two sons, Thomas and James A., who have both been Directors of his firm of many years and both Past Masters of the Worshipful Company of gunmakers, and who will continue the business at the present address.
>
> The funeral took place on Wednesday at Folkstone, and a memorial service was held at St. George's Hanover Square, London, on Thursday 4th inst., at noon, being attended by a large number of friends and representatives of the gunmaking industry.

Athol had essentially run the firm from the late 19th century to the late 1920s. He had guided Purdey's through the difficult war period and continued to ensure that Purdey's remained throughout the world as an institution for best guns. He died intestate. His wife, Mabel, died shortly after him, in one of the flats in Audley House on 5 September 1939. She was cremated and her ashes were buried alongside her husband's in the grounds of the Ashford Crematorium.

With falling gun orders and the certainty of war on the horizon, Purdey could draw on their experience of war economy, a depressing 25 years earlier. There were no illusions of a short, sharp war – this would be another total war. On account of this, very few guns were produced in the 1939-45 period. A small amount of sporting gun activity was undertaken, mainly due to the age of one or two craftsmen who found it difficult to adapt to the entirely new production output at Purdey's – gunmakers like Charlie Lane, Ben Delay and Fred Williams.

To Harry Lawrence, great credit must be given for his role, not only in guiding Purdey's through the difficult war period, but for his contribution to war production. His services were officially recognised and he was awarded the M.B.E. for his war work at the end of the war. In 1938, Harry actively sought out alternative work for Purdey's as the European situation worsened. He found a firm named Aircraft Materials near King's Cross Station that required a pop-rivet tool. Monocoque Aircraft Design with stressed skin construction had just been developed and rivet guns were required in their thousands for unskilled labour to build fuselages, etc. Mr. Gould at Aircraft Materials had invented such a tool but it was left to Harry Lawrence to develop and make the prototypes. Eventually thousands were produced in the Irongate Road factory.

Tom Purdey was informed that the B.S.A. factory in Birmingham was having difficulty coping with the re-

A Purdey beanfeast in 1939. An outing from Marlow to Windsor.

armament programme. There was a shortage of skilled workers to make the necessary gauges for the Lee-Enfield Mk. IV rifle. Harry visited Mr. J Leake of B.S.A. in 1938 and realised immediately that gauge-making was eminently suitable for Purdey craftsmen. As a result Purdey's received a contract to manufacture such gauges.

In the quest for lebensraum, the Germans nourished designs on their next victim, Poland. With the volte face over appeasement on account of Germany's seizure of Czechoslovakia in March 1939, Britain had guaranteed to help Poland in the event of German attack. Hitler's stumbling block to such an attack, Russia, was removed when an astonished world was told of the Russo-German Pact of August 1939. Hitler was free to attack Poland and this he did on 1 September 1939. The British ultimatum to Germany to stop the attack on Poland expired at 11.00 a.m. on 3 September 1939. No response being forthcoming, Great Britain was once again at war with Germany.

Purdey's were already on a war footing with the manufacture of gauges and the pop-rivet guns. Now with the declaration of war, the manifestations of war were everywhere. The threat of massed air attack, amply demonstrated in the Spanish Civil War at Guernica, caused an immediate proliferation at Audley House and at Irongate Wharf of black-out curtains and sticky tape across windows. Buckets filled with sand and stirrup pumps were on hand to deal with incendiary bombs. Thousands of P14 rifles, preserved since World War One by a liberal coating of thick grease, were delivered to the factory for de-greasing and checking, a thoroughly unpleasant and dirty job.

The threat of invasion was real and the Local Defence Volunteers were set up, later re-named the Home Guard. To equip this force, the Ministry of Supply was empowered to take over stocks of weapons from gunmakers. In addition to various other makes held in the gun room, Purdey was forced to sell guns Nos. 11728, 12717 and rifle No. 16274 to the War Department. I wonder where they ended up?

The gauge-making side of business proved to be an outstanding success, so much so that the premises in Irongate Wharf were not large enough. The Ministry of Supply stepped in and requisitioned a large factory from Rio Truck in the Great West Road, Brentford on the western outskirts of London. The majority of Purdey's skilled craftsmen transferred there to concentrate on gauge manufacture. Harry Lawrence was put in charge of the factory, while his father, Ernest Lawrence, remained at Irongate Wharf.

At the Great West Road factory, the Purdey gunmakers made a variety of gauges and moulds. They made complicated receiver gauges, special tools and gauges for cartridge manufacture, such as the 17-pounder anti-tank gun and plastic moulds for aircraft electrical equipment. Demand was such that many extra staff had to be taken on, working day and night shifts. By early 1944, there were 52 gauge and tool makers, including 8 women, working at this factory. At the old Irongate Factory there were 49 workers, by far the majority being women. Nine men worked at Irongate, only two, Charlie Lane the finisher and Ben Delay senior, being involved in Purdey gun work. The premises had even expanded at Irongate, an adjoining warehouse being rented

Bomb damage in South Audley Street near Purdey's, 1941.

for the manufacture of rifle chamber caps. The workers in each factory could volunteer for fire watch duties, being paid an extra 5s per week. This entailed staying up overnight and being ready to douse any incendiaries. Cartridge manufacture under Ralph Lawrence and Bill Leeper continued throughout the war in Audley House. Food imports were curtailed due to enemy action and the nation had to resort to increased home production. Marginal land and age old pasture were put to the plough and vermin control was essential. Although cartridge manufacture was encouraged for such purposes by the Government, the quality of cartridges was poor with their inferior brown cases and wads.

In the Autumn of 1940, the Luftwaffe changed its tactics and began bombing British cities in an attempt to sap the will of the people. London was particularly badly hit in the Blitz that lasted from September 1940 to May 1941. Night after night waves of bombers disgorged their loads causing severe damage and dislocation to the capital. Purdey's were no exception and experienced severe damage during a raid of

The portrait of Jim Purdey presented to him on his 50th birthday, 30 September 1941. The label states 'JAMES ALEXANDER PURDEY – Eldest son of Athol Stuart Purdey, Father of James Oliver Kinloch Purdey and William Purdey. Born 1891, Freedom 1913, Court 1928. Died 1963. Master 1931.'. 'Presented to Captain James Purdey, late 21 and 12th Lancers on his fiftieth birthday, 30 September 1941 by the Directors and Employees of James Purdey & Sons Ltd.' 'W Smithson Broadhead 1941.' (*See plate 62 in colour section.*)

15/16 April 1941 when a stick of bombs straddled South Audley Street and Mount Street. These were high explosive bombs designed to de-house. All the windows in Audley House were broken and the slates blown off the roof. Fortunately there was no fire. Work ceased in Irongate the next day as the men were taken from the factory to cover the roof with tarpaulins and board up the windows. The scars of these bomb blasts are still evident today, the columns on the outside of Audley House displaying the shrapnel damage inflicted. A brass plaque proclaims that the bombs exploded at 1.00 a.m., 16 April 1941. Even inside the front shop, a piece of shrapnel has been preserved embedded in the wall. This wouldn't be the last time that Purdey's would be bombed, an I.R.A. bomb exploding on 29 October 1975.

Jim Purdey would celebrate his 50th birthday on 30 September 1941 and to mark the event a party was held in the Connaught Rooms. The workmen were given the day off to attend the party. An oil portrait of Jim had been commissioned from the painter W Smithson Broadhead, all of the workers contributing a small sum to its cost (see plate 62). Several of Jim's friends and relatives attended as well and the portrait was presented.

On 23 July 1943, the nephew of Harry Lawrence, Lawrence Salter, joined Purdey's aged fourteen as an apprentice toolmaker at the Great West Road factory. At the end of the war he was transferred to the gunmaking factory at Irongate where he learned his trade as an actioner under his uncle, Ernest Lawrence. In 1967 he became a director, on 23 January 1968 assistant managing-director and on 23 April 1970 managing-director. He became Master of the Gunmakers' Company on two occasions, 1976 and 1986.

In October 1943, Cecil Purdey was admitted to the Princess Beatrice Hospital, Old Brompton Road for an operation for a stomach ulcer. The operation was not a success and he died there on 30 October 1943. He was 78 and had been living temporarily at the Balholm Hotel, Paignton, Devon. In his will he left £16,019.8s.9d, all of it passing to his wife Harriet. Cecil had come into the Purdey business by default due to the illness of his younger brother James in the 1880s. He was always regarded as the lesser partner to his elder brother Athol and only enjoyed a one-third share of the business as opposed to Athol's two-thirds. As such he never appeared in the limelight in comparison to Athol. So ended the third generation of Purdey's, James Purdey the Elder, his son James Purdey the Younger, his sons Athol and Cecil Purdey.

In November 1943, Lord Portal and Major Miller-Mundy sold their preference shares in Purdey to Cobbold & Co. of Ipswich. Ivan Cobbold had been a friend and customer of Purdey's for some time and with his financial backing and personal interest in the firm, the future of Purdey's looked secure. Cobbold at this time was a colonel in the Scots Guards. On Sunday 18 June 1944, he attended a service in the Guards' Chapel. Hitler had intensified his terror campaign on London using pilotless flying bombs, the V1, launched from across the Channel. One of these bombs hit the Guards' Chapel, several people being killed including Ivan Cobbold.

Following the invasion of 6 June 1944, the German war machine was gradually pushed out of France and the Low Countries. By late 1944, it was obvious that the war would end in the not too distant future. The government began to reduce its contracts with the result that some of the women in the Irongate Wharf factory were made redundant. In April 1945, most of the Air Ministry contracts ended, with more workers being laid-off. On 7 May 1945, the German forces surrendered unconditionally. The amount of skilled work contributed by Purdey's to war production was officially recognised. Harry Lawrence was awarded the MBE for his efforts in re-organising and running the factory and Fred Williams, an actioner, the BEM. Fred Williams had been with Purdey's since the 1880s and was the oldest actioner with the firm by the war period. He was one of the few gunmakers who had continued to work on guns throughout the war.

Purdey's faced a difficult dilemma. They possessed skilled gunmakers who could rapidly revert to the trade they new best, gunmaking. Several guns had been ordered during the war and once the factory had been reorganised, gunmaking could once again commence. At the same time, Purdey's had built up during the war, a pool of skilled toolmakers to make moulds, gauges, etc. Due to the devastation caused by the war, skilled toolmakers would be in demand post war.

The trauma caused by World War Two, not only in personal terms but in economic and political upheaval was immense. Much of Europe lay in ruins and the greyness of post-war Europe and the austerity of post-war Britain were not conducive to a healthy demand for a luxury product like

A pen-and-ink drawing of Audley House by Fletcher drawn in early 1945. Note the as yet unrepaired windows damaged in the 1941 bombing.

best guns. The Labour Government, with Clement Attlee at the helm, returned to power in 1945, was intent on creating a socialist, just, Britain as had been promised but never delivered to the returning heroes of 1918. The upshot was that a high taxation policy, including a highly progressive income tax, was created that diminished the disposable income of Purdey customers. This high re-distributive taxation along with the Labour Party's commitment to nationalisation and policy of social justice, was either doctrinaire or altruistic depending upon perspective. Not only did these policies reduce demand for Purdey guns, they also created an air of pessimism for the future of the firm in general. Increased wage demands during the war had pushed up labour costs to the extent that a basic Purdey gun would cost £230 in 1945. By mid-1946 this price was adjusted to £280. This price was too high for an American market likewise exhausted by the debilitating effect of a major war.

This Age of Austerity and pessimism manifested itself in a major cancellation of gun orders in 1946. Over one-third of the orders taken during the war were cancelled. The future looked bleak. In March 1946, the Cobbold shares were sold to Sir Hugh Seely who had been Under-Secretary for Air during the war. Sir Hugh, later Lord Sherwood, became a director and owner of Purdey's and great credit must be given to him for his vision in this difficult era. As early as 1943, Cecil Purdey had suggested at a board meeting that perhaps the future of Purdey's lay in tools and moulds and not in guns. Now with the cancellation of orders, the policies of the Labour government and the cost of the Purdey gun for the American market, Tom Purdey again raised the question about which direction the firm should take. Jim Purdey, by now living permanently in the home country of his wife, New Jersey, USA, agreed with Tom. Tom suggested that Purdey's should invest in machines and concentrate all their efforts in tool and mould manufacture. The gunmaking side would be dropped and the gunmakers transferred as they had done so during the war to toolmaking.

Lord Sherwood disagreed. His view was that Purdey's had a worldwide reputation in building guns, that this was what the firm excelled in and just because high profits had been made in toolmaking during the war it did not necessarily mean that this would continue in the future. Toolmaking firms were relatively common and competition intense – there was only one Purdey and just because things were difficult at present, that fact should not be forgotten. Lord Sherwood's opinion won the day and although there were difficult periods ahead, with the benefit of hindsight, his decision was absolutely correct.

In the meantime it was decided to keep both options open. The gunmakers continued building guns in the old Irongate Wharf factory. The lease on the Great West Road factory, where the toolmaking took place, expired in 1946 and new premises were found for the toolmakers quite near the gunmakers at Irongate Wharf Road. The Purdey toolmaking business would continue until 1961.

Tom and Jim Purdey in the Long Room in the late 1940s.

Sir Hugh Seely (Lord Sherwood), bought Purdey's 1946, chairman 1955, died 1 April 1970.

Chapter nine

FROM AUSTERITY TO RENAISSANCE

The post-war austerity would have a marked effect on a firm like Purdey's for a long time. European gun demand was far less, meaning lower annual gun production. The 1920s and 1930s had seen average annual output of around 200 guns, whereas the post-war period saw this figure drop to around 70. The American market assumed far greater importance and an astute move by Purdey in 1948 meant that Purdey's could gain a greater foothold there. On 1 January 1949, Purdey's bought the business of James Woodward & Son and with it the rights to manufacture the very successful Woodward O/U. On Tom Purdey's various trips to the USA in the immediate post-war period, he had frequently been asked about O/U guns, but there were reservations about the pre-war Purdey O/Us.

The founder of the business, James Woodward, began work with Charles Moore in 1827 at 77 St. James's Street. By the mid 1840s, Woodward was taken into partnership with Charles Moore, the firm trading as Moore & Woodward. Around 1850 the firm became known as James Woodward and in 1872 the firm was re-named James Woodward & Sons in reference to his two sons James and Charles. In 1937 the firm moved to 29 Bury Street. Woodwards had established a reputation for building particularly finely finished and elegant guns and in addition they had patented and developed a highly successful O/U gun.

O/U guns had developed in Germany and several British makers at the beginning of the 20th century patented their own designs. Most of these designs resulted in heavy, clumsy guns that did not appeal to the shooting public. The exception to this was the Boss over-and-under gun, a masterpiece of simple ingenuity with very elegant proportions. John Robertson, the proprietor of Boss, patented this O/U gun in patents Nos. 3307 and 3308 of 10 February 1909 and it was an immediate success, revolutionalising the over-and-under gun.

Some four years later James Woodward patented a very similar design to the Boss O/U. patent no. 4986 of 27 February 1913, taken out in the names of Charles Woodward, William Evershed, the manager of the firm and Charles Hill, all giving Woodward's address in the patent – 64 St. James's Street – created the Woodward O/U gun. Like the Boss O/U gun the Woodward design incorporated the barrel lumps on either side of the lower barrel (figure 6, part 10). The rear lumps had slots cut out to lock the barrels. The curved surfaces on both lumps provided a very secure locking mechanism. In the patent, Woodward stressed the main virtue of his patent which was the interlocking tongue and grooves for lateral strength. There were two pairs of tongue and grooves. The first pair were placed on the front barrel lump to lock the action (figure 6, parts 10 and 11, and figure 3, parts 12

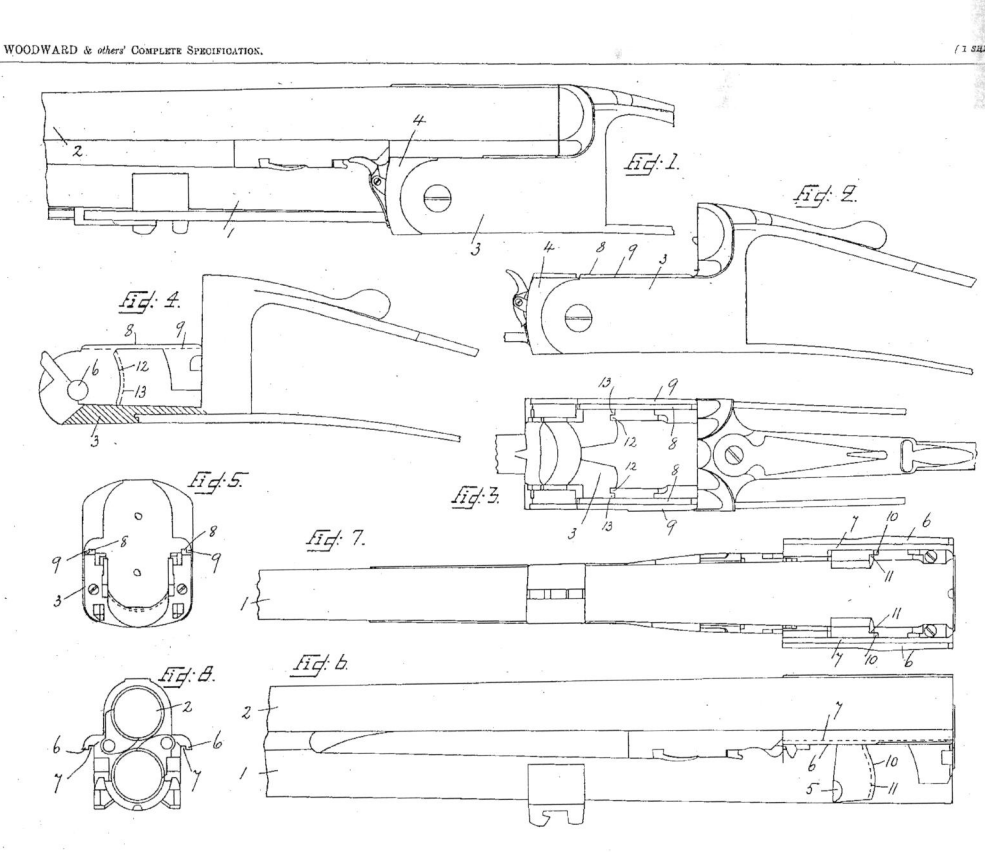

Patent no. 4986 of 27 February 1913 that created the Woodward O/U gun.

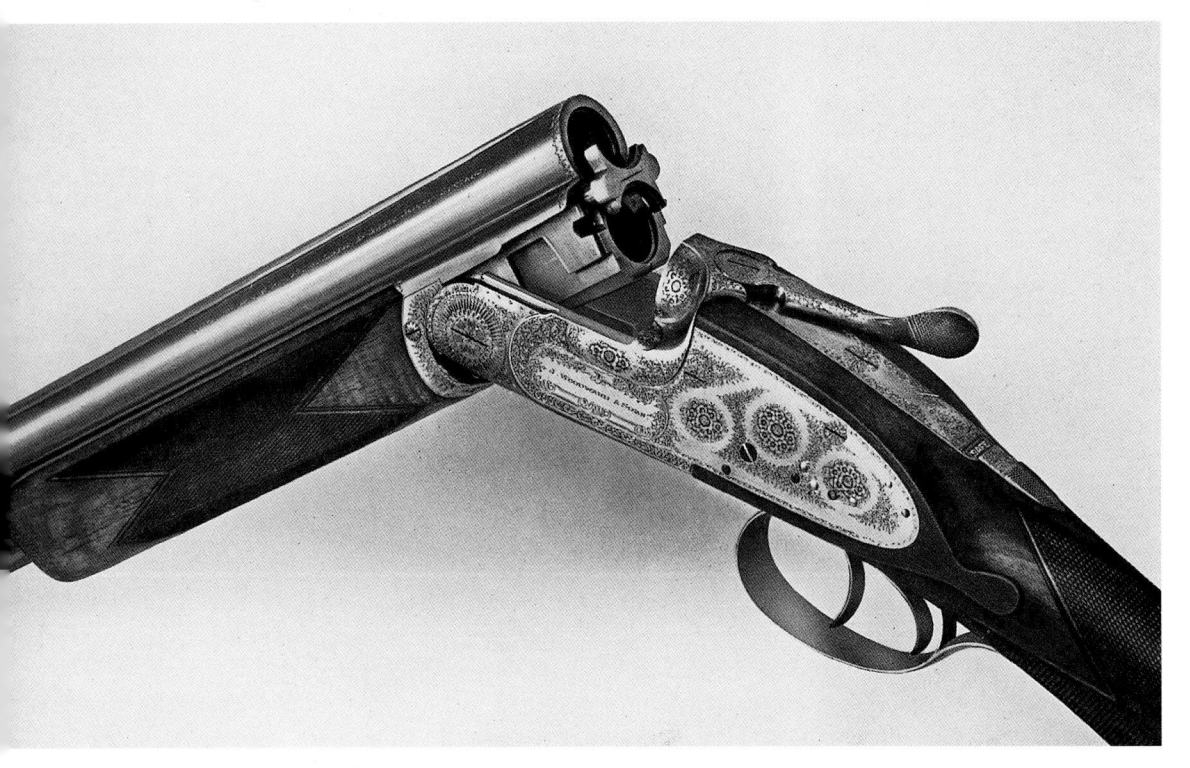

A Woodward O/U built in the 1920s showing the lumps on the lower barrel.

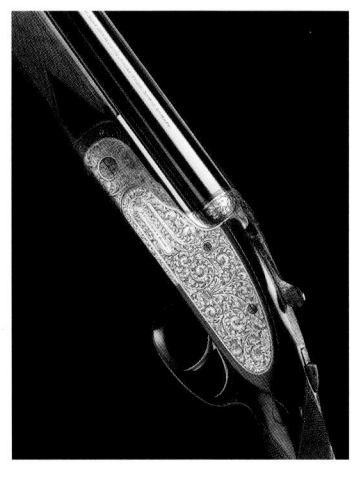

An early O/U gun, 12-bore No. 26212 sold in August 1951. The detonating is carved with oak leaves and acorns and the engraving is of foliate scroll. Hold open top lever, cocking indicators and barrels with matt top rib. Weight 7lb 9½oz. This gun was stocked by Harold Delay, put together by Warlow and engraved by Harry Kell. (*See plate 63 in colour section.*)

Ernest Douglas Lawrence.

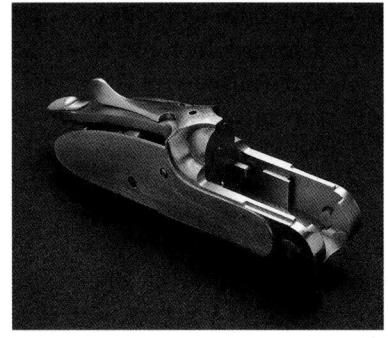

Prototype O/U .410 action built by Ernest Lawrence.

and 13). The second pair were placed on either side of the barrels, again to lock in the action (figure 8, parts 6 and 7 and figure 5, parts 8 and 9).

The end result was a very strong O/U action and in addition a very slim action was created due to the lumps being placed on either side of the barrels. Both these factors coupled with the high quality of Woodward guns ensured that the Woodward O/U was a resounding success.

The Woodward O/U along with the Boss O/U were regarded as the finest designs of their time, both models being of slim, elegant proportions, very light in weight yet very strong. The pre-war Purdey O/U based on the Edwinson Green gun did not stand comparison and when Purdey's were offered Woodward in 1948 it was an offer that they could not refuse, particularly when the Woodward and Boss O/Us were so successful in the American market.

Woodwards felt keenly the effects of the post-war economy, producing around three guns per year, so small an amount that the firm could not survive. In addition, Charles Woodward wanted to retire and approached Tom Purdey to negotiate a sale. The agreement was signed on 1 October 1948, the sale to conclude on 1 January 1949. For the price of £444.14s.6d (£300 for the goodwill of the business and £144.14s.6d for the stock and trade), Purdey bought the goodwill of the business, the name of James Woodward & Son, the names and addresses of customers, various part-finished Woodward guns and, most important of all, the 'right' (exercisable at their own discretion) to manufacture the 'Woodward Over-and-Under Gun' and to use the name 'Woodward'.

Upon the conclusion of the sale, Purdey's made certain modifications to the Woodward over-and-under, such as re-designed firing pins, different types of sidelock, use of Purdey's safety and top lever. It was primarily Harry Lawrence's younger brother, Ernest Douglas Lawrence, who made these modifications and took over the building of the action, the cocking and the ejector. Ernest Lawrence had taken up his apprenticeship as an actioner with Purdey's in 1927 and at the beginning of the war in 1939 joined the navy and served on *H.M.S. Carlisle*, *H.M.S. Kimberley*, *H.M.S. Capel* and *H.M.S. Nelson*. He came out of the navy in 1946 and re-joined Purdey's.

The first O/U gun built to Woodward's design was No. 25950, a 12-bore weighing 7lb 9oz delivered in 1950. From then onwards, O/Us began to be produced in increasing quantities and to date some 447 have been delivered. The Woodward side-by-side was discontinued and it is only very recently that Purdey resurrected this gun, producing it under the Woodward name.

In January 1948, Ernest Charles Lawrence, the factory manager, retired. He had joined Purdey's in 1898 and had become factory manager in 1914.

FROM AUSTERITY TO RENAISSANCE

Tom Purdey and Ernest Charles Lawrence in the Long Room on the occasion of Ernest Lawrence's retirement, January 1948.

The Hon. Richard Beaumont, Chairman of Purdey's 1971-94. A portrait of him as a Midshipman R.N.V.R. painted by Oswald Birley, 1945.

In early 1949, Richard Beaumont joined Purdey's after war service with the Royal Naval Volunteer Reserve and subsequent demobilisation in 1947. His uncle was Lord Sherwood, the owner and a director of Purdey's. The Hon. Richard Beaumont, born in 1926, would play a big role in Purdey's over the next forty years. He became a director on 25 March 1953, chairman on 26 July 1971 and was Master of the Gunmakers' Company in 1968 and 1984. Like James Purdey the Elder and Tom and Jim Purdey, he delved into authorship with his popular and original history of Purdey's: *Purdey's, The Guns and the Family*, first published in 1984.

The year 1950 saw the Purdey factory on the move again for the fifth time. The factory had been at No. 2 Irongate Wharf since 1900 and this time the move was not very far, to 20/22 Irongate Wharf. Here the factory would remain until 1971 when it moved, again close by, to North Wharf Road (Bishop's Bridge Road).

A change of a more permanent nature was the cessation in 1951 of Purdey hand-loaded cartridges in Audley House. Hand-loaded cartridges had been produced in their millions by Purdey, more recently under the direction of Ralph Lawrence in Audley House. However new powders introduced by I.C.I. replacing the traditional Schultze, EC and Diamond powders meant that they were too difficult to handle and all Purdey cartridge loading was transferred to Imperial Metal Industries, a subsidiary of I.C.I. As a result Ralph Lawrence went to work for the Gunmakers' Company in 1950 as Assistant Proof Master at the Proof House. On 18 March 1952, tragedy struck when he put down a recently loaded rifle to answer the phone. Something caught the trigger and the rifle discharged, killing him through the neck. Shortly after this, on 22 November 1953, his father, Purdey's long-standing factory manager, Ernest Charles Lawrence, died aged 82. On a more positive note, Harry Lawrence became a director of Purdey in 1951 and would become managing-director in 1954.

To capitalise on the essential American market, Tom Purdey made several trips there in the 1950s. A typical trip would last about six weeks and he would stay at such places as the Statler Hotel, St. Louis, the Blackstone Hotel, Chicago, the Mary Hopkins Hotel, San Francisco and the Ambassador

Tom Purdey in the Long Room in the year 1950, inscribed 'To Harry (Lawrence) from two old gunmakers TP 1950'. (Tom is holding flintlock gun No. 86.)

147

Hotel, Los Angeles. These trips were always well publicised in advance and resulted in much needed gun orders, particularly for O/Us. American gun demand differed considerably from the traditional British style in that American customers tended to specify more ostentatious engraving. Purdey's in-house engravers had always concentrated on traditional rose and scroll and more flamboyant work was given out to engravers like Harry Kell. One of Kell's apprentices, Ken Hunt, had been taken on by Purdey's in 1950 and so popular was his work, particularly with the Americans, that his skills were frequently in demand. Hunt actually trained and worked in Kell's workshop remaining there until National Service called in 1957. By the end of his National Service in 1959, Kell had died and Hunt briefly returned to Purdey's in that year, later going freelance to become one of the leading engravers in the second half of the 20th century.

Continuing the tradition begun by the Prince of Wales in 1868, the new Queen of Great Britain, Queen Elizabeth II, granted Purdey's the Royal Warrant of Appointment on 15 July 1955 followed by her husband the Duke of Edinburgh on 2 January 1956.

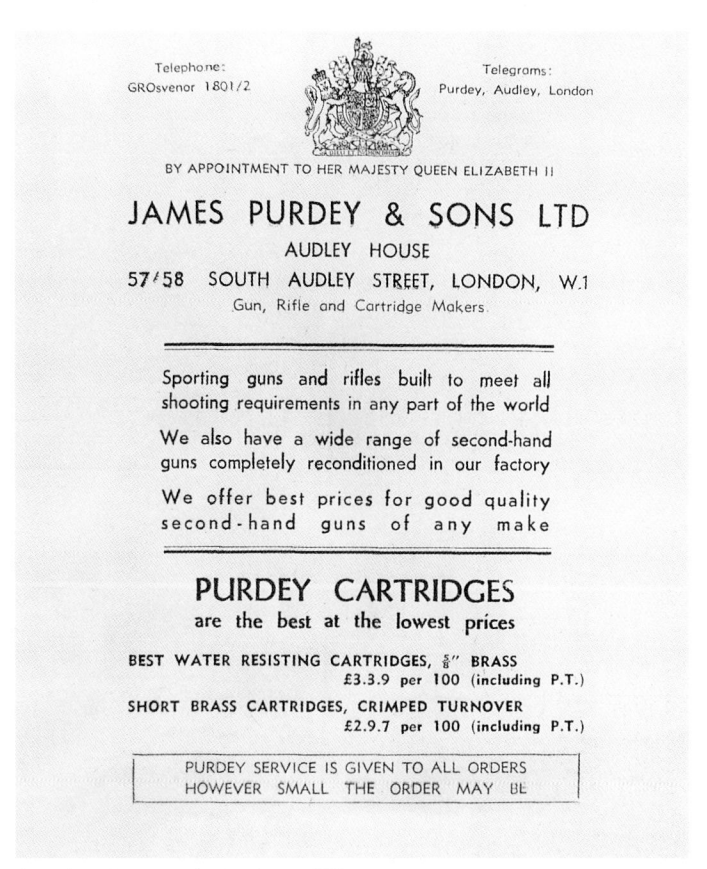

An advertisement dating from 1955.

Audley House 1953, decorated for the coronation of Queen Elizabeth II. Note the unrepaired Luftwaffe 1941 bomb damage on the entrance pillars.

TOM PURDEY 1897-1957

Tom Purdey had always been, to use that most hackneyed phrase, a character, a *bon viveur* and a man who enjoyed batchelor life to the full, unencumbered by family. He was famous for his rages, yet charming, erudite and interesting. He was knowledgeable about music, prose and verse and on a human side full of compassion and humour. He was infamous for his love of whisky. Such a life of good living took its toll and in late 1954 Tom entered a private nursing home for an operation. He never really regained full strength after this and it became apparent that he could not give all his energies to Purdey's. On 1 May 1955 Tom was made president of the company, granted a pension and given a cottage, Fern Cottage at Chilham in Kent. Here Tom enjoyed his retirement, occasionally coming up to Purdey's.

One year later in 1956, it was obvious that Tom was very ill suffering from cancer. He went into Canterbury Hospital for another operation in the spring of 1957, but did not recover and died there on 5 March 1957, his death certificate stating 'cancer of the colon'. He was 59 years of age. Tom was cremated at Ashford crematorium and his ashes were placed in the crematorium grounds beside his mother and father, Mabel and Athol Purdey.

In Tom's will dated 24 October 1956, he left the whole of his property amounting to £3,653.14s.9d to Harry Lawrence. He expressed the wish that, out of his estate Harry should 'give some suitable item of my personal property to each of my personal friends and my friends on the staff of James Purdey & Sons Limited as a memento of the respect and friendship which has always existed between us'. With Tom's death, the last direct family link with Purdey ended for a considerable period. Although his brother Jim and Jim's son Jok remained shareholders, they were not involved in the day-to-day running of the firm. Today the direct family link has been re-established with Jim Purdey's grandson, Richard Purdey, playing a role in the running of the business as chairman.

FROM AUSTERITY TO RENAISSANCE

Tom Purdey had run the firm in difficult times, the inter-war depression, World War Two and the post-war disruption. Thanks to his charm and personality and visits to America, Purdey gained a firm in-road there so vital to its future survival. He was fiercely proud of the Purdey name and it is thanks to him that he kept the tradition of the firm intact through several changes of ownership in such turbulent times. Unlike his ancestors Tom never had his portrait painted in his lifetime. In 1959 his portrait was commissioned from Robert Swan using several photographs. Today this portrait hangs in the Long Room and the label states 'Thomas Donald Stuart Purdey, Son of Athol Stuart Purdey. Born 1897. Freedom 1919. Court 1925. Master 1928, 1940, 1951. Died unmarried 1957 aged sixty years' (see plate 64).

Tom Purdey by Robert Swan 1959. (*See plate 64 in colour section.*)

Thanks to the sales trips abroad, the O/U gun and the healthy American market, Purdey gun production remained steady at around 60 to 70 guns per year in the 1950s. Profits were good and the gloom of the late 1940s dissipated. However the other side of the Purdey business, the mould making, painted a different picture. By the late 1950s the mould factory was trading at a loss and it became apparent that the gun profit was subsidising mould making. With the future of the gun business looking healthy, Purdey decided to close down the mould business, final closure occurring in 1961. Mould making had been an interesting interlude, offering good profits during the war yet open to great competition from other such firms in normal times. With the benefit of hindsight, the proposal to concentrate on moulds only after the war was quite rightly over-ruled. There was relief that Purdey's had returned to where their reputation and specialisation excelled.

With Tom Purdey gone, the sales trips abroad were made by Harry Lawrence and Richard Beaumont all resulting in a constant stream of orders. Jim Purdey was by now living in America and it was there that he died in 1963 aged 72 at Holmchel, New Jersey on 25 July 1963, having been ill for some time. Due to thrombosis he had had both legs amputated. His son, Major James Oliver Kinloch (JOK) Purdey (see plate 65), whilst carrying on the Purdey name, did not really take part in the business, although he remained close to it.

Major James Oliver Kinloch (JOK) Purdey 1918-84, son of James Purdey IV and father of Richard Purdey. (*See plate 65 in colour section.*)

A group of long-standing Purdey gunmakers. Left to right: Bob Heath, barrel-maker; Ben Delay, actioner; Harry Lawrence; Bill Geekie, finisher; Bert Price, finisher; Bob Thomson, finisher. A photograph taken in the 1960s.

Lawrence Salter, managing-director of Purdey's 1970-94.

Robin Nathan and Don Hazells in the front shop, Audley House 1965. Robin, as shop manager, is still with Purdey's today.

Harry Lawrence's nephew, Lawrence Salter, who had joined Purdey's as an apprentice on 23 July 1943 became assistant managing-director on 20 January 1968 and managing-director on 23 April 1970 and was Master of the Gunmakers' Company on two occasions in 1976 and 1986. In the late 1970s, it would be Lawrence Salter who re-designed the new Purdey single-trigger, developing the bobweight inertia single-trigger that is used today. He retired in 1994.

One interesting use of the Long Room in the late 1960s was as a Committee Room to thrash out proposals for the new shotgun certificate that was introduced in 1968. Firearms in Great Britain had been subject to strict laws for many decades, but shotguns could be openly purchased by anyone over fourteen. The increase in armed crime, particularly the prevalent use of shotguns, meant that the public and Government demanded greater control. Harry Lawrence put forward the suggestion that a committee of the Gun Trade Association and Home Office officials use the Long Room as a convenient meeting place. The end result was the introduction in 1968 of the shotgun certificate stipulating that only holders of the certificate granted by the police could purchase shotguns.

On 1 April 1970, the chairman of Purdey's, Lord Sherwood, died at Brook Hill, Isle of Wight aged 71. He had been Under Secretary of State for Air 1941-45 and was a noted Liberal M P. He had bought the Purdey shares from the estate of Ivan Cobbold and became owner of Purdey's on 12th March 1946, subsequently becoming chairman on 1 May 1955 until his death in 1970. His brother, a director of Purdey's, Sir Victor Seely took over the chairmanship, relinquishing it to Richard Beaumont on 26 July 1971. Credit must be given to Lord Sherwood for insisting in the dark immediate post-war years to retain the gun side of the business and not to change entirely over to mould manufacture.

In 1970 the landlords of the factory at 20-22 Irongate Wharf informed Purdey's that they intended to re-develop the site. The Purdey factory had been at this address since 1950 and in Irongate Wharf itself since 1900. The old factory was demolished and the Metropolitan Hotel now stands on the site, rumour having it that a pair of scrap Purdey barrels lie buried beneath the foundations as a tribute to the old factory. New premises were found close by and in 1971 the new factory opened at 57 North Wharf Road (off Bishop's Bridge Road). Here the factory would remain until its present move to Felgate Mews in 1979.

A visit by the Duke of Edinburgh to the factory in Irongate Wharf in the early 1960s. He is seen talking to Peter Delay, actioner. He had in fact met three generations of the Delay family on his visit, Ben Delay Snr., his two sons, Ben and Harold and grandson Peter.

FROM AUSTERITY TO RENAISSANCE

THE SPIRAL OF THE SEVENTIES.

The vagrancies of politics and economics had certainly affected Purdey's in the first half of the 20th century. However of all the difficult times experienced by the firm, probably the inflation of the late 1960s and 1970s caused it the greatest problem and threat.

The 1960s had witnessed increasing affluence for most people, secure jobs and high wages. One side effect of this prosperity was a gradual inflation, culminating in rampant inflation by the early 1970s. Spiralling wages meant that many Purdey gunmakers left the firm to seek better reward elsewhere. To retain their gunmakers, Purdey's raised wages and consequently the price of new guns had to be increased. But orders for new guns were on a fixed price basis, of great attraction to Americans benefiting from the inflation.

Such a situation was disastrous to Purdey. Take for example an O/U gun ordered at a fixed price of £1,500 in 1969. Delivery was about four years due to the lack of gunmakers and when the gun was delivered at its original fixed price it had actually cost about £2,500 to build. Obviously this situation, if it continued, would result in bankruptcy. In the early 1970s inflation averaged about 25% per year, peaking in 1974 to 32%. Prices continually had to be increased on account of this, e.g. the cost of a side-by-side in 1968 was £1,100, 1970 £1,500, 1971 £2,000, 1976 £4,500. By the early 1970s Purdey had to introduce surcharges upon delivery and later on wrote into order contracts an open-ended escalation clause. By 1976, as a result of these measures and a diminution of inflation, matters eased, craftsmen returned and delivery times were cut. The period had been a vicious spiral, inflation equalling higher wages, craftsmen leaving, lengthy delays, higher prices, customer antagonism, low production and poor profits. Such conditions manifested themselves in occasional guns not up to the usual Purdey standard.

In 1970, Harry Lawrence, by now aged 70, retired as managing-director, although he still remained a director and was retained as an adviser. In his place, his nephew, Lawrence Salter, was appointed managing-director. In reality Harry Lawrence never retired (see plate 66). He continued working with Purdey's until his death in 1984 and in his later years

Harry Lawrence and Eugene Warner, Long Room 1965.

Harry Lawrence, MBE 'in retirement' in the Long Room in the early 1980s. (*See plate 66 in colour section.*)

spent a considerable amount of time cataloguing, naming and sorting out various Purdey photographs and documents that have been of great assistance to me. Harry died on 28 July 1984 aged 84.

Harry Lawrence had played a pivotal role in Purdey's in the 20th century. He commanded great respect from everyone, was a first-class craftsmen and possessed great knowledge of all aspects of gun manufacture. From the beginning of his apprenticeship in 1914, his contribution to Purdey's was immense, whether it be building the miniature guns, managing the factory, or re-organising for war production. Such devotion to Purdey's was summarised in an article that appeared in the *Shooting Times* of 5 March 1964.

> Lawrence is managing-director not only in name but in deeds. He is at the factory at eight o'clock every morning to deal with any technical problems or points awaiting his decision. He still retains his own bench there and takes both a personal and if need be, an active part in the day to day work of the factory... Lawrence's daily visit to the factory is however only the beginning of his day. At about eleven o'clock, he arrives at Audley House and his day's work there is rarely finished before 7.00 p.m. After fifty years' work, one cannot but feel admiration for such sustained devotion to the gunmaker's craft, the name of Purdey and all that it stands for...

Audley House had experienced the bombs of the Luftwaffe in 1941, yet in more peaceful times suffered bombing again. At 9.30 p.m. on 29 October 1975, an IRA bomb exploded in the restaurant opposite the shop. The blast was considerable and blew in all the windows and ornamental railings.

In December 1977, Richard Beaumont's cousin, Nigel Beaumont, joined the firm. A university graduate, Nigel was a practical man intent on using his hands as well as his brain. He trained in the factory as an actioner under Ben Delay for four years and in addition learned all other aspects of gun manufacture such as stocking and barrel-making. In 1982 he was made a director of the firm and in 1994 managing-director upon the retirement of Lawrence Salter. In 1979 the factory was on the move yet again, transferring from North Wharf Road to Felgate Mews. The official opening of this factory was on 30 October 1979 and it is still at this location that Purdey guns are made today.

In the late 1970s Purdey's replaced their original gate

James Purdey & Sons Ltd.

(Incorporating James Woodward & Sons)

BY APPOINTMENT TO
HER MAJESTY QUEEN ELIZABETH II
GUN AND CARTRIDGE MAKERS

BY APPOINTMENT TO
H.R.H. THE DUKE OF EDINBURGH
GUN MAKERS

GUN, RIFLE & CARTRIDGE MAKERS

DIRECTORS:
HON. RICHARD BEAUMONT
(Chairman)
LAWRENCE SALTER
(Managing Director)
SIR ARTHUR COLLINS, KCVO
LORD TRYON
H. L. C. GREIG, CVO
C. H. LAWRENCE, OBE

Registered Office
AUDLEY HOUSE
57-58 STH AUDLEY STREET
LONDON W1Y 6ED

Tel: 01-499 1801/2. Grams: Purdey, London W1

SHOOTING SCHOOL
AT WEST LONDON SHOOTING
GROUNDS,
NORTHOLT, GREENFORD,
MIDDLESEX

REGISTERED IN ENGLAND
COMPANY Reg. No. 208758

An advertisement from 1980.

The damage caused by the IRA bomb in October 1975.

A part-finished gate single-trigger.

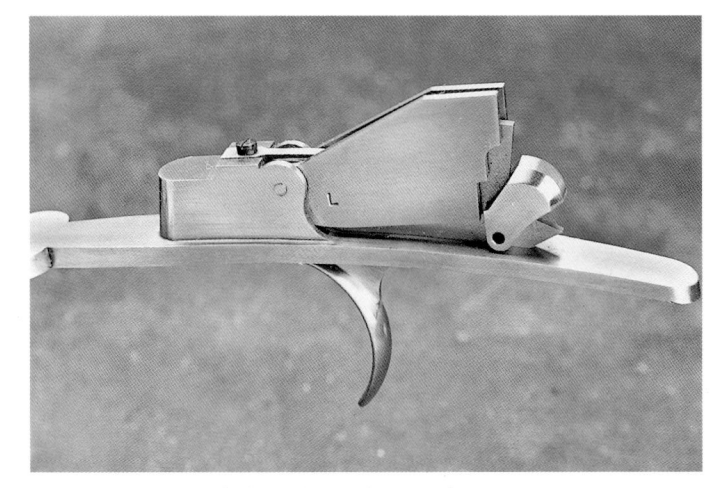

Lawrie Salter inertia bobweight single-trigger.

trigger with Lawrence Salter's inertia bobweight single-trigger. The gate single-trigger was complicated and expensive to make involving many parts. In addition it took up a lot of space in the gun and required expert regulation to make it work properly. Although it was a perfectly reliable single-trigger, its one defect was that it was slow in operation causing some outside gunmakers to make alterations to it thereby upsetting its regulation. This single-trigger continued on O/Us until the late 1980s. The gate trigger's replacement, the inertia, bobweight single-trigger was perfected by Lawrence Salter, Purdey's managing-director. Although termed an inertia single-trigger, it is in reality more mechanical than inertia. Its great virtue was in its simplicity requiring only six parts. When the gun fires, the gun recoils taking the bobweight with it. As the gun hits the sportsman's shoulder, it bounces off and leaves the bobweight behind. This negates the second involuntary pull that occurs at this moment. As the gun settles down, the bobweight moves forward and allows the second barrel to fire. Although non-selective, this trigger is very reliable, is simpler to make and is in high demand today. Another change in this era was in the re-adoption of the traditional intercepting safety sear in preference to Ernest Lawrence's locking sear.

In the 1980s some very longstanding members of Purdey staff took retirement. In 1985 Chris Gadsby the factory manager retired after some 56 years service. Chris Gadsby had begun his apprenticeship as a finisher under Archie Turvey in 1929. One of the most remarkable longstanding Purdey employees was Eugene Warner who retired in Christmas, 1989 aged 93 after some 72 years service with Purdey. Eugene Warner had been a sergeant in the Royal Artillery during World War One and severely wounded on Christmas Day, 1916. On crutches he joined the accounts department of the firm on 23 July 1918, responsible for keeping the firm's ledgers and accounts. On 7 August 1986, to celebrate his 90th birthday, a party was held in the Long Room. Eugene Warner died on 12th February 1992.

Purdey's have been so long established in Audley House, that the premises are on some of the official tourist maps of London. To commemorate the fact that Purdey's are one of the few London businesses to have traded on the same site for over 100 years, a Green Plaque was mounted on the wall of the building. The plaque was unveiled in a ceremony by Dame Shirley Porter on 30 April 1992, the plaque reading 'James Purdey the Younger 1828-1909 Gunmaker, built these premises in 1880 to house his new showroom and workshops'.

THE VENDOME TAKEOVER 1994

James Purdey had been a family run firm from its beginning in 1816 to the creation of the limited company in 1925. Upon the formation of this limited company, the firm had undergone various changes of ownership culminating in the most recent change, their acquisition by Vendome PLC on 5 October 1994. Vendome is a French luxury goods consortium that was founded in 1993 owning such companies as Dunhill, Cartier, watchmakers Baume & Mercier and Puget, Montblanc pens and the fashion and perfume houses Chloe and Karl

Richard Purdey (chairman), grandson of James Purdey IV and great grandson of Athol Purdey. (*See plate 67 in colour section.*)

Lagerfield. Shortly after the takeover, Richard Beaumont retired as chairman becoming president of Purdey's and in his place Richard Purdey took over. Since Tom Purdey's death in 1957, there had never really been a direct involvement of a Purdey in the running of the firm. So it was heartening to see a Purdey once more at the helm. Richard Purdey is the grandson of James Purdey IV and great-grandson of Athol Purdey.

Vendome made a major investment in Purdey that has ensured that Purdey entered the Millennium with renewed vigour. Thanks to Vendome's commitment, the Purdey machine shop includes the very latest technology, the computerised machines that are of great assistance to the gunmakers. The firm has become more marketing orientated with a new logo, the single word 'Purdey' and has re-designed the interior of Audley House to make it more welcoming. The name of James Woodward has been resurrected again. The last Woodward was produced in 1948 with gun No. 7184 and now Purdey's offer Woodward guns again continuing from that serial number built to Woodward specifications at the same prices as Purdey guns. The first such guns were completed in the Purdey factory in 1997, Woodward O/Us built to the original design and side-by-sides on offer. The side-by-side Woodward is a conventional cocking non self-opener built to patent no. 397 of 29 January 1881 by John Thomas Rogers and John Rogers. The Rogers are listed in the trade directories as gun action filers of 78 Lower Tower Street, Birmingham. Their patent became the standard British gun trade sidelock action in which the locks were cocked by the drop of the barrel. As such the Woodward gun is easier to close than the Purdey. As per the original Woodwards, the new examples have arcaded fences, T-shaped safeties, tight scroll engraving and the name in an engraved parchment banner.

In the summer of 1999, for the first time in the history of the company, a Purdey shop outside Audley House was opened at 844 Madison Avenue, New York selling guns, clothes and accessories. There are plans to open a similar establishment in Paris. When the takeover was first announced, the gun world shuddered at the thought that the new investment might downgrade the gun side of Purdey's and concentrate on the clothing and accessory side. Nothing could be further from the truth. Guns are and will remain the core of the Purdey business. Demand is healthy and production has expanded to around 65 to 80 guns per year. Although the clothing and accessories side of the business will expand, the name 'Purdey' is still synonymous throughout the world with best guns and everything will support that goal.

'There is no gunmaker personally better known that Mr. Purdey; there is none less written about,' wrote G T Teasdale-Buckell in *Experts in Guns and Shooting* in 1900. Purdey's have a powerful sense of history, a powerful image and a powerful prestige – they are and will remain Purdey Gun and Rifle Makers.

Shop manager, Robin Nathan, examining a Dimension Book in the front shop of Audley House. Behind him are the sales ledgers and Dimension Books. (*See plate 69 in colour section.*)

Peter Blaine (gun sales), Tony Sinnett (general manager), Nigel Beaumont (managing-director), Long Room, March 2000. (*See plate 70 in colour section.*)

Pinfire gun No. 6829 built in 1864 being weighed today with its relevant entry in the Dimensions Book shown. (*See plate 68 in colour section.*)

Chapter ten

THE PURDEY WAY

The best guns of all the famous makers over the years are very similar in quality, style and craftsmanship. Their manufacturing techniques resembled each other and all were built in roughly the same manner. However each maker had different subtle methods to create best guns and in Purdey's a process evolved over the centuries known as 'the Purdey way'.

The Purdey way refers primarily to the organisation and specialisation of various craftsmen that differs from other makers. The early Dimensions Books until 1877 gave the initial of the gunmaker responsible for building each part of the Purdey gun. After 1877, an entirely new type of Dimension Book came into being that listed only two specialisations, 'stocked' and 'put together'. The reason behind listing only two specialisations is due to the Purdey way.

In building a Purdey gun, the stocker was of far greater importance than in any other gunmaking firm. Purdey stockers were trained to perform a variety of tasks to such an extent that the whole gun revolved around them. The origins of these tasks can probably be traced back to James Purdey the Elder right at the beginning of his career. Not only was he a stocker at Forsyth's, he was also a lock filer. Since he worked in wood and metal, he founded the tradition that a Purdey stocker would do far more than work simply with wood. This partly explains why Purdey stockers like Frederick Beesley and John Robertson were able to invent and build such complicated patents.

The stockmaker had a great deal of metal work to do, filing the trigger plate, drilling the top strap, cutting out the fore-end loop and filing and fitting the fore-end snap and bolt, filing and fitting the safety work, stamping on the gun number, filing chamfers on all parts that would come into contact with the wood, etc. In total, before he had even begun to touch the stock, the stocker had fourteen to fifteen hours metal work to do. Only after he did this could he begin to inlet the various parts into the stock. The stock by this point would only be a rough blank and he now had to shape it to its final form. After finishing and testing at the shooting ground, the stocker balanced the gun, chequered it and fitted the gold or silver oval.

Putting together refers to the final finishing of the gun.

A group of Purdey gunmakers in the factory at 37 North Row *circa* 1890. Left to right: Standing: Stentiforth (stocker); 'Tiger' Mayo (barrels); Harry Gatrell(ejectors); Lees. Sitting: Fred Smith (actioner); Sol Prentice (actioner); Harry Leggett (stocker). In front: J Taylor (stocker).

Purdey guns have always been finished to a very high standard to create the unrivalled finish that has always distinguished them. Finishing is a two-part process involving about 75 hours of work. In the first part, the finisher regulated the joint, locks, sears and trigger mechanism to ensure everything fitted together and worked properly. Then the gun went to the shooting ground for testing and choke alterations.

In the second half of the finishing process, the gun received its final polishing, blacking and blueing.

If a boy wanted to become a gunmaker, conditions regarding his apprenticeship were very strict in the first half of the 19th century. Apprenticeships lasted seven years and the apprentice was bound in servitude to his master. It appears that apprentices received no pay and had to pay their master 'Consideration money' for his tuition. In return, the master would house, feed, clothe and instruct the boy in the art of gunmaking. This apprenticeship system was devised by the Guilds, early trade union organisations applying to the skilled trades. The Guilds insisted on such restrictive practices and on such a long apprenticeship to restrict the supply of skilled labour thereby forcing up wage rates. The original Indenture of James Purdey the Younger survives dated 14 July 1843 to show how strict apprenticeships were (see plate 71).

THIS INDENTURE Witnesseth

James Purdey the Younger Son of James Purdey Oxford Street in the County of Middlesex Gunmaker doth put himself Apprentice to his said Father James Purdey Citizen and Gunmaker of London, to learn his Art; and with him, after the Manner of an Apprentice to serve from the Day of the Date hereof, until the full End and Term of Seven Years, and from thence next following, to be fully complete and ended. During which Term, the said Apprentice his said Master faithfully shall serve, his Secrets keep, his lawful Commands everywhere gladly do. He shall do no Damage to his said Master, nor see it to be done of others; but that he to the utmost of his power shall let, or forthwith give Warning to his said Master, of the same. He shall not waste the Goods of the said Master, nor lend them unlawfully to any. He shall not commit Fornication, nor contract Matrimony within the said Term. He shall not play at Cards, Dice, Tables, or any other unlawful Gains, whereby his said Master may have any Loss. With his own Goods or others, during the said Term, without Licence of the said Master, he shall neither buy nor sell. He shall not haunt Taverns or Playhouses, nor absent himself from his said Master's Service Day nor Night unlawfully. But in all things as a faithful Apprentice he shall behave himself towards the said Master, and all his during the said Term. And the said Master, in Consideration of the Natural love and affection which he beareth towards his said son James Purdey his said Apprentice, in the same Art and Mystery which he useth, by the best means that he can, shall teach and instruct, or cause to be taught and instructed; finding to his said Apprentice, Meat, Drink, Apparel, Lodging, and all other Necessaries according to the Custom of the City of London, during the said Term.

As the century progressed and industrialisation proceeded apace in Britain, apprenticeship conditions eased. This was mainly done to attract youths who might otherwise have found ready money in factories. The Indenture of a Purdey gunmaker, George Denholm dated 21 March 1882 is a good example to illustrate the change. Denholm was apprenticed 'to learn the art of stocking, screwing and finishing of guns' to the Purdey stocker James Lumsden of 5 Park Villas, Park Road, Crouch End, Hornsey. The apprenticeship was seven years and although there were the usual stipulations about serving his master faithfully, the big change was in money and independence.

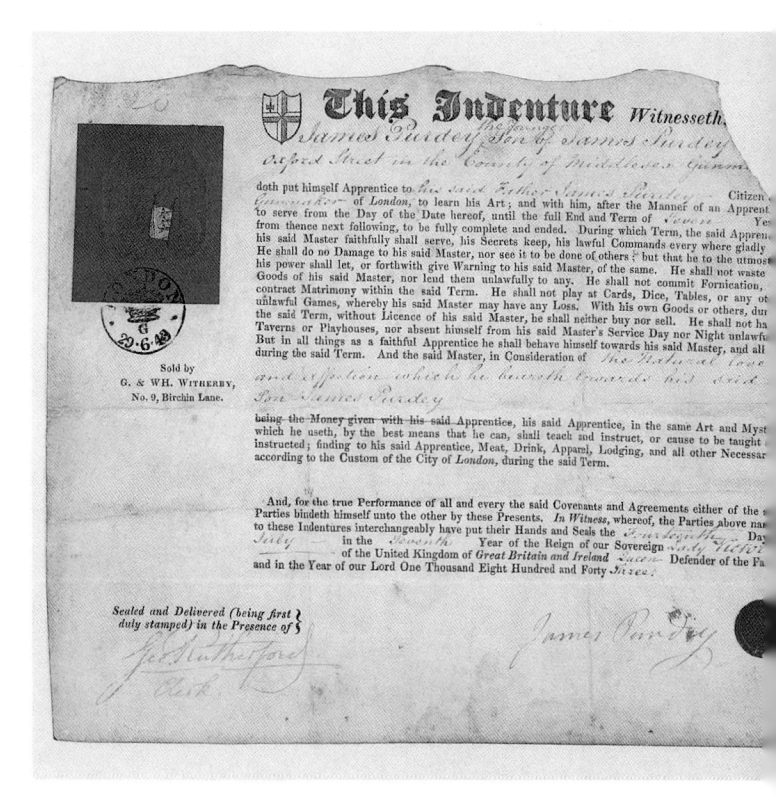

The Indenture of James Purdey the Younger dated 14 July 1843. Note that no Consideration money was given by the apprentice to his master, due to the family connection, but no wages are mentioned and that the master would house, feed and clothe him. (*See plate 71 in colour section.*)

'During the said term seven years the said George James Denholm shall receive no wages during the first year, two shillings and sixpence per week during the second year, five shillings per week during the third year, seven shillings and sixpence per week during the fourth year, twelve shillings per week during the fifth year, eighteen shillings per week during the sixth year and twenty five shillings per week during the seventh and last year signed by the said James Lumsden his Apprentice in the Art, Trade, or Business of Stocking, Screwing and finishing of guns. By the best means in his power shall teach and instruct or cause to be taught and instructed The hours of work for the said apprentice shall be those the said appointed by James Purdey the employer of the said finding the said Apprentice sufficient Meat, Drink, Lodging, and all other necessaries during the said term James Lumsden and if from any cause the said James Lumsden during the term of this Indenture should leave the employment of the aforesaid James Purdey, Gunmaker of Oxford Street, London, then the said apprentice George James Denholm shall become bound by this Indenture to the said James Purdey or any person he may appoint until the termination of this Indenture.'

The Consideration money has gone, the apprentice receives pay and he is bound to Purdey not his master.

Fully-trained gunmakers received good wages in the 19th and 20th centuries. Theirs was a skilled trade in demand and as such employers had to pay out reasonable wages. In the 19th century the average weekly rate of pay was around £2–£3 per week. The gunmakers were on piecework, paid by the amount of work they did. There was no point in rushing work as the viewer inspected all stages and would reject any substandard work. Many Purdey guns will be found with the craftsman's initials stamped on various parts. This was done primarily to help identify who made the part if there was any question about its quality or fault. Appendix 6 lists Purdey gunmakers over the years to help identify such initials.

The completion of an apprenticeship was always observed by the men in the factory. At the stroke of mid-day on the day of completion, every gunmaker in the factory hammered something metal for about ten minutes. Rude notices were put all over the apprentice's bench. During lunchbreak, a prodigious amount of refreshment was produced by the apprentice and consequently little work was done in the afternoon. Being on piecework, this loss of production could be made up on the following days. If the apprentice's parents could not afford the refreshment, there would be a whip-spring in his later years, he nodded off at his bench, but kept on polishing and wasted the spring. In total he gave around 75 years service to Purdey's. A relative, possibly his son, George Robins was also a hardener, dying in 1925. Many sons followed in their fathers' footsteps giving long continuity of service. For instance, Henry Dean was a stocker in the last quarter of the 19th century and his sons, Arthur and Phillip Dean, stockers in the 20th century. Arthur Dean stocked all of the King George V hammer-guns from 1905 onwards and most of the guns for the royal family until the time of his death in 1947. Phillip Dean, apprenticed in 1902, worked as a stocker until his death in 1959. Another long standing family were the Astons, father and son, barrel-makers. Aston Snr. had begun with Purdey's in the 1850s and his son, Harry Aston, continued until the 1930s. Harry Aston dressed well and gave the impression that he owned Purdey's. At work he changed in to the dirtiest of clothes but produced some very skilled work such as building all the double rifle barrels. The Delays likewise gave very long service. Ben Delay Snr. began as a stocker just before World War 1 and his sons, Ben and Harold, continued the tradition right up through this century. The longest serving of all, were, of course, the Lawrence family beginning in the 1880s and continuing at Purdey's for over a century.

round to help out. When Harry Lawrence came out of his apprenticeship in 1921, it cost his father eight bottles of whisky and six bottles of gin plus countless bottles of beer.

A great many gunmakers built up incredible lengths of service at Purdey's. J Lucas, the engraver, served Purdey's for 60 years. Abbe Robins, the hardener, began around 1825 and worked until he was 92, retiring in 1901. Whilst polishing a

A Purdey beanfeast of May 1914.
Left to right: *Seated with driver*: Charlie Sadler (ejectors); Wesley Nobbs (actioner). *Standing behind*: Syd Smith (ejectors); Joe Thomson (actioner); Fred Williams (actioner); Percy Wilkes (actioner). *Behind them on brake*: W Russell (finisher); G Woolman (engraver); Jim Gorman (cartridge loader); Bill Geekie (finisher); R Thomson (finisher) *Standing in front*: W Hopewell (finisher); Walter Warren (engaver); Sam Smallwood (shooting coach); W Egginson (finisher); W Griffiths (finisher).

Purdey gun production differed from several other makers in that their guns were built entirely on the premises. Many other makers, usually in smaller concerns, put out to the trade work like stocking and actioning. For example, John Robertson in the 1870s and 1880s was a leading outworker to the trade, working first of all from 101 Great Titchfield Street from 1873 to 1882 and then from 4 George Yard, Wardour Street. His records show that he was stocking and actioning guns for Stephen Grant, Joseph Lang, Henry Atkin, Boss & Co., Holland & Holland, etc. Purdey's, being such a large firm with good premises and a large workforce built all their guns *in situ*. The exception to this was, in the very early days, when James Purdey the Elder had just established his business and used outworkers like Thomas Boss. The other exception was the A to E quality era in the late 19th century when there was no pretence where the lower quality guns were built.

Engraving of guns was one area where specialists might have to be employed. In the 19th century the early open style and later bouquet and scroll types of engraving were craftsmen orientated. Purdey's used their own skilled engravers in the second half of the 19th century like Lucas and Mace – Mace engraving from around 1850 to around 1880 and Lucas from around 1855 to 1915. From the 1880s until the 1930s, Walter Warren did much of the fine scrollwork on Purdey guns. He had several pictures accepted by the Royal Academy, and whilst still an apprentice, won first prize in a competition for the best sketch of the front page of the old original magazine *Punch*. He produced some very fine rose and scroll engraving.

In the closing decades of the 19th century, the burgeoning American and existing Eastern market demanded more ostentatious decoration than the traditional rose and scroll. Carved, chiselled and pictorial work was specified. This was beyond the capabilities of Purdey in-house engravers and more specialist firms had to be sought out. In addition, the vastly increased output of the late 19th century meant that the Purdey in-house engravers could not cope with the volume of guns produced.

The better type of Dimension Book introduced in 1877 did not list engravers unlike the earlier Dimension Books. However we are fortunate in that from 1893 onwards, factory workbooks exist that were kept in the factory and detailed the surname of all the gunmakers involved in building a particular gun. (There are unfortunately many volumes missing.) With these workbooks we have quite conclusive evidence as to who the engravers were.

They show how outside engravers were increasingly used to cope with the increased volume and complexity of engraving by the turn of the century. The first available workbook of 1893 lists not only Lucas and Warren but Sanders as well. Thomas Sanders had established his engraving business in Soho at 13 Dean Street in 1862, moving to 6 Greek Street in 1866 and later on to 142 Wardour Street. Sanders had a small workforce of engravers who engraved guns for much of the London Trade. It was into this business that Henry Kell (c 1860-1929) was apprenticed around 1875, later on becoming a partner. Henry Kell took over the business in 1919 and re-named it Henry Kell & Son. The business moved in 1921 to 38a Broad Street, Soho, moving again to 45 Broadwick Street in 1937, remaining there until 1957. Henry's son, Harry (1880-1958) was apprenticed to his father around 1894, taking over the business when his father died in 1929. By 1957, Harry Kell's health was failing; he closed the business and went to work in the Purdey factory, dying one year later in 1958. To Harry Kell great credit must be given for his execution of the new genre of gun engraving, the game and animal scenes.

A 1920 workbook lists Walter Warren, Woolman (Purdey engraver), Kell and Haynes (A C Haynes, 23 Lisle Street, Leicester Square). Of all these engravers in the first half of the 20th century, Kell is by far the most often encountered. In the immediate post-World War Two period Harry Kell engraved virtually all the Purdey guns. One of Harry Kell's apprentices, Ken Hunt, was taken on by Purdey's in 1950 and his skills were such that he was in high demand from customers for his skilful artistic engraving and inlay work. Today Purdey's have their own engravers for traditional rose and scroll and, for more specialist work, ouside engravers such as Ken Hunt, Simon Coggan, Cecile Flohiment, Stephen Kelly and Brown Brothers.

A corner of the repair shop at No. 2 Irongate Wharf 1920s. Left to right: Bill Rouse (repairs), Jimmy Colle (ejectors) and Ben Delay Sr. (actioner).

Opposite: The barrel shop at No. 2 Irongate Wharf, 1950. 1. Dan O'Brien (hardener); 2. Arthur Wilkes (barrels); 3. Brian Frost (apprentice – barrels); 4. Bob Heath (barrels); 5. Jack Aldous (barrels); 6. Alf Harvey (barrels); 7. George Wood (barrels).

THE PURDEY WAY

A Purdey beanfeast to Worthing 1936. This group comprised gunmakers with over 25 years service to Purdey's. Left to right: *Back row* (5): Tom Blogg (cartridge loader), Frank Winter (actioner), Fred Scales (stocker), Tom Davidson (actioner). *Fourth row* (4): Bob Thomson (finisher), Charlie Sadler (ejectors), Harry Lawrence (actioner), Archie Turvey (finisher), Arthur Dean (stocker). *Third row* (3): Arthur Wilkes (barrels), Maurice Timbers (actioner), Bill Rouse (repairs), Bill Johnston (porter), Jack Apted (stocker), Bill Bayliss (machinist), Charlie Waite (repairs), Bill Geekie (finisher). *Second row* (2): Alf Warren (finisher/inspector, Audley House), Fred Williams (actioner), Ernest Lawrence (factory manager), Sam Simons (barrels), Bill Hill (barrels), Bill Leeper (cartridge loader), Jimmy Colle (ejectors and single-triggers). *Front row* (1): Alf Smith (ejectors), Percy Wilkes (actioner), Syd Smith (ejectors).

Harold Delay, stocker. Irongate Wharf *circa* 1965.

Ken Hunt, engraver. Irongate Wharf *circa* 1965.

Bill Geekie, finisher. Irongate Wharf *circa* 1965.

Ben Delay, actioner. Irongate Wharf *circa* 1965.

THE PURDEY WAY

Building a Purdey gun today differs very little from the techniques of the last century. The major change has been in the adoption of the latest C.N.C. (Computer Numerical Controlled) technology. It must be emphasised that this technology is in support of the craftsman and in no way takes over from the skills of the gunmaker developed through years of practice. There are about 35 gunmakers compared to 2 C.N.C. operators. Each gun, apart from matched pairs, is completely individual and built to the exact demands of the customer.

Purdey gunmakers begin their apprenticeship at the age of sixteen. Each apprentice is trained in one of the individual skills that goes towards the making of a Purdey gun. An apprenticeship lasts five years and upon completion the gunmaker is then entitled to stamp his initials on the part of the gun he creates. There are seven distinct areas in the creation of a gun: barrel-making, action-making, lock and trigger ('furniture') making, ejector-making, stocking, engraving and finally finishing. With the exception of bought-in rough barrel tubes, Purdey guns are made entirely on the premises.

Purdey's have invested in the very latest C.N.C. technology to support their craftsmen. There are four C.N.C. controlled E.D.M. (Electro Destruction Machining) machines. Two of these machines are spark-eroders and the other two wire-cutters. Take for example the steel forging that is required for the gun action. The exact dimensions of the gun action will be fed into the computer. The steel forging is placed in the wire-cut machine and an electrical charge passed through the wire. Like a fretsaw, the wire burns out the shape of the action from the steel ingot to a tolerance of less than one-thousandth of an inch. The spark-eroders work on the same principle and electrically erode metal to cut out such examples as action housings or fore-end irons. These E.D.M. machines work slowly and run 24 hours per day. The tools used in the spark-eroding machines wear out fairly rapidly and two C.N.C. milling machines re-make the tools required. These machines help to take the hard slog out of gunmaking and produce very accurate parts, ready for the gunmaker to apply his skills.

The building of a gun begins with the barrels. All barrels are of chopper-lump construction. The tubes are supplied to very precise measurements to within four-thousandths of an inch. The barrel maker then files the tube to the description of the gun, whether it be rifle, lightweight gun, etc. This is done with the use of gauges to measure the external dimensions over the length of the barrel to ensure it conforms to Purdey measurements. The filed barrel must be perfectly round. This process is known as 'striking up'. The tube is regularly checked for straightness inside, a process determined by the barrel maker's eye only. Similarly the outside of the barrel is checked. When both barrels are struck up, they are brazed together at the lumps and muzzles using silver solder. The ribs are wired onto the barrels and are tinned on using tin solder and pine resin with flux. The internal barrel bores are finished by lead lapping. A lead lap is a lead plug about nine inches long with abrasive on it. This plug rotates up and down the barrel to give the exact internal barrel dimension and to impart a very high degree of finish. The lead laps are made in the factory. Modern honing machines create rough chokes. The barrel lumps are then machined and split into two, forward and rear lump, the ejector luggers fitted and the barrels chambered. The barrels are then numbered and the individual gun is on its way.

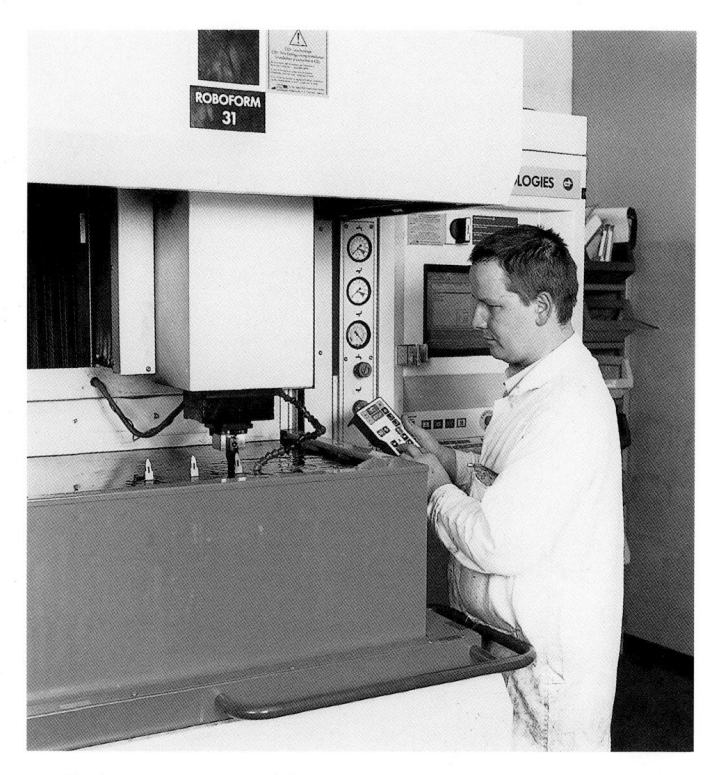

Ian Clarke operating one of the C.N.C. controlled E.D.M. machines. Note the three tangs being destructed in the fluid.

With the barrels made, the actioner can get to work. The action is the 'engine' of the gun including all the parts to make it work, the lever, the bolt, the locks, etc. The actioner will pick up from the machine shop the relevant accurately cut

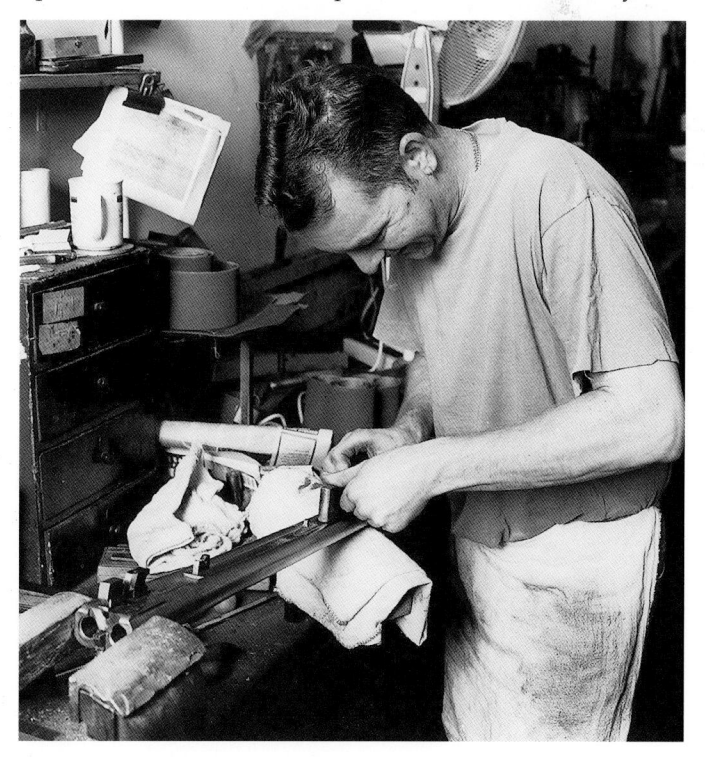

Scott Wood striking up a pair of barrels.

forgings. His first task is to fit the bolt. Smoke blacking is used to ensure a perfect fit of all parts in the gun. A flame emitting black soot is played over the part. When the part is fitted any high point is immediately apparent on the soot and can be filed to fit. The barrel lumps are dressed to prepare them for jointing as are the action slots. One of the most precise jobs is that of joining, fitting the barrels to the action to a very high degree of precision. Guns must be capable of firing hundreds of thousands of rounds with no play in the action. The top strap is then bent to the customer's measurements and filed to its correct shape. The locks are fitted as are the disc set strikers. The top lever, spindle and safety work can then be fitted. After this the fore-end is fitted and the final barrel joint created, cutting out the hook from the front lump and fitting the crosspin. The strikers are put in and the gun detonated. 'Detonating' refers to the carving and finishing of the action. In total, actioning the gun will have taken around 120 hours. O/U construction follows the same procedure.

Keith Ackerman, actioner.

While the gun is being manufactured, the furniture is constructed. 'Furniture' is the term given to the locks and triggers. Again this work is all done in the factory. The lockmaker will file the plate, make the bridle, sear and springs, etc. Some locks are pinless to give an uninterrupted plate for engraving. Today Purdey's have returned to their original type of lock with traditional intercepting safety sear. Customers have a choice of double-trigger, single-trigger or spring-bladed front-trigger (the front-trigger is articulated to alleviate damage to the back of the trigger finger on discharge of the second barrel). The type of single-trigger employed by Purdey's since the late 1970s is the inertia bobweight single-trigger perfected by Lawrence Salter, the managing-director of Purdey's in that era.

With the gun now jointed, the ejectors are fitted. Purdey's still used the original Wem ejector of 1888 with the modification introduced by Ernest Lawrence in the 1930s, the substitution of the crossbar with a central lifting lever. In addition to the ejector mechanism, the ejector craftsmen have to fit the cocking system into the action.

The gun is now ready for stocking. As previously stated, Purdey stockers are required to do much metalwork, fitting the trigger-plate, hanging the triggers, fitting the safety, fitting pins and doing some fore-end work, etc. After the metalwork has been completed, the stocker will receive the blank and rough shape it. The stock is then headed up. 'Headed up' means fitting the stock into the action. To make this difficult task as accurate as possible, the action and locks are coated in resin to create a precise mould of their shape. This mould is placed in a duplicating machine, a machine rather like a large pantograph that then copies the mould and cuts out the shape into the stock. The stocker will have to fine-finish the rough cut and then fit the trigger-plate. The stock is then made off. 'Making off' refers to the carving of the final shape of the stock to the customer's dimensions. The stock will be rough-bored in the butt to create the weight demanded by the customer. The fore-end is made in a similar way. At this stage the gun might be checkered, although this is sometimes done in the finishing process.

Mark McCarthy, stocker.

Now comes the most personal part of the gun, the engraving. A complete range of engraving is on offer. 'Standard fine' refers to the classic rose-and-scroll engraving introduced by Lucas and Mace in the 1860s, so typical of the Purdey gun that it is known today as 'Purdey engraving'. Standard fine is the most commonly asked for and is inclusive in the price of the gun. Other engraving styles include large

THE PURDEY WAY

scroll, with or without game scenes, gold inlays and carving. Purdey's use their own engravers for standard fine, but for more flamboyant engraving, specialist engravers are employed.

Paul Chung, engraver.

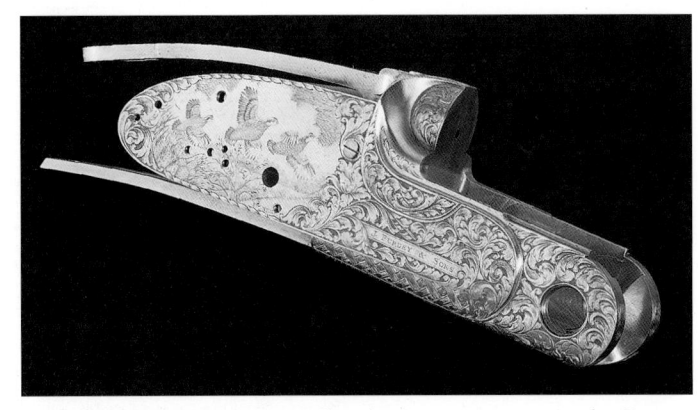

O/U action No. 29596, large scroll and game scene engraving by Simon Coggan. (*See plate 72 in colour section.*)

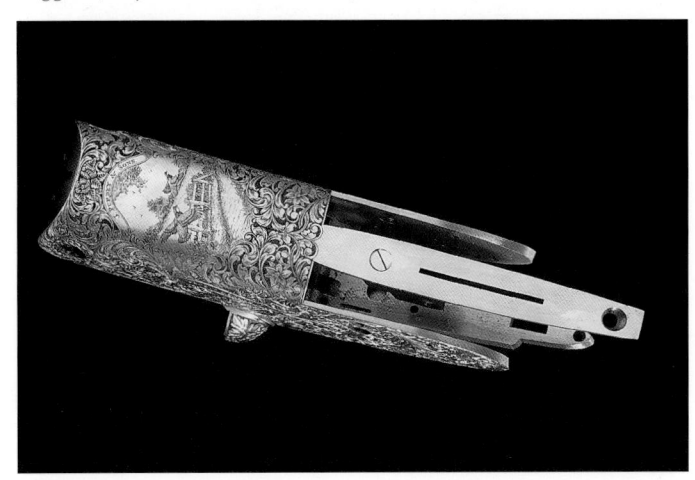

Recently completed gun No. 29687, large scroll and game scene engraving by Simon Coggan. (*See plate 73 in colour section.*)

The gun is now ready to be hardened. There are two types of hardening. The traditional case hardening using crushed bone is known as pack hardening. Pack hardening imparts a myriad of colours to the metal. The other type of hardening is cyanide hardening that gives the metal a dull finish.

After hardening the gun goes to the finisher. Finishers play a major part in the Purdey gun. They must be well-versed in all the stages of construction and must impart the high standard of finish that is the by-word for the make. Finishing is a two-part process. The first part involves regulating the gun, to make everything work properly, and the second part is to finish the gun inside and out. When the gun returns from the hardener, a slight distortion of metal always occurs. In regulating, the finisher must ensure that the joint is the correct interference fit, the ejectors work properly, the single-trigger functions, etc. In the factory itself, the finisher will fire several rounds to check this. About forty hours are spent in this first part of finishing. The gun is then sent to the shooting ground for pattern tests.

Upon return, the second part of finishing takes place. The stock is prepared and the grain flatted. The wood is buffed using a chamois leather to make it shine. To give it good colour, red oil (a mixture of linseed oil and alkanet root) is rubbed in. After this the famous Purdey slacum oil is applied to the stock. This mixture was reputedly invented in the closing decades of the 19th century by Ernest Lawrence, the factory manager. Slacum oil imparts a wonderful shine to the stock and has achieved legendary status, no doubt in part due to the secrecy of its ingredients. I asked Bob Nichols, the Purdey finisher today, what was in it, but the enigmatic smile and the twitch of the nose was the only answer received! The slacum oil is applied lightly with a rag and left to dry for two hours. It is then wiped off. About fifteen to twenty coats of slacum are applied over three weeks. Rottenstone is also applied to cut back the shine. In total, it takes about five weeks

Darren Williams, finisher, rubbing in the slacum oil.

to polish a stock. The end result is a very hard, durable and waterproof high-gloss finish deep within the wood.

The gun is also completely stripped and all internal work polished to a very high standard. The trigger guard, top lever, etc. are blacked, as are the barrels. The completed gun is again tested, the finisher firing about two hundred rounds to complete his test. From beginning to end, a side-by-side takes twelve to eighteen months to make and an O/U eighteen to twenty-four months. The gun is then delivered to Audley House for inspection, fitted into its case and delivered to the customer.

Joel Kutock, polishing an action.

Chapter eleven

LATER BREECH-LOADING GUNS AND RIFLES

The year 1886 saw the watershed when more hammerless guns were produced than hammer guns. With the addition of the efficient Purdey ejector in 1888, hammerless guns produced since that date have changed little. Damascus barrels were phased out in the early years of this century, barrel lengths became shorter due to the nitro powders, and there were subtle changes to the ejector, third fastening and single-trigger. With the purchase of Woodward in 1948, and the modifications to this action by Purdey's, O/Us have become popular. Smaller bore sizes are also more in demand.

An early Beesley gun No. 11837, a double-barrel 12-bore self-opening non-ejector gun sold on 3 July 1884 to F Simpson. Note the carved acanthus fences so popular in the 1880-1914 period. (See plate 74 in colour section.)

The decorative style of weapons has changed from the traditional rose-and-scroll type of engraving. Engraving has been elevated to an art form, with carving, chiselling and precious metal application. One interesting change is that many Purdey guns are bought for investment purposes only.

One big change since 1886 has been in the price of Purdey guns. In the 19th century there was little difference between the cost of a Purdey gun in 1830 and its equivalent in 1890 due to a more stable economy. However, in the 20th century gun prices have rocketed due to a very different economy with resultant inflation.

Year	Hammerless ejector	Other types	
1900	£92 2s	Hammerless rifle	£94 10s
		Hammer gun	£75 12s
1920	£92 8s		
1930	£130	Hammerless rifle	£155
		O/U gun	£175
		Single trap gun	£115
		Oak & leather case	£12 10s
		Single-trigger	£10 10s
		Chased relief work	£80 approx.
1940	£150.10s		
1950	£375	O/U gun	£475
1960	£653 2s 6d.	O/U gun	£831 5s
		Hammerless rifle	£650
1970	£1500	O/U gun	£2000
1971	£2000		
1976	£4500		
1978	£7500		
1983	£11,000 + VAT.	O/U gun	£17,500 + VAT.
1993	£27,500 + VAT.	O/U gun	£32,500 + VAT.
2000	£34,500 + VAT.	O/U gun	£44,000 + VAT.

Whenever the Beesley hammerless action was patented in 1880, there was no immediate rush to buy the new hammerless guns. Gradually in the early 1880s they became more in demand. No. 11837 illustrated is a typical early Purdey hammerless gun sold on 3 July 1884 to F Simpson. Purdey and Beesley got the design just right. The shape of the locks and their fit to the action combined with the use of a top

Above: The record in the Dimension Book for No.11837. Boulter, barrels; Glaysher, stocker; put together by Blanton.

Below: The record in the Dimension Book for Nos. 15082/3. Stocked by Taylor and put together by Matthews and Wilkes.

lever established the style of the Purdey hammerless gun that is so admired today. The locks have fine rose-and-scroll engraving and the action fences are carved with acanthus foliage. This carving of fleur-de-lys, fern leaves and acanthus leaves was very popular in the 1880-1914 period and was most probably executed by the Purdey actioner Arthur Roberts. The gun has 29 1/2-inch Damascus barrels and is a non-ejector as the Wem ejector was not patented until 1888. A small number of early Beesley hammerless guns still employed the Daw lever that was used on the hammer guns of the 1860s.

In the 1860s muzzle-loading production died out rapidly with the introduction of the breech-loader. The same thing did not happen to hammer guns whenever the hammerless action arrived in 1880. On the contrary, hammer guns were refined and produced in fair numbers until World War One. Even after this war, hammer guns, albeit in much reduced quantities, were still constructed mainly for live pigeon shooters. The reason why hammer guns persisted was traditional. Since time immemorial, guns always had hammers and their disposal would take some time to break that tradition. It is interesting that the great shots of the late 19th century, Sir Harry Stonor, Lord Ripon, Lord Walsingham and King George V, all persisted in using hammer guns and no doubt this had an influence too. Nos. 15082/3 are very typical of the hammer gun at its ultimate development. This pair were tested on 17 October 1894 and sold to Robert Pryor. They are 12-bore top-lever ejector guns. The isolated back action locks and hammers are unmistakenly 'Purdey' and are finely scroll engraved. The actions are likewise engraved. They weigh 6lb 13oz each.

In the flintlock period, single-barrel guns were more common than double-barrel guns. In the percussion period, the double-barrel gun rose to prominence and single-barrel production dropped dramatically. In the early breech-loading period, very few single-barrels were built, mostly of lesser quality for boys and keepers. In the hammerless period, single-barrel guns are very rare indeed. They are mostly E quality guns produced elsewhere and finished by Purdey. No. 15339 (see plates 76 and 77) is the rarest of all Purdey guns I have ever studied – a best quality single-barrel 16-bore hammerless non-ejector gun. The Dimension Books can sometimes be vague. When 'Single' is written and nothing else, this means an E quality gun. The best guns always have full details. There are about two other single-barrels with details written about them, but without examination it is difficult to ascertain their quality. There were probably no more than two or three best quality single-barrel hammerless guns made. In the 1920s, single-barrel best quality trap guns were constructed, but they were for a specialised purpose.

No. 15339 was sold on 2 August 1895 to Edward Balfour of Balbirnie House, Markinch, Fife. He bought it for his son Robert 'Jack' Balfour to learn to shoot. 'Jack', born in 1883, was aged twelve when the gun was delivered. Jack subsequently joined the Scots Guards and as a young captain was killed very early on in the First World War, dying in Flanders on 28 October 1914. Edward Balfour's second son, 'Bill' Balfour born in 1884, also learned to shoot with the gun, as did his third son John Balfour, born in 1895. Tragedy struck the family again when John Balfour was killed in action at Arras in 1918.

The left-hand lockplate contains the mechanism, the right-hand plate is a dummy to maintain symmetry. Both lockplates and action have fine rose and scroll engraving and a cocking indicator is fitted to the left-hand plate. The 28-inch barrel is engraved 'Made of Sir Joseph Whitworth's Fluid Compressed Steel, J Purdey & Sons, Audley House, South Audley Street, London'. On the bottom of the action 'Purdey's Patent' is engraved. This engraving first appeared in 1863, referring to the snap action patent of that year and continued long after the expiry of that patent in 1877. The gun is contained in its original oak and leather case, with snap cap, ivory box containing a spare striker, Moroccan leather cleaning pouch containing a pull-through, ebony cleaning rod handle, tool for extracting a jammed cartridge, ebony handled wad rammer, ebony handled turnscrew and an ebony handled disc-set-striker removal tool.

During the muzzle-loading period, Purdey's built large numbers of rifles. In the early breech-loading period, hammer rifles were not produced in such relative quantities. The

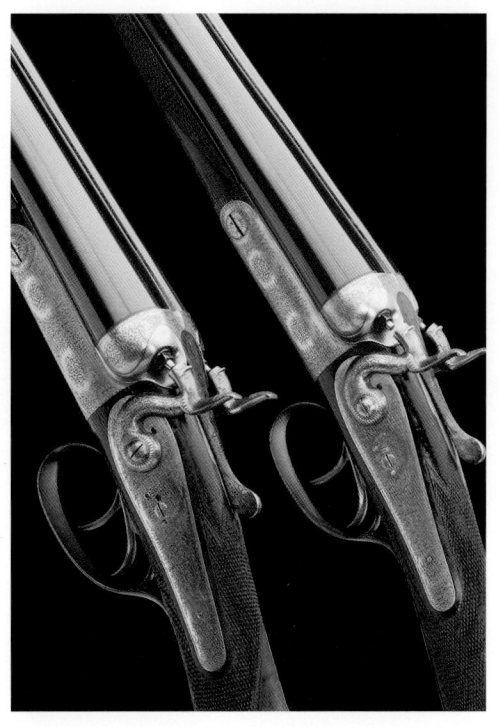

A pair of 12-bore hammer ejector guns Nos. 15082/3 tested in October 1894 and sold to Robert Pryor. Engraved by Sanders. (*See plate 75 in colour section.*)

The record in the factory workbook for Nos. 15082/3. The gunmakers were: Simons, barrels; Page; Phillips, actioner; Smith, luggers; Wilkin, levers and detonating; Taylor, stocking; Nobbs, hammers; Gatrell, ejectors; Sanders, engraving; Matthews and Wilkes, finishing.

'Jack' Balfour *circa* 1910 after he had learned to shoot with No. 15339.

No. 15339 in its original oak and leather case containing all its original accessories. (*See plate 76 in colour section.*)

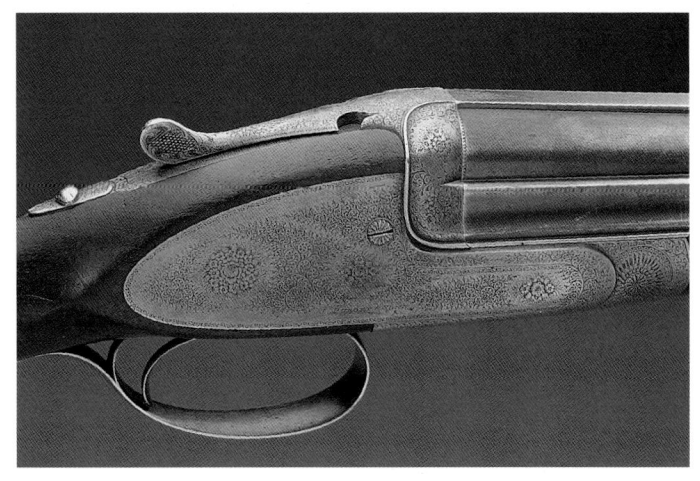

Single-barrel 16-bore hammerless non-ejector gun No. 15339 sold on 2 August 1895 to Edward Balfour of Balbirnie House, Markinch, Fife. This single-barrel hammerless gun is extremely rare, probably only one or two others being made. Engraved by Lucas. (*See plate 77 in colour section.*)

The left-hand plate containing the sidelock.

Left: The underside of the action showing the very fine scroll engraving of J Lucas.

Opposite: The record in the Dimension Book for No. 15339. Note beside 'Name', 'E Balfour Esq. for Son, Dec'sd.' Stocked by Dean and put together by Homer.

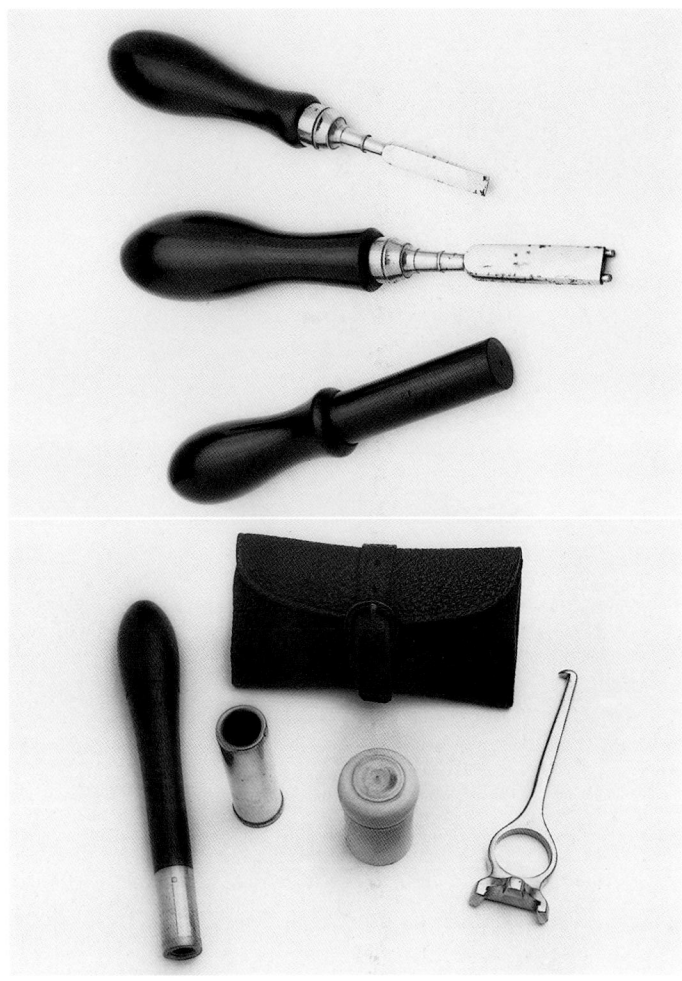

The original accessories of No. 15339. From top to bottom: turnscrew, disc-set-striker remover, wad rammer, Moroccan leather cleaning pouch, cleaning rod handle, snap cap, striker box, cartridge extractor.

The Charges label pasted in the lid.

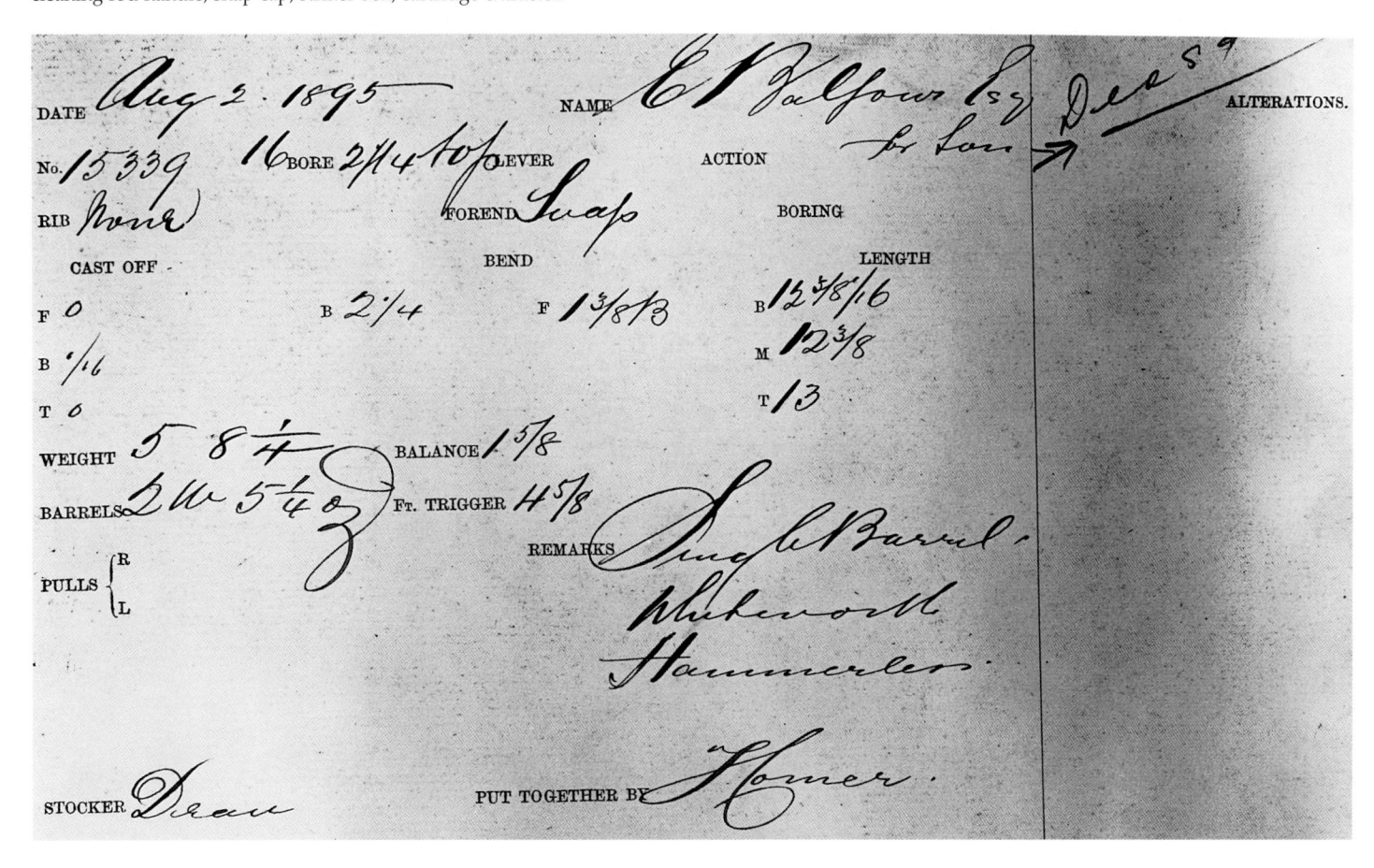

The record in the factory workbook for No. 15339. The gunmakers were: Meers, barrels; Fullalove, levers and detonating; Dean, stocker; Smith, luggers; Nobbs, actioner; Lucas, engraver; Homer, finisher.

majority of hammer rifles were of lesser quality. In the hammerless period, rifle production declined even further and best quality hammerless rifles are relatively uncommon. Such a best hammerless rifle is illustrated (see plate 78). No. 15451 is a double-barrel .303 self-opening, sidelock, hammerless, non-ejector rifle with a Jones spring assisted underlever sold on 20 June 1896 to Weller Poley.

The record in the Dimension Book for No. 15451.

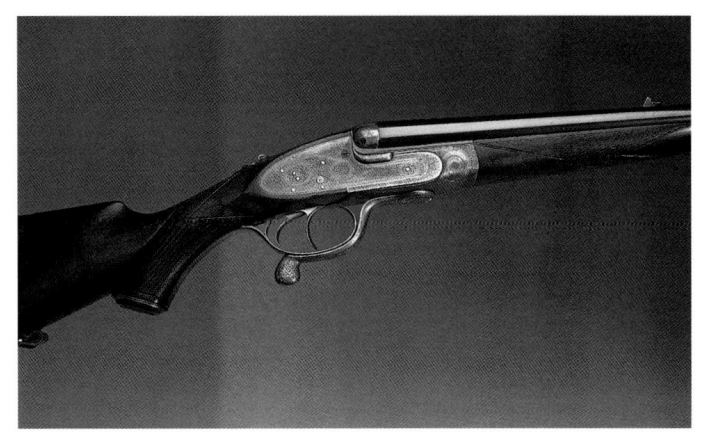

A .303 self-opening, sidelock, non-ejector rifle No. 15451 with spring-assisted Jones underlever sold on 20 June 1896 to Weller Poley. (*See plate 78 in colour section.*)

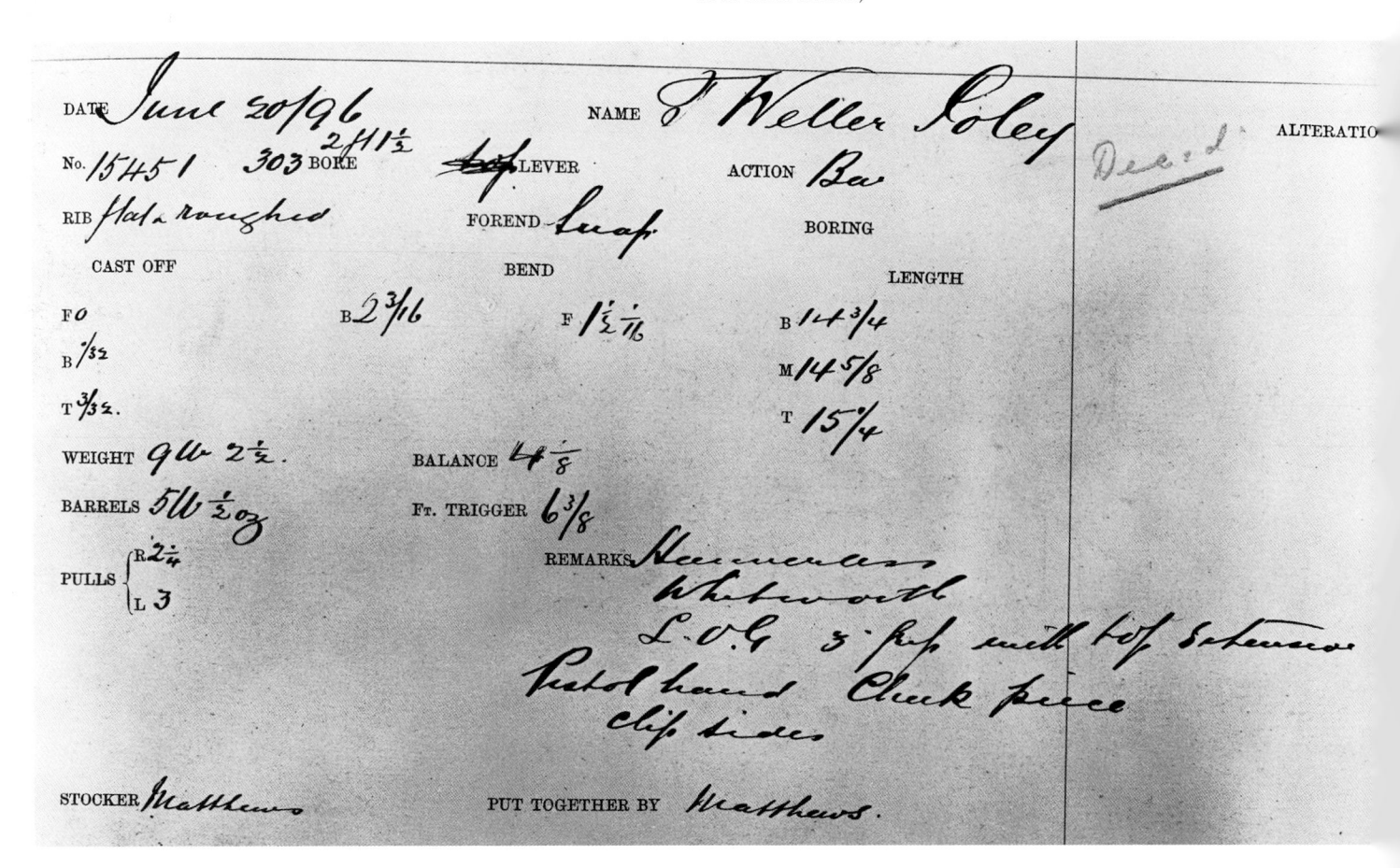

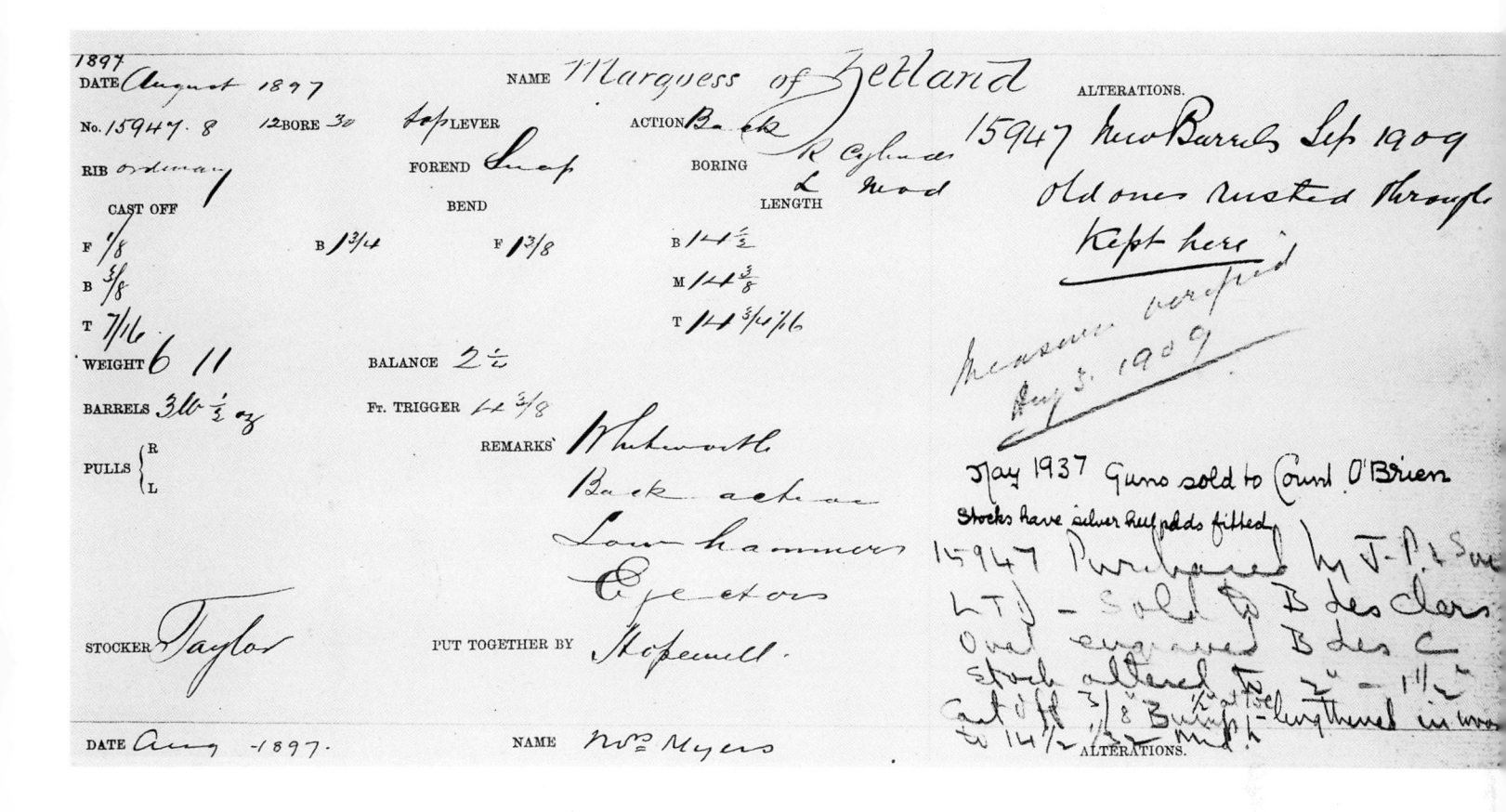

The record in the Dimension Book for Nos. 15947/8. Stocked by Taylor and put together by Hopewell. Note under 'Alterations': '15947 New Barrels Sep 1909 old ones rusted through Kept here.'

Right: A 12-bore top lever hammer ejector gun No. 15948, the No. 2 gun of a pair sold in August 1897 to the Marquess of Zetland. This gun is unusual in this period in having locks that are not of the isolated type. (*See plate 79 in colour section.*)

Another hammer ejector gun is illustrated. No. 15948 is the No. 2 gun of a pair of 12-bore top lever hammer ejector guns sold in August 1897 to the Marquess of Zetland, Aske, Richmond. The fine rose and scroll engraved back action locks are unusual in this period in that they are not of the isolated type. This gun shows an early use of the articulated front trigger. The barrels are 30 inches long.

No. 16472, illustrated right is a .303 double-barrel hammerless, top lever, self-opening, non-ejector rifle sold in August 1907 to Elim Pavlovich Demidov-San-Donato. He was an enthusiastic hunter who published various books on hunting, *Hunting Trips in the Caucasus*, 1898, *After Wild Sheep in the Altai and Mongolia*, 1900 and a *Shooting Trip to Kamchatka*, 1904. In 1914 he was appointed Russian Ambassador to Athens. The action has sideclips, third fastening and a bolted automatic safety. The locks have cocking indicators and the whole rifle has fine rose-and-scroll engraving. The stock has a pistol-grip, cheek-piece and sling swivels. The 25½-inch chopper-lump barrels are of Whitworth steel and have a matt file cut rib and open sights.

A .303 top lever, sidelock, self-opening, non-ejector rifle No. 16472 sold in August 1907 to Prince Demidov. Shown insert is the gold oval with the Demidov crest. (*See plate 80 in colour section.*)

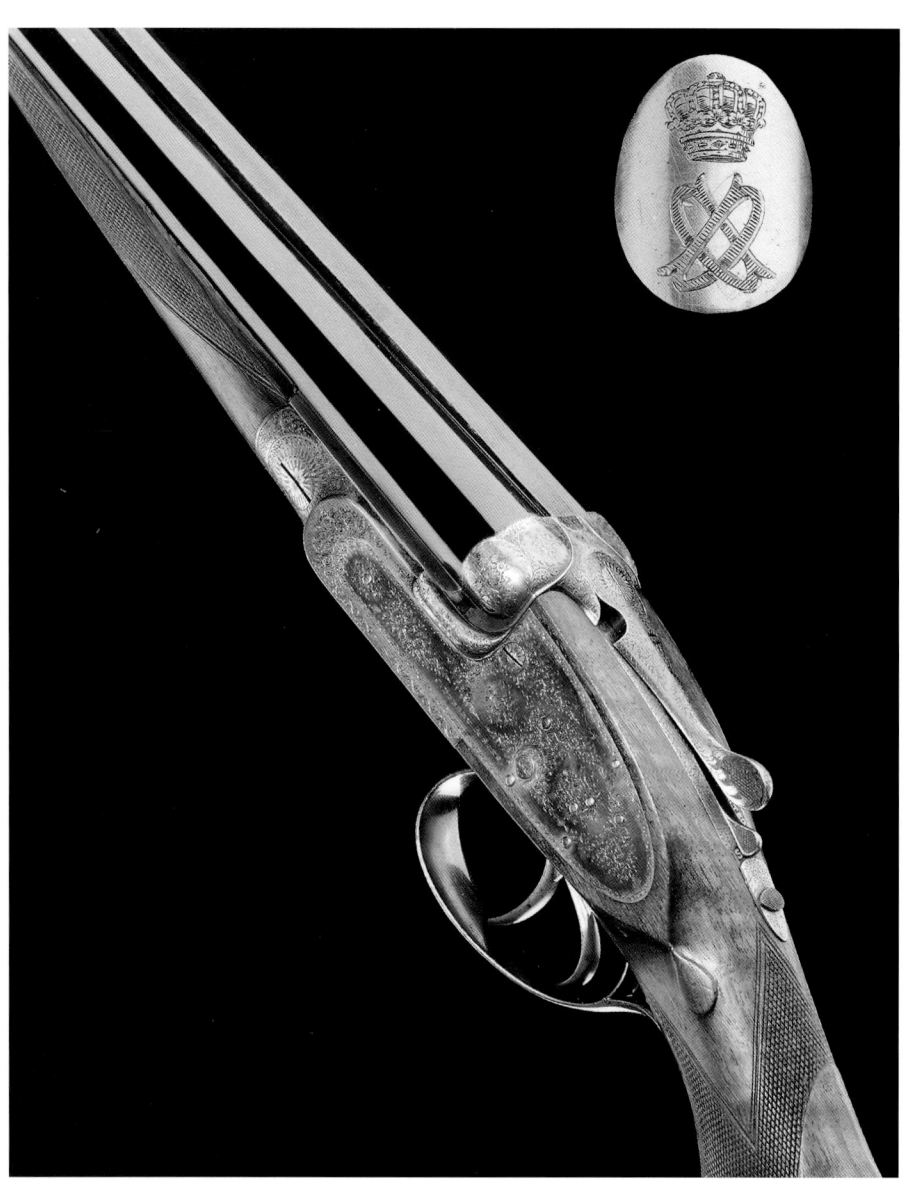

Below: The record in the Dimension Book for No. 16472. Note 'Barrels sand blasted all over to dull them.'

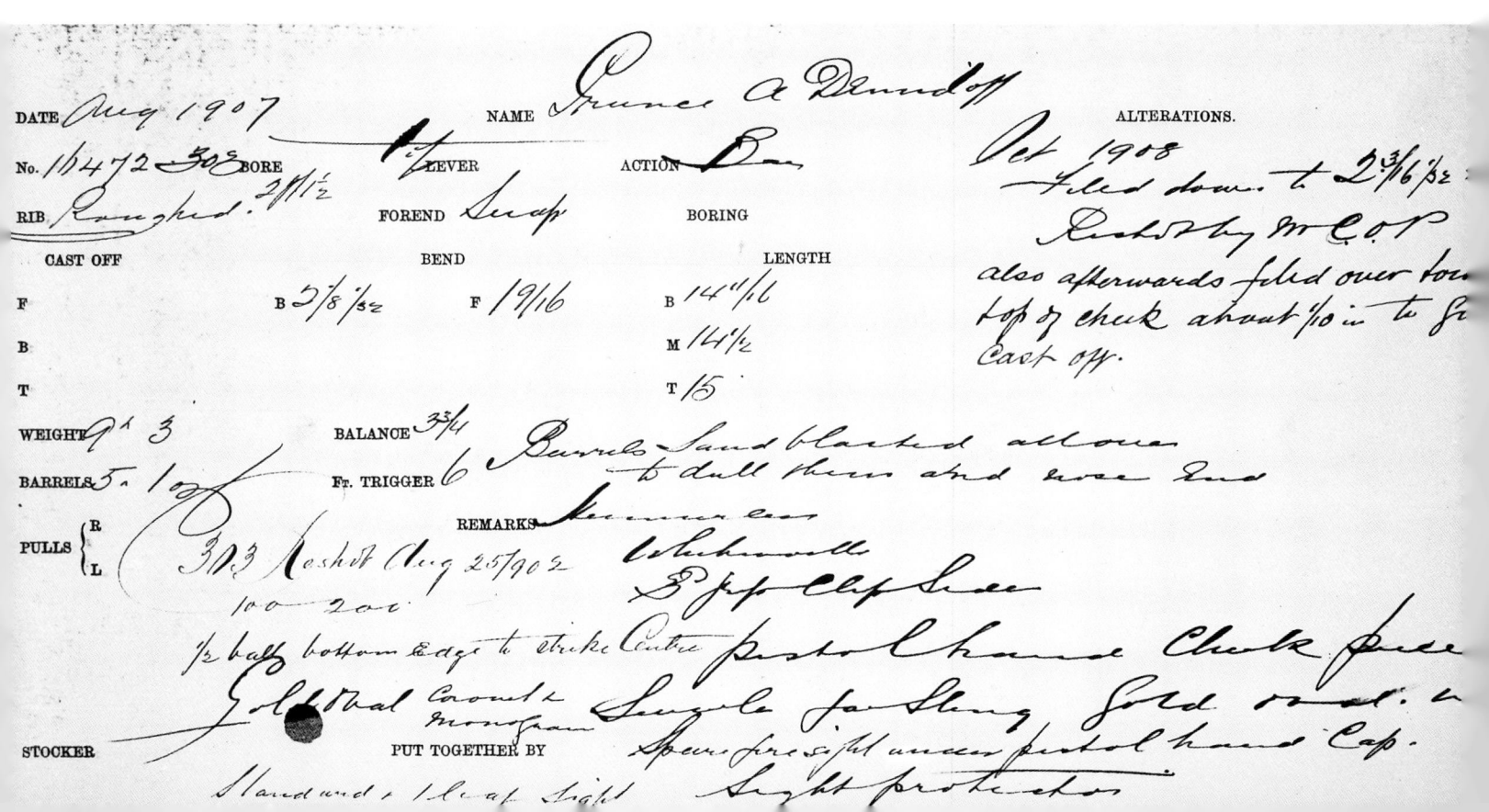

A very rare combination gun is shown (see plate 81). Combination guns, in which one barrel is a smooth bore shotgun barrel and the other barrel is a rifle barrel, had been produced in muzzle-loading days. The object behind the arrangement was to be able to offer an immediate option to a sportsman in a wild country such as Africa or India. The combination gun obviated the necessity to carry both rifle and shotgun on long trips. They have always been uncommon. Purdey's produced a mere handful of such weapons and hence gun/rifle No. 19658 is a very rare commodity. No. 19658, a top lever, self-opening, sidelock ejector gun/rifle, was sold on 15 December 1909. It is unusual in that it has two pairs of barrels. The first pair of barrels are 16-bore, 28-inch chopper-lump, Whitworth steel barrels with game rib. The gun with these barrels weighs 6lb 5oz. The second set of barrels, again 28-inch long chopper-lump Whitworth steel, are the combination barrels. One barrel is a 16-bore shotgun barrel, with a rifled choke, the other is a .400 (3-inch light) rifle barrel. This pair of barrels have a matt file cut rib and open sights. With these on, the gun/rifle weighs 7lb 8oz. Each set of barrels has its own fore-end. The action has sideclips, the third fastening and the fences are carved with oak leaves and acorns in yet another variation of this popular turn of the century carving. The gun has fine rose-and-scroll engraving and cocking indicators are fitted.

Below: The record in the Dimension Book for No. 19658. Note 'a pair of Extra Bls Right 16 Rifled Choke Left 400 Cordite 28 inches long. Weight 4lbs. 2 1/2 oz.' Stocked by Dean and put together by Anderson.

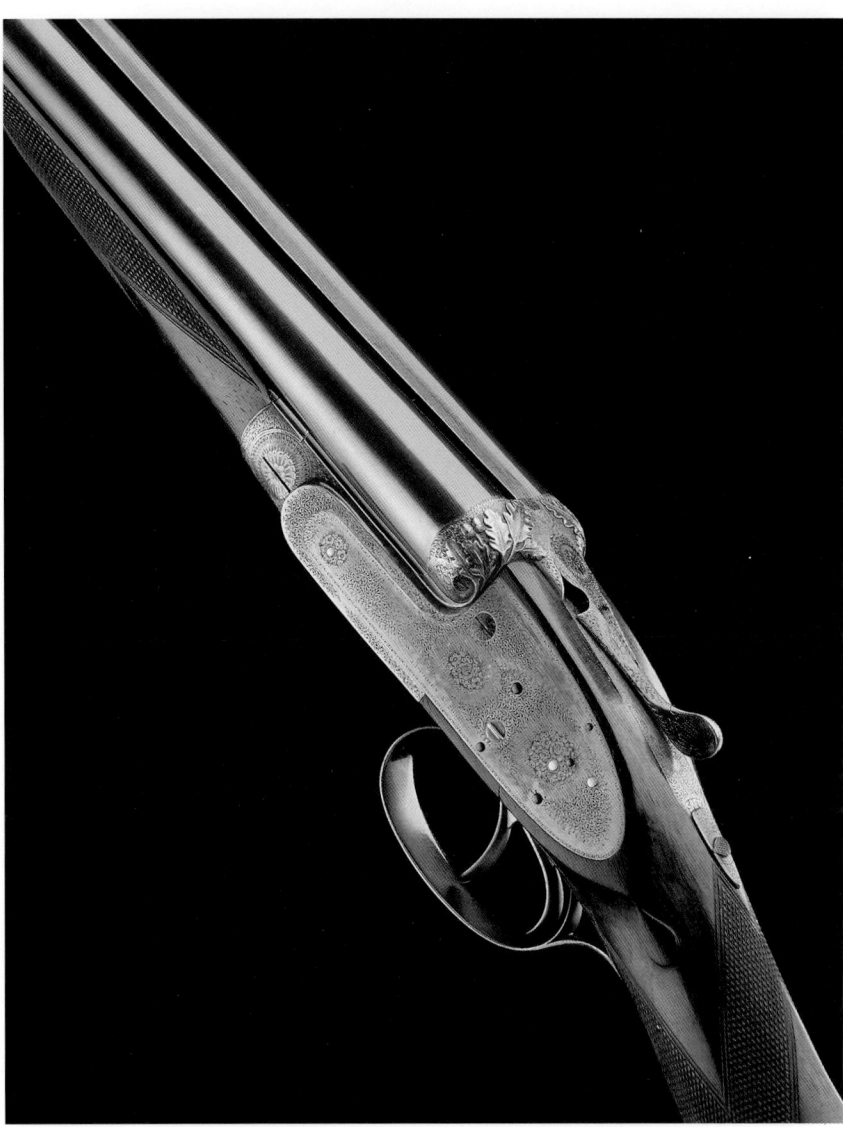

A very rare self-opening, sidelock, combination gun/rifle No. 19658 sold on 15 December 1909. Two pairs of barrels were supplied, the first pair being 16-bore shotgun barrels, the second pair being combination 16-bore shotgun/.400 rifle barrels. (*See plate 81 in colour section.*)

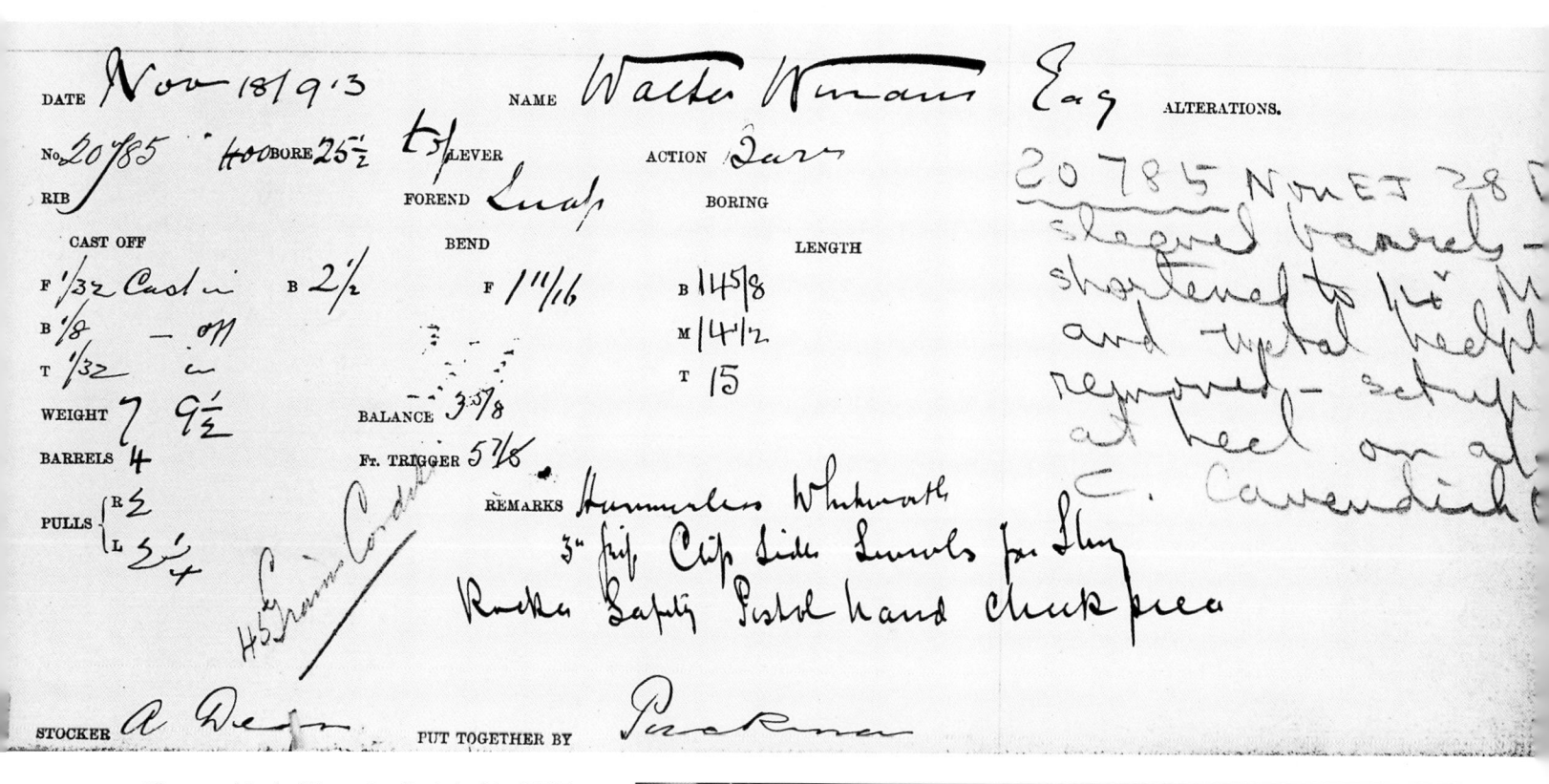

The record in the Dimension Book for No. 20785. Stocked by Dean and put together by Packman.

A rifle in a similar calibre is illustrated. There was a trend in the late 19th century to move away from the bigger calibres. James Purdey the Elder had promoted this with his two groove muzzle-loading Express rifles in the 1850s and 1860s. The introduction of breech-loaders continued this trend. The breech-loading rifle could employ a larger charge thereby creating a higher velocity and flatter trajectory. No. 20785 is a .400 (3-inch light) top lever, hammerless, self-opening, non-ejector rifle. It was sold on 18 November 1913 to Walter Winans (1852-1920), the world-famous rifle and revolver shot and horse-breeder. Using this rifle, Winans won the Running Deer Competition at Bisley. He wrote several books on rifle and revolver shooting as well as on deer breeding. The fine rose and scroll engraved action has sideclips, the third fastening, cocking indicators and a bolted automatic safety. The stock has a pistol-grip and cheek piece. The rifle is now converted to a 28-bore smooth bore.

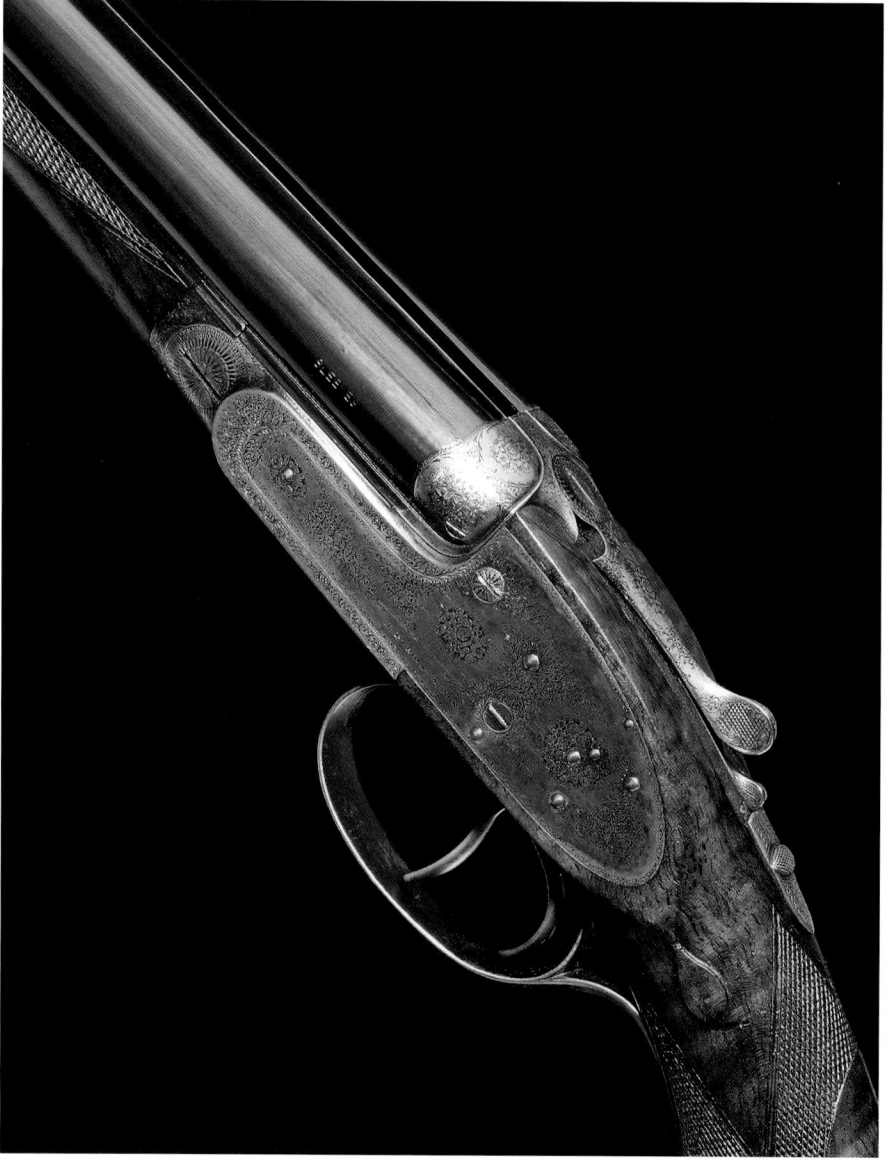

Right: A .400 (3-inch light) sidelock, self-opening, non-ejector rifle No. 20785 sold on 18 November 1913 to Walter Winans, the world-famous rifle and revolver shot. (*See plate 82 in colour section.*)

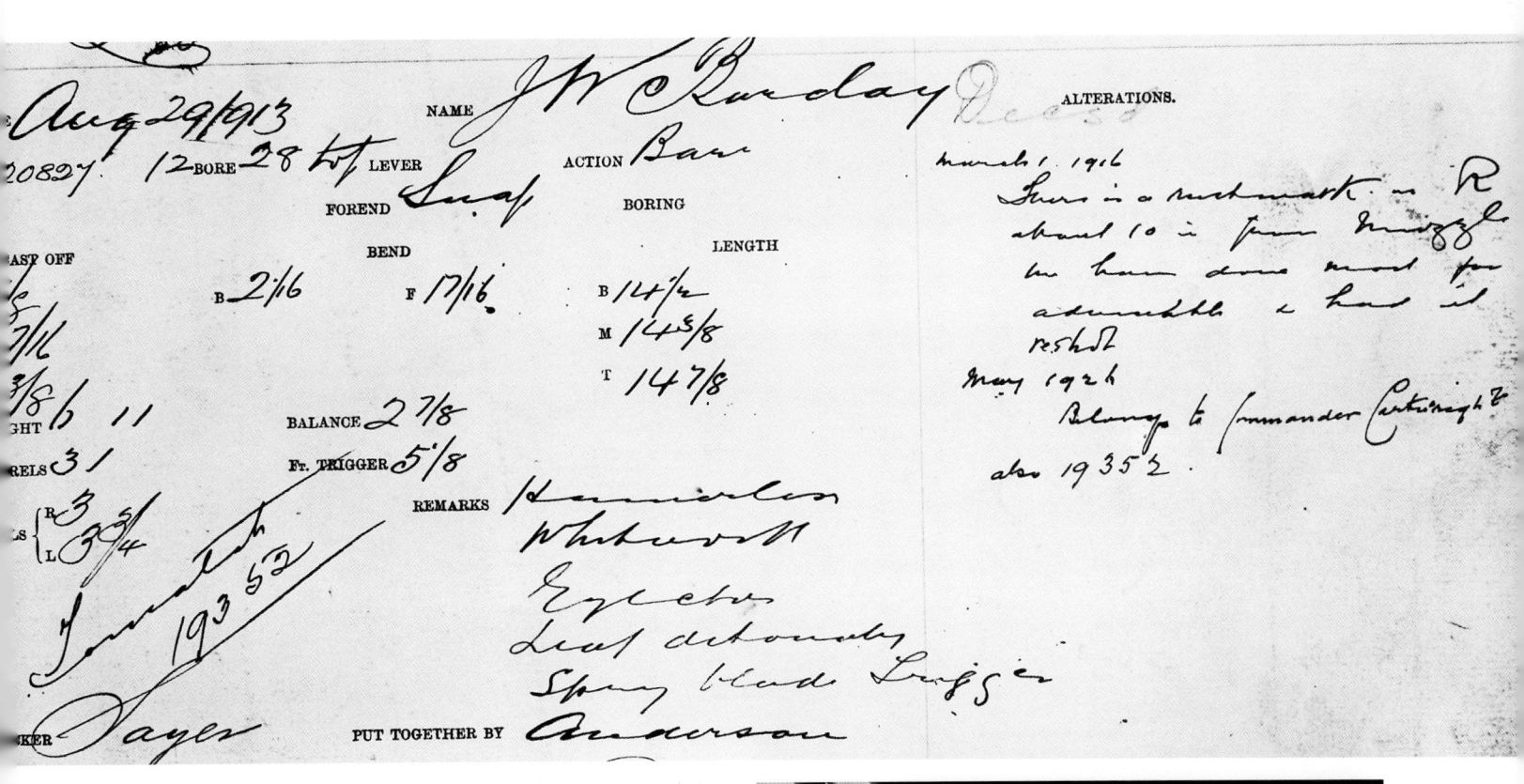

The record in the Dimension Book for No. 20827. Note beside 'Remarks': 'Leaf detonating.' Stocked by Sayer and put together by Anderson.

Illustrated is a very handsome 12-bore sidelock ejector gun No. 20827 sold on 29 August 1913 to J W Barclay. No. 20827 is the No. 2 gun of a pair. The action and locks have fine rose-and-scroll engraving and the fences are carved with acanthus leaves. The locks have cocking indicators and an articulated front trigger is fitted. The 28-inch chopper-lump barrels are of Whitworth steel.

After World War I, Purdey reverted fairly quickly to gun production. The 1920s saw varying fortunes as Purdey's followed the economic climate of booms and troughs. Gun design changed slightly after World War I to create the hammerless ejector as it is styled today. The fern and acanthus leaf carving on the actions disappeared and barrels gradually became shorter at 28 inches. Nos. 22349/50 (see plate 84) were sold in July 1923 to S Hill-Wood. They were tested on 11 August 1922. Nos. 22349/50 are a pair of 12-bore, top lever, self-opening, ejector guns with best rose-and-scroll engraving and 30-inch chopper-lump Whitworth barrels.

A pair of 12-bore, self-opening, sidelock, ejector guns Nos. 22349/50 sold in July 1923 to W Hill-Wood. (*See plate 84 in colour section.*)

A 12-bore self-opening, sidelock ejector gun No. 20827 sold on 29 August 1913 to J W Barclay. (*See plate 83 in colour section.*)

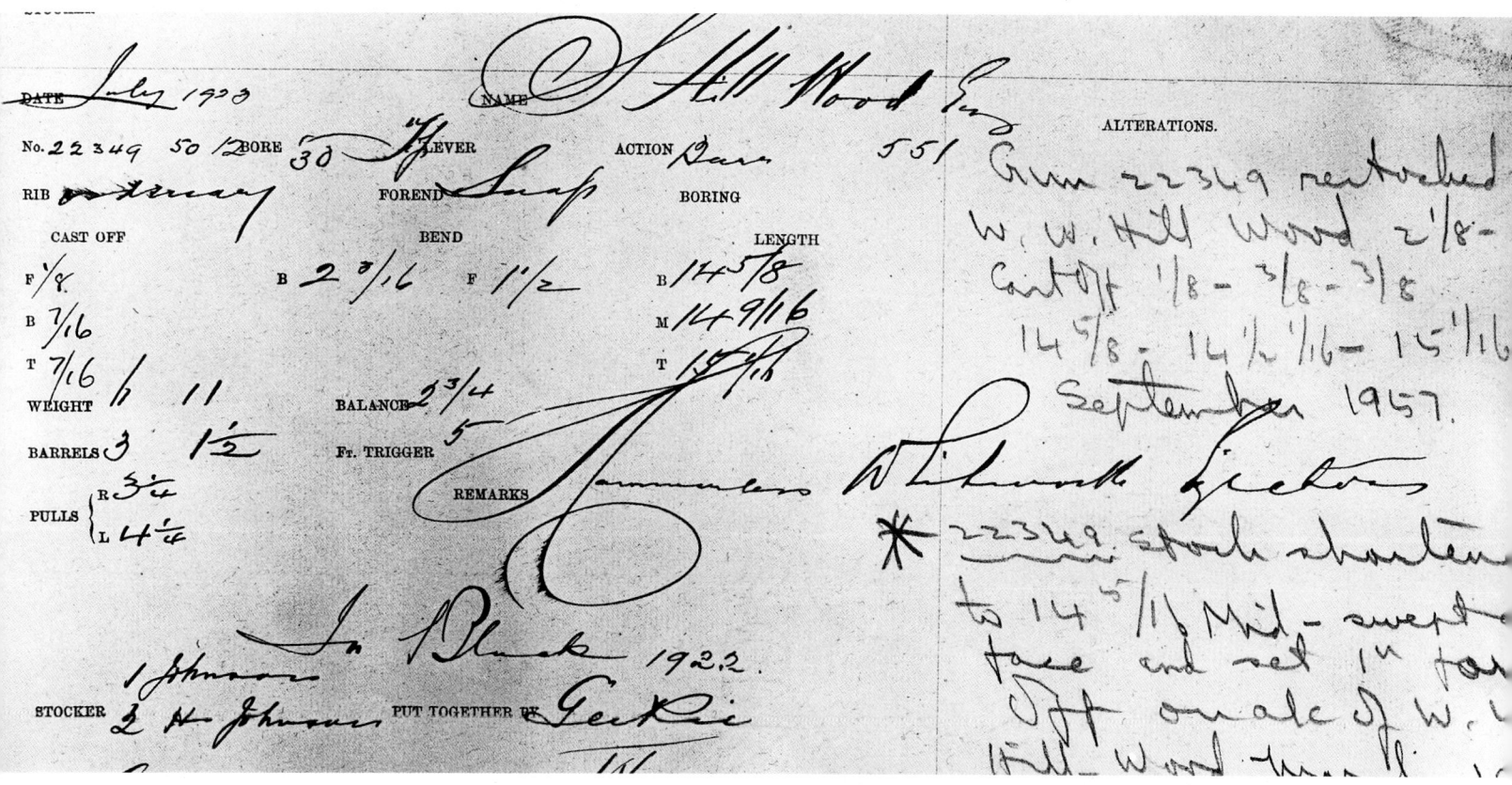

The record in the Dimension Book for Nos. 22349/50. Stocked by Johnson and put together by Geekie. Note 'In Black 1922', in reference to the guns being tried out before final finishing.

The rifle illustrated (see plates 85/86) is a very rare and unusual double rifle in that it is fitted with electric night sights, only about four other examples being known. No. 23289 is a .450 double rifle sold on the 28 July 1927 to the Maharaja Rewa. (He is responsible for the .577 Rewa cartridge that bears his name.) The barrels are 26 inches long and have a smooth concave rib. They are engraved 'J Purdey & Sons, Audley House, South Audley Street, London. Made of Sir Joseph Whitworth's Fluid Compressed Steel' and in gold 'Maharaja Rewa 1927.' The self-opening action is reinforced and the top strap extends to the comb for extra strength. The action has side clips and the third fastener. The stock has a pistol grip and a cheek-piece. Where the gun is very unusual is in its electrified sighting system. The Maharaja Rewa shot big game at night and asked for an illuminated sight. There are 100yd fixed and 200 and 300 yd folding sights and a non adjustable flip-up peep sight on the top lever. By releasing a small locking lever, the rear sight can lift up. Underneath the sight is a small bulb assembly; the muzzle end reveals a similar set up. A large screw tapped into the end of the barrel, upon removal, contains another small bulb. Small pinholes were drilled in both front and rear sights to obtain the light from these bulbs. Due to the technology of the period external batteries had to be used. Both positive and negative connections were made on the front swivel. The front swivel rotated to complete the circuit and switched the light on. A rifle like this was very difficult to make as very thin wires had to run under the rib to the rear sight. The rifle was stocked by Jack Apted, put together by Miles and engraved by Kell.

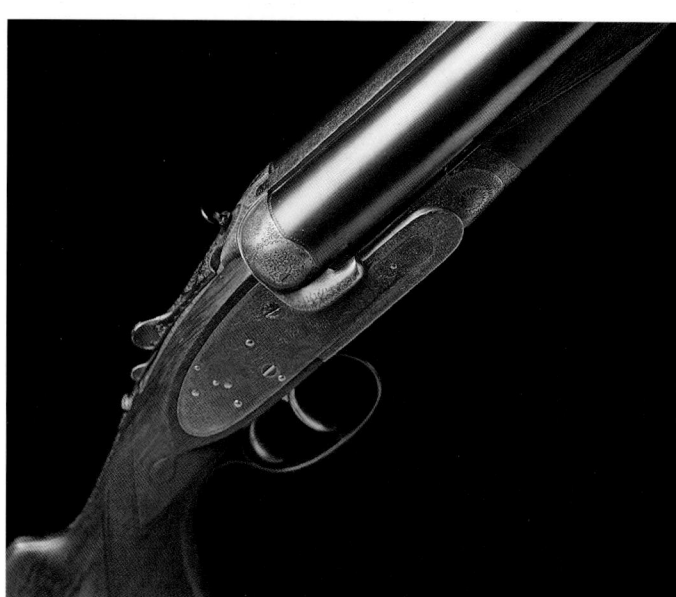

Double .450 rifle No. 23289 sold on the 28 July 1927 to the Maharaja Rewa. The rifle is very unusual in that it has electric night sights. (*See plate 85 in colour section.*)

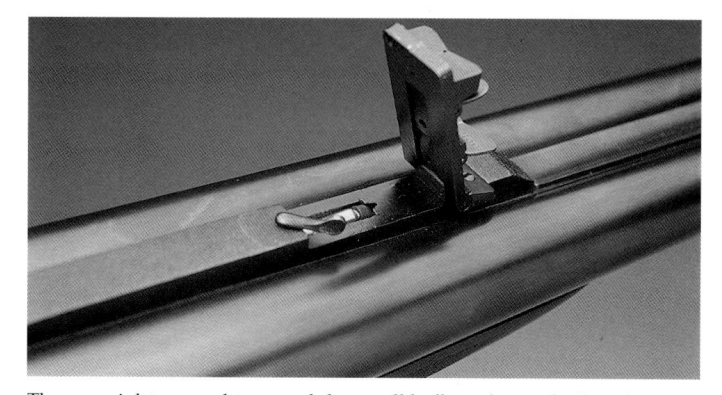

The rear sight opened to reveal the small bulb underneath. (*See plate 86 in colour section.*)

The record in the factory workbook for No. 23306. The gunmakers were: Simons, barrels; Hughes, actioner; Redston, ejectors; Apted, stocker; Sumpter, barrel boring; Gosling, finisher.

The sport of live pigeon shooting had been banned in Britain since 1922. However it still continued to flourish abroad and Purdey's Dimension Books of the 1920s are full of orders for pigeon guns. A very typical 1920s pigeon gun is illustrated No. 23306 is a 12-bore, top lever, self-opening, sidelock ejector gun sold on 13 July 1927 to Purdey's American agent, Abercrombie and Fitch. It was tested on 8 June 1927. This gun possesses all the classic pigeon gun features. The chopper-lump 30' Whitworth steel barrels are chambered for the 2 $^{3}/_{4}$-inch cartridge and the top rib is matt file cut. For extra strength, the fine rose and scroll engraved action has sideclips and the third fastening. The gun is heavier than a normal game gun and weighs 7lb 7oz.

In 1928 King George V suffered serious illness. He was very debilitated and had to give up temporarily one of his great passions, shooting. It was on account of this illness, that Purdey's made him the lightweight, wooden electric gun in 1929 for indoor practice. The King had always shot with hammer ejector guns. Out of interest Purdey's built the following guns for King George V:

Nos. 1149 3/4, a pair of 16-bore hammer guns sold on 21 December 1882 when he was then Prince George.
Nos. 14770/ 1/2, a trio of 12-bore hammer ejector guns sold in August 1894 when he was the Duke of York.
Nos. 18449/50/51, a trio of 12-bore hammer ejector guns sold on 4 May 1906 when he was Prince of Wales.
Nos. 2079 1/2/3, a trio of 16-bore hammer ejectors sold on 18 October 1913.
Nos. 2389 1/2, a pair of 20-bore hammer ejectors tested on 9 July 1929.
Nos. 2418 1/2, a pair of 12-bore hammer ejectors sold in July 1930.

A 12-bore, self-opening, sidelock, ejector pigeon gun No. 23306 sold on 13 July 1927 to Abercrombie and Fitch, probably engraved by Warren. This gun displays many pigeon gun features, 2 $^{3}/_{4}$-inch chambers, file cut rib, sideclips, third fastening and is of greater weight. (*See plate 87 in colour section.*)

Due to the effects of his illness, King George V required far lighter guns. Accordingly, Purdey's built him a pair of light 20-bore, top lever hammer ejector guns. Nos. 2389 1/2 were presented in 1929 to King George V. They weighed only 5lb 12oz. The fine rose and scroll engraved actions have sideclips and retain virtually all their original hardening colour. The highly figured pistol-grip stocks are perfectly matched and have recoil pads. The 28-inch chopper-lump barrels are of Whitworth steel. In the relevant entry in one of the Dimension Books, a single word is written 'returned'. For some reason King George V did not like these guns and returned them to Purdey's. I presume it was because they were 20-bore. He then bought the pair of 12-bore hammer ejectors Nos. 24818/2 in July 1930, a very lightweight pair weighing only 5lb 10$^{1}/_{2}$ oz.

The record in the factory workbook for Nos. 2389 1/2. The gunmakers were: Simons, barrel maker; Fullalove, actioner; Williams, actioner; Sidney, luggers; Dean, stocker; Sumpter, barrel boring.

King George V 20-bore hammer ejectors guns Nos. 2389 1/2 presented in 1929. The word 'returned' is entered in the Dimension Books, as the king did not like them. Probably engraved by Kell. (*See plate 88 in colour section.*)

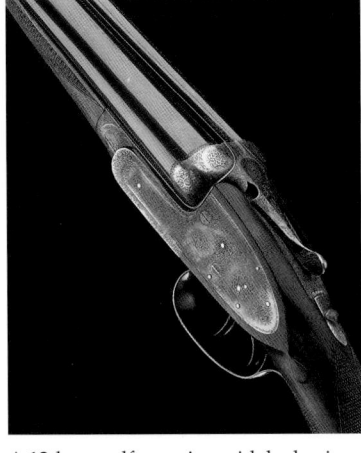

A 12-bore self-opening, sidelock, ejector gun No. 25968 sold in March 1947. Engraved by Kell. (*See plate 89 in colour section.*)

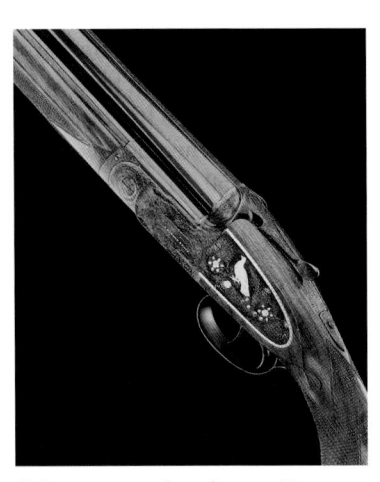

12-bore over-and-under gun No. 26619 tested on 29 December 1956. Engraved by Harry Kell. (*See plate 90 in colour section.*)

The period after World War II presented severe difficulties for Purdey's due to political and economic devastation caused by the war. Gun production was low, less than 100 guns being produced each year. The quality of workmanship did not diminish at all as No. 25968 shows (see plate 89). No. 25968 is a 12-bore, self-opening, sidelock ejector gun tested on 14 January 1947 and sold in March 1947. The fine scroll engraved action has sideclips and the locks have cocking indicators. The chopper-lump barrels are 28-inches long. The gun remains in superb original condition. Stocked by Harold Delay, put together by Geekie and engraved by Kell.

With the purchase of Woodward in 1948 and the subsequent modifications by Ernest Lawrence to their O/U gun, O/Us began to be produced in increasing quantities in the 1950s. Over and under gun No. 26619 (see plate 90) is a 12-bore sidelock ejector with $2^{3}/_{4}$-inch chambers tested on 29 December 1956. The 30-inch barrels are bored full choke, have a ventilated top rib and intermediate bead sight. The action has a hold open top lever, cocking indicators and 'standard fine engraving' by Harry Kell with gold encrusted clay pigeon on one lockplate and a bird on the other. Originally a single-trigger, this gun was converted to a two-trigger in 1968. The gun was stocked by Harold Delay.

A superb pair of 12-bore sidelock ejectors are shown (plate 91). Nos. 2700 1/2 were tested on 11 January 1963 and sold in October 1964. The 'standard fine engraving' was by Geoffrey Casbard who had been apprenticed to Purdey's in 1955 and like Ken Hunt before him, went directly to Harry Kell to learn his craft. He finished his apprenticeship in 1960 and worked again for Purdey's between 1963 and 1970. They were stocked by Harold Delay and put together by Chapman. They are contained within their original oak and leather double case with all accessories.

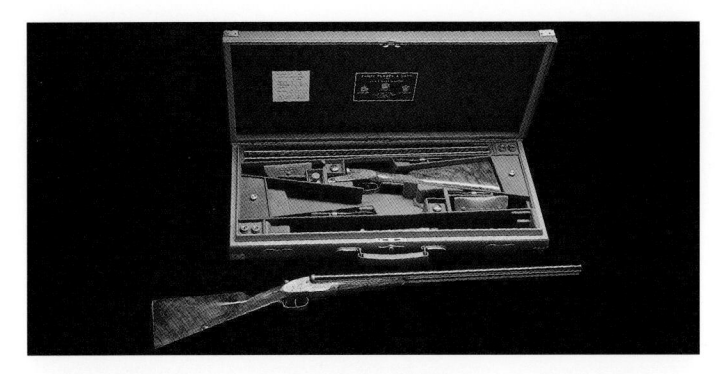

A pair of 12-bore sidelock ejectors Nos. 27001/2 tested on 11 January 1963, contained in their original oak and leather case. Engraved by Casbard. (*See plate 91 in colour section.*)

No. 27379 shown below is a 20-bore over-and-under gun with single-trigger tested on 30 October 1967. This gun has two sets of barrels, the first pair being 28 inches long and bored $^3/_8$ and $^7/_8$ choke, the second pair being 26 inches long and bored improved cylinder and $^1/_4$ choke. The action has a hold open top lever, cocking indicators and the lockplates and underside of the action are engraved with pheasant and quail enclosed by foliate scrolls. Ken Hunt did the engraving and signed both locks 'K C Hunt'. The gun was stocked by Harold Delay and put together by Geekie.

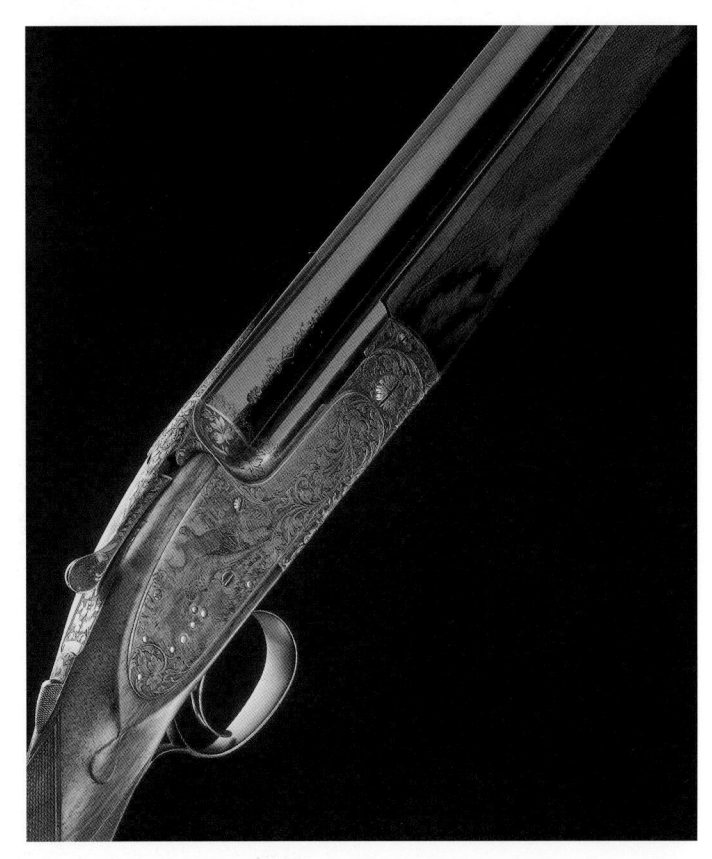

20-bore over-and-under gun No. 27379 tested on 30 October 1967. This gun has two sets of barrels. Engraved by Ken Hunt. (*See plate 92 in colour section.*)

12-bore sidelock ejector gun No. 27699 illustrated in plate 93 was tested on 5 March 1970. The 28-inch barrels are bored improved cylinder and half choke. The lockplates, engraved by Ken Hunt, are signed 'K C Hunt' and display grouse and pheasant within bold scrollwork. The relevant entry in the

12-bore sidelock ejector gun No. 27699 tested on 5 March 1970. Engraved by Ken Hunt. (*See plate 93 in colour section.*)

Dimension Book states 'large scroll with game scenes'. The action and locks are cyanide finished. Stocked by C O'Brien and put together by Chapman.

A very ornate 12-bore sidelock ejector No. 28147 is illustrated overleaf. No. 28147 was tested on 24 November 1977 and the Dimension Book states 'special engraving by K Hunt'. As to the gun itself, the 27-inch barrels are bored full choke and chambered for 2 $^3/_4$-inch cartridges. The lockplates, action body and furniture are spectacularly encrusted in gold. The underside of the action body displays the head of the Green Man, the fences have female demi-figures, the top lever a lion amid thunderbolts, the trigger guard a head within a sunburst plus a great amount of other exotic work. The trigger plate is signed 'K C Hunt ENG 78'. To complement this extraordinary gun, the whole is contained in an oak and crocodile skin lined case with deluxe accessories. The gun was stocked by C O'Brien and put together by Swanson.

Throughout their history, Purdey's have rarely made trios of guns and even more rarely quartets. Nos. 28156/7/8/9 illustrated overleaf are a rare quartet of 12-bore sidelock ejector guns. Tested on 18 March 1976, they have 28-inch barrels, cocking indicators and 'standard fine engraving'. They are chambered for 2 $^3/_4$-inch cartridges. The guns are cased as pairs.

12-bore single-trigger over-and-under gun No. 28589 is shown overleaf. This gun was tested on 5 February 1986. It

A spectacular gold encrusted 12-bore sidelock ejector No. 28147 tested on 24 November 1977. Engraving by Ken Hunt. (*See plate 94 in colour section.*)

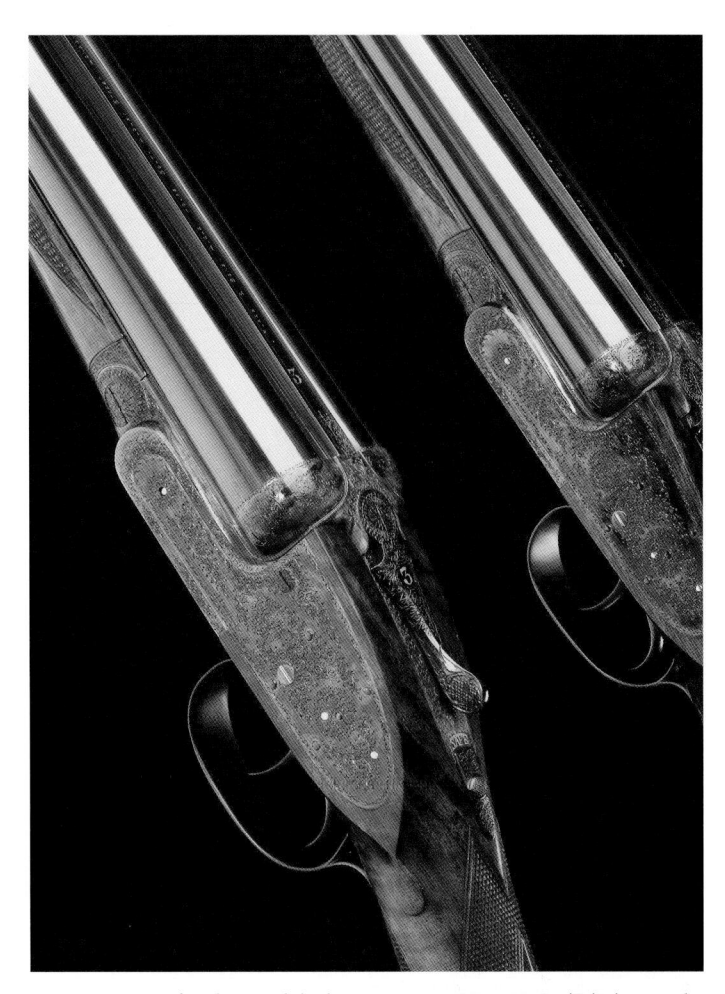

A rare quartet of 12-bore sidelock ejector guns Nos. 28156/7/8/9 tested on 18 March 1976. The No. 3 and 4 guns are shown. Purdey's made very few quartets of guns. (*See plate 95 in colour section.*)

weighs 7lb 10oz, has 28-inch barrels, a single-trigger, rolled edge trigger guard, hold open top lever, beetle backed safety and cocking indicators. It was stocked by A Davies and D Josey and put together by Bob Nicholls. The engraving is by W P Sinclair and shows scenes of pheasants and pintails surrounded by a acanthus scrollwork. 'J Purdey & Sons' is gold inlaid on the action. The trigger-plate is signed 'W P Sinclair'. The gun has cyanide hardening.

Purdey's have produced relatively few hammerless rifles. If hammerless rifles are relatively rare, then pairs of hammerless rifles must be priceless. Nos. 29181/2 are such a pair, sold on 2 December 1998. Both rifles are identical apart from the engraving. They have 24-inch barrels and are

.300 double-barrel hammerless rifle No. 29181, the No. 1 of the pair sold in 1998 with 'standard fine engraving'. (*See plate 97 in colour section.*)

12-bore over-and-under gun No. 28589 tested on 5 February 1986. Engraved by W P Sinclair. (*See plate 96 in colour section.*)

LATER BREECH-LOADING GUNS AND RIFLES

chambered for the .300 H & H cartridge. The superb figured stocks have pistol grips and cheek-pieces. Each rifle weighs 9lb 5oz. The actions have sideclips and the third fastening. No. 29181 (see plate 97) has 'standard fine engraving' whereas No. 29182 (see plate 98) has incredible leopard scene engraving by Stephen Kelly.

A recently completed 20-bore O/U gun No. 29424 is illustrated (see plates 99 and 100). Nos. 29424/5 are a pair of 20-bore O/Us sold in April 1998. They have 28-inch barrels, chambered for the 2 ³/₄-inch cartridge and have single-triggers. The engraving and gold inlay work is quite superb being the work of Philip Coggan.

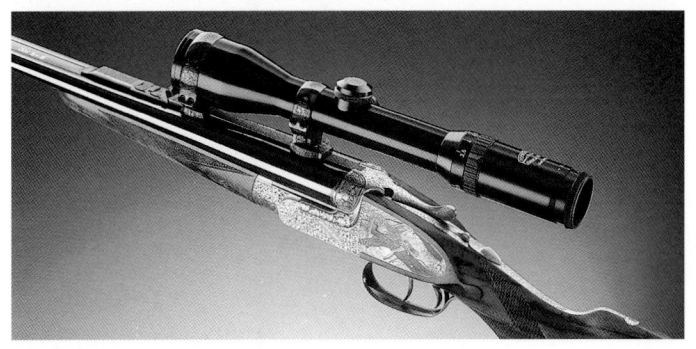

The underside of the action of No. 29424 featuring the engraving and inlay work of Philip Coggan. (*See plate 100 in colour section.*)

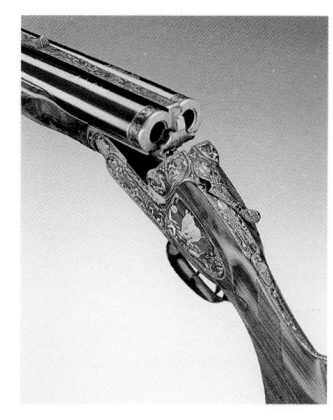

Double-barrel hammerless .600 rifle No. 29601 sold in 1997. Engraving and carving by Cecile Flohiment. (*See plate 104 in colour section.*)

.300 double-barrel hammerless rifle No. 29182, the No. 2 of the pair with leopard scene engraving by Stephen Kelly. (*See plate 98 in colour section.*)

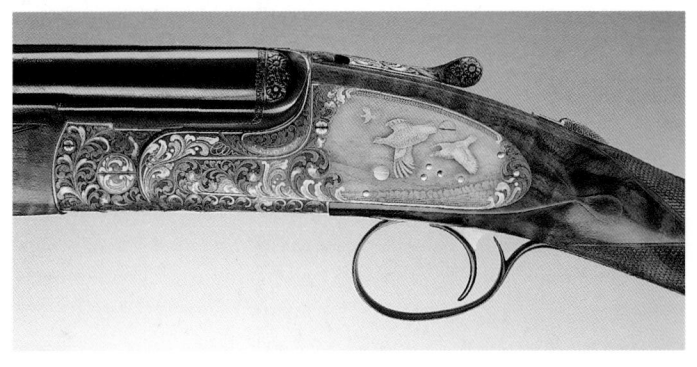

No. 29424 the No. 1 gun of a pair of 20-bore O/Us sold in 1998. The engraving and gold inlay work is by Philip Coggan. (*See plate 99 in colour section.*)

Another rifle, No. 29530 sold in 1997 is shown (plate 101). No. 29530 is a .375 H & H double-barrel hammerless rifle with 'standard fine engraving'. The barrels are 23 inches long and the entire rifle weighs 9lb 11 ¹/₂ oz. The action has side-clips and the third fastening. A spring bladed front trigger is used and the heelplate is leather covered. A Zeiss 1.5-6 x 42 scope is mounted. The rifle was stocked by R Bailey and put together by J MacDonald.

Another rare rifle, No. 29601 is illustrated (see plates 102-104). No. 29601 is a double-barrel hammerless .600 double rifle

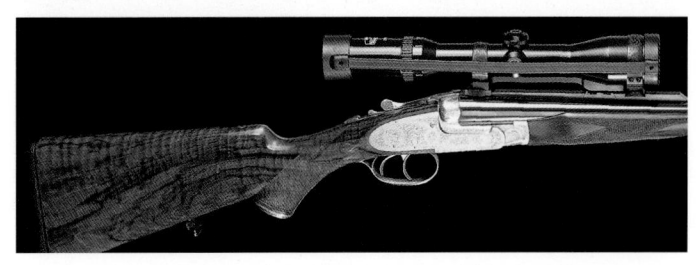

.375 double-barrel hammerless rifle No. 29530 with Zeiss 1.5-6 x 42 scope. (*See plate 101 in colour section.*)

sold in 1997. The barrels are 24 inches long with the third fastening and the action has sideclips. The tops strap extends to the comb for extra strength. This rifle weighs a massive 15lb 1oz. The engraving is spectacular being the work of Cecile Flohiment. The locks, action, trigger-guard, etc. are carved and gold encrusted displaying big game scenes. The rifle was stocked by D Bailey and put together by J MacDonald.

The underside of No. 29601 showing the gold-encrusted elephant. (*See plate 102 in colour section.*)

A spectacularly inlaid gun No. 29660 is shown (see plates 105 and 106). No. 29660, sold in 1997 is a 28-bore hammerless ejector sporting gun with 28-inch barrels, bored half choke and full choke and chambered for the 2 ³/₄-inch cartridge. The gun features the third fastening, side clips and a single trigger. What makes No. 29660 very special is the quite spectacular inlay work of Brown Brothers. The lockplates have chiselled mythical and allegorical figures on a gold background and are signed 'J P Brown'. The action, top lever, etc. have deeply chiselled scrollwork, again within a gold background. The gun is contained in a sumptuous rosewood case lined in tooled blue leather with deluxe accessories.

The final gun illustrated (overleaf) is No. 30,000, the Millennium Gun. This very special gun is a 28-bore ultra round bar sidelock ejector. The 28-inch barrels have 2 ³/₄-inch chambers and are bored ¹/₂ and full choke. The barrels are inlaid in gold with the wording 'The Millennium Gun.' A single trigger is fitted and the stock has a semi-pistol grip with metal cap. The action lock and trigger guard are profusely inlaid with different colours of gold, executed byn Ken Hunt.

181

The chiselled mythical and allegorical work of Brown Brothers on No. 29660. (*See plate 106 in colour section.*)

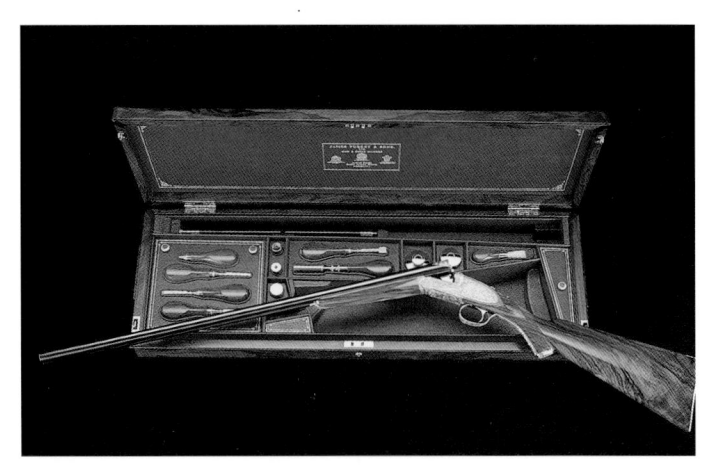

No. 29660 in its blue leather lined rosewood case complete. (*See plate 107 in colour section.*)

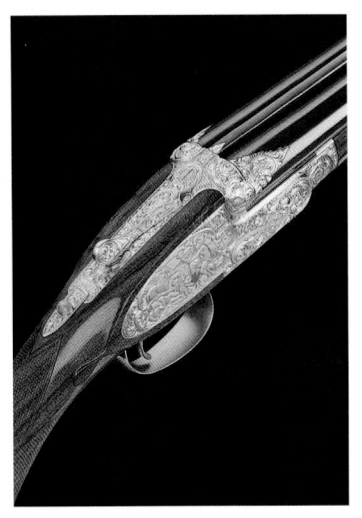

No. 29660, a 28-bore gun sold in 1997 engraved and inlaid by Brown Brothers. (*See plate 105 in colour section.*)

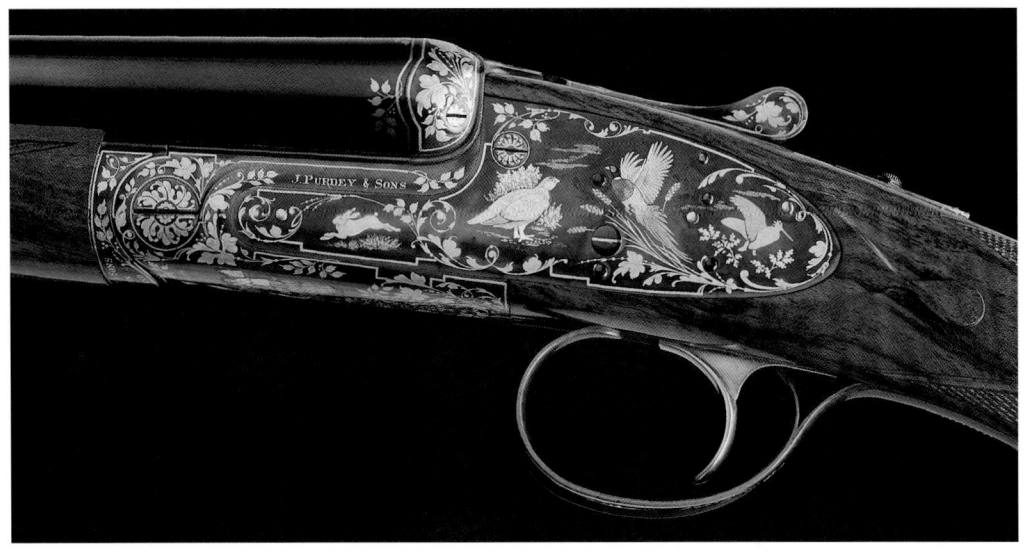

The Millennium Gun, No. 30,000, a 28-bore round bodied sidelock ejector with spectacular different coloured gold inlay by Ken Hunt. (*See plate 108 in colour section.*)

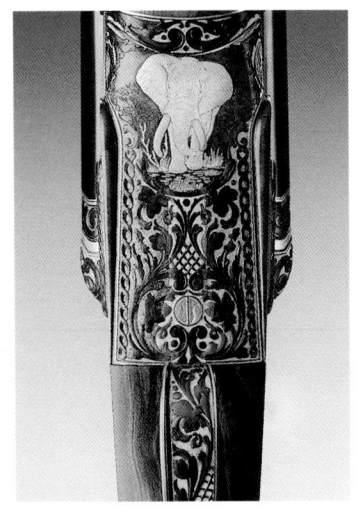

The action of 29601. (*See plate 103 in colour section.*)

The underside of No. 30,000. (*See plate 109 in colour section.*)

APPENDICES

Appendix 1

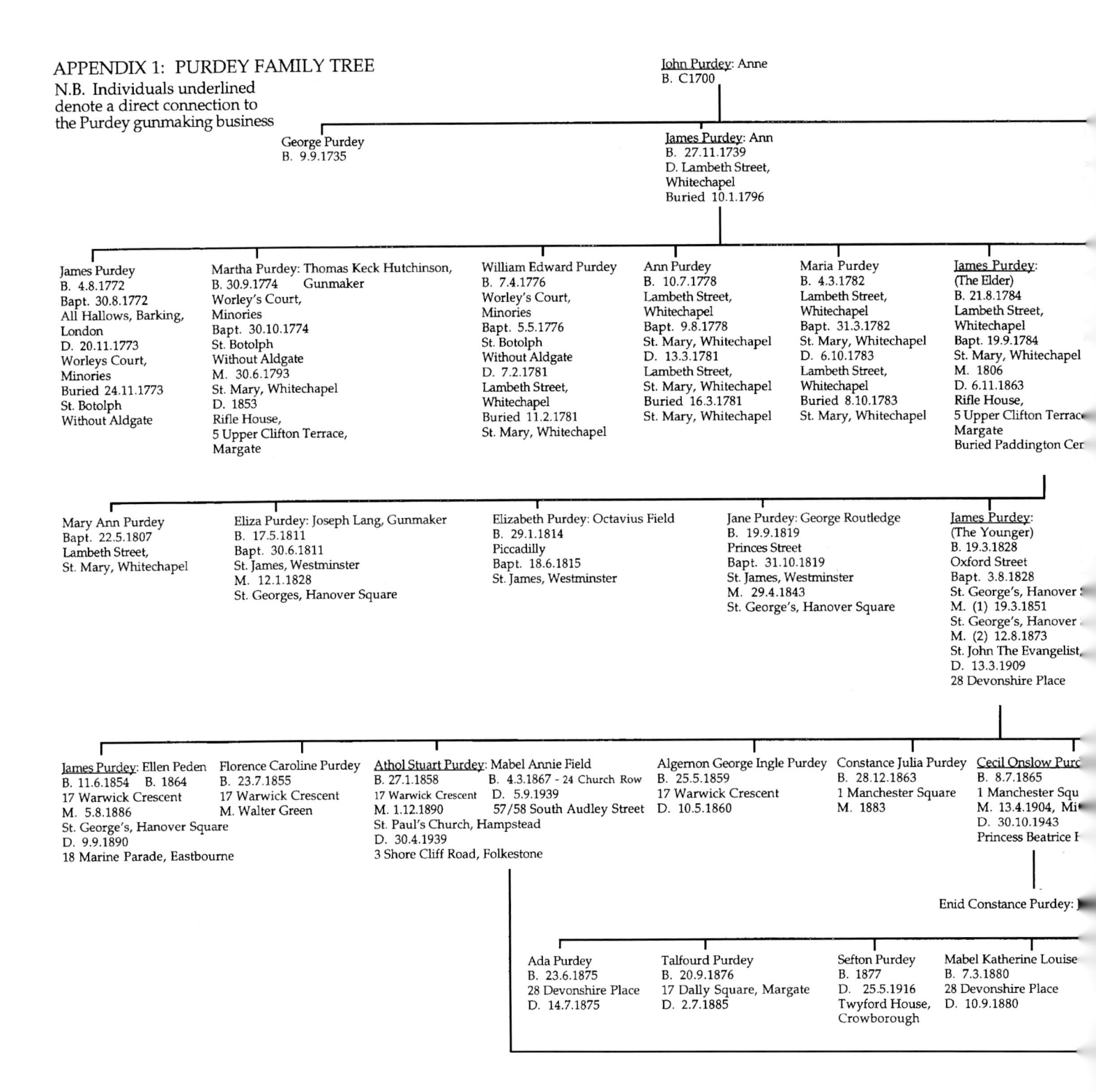

PURDEY FAMILY TREE

APPENDIX 1: PURDEY FAMILY TREE
N.B. Individuals underlined denote a direct connection to the Purdey gunmaking business

John Purdey: Anne
B. C1700

- **George Purdey**
  B. 9.9.1735

- **James Purdey**: Ann
  B. 27.11.1739
  D. Lambeth Street, Whitechapel
  Buried 10.1.1796

Children of James Purdey and Ann:

James Purdey
B. 4.8.1772
Bapt. 30.8.1772
All Hallows, Barking, London
D. 20.11.1773
Worleys Court, Minories
Buried 24.11.1773
St. Botolph
Without Aldgate

Martha Purdey: Thomas Keck Hutchinson, Gunmaker
B. 30.9.1774
Worley's Court, Minories
Bapt. 30.10.1774
St. Botolph Without Aldgate
M. 30.6.1793
St. Mary, Whitechapel
D. 1853
Rifle House,
5 Upper Clifton Terrace, Margate

William Edward Purdey
B. 7.4.1776
Worley's Court, Minories
Bapt. 5.5.1776
St. Botolph Without Aldgate
D. 7.2.1781
Lambeth Street, Whitechapel
Buried 11.2.1781
St. Mary, Whitechapel

Ann Purdey
B. 10.7.1778
Lambeth Street, Whitechapel
Bapt. 9.8.1778
St. Mary, Whitechapel
D. 13.3.1781
Lambeth Street, St. Mary, Whitechapel
Buried 16.3.1781
St. Mary, Whitechapel

Maria Purdey
B. 4.3.1782
Lambeth Street, Whitechapel
Bapt. 31.3.1782
St. Mary, Whitechapel
D. 6.10.1783
Lambeth Street, Whitechapel
Buried 8.10.1783
St. Mary, Whitechapel

James Purdey: (The Elder)
B. 21.8.1784
Lambeth Street, Whitechapel
Bapt. 19.9.1784
St. Mary, Whitechapel
M. 1806
D. 6.11.1863
Rifle House,
5 Upper Clifton Terrace, Margate
Buried Paddington Cer[metery]

Children of James Purdey (The Elder):

Mary Ann Purdey
Bapt. 22.5.1807
Lambeth Street,
St. Mary, Whitechapel

Eliza Purdey: Joseph Lang, Gunmaker
B. 17.5.1811
Bapt. 30.6.1811
St. James, Westminster
M. 12.1.1828
St. Georges, Hanover Square

Elizabeth Purdey: Octavius Field
B. 29.1.1814
Piccadilly
Bapt. 18.6.1815
St. James, Westminster

Jane Purdey: George Routledge
B. 19.9.1819
Princes Street
Bapt. 31.10.1819
St. James, Westminster
M. 29.4.1843
St. George's, Hanover Square

James Purdey: (The Younger)
B. 19.3.1828
Oxford Street
Bapt. 3.8.1828
St. George's, Hanover [Square]
M. (1) 19.3.1851
St. George's, Hanover [Square]
M. (2) 12.8.1873
St. John The Evangelist,
D. 13.3.1909
28 Devonshire Place

Children of James Purdey (The Younger):

James Purdey: Ellen Peden
B. 11.6.1854   B. 1864
17 Warwick Crescent
M. 5.8.1886
St. George's, Hanover Square
D. 9.9.1890
18 Marine Parade, Eastbourne

Florence Caroline Purdey
B. 23.7.1855
17 Warwick Crescent
M. Walter Green

Athol Stuart Purdey: Mabel Annie Field
B. 27.1.1858   B. 4.3.1867 - 24 Church Row
17 Warwick Crescent   D. 5.9.1939
M. 1.12.1890   57/58 South Audley Street
St. Paul's Church, Hampstead
D. 30.4.1939
3 Shore Cliff Road, Folkestone

Algernon George Ingle Purdey
B. 25.5.1859
17 Warwick Crescent
D. 10.5.1860

Constance Julia Purdey
B. 28.12.1863
1 Manchester Square
M. 1883

Cecil Onslow Pur[dey]
B. 8.7.1865
1 Manchester Squ[are]
M. 13.4.1904, Mi[...]
D. 30.10.1943
Princess Beatrice [...]

Enid Constance Purdey: [...]

Children of Athol Stuart Purdey and Mabel Annie Field:

Ada Purdey
B. 23.6.1875
28 Devonshire Place
D. 14.7.1875

Talfourd Purdey
B. 20.9.1876
17 Dally Square, Margate
D. 2.7.1885

Sefton Purdey
B. 1877
D. 25.5.1916
Twyford House, Crowborough

Mabel Katherine Louise
B. 7.3.1880
28 Devonshire Place
D. 10.9.1880

184

```
                    ┌─────────────────────────────────────────────────────────────────────┐
                    │                                                                     │
        James Alexander Purdey:   (1) Hariot Patricia Kinloch   (2) Beatrice Oliver      Thomas Donald Stuart Purdey
        B. 30.9.1891                  B. 1892                                              B. 22.3.1897
        67 Canfield Gardens           D. 26.12.1947              (3) Mary La Boyteaux      67 Canfield Gardens
        M. (1) 14.4.1917                                             D. 1965               D. 5.3.1957
        St. Paul's Church, Knightsbridge                                                   Canterbury Hospital
        M. (2) 22.9.1923
        Dar es Salaam                                             William Purdey
        M. (3) 28.8.1930                                          B. 1937
        Riverfields, New Jersey                                   5 Wellington Square
        D. 25.7.1963
        Holmchel, New Jersey
```

James Oliver Kinloch Purdey: (1) Barbara Allen   (2) Marjorie Marshall-Smith   (3) Janet Hodsoll
B. 26.1.1918   B. 16.7.1918   D. 1980   M. 1981
Farm House, Old Windsor
M. (1) 1941
Grosvenor Chapel,
South Audley Street
M. (2) 1947
M. (3) 1981
D. 24.9.1984
Farnham

Charles James Richard Purdey: Gun Rigmor Margaretha   Rosemary   Alexandra
B. 28.2.42   Nidle, Lidköping (Sweden) B. 1948   B. 1949
Hove
M. 1968

Annika Louise Purdey   Kristina Alexandra Purdey
B. 2.6.1969   B. 22.2.1971
Lidköping (Sweden)   Tunbridge Wells

Purdey
.1740
ster Street,
y, Whitechapel
1.8.1740

Susannah Purdey
B. 26.2.1786
Lambeth Street,
Whitechapel
Bapt. 26.3.1786
St. Mary, Whitecha
D. 1786
Lambeth Street
Buried 6.8.1786
St. Mary, Whitecha

.1790
1860
ottage, Queen's Road,
ter
Paddington Cemetery

line Elizabeth Thomas (2) Julia Haverson
. 20.4.1831   B. 10.7.1854
Marylebone, All Souls   Barking Road,
.1870   Plaistow
ington House Asylum   D. 5.1.1911
                           Harrow Weald

anny Turner   Percy Purdey: Marion
              B. 24.8.1869
              28 Devonshire Place

d Purdey   Lionel Bateson Purdey
1881   B. 16.2.1886
nshire Place 28 Devonshire Place
1885   D. 1959

Appendix 2

DIARY OF EVENTS IN PURDEY HISTORY

Date	Event
c1700	John Purdey travels from Scotland to London
27 November 1739	James Purdey born to John and Anne
c1760	James Purdey works as a blacksmith in the Minories
c1770	James Purdey marries Ann
30 September 1774	Martha Purdey born to James and Ann, Worley's Court, The Minories
21 August 1784	James Purdey (the Founder) born to James and Ann, Lambeth Street, Whitechapel
30 June 1793	Martha marries Thomas Keck Hutchinson, gunmaker, St. Mary's, Whitechapel
10 January 1796	James Purdey (the Blacksmith) buried St. Mary's, Whitechapel
21 August 1798	James Purdey apprenticed to Thomas Keck Hutchinson
August 1805	James Purdey completes his apprenticeship
1805	James Purdey joins Joseph Manton, gunmaker
1806	James Purdey marries Mary
1808	James Purdey joins Alexander Forsyth, gunmaker
31 December 1812	James Purdey admitted to the freedom of the Gunmakers' Company
Spring, 1816	James Purdey sets up his own business at 4 Princes Street, Leicester Square
3 February 1818	Wyatt's patent for safety gun lock used by Purdey
1820	First Purdey gun recorded in the Dimension Books – No. 206, probably percussion
Late 1826	Purdey moves to 315 Oxford Street, Joseph Manton's old premises
Mid-1827	Shop number changed to 314 $^1/_2$ Oxford Street
12 January 1828	Eliza Purdey marries Joseph Lang, gunmaker, St. George's Church, Hanover Square
19 March 1828	James Purdey (the Younger) born 314 $^1/_2$ Oxford Street
1841	James Purdey elected Master of the Gunmakers' Company
14 July 1843	James Purdey the Younger apprenticed to his father, James Purdey the Elder
1851	Probable first Express rifle No. 4700
19 March 1851	James Purdey the Younger marries Caroline Thomas, St. George's, Hanover Square
1852	Board of Ordnance rifle trials
	Purdey granted registered design no. 3135, self-expanding bullet
1853	Martha Hutchinson (née Purdey) dies at Margate
11 June 1854	James Purdey III born 17 Warwick Crescent
1857	Probable first breech-loader No. 5305
1 January 1858	James Purdey the Younger obtains full control of the business
27 January 1858	Athol Purdey born at 17 Warwick Crescent
5 February 1860	Death of James Purdey the Elder's wife, Mary, at Rifle Cottage, Queen's Road
27 December 1860	James Purdey the Younger admitted to the Freedom of the Gunmakers' Company
5 February 1861	First patent taken out by James Purdey the Younger (patent no. 302 Turnover Tool)
2 May 1863	The Purdey bolt patent no. 1104
6 November 1863	James Purdey the Elder dies at Rifle House, 5 Upper Clifton Terrace, Margate
1865	Probable first centre-fire No. 6992
8 July 1865	Cecil Purdey born at 1 Manchester Square
c1868	Purdey family moves to 28 Devonshire Place

DIARY OF EVENTS IN PURDEY HISTORY

12 February 1868	Purdey's receive the Royal Warrant of Appointment from the Prince of Wales
7 January 1870	James Purdey the Younger's wife, Caroline, dies
12 August 1873	James Purdey marries (second) Julia Haverson in Penge
1874	James Purdey the Younger elected Master of the Gunmakers' Company
c1875	Athol Purdey joins the firm
28 June 1877	James Purdey III admitted to the Freedom of the Gunmakers' Company
21 December 1877	The name of the firm is changed to James Purdey and Sons
30 January 1878	The Third Fastening, patent no. 397
29 March 1878	Purdey's receive the Royal Warrant of Appointment from Queen Victoria
13 November 1879	Athol Purdey admitted to the Freedom of the Gunmakers' Company
Late 1870s	Introduction of A, B, C, D, E quality guns and rifles
1879	James Purdey buys the leases on 57-60 South Audley Street
3 January 1880	Frederick Beesley's patent no. 31, the Spring Cocked, Self-Opening, Hammerless Gun
1880	Probable first Beesley hammerless gun No. 10743
1 October 1880	London County Council re-numbers 314 $1/2$ Oxford Street as 287/289 Oxford Street
1 December 1881	Lease acquired on 37 North Row, first Purdey factory
1882	James Purdey the Younger elected Master of the Gunmakers' Company
1 January 1883	James Purdey and Son move to Audley House, 57-58 South Audley Street
2 March 1883	William Nobbs ejector patent no. 1137
Early 1880s	Adoption of Whitworth's fluid compressed steel
5 August 1886	Marriage of James Purdey III to Ellen Peden
29 February 1888	The Wem ejector (the Purdey ejector) patent no. 3100
Late 1880s	Cecil Purdey joins the firm
1890	Athol Purdey elected Master of the Gunmakers' Company
9 September 1890	James Purdey III dies at 18 Marine Parade, Eastbourne
1 December 1890	Athol Purdey marries Mabel Field, St. Paul's Church, Hampstead
30 September 1891	James Alexander Purdey (James IV) born at 67 Canfield Gardens, Hampstead
1892	James Purdey re-develops 84 Mount Street
1892	James Purdey the Younger elected Master of the Gunmakers' Company
6 July 1894	William Nobbs single-trigger patent no. 13130
22 March 1897	Thomas Donald Stuart Purdey born 67 Canfield Gardens
17 August 1897	First patent of Athol Purdey, patent no. 19027, hand protector
1899	Athol Purdey elected Master of the Gunmakers' Company
1900	Factory moves to No. 2 Irongate Wharf, Paddington
29 May 1901	Purdey's receive the Royal Warrant of Appointment from King Edward VII
1 March 1902	Purdey's receive the Royal Warrant of Appointment from the Prince of Wales
1902	Cecil Purdey elected Master of the Gunmakers' Company
3 July 1904	Probable last sale of a muzzle-loader No. 18198
15 December 1906	Beginning of the single trigger patent dispute
1908	Athol Purdey elected Master of the Gunmakers' Company
13 March 1909	James Purdey the Younger dies at 28 Devonshire Place
1909	James Purdey IV joins the Royal Military College, Sandhurst
1 March 1910	Single-trigger patent no. 5150
5 January 1911	Julia Purdey dies at Harrow Weald
1 February 1911	Purdey's receive the Royal Warrant of Appointment from King George V
3 October 1911	Single trigger patent no. 21822
1911	Cecil Purdey elected Master of the Gunmakers' Company
8 May 1913	James Purdey IV admitted to the Freedom of the Gunmakers' Company
27 January 1914	Harry Lawrence begins his apprenticeship
7 March 1914	Ernest Charles Lawrence becomes factory manager
12 November 1914	Tom Purdey joins the Royal Military College, Sandhurst
27 February 1915	Athol Purdey's muzzle-protector patent no. 3188
21 March 1915	Lieutenant Tom Purdey posted to France
14 April 1917	James Purdey IV marries Patricia Kinloch at St. Paul's Church, Knightsbridge
26 January 1918	James Oliver Kinloch Purdey born Farm House, Old Windsor
6 November 1919	Tom Purdey admitted to the Gunmakers' Company
26 May 1920	Purdey's receive the Royal Warrant of Appointment from the Prince of Wales
June 1920	Tom Purdey joins Purdey's
1921	Athol Purdey elected Master of the Gunmakers' Company

APPENDICES

1923	Probable first single-barrel trap gun No. 22417
1923	Probable first O/U gun No. 22564 on the Edwinson Green design
1923	Queen Mary Doll's House guns Nos. 22491/2
1923	Cecil Purdey elected Master of the Gunmakers' Company
22 September 1923	James Purdey IV second marriage to Bee Oliver, Dar-es-Salaam, Tanganyika
2 October 1925	Formation of a limited company 'James Purdey & Sons Ltd.'
1925	James Purdey IV joins Purdey's
26 February 1926	Tom Purdey's shooting stick patent no. 5523
30 July 1926	Tom Purdey's shooting stick patent no. 19052
1927	Purchase of the shooting ground at Eastcote, South Harrow
1928	Tom Purdey elected Master of the Gunmakers' Company
13 May 1929	Electric cartridge patent no. 14943
23 May 1929	Athol Purdey's walking stick patent no. 15985
Late 1920s	Retirement of Athol Purdey
28 August 1930	James Purdey IV third marriage to Mary La Boyteaux, Riverfields, New Jersey
1930s	Re-designed ejector mechanism
1931	Jim Purdey elected Master of the Gunmakers' Company
1934	Cecil Purdey elected Master of the Gunmakers' Company
1935	Miniature hammer ejector guns No. 25000/1 presented to King George V
1936	Eastcote shooting ground sold, West London Shooting Grounds at Northolt used instead
1936	Publication of *The Shot Gun* by T D S Purdey and Captain J A Purdey
30 June 1938	Purdey's receive the Royal Warrant of Appointment from King George VI
1938	Long Room rebuilt
1938	Gauge making and pop rivet gun manufacture commences
30 April 1939	Athol Purdey dies at 3 Shorecliffe Road, Folkestone
1939	Factory taken over on the Great West Road for gauges and moulds
5 September 1939	Mabel Purdey dies at Audley House
1940	Tom Purdey elected Master of the Gunmakers' Company
1941	Jim Purdey elected Master of the Gunmakers' Company
16 April 1941	Audley House hit by a German bomb
23 July 1943	Lawrence Salter joins Purdey's
30 October 1943	Cecil Purdey dies at the Princess Beatrice Hospital, Old Brompton Road
1945	Harry Lawrence awarded the MBE and Fred Williams the BEM
1946	Toolmakers transfer to Irongate Wharf Road
1 January 1948	Ernest Charles Lawrence retires
1 October 1948	Agreement signed with James Woodward & Sons
1 January 1949	Sale concludes of Woodward to Purdey's
1949	Purdey's make modifications under Ernest Douglas Lawrence to the Woodward O/U
1949	Richard Beaumont joins Purdey's
1950	First Purdey/Woodward O/U delivered No. 25950
1950	Factory moves to 20/22 Irongate Wharf
1951	Cessation of Purdey hand-loaded cartridges in Audley House
1951	Tom Purdey elected Master of the Gunmakers' Company
18 March 1952	Ralph Lawrence killed in an accident in the London Proof House
25 March 1953	Richard Beaumont becomes a director
22 November 1953	Ernest Charles Lawrence dies
1954	Harry Lawrence becomes managing-director
1 May 1955	Tom Purdey retires and is made President of firm and Lord Sherwood becomes chairman
15 July 1955	Purdey's receive the Royal Warrant of Appointment from Queen Elizabeth II
2 January 1956	Purdey's receive the Royal Warrant of Appointment from the Duke of Edinburgh
1956	Victor Seely elected Master of the Gunmakers' Company
5 March 1957	Tom Purdey dies at Canterbury Hospital
1961	Mould making side of the business closes down
1962	Harry Lawrence elected Master of the Gunmakers' Company
25 July 1963	James Purdey IV dies at Holmchel, New Jersey
1964	Victor Seely elected Master of the Gunmakers' Company
1966	J O K Purdey elected Master of the Gunmakers' Company
1968	Richard Beaumont elected Master of the Gunmakers' Company
1 April 1970	Lord Sherwood dies Brook Hill, Isle of Wight and Sir Victor Seely becomes chairman

DIARY OF EVENTS IN PURDEY HISTORY

23 April 1970	Lawrence Salter becomes managing-director upon the retirement of Harry Lawrence as managing-director
1971	Factory moves to 57 North Wharf Road
26 July 1971	Richard Beaumont becomes chairman after Sir Victor Seely relinquishes the position
29 October 1975	IRA bomb damages Audley House
1975	Lawrence Salter elected Master of the Gunmakers' Company
December 1977	Nigel Beaumont joins Purdey's
Late 1970s	Lawrence Salter designs the new inertia bobweight single-trigger
30 October 1979	Official opening of the new factory at Felgate Mews
1982	Nigel Beaumont becomes a director
1984	Publication of *Purdey's, The Guns and The Family* by Richard Beaumont
1984	Richard Beaumont elected Master of the Gunmakers' Company
28 July 1984	Harry Lawrence, MBE, dies
24 September 1984	James Oliver Kinloch Purdey dies at Farnham
1985	Chris Gadsby, the factory manager retires
1985	Ernest Douglas Lawrence elected Master of the Gunmakers' Company
1986	Lawrence Salter elected Master of the Gunmakers' Company
Christmas, 1989	Eugene Warner retires after 72 years service
30 April 1992	Green plaque unveiled on Audley House
1994	Lawrence Salter retires as managing-director and Nigel Beaumont takes over
5 October 1994	Purdey's are taken over by Vendome PLC
1994	Richard Beaumont retires as chairman and becomes president of Purdey's. Richard Purdey takes over as chairman
Mid 1990s	Production recommences of Woodward O/Us and side-by-sides
Summer, 1999	Purdey's shop at 844 Madison Avenue, New York opens
2000	Millennium gun No. 30000 produced

Appendix 3a

PURDEY SERIAL NUMBERS AND DATING

It must be stated from the outset that dating a gun or rifle is not a straightforward procedure. When do you date it from – its order, its date of completion, its date of sale? Weapons took many months to make, some, notably rifles and pistols, took longer to make than others and some took months if not years to sell. For these reasons it is wise not to be dogmatic about precise dating.

Purdey's possess a vast array of archive material dating back to 1818. An entire wall in the main shop in Audley Street displays records! Consequently it might be assumed that the dating of Purdey's is a simple task. Unfortunately this is not the case. Due to the long established nature of the business, records have varied over the years, and in addition some records are missing. Differing records have to be used for particular periods.

SALES LEDGERS 1818 – THE EARLY 1860s

The Dimension Books in this period are of little use in assisting with the dating of weapons. They give only gun details and owner. No helpful dates are given. Dates do appear but have been added considerably later on and cannot be relied upon.

The main types of record that must be used in this period are the sales ledgers – these show the accounts of Purdey customers in great detail but give only the date of sale of a particular gun, not when it was built. Some guns were sold very soon after they were made, others such as stock guns, that would remain in the shop awaiting a customer, might take longer. Rifles and pistols were more complicated to make and they tended to lag behind expected serial number placement. Some weapons do not appear in the sales ledgers at all and estimates of sale have had to be calculated. Although the first sales ledger bears the date 1818 on the spine and there are accounts from that date, it is apparent that like the first Dimension Book, the ledger was begun probably in the mid 1820s and filled in retrospectively. The first serial number, No. 567, of a gun in a customer's account dates from 15 January 1824. Serial numbers were often not quoted and it isn't until the late 1820s that they appear with frequency. Consequently pre-1824 reasoned analysis must be used.

1816	Nos. 1-12
1817	Nos. 13-40
1818	Nos. 41-90
1819	Nos. 91-165
1820	Nos. 166-250
1821	Nos. 251-340
1822	Nos. 341-440
1823	Nos. 441-560
1824	Nos. 561-725
1825	Nos. 726-890, 907, 917, 919
1826	Nos. 891-906, 908-916, 918, 920-994, 996, 999-1002, 1004, 1007-1008, 1010-1015, 1018-1030, 1032-1047, 1049-1062, 1064-1067, 1069-1073, 1075-1079, 1084-1089, 1098-1099, 1102-1103, 1108, 1112, 1120-1121, 1144
1827	Nos. 995, 997-998, 1003, 1009, 1016-1017, 1031, 1063, 1068, 1074, 1080-1083, 1090-1097, 1100-1101, 1104-1107, 1109-1111, 1113-1115, 1117-1119, 1122-1137, 1140-1143, 1145-1147, 1149-1157, 1160-1177, 1179-1185, 1187-1205 1207-1224, 1226-1230, 1232-1233, 1235-1238, 1240-1257, 1259-1285, 1287, 1290-1297, 1299-1303, 1305-1311, 1313, 1317, 1319-1321, 1323-1324, 1326-1327, 1329-1330, 1332-1334, 1337, 1343, 1345-1349, 1362, 1364, 1525
1828	Nos. 1005-1006, 1048, 1116, 1138, 1158-1159, 1178, 1186, 1231, 1234, 1239, 1286, 1288-1289, 1298, 1304, 1312, 1314-1316, 1318, 1322, 1325, 1328, 1331, 1335-1336, 1338-1342, 1344, 1350-1353, 1355-1361, 1363, 1368-1374, 1376-1414, 1416-1426, 1428-1432, 1435-1438, 1440, 1443-1452, 1454-1455, 1457-1478, 1480-1501, 1503-1511, 1513-1524, 1526-1537, 1539-1549, 1552-1559, 1561-1567, 1569-1583,

1585-1599, 1601, 1604, 1607-1609, 1612- 1614, 1624, 1631

1829 Nos. 1139, 1148, 1206, 1225, 1258, 1354, 1367, 1375, 1415, 1433-1434, 1441-1442, 1453, 1479, 1502, 1512, 1538, 1550-1551, 1560, 1568, 1584, 1600, 1602-1603, 1605-1606, 1610-1611, 1615-1623, 1626-1630, 1632-1656, 1658-1664, 1666-1684, 1686, 1688-1693, 1696-1705, 1707-1709, 1712-1715, 1717-1751, 1753-1760, 1762-1838, 1844, 1847-1849, 1851-1852, 1854-1870, 1877, 1886

1830 Nos. 1366, 1427, 1625, 1657, 1694-1695, 1752, 1761, 1839-1841, 1843, 1845-1846, 1853, 1871-1876, 1878, 1880- 1882, 1884-1885, 1887-1890, 1892-1893, 1895, 1899-1916, 1921-1930, 1934-1936, 1938, 1940, 1942-1961, 1963- 1998, 2000-2002, 2004-2006, 2009-2011, 2016-2018, 2020-2021, 2023-2025, 2028, 2030-2038, 2043, 2047, 2051-2056, 2069, 2133

1831 Nos. 1365, 1439, 1665, 1685, 1687, 1706, 1710-1711, 1716, 1842, 1850, 1879, 1883, 1891, 1894, 1896-1897, 1919, 1931-1933, 1939, 1941, 1999, 2003, 2007, 2012-2015, 2019, 2022, 2026-2027, 2029, 2039-2042, 2044-2046, 2048- 2050, 2058-2068, 2070-2075, 2080-2082, 2085-2086, 2098-2100, 2102-2107, 2110-2118, 2120-2122, 2124-2126, 2128, 2131, 2135-2138, 2141-2142, 2144-2152, 2154-2155, 2160-2162, 2165-2178, 2180-2181, 2183, 2186-2191, 2193-2198, 2210-2219, 2221-2232, 2237-2238, 2240, 2244-2248, 2256-2257, 2272, 2283-2284

1832 Nos. 1917-1918, 1920, 1937, 2008, 2076-2079, 2089-2091, 2101, 2108, 2119, 2123, 2127, 2129, 2139-2140, 2143, 2156-2157, 2179, 2182, 2184-2185, 2199-2209, 2220, 2234-2236, 2239, 2241-2242, 2250-2251, 2253-2255, 2259, 2261-2263, 2266-2267, 2269-2271, 2273-2274, 2280-2282, 2285, 2287-2291, 2293, 2297-2306, 2308-2312, 2314-2317, 2319-2330, 2332-2334, 2337, 2340-2351, 2353-2361, 2365-2366, 2369-2371, 2375-2376, 2379-2393, 2398-2400, 2403-2404, 2410

1833 Nos. 1456, 1898, 2057, 2083-2084, 2087-2088, 2092-2093, 2096-2097, 2109, 2134, 2153, 2158-2159, 2243, 2249, 2252, 2258, 2260, 2264, 2268, 2275-2277, 2286, 2292, 2294, 2307, 2313, 2318, 2335-2336, 2338-2339, 2352, 2363- 2364, 2368, 2372-2374, 2377, 2394-2397, 2401-2402, 2405, 2407-2409, 2412, 2415-2417, 2421-2422, 2425, 2428- 2439, 2441-2444, 2446-2448, 2451-2453, 2459-2468, 2470-2493, 2495-2496, 2498-2500, 2502-2512, 2514, 2516, 2519-2523, 2527-2530, 2537, 2542-2546, 2549-2550

1834 Nos. 2094-2095, 2130, 2132, 2265, 2278-2279, 2331, 2367, 2406, 2411, 2418, 2426-2427, 2445, 2454-2458, 2469, 2497, 2501, 2515, 2517-2518, 2524-2526, 2531-2536, 2538-2541, 2547-2548, 2551-2552, 2554-2555, 2557-2566, 2568-2581, 2584-2585, 2591, 2593-2597, 2600-2602, 2604-2607, 2609, 2612-2614, 2617-2619, 2621, 2625-2627, 2632-2634, 2636-2669, 2671-2681, 2683, 2689, 2691-2696, 2700

1835 Nos. 2192, 2233, 2295-2296, 2362, 2378, 2413-2414, 2494, 2553, 2556, 2567, 2582-2583, 2257-2590, 2592, 2598, 2608, 2610-2611, 2620, 2624, 2628-2631, 2635, 2670, 2682, 2685-2687, 2690, 2697-2698, 2701-2704, 2707-2708, 2712-2713, 2716-2718, 2720-2724, 2726-2738, 2741-2742, 2744-2745, 2747- 2755, 2757-2780, 2782-2796, 2798-2801, 2803-2815, 2818, 2820-2823, 2825-2828, 2830-2831, 2834, 2839-2840

1836 Nos. 2163-2164, 2419-2420, 2423-2424, 2449-2450, 2513, 2586, 2622-2623, 2684, 2705-2706, 2711, 2719, 2725, 2739-2740, 2743, 2746, 2756, 2781, 2797, 2802, 2816-2817, 2819, 2824, 2832, 2843-2853, 2855, 2858-2894, 2896-2916, 2920-2924, 2928-2931, 2937-2941, 2967, 2970-2971, 2977, 3087

1837 Nos. 2440, 2615-2616, 2688, 2709-2710, 2829, 2833, 2835-2836, 2917-2919, 2925, 2927, 2932-2936, 2942-2955, 2959, 2964-2966, 2969, 2972, 2975, 2978-2988, 2991-3003, 3005, 3007-3020, 3022-3023, 3026, 3028, 3030-3036, 3038, 3042-3067, 3069-3073, 3075-3080, 3093, 3098

1838 Nos. 2714, 2841-2842, 2854, 2856-2857, 2960-2961, 3004, 3006, 3024, 3027, 3029, 3039-3041, 3074, 3081-3086, 3088-3091, 3094-3097, 3100-3101, 3107-3108, 3110-3119, 3121, 3123-3125, 3127, 3130-3141, 3143- 3144, 3146, 3148-3153, 3158-3161, 3163-3170, 3172-3178, 3180, 3182-3186, 3189-3191, 3193-3198, 3200-3205, 3208-3211, 3213-3214, 3216-3220, 3222-3223, 3226-3228, 3231-3233, 3244-3245, 3248-3249, 3251-3252, 3270

1839 Nos. 2599, 2958, 2968, 2976, 3021, 3025, 3037, 3068, 3099, 3104-3106, 3122, 3145, 3147, 3162, 3171, 3179, 3181, 3192, 3199, 3206, 3221, 3224-3225, 3229-3230, 3234, 3236-3243, 3247, 3250, 3254, 3256-3257, 3260-3266, 3271- 3277, 3279-3282, 3286, 3288-3289, 3296-3308, 3311, 3314-3317, 3320-3323, 3327, 3329-3334, 3336-3342, 3345-3372, 3380, 3385-3386, 3494-3495

1840 Nos. 2603, 2926, 3120, 3126, 3128-3129, 3156-3157, 3187, 3207, 3212, 3235, 3246, 3255, 3267-3269, 3278, 3284-3285, 3287, 3292-3295, 3309-3310, 3312-3313, 3324-3326, 3328, 3343-3344, 3373-3375, 3383-3384, 3387, 3389- 3391, 3394-3395, 3397-3400, 3404, 3406-3409, 3412-3420, 3422-3428, 3430-3432, 3434-3435, 3437-3451, 3453- 3467, 3480, 3485-3486, 3490-3493, 3496, 3499-3501

1841 Nos. 1962, 2956, 3102-3103, 3109, 3142, 3259, 3283, 3318-3319, 3335, 3376-3379, 3381-3382, 3388, 3392-3393, 3396, 3401-3403, 3405, 3421, 3429, 3433, 3436, 3452, 3468-3475, 3477-3478, 3481, 3484, 3497-3498, 3502-3507, 3509-3515, 3520-3524, 3526, 3528, 3531-3536, 3540-3550, 3553-3554, 3556, 3559, 3562-3563, 3565-3587, 3589- 3590, 3595-3596, 3599-3601, 3603-3606

1842 Nos. 2895, 2957, 3253, 3476, 3479, 3482-3483, 3489, 3508, 3525, 3537-3538, 3552, 3557-3558, 3560-3561, 3564, 3588, 3591-3594, 3597-3598, 3607-3615, 3618-3622, 3624-3628, 3630-3631, 3634-3636, 3638-3643, 3645-3650, 3653-3659, 3661-3671, 3673-3674, 3677, 3679-3687, 3689-3696, 3700-3702, 3721

1843 Nos. 2973-2974, 2989-2990, 3092, 3617, 3637, 3644, 3651-3652, 3660, 3688, 3697-3699, 3704-3710, 3713-3714, 3717-3718, 3722-3730, 3732-3735, 3737-3740, 3743-3746, 3748-

APPENDICES

3757, 3762-3771, 3773, 3778-3781, 3784-3785, 3787-3789, 3792-3794, 3796-3797, 3799, 3803- 3807, 3809-3810, 3812-3817, 3819-3821, 3823-3824, 3834-3835, 3997

1844 Nos. 3154-3155, 3516-3517, 3529-3530, 3602, 3623, 3672, 3675-3676, 3678, 3703, 3711-3712, 3715-3716, 3720, 3731, 3736, 3742, 3747, 3758-3761, 3772, 3774-3777, 3790-3791, 3795, 3798, 3800-3802, 3808, 3822, 3825, 3827- 3829, 3831-3833, 3836-3840, 3845-3849, 3851-3862, 3864-3867, 3870-3876, 3878-3879, 3883-3888, 3890-3898, 3900-3903, 3905-3913, 3915-3919, 3923, 3925-3926, 3937-3938, 3943-3944

1845 Nos. 2699, 2962-2963, 3188, 3215, 3258, 3551, 3632-3633, 3741, 3783, 3786, 3826, 3830, 3863, 3877, 3880-3882, 3889, 3904, 3914, 3920, 3929-3936, 3939-3942, 3946, 3949-3951, 3955-3962, 3964, 3966-3967, 3969-3985, 3987- 3995, 3998-4006, 4008-4012, 4014-4027, 4029-4035, 4037-4039, 4046-4052

1846 Nos. 2715, 3488, 3629, 3811, 3818, 3850, 3921-3922, 3924, 3927, 3945, 3947-3948, 3952-3953, 3996, 4007, 4013, 4028, 4036, 4040-4043, 4045, 4054-4088, 4090-4095, 4097-4109, 4113-4131, 4134-4136, 4138-4139, 4142, 4146- 4148, 4186, 4193, 4204, 4238

1847 Nos. 3487, 3527, 3539, 3616, 3899, 3954, 3963, 3965, 3968, 3986, 4044, 4053, 4096, 4110-4112, 4132-4133, 4137, 4140-4141, 4143-4145, 4149-4158, 4162-4163, 4166, 4171-4176, 4178-4183, 4185, 4187-4188, 4191-4192, 4194, 4197-4202, 4205-4209, 4211-4214, 4217-4229, 4231-4237, 4239-4247, 4249-4250, 4265

1848 Nos. 3782, 3843-3844, 3868-3869, 3928, 4161, 4165, 4184, 4189-4190, 4195, 4203, 4215, 4230, 4253-4264, 4266- 4286, 4288-4290, 4294, 4298-4304, 4306, 4308-4309, 4312-4313, 4315-4330, 4332, 4335-4338, 4340-4350, 4353, 4362-4363, 4374-4377, 4382-4383, 4386-4388, 4408, 4424, 4432-4438, 4448-4450

1849 Nos. 4089, 4159-4160, 4165, 4167-4170, 4216, 4248, 4251-4252, 4287, 4291-4293, 4295-4297, 4305, 4307, 4311, 4314, 4339, 4352, 4355-4359, 4364, 4366-4370, 4372-4373, 4378-4381, 4384-4385, 4389-4391, 4394-4401, 4405-4407, 4409-4416, 4418-4423, 4425, 4427-4428, 4430-4431, 4439-4441, 4444-4447, 4451-4453, 4455-4457, 4459-4468, 4471

1850 Nos. 3290-3291, 3410-3411, 3518-3519, 3555, 3719, 4177, 4196, 4210, 4310, 4331, 4333-4334, 4351, 4360-4361, 4365, 4371, 4392-4393, 4402-4404, 4410, 4426, 4429, 4443, 4454, 4458, 4469-4470, 4472-4473, 4476-4497, 4499- 4502, 4504-4512, 4514-4521, 4523-4538, 4555-4557, 4559-4560, 4569-4579, 4584-4587, 4591

1851 Nos. 4354, 4498, 4513, 4522, 4539-4554, 4561-4564, 4566, 4582-4583, 4588-4589, 4593-4599, 4601, 4604-4609, 4614-4624, 4626-4631, 4634, 4636-4644, 4646-4647, 4649-4683, 4685-4690, 4692, 4699, 4801

1852 Nos. 4442, 4558, 4567-4568, 4590, 4592, 4602, 4610-4611, 4625, 4645, 4691, 4693-4698, 4700-4703, 4705-4710, 4713-4719, 4721-4724, 4726-4728, 4730-4733, 4735-4750, 4752, 4755-4760, 4763-4764, 4767-4775, 4778, 4781-4784, 4790, 4792

1853 Nos. 4580-4581, 4612, 4635, 4684, 4704, 4711-4712, 4720, 4725, 4729, 4734, 4753-4754, 4761-4762, 4766, 4776-4777, 4779-4780, 4785-4787, 4793-4800, 4802-4806, 4808-4812, 4816-4819, 4822, 4825-4829, 4831-4847, 4849-4890, 4892-4895, 4898, 4900-4901, 4907-4909, 4911-4913

1854 Nos. 4475, 4565, 4613, 4648, 4751, 4789, 4807, 4813-4815, 4820-4821, 4823, 4848, 4891, 4899, 4902-4906, 4910, 4914-4956, 4958-4975, 4977-4995, 4998-5005, 5013, 5015-5017

1855 Nos. 4633, 4791, 4976, 4996-4997, 5006-5012, 5014, 5019-5022, 5024-5031, 5034-5049, 5051-5055, 5057-5075, 5077-5102, 5104-5107, 5109-5110, 5113-5116, 5118, 5120-5121, 5123-5128, 5135, 5190

1856 Nos. 4603, 4765, 4788, 4824, 4830, 4896, 4957, 5018, 5023, 5032-5033, 5056, 5076, 5103, 5108, 5111-5112, 5117, 5119, 5122, 5129-5134, 5136-5189, 5191-5223, 5225-5250, 5253, 5256-5257, 5335

1857 Nos. 4474, 4600, 4897, 5050, 5224, 5251-5252, 5254-5255, 5258-5282, 5284-5310, 5312-5322, 5324-5334, 5336- 5355, 5358-5375, 5378-5381, 5383-5387, 5390-5391, 5393-5394, 5396-5397, 5399, 5542-5543

1858 Nos. 4632, 5356-5357, 5376-5377, 5382, 5388, 5392, 5395, 5398, 5400-5401, 5403-5428, 5430-5432, 5434-5440, 5442-5443, 5445-5466, 5468-5514, 5517-5523, 5525-5529, 5531-5535, 5539, 5544-5549, 5551-5555, 5557-5563, 5570-5571, 5575

1859 Nos. 3841-3842, 4503, 5389, 5402, 5429, 5433, 5441, 5444, 5515-5516, 5524, 5536-5538, 5540-5541, 5550, 5556, 5564-5569, 5573-5574, 5576-5630, 5632-5654, 5656-5685, 5687-5694, 5696-5701, 5703-5722, 5724-5755, 5757-5765, 5769-5771, 5779-5780, 5868

1860 Nos. 5283, 5311, 5467, 5572, 5631, 5655, 5686, 5695, 5702, 5723, 5756, 5766-5768, 5772-5778, 5781-5789, 5791- 5795, 5797-5801, 5803-5808, 5810-5832, 5834-5844, 5846-5867, 5869-5887, 5889-5895, 5897-5899, 5901-5972, 5974-5976, 5979-5984, 5987-5990, 5993, 5995-5997, 6003-6004, 6006, 6011, 6016, 6033, 6159-6160

1861 Nos. 5530, 5790, 5796, 5809, 5896, 5900, 5973, 5978, 5985-5986, 5991-5992, 5994, 5998, 6000-6002, 6005, 6007- 6010, 6012-6015, 6017-6031, 6034-6042, 6044-6061, 6063-6104, 6106-6116, 6118-6143, 6145-6158, 6161, 6163, 6165-6171, 6174-6177, 6179-6180, 6182-6183, 6185-6189, 6191-6197, 6199-6206, 6209-6211, 6213-6214, 6216-6217, 6219, 6221, 6223, 6225-6227

1862 Nos. 5323, 6144, 6162, 6181, 6184, 6190, 6207- 6208, 6212, 6218, 6220, 6222, 6224, 6228-6229, 6231-6234, 6236- 6239,

6243-6253, 6255-6268, 6270-6359, 6361-6375, 6378-6395, 6397-6399, 6401-6411, 6413-6415, 6418-6424, 6485

1863 Nos. 5833, 5888, 5977, 5999, 6043, 6062, 6105, 6117, 6164, 6178, 6198, 6215, 6230, 6235, 6240-6242, 6254, 6269, 6360, 6376-6377, 6396, 6400, 6412, 6425-6484, 6486-6548, 6550-6584, 6587-6598, 6600-6612, 6614-6615

1864 Nos. 6032, 6416-6417, 6549, 6585-6586, 6599, 6613, 6616-6632, 6635-6708, 6712-6718, 6722-6755, 6757-6763, 6765-6785, 6787-6789, 6791-6792, 6794-6796, 6799-6803, 6805, 6807-6819, 6821-6824, 6827-6829, 6831-6843, 6845-6855, 6857-6858, 6860-6866, 6868-6869, 6872-6874, 6876-6880, 6883-6886, 6890, 6893, 6896, 7006-7007

BARREL RECORDS: EARLY 1860s – PRESENT DAY

Dating from the early 1860s, Purdey's possess barrel records that give a far more accurate dating procedure for guns. These barrel records record in strict numerical progression of serial numbers, the details of the pattern tests that were carried out on shotguns. The date of the test is invariably recorded. Guns being tested were in the closing stages of manufacture and after testing would undergo final finishing and balancing. Rifles were obviously not subjected to such tests, yet many are listed just as 'rifles' in the numerical progression of serial numbers. Hence it is reasonable to assume that the dates of manufacture of rifles closely followed that of the shotguns. Each year a small handful of guns were tested beyond the date I have given.

1865 Nos. 6633-6634, 6709-6711, 6719-6721, 6756, 6764, 6786, 6790, 6793, 6797-6798, 6804, 6806, 6820, 6825-6826, 6830, 6844, 6859, 6867, 6870-6871, 6875, 6881-6882, 6887-6889, 6891-6892, 6894-6895, 6897-7005, 7008-7094, 7096-7150, 7153-7155, 7171

1866 Nos. 7095, 7151-7152, 7156-7170, 7172-7358, 7361-7367, 7369-7372, 7374-7376, 7378-7382, 7384, 7389-7390, 7394-7400

1867 Nos. 6856, 7359-7360, 7368, 7373, 7377, 7383, 7385-7388, 7391-7393, 7401-7602, 7610, 7621-7622, 7653

1868 Nos. 5845, 6172-6173, 7603-7609, 7611-7620, 7623-7652, 7654-7835

1869 Nos. 5802, 7836-8103, 8106-8107, 8111

1870 Nos. 8104-8105, 8108-8110, 8112-8364, 8374

1871 Nos. 8365-8373, 8375-8563, 8566-8583, 8587-8590

1872 Nos. 8564-8565, 8584-8586, 8591-8817, 8822-8829, 8831-8837, 8840-8844, 8849-8852, 8864, 8908

1873 Nos. 8818-8821, 8830, 8838-8839, 8845-8848, 8853-8863, 8865-8907, 8909-9089

Pages from a barrel book of the early 1860s. Of interest is 12-bore pinfire gun No. 6829 illustrated in plate 68. Batham and Smith were two of the gun testers of the period.

1874 Nos. 9090-9099, 9101-9320, 9322-9323, 9328-9330, 9337

1875 Nos. 9100, 9321, 9324-9327, 9331-9336, 9338-9352, 9354-9509, 9511-9520, 9522-9537, 9539-9546, 9548-9554, 9556-9562.

1876 Nos. 9353, 9510, 9521, 9538, 9547, 9563-9582, 9585-9739, 9741-9759, 9761-9784

1877 Nos. 9555, 9583-9584, 9740, 9760, 9785-10107

1878 Nos. 10108-10356, 10358-10363, 10366-10388

1879 Nos. 10357, 10364-10365, 10389-10625, 10627-10639, 10641-10642

1880 Nos. 10626, 10640, 10643-10885

1881 Nos. 10886-11106, 11110-11113, 11115, 11119, 11123-11124

1882 Nos. 11108-11109, 11114, 11116-11118, 11120-11122,

APPENDICES

11125-11420, 11422-11430

1883 Nos. 11421, 11432-11710, 11712-11724, 11726-11732, 11734-11753, 11755-11781

1884 Nos. 11711, 11725, 11733, 11754, 11782-12058, 12063

1885 Nos. 12059-12062, 12064-12330, 12336-12338, 12341-12345

1886 Nos. 12331-12335, 12339-12340, 12346-12616

1887 Nos. 12617-12925

1888 Nos. 12926-13223

1889 Nos. 13224-13510

1890 Nos. 13511-13851

1891 Nos. 13852-14259

1892 Nos. 14260-14605

1893 Nos. 14606-14922

1894 Nos. 14923-15185

1895 Nos. 15186-15509

1896 Nos. 15510-15809

1897 Nos. 15810-16139

1898 Nos. 16140-16479

1899 Nos. 16480-16827

1900 Nos. 16828-17126

1901 Nos. 17127-17439

1902 Nos. 17440-17744

1903 Nos. 17745-18073

1904 Nos. 18074-18320

1905 Nos. 18321-18599

1906 Nos. 18600-18893

1907 Nos. 18894-19204

1908 Nos. 19205-19488

1909 Nos. 19489-19732

1910 Nos. 19733-20007

1911 Nos. 20008-20306

1912 Nos. 20307-20586

1913 Nos. 20587-20967

1914 Nos. 20968-21270

The period 1915-18 presents difficulties due to the dislocation caused by World War One. Guns were completed and tested erratically, hence the block 1915-18 must be used.

1915-18 Nos. 21271-21503 (guide only)

The year 1919 also presents problems. Many guns were part finished and tested during the war, but were not completed until after the war.

1919 Nos. 21504-21701 (guide only)

1920 Nos. 21702-22001

1921 Nos. 22002-22215

1922 Nos. 22216-22444

1923 Nos. 22445-22636

1924 Nos. 22637-22828

1925 Nos. 22829-22992

1926 Nos. 22993-23221

1927 Nos. 23222-23480

1928 Nos. 23481-23778

1929 Nos. 23779-24076

1930 Nos. 24007-24334

Due to the onset of world depression around 1930, dating of guns in the period 1931-34 is very difficult due to cancelled orders and stockpiled guns. This period must be given as a block on account of this. Even after 1934, chronology of serial numbers is haphazard due to the aftermath of the depression and hence serial numbers given must be used as a guide.

1931-34 Nos. 24335-24871 (guide only)

1935 Nos. 24872-25088

1936 Nos. 25089-25265

1937 Nos. 25266-25479

1938 Nos. 25480-25663

1939   Nos. 25664-25767 (guide only)

The Second World War period caused more dislocation than any other period. Very few guns were produced and again a block must be given and used as a guide.

1940-45 Nos. 25768-25830 (guide only)

The post-war period saw another period of instability as guns ordered or begun before or during the war were delivered. A block must be given and used as a guide. Occasionally a weapon will be found with the suffix 'A' denoting that it was bought in and finished by Purdey, e.g. No. 25926A is a 7mm Mauser rifle.

1946-49 Nos. 25831-26173 (guide only)
1950   Nos. 26174-26234
1951   Nos. 26235-26318
1952   Nos. 26319-26389
1953   Nos. 26390-26443
1954   Nos. 26444-26500
1955   Nos. 26501-26562
1956   Nos. 26563-26636
1957   Nos. 26637-26680
1958   Nos. 26681-26778
1959   Nos. 26779-26828
1960   Nos. 26829-26910
1961   Nos. 26911-27020
1962   Nos. 27021-27089
1963   Nos. 27090-27169
1964   Nos. 27170-27256
1965   Nos. 27257-27337
1966   Nos. 27338-27434
1967   Nos. 27435-27528
1968   Nos. 27529-27618

The late 1960s and 1970s are very difficult to date due to the high inflation of the era resulting in cancelled orders and lengthy delays. Dates given must be used as a guide only.

1969   Nos. 27619-27690
1970   Nos. 27691-27750
1971   Nos. 27751-27795
1972   Nos. 27796-27840
1973   Nos. 27841-27940
1974   Nos. 27941-28040
1975   Nos. 28041-28090
1976   Nos. 28091-28168
1977   Nos. 28169-28245
1978   Nos. 28246-28311
1979   Nos. 28312-28402
1980   Nos. 28403-28460
1981   Nos. 28461-28522
1982   Nos. 28523-28584
1983   Nos. 28585-28710
1984   Nos. 28711-28778
1985   Nos. 28779-28825
1986   Nos. 28826-28874
1987   Nos. 28875-28947
1988   Nos. 28948-29039
1989   Nos. 29040-29107
1990   Nos. 29108-29187
1991   Nos. 29188-29291
1992   Nos. 29292-29392
1993-
2000   Nos. 29393-Millennium gun No. 30000

Appendix 3b

WOODWARD SERIAL NUMBERS AND DATING

James Purdey and Sons hold the records of the Woodward guns and rifles. James Woodward's Dimension Books list the date of sale only of a particular weapon and as such sale dates can vary. The sale dates listed below show when the majority of guns were sold. Some guns will be found beyond these sale dates.

Woodward's records begin at gun No. 2000. However no detail at all is given until No. 2886 (sold 27 January 1876 – a sale far later than when the gun was built). There is another gap to No. 2935 (20 July 1874 – another late sale), then another gap to No. 3058, 27 July 1870 (probably a near correct date), another gap to No. 3235 (6 August 1875 – late sale), another gap to No. 3270 (29 May 1874 – late sale), then spasmodic entries until No. 3380 of 18 November 1875. The Dimension Book is then complete.

After the sale of Woodward in 1948 no Woodwards were built until 1997 when Purdey's produced Nos. 7185/6. Purdey's are now beginning to re-manufacture Woodwards to their original specification, both side-by-sides and O/U's. The chronology of serial numbers will continue.

Year	Numbers	Year	Numbers	Year	Numbers
1874	Nos. – 3433	1905	Nos. 5854-5912	1936	Nos. 7069-7082
1875	Nos. 3434-3473	1906	Nos. 5913-5970	1937	Nos. 7083-7117
1876	Nos. 3474-3536	1907	Nos. 5971-6022	1938	Nos. 7118-7127
1877	Nos. 3537-3602	1908	Nos. 6023-6093	1939	Nos. 7128-7150
1878	Nos. 3603-3655	1909	Nos. 6094-6160	1940	Nos. 7151-7160
1879	Nos. 3656-3717	1910	Nos. 6161-6213	1941-46	Nos. 7161-7177
1880	Nos. 3718-3757	1911	Nos. 6214-6296	1946-48	Nos. 7178-7184
1881	Nos. 3758-3808	1912	Nos. 6297-6340		
1882	Nos. 3809-3882	1913	Nos. 6341-6382	The last Woodward No. 7184 was sold on 21 June 1948.	
1883	Nos. 3883-3963	1914	Nos. 6383-6440		
1884	Nos. 3964-4039	1915	Nos. 6441-6454		
1885	Nos. 4040-4117	1916	Nos. 6455-6460	1997	No. 7185-
1886	Nos. 4118-4173	1917	Nos. 6461-6467		
1887	Nos. 4174-4243	1918	Nos. 6468-6480		
1888	Nos. 4244-4328	1919	Nos. 6481-6497		
1889	Nos. 4329-4387	1920	Nos. 6498-6570		
1890	Nos. 4388-4499	1921	Nos. 6571-6622		
1891	Nos. 4500-4627	1922	Nos. 6623-6658		
1892	Nos. 4628-4719	1923	Nos. 6659-6703		
1893	Nos. 4720-4794	1924	Nos. 6704-6744		
1894	Nos. 4795-4904	1925	Nos. 6745-6764		
1895	Nos. 4905-5003	1926	Nos. 6765-6796		
1896	Nos. 5004-5097	1927	Nos. 6797-6832		
1897	Nos. 5098-5233	1928	Nos. 6833-6880		
1898	Nos. 5234-5327	1929	Nos. 6881-6909		
1899	Nos. 5328-5427	1930	Nos. 6910-6955		
1900	Nos. 5428-5513	1931	Nos. 6956-6979		
1901	Nos. 5514-5615	1932	Nos. 6980-6996		
1902	Nos. 5616-5713	1933	Nos. 6997-7020		
1903	Nos. 5714-5763	1934	Nos. 7021-7049		
1904	Nos. 5764-5853	1935	Nos. 7050-7068		

Appendix 4a

MUZZLE-LOADING GUN, RIFLE AND PISTOL PRODUCTION

It must be stressed that the production figures given are not as accurate as could be hoped for. In the first Dimension Book, from gun No. 273 to No. 9165 of 1874, the very early records contain little or no detail, sometimes just recording the serial number and nothing else. Gradually in the 1820s more detail was entered until by the 1830s full detail was given, within the parameters explained in chapter two. This Dimension Book was probably begun around 1826 when Purdey's moved to Oxford Street and when, in late 1826, Purdey serial numbers were in the range 960-1000. It is apparent that details of pre-Oxford Street weapons were filled in retrospectively when such weapons came back for repair or resale and this accounts for the frugal nature of the early entries. Types of ignition system, flintlock or percussion, are often not recorded making it impossible to give an accurate breakdown of such ignition types. Nevertheless this appendix does give a good idea of relative production figures for differing types of weapons.

SPORTING GUNS

The double-barrel sporting gun was the mainstay of Purdey's. Around 3,500 were produced in the muzzle-loading era in all manner of bore sizes, 5, 6, 7, 8, 9, 10, 11, 12, 12 $^1/_2$, 13, 13 $^1/_2$, 14, 14 $^1/_2$, 15, 16, 17, 17 $^1/_2$, 18, 18 $^1/_2$, 19, 20, 21, 22, 23, 24, 25, 26, 27, 28, 30, 32. 14- and 16-bore tended to be the most popular. By far the majority of sporting guns had front action locks in comparison to the early breech-loaders which had back-action locks. Due to the lack of information in the early part of the Dimension Book, the number of flintlock shotguns cannot be assessed, although a credible guess would be over 300. The earliest surviving flintlock gun is No. 14 of 1816/17. The earliest surviving percussion gun is No. 349, a double-barrel 14-bore gun built in 1822. 'Keepers' Guns' of lesser quality were also built, priced around £20.0s.0d. for a double as opposed to around £52.10s.0d. for a best gun. Combination guns described as 'rifle and shot' were built with one smooth bore barrel and one rifled barrel. The 'pistol grip' appeared during the 1830s and this is frequently encountered in the records. Double guns were always built in far greater quantities than single guns, right from the establishment of the business, and by the early 1850s very few single guns were being produced. It was in this period that pairs of guns became far more common. The breech-loader upon its perfection, succeeded the muzzle-loader rapidly in the late 1850s and by 1863 muzzle-loading production had tailed off rapidly. Probably the last muzzle-loader built was 14-bore double gun No. 18198 sold on 3 July 1904 to Charles Gordon, a well known eccentric collector of muzzle-loaders in the swansong of the 19th century.

Type of sporting gun	Numbers built
Double-barrel sporting guns	3,508
Single-barrel sporting guns	324
Duck guns – 8-bore and over (within the totals)	35
Keepers' guns (within the totals)	17

RIFLES

Until the late 1830s, the single rifle was more common than the double rifle. From the 1840s onwards the double rifle rose to prominence and single rifle production declined. A great many rifles were supplied with extra shotgun barrels. 'Small' or 'pea' rifles, more commonly known today as 'rook and rabbit' rifles were produced in small-bore sizes of 60- to 100-bore. Some of these 'pea' rifles were double-barrelled. Often the calibre of a 'small' or 'pea' rifle is not given. 'Keepers' rifles' of lesser quality occasionally appear priced around £26 for a single as opposed to the normal price of £42 Express rifles are not specifically mentioned in the Dimension Books and as such it would be imprudent to attempt to create a separate category.

The earliest recorded rifle is No. 505 a single-barrel 14-bore sold to the 4th Duke of Atholl for £31.10s. on 12 July 1823. The first recorded double rifle is No. 1031 recorded in the ledgers as a 'double shotgun with an extra pair of rifle barrels, the shotgun barrels not numbered' – sold on 5 February 1827 for £82 The only recorded flintlock rifle is No. 1186 sold for £20 to Joseph Lang the dealer on 9 May 1828, although it was probably made in 1827. No. 4700 is probably the first Express rifle, a two-groove single 16-bore sold for £20 on 22 October 1856. It is recorded in the Dimension Book as 'experimental 2 groove new 2'6-inch barrel pointed ball 16-bore'. Being a 16-bore it does not technically fit into the accepted concept of the Express, as Express rifles were generally of smaller bore. The rifle was actually built in late 1851, probably being retained for experimental purposes and not sold until later in 1856 (see illustration on page 30).

No. 4703 was the first true Express rifle, a double-barrel 40-bore sold for £84 on 8 October 1852. The probable last muzzle-loading rifle listed in the Dimension Books is No. 15331, a 32-bore back action, with Whitworth steel barrels, sold in April 1896 to Charles Gordon

Type of rifle	Numbers built
Single-barrel rifles	496
Double-barrel rifles	809
Small or Pea rifles	80

PISTOLS

Although Purdey built a vast array of pistols, carriage, duelling, target, cavalry, multi-barrelled, pocket and holster pistols, the Dimension Book often does not record type. 'Small double pistol', or 'Pr. of best pistols' is a common, vague description. Regularly 'duelling pistol' is recorded, yet this description is known to have a wide interpretation to include target pistols as well. Some pistols such as pocket pistols were bought 'in the white' from suppliers and finished by Purdey. They do not have serial numbers in line with normal Purdey production and hence do not appear in the Dimension Books. Due to the lack of detail in the pistol records, it is impossible to give exact production figures for each type of pistol produced. By far the majority of pistols, both single and double, were built and sold as pairs. Muzzle-loading pistol production ceased in the 1860s, the anachronism again being left to Charles Gordon who bought Nos. 17071/2 a pair of double 40-bore muzzle-loading back action pistols with Whitworth barrels, in December 1901.

Type of pistol	Numbers built
Double-barrel pistols	161
Single-barrel pistols	199
Multi-barrel pistols	10

Appendix 4b

EARLY BREECH-LOADING GUN AND RIFLE PRODUCTION 1857-79

It is possible to give more accurate figures for this appendix due to further detail in the first Dimension Book from the 1830s onwards. From this period all serial numbers are recorded and the type of weapon entered. The second Dimension Book begins at gun number 9001 of 1873 (there was a slight overlap between the first and second Dimension Books) and finishes at number 11988 of 1884. An entirely new type of Dimension Book appeared with number 9841 in 1877, that in addition to gun details gave for the first time the date of sale as well.

A natural break occurs by the end of the year 1879. In January 1880, Beesley patented his famous hammerless action and the patent was purchased by Purdey. From 1880 onwards the hammerless gun as we know it today began to be produced in increasing quantities.

The first pinfire produced was a 13-bore shotgun No. 5305 produced in 1857 but not sold until 26 October 1864 to F Soames. The first pinfire rifle produced was a single-barrel 40-bore No. 5306 again produced in 1857. The first recorded sale of a pinfire was 12-bore shotgun No. 5462 sold on 3 May 1858 to W Bromley-Davenport. Very few pairs of pinfires were sold on account of the fact that most sportsmen would wait to try the new system out before investing in a pair. I can find only one record of a single-barrel pinfire shotgun – No. 6421, a 12-bore sold on 8 November 1862, and only five single-barrel pinfire rifles – No. 5306 (1857), No. 6013 (1861), No. 6305, No. 6370 and No. 6392, all of 1862. The probable last pinfire built was 12-bore shotgun No. 16056 sold in May 1898, again to Charles Gordon.

The first recorded centre-fire was 12-bore shotgun No. 6992 built in 1865 and sold to F J Parkes. Only one year later centre-fires reigned supreme and vastly outnumbered pinfires. The first recorded centre-fire rifle was a double-barrel 70-bore sold to Colonel H Johnson in 1866. Again only one year later in 1867 far more centre-fire rifles were being built than pinfires. Very few single-barrel centre-fire guns were built.

The first recorded hammerless gun was 12-bore gun No. 10106 tested on the 26 September 1877 and sold to G W Amory on 27 July 1880. Hammerless guns were uncommon in the 1870s and it would not be until 1886 that more were produced than hammer guns

Type of pinfire	Numbers built
Double-barrel sporting guns	1110
Single-barrel sporting guns	1
Double-barrel rifles	129
Single-barrel rifles	5
Bastin/Purdey shotguns	34
Bastin/Purdey rifles	7
Type of centre-fire	
Double-barrel hammer shotguns	2802
Single-barrel hammer shotguns	26
Double-barrel hammer rifles	312
Single-barrel hammer rifles (including single Pea rifles)	27
Double-barrel hammerless shotguns	31
Purdey/Henry rifles	41

Appendix 4c

BREECH-LOADING GUN AND RIFLE PRODUCTION 1880-2000

Hammer shotguns continued to be made in large numbers towards the close of the 19th century. By the turn of the century, most hammer guns were hammer ejectors used for live pigeon shooting. The last hammer guns built were the miniature guns Nos. 25000/1 built for King George V in 1935, although there is a vague record of a later hammer gun No. 25015 of 1935.

The first recorded Beesley hammerless gun was No. 10743 of 1880. The year 1886 was the watershed year for the changeover to hammerless guns, and from this date on hammerless guns reigned supreme. The first record of the Wem ejector was No. 13501 of 1888.

The single-barrel shotguns listed were of second quality. Only one or two were best quality. The specialist single-barrel trap guns were all best quality.

Hammer rifles continued to be made well after the 1880s. The first recorded Beesley hammerless rifle was No. 10905 built in late 1880, early 1881. The first O/U built to Edwinson Green's patent was No. 22564 of 1923. The first O/U built to Woodward's design was No. 25950 of 1950. From then on O/U's were increasingly built. The single trigger made its appearance in the 1920s but only really became popular after the war. Production figures given include all the second quality weapons.

Type of weapon	Numbers built
Double-barrel hammer shotguns (including hammer ejectors)	1,625
Single-barrel shotguns (both hammer and hammerless)	81
Single-barrel trap guns	59
Double-barrel hammerless shotguns	14,558
Double-barrel hammer rifles	327
Single-barrel rifles (all calibres and types, hammer, hammerless, bolt-action)	209
Double-barrel hammerless rifles	419
O/U guns (pre-war Green design)	27
O/U guns (post-war Woodward design)	447
Single-triggers (within the above figures)	1,072

Appendix 5

ANALYSIS OF GUN DEMAND 1816-2000

In constructing the following graph, the same sources of information have been used as per Appendix 3.

It is apparent that Purdey's business' established in 1816, rapidly drew customers. Due to the lack of detail in the records regarding ignition systems, flintlock and percussion, it is impossible to state when the watershed change from flintlock to percussion occurred. Most probably it was in the early 1820s. Due to Purdey's promotion and success of the percussion gun, demand grew rapidly for the new system in the late 1820s, particularly after the move in 1826 to larger premises in Oxford Street. By the 1830s most sportsmen would have bought the new percussion guns and demand settled to a steady pattern. On the advent of breech-loading in the late 1850s, demand rocketed as sportsmen were intent on purchasing the new system. The year 1860 was the watershed.

In 1859, 109 muzzle-loading shotguns and 67 breech-loading shotguns were sold. One year later in 1860, 69 muzzle-loading shotguns and 117 breech-loading shotguns were sold.

Steady demand continued throughout the 1870s. The 1880s and 1890s saw a massive increase in sales due to three factors; the introduction of the hammerless gun, the arrival of A-E quality guns, and the terrific popularity of shooting. The year 1891 saw Purdey's break the 400 sales mark for the first and only time. High sales continued until World War One when gun production plummeted due to Purdey's involvement in war work and the contraction of gun orders caused by war dislocation.

The immediate post-war years saw a fluctuation in demand. The post-war boom of 1920 saw a return to normal, yet the early 1920s saw a recession. The period until 1930

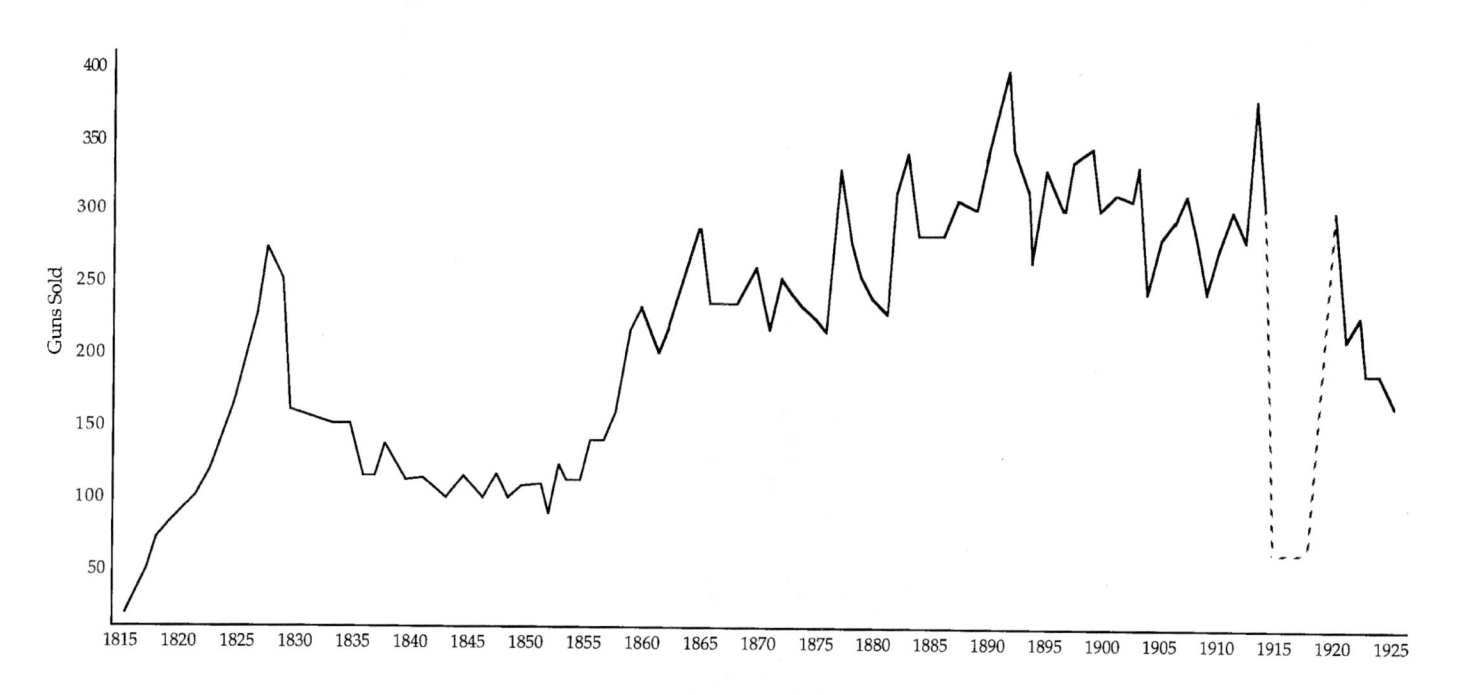

The broken lines indicate difficult periods when gun production and sales were erratic

witnessed buoyant demand particularly from the American market. The Great Depression, heralded by the Wall Street Crash of 1929, resulted in a severe curtailment of gun orders and gun production dropped dramatically. By the mid 1930s economic recovery was occurring and demand increased. World War Two resulted in the virtual curtailment of gun production as total war necessitated re-allocation to war production. The devastation caused by the war meant that post-war recovery was very slow. Due to changed economic and political circumstances, post-war gun demand could never be as great as in preceeding periods. From the 1950s to the present day, gun production has averaged out at round 60-70 guns per year. One big change in demand in recent years has been in the renaissance of the O/U gun, sales of this type accounting for a far higher percentage of annual production than in the past.

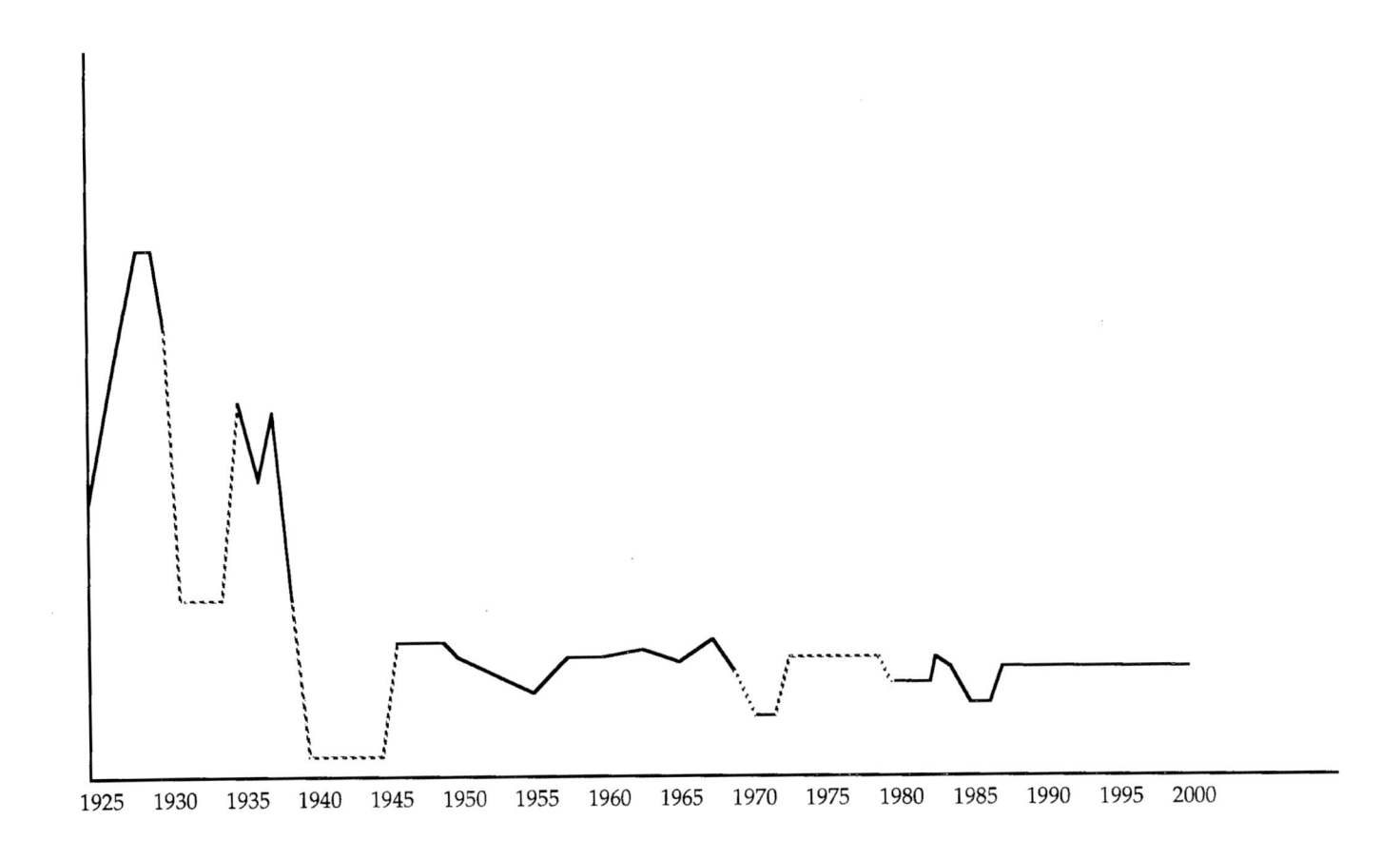

Appendix 6

PURDEY GUNMAKERS

On the various parts of Purdey guns, stamped initials will often be found, the 'signature' of the gunmaker involved. This appendix should help in identifying such gunmakers.

Due to the fact that no wage books exist pre-1863, the Dimension Books must be used to identify particular workers before this time. Only an initial is given, which obviously makes recognition difficult. Very occasionally a surname appears in full. Pre-1863, the following names of Purdey gunmakers, suppliers and outworkers can be deduced.

1820s

Charles Lancaster, barrel maker, 10 Craven Buildings, Drury Lane until *c.*1818 and Great Titchfield Street in the early 1820s. Barrels stamped 'CL'.

William Fullerd, barrel maker, 56/57 Compton Street, Clerkenwell. Barrels stamped 'WF'.

Thomas Evans, barrel maker, Circencester Place, Paddington and from 1859 at 9 Charlotte Mews, Tottenham Court Road. Barrels stamped 'TE'.

Thomas Boss, stocker, screwing together, making off, 3 Bridge Road, Lambeth.

Robert Bagnall, stocker, screwing together, making off.

Henry Atkin, stocker, screwing together, making off.

Peter Gumbrell, engraver, King Street, Golden Square and after 1839, 4 Little Marlborough Street.

1840s and 1850s

Thomas Parkin, barrel maker, 5 Meards Court, Soho. Barrels stamped 'TP'.

H Glaysher, stocker.

Henry Atkin, stocker.

Tregale, stocker.

Henry Lewis, stocker.

Peter Gumbrell, engraver, 4 Little Marlborough Street

Jack Sumner, engraver, 10 Queen Street, Soho.

'STOCKERS' WORKBOOK 1863-66'

There is a 'stockers' workbook 1863-66' in existence that gives the names of all the stockers who worked in this period:

Henry Atkins, Henry Lewis, Tregale, Carver, H Glaysher, John Robertson (worked for Purdey's 1864-73, later bought Boss & Co. in 1891), T Jones, J Lumsden, Frederick Beesley.

Within the 'stockers' workbook', a small section is devoted to 'lock orders', that lists the main suppliers of Purdey locks.

Joseph Brazier, Wolverhampton (stamped on the inside of the lock 'IB'), J Grainger, Wolverhampton (stamped on the inside of the lock 'JG').

The earliest surviving wage books date from 1863. Purdey's possess from this date on, a comprehensive collection of wage books to the present day. Selective years are given in the following pages with the specialisation of the gunmaker when known. A complicating factor is that usually only a surname is given. A great many sons followed their fathers into Purdey's and it is often difficult to distinguish between father and son and their respective specialisations. Average weekly wage is also given. Due to the fact that the gunmakers were on piece-work, this wage could vary considerably each week.

JUNE 1863

G Aston – head barrel maker	£10. 4s. 0d.
Henry Atkin – stocker	£2. 0s. 0d.
J Apted – finisher	£2. 17s. 0d.
Bissell	£4. 3s. 0d.
Batham – gun tester	£2. 0s. 0d.
Boulter – barrel maker	£2. 2s. 0d.
Denholm	£2. 10s. 0d.
J Goff	£3. 0s. 0d.
Hewson	£2. 7s. 6d.
Harbrol	£2. 2s. 0d.
Hawkes – finisher	£1. 4s. 0d.

Henry Lewis – head stocker	£7. 5s. 0d.	Heasman	£4. 2s. 0d.
James Lewis	£1. 12s. 0d.	J Harris – nipples and plungers, levers	£3. 4s. 6d.
J Lucas – engraver	£4. 16s. 6d.	Hawkes	£1. 8s. 0d.
F Mayo – actioner	£3. 3s. 0d.	Hawkes Snr. – finisher	£1.15s. 0d.
Marchin(?)	£3. 0s. 0d.	Horsley – stocker	£1. 7s. 6d.
Milsted	£2. 10s. 0d.	Hook	7s. 0d.
J Mace – engraver	£2. 0s. 0d.	T Jones – stocker	£4.12s. 6d.
Norman	£2. 4s. 0d.	Jackson	£2.16s. 0d.
J Prentice	£3. 7s. 8d.	Henry Lewis – head stocker	£4. 0s. 0d.
G Prentice – cocking	£4. 5s. 4d.	N Lewis – percussioning	£2. 11s. 6d.
F Phillips – actioner	£2.10s. 0d.	J Lewis	£2. 5s. 0d.
Portlock	£3. 4s. 6d.	J Lucas – head engraver	£8. 0s. 0d.
Purves	£1. 4s. 0d.	G Lubbock – shop manager	£3. 5s. 0d.
Pike	£1. 0s. 0d.	James Lumsden – stocker	£4.13s. 6d.
Ridley	£2.10s. 0d.	F Mayo – actioner	£4.13s. 0d.
Abbe Robins – hardening	£3.10s. 0d.	Mace	£2.15s. 0d
Sanger	£2. 7s. 0d.	J Mace Snr. – engraver	£4. 7s. 3d.
E Sanger	£3.10s. 0d.	A Meers – barrel maker	£2.10s. 0d.
Smith Jnr.	£2.10s. 0d.	E Meers	£2. 4s. 3d.
John Smith – gun tester	£2.12s. 0d.	F Meers	£2. 4s. 8d.
Schofield	£3. 6s. 0d.	G Prentice – cocking	£3. 2s. 0d.
Suffolk	£2. 8s. 0d.	J Prentice	£4.15s. 0d
Titterton	£1. 7s. 0d.	A Phillips – actioner	£6. 8s. 0d.
Tregale – stocker	£4. 5s. 6d.	H Phillips	£5. 0s. 0d.
William Webster	£4.13s. 0d.	F Phillips – percussioning	£3. 5s. 4d.
Weston	£2.10s. 0d.	Potter	£2. 1s. 0d.
John Webster	£2. 0s. 0d.	J Purves	£1. 4s. 0d.
L Wasdell – finisher	£2.10s. 0d.	Pike	£1. 4s. 0d.
Wyburn	£1. 4s. 0d.	Abbe Robins – hardening	£4. 15s. 9d.
		J Ridout	16s. 0d.

In addition to the above gunmakers, other people were employed by Purdey's.

Sarah Davies	£1. 0s. 0d.	Reffell	16s. 0d.
(a house servant who kept 314 ½ Oxford Street)		George Roberts – barrel maker	£1. 9s. 2d.
Mr. Jump	£2. 3s. 0d	Sanger	£2. 2s. 0d.
Mrs. Titterton	8s. 0d.	C Smith – actioner	£3. 4s. 0d.
		H Schmidt – levers, luggers	£3. 12s. 6d.
		Sharp	18s. 0d.
		Sandford	£1. 7s. 0d.
		Terry	£1. 15s. 0d.
		Virgo – levers	£2. 17s. 6d.
		Webster	£2. 0s. 0d.

MAY 1875

G Aston – head barrel maker	£3. 2s. 0d.	J Webster	£2. 2s. 0d.
J Apted – finisher	£2.14s. 1d.	L Wasdell – finisher	£2. 5s.10d.
Frederick Beesley – stocker	£4. 0s.10d.	Wyburn	£1. 6s. 0d.
Boulter – barrel maker	£2.10s. 0d.	Walker	£1.17s.11d.
Batham – gun tester	£2. 0s. 0d.	S Wheatley	£2. 10s. 0d.
H Batham	£1. 5s. 6d.	Walton	£1. 18s. 0d.
Crisp – actioner	£4. 0s. 0d.	Wright	14s. 0d.
Clarke	£2.12s. 0d.	Charlie Wilkes – viewer	£2. 0s. 0d.
Crocker	16s. 0d.		
Denholme	£2.15s. 0d.	**JANUARY 1889**	
Emerson	£1. 2s. 0d.		
J Farnell – stripping	£2.10s. 0d.	J Apted – finisher	£2. 15s. 0d.
Flowers	£2. 4s. 3d.	G Aston – head barrel maker	£5. 2s. 0d.
H Glaysher – stocker	£4. 7s. 0d.	Batham Snr. – gun tester	£2. 0s. 0d.
E Glaysher	£1.18s. 0d.	Batham Jnr.	£1.12s. 0d.
J Goff	£1.10s. 0d.	G Bilston	£2. 7s. 0d.
Harbrol	£1. 5s. 0d.	W Bilston	£2. 7s. 0d.
Henson – stocker	£1. 7s. 6d.	Bird	£1.13s. 0d.
Hutchinson – barrel maker	£5. 2s. 0d.	Blanks	£2.10s. 0d.

H Blanton – finisher	£2. 8s. 9d.	**Shop assistants**	
Clark	£1.14s. 3d.	Charles Butler	£3. 3s. 0d.
Colina	14s. 0d.	Charles Clark	£1.13s. 0d.
Crisp – actioner	£2.10s. 6d.	Nash	18s. 0d.
H Dean – stocker	£3.10s. 0d.	Page	£1.10s. 0d.
W Delaney	£1.12s. 2d.	Read	10s. 0d.
G Farnell – stripping	£2.14s. 6d.	George Tillson	£2. 8s. 0d.
G Gear – barrel maker	£2.18s. 6d.	William Youngman	£3. 0s. 0d.
W Gerrard – cartridge loader	£1. 8s. 9d.		
H Glaysher – stocker	£2.18s. 6d.	**Apprentices and other trades**	
Bill Hill – barrel maker	£2. 5s. 0d.	Flower	7s. 0d.
E Hodges – barrel maker	£2.10s. 6d.	Jim Gorman – cartridge loader	17s. 0d.
Hopewell – finisher	£2. 5s. 0d.	Chas Gorman	15s. 0d.
H Horsley – stocker	£3. 1s. 6d.	Hayson	12s. 0d.
Bob Horscroft – repairs	£1. 4s.11d.	Kippen – cartridge loader	12s. 6d.
Howell – finisher	£3.15s. 0d.	Meek	5s. 0d.
John Hutchinson – barrel maker	£2.10s. 0d.	Murray Jnr.	8s. 0d.
H W Johnson – stocker	£3. 6s. 6d.	Nobbs	10s. 2d.
Thomas Lawrence – actioner	£2. 4s.10d.	Rigartsford	17s. 3d.
C Leggett – detonating	£2.15s. 0d.	Taylor	15s. 0d.
Lewis	£1. 3s. 0d.	White	14s. 0d.
J Leeper – carpenter	£2. 2s. 8d.	Poole	12s. 0d.
J Lucas – head engraver	£7. 3s. 6d.	Mr. Cecil	15s. 0d.
James Lumsden – head stocker	£8. 5s. 0d.	Zieschary	10s. 0d.
J Maddox	£3.13s.11d.	Terkelsen	£2.10s. 0d.
W R Marnes	£1. 4s. 6d.		
Matthews – actioner	£2.10s. 0d.	**JUNE 1912**	
J Matthews – stocker	£1.19s.10d.		
Mayo Snr. – actioner	£2. 0s. 0d.	**Gunmakers**	
F Mayo – barrel maker	£3.10s. 6d.	Jack Apted – stocker	£3. 7s. 0d
A Mayo	£1. 3s. 0d.	Alec Anderson – finisher	£2. 8s. 4d
A Meers – barrel maker	£2. 7s.10d.	Harry Aston – barrel maker	£5. 8s. 6d
H Meers	£2. 2s. 0d.	J Bartholomew – finisher	£1.10s. 0d
D Murray – cartridge loading	£1. 7s. 0d.	Barrett – finisher	£1.15s. 9d
William Nobbs Snr. – detonating/safety	£5.16s. 6d.	Bill Bayliss – engineer	£1.16s. 0d
Wesley Nobbs – actioner	£2. 5s. 0d.	Bishop – finisher	£2.10s. 0d
W Palmer	£1.12s. 0d.	T Blogg – engineer	£1. 8s. 6d
S Pearsall	£2.14s. 6d.	W Burbidge – shooting ground	£2. 0s. 0d
A Phillips – actioner	£4. 5s. 0d.	William Clark – engineer	£3. 0s. 0d
F Phillips – percussioning	£3.17s. 6d.	Jimmy Colle – ejectors	£2.18s. 0d
Pike – shooting ground	£1.10s. 0d.	W Cooper – barrels	£1.17s. 4d
G Prentice – cocking	£1.10s. 0d.	Tom Davidson – actioner	£3. 7s. 6d
Sol Prentice – actioner	£3. 4s. 0d.	H Dean Sr. – stocker	£2.15s. 0d
J Ridout	£1. 6s. 4d.	Arthur Dean Jr. – stocker	£4. 6s. 0d
George Roberts – barrel maker	£2. 2s. 0d.	Phil Dean – stocker	£2. 8s. 0d
Abbe Robins – hardening	£3.14s. 8d.	W Dewen – ejectors	£2.10s. 0d
W Russell – finisher	£2.10s. 0d.	W Egginson – finisher	£2.10s. 0d
H Schmidt – levers, luggers	£3.10s. 0d.	Eves – finisher	£2. 8s. 8d
Smith – actioner	£2.19s. 6d.	Fred Eves – finisher	19s. 9d
Sparrow – repairs	£3.10s. 0d.	A Field – viewer	£4.10s. 0d
G Sturman	£1.14s. 5d.	Walter Forbes – stocker	£2. 8s. 0d
Tysall – actioner	£4.13s. 0d.	Alf Fullalove – actioner	£6.16s. 0d
Walter Warren – engraver	£2.14s. 4d.	Harry Gatrell – ejectors	£3. 6s. 0d
William Wem	£2.15s. 0d.	Bill Geekie – finisher	£1.11s. 0d
Fred Williams – actioner	£3. 5s. 0d.	W Gerrard – cartridge loader	£1.15s. 0d
S Wheatley – factory manager	£4. 0s. 0d.	Jim Gorman – cartridge loader	17s. 3d
Charlie Wilkes – viewer	£1.14s. 2d.	W Griffiths – finisher	£2.15s. 0d
W Wilkes – barrel maker	£2. 4s. 0d.	Jerry Hawkes – finisher	£2. 5s. 0d
		Joe Hayes – repairs	£1. 8s. 0d

Henson – stocker	£3. 2s. 0d	
Henderson – repairs	£2. 5s. 0d	
Bill Hill – barrel maker	£7. 6s. 6d	
W Hopewell – finisher	£2.10s. 0d	
H Horsley – stocker	£3. 1s. 0d	
Bob Horscroft – repairs	£2. 0s. 0d	
Fred Hughes – actioner	£8.16s. 0d	
H W Johnson Sr. – stocker	£3. 3s. 0d	
Johnson Jr. – stocker	£3. 5s. 0d	
E Johnson – stocker	£3. 3s. 0d	
A Kippen – cartridge loader	£1. 6s. 0d	
C Lane – finisher	£2.10s. 0d	
Ernest Lawrence – finisher	£2.15s. 0d	
Leeper Sr. – carpenter	£2. 5s. 0d	
Bill Leeper Jr. – cartridge loader	£1.12s. 6d	
Harry Leggett – stocker	£2.15s. 0d	
J Lucas – engraver	£5. 4s. 6d	
James Lumsden Sr. – stocker	£5. 9s. 6d	
Lumsden Jr. – stocker	£2.15s. 0d	
Charlie Matthews – stocker	£3. 4s. 6d	
F Mayo – barrel maker	£1.17s.10d	
D Murray – cartridge maker	£1.11s. 0d	
Wesley Nobbs – actioner	£3. 6s. 0d	
Nobbs Jr. – actioner	£2.14s. 6d	
Packman – engineer	£2. 4s. 3d	
A Phillips – actioner	£2.12s. 6d	
Pike – shooting ground	£1.17s. 0d	
Price – hardener	£2.17s. 6d	
Purvis –	£1. 2s. 0d	
George Roberts Sr. – barrel maker	£2. 5s. 6d	
Arthur Roberts Jr. – barrel maker	£4. 2s. 0d	
Abbe Robins – hardener	£2.19s. 6d	
Bill Rouse – repairs	£1.17s. 0d	
W Russell Sr. – finisher	£3.14s. 8d	
Russell Jr. – actioner	£3. 0s. 0d	
Charlie Sadler – ejectors	£1.15s. 0d	
Sam Simons – barrel maker	£5.15s. 6d	
Sam Smallwood – shooting ground	£1.18s. 0d	
Alf Smith – ejectors	£3.14s. 6d	
E Smith – actioner	£1.18s. 0d	
Fred Smith – actioner	£2.10s. 0d	
Syd Smith – ejectors	£3.16s. 0d	
Henry Sparrow – repairs	£2.14s. 6d	
Stanley – actioner	£2.10s. 6d	
Frank Taylor – painter	£1.15s. 0d	
Joe Thompson – actioner	£6. 4s. 0d	
Maurice Timbers – actioner	£2.15s. 0d	
Tombs – barrel maker	£2. 0s. 0d	
Walter Warren – engraver	£2.14s. 9d	
Warren Jr. – Repairs	£2.15s. 0d	
Joe Watts – barrel maker	£3. 0s. 0d	
Fred Williams – actioner	£4.12s. 0d	
Arthur Wilkes – barrel maker	£2. 0s. 0d	
Charlie Wilkes – viewer	£2.10s. 0d	
Frank Wolfe – engineer	£1. 9s. 5d	
Wheatley – factory manager	£3. 0s. 0d	

Front shop

Youngman	£2. 3s. 0d
Charles Butler	£4. 0s. 0d
Clarke	£2. 5s. 0d
Page	£3. 3s. 0d
Poole	17s. 0d
Nash	£2.13s. 0d
George Tillson	£3.15s. 0d

Apprentices and other trades

Bradley	£1. 2s. 6d
Field	£1.11s. 0d
Hamilton – shooting ground	£1. 5s. 0d
Hemmington	18s. 0d
Johnstone	£1. 6s. 0d
Simpson	£1. 3s.10d
Charlie Waite – repairs	£1. 0s. 6d
Lovett	15s. 6d
Mr. Cecil	£3.10s. 0d
Scales	£2. 8s. 0d
Booth – Porter	7s. 1d

MARCH 1936

Gunmakers

J Aldous – barrel maker	£2.18s. 4d
Jack Apted – stocker	£4.15s. 3d
Bill Bayliss – machinist	£ 4. 8s. 4d
Bluck – stocker	£ 4. 3s. 4d
Jimmy Colle – ejectors	£ 3. 2s. 6d
Tom Davidson – actioner	£ 3. 5s. 0d
Arthur Dean – stocker	£ 4.18s. 1d
Philip Dean – stocker	£ 4.19s. 8d
Ben Delay – actioner	£ 4. 2s. 9d
Harold Delay – stocker	£ 3.13s. 4d
F Edge – ejectors	£ 4.10s. 3d
Bill Geekie – finisher	£ 4.15s. 9d
Arthur Hamilton – machinist	£ 3. 3s. 4d
Alf Harvey – barrel maker	£ 3.15s. 8d
Bob Heath – barrel maker	£ 3.12s. 6d
Bill Hill – barrel maker	£ 7.11s. 9d
Len Howard – actioner	£ 4. 3s. 4d
Fred Hughes – actioner	£ 4. 7s.10d
Alfred Jelffs – repairs/barrel blacking	£ 3.18s. 4d
Johnson – stocker	£ 3. 8s. 4d
Charlie Lane – finisher	£ 4. 8s. 9d
H E Larman – machinist	£ 3. 3s. 4d
Ernest Lawrence – factory manager	£10. 0s. 0d
Harry Lawrence – actioner	£ 4.18s. 4d
Ernest D Lawrence – actioner	£ 3. 5s. 0d
Harry Leggett – stocker	£ 3. 6s. 8d
J Lovett – engraver	£ 3. 8s. 4d
H Mallett – actioner	£ 4.18s. 9d
G May – finisher	£ 3.18s. 4d
M Miles – finisher	£ 4. 8s. 4d
Bert Price Sr. – polisher/hardener	£ 5. 5s. 0d
Price Jr. – finisher	£ 4. 6s. 7d
Rixon – machinist	£ 2.10s. 0d
Charlie Sadler – ejectors	£ 3.10s. 0d
Fred Scales – stocker	£ 4. 5s. 4d
Gus Shackell – stocker	£ 4.14s. 6d

Sam Simons – barrel maker £ 8.10s. 8d
Alf Smith – ejectors £ 4.19s. 3d
Syd Smith – ejectors £ 4.13s. 7d
W Sumpter – barrel maker £ 4. 2s. 6d
Bob Thomson – finisher £ 3.17s. 6d
Maurice Timbers – actioner £ 5. 2s. 6d
Archie Turvey – finisher £ 4.19s. 9d
Jack Warlow – finisher £ 4.11s.11d
Whitehouse – actioner £ 3.18s. 4d
Arthur Wilkes – barrel maker £ 5.10s. 6d
Percy Wilkes – actioner £ 4.16s.10d
Fred Williams – actioner £ 6. 1s. 2d
Frank Winter – actioner £ 4.18s. 6d
George Wood – ejectors £ 2.13s. 4d
Bert Woolmer – actioner £ 5. 0s. 4d

Apprentices
W Field – ejectors £1.18s. 4d
P Sumpter Jr. – actioner £2.13s. 3d
Chris Gadsby – finisher £1.15s. 0d
H Bellamy – actioner 13s. 9d
Bowens 8s. 9d
Daw £1.13s. 5d
Ashmore 8s. 9d
Rogerson 8s. 5d
Martin 9s.10d
Richmond 8s. 9d
F Hughes – actioner 9s.10d
Allen 9s.10d
Dan O'Brien – hardener 9s.10d
D Carnack 9s.10d
Netherray 9s.10d
Carnack 8s. 9d

Repairs
Ben Delay Sr. £4. 3s. 4d
Joe Megroff £2.18s. 4d
Warren Jr. £3.18s. 4d
Charles Waite £2.18s. 4d
Bill Rouse £3. 0s. 0d

Cartridge loading
F Hirst £2. 2s. 0d
Bill Leeper £2.18s. 4d
Ralph Lawrence £2.10s. 0d
O'Brien £1.18s. 4d
W Thomas 14s.10d
D Thomas £1. 3s. 0d

Shooting grounds
Bill Morgan £4.10s. 0d
Morgan Jr. £3. 5s. 0d
W Percy £2.18s. 4d
T Wilson £1.13s. 4d

Others
T Blogg – cartridge loader £2.18s. 4d
Bill Johnston – porter £2. 5s. 0d
G Hirst £2.10s. 0d

L Witts £2.15s. 0d
Ewing £1.18s. 7d
Hill £2. 0s. 0d

Salaries
Mr. G Green – front shop £3. 0s. 0d
Mr. Richardson – front shop £5. 0s. 0d
Mr. Graham Tollett – front shop £4. 5s. 0d
Mr. Eugene Warner – front shop £4.10s. 0d
Mr. Ted Howes – front shop £4.10s. 0d
Mr. Buvyer – front shop £2. 5s. 0d
Mr. Gilbert – front shop £1.15s. 0d
Mr. Watson – front shop £5. 0s. 0d

Secretary
Mr. George Tillson £5. 0s. 0d

28 NOVEMBER 1952

Gunmakers Irongate
J Aldous – barrel maker £10. 4s. 0d
Anstead £ 4.13s.11d
P Chapman – finisher £ 3.17s. 8d
Ted Comben – barrel maker £ 9.11s. 4d
T Corney – actioner £ 5.19s. 9d
Cox £ 1.17s. 11d
Philip Dean – stocker £ 9.18s. 0d
Ben Delay – actioner £13. 2s. 8d
Harold Delay – stocker £14.16s. 4d
Downey – polisher £ 6. 0s. 0d
Jimmy Dudden £ 9. 9s.11d
A Dudley – finisher £ 3. 0s. 1d
F Edge – ejectors £ 9.18s. 0d
W Field – ejectors £10. 8s.11d
Walter Fillingham – machinist £ 9. 9s.11d
Brian Frost – barrel maker £ 2. 3s. 4d
Chris Gadsby – finisher and asst. factory manager £11. 5s. 0d
Bill Geekie – finisher £13. 3s. 5d
D Harding £ 8. 7s. 5d
R Harlow – actioner £ 2. 8s. 5d
Alf Harvey – barrel maker £ 9.19s. 9d
Bob Heath – barrel maker £ 7.18s. 6d
F Hirst – repairs £11. 2s. 0d
Ken Hunt – engraver £ 3. 5s. 0d
Ernest D Lawrence – actioner £12. 9s. 0d
Jim May – viewer £11. 0s. 0d
Mills £ 4. 2s. 7d
Dan O'Brien – hardener £11.14s. 0d
R G O'Brien £ 9.19s. 5d
Bill O'Brien – stocker £11. 5s. 2d
A J Price Jr. – finisher £10. 3s. 5d
J Rogers – actioner £10. 5s. 1d
Lawrie Salter – actioner £ 9.11s. 4d
Colin Smith – finisher £ 4. 4s. 1d
Sorrell – stocker £ 2. 3s. 4d
Maurice Timbers – actioner £10.10s. 1d
Jack Warlow – finisher £ 9.16s. 7d
Arthur Wilkes – barrel maker £ 7. 9s. 6d
Fred Williams – actioner £ 2. 3s. 4d

George Wood – barrel maker — £11.10s. 9d
Cook
Peter Nelson – actioner

Salaries
Mr. Graham Tollett — £10.10s. 0d
Mr. Eugene Warner — £10.10s. 0d
Mr. Leonard Lowe — £ 8.10s. 0d
Mr. D Hazells — £10. 0s. 0d
Mr. Ruggles — £ 4.10s. 0d
Mr. Malcolm — £ 6. 0s. 0d
Mr. L Wardle — £ 6. 0s. 0d

Repairs Audley House
Ben Delay Sr. — £10. 2s. 4d
Joe Megroff — £ 5. 7s. 7d
R Thomson – finisher — £ 8. 5s. 8d
Thomas Woodward — £ 7. 1s. 0d

Cartridge shop
S Coleman — £ 6.10s. 0d

Others
Bill Morgan – shooting ground — £ 9. 0s. 0d
H Smith — £ 6.17s. 8d
J P Reilly — £ 7.16s. 5d
P Aylward — £ 7.10s. 9d
G A Grun — £10. 0s. 0d

Irongate moulds (toolmakers)
H Bellamy — £ 9.13s. 6d
C Carter — £10. 5s. 4d
C E Chase — £ 8.15s. 0d
Clancy — £ 2.11s. 4d
Coltman — £ 5. 7s. 7d
G Dew — £ 9.11s. 3d
Edwards — £ 9.13s. 4d
Glascow — £ 3.17s.11d
A Hamilton — £ 8.12s. 4d
R Hastings — £ 2. 7s. 8d
L Hemmings — £12.10s. 0d
R Hepburn — £11.13s. 1d
Hollingsworth — £ 6. 2s. 0d
A Howard — £ 9.18s. 0d
Frank Hughes — £11.13s. 1d
A Jenn — £ 4. 8s.11d
D Lloyd — £ 4.12s. 1d
J Lumsden — £ 5.18s. 1d
H McIntyre — £10. 4s. 8d
Moynihan — £ 2. 7s. 1d
J Netherway — £11.11s. 5d
Roberts — £ 7. 9s. 2d
G Steff — £11. 4s. 7d
P Sumpter — £11.13s. 1d
Twineham — £10.14s. 3d
R White — £11. 5s.11d
A Wilson — £ 9.10s. 8d
Bert Woolmer — £12.10s. 4d

Appendix 7

TRADE LABELS

(All sizes approximate due to hand cutting). Date is given as a guide only as existing stocks would be used before new labels were ordered.

Small 4 Princes Street label 3 x 1 1/2 inches. Black ink. In use from 1816-26.

315 Oxford Street label 7 1/2 x 5 3/4 inches. Blue ink. In use 1826 to early 1827.

APPENDICES

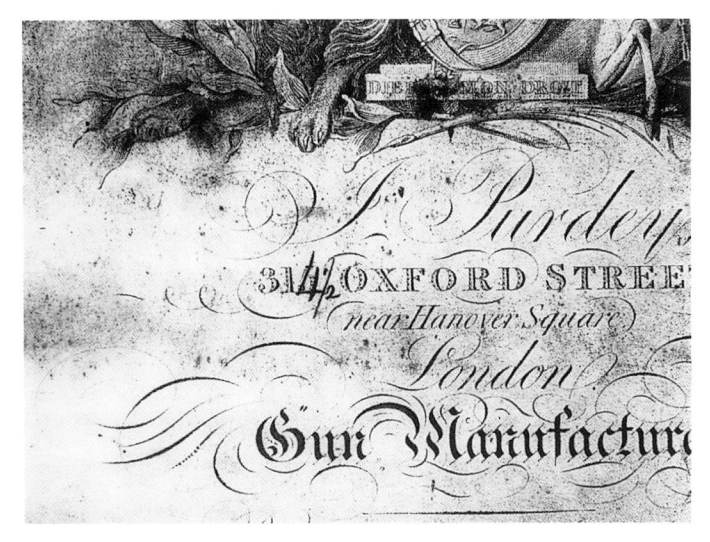

Handwritten alteration to the 315 Oxford Street label to read 314 $^1/_2$ Oxford Street. 7 $^1/_2$ x 5 $^3/_4$ inches. Blue ink. In use mid to late 1827.

The small 314 $^1/_2$ Oxford Street label. 3 x 1 $^1/_2$ inches. Blue green ink. A very rare label in use pre-1877.

314 $^1/_2$ Oxford Street label. 7 $^1/_2$ x 5 $^3/_4$ inches. Blue ink. In use from late 1827 to 1877. This label was often cropped from the 1840s onwards by removing the last two lines, the 'Patentee for the safety Gun Locks' and 'N B removed from Princes Street, Leicester Square'.

TRADE LABELS

The cropped 314 $^1/_2$ Oxford Street label. 6 $^1/_2$ x 4 $^1/_2$ inches. Blue ink. In use from the 1840s to 1877.

314 $^1/_2$ Oxford Street label revised to include Purdey's two sons, James and Athol, into the business. Black ink. In use 1878 to 1882.

Audley House, South Audley Street label. 4 x 2 1/2 inches. Black ink. In use 1883-1901.

Audley House, South Audley Street label. 4 1/2 x 3 inches. Black ink. In use 1901-11.

TRADE LABELS

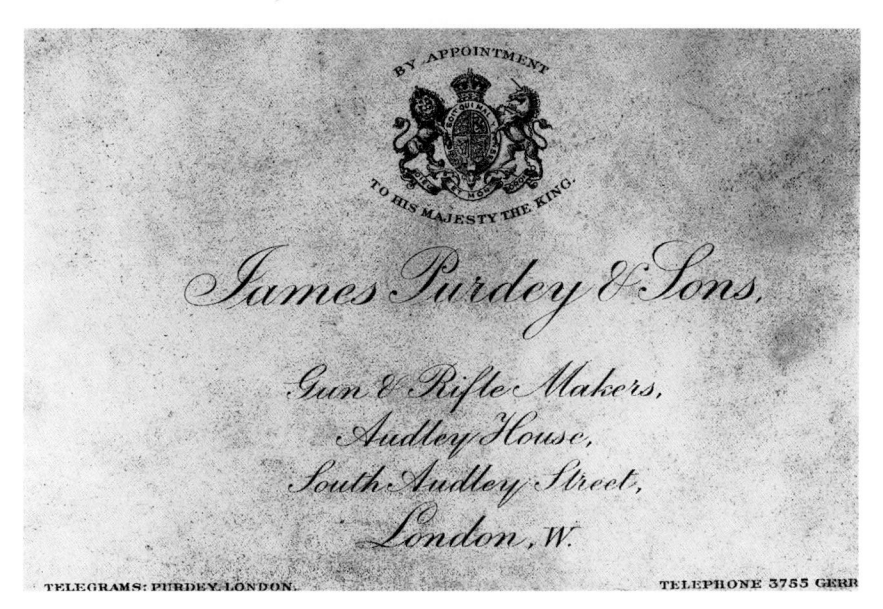

Audley House, South Audley Street label. 4 1/2 x 3 1/2 inches. Black ink.
In use, early period 1911-21.

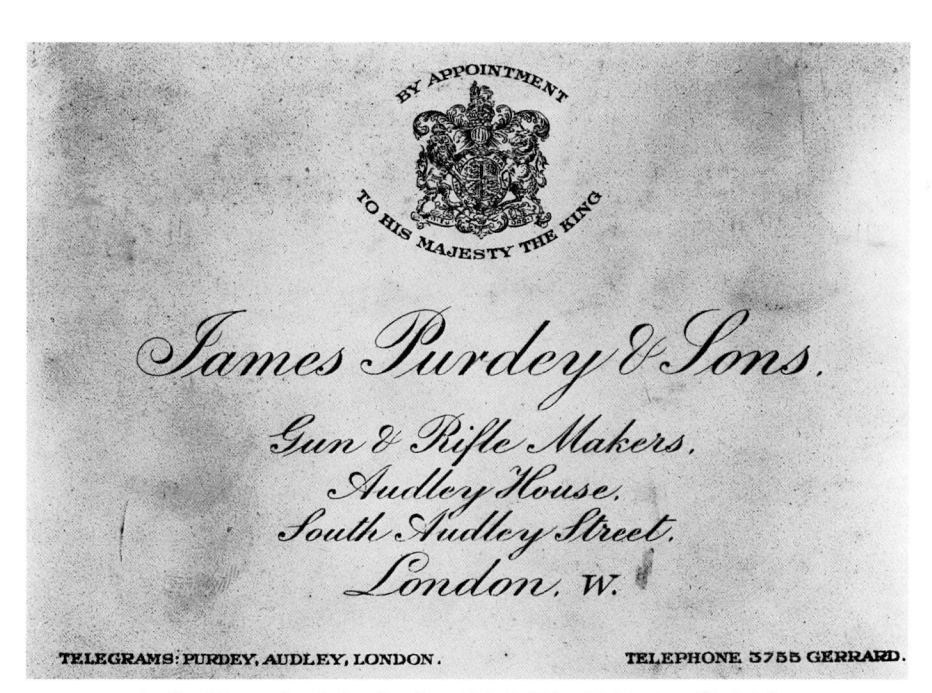

Audley House, South Audley Street label. 4 3/4 x 3 1/2 inches. Black ink.
In use, later period 1911-21.

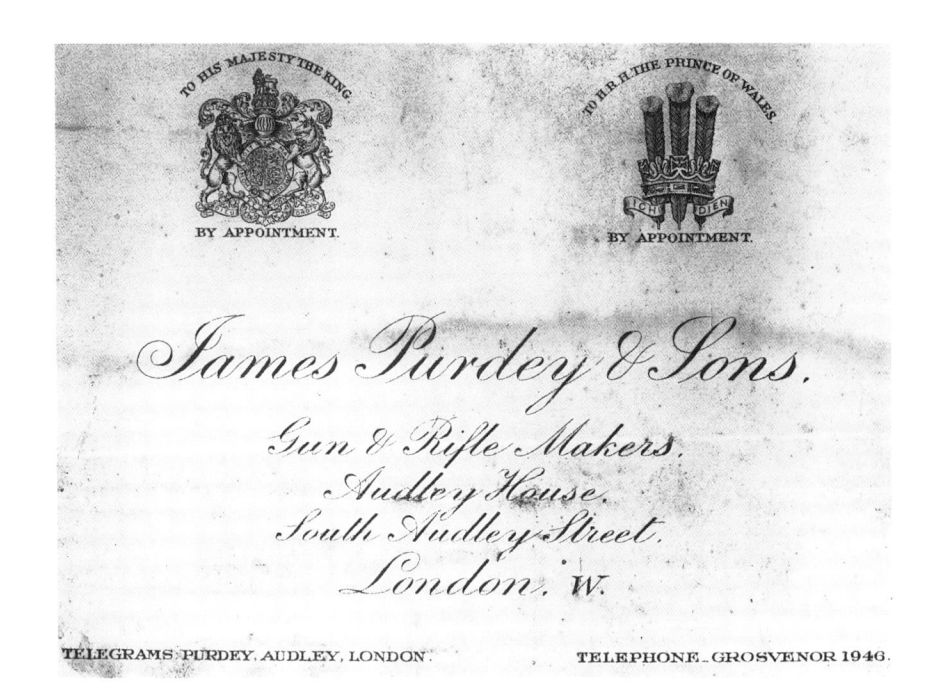

Audley House, South Audley Street label. 4 ½ x 3 ½ inches. Black ink.
In use, early period 1921-38.

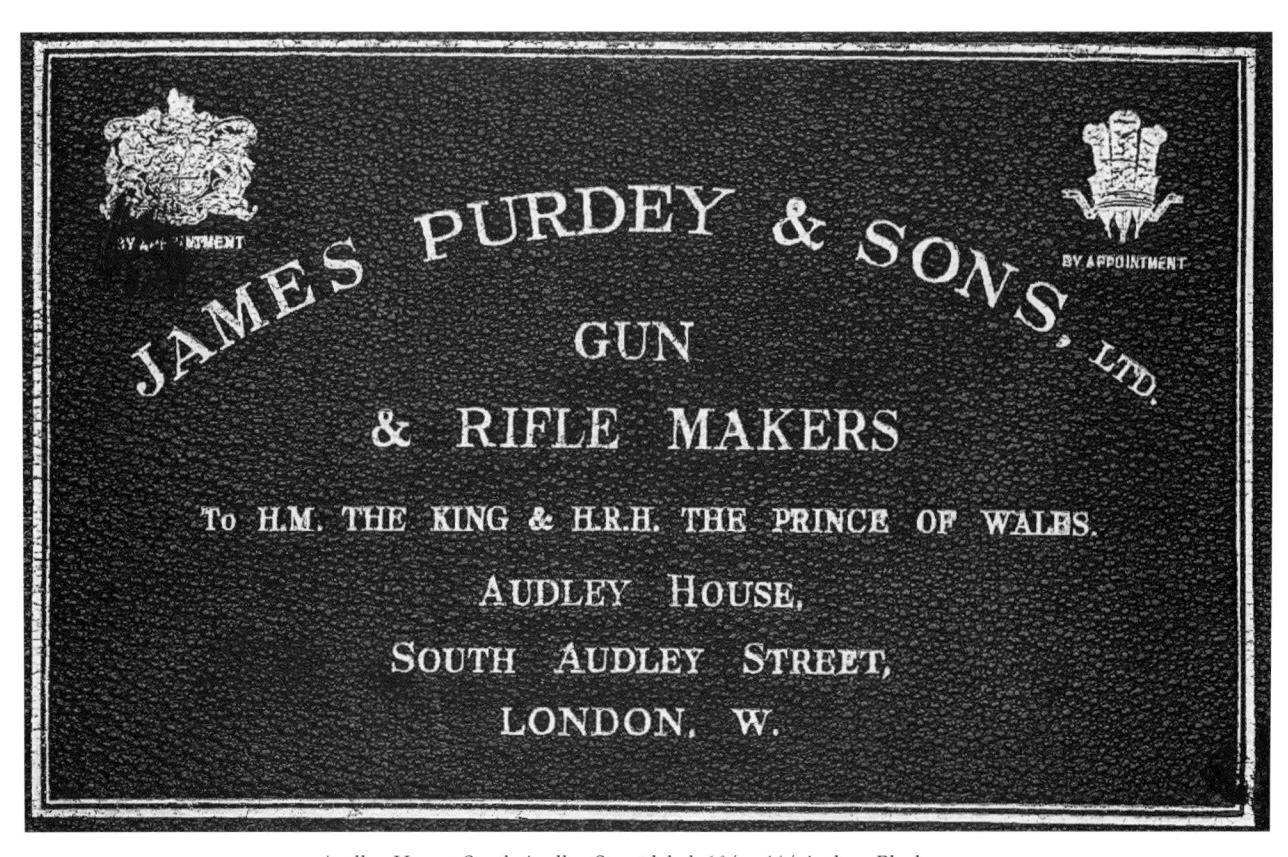

Audley House, South Audley Street label. 6 ¾ x 4 ¼ inches. Black leather. In use, later period 1921-38.

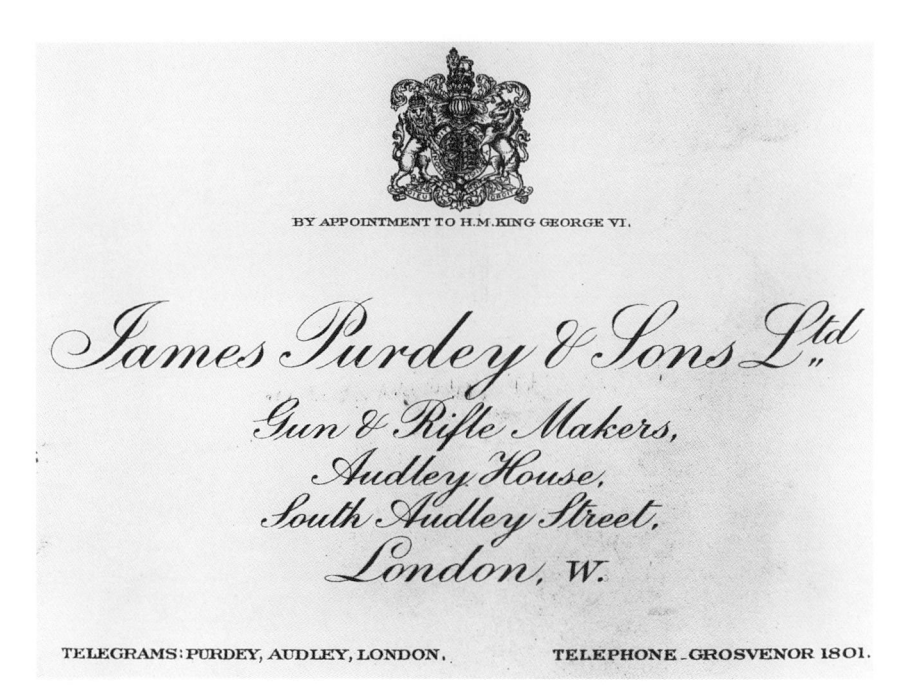

TRADE LABELS

By Appointment to H.M. King George VI.

James Purdey & Sons Ltd
Gun & Rifle Makers,
Audley House,
South Audley Street,
London, W.

TELEGRAMS: PURDEY, AUDLEY, LONDON.   TELEPHONE – GROSVENOR 1801.

Audley House, South Audley Street label. $4\frac{1}{2} \times 3\frac{1}{2}$ inches. Black ink. In use 1938-55.

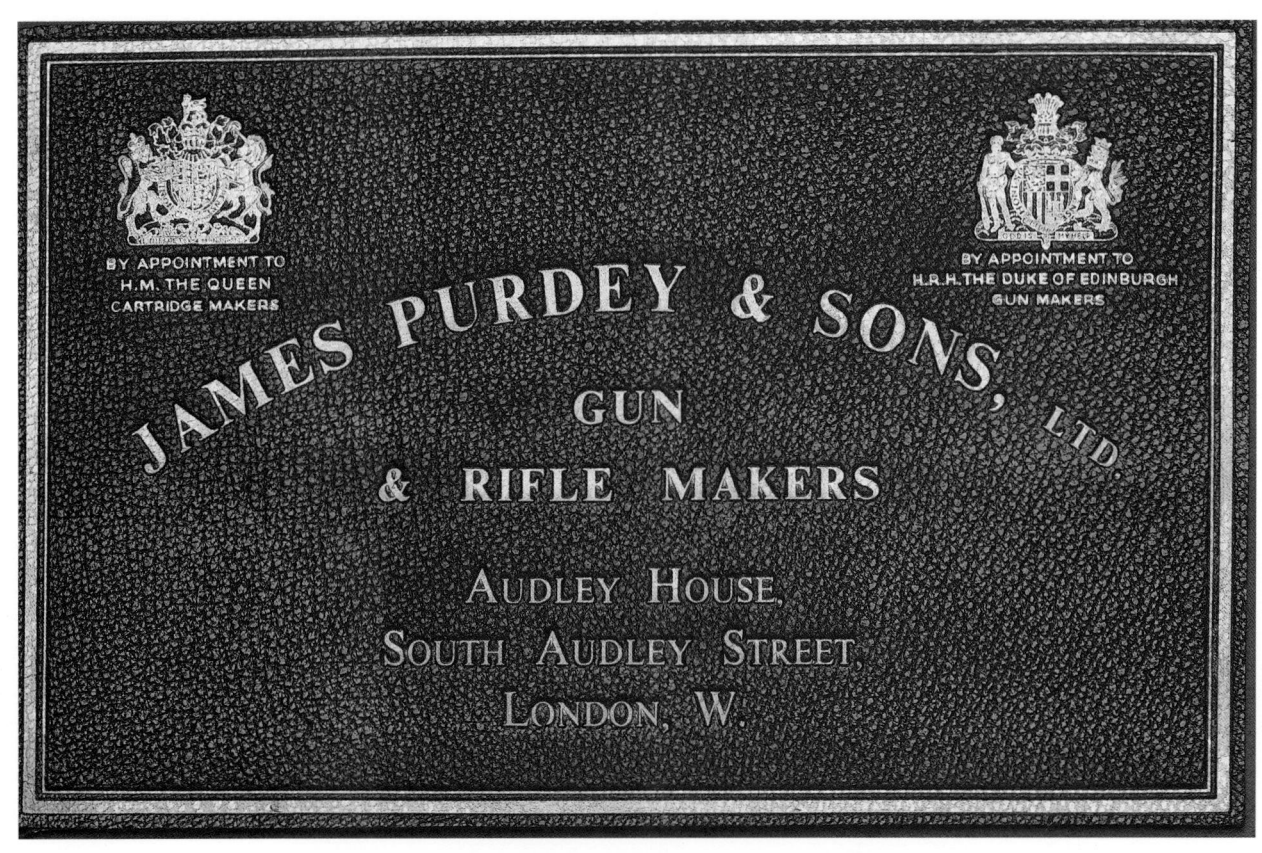

JAMES PURDEY & SONS, LTD.
GUN & RIFLE MAKERS
AUDLEY HOUSE,
SOUTH AUDLEY STREET,
LONDON, W.

BY APPOINTMENT TO H.M. THE QUEEN CARTRIDGE MAKERS

BY APPOINTMENT TO H.R.H. THE DUKE OF EDINBURGH GUN MAKERS

Audley House, South Audley Street label. In two sizes, $6\frac{3}{4} \times 4\frac{1}{4}$ inches and $5\frac{1}{4} \times 3\frac{1}{4}$ inches. Black leather. In use, early period 1955-81.

Later use of the same label with Queen Elizabeth's Warrant changed to
'By Appointment to HM The Queen, Gun & Cartridge Makers'.

Audley House, South Audley Street label. Two sizes, 7 x 4 ¹/₂ inches and
5 ¹/₂ x 3 ¹/₂ inches. Black leather. In use 1981-86.

TRADE LABELS

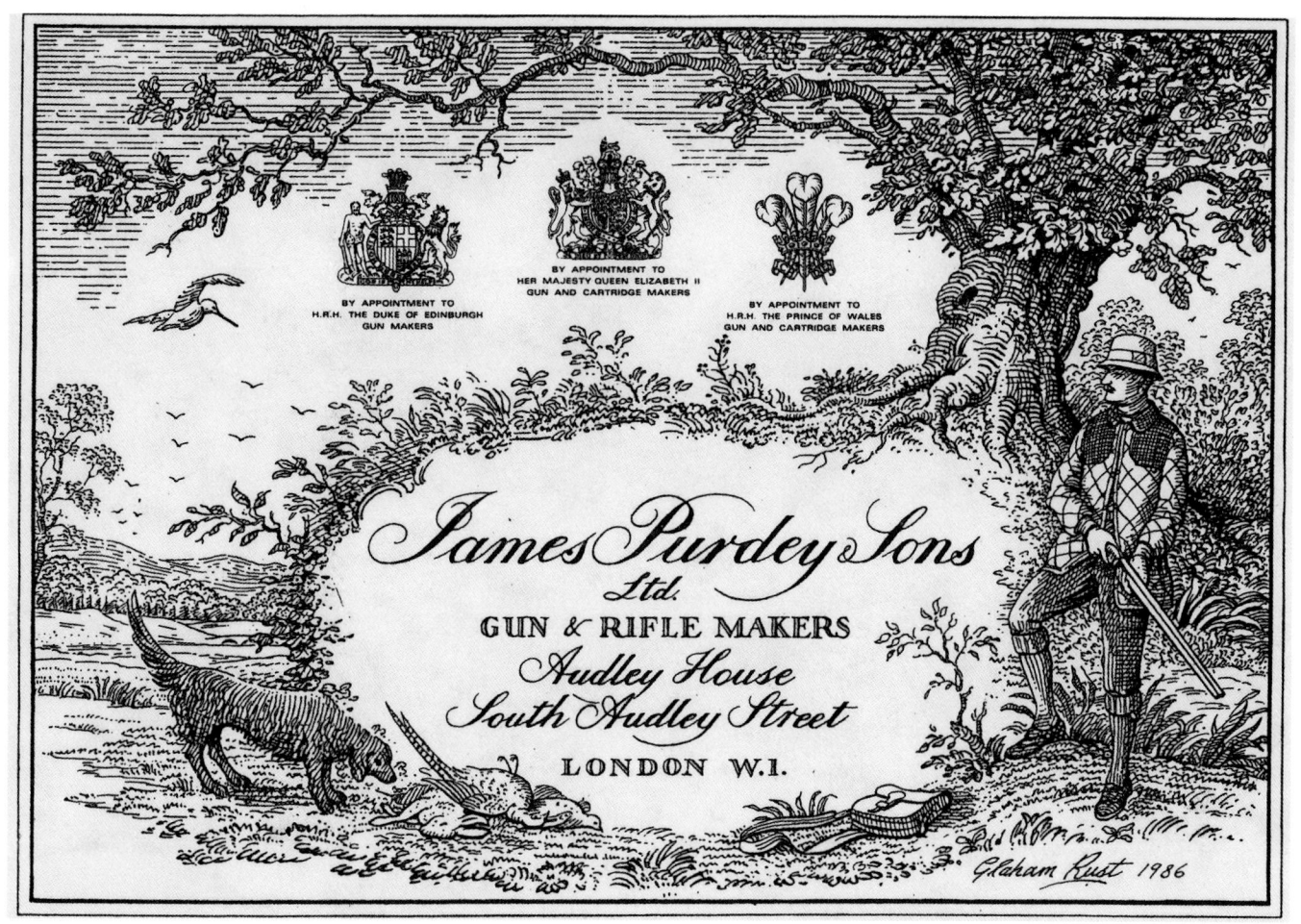

Audley House, South Audley Street label. 7 1/4 x 5 inches. Buff paper label. In use 1986-91.

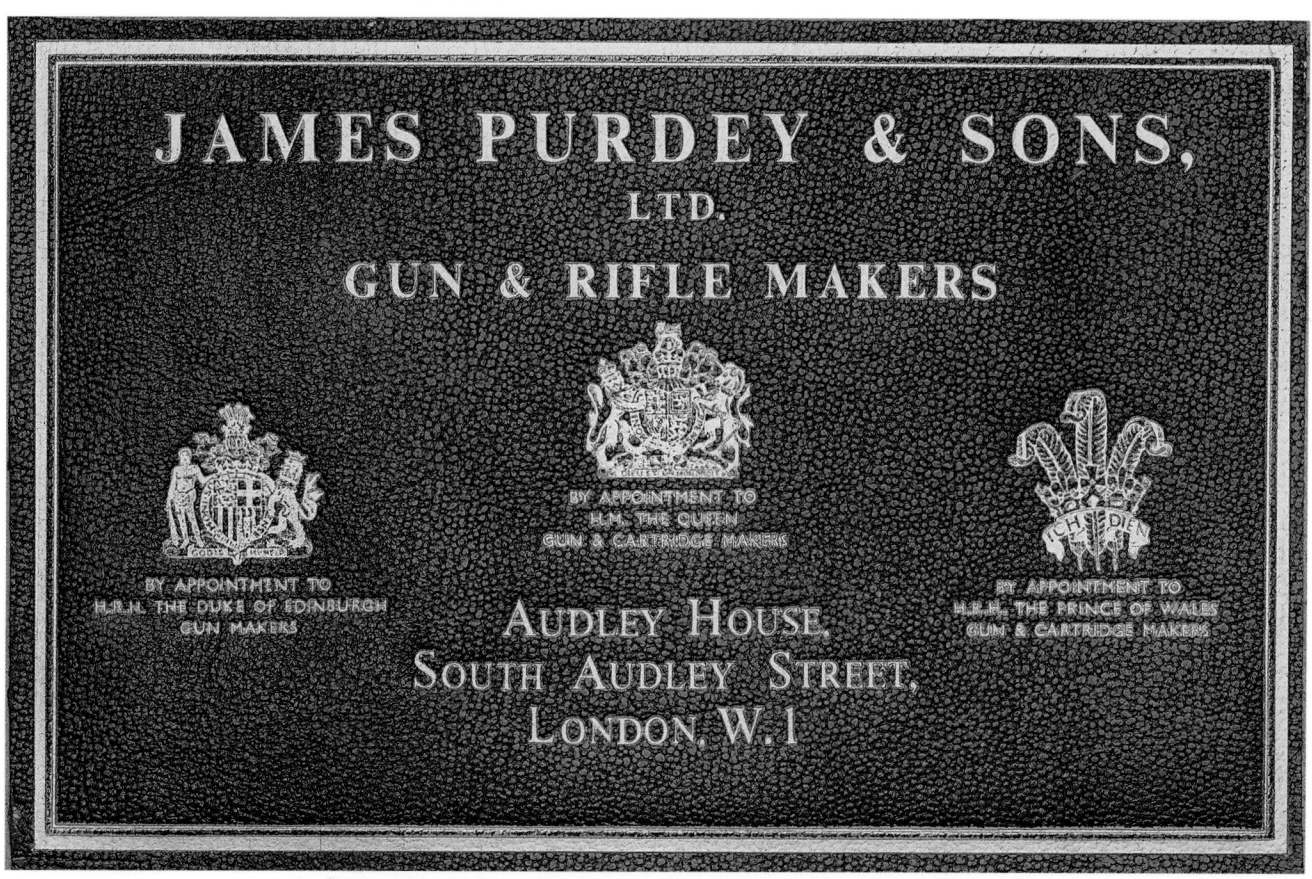

Audley House, South Audley Street label. In two sizes, 7 x 4 1/2 inches and 5 1/2 x 3 1/2 inches. Black leather. In use 1991-present day. Prince of Wales feathers altered.

Appendix 8

JAMES PURDEY AND SONS PATENTS

During the 19th and 20th centuries, a total of sixteen patents have been granted to three generations of Purdeys. The object behind a patent was to give an inventor a monopoly on his invention for a maximum period of fourteen years to exploit and profit from it. The inventor first of all applied for a Provisional Specification. This was a very general description of the invention. The title of the invention was often kept deliberately vague so as not to alert potential competitors as to the nature of the invention. Within nine months, the inventor then had to submit a Complete Specification in which the invention had to be described in detail, accompanied by drawings. The inventor had to pay fees to obtain the grant of patent. These fees were not cheap. In addition to an initial fee, subsequent fees had to be paid if the patentee wished his patent to remain in force for the full fourteen years. As well as these fees, a patent agent would have to be employed to draft and draw the patent. Consequently patents were not entered into lightly and this helps to explain why Frederick Beesley in the early years of his business was keen to sell his patent to James Purdey.

The Certificate of Renewal for Beesley's patent no. 31 of 3 January 1880. The renewal for one year in 1892 cost £20. 'Newton and Son' were the patent agents.

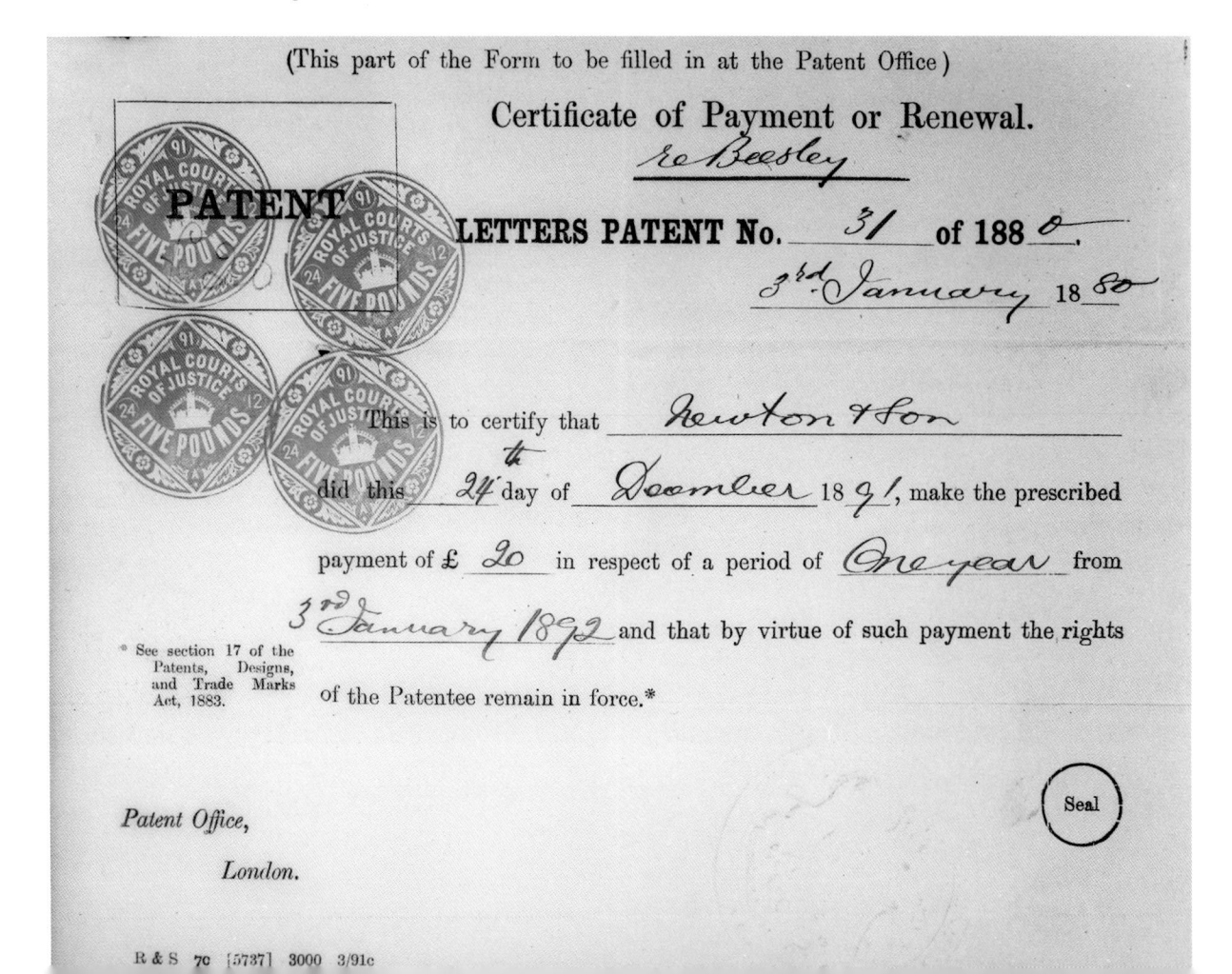

JAMES PURDEY AND SONS PATENTS

THE PURDEY PATENTS

(THE DESCRIPTION IS MY INTERPRETATION OF THE PATENT)

PROVISIONAL PATENT NO	PATENTEE & DATE	TITLE	DESCRIPTION
No. 302 – 5 February 1861	James Purdey	'Improved Apparatus For Ramming and Turning Over Breech-Loading Cartridges'	Turnover tool
No. 1104 – 2 May 1863	James Purdey	'Improvements in Breech-Loading Firearms'	Double bolt snap action (the Purdey Bolt)
No. 424 – 14 February 1865	James Purdey	'Improvements in Breech-Loading Firearms'	Rocking lever snap action, retractable strikers, cartridge pins, extractors, slide-action extractors
No. 1464 – 25 May 1866	James Purdey	'An Improvement in Breech-Loading Firearms'	Loaded indicators
No. 2319 – 23 July 1868	James Purdey	'Improvements in Firearms'	Adjustable elevation for the breech
No. 3118 – 28 November 1870	James Purdey	'An Improvement in the Action of Breakdown Guns with a Snap Fastening'	Trigger safety lock
No. 2952 – 3 November 1871 (This patent was never proceeded with as a complete specification)	James Purdey	'An Improvement in the Construction of Rifled Breech-Loading Firearms'	Rifled tube
No. 397 – 30 January 1878	James Purdey	'Improvements in Breech-Loading Firearms'	Third fastening
No. 22618 – 22 November 1894	James Purdey	'Firearms'	'Abandoned/Void'
No. 19027 – 17 August 1897	A S Purdey	'An Improved Hand Protector for Sportsmen'	Padded left-hand glove
No. 5955 – 17 March 1908	A S Purdey	'Shotguns'	'Abandoned/Void'
No. 5150 – 1 March 1910	J Purdey & Sons & William George Clark	'Improvements in Single Trigger Double Barrelled Guns'	Single trigger
No. 21822 – 3 October 1911	J Purdey & Sons & William George Clark	'Improvements in Single Trigger Double Barrelled Guns'	Single trigger
No. 2608 – 18 February 1915	A S Purdey	'Rifles'	'Abandoned/Void'
No. 3188 – 27 February 1915	A S Purdey	'Improvements in Muzzle Protectors for Rifles'	Muzzle protector
No. 5523 – 26 February 1926 (This Patent was never proceeded with as a complete specification)	James Purdey & Sons & T D S Purdey	'Improvements in and Relating to Shooting Seats or Sticks for Facilitating the Loading of Sporting Guns'	Cartridge holders
No. 19052 – 30 July 1926	James Purdey & Sons & T D S Purdey	'Improvements in or Relating to Cartridge Holders'	Cartridge holders
No. 14943 – 13 May 1929	J Purdey & Sons & Ernest Charles Lawrence	'Light Projecting Dummy Cartridge for Shotguns'	Electric cartridge
No. 15985 – 23 May 1929	A S Purdey	'Walking Stick Adapted for Shooting Practice'	Walking stick

APPENDICES

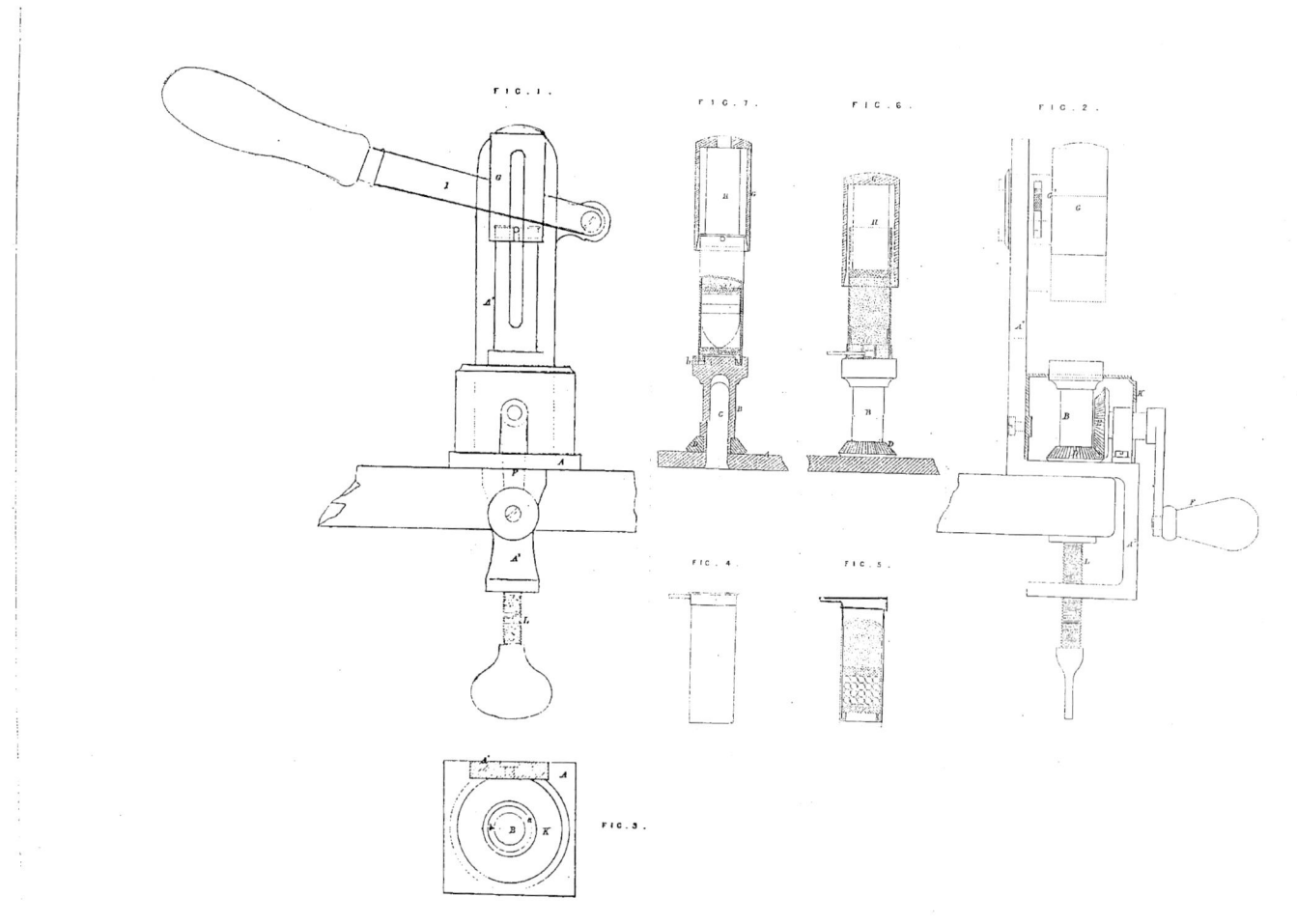

Above: Provisional patent no. 302 – 5 February 1861 – Turnover Tool

Below: Provisional patent no. 1104 – 2 May 1863 – Double Bolt Snap Action (The Purdey Bolt)

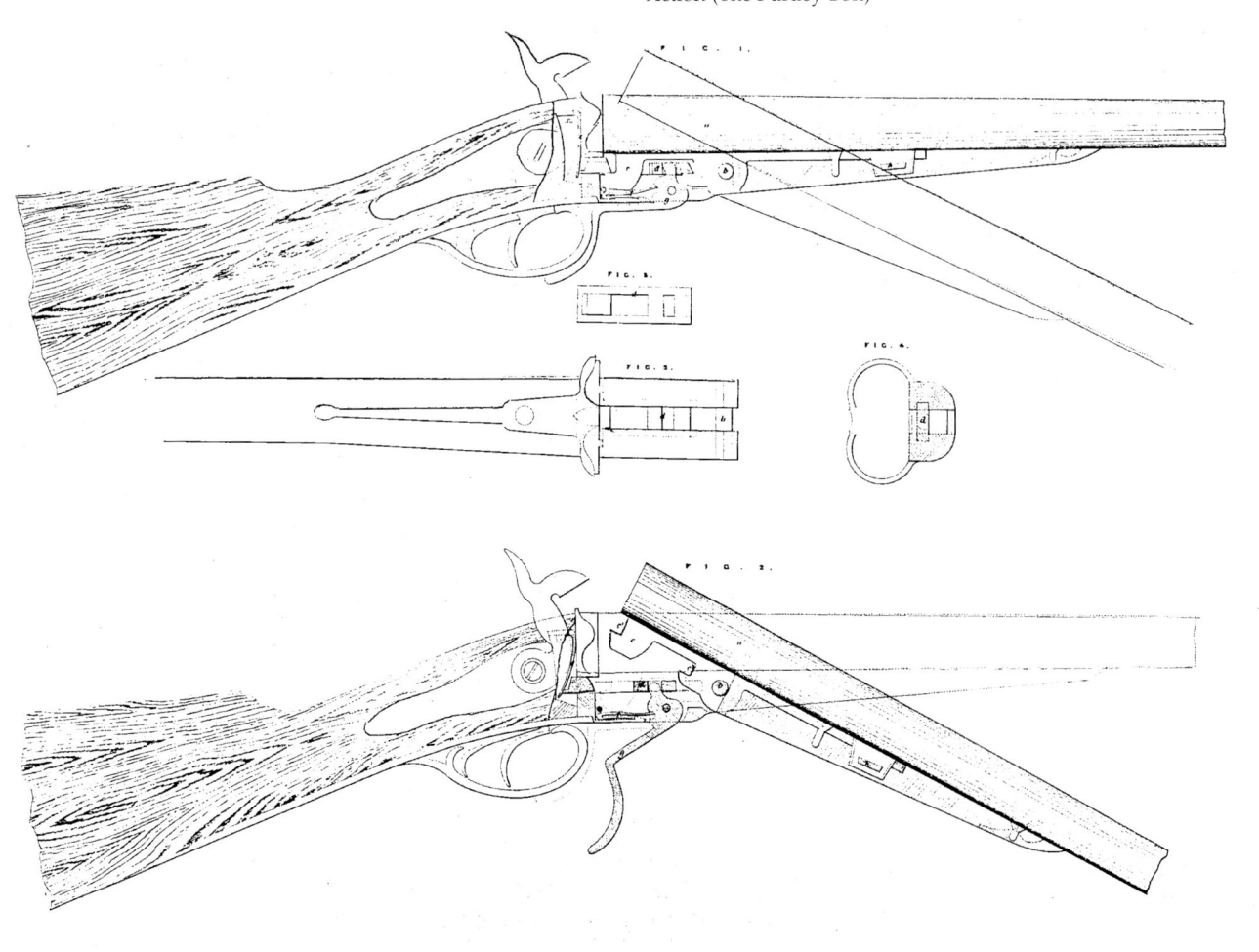

Patent no. 302
This was the first machine to produce a really effective turnover on cartridges. Figure 1 is the front view and figure 2 the side view. The previously loaded cartridge was placed, primer head down, on top of spindle B (figure 6). It was then compressed using lever (I) with the cylinder (G). The cartridge was then reversed (figure 7) and the open end placed in the groove in the spindle head (B). A small steel projection (b) protruded into this head. Crank lever (F) is rotated and the steel projection (b) bears upon the edge of the cartridge and turns it inwards to effect the turnover.

Patent no. 1104
This patent concerns the famous Purdey bolt that has been in continuous production all over the world since 1863. The patent illustrates the first pattern thumb-hole under lever (g). Two notches (c1) and (c2) are cut in the barrel lumps to receive the sliding bolt (d). When the barrels are closed, the lump at (c2) will force back bolt (d). Upon closure the spring will drive forward the bolt to lock the barrels at the two notches (c1) and (c2). This patent illustrates two springs (e) and (f). The most common thumb-hole, the second pattern, uses a single spring with two limbs on either side of the triggerwork.

Patent no. 424
This was a long complicated patent comprising five different improvements. In the first improvement (figure 3) a locking bolt (a) has cut outs to match the barrel lump (b). Upon closure, the barrel lump (b) pushed the locking bolt (a) forward, whereupon a spring powered vertical wedge (d) descends and locks the bolt. To release the mechanism, a button (i) on the rocking lever (e) is depressed, this lifts the wedge, rotates the bolt and the barrels lift. Figure 7 shows how the mechanism could be applied to the Daw lever. In the second improvement, relating to early centre-fire weapons (figures 8, 9 and 10) the striker (r) is attached by a pin working in the rear of the hammer, to the hammer itself. When the hammer is drawn back to full cock, the striker is automatically retracted. The striker remains in this position even when the hammer is drawn to the full cock due to the curved form of the groove in the rear of the hammer. A third improvement (figures 11 and 12) shows a centre-fire cartridge with a pin attached to pull it out. A fourth improvement (figures 13 and 14) shows an extractor system. When the barrels are opened, a small spring powered lever (x) pushes against the extractor lever (w) to push out the extractors (v). A fifth improvement shows cartridge extractors for the Bastin slide action breech-loader (figure 9). When the loaded barrels are pushed back to close the gun, the extractor lever (w) is moved back and by means of a spring clicks into place to lock the cartridge rim. When the barrel is pushed forward, the extractor lever (w) holds the rim of the cartridge assisted by a nib (y) at the top of the breech. There were two extractors and two levers so that if one cartridge had not been fired, the relevant lever (w1)

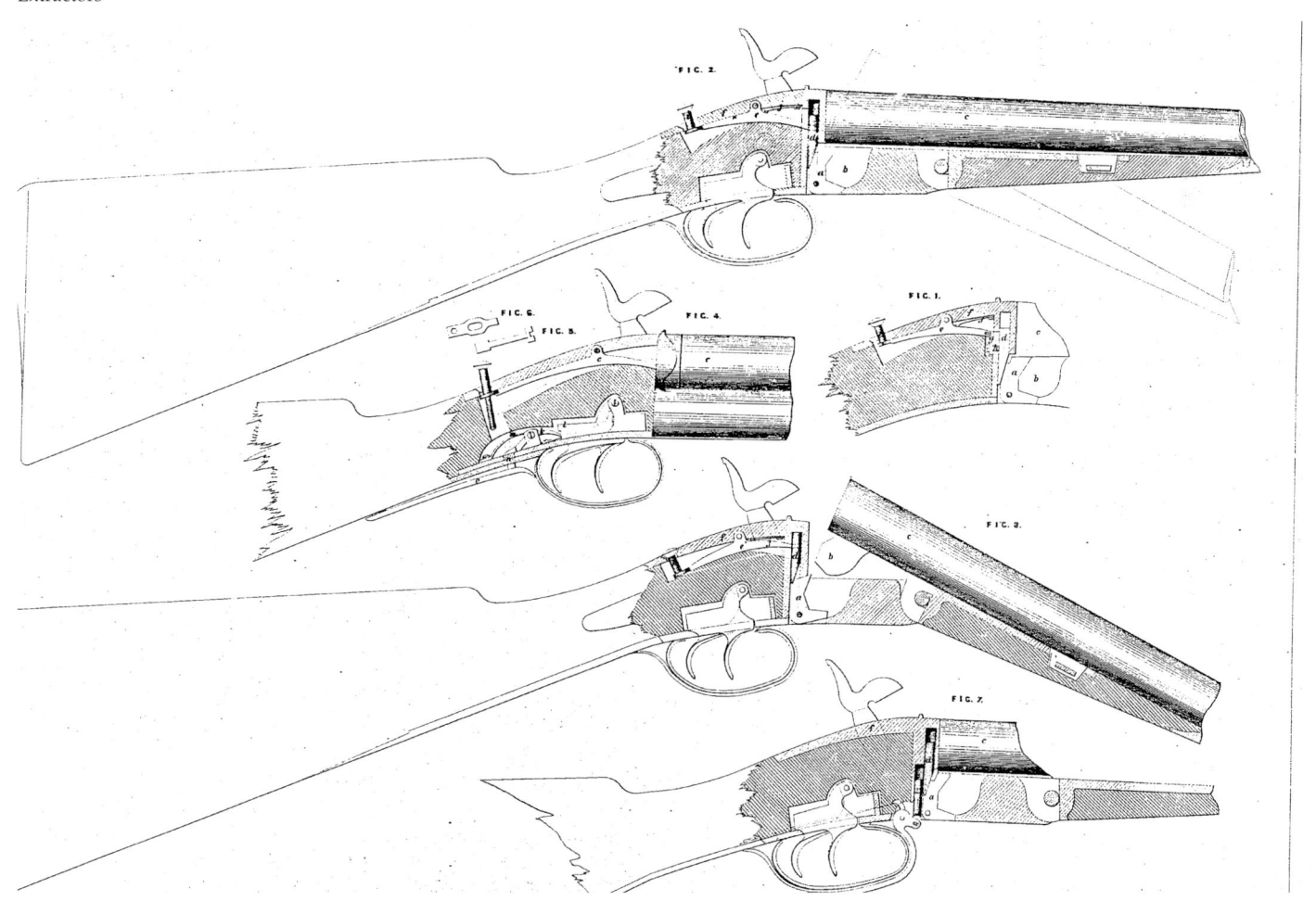

Provisional patent no. 424 – 14 February 1865 – Rocking Lever Snap Action, Retractable Strikers, Cartridge Pins, Extractors, Slide Action Extractors

APPENDICES

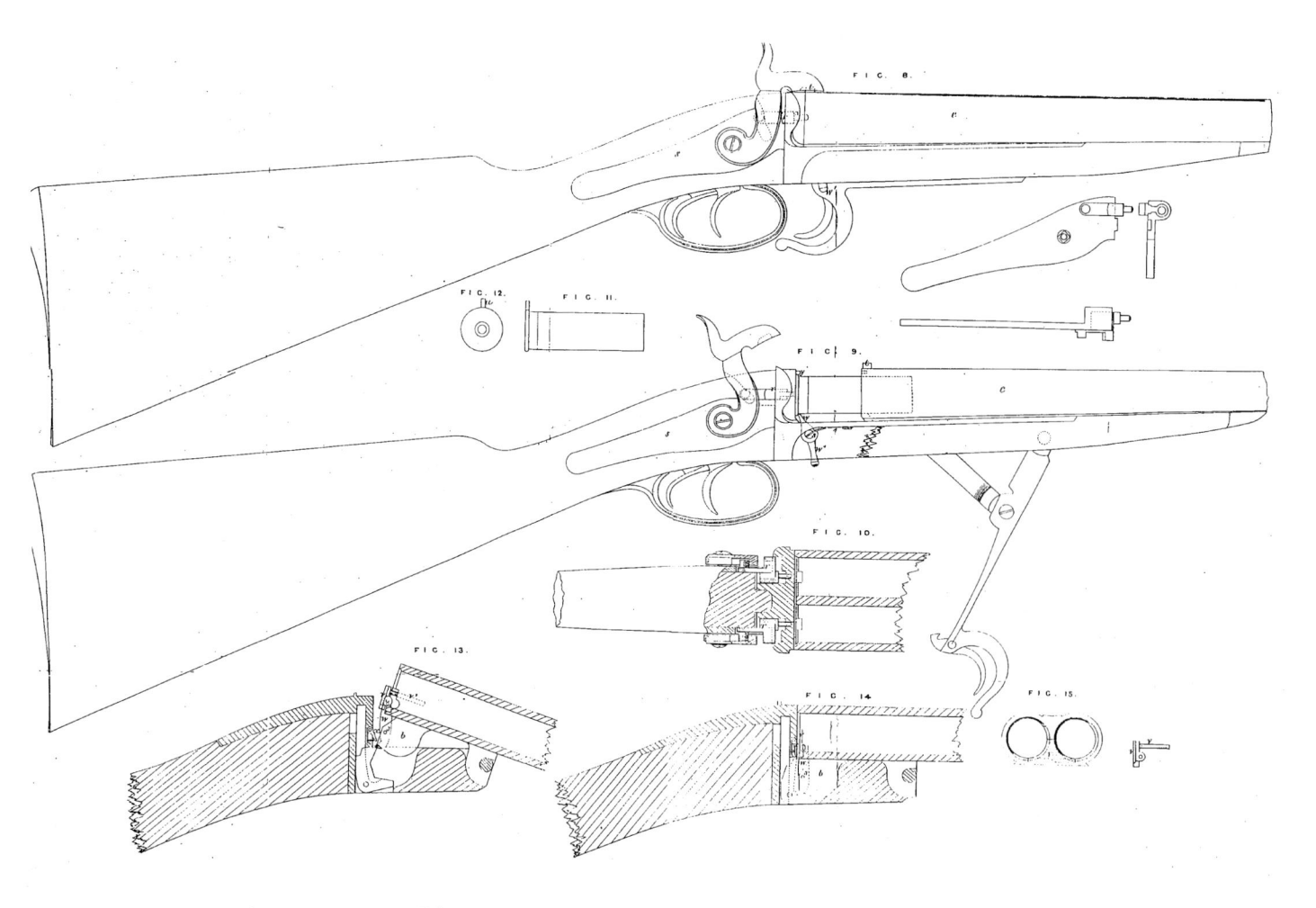

Above: Sheet 2 Provisional patent no. 424 – 14 February 1865.

Below: Provisional patent no. 1464 – 25 May 1866 – Loaded Indicators

PURDEY'S SPECIFICATION.

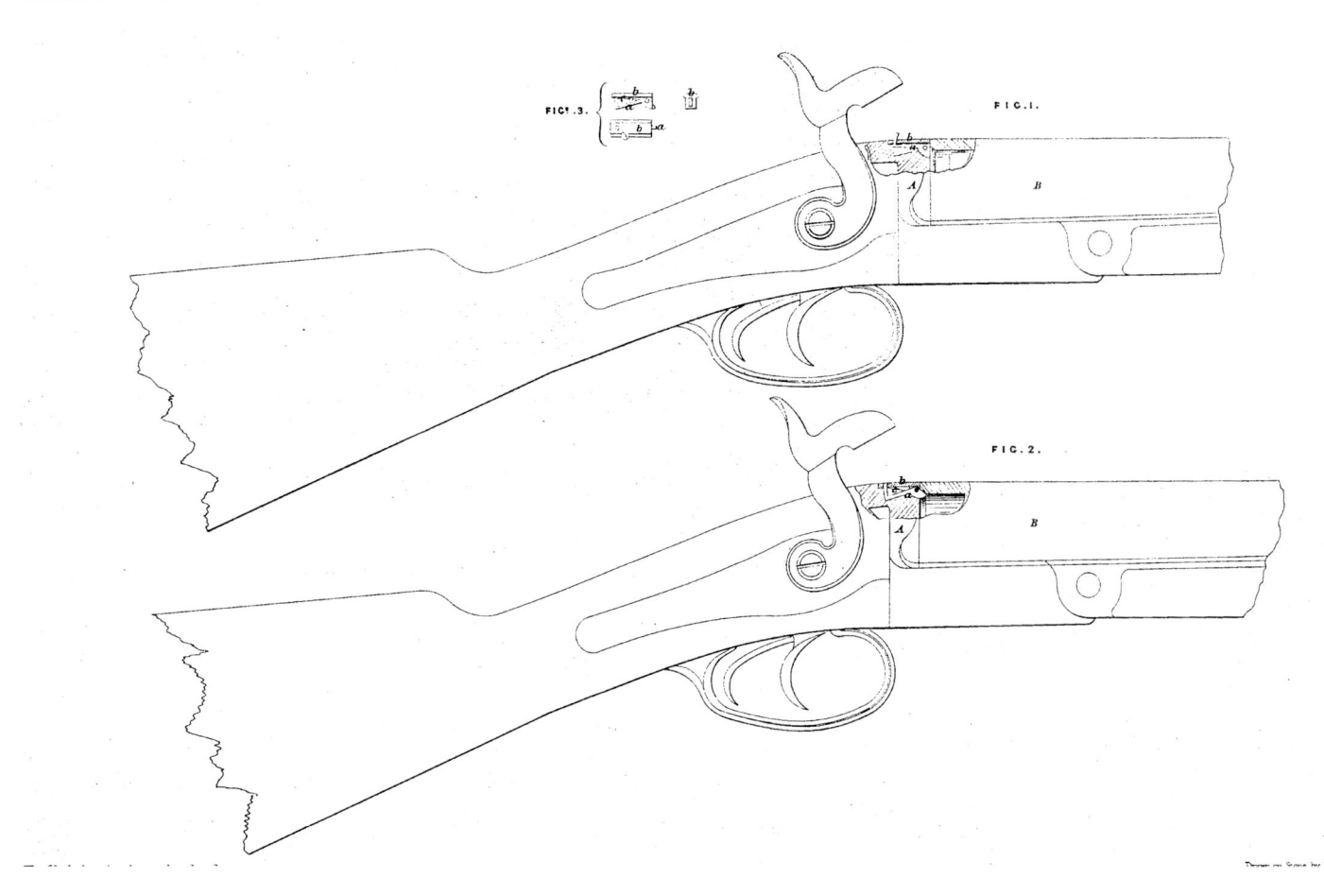

projecting beneath the stock, could be manually pushed back to release the point of the extractor from the rim of the cartridge.

Patent no. 1464
In flintlock, percussion and pinfire guns, it was visually apparent when a gun was loaded and ready to fire. In the newly introduced centre-fire, since the cartridge was totally enclosed, there was no means of seeing this. In this patent, James Purdey invented a loaded indicator to show when a cartridge was present in the breech. Figure 1 shows a charged barrel and Figure 2 an empty barrel. A small crank lever (a) locks on a small pin all contained in the top of the breech. Upon the closure of a loaded barrel, the head of the cartridge pushed the small projection of the lever on the action face to cause the other end to pop out of the top of the breech. A small spring (c) would return the crank lever to its original position upon removal of the cartridge.

Patent no. 2319
Joseph Manton had introduced the elevated rib in patent no. 2966 of 15 September 1806 with the intention of throwing the centre of the charge of shot up to the object aimed, at the distance required. This elevated rib has been used to a greater or lesser extent since then on most shotguns. Some guns required, such as pigeon guns, a greater elevation than others. This invention attempted to give an adjustable elevation at the breech to suit the varying requirements of the user. A removable plate (c) would be regulated by means of an adjusting screw (d).

Patent no. 3118
This invention provided for a safety lock on the triggers to prevent a gun from being fired until it was properly closed and locked. Although the drawing shows a second pattern thumb-hole, a description was provided of the safety applied to a top lever. Figure 2 shows the bifurcated spring (F) that powered the bolt and thumb-hole. This bifurcated spring lay on either side of the triggers. In this invention, Purdey fitted a crossbar (f) to the spring. When the lever was pushed forward, or in any other position apart from closed, the spring (F) would be depressed and the crossbar (f) would engage in a slot in the trigger blade (E) to prevent the trigger being pulled. When the thumb-hole was closed, the spring would rise to its normal position and the crossbar would disengage from the trigger blade allowing the gun to fire.

Patent no. 2952
For some reason this patent was never proceeded with as a complete specification. Consequently only a brief description is given with no drawings. The object was to obtain a higher velocity of a bullet with less fouling and less stripping. In the invention, a rifle barrel was smooth bore for about 3/4 of its length. In the last six inches or so a rifled tube was inserted.

Below: Provisional patent no. 2319 – 23 July 1868 – Adjustable Elevation for the Breech

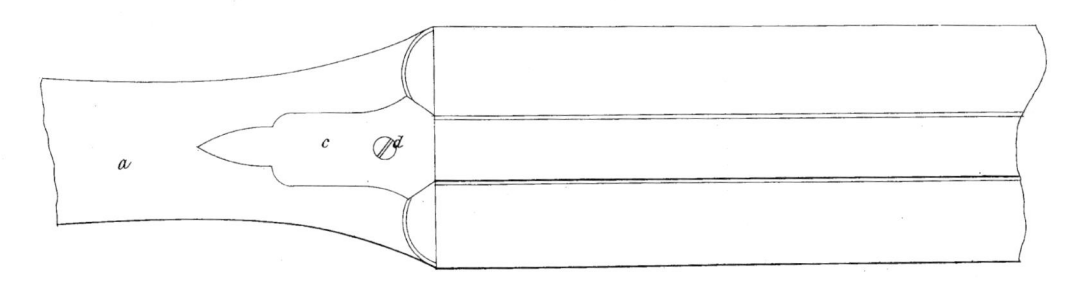

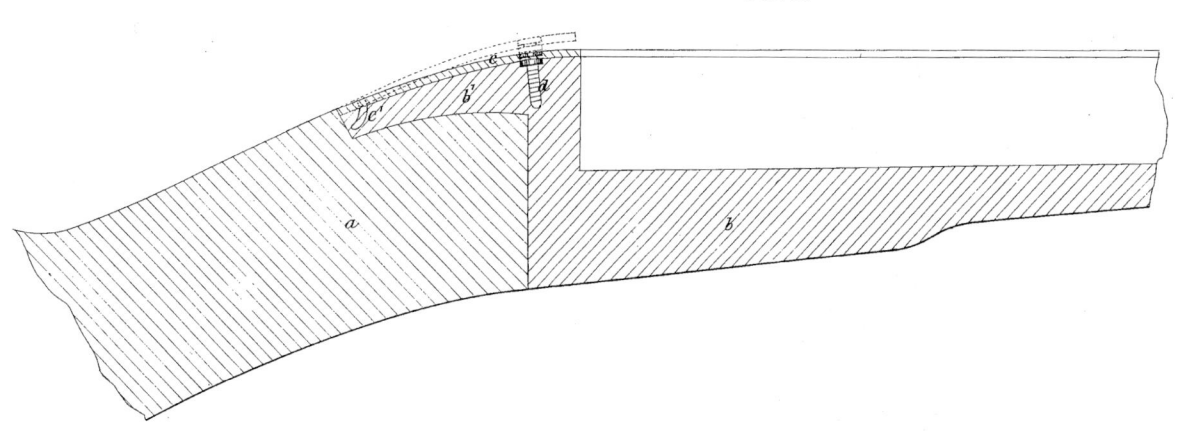

APPENDICES

AD.1870, Nov. 28, N° 3118,
PURDEY'S SPECIFICATION.

FIG. 1.

(1 SHEET)

FIG. 2.

FIG. 4.

FIG. 3.

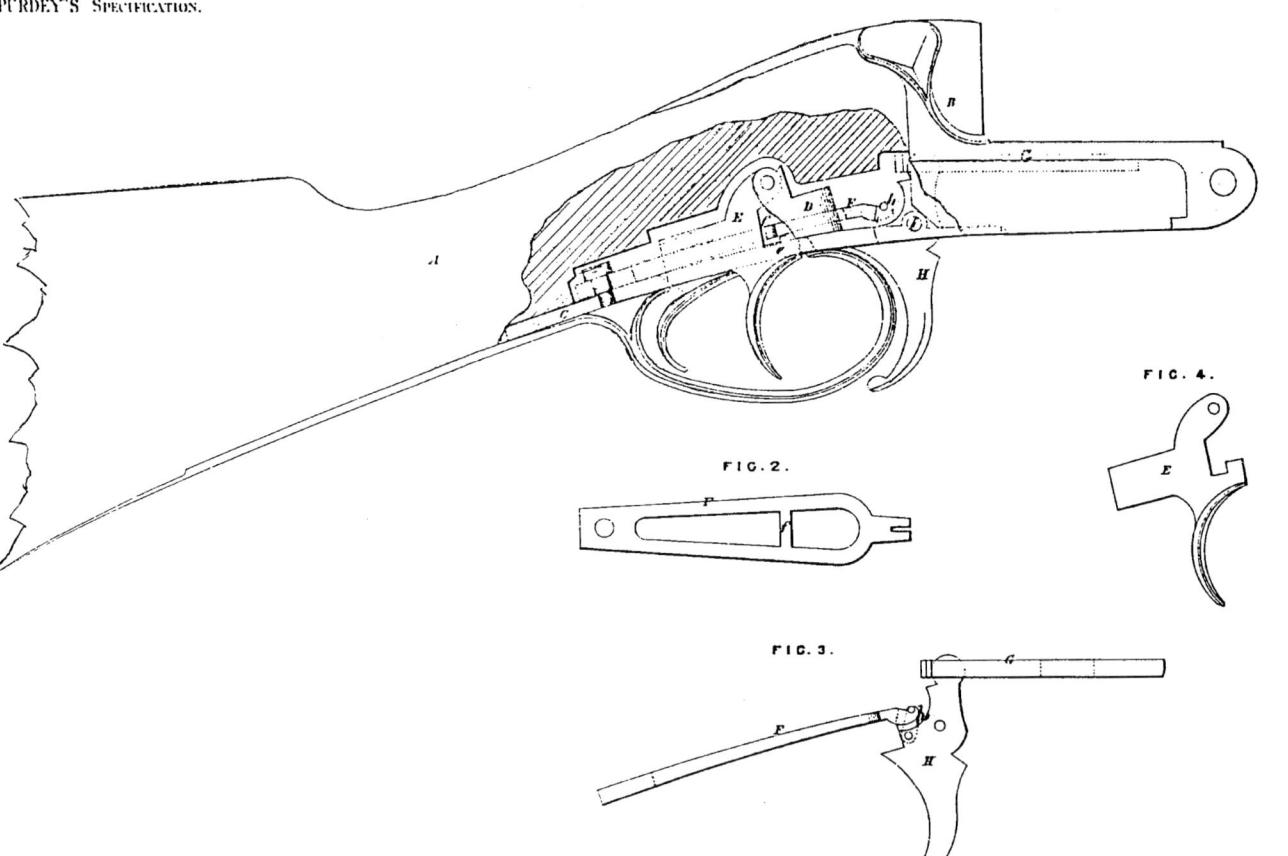

The filed drawing is partly colored.

London: Printed by George Edward Eyre and William Spottiswoode, Printers to the Queen's most Excellent Majesty. 1871.

Drawn on Stone by Malby & Sons

Above: Provisional patent no. 3118 – 28 November 1870 – Trigger Safety Lock

Below: Provisional patent no. 397 – 30 January 1878 – Third Fastening

AD.1878. Jan. 30. N° 397.
PURDEY'S SPECIFICATION.

(1 SHEET)

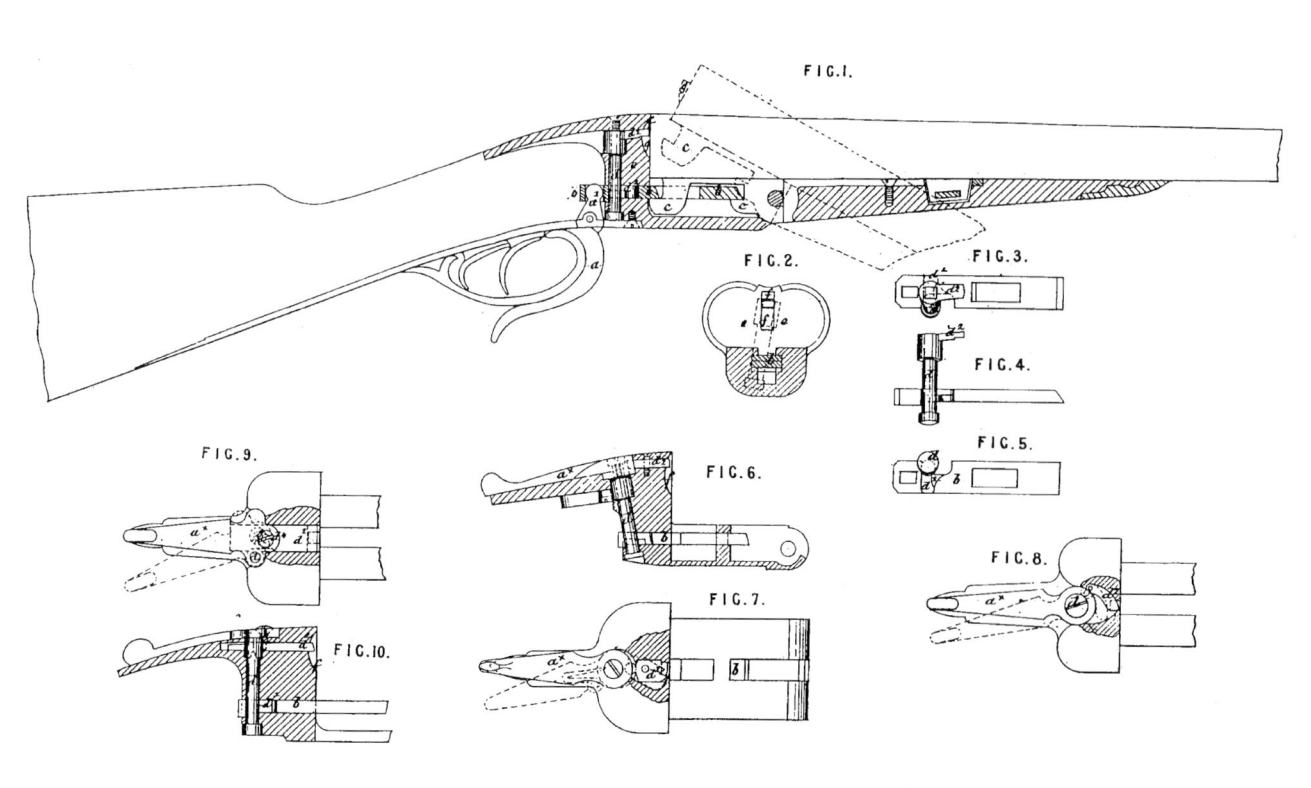

FIG. 1.

FIG. 2. FIG. 3.

FIG. 4.

FIG. 5.

FIG. 9. FIG. 6.

FIG. 8.

FIG. 10. FIG. 7.

London: Printed by George Edward Eyre and William Spottiswoode, Printers to the Queen's most Excellent Majesty. 1878.

Malby & Sons, Photo-Litho.

JAMES PURDEY AND SONS PATENTS

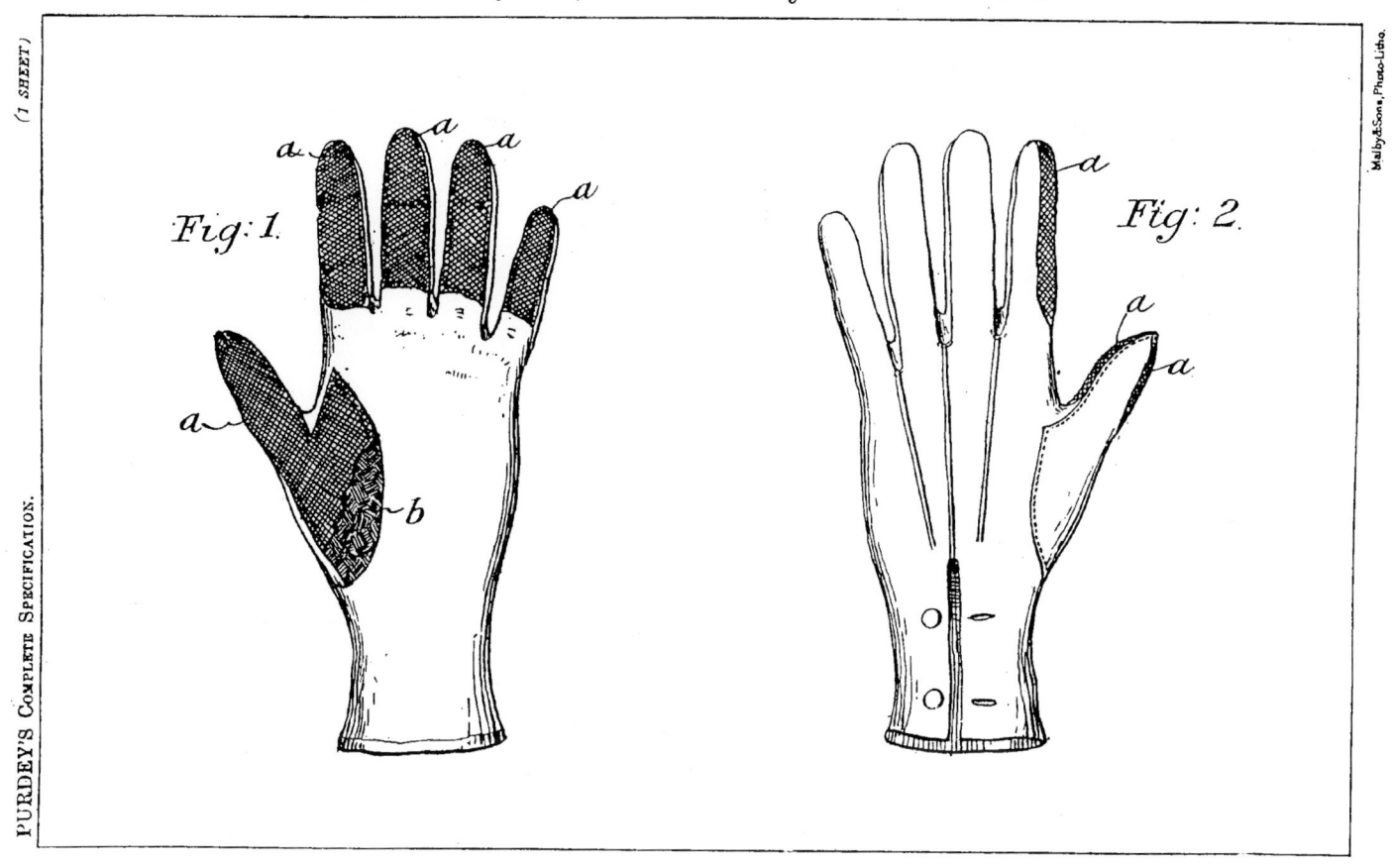

Above: Provisional patent no. 19027 – 17 August 1897 – Padded Left-Hand Glove

Below: Provisional patent no. 5150 – 1 March 1910 – Single Trigger

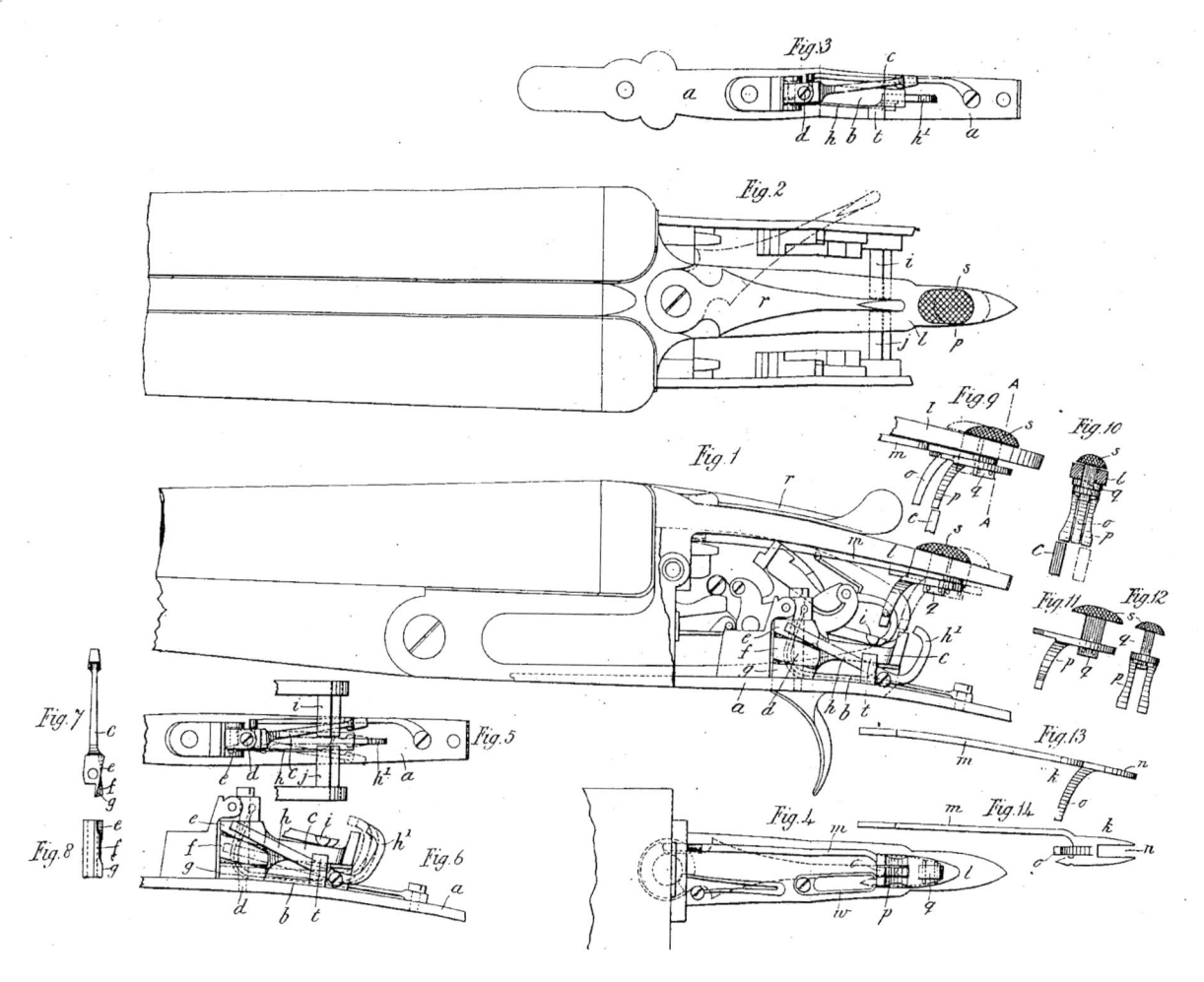

APPENDICES

The tube was tapered at its inner end to facilitate the bullet entering the grooves. The end result was supposed to be a far higher velocity for the bullet.

Patent no. 397
Although the Purdey bolt was perfectly secure for most purposes, a third fastening might be desirable in some circumstances where larger loads might be used, e.g. pigeon guns, wildfowling guns. In this patent, James Purdey invented an additional bolt, the 'Third Fastening' for such weapons. Two types of action are shown in the patent, a snap under lever (figure 1) and a top lever (figures 6-10). Both used essentially the same system of operation. The vertical spindle (d) had a small bolt (d2) attached to its upper part. When either opening lever is operated, the spindle (d) will turn withdrawing the standard Purdey bolt (b) as well as withdrawing the small upper bolt (d2) from the projection (g) on the rear end of the barrels. Upon closure, the small bolt (d2) will turn round to lock the projection on the rear of the barrels. This small additional bolt is known as the 'Third Bite' or 'Third Fastening'.

Patent no. 19027
This was Athol Purdey's first patent. During rapid fire, the barrels could become very hot and uncomfortable to hold. A left-hand glove was padded with a material like asbestos to afford protection.

Patent no. 5150
This was a system utilising a swinging arm. The swinging arm (c) is shown in figure 7 and figure 5. At the forward end of the arm there were three inclined planes (e, f, g). The movement of the arm was effected by a spring lever (h). Figure 5 shows the arm to the right and the gun ready to fire. Upon the first pull, the arm pushes up the lock sear (i), discharge takes place and under pressure of the spring lever (h) working on the inclines of the swinging arm (c), the arm moves to the central position between the two sears. The second involuntary pull saw the arm between the two sears. Upon relaxing the grip on the trigger, the arm was then pushed to the left by the inclined plane and upon the third pull, the arm pushes up the left lock sear (j) to discharge the left barrel.

Patent no. 21822
This was basically the same as the previous patent. Where it differed, was that in the swinging arm (a) there were only two inclines (e and f). With the swinging arm (a) on the right position under the right sear (d), discharge could take place on the first pull. The arm then moved to the centre powered by the spring lever working on the incline and the second

Provisional patent no. 21822 – 3 October 1911 – Single Trigger

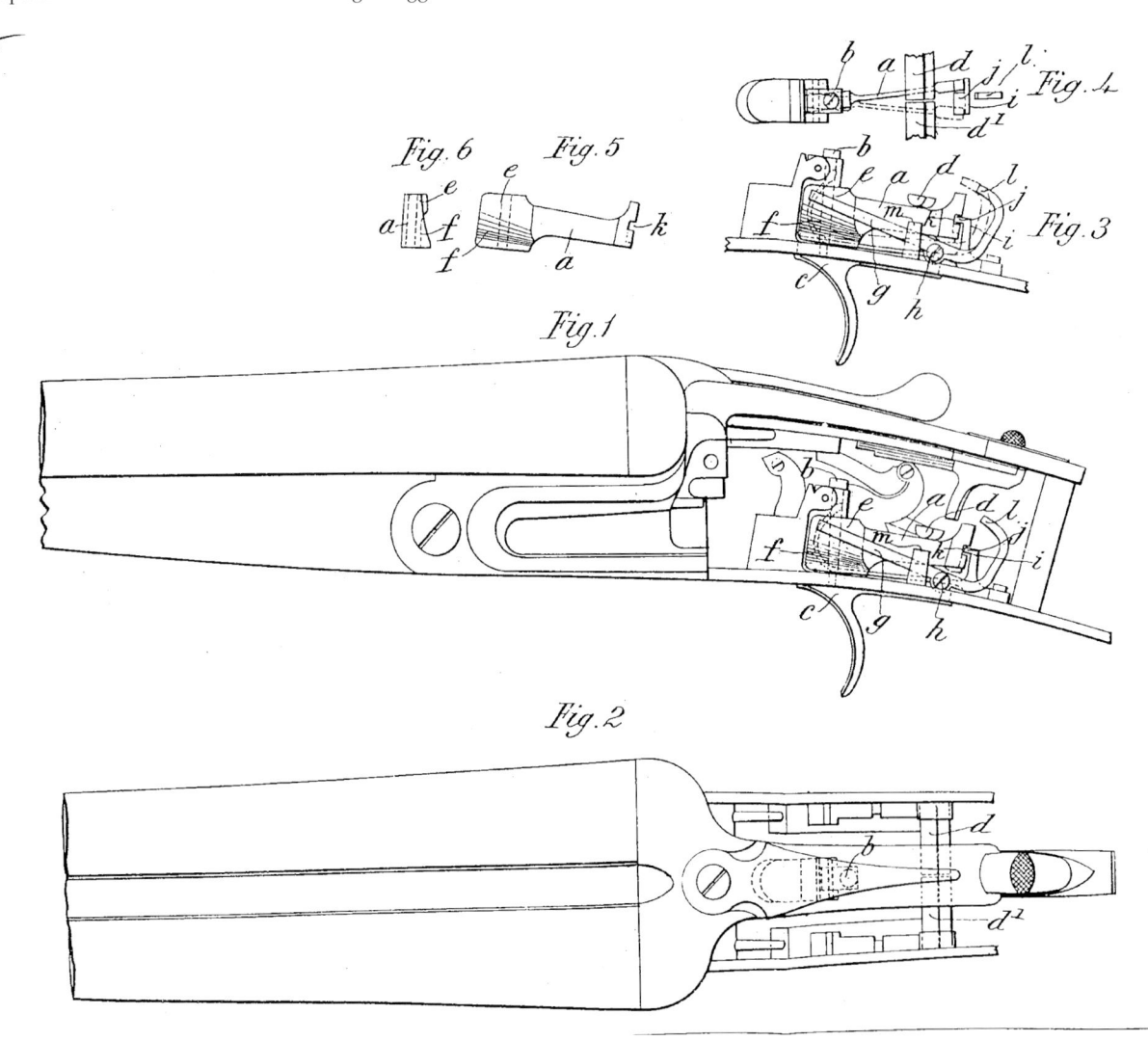

JAMES PURDEY AND SONS PATENTS

A.D. 1915, Feb. 27. N° 3188.
PURDEY'S COMPLETE SPECIFICATION.
(1 SHEET)

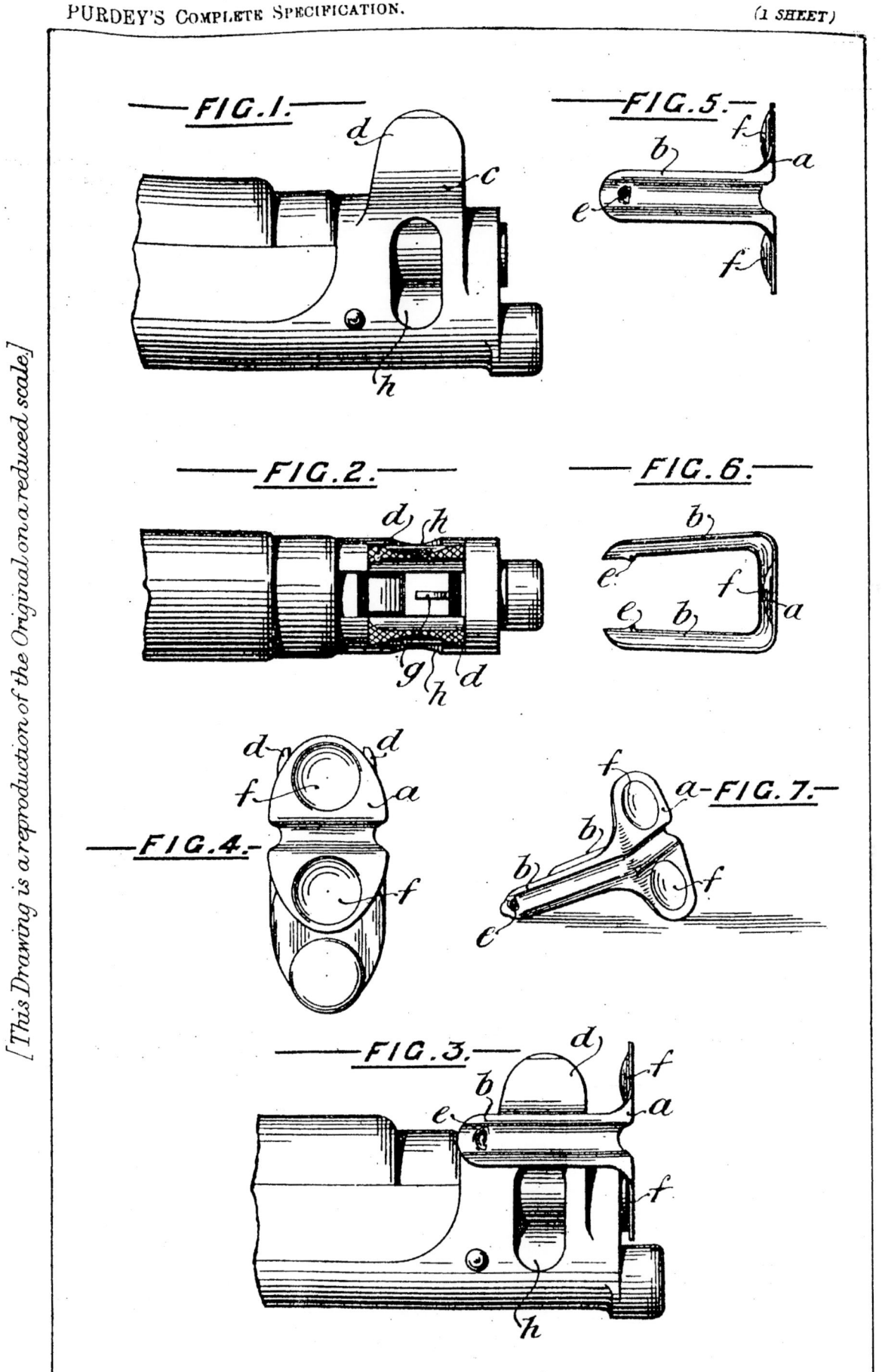

[This Drawing is a reproduction of the Original on a reduced scale.]

Provisional patent no. 3188 – 27 February 1915 – Muzzle Protector

involuntary pull took place. The arm was locked in this position by an interceptor (i). Upon relaxing the grip on the trigger, the arm was then pushed to the left by the spring powered inclined plane and when the trigger was pulled for the third time, the left sear (d1) would be lifted and discharge take place.

Patent no. 3188
This was designed to be used with the Lee Enfield service rifle. The device covered the muzzle to prevent ingress of mud, yet at the same time, offered little obstruction if the rifle was discharged without removing the protector. The protector was double-ended and could be used either way, one end blocking the sight to warn the soldier of its attachment.

Patent no. 5523
This patent remained as a Provisional Specification only, hence there are no drawings. In a shooting stick with a padded seat, the seat was formed with shallow holes to permit the insertion of cartridges, primer end uppermost. For thin leather seats, a flexible strip of leather with holes cut out for cartridges was attached above the seat.

Patent no. 19052
This was a very similar patent to patent no. 5523. A piece of leather, with holes cut out for cartridges, had clips on it for clipping over a shooting stick or shooting bag.

Patent no. 14943
The cartridge consisted of a long metal outer tube with a small projecting lens (2) at the front end. This cartridge was designed to fit into the barrel of a gun. Within this tube is fitted another tube containing at the front end, a light bulb (5) and two batteries (6) and at the rear end a tubular extension (7) about the size of an ordinary cartridge. This tubular extension contained a set of electrical contacts (8 and 13). When the gun is closed, the sliding sleeve (11) is pushed forward and the contact pin (13) comes into close proximity with the other contact (8). When the gun is fired, the striker pushes forward the contact pin (13) and electrical contact is made causing illumination to take place. Upon opening the gun, the sliding sleeve resumes its normal position and the circuit is broken.

Patent no. 15985
A normal walking stick was fitted with a folding trigger (3). This trigger made a realistic click upon being pulled due to the action of a spring (10) striking the block (4).

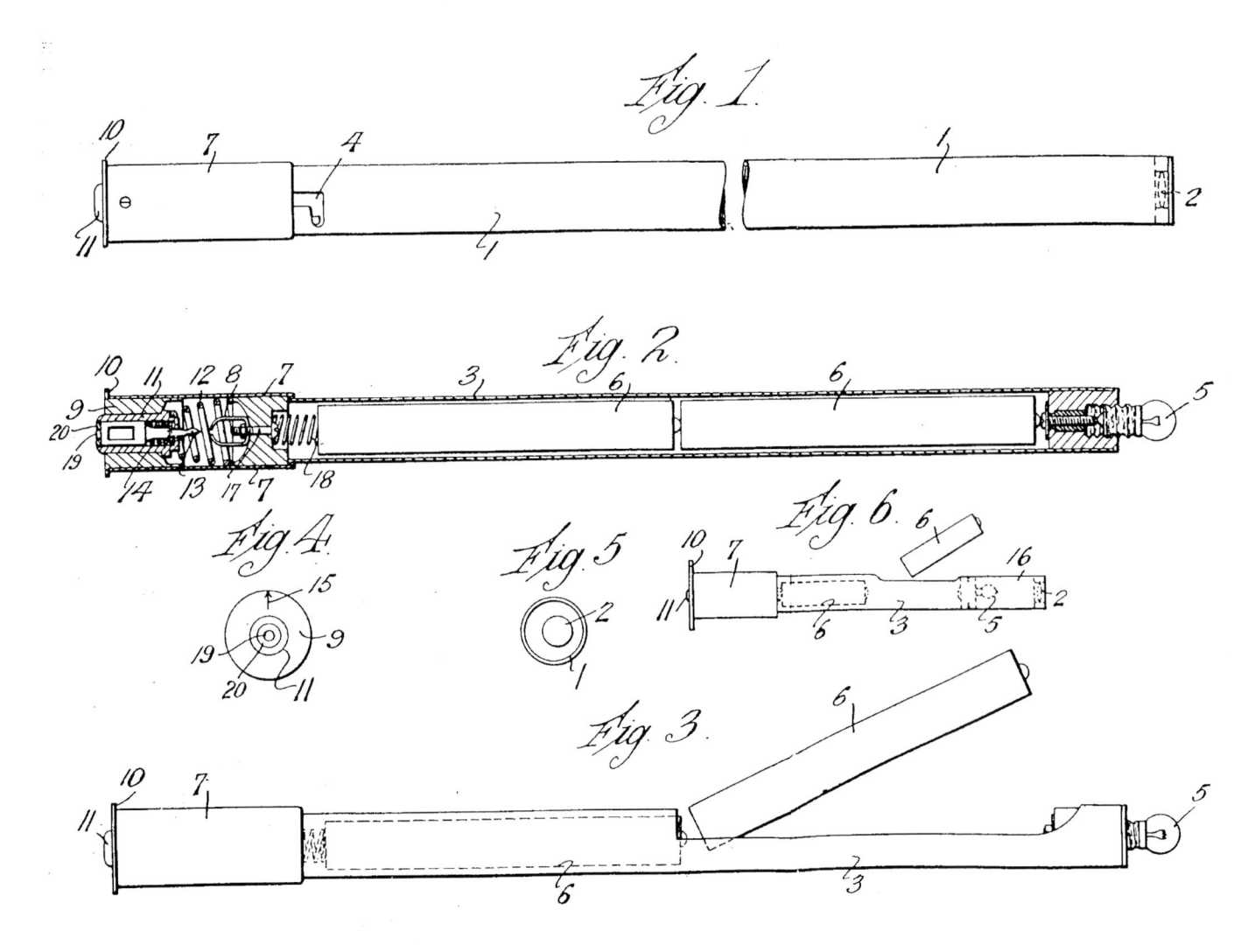

Provisional patent no. 14943 – 13 May 1929 – Electric Cartridge

JAMES PURDEY AND SONS PATENTS

271,570   COMPLETE SPECIFICATION   1 SHEET

Fig. 1.

Fig. 2.

Fig. 3.

Fig. 4.

[This Drawing is a reproduction of the Original on a reduced scale]

Charles & Read Ltd. Photo Litho.

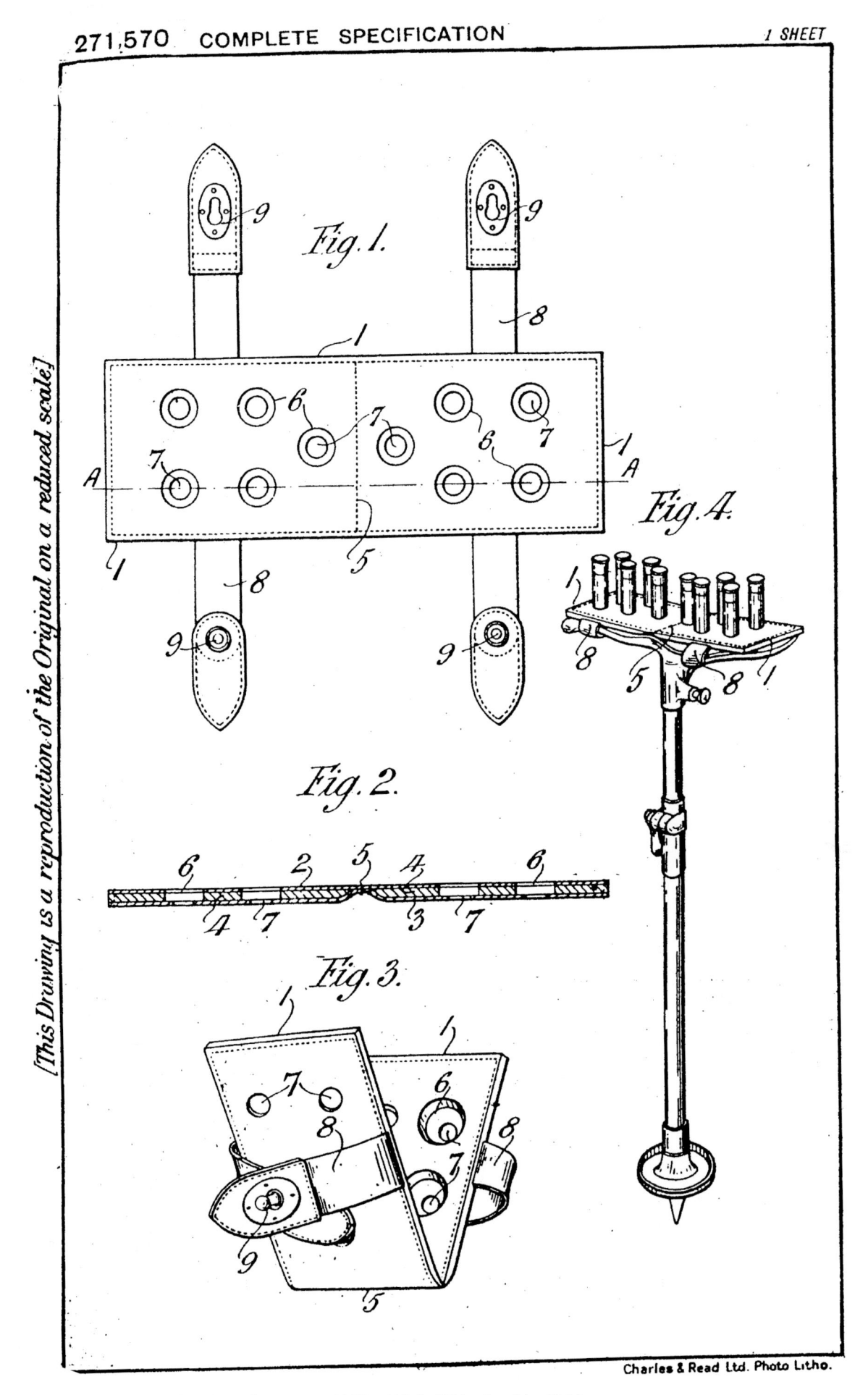

Provisional patent no. 19052 – 30 July 1926 – Cartridge Holders

APPENDICES

233,935 COMPLETE SPECIFICATION 1 SHEET

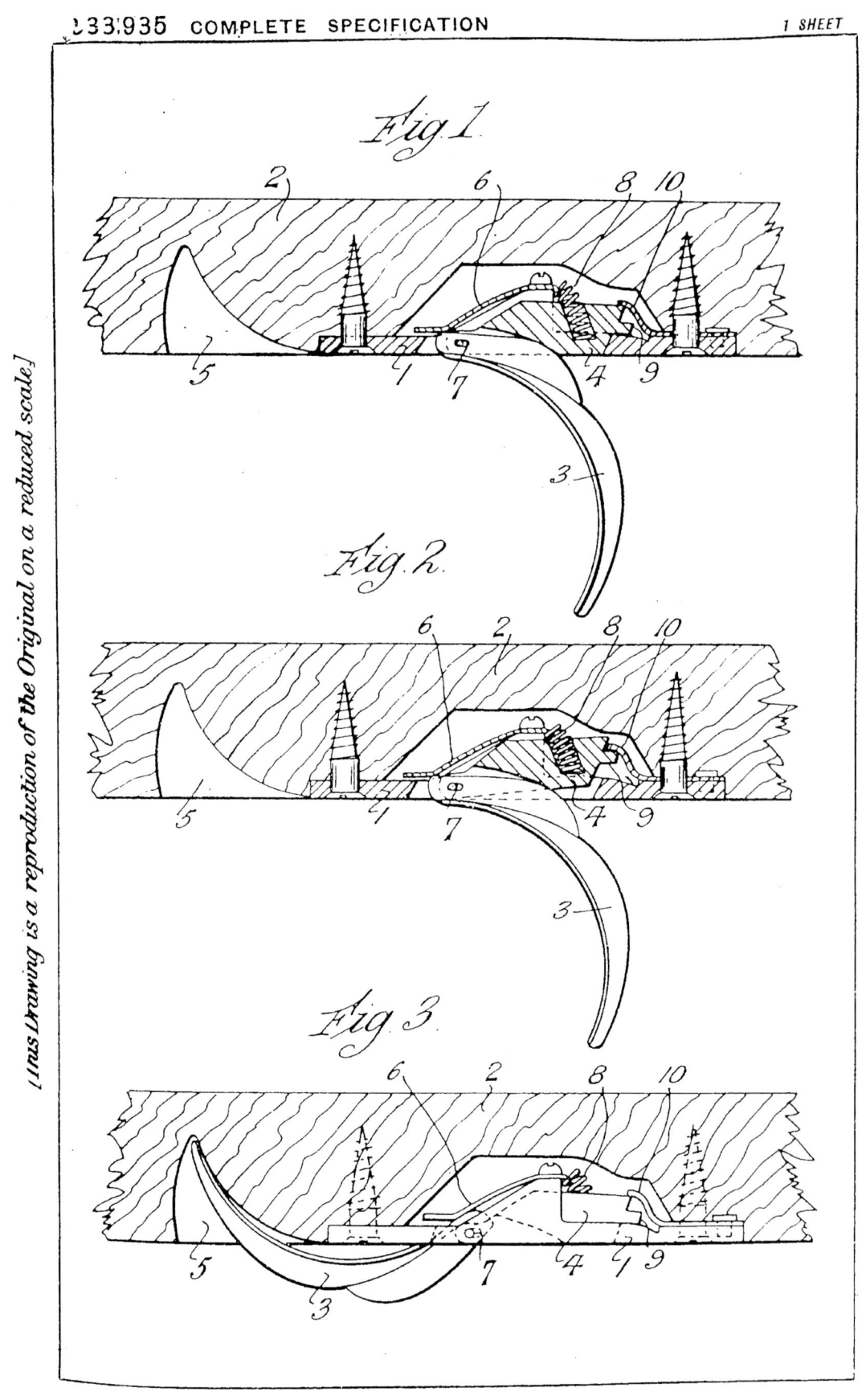

Fig. 1.

Fig. 2.

Fig. 3.

[This Drawing is a reproduction of the Original on a reduced scale.]

Charles & Read Ltd. Photo Litho.

Provisional patent no. 15985 – 23 May 1929 – Walking Stick

Appendix 9

TOM PURDEY'S NOTEBOOK 1921

Tom Purdey produced a notebook in the 1920s primarily to assist him on his trips abroad. The notebook consisted of drawings of all the parts of the Purdey gun, details on cartridge charges and patterns, how to measure for a gun, possible faults, gun prices, etc. The notebook is lengthy and I have reproduced the drawings only. Harry Lawrence did the drawings for the notebook.

RECEIPT OF ORDER IN FACTORY

At the end of the notebook is a detailed account of how a Purdey gun is made entitled: 'Receipt of Order in Factory'.

1. Reckonings to be made as to what weight and balance barrels are to be made, and what gauges to be used.
2. Type of action to be ordered; thickness of back and bar, weight, etc.
3. Barrels started making (2 tubes, top rib, bottom rib, stays and loop).
4. Barrels viewed.
5. Barrels passed out actioner plus action and fore-end machining (bolt, lever spindle, safety slide, and thumbpiece forgings; a pair of locks, lever, safety and 2 plunger springs, steel for pins and lugger machining).
6. Action viewed.
7. Barrels, action and fore-end, etc given out for ejectoring (2 mainsprings, 2 side springs and 2 ejector rod forgings, steel for cams, lifters etc).
8. Ejector viewed.
9. Furniture ordered and made. Same viewed.
10. Stock ordered and picked according to weight of gun and type required.
11. Given out for stocking (barrels, action etc., stock, fore-end wood, fore-end snap, tail pipe forging, furniture, pin forgings).
12. Viewed for stocking.
13. Gun stripped.
14. Stripping viewed.
15. Gun taken to pieces.
16. Action, etc. polished and burnished.
17. Engraving and inlaying.
18. Barrels bored for shooting.
19. Action, etc. hardened.
20. Given out to finisher to get into half-finished state.
21. Barrels smoothed and balanced.
22. Gun sent to Grounds for shooting to be tested and corrected.
23. Gun weighed and jigged (ie. for weight, balance and test of measurements).
24. Given out to stocker to bore stock according to previous test and to clean out locks, etc. and chequer.
25. Weight and balance retested.
26. Gun given back to finisher to finally finish, ie. barrels engraved, measured and browned, work blued, stock oiled, etc.
27. Gun viewed, alterations made.
28. Finally shot and tested.
29. Viewed by Office, more alterations.
30. Measurements finally checked, and weight and balance of gun and barrels booked.

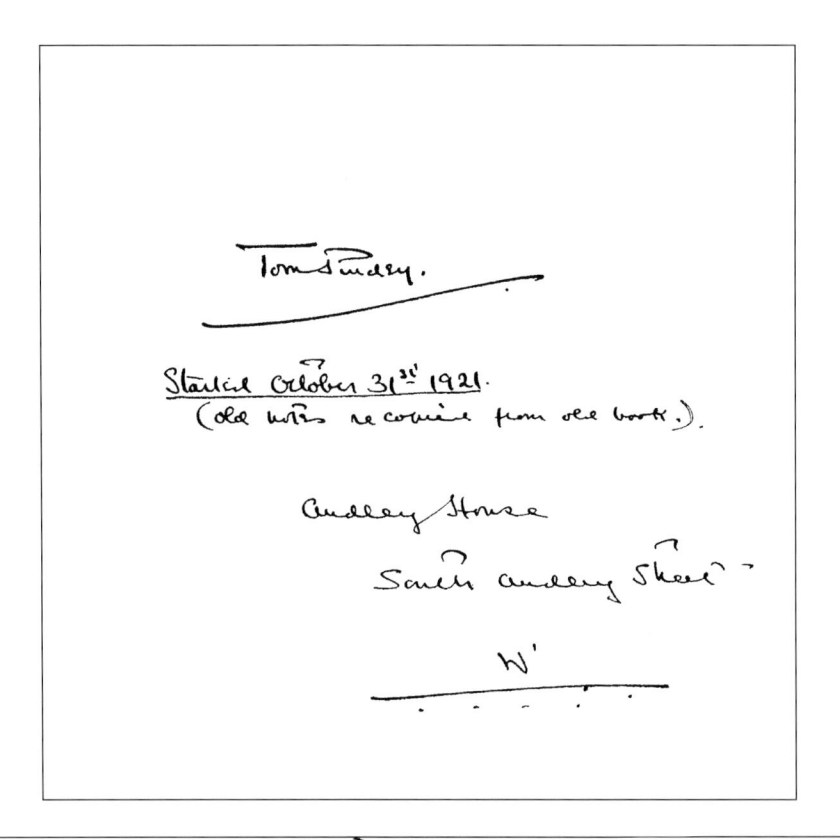

APPENDICES

Tom Purdey.

Started October 31st 1921.
(Old notes recovered from old book.)

Audley House
South Audley Street
W.

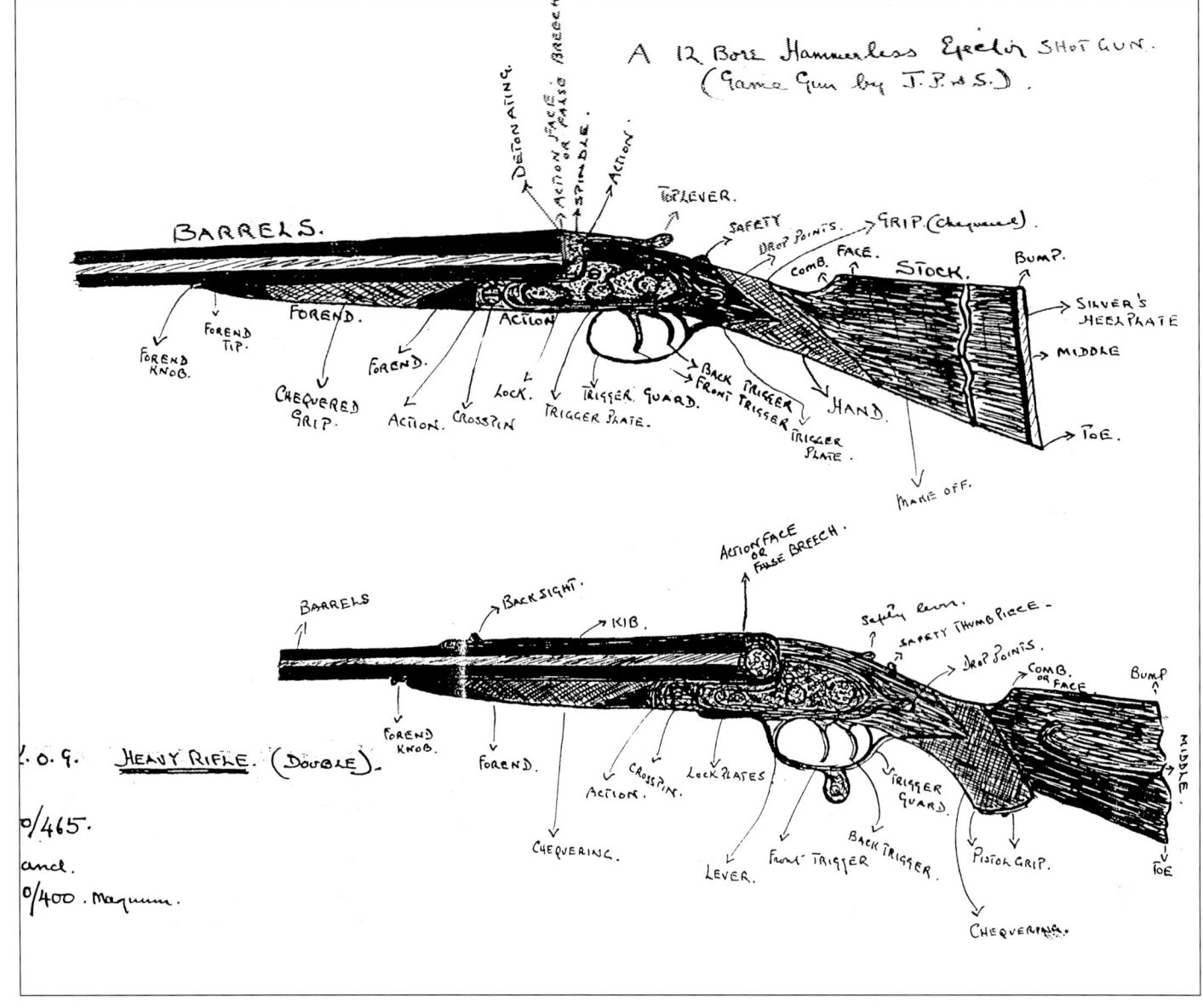

A 12 Bore Hammerless Ejector SHOT GUN.
(Game Gun by J.P. & S.)

Labels: Detonating; Action face or false breech; Spindle; Action; Top lever; Safety; Drop Points; Grip (Chequered); Comb. Face; Stock; Bump; Silver's Heel plate; Middle; Toe; Hand; Make off; Trigger Plate; Front Trigger; Back Trigger; Trigger Guard; Lock; Crosspin; Action; Forend; Chequered Grip; Forend Tip; Forend Knob; Barrels.

HEAVY RIFLE. (DOUBLE).
.465
and
.400 Magnum.

Labels: Barrels; Backsight; Rib; Action face or false breech; Safety lever; Safety Thumb Piece; Drop Points; Comb or Face; Bump; Middle; Toe; Pistol Grip; Back Trigger; Front Trigger; Trigger Guard; Lever; Lock Plates; Crosspin; Action; Chequering; Forend; Forend Knob.

The Parts of a Gun.

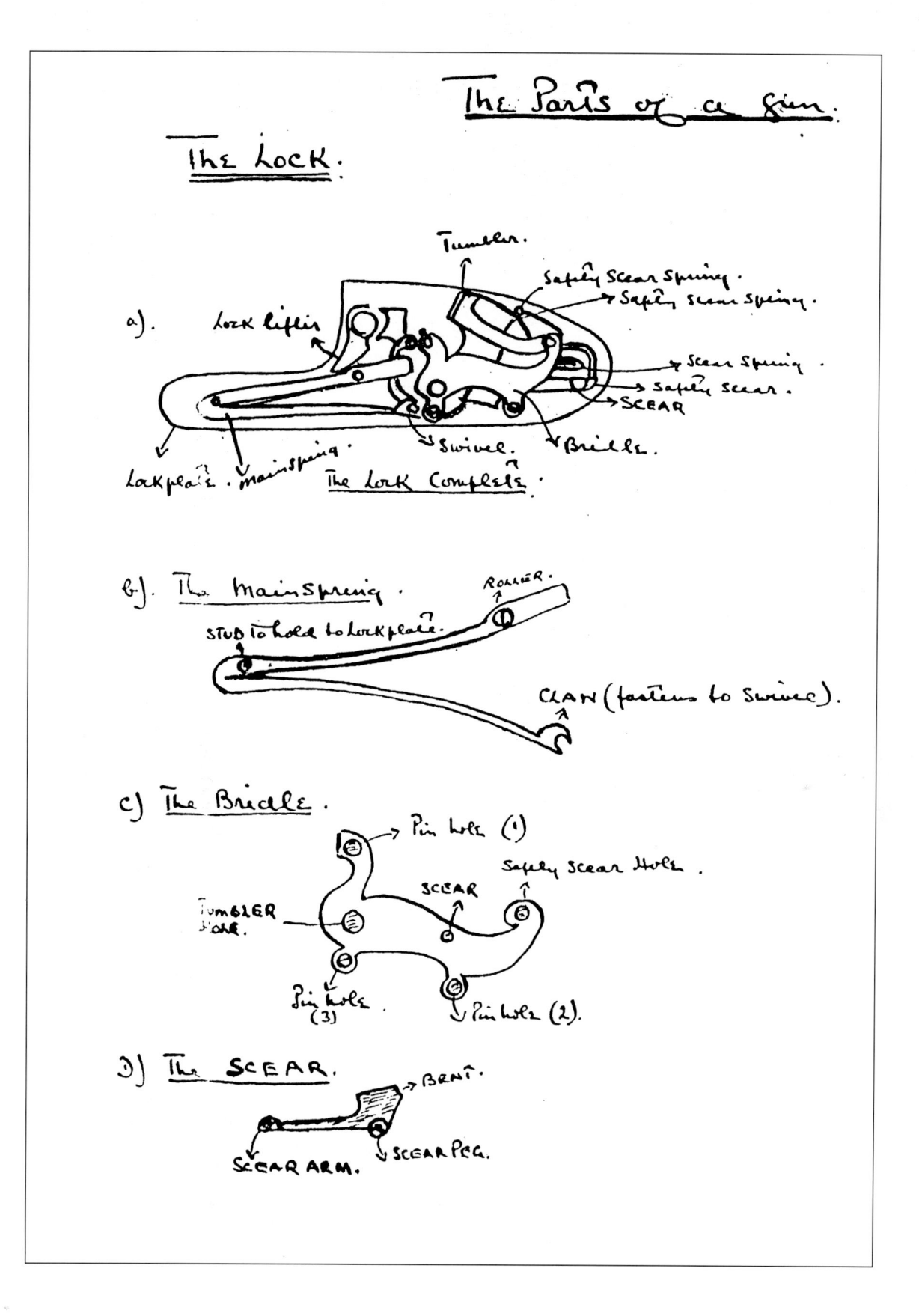

The Lock.

a). *The Lock Complete.*

Labels: Tumbler, Safety Scear Spring, Safety Scear Spring, Lock lifter, Scear Spring, Safety Scear, Scear, Lockplate, Mainspring, Swivel, Bridle.

b). **The Mainspring.**

Labels: Roller, Stud to hold to Lockplate, Claw (fastens to Swivel).

c) **The Bridle.**

Labels: Pin hole (1), Safety Scear Hole, Tumbler Hole, Scear, Pin hole (3), Pin hole (2).

d) **The Scear.**

Labels: Bent, Scear Arm, Scear Peg.

4 The PARTS of a gun. (cont'd)

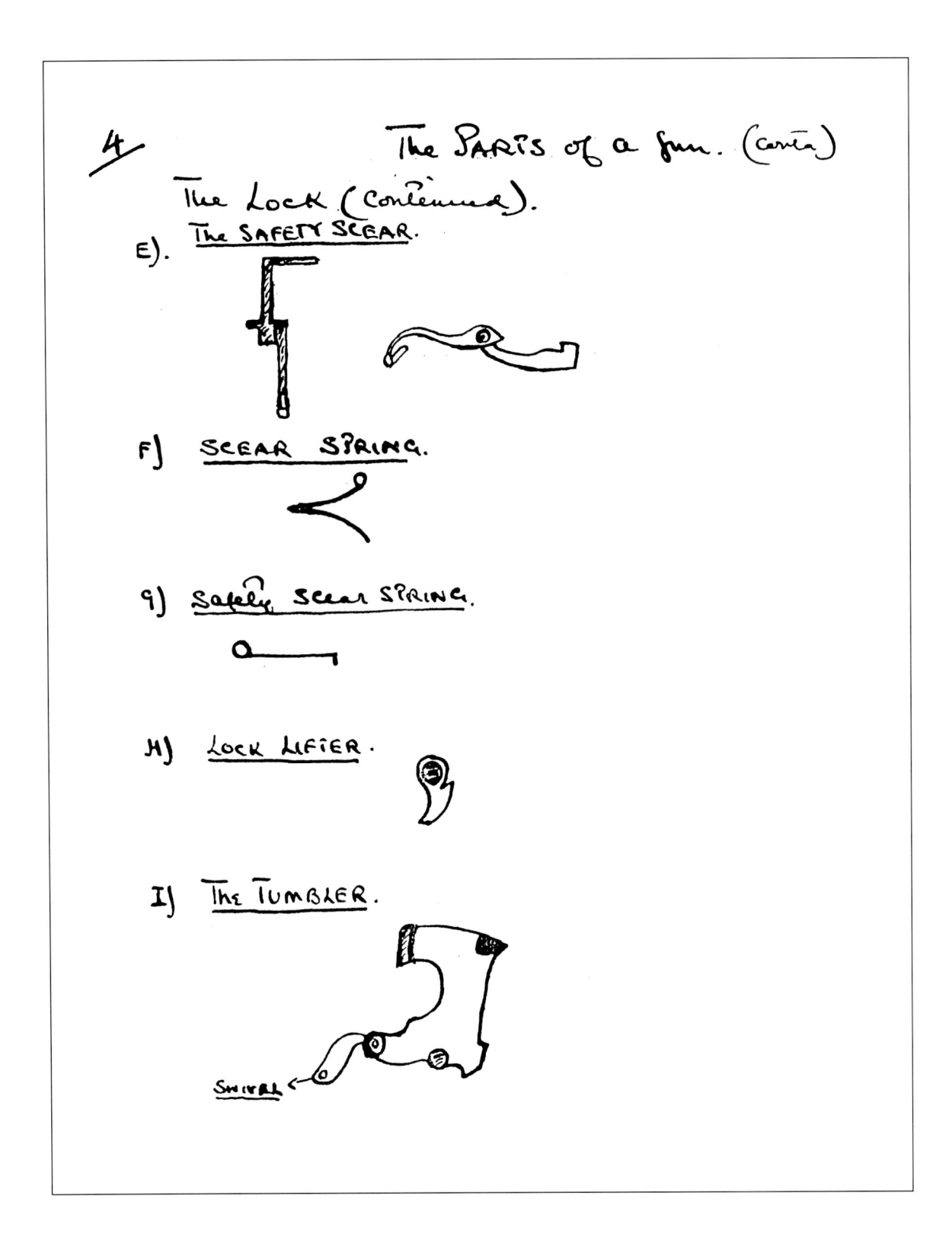

The Lock (continued).

E). THE SAFETY SCEAR.

F) SCEAR SPRING.

G) Safety SCEAR SPRING.

H) LOCK LIFTER.

I) THE TUMBLER.

SWIVEL

The Parts of a Gun.

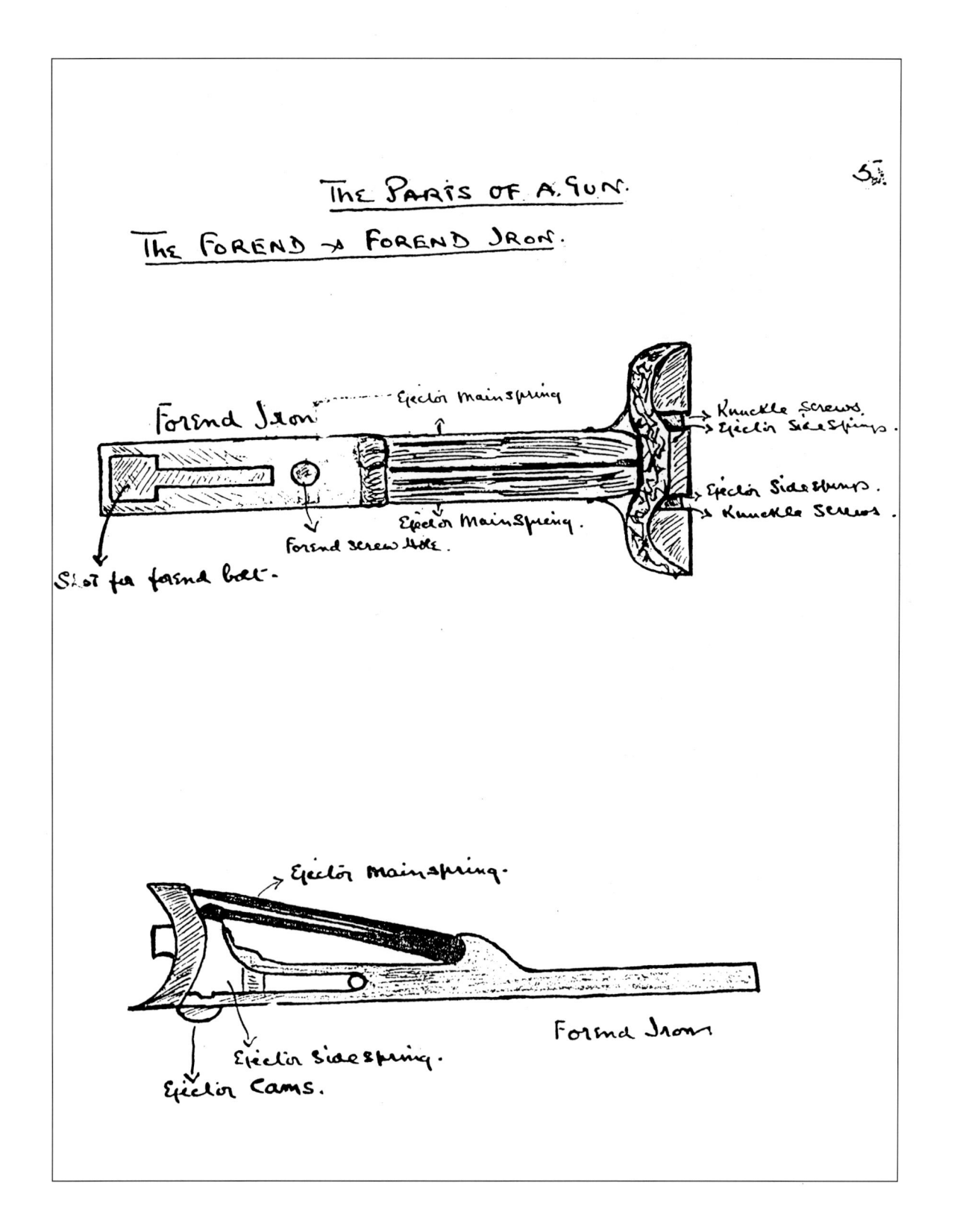

The Forend & Forend Iron.

Forend Iron

- Ejector Mainspring
- Knuckle Screws
- Ejector Sidesprings
- Ejector Mainspring.
- Ejector Sidebumps.
- Knuckle Screws.
- Forend screw hole.
- Slot for forend bolt.

- Ejector Mainspring.
- Forend Iron
- Ejector Sidespring.
- Ejector Cams.

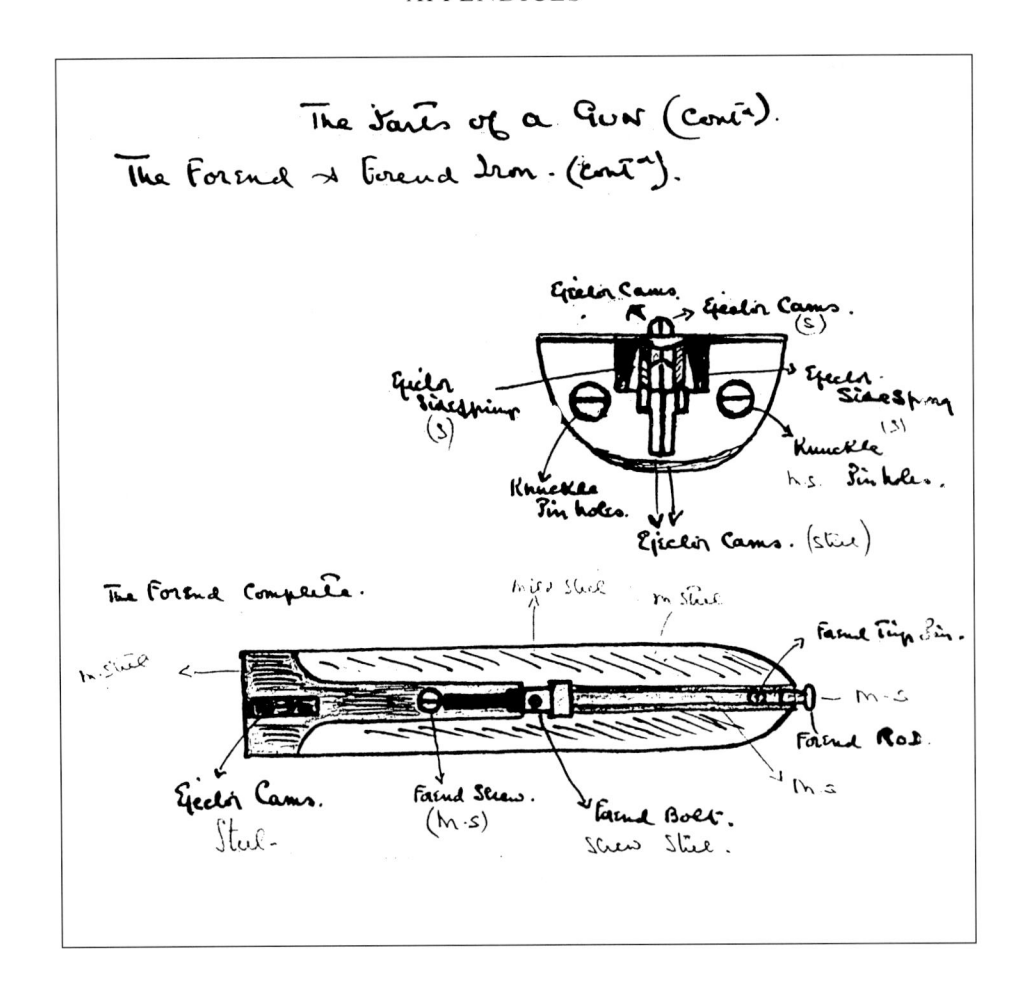

APPENDICES

The Parts of a Gun (Cont'd).
The Forend & Forend Iron. (Cont'd).

[Diagram of forend iron showing: Ejector Cams, Ejector Cams (S), Ejector Sidespring (S), Ejector Sidespring (S), Knuckle Pin holes, Knuckle Pin holes, Ejector Cams (steel)]

The Forend Complete.

[Diagram of complete forend showing: Mild Steel, m. Steel, Forend Tip Pin, M-S, Forend Rod, M-S, Ejector Cams Steel, Forend Screw (M-S), Forend Bolt Screw Steel.]

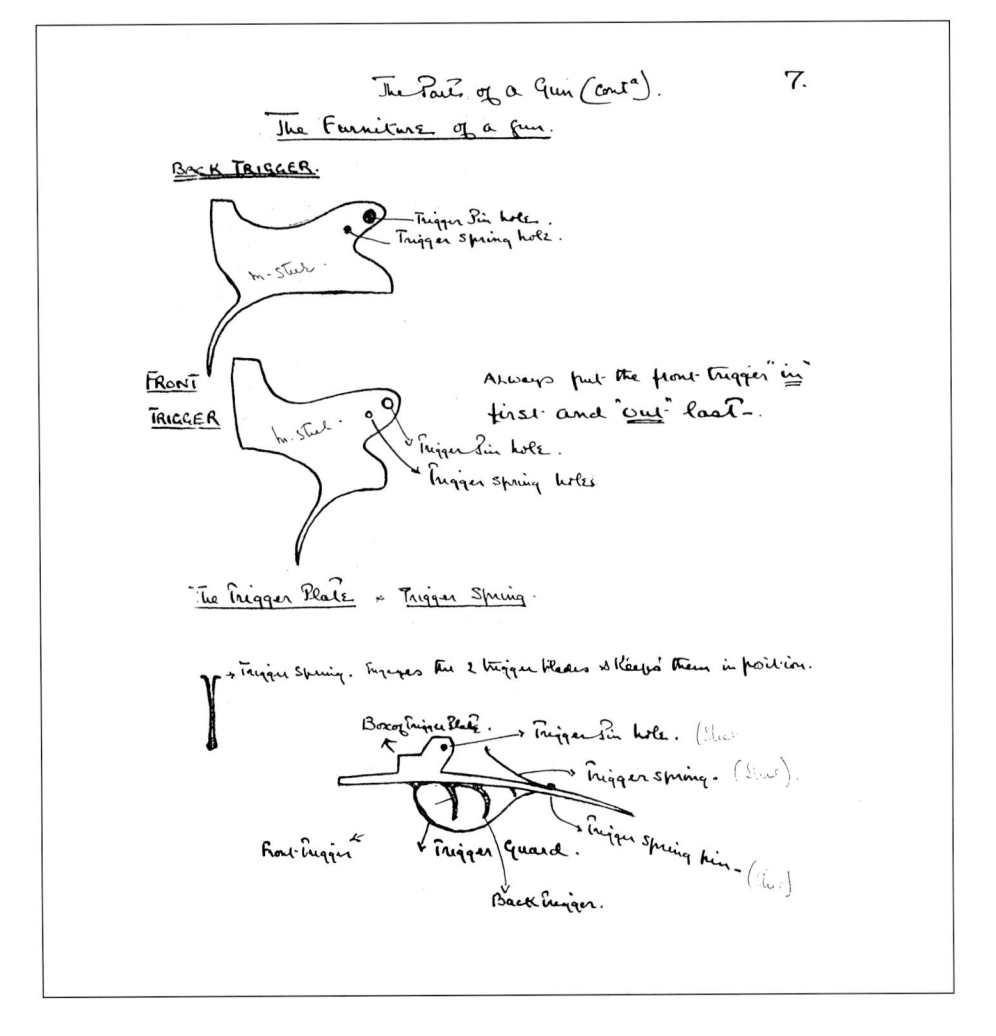

The Parts of a Gun (Cont'd). 7.
The Furniture of a Gun.

BACK TRIGGER.

[Diagram of back trigger: m-Steel, Trigger Pin hole, Trigger spring hole.]

FRONT TRIGGER

[Diagram of front trigger: m-Steel, Trigger Pin hole, Trigger spring hole.]

Always put the front trigger "in" first and "out" last.

The Trigger Plate & Trigger Spring.

→ Trigger Spring. Engages the 2 trigger blades & keeps them in position.

[Diagram showing: Box of Trigger Plate, Trigger Pin hole (steel), Trigger spring (steel), Trigger spring pin (m.s), Front Trigger, Trigger Guard, Back Trigger.]

TOM PURDEY'S NOTEBOOK 1921

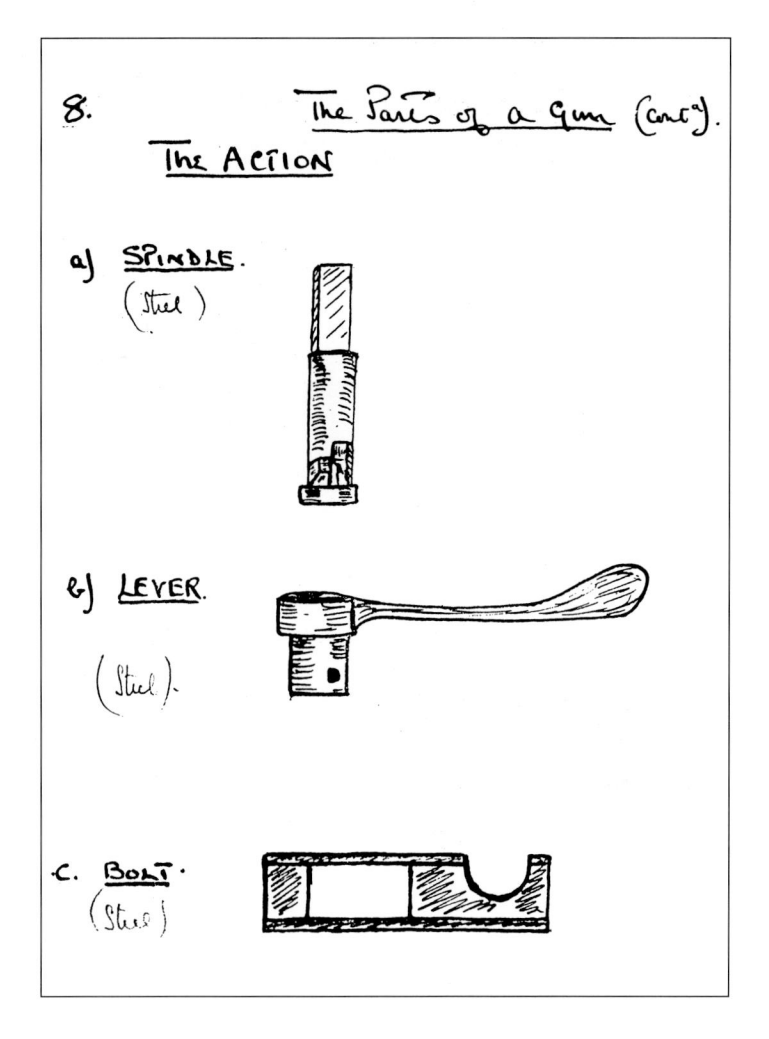

8. ___The Parts of a Gun (cont'd)___

___The Action___

a) ___SPINDLE___.
(Steel)

b) ___LEVER___.
(Steel).

c. ___BOLT___.
(Steel)

The parts of a gun (cont'd).

___The Action___ (cont'd).

D. ___The Disc___. (Steel)
Disc Keyhole → ⊙ ← disc keyhole
→ Plunger Hole.

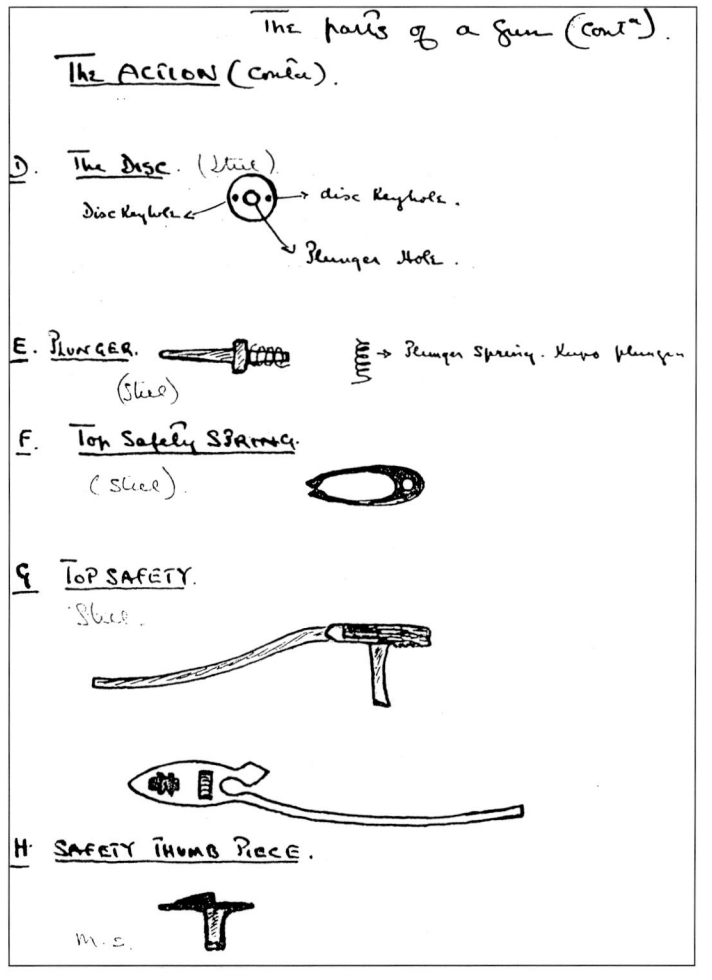

E. ___Plunger___.
(Steel) → Plunger Spring. keeps plunger

F. ___Top Safety Spring___.
(Steel)

G. ___Top Safety___.
Steel.

H. ___Safety Thumb Piece___.
M.S.

10.   The Parts of a Gun (Cont'd).

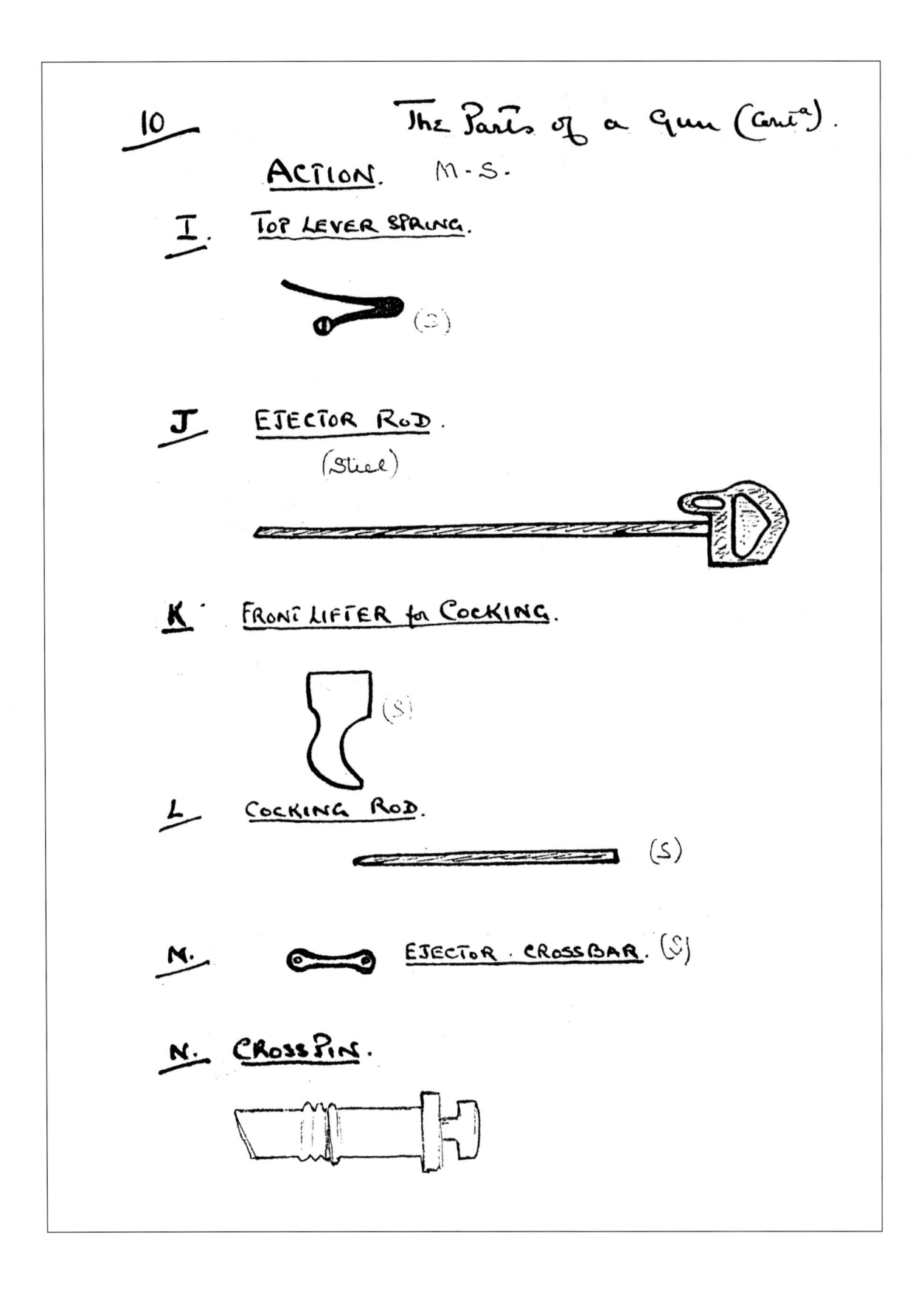

ACTION. M·S.

I. TOP LEVER SPRING.

J. EJECTOR ROD.
(Steel)

K. FRONT LIFTER for COCKING.

L. COCKING ROD.

M. EJECTOR CROSSBAR. (S)

N. CROSS PIN.

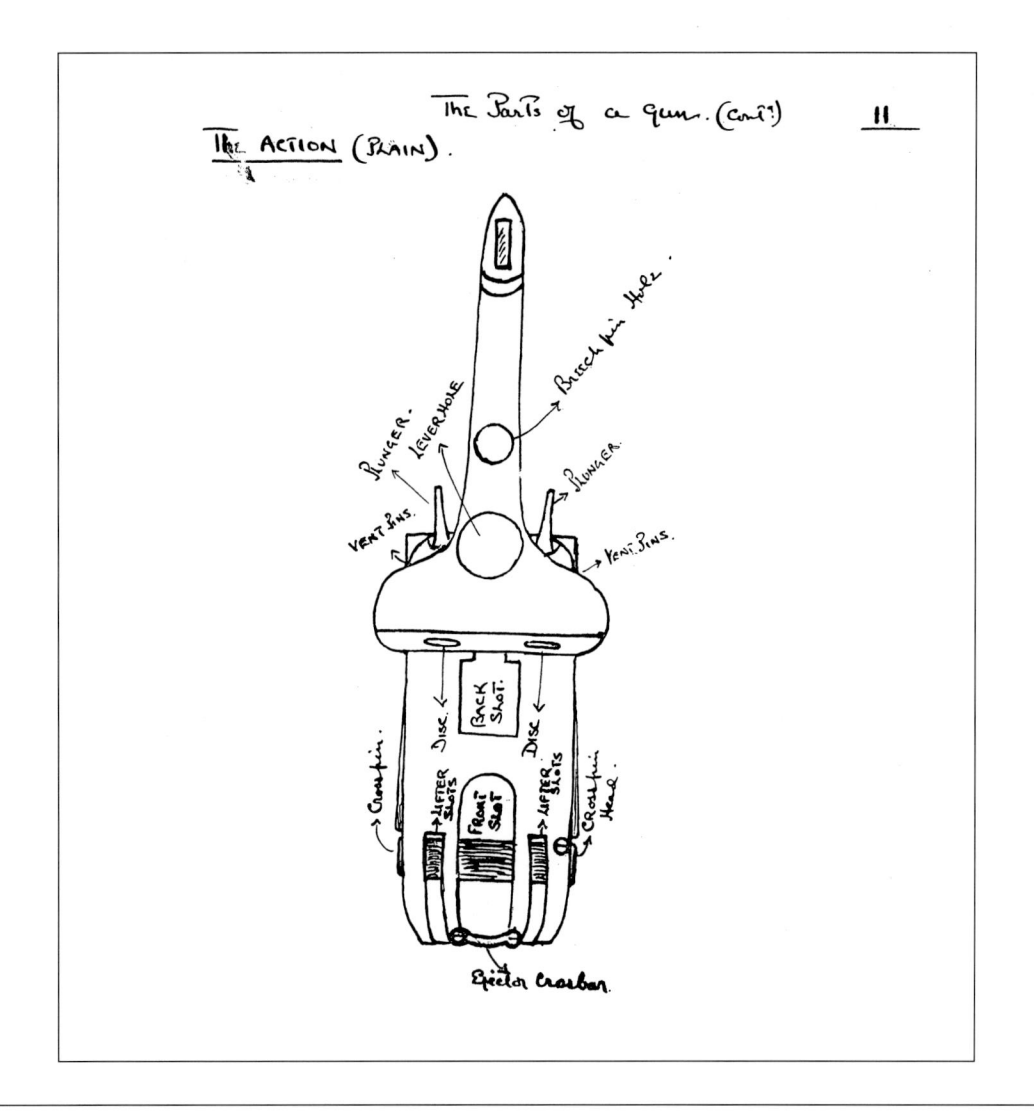

TOM PURDEY'S NOTEBOOK 1921

The Parts of a gun. (Cont?) 11

THE ACTION (PLAIN).

- Plunger.
- Lever Hole.
- Vent Pins.
- Breech Pin Hole.
- Plunger.
- Vent Pins.
- Crosspin.
- Disc.
- Back Shot.
- Disc.
- Crosspin Hole.
- Lifter Slots.
- Front Shot.
- Lifter Slots.
- Ejector Crossbar.

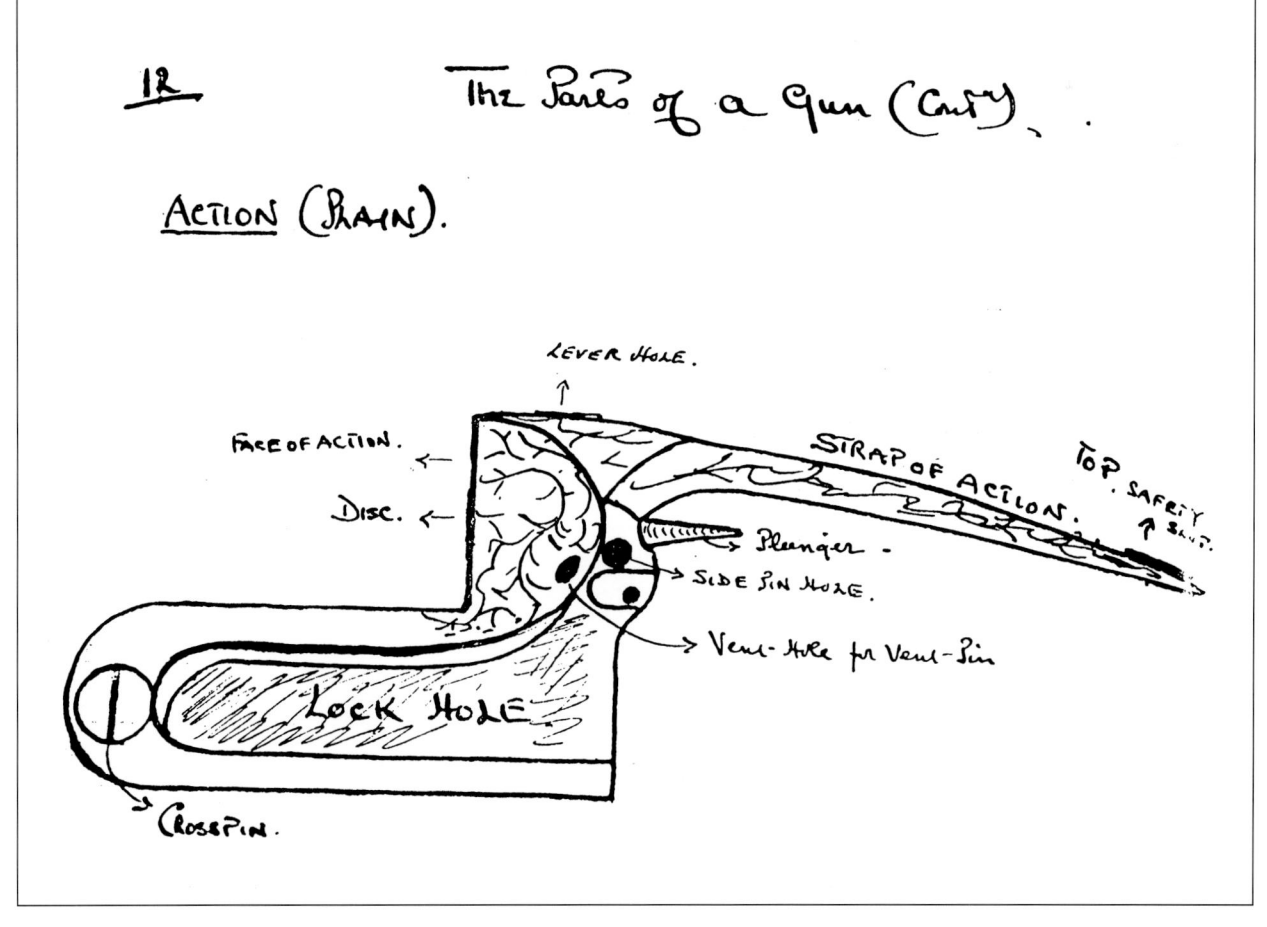

12 The Parts of a Gun (Cont?).

ACTION (PLAIN).

- Lever Hole.
- Face of Action.
- Strap of Action.
- Top Safety Shot.
- Disc.
- Plunger.
- Side Pin Hole.
- Vent-Hole for Vent-Pin.
- Lock Hole.
- Crosspin.

Appendix 10

PURDEY MASTERS OF THE WORSHIPFUL COMPANY OF GUNMAKERS

Since 1841 the Purdey family or members of the Purdey firm have provided twenty-eight Masters of the Worshipful Company of Gunmakers. Only the Barnett family of gunmakers has bettered this total, providing thirty Masters between 1761 and 1843.

1841	James Purdey the Elder.
1874	James Purdey the Younger.
1882	James Purdey the Younger
1890	Athol Stuart Purdey
1892	James Purdey the Younger
1899	Athol Stuart Purdey
1902	Cecil Onslow Purdey
1908	Athol Stuart Purdey
1911	Cecil Onslow Purdey
1921	Athol Stuart Purdey
1923	Cecil Onslow Purdey
1928	Thomas Donald Stuart Purdey
1931	James Alexander Purdey
1934	Cecil Onslow Purdey
1940	Thomas Donald Stuart Purdey
1941	James Alexander Purdey
1951	Thomas Donald Stuart Purdey
1954	Charles Harry Lawrence
1956	Victor Basil John Seely
1962	Charles Harry Lawrence
1964	Victor Basil John Seely
1966	James Oliver Kinloch Purdey
1968	The Honourable Richard Blackett Beaumont
1975	Ernest Douglas Lawrence
1976	Lawrence Peter David Salter
1984	The Honourable Richard Blackett Beaumont
1985	Ernest Douglas Lawrence
1986	Lawrence Peter David Salter

SELECT BIBLIOGRAPHY AND SOURCES

BIBLIOGRAPHY:

The Badminton Library, *Shooting Field and Covert* – Lord Walsingham & Sir Ralph Payne-Gallwey, London 1900.

Boss & Co., Builders of Best Guns Only – Donald Dallas, Quiller Press, London 1995.

The British Shotgun Volume I – I N Crudgington & D J Baker, Barrie & Jenkins, London 1979; The British Shotgun Volume II – Ashford, Sledfield 1989.

Early Percussion Firearms – Lewis Winant, Herbert Jenkins, London 1959.

The Early Purdeys – Patrick Unsworth, Christie's, London 1996.

Experts on Guns and Shooting – G T Teasdale-Buckell, London 1900.

Forsyth & Company, Patent Gunmakers – W Keith Neal & D H L Back, G Bell & Sons, London 1969.

Game Guns and Rifles – Richard Akehurst, G Bell & Sons, London 1969.

The Gun and its Development – W W Greener, Cassell & Co., London 1910.

Instructions to Young Sportsmen, Etc., – Colonel Peter Hawker, Longman, Brown, Green & Longman, London 1833.

Letters to Young Shooters – Sir Ralph Payne-Gallwey, Longmans, Green & Co., London 1892.

London Gunmakers – Nigel Brown, Christie, Manson & Woods, London 1998.

The Mantons, Gunmakers – W Keith Neal & D H L Back, Herbert Jenkins, London 1967.

The Modern Shooter – Captain Richard Lacy, Whittaker & Co., London 1842.

The Modern Shotgun – Major Sir Gerald Burrard, Herbert Jenkins, London 1931

The Modern Sportsman's Gun and Rifle – J H Walsh, London 1884.

Purdeys, the Guns and the Family – Richard Beaumont, David & Charles, Devon 1984.

The Shotgun and Sporting Rifle – J H Walsh, Routledge, Warne & Routledge, London 1862.

MAGAZINES AND PERIODICALS:

Arms and Explosives
The Country Gentleman
The Field
Land and Water
Rod and Gun
The Shooting Times
The Sporting Magazine
The Sporting Mirror Advertiser
The Times
The Turf, Field and Farm

SOURCES:

1st Avenue house, High Holborn, London
The British Library, Euston Road, London
The Dimensions Books, sales ledgers and all other archives of James Purdey & Sons
English Heritage, Savile Row, London
Family Records Centre, Islington, London
The Guildhall Library, Aldermanbury, London
The London Metropolitan Archives, Northampton Road, London
The Mitchell Library, North Street, Glasgow
The National Library of Scotland, George IV Bridge, Edinburgh
Newspaper Library, Colindale Avenue, London
The Patent Office, Newport
The Public Record Office, Kew, London
Westminster City Archives, St. Ann Street, London

INDEX

acanthus detonating	167, 175	
A, B, C, D, E quality guns and rifles	74-80, 109, 131, 158, 167, 201	
Adams, William	82, 83	
adjustable breech elevation	62, 63	
Albert, Prince	26, 49	
Allport, Samuel B	74, 76	
Anson & Deeley Action	85	
apprenticeship	4, 6, 20, 21, 156, 157, 161	
Apted, John	81	
Arms and Explosives	120	
Ashburton, Lord	113, 122	
Aston	63, 157	
Atkin, Henry	16, 27, 110, 158	
Audley House		
Move to	100-103	
Coronation 1937	138, 139	
Bombing 1941	141, 142	
I.R.A. bomb 1975	151, 152	
Green Plaque 1992	153	

back action locks 60, 61
Badminton Library - Shooting -
  (Walsingham, Payne-Gallwey) 9, 110
Bagnall, Robert 15
Baker, John 20
Baker, William 120
bar-in-wood action 61
Barnett, gunmaking family 27
barrel records 193
base wad 49
Bastin slide action 51, 62, 91, 92
Beaumont, Nigel 151, 154
Beaumont, Richard 147, 150, 151, 153
Beckwith, W A 7, 15
Beesley, Frederick 84-88, 155
Beesley self-opening action 85-88
Bentinck, Lord Henry 31, 32
"black book" 13, 14
"black in the" 110, 111, 176
black lacquered stocks 25, 26, 54
blacksmiths 1, 4.
Blaine, Peter 154
Blissett, Isaac 20
Board of Ordnance Trials 1852 28, 29
bobweight single-trigger 121, 150, 151, 152, 153, 162
bombing 1941 141, 142
Boss, Thomas 5, 15, 16, 37, 158
Boss & Co. 27, 58, 82, 112, 119, 120, 130, 145, 146

British Empire 23, 26, 76
Brown brothers 158
browning barrels 15
bullet swage 41, 43

campaign pistols 25
Cape rifle 30
cartridge sales and loading 109, 141, 147
Casbard, Geoffrey 178, 179
centre-fire 59-63
Charlotte Mews 27, 100
choke boring 71, 73, 161
chopper lump barrels 161
Clark, William George 121
C.N.C. technology 161
Cobbold, Ivan 142, 143
Coggan, Simon and Philip 158, 163
Collins, James 20
combination guns 173, 197
Commission of Bankruptcy 17
consideration money 4, 6, 20, 21, 156
conversion of muzzle-loaders
  to breech-loaders 22, 40
copper cap 12, 13
Country Gentleman 122
cyanide hardening 163

Daw, G.H. 58, 60, 81
Daw lever 57, 60, 83
Dean, Arthur, Henry and Philip 126, 157
de Brante lever 57, 81
de Grey, Earl (Lord Ripon) 109, 110
Delay, Ben and Harold 136, 140, 149, 150, 157, 160
Delvigne, Capt. Gustave 29
Depression, Great 1929 134, 135
detachable hammer noses 47, 48
detonating 15, 162
detonating compound 5, 11, 12
Devonshire Place 59, 100, 121
Diamond powder 147
Dimension Books 12-15, 28, 66, 83, 84, 190
"Dora" 129
Dougall, J D 58
duelling pistols 21, 24, 25, 198

Early Percussion Firearms
  (Winant) 12
East India Company 26
Eastcote shooting ground 132, 133, 135
ebonised finish 25, 26
E C powder 109, 147
Edinburgh, Duke of 148, 150
ejectors 104-106
electric cartridges 133, 134
electric night sight 176
electric spotter gun 133, 134
Elizabeth II, Queen 148
Ellis, Richard 74, 75, 98, 99
Enfield rifle 29
escutcheons 16
Evans, Thomas 27
Evans, William 8, 113, 114
exhibitions (19th century) 81
Experts on Guns and Shooting
  (G T Teasdale-Buckell) 107, 122, 154
Express rifle 23, 29-31, 40-45

Felgate Mews factory 151
fern leaf detonating 167, 175
Field, Mabel 108, 109, 140
Field, The 52, 54, 71, 73, 120, 122, 133
Field Trials 1858/9 52
firing pins 62, 63, 93
flash guard 10
Flohiment, Cecile 158
Forsyth Patent Gun Company 5
Forsyth, Rev. Alexander 5, 6, 8, 11, 155
four-barrel gun 95-97
"Foxholes" shooting ground 26
Franz-Ferdinand, Archduke 125
Fullerd, William 15, 27
fulminates 5
"furniture" 161, 162

Gadsby, Chris 153
Gass, D 20
gate single-trigger 121, 151-153
gauge making 141, 144
Geekie, Bill 160
George V, King 113, 133, 134-137, 177, 178
George VI, King 138, 139
Gibbs & Pitt 81, 82
Glaysher, Henry 27
Gloucester, Duke of 26

242

INDEX

gold medals	81	
Gordon, Charles	25, 46, 47, 48, 52, 197, 198	
gothic script	9, 35, 36, 37	
Grant, Stephen	58, 73, 82, 158	
gravitating stop	10	
Greatorex, Samuel and Thomas	8	
Great Exhibition 1851	49	
Great West Road factory	141,142	
Grey Coat Place	6	
Green, Edwinson	130, 146	
Greener, W W	29, 30, 73, 86, 106	
grip tail guard	40, 41	
Grubb, Joseph G	81	
Gumbrell, Peter	14, 16	
Gun and its Development The, (W W Greener)	86, 106	
Gun Club, The	71-73	
Gunmakers' Company	5, 6, 27, 54, 55, 69, 123, 129	

hair trigger	23
hammer design	23, 24, 61
hammerless actions	81-88
hand-loaded cartridges	147
Hanover Square	17, 19
hardening	163
Hardinge, Viscount	29
Hatch, Martha	53, 54
Haverson, Julia	68, 123
Hawker, Col. Peter	4, 7, 8, 9, 11, 21
Haydon, Benjamin Robert	8, 10
Haynes, A .C.	158
"headed up"	162
Henry, Alexander	58, 76
"highland handle"	128
Hodges, E C	124
Holland, H J	58
Holland & Holland	70, 158
Hornsey Wood House	26, 52, 71
Horwood, Richard	7
Houllier	49
Hunt, Ken	148, 158, 160
Hutchinson, Thomas Keck	2, 3, 4, 27
Hutton sight	128

income tax	7
Indentures	156, 157
indicators	62 ,63
Instructions to Young Sportsmen (Hawker)	4, 8, 9, 11, 21
intercepting safety sear	137, 153
Irongate Wharf factory	118, 144, 147, 150
isolated locks	61

Jackson, Thomas	58
Jacobite uprisings	1
Jones, Henry, Patent No. 2040	50, 51, 56, 58
Jones, William	74
keepers' guns	22, 76, 197

Kell, Harry	64, 136, 148, 158
Kelly, Stephen	158
Krupp steel	107

La Boyteaux, Mary	131
Lacy, Captain	12, 26
Lancaster, Alfred	58
Lancaster, Charles	15, 27, 73, 96, 97
Land and Water	1, 18, 71, 75, 102, 103, 106
Lane, Charlie	140
Lang, Joseph	6, 20, 21, 49, 158
law suits	6, 8
Lawrence, Ernest Charles	105, 106, 121, 123, 124, 128, 129, 133, 137, 146, 147, 162, 163
Lawrence, Ernest Douglas	124, 125, 146
Lawrence, Harry	121, 124, 125, 127, 129, 130, 136, 140, 142, 147, 148, 150, 151, 157
Lawrence, Ralph	125, 147
Lawrence, Thomas	123, 124
lead lapping	161
Ledgers, Sales	14, 190
Lee Enfield rifle	128, 141
Lefaucheux, Casimir	49, 60
Leinegen, Prince	13, 26
Letters to Young Shooters (Payne-Gallwey)	59
lever-over-guard	51
Lewis gun	128
Lewis, Henry	16, 27, 63, 66
Limberry, Matthew	2
Limited Company 1925	131
live pigeon shooting	71, 72
locks, front action	22
locks jointed	15, 16
long-guard-lever	51, 90, 95
Long Room	102, 103, 138, 150
Lubbock, George	32, 84
Lucas, J.	63, 64, 114, 116, 157, 158, 162
Lumsden, James	156

Mace, J.	64, 158, 162
Madison Avenue	154
"making off"	15, 162
Manton, John	4, 11, 21, 118
Manton, Joseph	4, 5, 6, 8, 9, 10, 11, 12, 15, 16, 19
Mary, Queen, Dolls' House guns	124, 130, 136
Millennium guns	182
Minié, Claude-Etienne	28, 29
Minories,the	1, 2, 3, 6
Modern Shooter, The (Lacy)	12, 26
Modern Sportsman Gun and Rifle, The (J H Walsh)	58, 86
Moore, Charles	15, 145
Moore and Grey	58, 85
Moore and Sons	46
Morgan, William	132
mould making	141,142,143,144,149
Mount Street	101, 102,128

multi-groove rifling	23, 25, 30, 40, 41
Murcott, Theophilus	81
muzzle protectors	128

Napoleonic Wars	6, 7
Nathan, Robin	150, 154
Neal and Back	11
Needham, Joseph	104
"new pattern handles"	25
Newton and Son, Patent Agents	119, 121, 218
Nobbs, William	104 ,105 , 18, 119
Nock, Henry	5
Nock, Samuel	27
Norlands, shooting ground	26
Norman sight	128
North Row factory	100, 101, 103, 109, 118
North Wharf Road factory	147,150, 151

Old Hats Club, the	26
Oliver family	131, 135
Osborne, Charles	74
Oxford Street, move to 314 $^1/_2$	17-19
Oxford Street, "move" to 287/289	100
Over-and-under guns	124, 130, 145, 146, 153

P 14 rifle	141
pack hardening	163
Paddington Cemetery	52, 53, 121, 123
Paddison, James	107
Pape, W.R.	71, 73
Parkin, Thomas	27
Patents, Purdey	
No. 302, 1861	55, 220, 221
No. 1104, 1863	55-59, 220, 221
No. 424, 1865	62, 221, 222
No. 1464, 1866	62, 63, 222, 223
No. 2319, 1868	62, 63, 223
No. 3118, 1870	70, 223, 224
No. 2952, 1871	70, 223
No. 397, 1878	70, 224, 226
No. 19027, 1897	113, 225, 226
No. 5150, 1910	121, 225, 226
No. 21822, 1911	121, 226, 228
No. 3188, 1915	128, 227, 228
No. 5523, 1926	131, 228
No. 19052, 1926	131, 132, 228, 229
No. 14943, 1929	133, 134, 228
No. 15985, 1929	133, 134, 228, 230
Patent dispute 1906	118-121
Paton, Edward	58
Pauly, Samuel	49, 60
Payne-Gallwey, Sir Ralph	9, 33, 59, 112
pea rifles	23, 197
pegs	15
pellet lock	4 ,6, 11, 12
percussion system	5, 6, 11-13, 17, 21
Perkes, Thomas	74, 104

INDEX

pinless locks	162
plug bullet	29
pocket pistols	25
poincons	35, 36, 37, 38
pop rivet guns	140
post war slump 1815	7
Pottet, Clement	60
Princes Street	7-9, 17
Purdey, Athol	
birth	28
school	68
admission to the Gunmakers' Company	69
marriage	108, 109
70th birthday	133
retirement	133
death	139
obituaries	139, 140
Purdey Bible	4, 20
Purdey bolt	55-59
Purdey, Cecil	
birth	59
joins Purdey	107, 108
death	142
Purdey Cup	73
Purdey-Henry rifle	76, 77
Purdey, James the Blacksmith	1-4
Purdey, James the Elder	
birth	2, 3
apprenticeship	4
marriage	4
joins Mantons	4, 5
joins Forsyth	5, 6
admission to the Gunmakers' Company	5, 6
establishment of business	7-9
safeguard 1818	10, 11
Oxford Street 314 1/2 move to	17-19
debts	32-34
death	52-54
will	53, 54
Master of the Gunmakers' Company	27
Purdey, James the Younger	
birth	17, 20
apprenticeship	20
admission to the Gunmakers' Company	54, 55
marriage (1)	27, 28
Express rifle	29-31
takes control 1858	31-34
obituary	54, 121 122
Master of the Gunmakers' Company	54
marriage (2)	68
death	121
will	121, 122
Purdey, James III	
birth	28
apprenticeship	59
admission to Gunmakers' Company	69
marriage	107
death	108
Purdey, James IV	
birth	109
school	118
joins army	123
admission to Gunmakers' Company	123
war service	127
marriage (1)	127
marriage (2)	131
joins Purdey	131
marriage (3)	131
50th birthday	142
death	149
Purdey, James Oliver Kinloch	127, 149
Purdey, John	1
Purdey, Martha	2, 3, 27
Purdey nipple	38
Purdey, origins	1
Purdey, Percy	59, 108
Purdey, Richard	153
Purdey, Sefton	68, 121
Purdey & Sons	28, 69, 70, 107
Purdey & Sons Ltd.	131
Purdeys, the Guns and the Family (Beaumont)	147
Purdey, Tom	
birth	109
school	118
joins army	126, 127
joins Purdey	129
admission to the Gunmakers' Company	129
trips to America	147, 148
death	148
will	148
Purdey, William	131
putting together	155, 156
Red House, the	26, 71
Redman, Richard	74
redundancy, gunmakers	134
Register of Apprentice Bindings	4, 20, 21
regulating	163
Reilly, E.M.	67
rifle and shotguns	22
Rigby, John	58
Rimington-Wilson, R H R	113
Riviere, Isaac	18
Roberts, Arthur	126
Robertson, John	83, 119, 120, 121, 145, 155, 158
Robins, Abbe	15, 157
Robinson, Lt. Leefe	128
Rogers, John, Thomas and John	153, 154
rook and rabbit rifles	23, 197
rose-and-scroll engraving	61, 64
safeguard, patent 1818	10, 11
safety bolt	23
safety locking sear	137, 153
Salter, Lawrence	121, 125, 142, 150, 162
Sanders, Thomas	158
Sandwell, Stephen	2
Sarajevo assassination	125
Schneider, Eugene	60
Schultze powder	109, 147
Scott top lever and spindle	56-59
Scott, W & C	56-59, 74, 87
screwing together	15, 16
scroll lever	57
sea monster engraving	9, 10, 35, 36, 37, 38
second hand guns	20
secret bite	70
Seely, Sir Hugh (Lord Sherwood)	143, 144, 150
Seely, Sir Victor	150
self expanding bullet	28-29
shooting stick	131-132
Shooting Times, The	120, 139, 140, 151
Shotgun and Sporting Rifle The (J H Walsh)	30, 31
Shotgun Certificate 1968	150
Shotgun The (T D S and J A Purdey)	137
Silver Jubilee miniature guns 1935	124, 135-137
single grip	50
single triggers	118-121, 150, 151, 152, 153, 162
Sinnett, Tony	154
skeletal shoulder stock	39
slacum oil	163
smallpox	2, 3
Smith, A. & Son	74
Smith, George	58
Smith, S & C	58
smoke blacking	162
snap action	55-59
snipers rifles	128
Southgate ejector	104
spade grip trigger	128
Sporting Magazine, The	10
Sporting Mirror Advertiser, The	88
spring bladed front trigger	162
"standard fine engraving"	162, 163
Stanton's rebounding lock	63
steel funnel	41, 42, 43
stirrup ramrods	39
Stonor, Sir Harry	111, 112, 113
"striking up"	161
Sumner, Jack	27, 64
Tallis, John	17, 18
target pistols	24, 25
Teasdale-Buckell, G T	107, 122, 154
Templeman, James	118
third fastening	70, 83
Thomas, Caroline	27, 28, 68
Thorn, Henry	96
throat-hole cocks	10, 35, 36
thumb-hole lever	56, 57, 70, 92, 93, 94, 95
Tower of London	1
trade labels	8, 19
Trafalgar, Battle of, 1805	4
trap gun, single	124, 130
Tregale	27
trigger guards	25
truss manufacture	15
tube lock	4, 12

INDEX

tuberculosis	68, 107, 108	Walsingham, Lord	9, 110, 111	Wilkinson	58
Turf, Field and Farm, The	73	Wardour Street	7	Willesden Cemetery	52, 53, 108
two groove rifle	23, 29-31	Warner, Eugene	151, 153	Williams, Fred, MBE	140, 142
		Warrants of Appointment, Royal	73, 74	Williams, William	6
		Warren, Walter	64, 158	Winans, Walter	174
		Waterloo, Battle of, 1815	7	Winant, Lewis	12
Vendome PLC	153	Wem, William	104, 105, 106, 162	Woodward, James	124, 130, 145, 146, 153, 154
Vickers gun	128	Westley-Richards	39, 58		
Victoria, Queen	23, 26	West London Shooting Grounds	135	Woolman	158
Wales, Prince of	67, 73, 74	Westminster, Duke of	100	Wyatt, Matthew Cotes	10, 11, 36, 39
Wall Street Crash, 1929	134	Wheatley, S	84, 123		
Walsh, J H	30, 31, 52, 58, 86	Whitworth steel	25, 106, 107		